Better
Homes
and Gardens.

Better Homes and Gardens®

ANNUAL•
Recipes
1998

Better Homes and Gardens® Books
Des Moines, Iowa

Double-Chocolate Lava Baby Cakes (page 246)

*M*ost *things can be replaced. Time can't. As our busy lives become more complicated it gets harder to eke out time to enjoy life's little pleasures—like meals shared with family and friends.*

That's why we spent the past year creating the best ways to simplify all the efforts that go into serving memorable meals. The delicious results are featured here in this 1998 collection of all the food ideas found in Better Homes and Gardens *magazine, including one of our newest features, Nutrition In No Time. In our Test Kitchen, we simplified or eliminated unnecessary cooking steps in the recipes and added timesaving hints, such as shopping tips, ingredient substitutions, menu ideas, and preparation times. We also tested and tasted dozens of new recipes for this book. You can locate them easily in the "new recipe" index on page 321.*

Cooking and mealtimes have the power to draw people together. May the ideas within these pages inspire good food, good times, and great memories with your family and friends for years to come.

Nancy Byal

Nancy Byal, *Editor*

A Team of Experts

*A*ll recipes are not created equal. What sets Better Homes and Gardens magazine recipes apart is the attention to detail provided by our full-time team of food experts.

They shepherd each recipe through development, followed by evaluation in our Test Kitchen. Then they oversee photography and writing. Throughout each step, team members check to make sure every recipe will be successful in your kitchen.

Jeanne Ambrose (below right) makes sure the finished products match their written descriptions. On location, she is helped by editorial assistant Karen Pollock, the prop storage expert. Karen makes sure all photo props have a shelf to call home in our enormous prop room. Editorial assistant Anna Anderson (right) has responsibility for overseeing our recipe

contests and typing recipes into our computer files. David Feder (bottom left), a registered dietitian and former restaurant chef, brings hands-on expertise to every project. Nancy Wall Hopkins (bottom center), senior food editor, supervises the content of each story, and is the resident expert on prop and photo styling. Richard Swearinger (below) writes many of our articles and lends his passion for baking to the team.

Together they continue the Better Homes and Gardens legacy of well-researched, beautifully photographed, and great-tasting food.

Better Homes and Gardens® Books

An Imprint of Meredith® Books

Better Homes and Gardens®
Annual Recipes 1998

Project Editor: *Jennifer Darling*
Contributing Editors: *Shelli McConnell, Joyce Trollope*
Associate Art Director: *Lynda Haupert*
Copy Chief: *Catherine Hamrick*
Copy and Production Editor: *Terri Fredrickson*
Editorial and Design Assistants: *Judy Bailey, Treesa Landry, Karen Schirm*
Test Kitchen Director: *Sharon Stilwell*
Illustrator: *Thomas Rosborough*
Electronic Production Coordinator: *Paula Forest*
Production Director: *Douglas M. Johnston*
Production Manager: *Pam Kvitne*
Assistant Prepress Manager: *Marjorie J. Schenkelberg*

Meredith® Books

Editor in Chief: *James D. Blume*
Design Director: *Matt Strelecki*
Managing Editor: *Gregory H. Kayko*
Executive Food Editor: *Lisa Holderness*

Vice President, General Manager: *Jamie L. Martin*

Better Homes and Gardens® **Magazine**

Editor in Chief: *Jean LemMon*
Executive Food Editor: *Nancy Byal*
Senior Editor: *Nancy Wall Hopkins*
Associate Editors: *David Feder, R.D.; Jeanne Ambrose; Richard Swearinger*
Editorial Assistants: *Karen Pollack, Anna Anderson*

Meredith® Publishing Group

President, Publishing Group: *Christopher M. Little*
Vice President, Consumer Marketing & Development: *Hal Oringer*

Meredith® Corporation

Chairman and Chief Executive Officer: *William T. Kerr*

Chairman of the Executive Committee: *E. T. Meredith III*

Our seal assures you that every recipe in
Better Homes and Gardens Annual Recipes 1998 has been
tested in the Better Homes and Gardens® Test Kitchen.
This means that each recipe is practical and
reliable, and meets our high standards of taste appeal.
We guarantee your satisfaction with this book for
as long as you own it.

Cover photograph: Nutmeg-Sour Cream Drop Cookies *(page 276)*
Page 1: Festive Cranberry-Apricot Pie *(page 275)*
Page 2: Double-Chocolate Lava Baby Cakes *(page 246)*

*Some of the images in this book are used by permission
of Zedcor, Inc., Tucson, AZ, from the 100,000 image and the
30,000 image DeskGallery® collections. 800-482-4567.*

All of us at Better Homes and Gardens® Books are
dedicated to providing you with the information and ideas you
need to create delicious foods. We welcome your comments
and suggestions. Write to us at: Better Homes and Gardens Books,
Cookbook Editorial Department, 1716 Locust Street, LN 112,
Des Moines, IA 50309-3023.

*If you would like to order additional copies
of this book, call 800-439-4119.*

CONTENTS

When this symbol appears with a recipe, rest assured that you can prepare the dish—start to finish—in 30 minutes or less.

Any recipe that bears this low-fat symbol has met our guideline of having no more than 10 grams of fat per serving (see page 8).

30 MIN.
LOW FAT

PRIZE
TESTED
RECIPE
WINNER

*This symbol is assigned
to recipes that are both
low in fat and can be
prepared—start to finish—
in 30 minutes or less.*

*The recipes that display this
blue-ribbon symbol have
earned top honors in our
monthly Prize Tested
Recipes contest.*

NUTRITION INFORMATION

With each recipe, we give you useful nutrition information you easily can apply to your own needs. First read "What You Need" (below) to determine your dietary requirements. Then refer to the Nutrition Facts listed with each recipe. You'll find the calorie count and the amount of fat, saturated fat, cholesterol, sodium, carbohydrates, fiber, and protein for each serving. In most cases, along with the Nutrition Facts per serving, you'll find the amount of vitamin A, vitamin C, calcium, and iron noted as a percentage of the Daily Values. The Daily Values are dietary standards set by the Food and Drug Administration. To stay in line with the nutrition breakdown of each recipe, follow the suggested number of servings.

HOW WE ANALYZE

The Better Homes and Gardens Test Kitchen computer analyzes each recipe for the nutritional value of a single serving.
- The analysis does not include optional ingredients.
- We use the first serving size listed when a range is given. For example: If we say a recipe "Makes 4 to 6 servings," the Nutrition Facts are based on 4 servings.
- When ingredient choices (such as margarine or butter) appear in a recipe, we use the first one mentioned for analysis. The ingredient order does not mean we prefer one ingredient over another.
- When milk is a recipe ingredient, the analysis is calculated using 2-percent (reduced-fat) milk.

WHAT YOU NEED

The dietary guidelines below suggest nutrient levels that moderately active adults should strive to eat each day. As your calorie levels change, adjust your fat intake, too. Try to keep the percentage of calories from fat to no more than 30 percent. There's no harm in occasionally going over or under these guidelines, but the key to good health is maintaining a balanced diet *most of the time*.

Calories:	About 2,000
Total fat:	Less than 65 grams
Saturated fat:	Less than 20 grams
Cholesterol:	Less than 300 milligrams
Carbohydrates:	About 300 grams
Sodium:	Less than 2,400 milligrams
Dietary fiber:	20 to 30 grams

LOW-FAT RECIPES

For recipes that meet our low-fat criteria, a main-dish serving must contain 10 or fewer grams of fat. For side dishes or desserts, the serving must contain 5 or fewer grams of fat. These recipes are flagged with a low-fat symbol.

JANUARY
Hidden Treasures

IN THIS CHAPTER

*Y*our parents always warned you not to play with your food, but how can you resist with food that has a playful twist. From appetizers to entrées to desserts, wrapped surprises such as Crepe Party Purses (chicken-filled packets), Curry Phyllo Triangles, Petite Spring Rolls, Chicken-Artichoke Turnovers, and Mandarin Beef Buns will delight eaters any day of the week. Entertain diners all the way through dessert with sweet packages that taste as good as they look, namely Fruit-Filled Napoleons and After-Dinner Wontons.

**30-minute recipes indicated in RED.
Low-fat and no-fat recipes indicated
with a ♥.
Photographs indicated in italics.
*All new in 1998.**

STUFFED JALAPEÑOS

Prep: 45 min. ◆ Bake: 8 min.

Not for the faint of palate! These party poppers are for those who like the heat.

1 small dried ancho pepper

❖❖❖

24 large fresh jalapeño peppers

❖❖❖

4 oz. ground raw turkey
3 cloves garlic, minced
1 tsp. ground cumin
¼ tsp. salt

❖❖❖

1 oz. cream cheese
1 Tbsp. snipped fresh cilantro

❖❖❖

2 beaten eggs
½ cup fine dry bread crumbs

1 With scissors, remove stem and cut open ancho pepper to remove seeds. Soak the pepper in hot water about 20 minutes or until softened.

2 Meanwhile, make a cut in each jalapeño pepper halfway through the stem end. Make a slit down the length of each pepper. This will make a T-shaped cut. Remove seeds and membranes.

3 In a large saucepan cook jalapeños in 1 cup boiling *water,* uncovered, for 2 to 3 minutes or until crisp-tender. Immediately drain and rinse with cold water. Drain and set aside.

4 Drain ancho pepper and finely chop. In a large skillet cook turkey, garlic, cumin, salt, and chopped ancho pepper until turkey is no longer pink.

5 Remove from heat; stir in cream cheese and cilantro. Using a small spoon, fill hollowed peppers with turkey mixture. Lightly press peppers back into their original shapes.

6 Dip stuffed peppers into beaten eggs; roll in bread crumbs to coat. (For a thicker, crunchier crust, give peppers a second coating of egg and bread crumbs. You'll need to increase the eggs to 4 and the bread crumbs to 1 cup.) Place on a foil-lined baking sheet. Bake in a 375° oven 8 to 10 minutes or until heated through. Makes 24 stuffed peppers.

TO MAKE AHEAD

Prepare stuffed peppers as directed, except do not bake. Place in a freezer container; freeze for up to 3 months. To serve, transfer the frozen peppers to a foil-lined baking sheet. Bake in a 350° oven for 25 minutes or until hot.

Nutrition facts per stuffed pepper: 34 cal., 1 g total fat (0 g sat. fat), 21 mg chol., 56 mg sodium, 4 g carbo., 1 g fiber, 2 g pro. *Daily values:* 3% vit. A, 76% vit. C, 1% calcium, 3% iron.

30 MIN.

BEAN BURRITO BITES

Start to finish: 30 min.

Each little cheese-and-bean tortilla holds big taste.

1 to 2 fresh jalapeño peppers, seeded and chopped
1 tsp. ground cumin
1 tsp. olive oil or cooking oil
1 15½-oz. can light red kidney beans, rinsed and drained
½ cup reduced-sodium chicken broth

8 7-inch flour tortillas

◆◆◆

6 oz. reduced-fat cream cheese (Neufchâtel), softened
1 large cucumber, cut into thin strips (2 cups)
1 small red sweet pepper, cut into thin strips (½ cup)
½ cup snipped fresh cilantro
Salsa
Cilantro sprigs (optional)

1 In a large nonstick skillet cook jalapeños and cumin in hot oil for 1 minute, stirring often. Add kidney beans; cook and stir for 4 minutes. Carefully stir in broth. Simmer, uncovered, for 10 minutes, stirring often. Set mixture aside.

2 Meanwhile, wrap tortillas in foil; heat in a 350° oven for 10 minutes. (When ready to fill tortillas, remove only half of them at a time, keeping remaining ones warm in the oven.)

3 For each burrito, spread 4 to 5 teaspoons of the softened cream cheese on a tortilla; spoon 2 tablespoons of the bean mixture on top, just below the center of the tortilla. Top with cucumber, red sweet pepper strips, and cilantro. Fold in sides until they meet; roll up. Cut each burrito in half; serve with salsa. If desired, garnish with cilantro sprigs. Makes 16 burrito appetizers.

Nutrition facts per burrito: 100 cal., 4 g total fat (2 g sat. fat), 8 mg chol., 167 mg sodium, 13 g carbo., 2 g fiber, 4 g pro. *Daily values:* 8% vit. A, 13% vit. C, 3% calcium, 7% iron.

CREPE PARTY PURSES

Start to finish: 50 min.

Flat crepes take on an added dimension when turned into small, chicken-filled packets called "purses." (See the photograph on page 39.)

1¼ cups milk
1 cup all-purpose flour
1 egg
1 tsp. olive oil or cooking oil
¼ tsp. baking powder
❖❖❖
6 green onions
❖❖❖
1 Tbsp. olive oil or cooking oil
1½ cups chopped cooked
    chicken breast
¼ tsp. ground white pepper
½ cup reduced-sodium chicken
    broth
⅓ cup dry white wine
1 5.2-oz. pkg. Boursin cheese
⅛ tsp. dried tarragon, crushed

1 For crepes, in a blender container combine milk, flour, egg, the 1 teaspoon oil, baking powder, and ¼ teaspoon *salt;* cover and blend until smooth. Heat a lightly greased nonstick 7-inch skillet over medium-high heat. Remove from heat. Spoon 2 tablespoons batter into center of the skillet; lift and tilt skillet to spread batter. Return to heat; cook about 1 minute or until light brown. Turn with a spatula; cook second side 30 seconds. Carefully slide finished crepe onto a paper towel-lined plate. Repeat with remaining batter, keeping crepes covered as you prepare them; set aside.

2 Clean green onions; trim and discard root ends. Thinly slice white parts; reserve 12 whole green top pieces. In a skillet bring ½ cup *water* just to boiling. Add onion tops; cook 30 seconds. Rinse with cold water and drain on paper towels; set aside.

3 In the same skillet heat the 1 tablespoon oil over medium-high heat. Add white parts of onions, the chicken, and white pepper; cook just until chicken is hot. Add broth and wine. Bring to boiling; reduce heat. Simmer, uncovered, for 5 to 7 minutes or until liquid is reduced by half. Add cheese and tarragon; cook and stir until cheese is melted. Strain mixture, reserving liquid for sauce and solids for crepe filling. Cover sauce; keep warm.

4 Spoon 2 tablespoons chicken mixture onto each crepe; pull up sides to make a "purse." Tie closed with a green onion top. Spoon 1 tablespoon sauce onto each plate; set a "purse" in center. If desired, garnish with *red sweet pepper pieces.* Makes 12.

Nutrition facts per purse: 147 cal., 7 g total fat (4 g sat. fat), 46 mg chol., 109 mg sodium, 9 g carbo., 0 g fiber, 9 g pro. *Daily values:* 6% vit. A, 2% vit. C, 4% calcium, 5% iron.

CURRY PHYLLO TRIANGLES

Prep: 30 min. ❖ Bake: 12 min.

You can make these crispy triangles ahead of time. Prepare as directed but do not bake; wrap and freeze for up to two weeks. To serve, bake as directed.

1 Tbsp. olive oil or cooking oil
8 oz. ground lamb
1 medium potato, peeled and
    chopped (1 cup)
½ cup finely chopped onion
4 to 5 tsp. curry powder
¾ tsp. dried thyme, crushed
1½ cups chopped tomato
½ cup snipped fresh parsley
❖❖❖
¼ cup olive oil or cooking oil
10 sheets frozen phyllo dough,
    thawed (18×14 inches)

1 In a large nonstick skillet heat the 1 tablespoon oil. Add lamb, potato, and onion; cook until lamb is no longer pink. Drain off fat. Stir in 2 to 3 teaspoons of the curry powder, ½ teaspoon of the thyme, and ½ teaspoon *salt.* Cook and stir for 1 to 2 minutes. Add tomato; reduce heat. Cook, covered, for 5 minutes. Remove from heat. Stir in parsley; set aside.

2 Combine the ¼ cup oil, remaining curry powder, and remaining thyme. Brush one sheet of phyllo with some of the oil mixture; place a second sheet on top. (Cover remaining phyllo with plastic wrap to prevent drying.) Lightly press the 2 sheets together and cut lengthwise into 5 strips, each 3¼ inches wide.

3 Spoon a rounded tablespoon of lamb mixture 1 inch from end of each strip. Fold each strip into a triangle by bringing a corner over filling to line up with other side of strip. Continue folding along strip as you would fold a flag. Repeat with remaining ingredients. Arrange triangles on a greased baking sheet. Brush tops lightly with oil mixture. Bake in a 375° oven 12 minutes or until golden. If desired, garnish with *sliced green onion.* Makes 25.

Nutrition facts per triangle: 74 cal., 4 g total fat (1 g sat. fat), 6 mg chol., 87 mg sodium, 6 g carbo., 0 g fiber, 2 g pro. *Daily values:* 1% vit. A, 7% vit. C, 4% iron.

RIGHT-BITE FINGER SANDWICHES

Prep: 30 min. ◆ Bake: 55 min.
Chill: 2 hr.

Use different types of bread, such as sourdough and pumpernickel, for visual and flavor variety.
(See the photograph on page 38.)

1 beaten egg
½ cup bottled barbecue sauce
  or catsup
1 to 2 Tbsp. Worcestershire
  sauce
1 cup soft bread crumbs
½ cup finely chopped onion
2 to 3 fresh serrano peppers,
  seeded and finely chopped
1 tsp. dried oregano, crushed
1¼ lb. lean ground beef
◆◆◆
12 slices bread
◆◆◆
24 to 36 purchased thin,
  lengthwise pickle slices
  Arugula or other leafy greens

1 In a large mixing bowl stir together the egg, ¼ cup of the barbecue sauce or catsup, and the Worcestershire sauce. Stir in bread crumbs, onion, serrano peppers, and oregano. Add beef to bread crumb mixture and mix well. Press mixture into an ungreased 8×4×2-inch loaf pan. Bake in a 350° oven about 55 minutes or until no pink remains. Cool in pan on a wire rack. Carefully remove from pan. Cover and chill for 2 hours.

2 Trim crusts from bread. Spread 6 of the slices with remaining barbecue sauce or catsup. Cut meat loaf crosswise into 6 equal slices. Place a slice of meat on each barbecue-sauced bread slice.

THE CLEVER COOK

FREEZING LEFTOVER WINE

When you aren't able to finish an entire bottle of wine, freeze the extra wine in ice-cube trays. After the wine is frozen, store the cubes in a self-sealing plastic bag. The frozen wine cubes then can be used to deglaze pans when making sauces.

Catherine M. Donnelly
Sea Girt, New Jersey

3 Top with pickle slices, arugula or other leafy greens, and remaining bread slices. Cut each sandwich into 3 lengthwise strips. Makes 18 finger sandwiches.

Nutrition facts per sandwich: 119 cal., 4 g total fat (1 g sat. fat), 32 mg chol., 461 mg sodium, 12 g carbo., 0 g fiber, 8 g pro. *Daily values:* 2% vit. A, 6% vit. C, 2% calcium, 9% iron.

QUICK-FIX FOCACCIA WEDGES

Prep: 20 min. ◆ Bake: 10 min.

Sweet caramelized onions and a puree of white beans pack rustic Italian flavors onto the already-prepared bread shells.
(See the photograph on page 38.)

3 medium onions, thinly
  sliced
¼ tsp. coarsely ground pepper
1 Tbsp. olive oil

¾ cup rinsed and drained
  canned white beans
½ cup dry white wine or
  reduced-sodium chicken
  broth
1 tsp. dried thyme, crushed
◆◆◆
4 6-inch Italian bread shells
  (such as Boboli)
  Red sweet pepper (optional)
  Fresh marjoram (optional)

1 In a skillet cook and stir onions and ground pepper in hot oil over medium-high heat 7 minutes or until onions turn brown. Remove onions; set aside. Add beans; cook 1 minute. Add wine and thyme; reduce heat. Simmer, uncovered, for 3 to 4 minutes or until liquid is reduced by half. Mash beans slightly.

2 On a baking sheet, spread bread shells with bean mixture; top with onions. Bake in a 450° oven for 10 minutes. Cut into wedges. If desired, garnish each wedge with red pepper and marjoram. Makes 16 wedges.

Nutrition facts per wedge: 108 cal., 3 g total fat (0 g sat. fat), 1 mg chol., 211 mg sodium, 16 g carbo., 1 g fiber, 4 g pro. *Daily values:* 2% vit. C, 3% calcium, 6% iron.

PORTOBELLO PIZZETTAS

Prep: 10 min. ◆ Bake: 12 min.

Omit the pepperoni to turn this into a great vegetarian appetizer.
(See the photograph on page 39.)

½ of a 10-oz. pkg. frozen
  chopped spinach
1½ cups shredded mozzarella
  cheese (6 oz.)

½ cup coarsely chopped turkey
   pepperoni or pepperoni
1 Tbsp. snipped fresh basil or
   1 tsp. dried basil, crushed
¼ tsp. coarsely ground pepper
12 portobello mushrooms
   (3 to 4 inches in diameter)
2 Tbsp. margarine or butter,
   melted
   Fresh basil (optional)

1 Thaw spinach and press out liquid; finely chop. In a bowl combine spinach, mozzarella cheese, pepperoni, basil, and pepper. Clean mushrooms; remove stems. On a lightly greased baking sheet, place mushrooms open side up; brush with margarine. Spoon 2 tablespoons spinach mixture into each mushroom.

2 Bake in a 350° oven about 12 minutes or until hot. (Or, to broil, place on the unheated rack of a broiler pan. Broil 4 inches from the heat for 3 to 4 minutes.) If desired, garnish with fresh basil. Makes 12 pizzettas.

Nutrition facts per pizzetta: 78 cal., 5 g total fat (2 g sat. fat), 16 mg chol., 201 mg sodium, 2 g carbo., 1 g fiber, 6 g pro. *Daily values:* 10% vit. A, 3% vit. C, 8% calcium, 5% iron.

LOW FAT VEGETABLE RIBBON MEATBALLS

Prep: 30 min. ◆ Bake: 30 min.

Far East in flavor, these party-perfect treats are great for serving large groups. (See the photograph on page 38.)

1 medium zucchini
1 medium yellow summer
   squash
1 medium red sweet pepper

1 lb. ground raw turkey
¾ cup soft bread crumbs
1 medium onion, finely
   chopped (½ cup)
6 cloves garlic, minced
1 Tbsp. snipped fresh basil
½ tsp. salt
¼ to ½ tsp. ground red pepper
⅓ cup hoisin sauce

1 Using a sharp vegetable peeler, slice zucchini and yellow squash lengthwise into wide, flat ribbons; set aside. Remove top and seeds from sweet pepper. Cut pepper into ¾- to 1-inch-wide strips. Trim flesh to make strips about ⅛ inch thick; set aside.

2 In a bowl combine turkey, bread crumbs, onion, garlic, basil, salt, and ground red pepper. Shape mixture into 1-inch balls; arrange in a shallow baking pan. Brush meatballs with half of the hoisin sauce. Bake in a 350° oven about 20 minutes or until no pink remains. Cool 15 minutes or until they are cool enough to handle.

3 Meanwhile, in a medium saucepan cook zucchini, yellow squash, and sweet pepper in boiling water, uncovered, 2 minutes. Drain and immediately rinse with cold water. Drain well. Wrap each ball with a ribbon of vegetable; secure with a toothpick.

4 Place wrapped meatballs on a clean, ungreased baking sheet. Brush with remaining hoisin sauce. Return to 350° oven; bake 10 minutes. Makes 40 meatballs.

Nutrition facts per meatball: 25 cal., 1 g total fat (0 g sat. fat), 4 mg chol., 78 mg sodium, 2 g carbo., 0 g fiber, 2 g pro. *Daily values:* 1% vit. A, 6% vit. C, 1% iron.

SERVE A CROWD WITH STYLE

Make entertaining the whole gang a breeze with these time-saving tips.

Team convenience and home-made foods. For appetizer parties, serve store-bought tortellini and meatballs with homemade sauces. Or, try bakery breads with freshly made spreads.

Say cheese. Offer a variety of cheeses in wedges or chunks, such as Gorgonzola, fontina, Brie, and Asiago, arranged on leaf-lined trays. Tuck in assorted crackers and baguette slices. Accent the trays with grape clusters.

Think big. Rather than prepare umpteen tiny finger foods, whip up dips, spreads, and mousses that can serve a crowd. Many of these spreadables can be made ahead. Set baskets of crackers or fresh vegetable crudités alongside and let guests help themselves.

Rent equipment. Peruse the Yellow Pages to find rental services for exactly the right piece of cooking or serving equipment.

Deliver direct. Sometimes large crowds seem to stay in places, so bring the goodies to the guests by passing hot appetizers and a few of the cold appetizers on trays.

Enlist help. Extra hands make a world of difference. Assign last-minute garnishing, food replenishing, and serving duties to your helpers. Keep the crew on hand for cleanup detail, too.

MANDARIN BEEF BUNS

Prep: 40 min. ◆ Rise: 20 min.
Bake: 15 min.

*Asian dim-sum appetizers
were the inspiration for these spicy
meat-filled sesame buns.
(See the photograph on page 39.)*

1 Tbsp. cooking oil
2 cups shredded cooked beef
   or pork
¼ tsp. crushed red pepper
1 cup chopped bok choy,
   Chinese cabbage, or green
   cabbage
2 Tbsp. grated fresh ginger
1 tsp. shredded orange peel
⅓ cup thinly bias-sliced green
   onions
¼ cup hoisin sauce
     ◆◆◆
1 16-oz. package hot-roll mix
     ◆◆◆
1 beaten egg
   Sesame seed

1 For filling, in a large skillet
heat oil over medium heat. Add
beef or pork and red pepper; cook
and stir for 3 minutes. Add bok
choy or other cabbage, ginger, and
orange peel. Cook and stir 2 to
3 minutes or until bok choy is wilted. Stir in green onions and hoisin
sauce. Remove from heat; cool.

2 Meanwhile, prepare the
hot-roll mix according to package
directions. Divide dough into
24 portions. Shape each portion
into a ball. On a lightly floured
surface roll or pat each ball into a
3½-inch circle.

3 For each bun, place about
1 tablespoon of the filling in the
center of a circle. Moisten edges
of dough with water and bring up
around filling, pinching the edges
together to seal (see below).

4 Arrange the filled buns,
seam sides down, on 2 lightly
greased baking sheets. Cover and
let rise in a warm place for
20 minutes. Brush buns with
beaten egg and sprinkle with
sesame seed. Bake in a 375° oven
about 15 minutes or until golden.
Serve warm. Makes 24 buns.

TO MAKE AHEAD

Prepare and bake buns as directed.
Remove from baking sheet and
cool for 30 minutes on a wire
rack. Wrap buns in heavy foil and
freeze for up to 1 month. To
reheat, leave the frozen buns in
foil wrap. Bake in a 325° oven
about 40 minutes or until buns
are heated through.

Nutrition facts per bun: 126 cal., 4 g total
fat (1 g sat. fat), 28 mg chol., 188 mg
sodium, 16 g carbo., 0 g fiber, 7 g pro.
Daily values: 3% vit. A, 5% vit. C, 6% iron.

PETITE SPRING ROLLS

LOW FAT

Start to finish: 40 min.

*Rice papers—sheets of pressed rice
paste—can be found in Asian specialty
markets or some large supermarkets.
(See the photograph on page 38.)*

4 oz. rice vermicelli (rice
   sticks)
1 cup shredded lettuce or
   Chinese cabbage
1 medium carrot, finely
   shredded
⅓ cup chopped honey-roasted
   peanuts or plain peanuts
     ◆◆◆
3 Tbsp. snipped fresh cilantro
1 Tbsp. snipped fresh mint
1 Tbsp. oriental fish sauce or
   soy sauce
2 tsp. cooking oil
1 tsp. toasted sesame oil
½ tsp. crushed red pepper
     ◆◆◆
16 6-inch rice papers
     ◆◆◆
⅓ cup bottled hoisin sauce
¼ cup bottled plum sauce
¼ cup water

1 In a large saucepan cook
vermicelli, uncovered, in boiling
water about 2 minutes or just
until limp. Drain; rinse with cold
water and drain well. Chop into
short pieces. In a large bowl combine the vermicelli, lettuce or
Chinese cabbage, carrot, and
peanuts.

2 In a bowl combine cilantro,
mint, fish sauce or soy sauce,
cooking oil, sesame oil, and red
pepper. Add herb mixture to
noodle mixture. Toss ingredients
together to thoroughly mix.

Menu

Petite Spring Rolls
(see page 14)

❖❖❖

Basil Chicken in Coconut-Curry Sauce over rice
(see right)

❖❖❖

Hot tea

❖❖❖

Almond cookies

3 Pour warm water into a large, shallow dish. Dip 1 or 2 rice papers at a time into water; gently shake off excess. Place the wet rice papers between clean, damp, 100-percent cotton kitchen towels; let stand for 10 minutes.

4 For each spring roll, spoon about 3 tablespoons of the noodle mixture onto a rice paper, just below center of paper. Tightly roll filled rice paper up from bottom, tucking in opposite sides as you roll. Repeat with the remaining papers and noodle mixture, covering rolls as you make them to prevent drying.

5 For sauce, in a bowl stir together the hoisin sauce, plum sauce, and the ¼ cup water. Spoon over spring rolls to serve. Makes 16 spring rolls.

Nutrition facts per spring roll: 143 cal., 2 g total fat (0 g sat. fat), 0 mg chol., 271 mg sodium, 26 g carbo., 1 g fiber, 4 g pro. *Daily values:* 10% vit. A, 1% vit. C, 3% iron.

PRIZE TESTED RECIPE WINNER

BASIL CHICKEN IN COCONUT-CURRY SAUCE

Start to finish: 50 min.

If you rummage in your cupboard, you'll find you have many of the spices that go in this spectacular curry sauce. It's the 1997 Grand Prize Winner in our Prize Tested Recipes® Contest.

4 skinless, boneless chicken breast halves (about 1 lb.)
½ tsp. each ground cardamom, cinnamon, cloves, coriander, and cumin, salt, and cracked black pepper
¼ tsp. ground turmeric
¼ tsp. chili powder

❖❖❖

1 large red onion, chopped
5 cloves garlic, minced
2 fresh jalapeño peppers, seeded and finely chopped
1 Tbsp. olive oil

❖❖❖

1 13½- or 14-oz. can unsweetened coconut milk
2 tsp. cornstarch
3 Tbsp. snipped fresh basil
1 Tbsp. finely chopped fresh ginger
Hot cooked rice
Fresh basil (optional)

1 Rinse chicken; pat dry. Cut into 1-inch pieces. Place chicken in a medium bowl. In a small bowl stir together the cardamom, cinnamon, cloves, coriander, cumin, salt, pepper, turmeric, and chili powder. Sprinkle spice mixture over chicken, tossing to coat. Cover and let stand at room temperature for 30 minutes or in the refrigerator for 1 to 2 hours.

HANDLING HOT PEPPERS

Because chili peppers, such as jalapeños, contain volatile oils that can burn your skin and eyes, avoid direct contact with them as much as possible. When working with chili peppers, wear plastic or rubber gloves. If your bare hands do touch the chili peppers, wash your hands well with soap and water.

2 In a large nonstick wok or skillet cook and stir onion, garlic, and jalapeño peppers in hot oil over medium-high heat 2 minutes. Remove onion mixture from wok. Add half of the chicken to wok. Cook and stir 2 to 3 minutes or until chicken is tender and no longer pink. Remove chicken from the wok. (If necessary, add additional oil.) Cook and remove the remaining chicken as above.

3 Combine coconut milk and cornstarch. Carefully add to wok or skillet. Cook and stir until bubbly. Return the chicken and onion mixture to wok. Stir in snipped basil and ginger. Cook and stir about 2 minutes more or until heated through. Serve over rice. If desired, garnish with fresh basil. Makes 4 servings.

Nutrition facts per serving: 361 cal., 25 g total fat (17 g sat. fat), 59 mg chol., 350 mg sodium, 11 g carbo., 1 g fiber, 24 g pro. *Daily values:* 1% vit. A, 24% vit. C, 3% calcium, 17% iron.

GREEK SAUSAGE AND VEGETABLE BAKE

Prep: 20 min. ◆ Bake: 40 min.

⅓ cup finely chopped celery
¼ cup finely chopped onion
6 Tbsp. butter
⅔ cup water
2 cups herb-seasoned stuffing mix

◆◆◆

8 oz. bulk sweet Italian sausage
3 leeks, chopped
1 medium zucchini or yellow summer squash, halved lengthwise and sliced
1 tsp. dried oregano, crushed
1 10¾-oz. can reduced-sodium condensed cream of celery soup
¼ cup feta cheese (1 oz.)

1 In a large skillet cook and stir celery and onion in hot butter until tender. Remove from heat; stir in water and stuffing mix. Reserve ½ cup of the mixture. Press remaining mixture into bottom and 2 inches up sides of a greased 1½-quart casserole.

2 Crumble sausage into the same skillet. Add leeks and cook and stir until sausage is brown. Drain off fat. Add zucchini or squash and oregano; cook and stir for 2 minutes. Remove from heat. Stir in the soup and feta cheese. Spoon into the stuffing-lined casserole. Sprinkle the reserved stuffing on top. Bake, uncovered, in a 350° oven about 40 minutes or until heated through. Makes 6 servings.

Nutrition facts per serving: 359 cal., 22 g total fat (10 g sat. fat), 59 mg chol., 1,004 mg sodium, 32 g carbo., 2 g fiber, 10 g pro. *Daily values:* 11% vit. A, 6% vit. C, 7% calcium, 15% iron.

ITALIAN BEEF AND SPINACH PIE

Prep: 25 min. ◆ Bake: 47 min.
Stand: 10 min.

This flavor-packed lasagna-without-noodles is a colorful entrée, thanks to all the veggies.

1 unbaked 9-inch pastry shell

◆◆◆

8 oz. lean ground beef
4 oz. ground mild Italian turkey sausage
¾ cup chopped red and/or yellow sweet pepper
½ cup sliced fresh mushrooms
1 clove garlic, minced
1 cup water
½ cup tomato paste
1½ tsp. dried Italian seasoning, crushed
½ tsp. salt

◆◆◆

1 10-oz pkg. frozen chopped spinach, thawed and well drained
⅔ cup light ricotta cheese
¾ cup shredded mozzarella cheese (4 oz.)
1 cup chopped tomato

1 Line pastry shell with a double thickness of foil. Bake in a 450° oven 8 minutes. Remove foil. Bake 4 to 5 minutes or until set and dry; remove from oven. Reduce oven temperature to 350°.

2 In a skillet cook beef, sausage, sweet pepper, mushrooms, and garlic until meat is brown and vegetables are tender. Drain off fat. Stir in water, tomato paste, Italian seasoning, and salt. Heat to boiling; reduce heat. Simmer, covered, for 10 minutes.

3 Meanwhile, in a medium bowl stir together spinach, ricotta cheese, and ¼ cup of the mozzarella cheese. Spoon the spinach filling into baked pastry shell. Top with meat mixture. Cover edge of pastry with foil to prevent over-browning. Bake in a 350° oven for 45 minutes. Remove foil. Top pie with tomato and remaining mozzarella cheese. Bake 2 minutes more or until heated through and cheese is melted. Let stand for 10 minutes. Cut into wedges. If desired, garnish with *fresh oregano*. Makes 8 servings.

Nutrition facts per serving: 290 cal., 16 g total fat (5 g sat. fat), 33 mg chol., 417 mg sodium, 22 g carbo., 2 g fiber, 16 g pro. *Daily values:* 34% vit. A, 51% vit. C, 12% calcium, 19% iron.

CHICKEN AND DRIED TOMATO PIE

Prep: 30 min. ◆ Bake: 35 min.

If you're looking to save yourself some calories and a few grams of fat, use the egg product and light dairy sour cream.

1¼ cups all-purpose flour
2 Tbsp. grated Parmesan cheese
⅓ cup butter
4 to 5 Tbsp. water

◆◆◆

½ cup snipped dried tomatoes (not oil-packed)
½ cup chopped onion
1 clove garlic, minced
1 Tbsp. olive oil

◆◆◆

3 beaten eggs or ¾ cup refrigerated or frozen egg product, thawed
1 cup milk
1 cup shredded Swiss cheese
2 Tbsp. all-purpose flour
⅓ cup regular or light dairy sour cream
2 tsp. snipped fresh oregano or ½ tsp. dried oregano, crushed
1 cup chopped grilled, roasted, or smoked chicken

1 In a mixing bowl combine the 1¼ cups flour and Parmesan cheese. Using a pastry blender, cut in butter until pieces are pea-size. Sprinkle 1 tablespoon of the water over part of the mixture; gently toss with a fork. Push moistened dough to side of bowl. Repeat using 1 tablespoon of the water at a time, until all the dough is moistened. Form dough into a ball. On a lightly floured surface, roll dough into a circle about 12 inches in diameter.

Transfer to a 9-inch pie plate. Trim pastry to ½ inch beyond edge of plate. Fold under extra pastry; crimp the edge. Line unpricked pastry shell with a double thickness of foil. Bake in a 450° oven for 8 minutes. Remove foil. Bake 4 to 5 minutes or until set and dry; remove from oven. Reduce oven temperature to 325°.

2 Soak tomatoes in warm water 15 minutes; drain and set aside. In a small skillet cook onion and garlic in hot oil until tender.

3 Mix eggs, milk, cheese, the 2 tablespoons flour, sour cream, and oregano. Stir in chicken and drained tomatoes. Spoon filling into baked pastry shell. Bake in a 325° oven for 35 to 40 minutes or until set. Let stand 10 minutes. Cut in wedges. Makes 6 servings.

Nutrition facts per serving: 435 cal., 26 g total fat (14 g sat. fat), 184 mg chol., 367 mg sodium, 27 g carbo., 1 g fiber, 22 g pro. *Daily values:* 25% vit. A, 4% vit. C, 25% calcium, 13% iron.

MEAT-STUFFED PHYLLO ROLLS

Prep: 25 min. ◆ Cool: 30 min.
Bake: 15 min.

12 oz. lean ground beef
8 oz. lean ground lamb
1 cup chopped onion
¼ cup all-purpose flour
2 Tbsp. snipped fresh dillweed or 1 tsp. dried dillweed
½ tsp. curry powder
⅛ to ¼ tsp. ground red pepper
1⅓ cups beef broth
¾ cup finely chopped pickled beets
⅓ cup golden raisins

◆◆◆

9 sheets frozen phyllo dough, thawed
⅓ cup butter, melted

1 Cook meat and onion until meat is brown. Drain fat. Stir in flour, dillweed, curry, red pepper, and ½ teaspoon *salt*. Add broth; cook and stir until bubbly. Cook and stir 1 minute more. Stir in beets and raisins. Cool 30 minutes.

2 Stack 3 sheets of phyllo, brushing each sheet with some of the butter. Cut stack in half crosswise. Place a generous ½ cup meat mixture near a short side of each phyllo stack. Roll up phyllo and filling, jelly-roll style, tucking ends in. Place seam-side down in a greased 15×10×1-inch baking pan. Repeat with the remaining phyllo, butter, and filling. Brush tops and sides with butter. Bake in a 400° oven 15 to 20 minutes or until golden. Makes 6 servings.

Nutrition facts per serving: 417 cal., 23 g total fat (11 g sat. fat), 88 mg chol., 712 mg sodium, 33 g carbo., 1 g fiber, 21 g pro. *Daily values:* 9% vit. A, 3% vit. C, 2% calcium, 20% iron.

Torn Turkey and Phyllo Pie

Prep: 20 min. ◆ Bake: 45 min.
Stand: 10 min.

Crisp, buttery layers of phyllo make a crust for the spinach and turkey filling. (See the photograph on page 41.)

- 2 medium leeks, thinly sliced
- 1 clove garlic, minced
- 1 Tbsp. butter or margarine
- 1 10-oz. pkg. frozen chopped spinach, drained
- 3 slightly beaten eggs
- 1 cup shredded mozzarella cheese (4 oz.)
- ⅔ cup milk
- 2 Tbsp. grated Parmesan cheese
- ¼ tsp. pepper
- 2 cups chopped, cooked turkey

◆◆◆

- 5 sheets frozen phyllo dough (18×14-inch rectangles), thawed
- 3 Tbsp. butter or margarine, melted

1 In a medium skillet cook leeks and garlic in 1 tablespoon butter or margarine until tender. Remove from heat. Stir in the spinach, eggs, mozzarella cheese, milk, Parmesan cheese, and pepper. Fold in turkey; set aside.

2 Lightly brush a sheet of phyllo with some of the melted butter; fold in half crosswise. Cover remaining phyllo with plastic wrap to prevent drying. Gently press folded phyllo into pie plate; allow ends to hang over edge. Repeat with 3 more sheets of phyllo and butter, staggering each sheet in pie plate to evenly cover bottom and sides.

Menu

Chicken-Artichoke Turnovers (see below)

◆◆◆

Salad of leaf lettuce, tomato wedges, shaved Parmesan cheese, and Italian vinaigrette

◆◆◆

Vanilla ice cream with sauteed apples and raisins

3 Spoon filling into pie plate. Fold ends of the phyllo toward the center of pie. Brush remaining sheet and fold in eighths. Cut folded phyllo into thin strips; sprinkle strips atop pie. Bake, uncovered, in a 375° oven 45 to 50 minutes or until a knife inserted near center comes out clean. Let stand for 10 minutes. Cut into wedges. Makes 8 servings.

Nutrition facts per serving: 257 cal., 15 g total fat (7 g sat. fat), 140 mg chol., 292 mg sodium, 12 g carbo., 2 g fiber, 19 g pro. *Daily values:* 33% vit. A, 7% vit. C, 17% calcium, 14% iron.

Chicken-Artichoke Turnovers

Prep: 30 min. ◆ Bake: 25 min.

Frozen patty shells offer a great shortcut for making these plump poultry packets.

- 1 10-oz. pkg. frozen patty shells
- ¼ cup light dairy sour cream
- 1 to 1½ tsp. chili powder
- 2 cloves garlic, minced
- 1 tsp. lemon juice
- 1½ cups chopped, cooked chicken
- ¾ cup shredded Monterey Jack cheese (3 oz.)
- ¾ cup coarsely chopped, drained artichoke hearts (half of a 14-oz. can)
- 1 4-oz. can diced green chilies, drained
- 2 green onions, thinly sliced
- 1 Tbsp. snipped fresh parsley

◆◆◆

Milk

1 Thaw patty shells; set aside. In a medium bowl stir together sour cream, chili powder, garlic, and lemon juice. Add chicken, Monterey Jack cheese, artichoke hearts, chilies, green onions, and parsley. Stir mixture to combine.

2 On a lightly floured surface roll out each patty shell to a 7-inch circle. Place about ½ cup filling on half of each circle. Moisten edges with water; fold other half of circle over filling. Press to seal with tines of a fork.

3 Place turnovers on an ungreased, foil-lined baking sheet. Cut a slit in the top of each turnover for steam to escape. Brush tops with milk. Bake in a 400° oven for 25 to 30 minutes or until golden. Makes 6 turnovers.

Nutrition facts per turnover: 367 cal., 23 g total fat (4 g sat. fat), 48 mg chol., 378 mg sodium, 22 g carbo., 1 g fiber, 18 g pro. *Daily values:* 8% vit. A, 17% vit. C, 13% calcium, 7% iron.

CRISP APPLE-RICE SALAD

Start to finish: 20 min.

Apples lend a refreshing crunch and contrast to the rice in this winning salad.

2 cups cooked brown and/or wild rice, chilled
2 cups chopped apple (about 2 medium)
1 cup thinly sliced celery
¼ cup shelled sunflower seeds
¼ cup dried currants
2 Tbsp. balsamic vinegar
1 Tbsp. olive oil
2 tsp. honey
2 tsp. brown mustard or Dijon-style mustard
2 tsp. finely shredded orange peel
1 clove garlic, minced

1 In a large salad bowl combine chilled rice, apple, celery, sunflower seeds, and currants. Stir together vinegar, oil, honey, mustard, orange peel, garlic, and ¼ teaspoon *salt.* Drizzle over rice mixture, tossing to coat. Serve immediately atop *radicchio* and *curly leaf lettuce,* if desired. Makes 6 side-dish servings.

▐ TO MAKE AHEAD ▌

Prepare salad as directed, except do not include apple. Cover and chill for up to 24 hours. Just before serving, chop apple and add to salad; toss. Serve as directed.

Nutrition facts per serving: 183 cal., 6 g total fat (1 g sat. fat), 0 mg chol., 133 mg sodium, 30 g carbo., 3 g fiber, 4 g pro. *Daily values:* 9% vit. C, 2% calcium.

BUTTERNUT SQUASH COMPOTE

Prep: 25 min. ◆ Bake: 1 hr.

A perfect way to get kids to eat their vegetables—squash candied along with fruit favorites. (See the photograph on page 41.)

1 2-lb. butternut squash, peeled, halved, seeded, and cut into 1½-inch chunks
¼ cup orange juice
¼ tsp. ground ginger
¼ tsp. ground nutmeg

◆◆◆

1 medium red or green tart apple, cored and cut into 1-inch chunks
1 medium pear, peeled, cored, and cut into 1-inch chunks
⅓ cup golden raisins
2 Tbsp. chopped pecans
2 Tbsp. margarine or butter, cut up
1 Tbsp. light-colored corn syrup
1 Tbsp. brown sugar
¼ tsp. salt

1 In a 2-quart casserole stir together squash, orange juice, ginger, and nutmeg. Bake, covered, in a 375° oven for 40 minutes.

2 Add fruits, pecans, margarine, corn syrup, brown sugar, and salt to squash mixture, stirring to coat. Bake, uncovered, for 20 minutes more or until squash is tender, stirring once or twice. Makes 6 side-dish servings.

Nutrition facts per serving: 168 cal., 6 g total fat (1 g sat. fat), 0 mg chol., 142 mg sodium, 31 g carbo., 4 g fiber, 2 g pro. *Daily values:* 79% vit. A, 39% vit. C, 4% calcium, 7% iron.

ASIAN-STYLE BEANS AND POTATOES

Start to finish: 25 min.

Five spice powder is a blend of cinnamon, star anise, fennel seed, Szechwan pepper, and cloves. You can purchase it in the spice section in supermarket or specialty stores.

1 lb. whole tiny new potatoes, quartered
1½ cups frozen cut green beans
2 stalks bok choy, cut into ¼-inch slices

◆◆◆

3 Tbsp. oyster sauce
½ tsp. five spice powder
⅛ tsp. pepper
¼ cup chopped honey-roasted peanuts

1 In a medium saucepan cook potatoes, covered, in boiling water for 10 minutes. Add green beans and bok choy. Return to boiling; reduce heat. Simmer, covered, about 5 minutes more or until potatoes are tender. Drain; return to saucepan.

2 Add the oyster sauce, five spice powder, and pepper to vegetables in saucepan. Stir to coat the vegetables with sauce; heat through. Transfer to a serving bowl. Sprinkle with peanuts. Makes 6 side-dish servings.

Nutrition facts per serving: 120 cal., 2 g total fat (0 g sat. fat), 0 mg chol., 305 mg sodium, 22 g carbo., 1 g fiber, 4 g pro. *Daily values:* 4% vit. A, 32% vit. C, 4% calcium, 12% iron.

MEXICANA COUSCOUS

Start to finish: 15 min.

Quick couscous helps put this dish, reminiscent of Spanish rice, on the table in no time.

¾ cup chopped onion
2 cloves garlic, minced
1 Tbsp. cooking oil
½ tsp. ground cumin

◆◆◆

1 cup reduced-sodium chicken broth
¾ cup loose-pack frozen peas
¾ cup coarsely chopped tomato or ¾ cup canned diced tomatoes
2 Tbsp. snipped fresh cilantro or 2 tsp. dried cilantro, crushed
¾ cup quick-cooking couscous
   Fresh cilantro sprigs (optional)

1 In a medium saucepan cook and stir onion and garlic in hot oil over medium heat until tender. Stir in cumin; cook for 30 seconds.

2 Carefully add the chicken broth, peas, tomato, and cilantro. Bring mixture to boiling. Stir in couscous; remove from heat. Cover and let stand for 5 minutes. Fluff with a fork. If desired, garnish with cilantro sprigs. Makes 6 side-dish servings.

Nutrition facts per serving: 134 cal., 3 g total fat (0 g sat. fat), 0 mg chol., 124 mg sodium, 23 g carbo., 6 g fiber, 4 g pro. *Daily values:* 15% vit. A, 13% vit. C, 1% calcium, 5% iron.

COUSCOUS

Granular semolina, known as couscous, is a grain product that's in the shape of very tiny beads. This commercially produced product made from ground semolina is a staple in North African cooking and can be used in recipes or served as a mild-tasting side dish in place of rice. Quick-cooking or regular couscous usually is found in the rice or pasta section of the supermarket or in a specialty food store.

---

30 MIN.
LOW FAT

SPICED RICE AND LENTILS

Start to finish: 30 min.

1 tsp. ground cumin
1 tsp. ground turmeric
¼ tsp. ground cardamom
¼ tsp. black or yellow mustard seed
¼ tsp. ground cinnamon
⅛ tsp. salt
⅛ tsp. ground red pepper
⅛ tsp. ground cloves

◆◆◆

1 Tbsp. olive oil
¾ cup long grain rice or basmati rice
3 cups water
¾ cup red lentils
½ cup mixed dried fruit bits or golden raisins
2 cups torn fresh spinach
½ cup plain yogurt

1 In a small bowl combine cumin, turmeric, cardamom, mustard seed, cinnamon, salt, red pepper, and cloves; set aside.

2 In a medium saucepan heat olive oil over medium heat. Add the spice mixture and cook for 1 minute. Stir in rice and carefully add water. Bring to boiling; reduce heat. Simmer, covered, for 10 minutes. Stir in lentils and fruit. Cook, covered, for 10 minutes more or until rice and lentils are tender. Stir in spinach. To serve, top each serving with a spoonful of yogurt. Makes 8 side-dish or 3 main-dish servings.

Nutrition facts per side-dish serving: 173 cal., 2 g total fat (0 g sat. fat), 1 mg chol., 70 mg sodium, 32 g carbo., 3 g fiber, 7 g pro. *Daily values:* 11% vit. A, 7% vit. C, 5% calcium, 17% iron.

FRUIT-FILLED NAPOLEONS

Prep: 20 min. ◆ Bake: 18 min.

Simple as well as elegant, each flaky pastry is filled with pudding, cream, or ice cream and crowned with fresh fruit.

½ of a 17¼-oz. pkg. frozen puff pastry (1 sheet), thawed
2 cups pudding, fruit-flavored yogurt, sweetened whipped cream, or softened ice cream
1 cup sliced kiwifruit, halved seedless grapes, berries, and/or orange slices
   Powdered sugar (optional)

1 On a lightly floured surface, unfold thawed pastry. Using a small sharp knife, cut pastry into

8 rectangles (each the same size). Place pastry rectangles on an ungreased baking sheet. Bake in a 375° oven about 18 minutes or until pastries are puffed and golden. Remove pastries from baking sheet and cool on a wire rack.

2 Just before serving, split each pastry rectangle in half horizontally. Spoon pudding, yogurt, sweetened whipped cream, or ice cream atop pastry bottoms. Top with fruit and pastry tops. If desired, dust tops with powdered sugar. Serve immediately. (If pastries are filled and held too long, they may get soggy.) Makes 8.

Nutrition facts per pastry with vanilla pudding, kiwifruit, and seedless red grapes: 266 cal., 13 g total fat (0 g sat. fat), 1 mg chol., 184 mg sodium, 35 g carbo., 1 g fiber, 3 g pro. *Daily values:* 4% vit. A, 67% vit. C, 8% calcium, 2% iron.

CHERRY AND CHOCOLATE HEARTS
Prep: 20 min. ◆ Bake: 18 min.

½ of a 17¼-oz. pkg. frozen
  puff pastry (1 sheet),
  thawed
¾ cup cherry pie filling
8 tsp. fudge ice-cream topping
2 Tbsp. chopped nuts

1 On a lightly floured surface, unfold thawed pastry. Using a 3½- to 4-inch heart-shaped cookie cutter, cut pastry into shapes, discarding pastry scraps or reserving for another use. Place pastry hearts on an ungreased baking sheet. Bake in a 375° oven about 18 minutes or until puffed and golden. Remove pastries from baking sheet; cool on a wire rack.

2 Just before serving, split each pastry heart in half horizontally. Spoon pie filling atop pastry bottoms. Add pastry top. Place hearts on dessert plates. Drizzle with fudge topping;* sprinkle with nuts. Serve immediately. Makes 8 pastry hearts.

***Note:** Heat fudge topping if too thick to drizzle.

Nutrition facts per filled pastry heart: 207 cal., 12 g total fat (1 g sat. fat), 0 mg chol., 123 mg sodium, 25 g carbo., 0 g fiber, 2 g pro. *Daily values:* 1% vit. A, 1% vit. C, 1% calcium, 1% iron.

LOW FAT

AFTER-DINNER WONTONS
Prep: 45 min. ◆ Bake: 12 min.

Baked fruit-and-nut-filled wontons add a light finish to a meal.

2 medium pears, peeled and
  shredded (about 1½ cups)
2 medium cooking apples,
  peeled and chopped
  (about 1⅓ cups)
3 Tbsp. dried tart red cherries,
  chopped
2 tsp. lemon juice
2 Tbsp. butter or margarine
3 Tbsp. Marsala or apple juice
2 Tbsp. finely chopped
  almonds
1 tsp. ground cinnamon
½ tsp. ground ginger
¼ cup maple-flavored syrup
◆◆◆
36 3¼-inch round wonton or
  pot sticker wrappers
◆◆◆
3 Tbsp. butter or margarine,
  melted
  Coarse granulated sugar or
  sifted powdered sugar

1 For filling, in a medium bowl toss together pears, apples, cherries, and lemon juice. In a large skillet cook fruit mixture in the 2 tablespoons butter or margarine over medium heat for 7 minutes; reduce heat. Stir in Marsala or apple juice, almonds, cinnamon, and ginger. Cook about 3 minutes more or until liquid has evaporated, stirring often. Stir in syrup; set aside.

2 For each wonton, spoon about 2 teaspoons filling into center of a wonton or pot sticker wrapper. Lightly moisten edges of wrapper with water. Fold top edge of wrapper over filling to opposite edge, making a half-moon (see below). Press edges together.

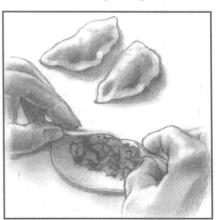

3 Arrange wontons on a greased baking sheet. Brush with melted butter or margarine. Sprinkle with coarse sugar, if using. Bake in a 350° oven 12 to 15 minutes or until golden. Remove from baking sheet and cool slightly on a rack. Sprinkle with powdered sugar, if using. Makes 36.

Nutrition facts per wonton: 60 cal., 2 g total fat (1 g sat. fat), 5 mg chol., 62 mg sodium, 9 g carbo., 0 g fiber, 1 g pro. *Daily values:* 1% vit. A, 1% vit. C, 2% iron.

CAPPUCCINO BROWNIE CUPS

Prep: 25 min. ◆ Bake: 25 min.
Cool: 2 hr.

Use brownie leftovers for parfaits, or crumble and sprinkle over ice cream.

¾ **cup butter or margarine**
¾ **cup granulated sugar**
½ **cup packed brown sugar**
½ **cup unsweetened cocoa powder**
2 **slightly beaten eggs**
1 **tsp. vanilla**

◆◆◆

1½ **cups all-purpose flour**
2 **Tbsp. instant coffee granules**
1 **tsp. baking powder**
1 **cup milk**
1 **cup finely chopped walnuts or pecans**

◆◆◆

1 **cup whipping cream**
2 **Tbsp. sifted powdered sugar**
1 **tsp. instant coffee granules**

◆◆◆

Ground cinnamon

1 Grease a 13×9×2-inch baking pan; set aside. In a large skillet heat and stir butter, sugars, and cocoa powder over medium heat until butter melts. Remove from heat; add beaten eggs and vanilla. Using a wooden spoon, beat lightly just until combined.

2 Combine flour, 2 tablespoons coffee granules, and baking powder. Add flour mixture and milk alternately to cocoa mixture, beating after each addition. Stir in walnuts or pecans.

3 Pour batter into prepared baking pan. Bake in a 350° oven 25 to 30 minutes or until a tooth-

pick inserted near center comes out clean. Cool on wire rack at least 2 hours.

4 Meanwhile, in a small bowl beat whipping cream, powdered sugar, and the 1 teaspoon coffee granules until stiff peaks form.

5 Using a cookie cutter, cut brownies into 2-inch circles. Using a measuring teaspoon, scoop out centers of brownie circles. Pipe or spoon cream mixture into brownies. Sprinkle with cinnamon. Makes 16 brownie cups.

Nutrition facts per brownie cup: 305 cal., 20 g total fat (10 g sat. fat), 71 mg chol., 134 mg sodium, 28 g carbo., 1 g fiber, 5 g pro. *Daily values:* 16% vit. A, 8% calcium, 9% iron.

LOW FAT

JELLY ROLL DAINTIES

Prep: 20 min. ◆ Bake: 8 min.
Cool: 1 hr.

Lemon curd, chocolate pudding, or ice cream are tasty filling alternatives for the fruit preserves.

¼ **cup all-purpose flour**
½ **tsp. baking powder**
2 **eggs**

◆◆◆

¼ **tsp. vanilla**
6 **Tbsp. granulated sugar**

◆◆◆

Sifted powdered sugar
Fruit preserves or other filling

1 Lightly grease a 15×10×1-inch jelly-roll pan. Line bottom with waxed paper; grease paper. Set pan aside. Combine flour and baking powder; set aside. Separate eggs; cover whites and set aside.

2 In a mixing bowl beat egg yolks and vanilla with an electric mixer on high speed until mixture thickens (about 5 minutes). Slowly add 3 tablespoons of the granulated sugar, beating on high speed until sugar is dissolved.

3 Wash beaters. In a clean bowl beat egg whites on medium speed until soft peaks form. Gradually add remaining granulated sugar, beating until stiff peaks form. Fold egg yolk mixture into beaten egg whites. Sprinkle flour mixture over egg mixture; fold in gently until combined.

4 Spread batter evenly in prepared pan. Bake in a 350° oven for 8 to 10 minutes or until cake springs back when lightly touched. Immediately loosen edges of cake from pan and turn cake out onto a towel sprinkled with powdered sugar. Carefully peel off waxed paper. Roll up towel and cake, jelly-roll style, starting from a short side. Cool on a rack at least 1 hour.

5 Carefully unroll cake and remove towel. Cut cake in half lengthwise. Cut each half crosswise into thirds. For each jelly roll, spread a cake square with 1 to 2 tablespoons fruit preserves or desired filling to within ½ inch of edges. Roll up the square and carefully slice in half crosswise. If desired, sprinkle tops of rolls with additional powdered sugar. Makes 12 miniature jelly rolls.

Nutrition facts per jelly roll: 100 cal., 1 g total fat (0 g sat. fat), 36 mg chol., 28 mg sodium, 22 g carbo., 0 g fiber, 1 g pro. *Daily values:* 1% vit. A, 1% calcium, 3% iron.

FEBRUARY
Simple Pleasures

IN THIS CHAPTER

Humble ingredients such as potatoes, noodles, and rice are the backbone of many richly flavored international dishes. Add ground lamb and feta cheese to potato skins and you have a savory Greek-style appetizer. Wasabi (Japanese horseradish) gives ordinary mashed potatoes a wake-up call. Chicken soup turns exotic when the noodles are the Asian soba or udon varieties. Rice pudding loses its old standby label with the addition of Indian spices, pistachio nuts, and dried apricots. This sweetest of months also is the time for pull-out-the-stops desserts, such as Raspberry Meringue Hearts or a layered Black Tie Cheesecake.

30-minute recipes indicated in RED.
Low-fat and no-fat recipes indicated with a ♥.
Photographs indicated in italics.
*All new in 1998.

LA BELLA BRUSCHETTA

The bruschetta (broo-SKET-ta), originally from the olive-growing regions of Italy, started out as the typical lunch of the olive grove workers—nearly as much a part of the olive harvest as the olives themselves. The classic bruschetta included olive oil and vegetables, such as sweet red peppers or plum tomatoes, and perhaps fresh mozzarella or creamy goat cheese.

Creating your own bruschetta is simple: Top thick slices of toasted or grilled crusty Italian bread with any ingredient you desire, savory or sweet, and enjoy.

SWEET RED PEPPER BRUSCHETTA

Start to finish: 10 min.

This classic bruschetta transports you to sun-drenched Tuscany from the first bite.

8 **bias-cut slices (about ¾ inch thick) Italian country bread or crusty sourdough bread**
½ **cup soft goat cheese (chèvre) or other spreadable soft white cheese**
¼ **cup purchased basil pesto**
1 **7-oz. jar roasted red peppers, drained and cut into ½-inch-wide strips**
  Snipped fresh herbs, such as basil, oregano, or thyme

1 Toast or grill bread slices. Spread each bread slice with some soft cheese. Spread pesto atop cheese and top each bruschetta with pepper strips. Garnish with snipped herbs. Serve immediately. Makes 8 bruschetta.

Nutrition facts per bruschetta: 190 cal., 11 g total fat (3 g sat. fat), 15 mg chol., 323 mg sodium, 18 g carbo., 0 g fiber, 6 g pro. *Daily values:* 9% vit. A, 74% vit. C, 3% calcium, 7% iron.

GREEK-STYLE POTATO SKINS
LOW FAT

Prep: 30 min. ◆ Bake: 50 min.

6 **large baking potatoes**
  ◆◆◆
8 **oz. ground lamb or ground raw turkey**
1 **6-oz. jar marinated artichoke hearts**
  ◆◆◆
2 **Tbsp. garlic-flavored oil**
½ **cup chopped red onion**
2 **plum tomatoes, chopped**
1 **cup crumbled feta cheese (4 oz.)**
2 **Tbsp. grated Parmesan cheese**
1 **Tbsp. tahini (sesame butter)**

1 Scrub potatoes and prick with a fork. Bake in a 425° oven for 40 to 45 minutes or until tender; cool. Cut each potato lengthwise into 4 wedges. Scoop out the inside of each potato wedge. Cover and chill fluffy white part of potatoes for another use.

2 In a skillet cook lamb or turkey until brown; drain fat. Drain the artichoke hearts, reserving 3 tablespoons liquid. Chop artichoke hearts.

3 Using a pastry brush, brush insides of potato wedges with garlic-flavored oil. Place potato wedges in a single layer on a large baking sheet. Sprinkle wedges with lamb or turkey, artichoke hearts, red onion, and tomato. Sprinkle with feta and Parmesan cheese. Bake, uncovered, 10 minutes. Meanwhile, stir together the tahini and reserved artichoke marinade. Drizzle atop hot potato wedges. Makes 24 wedges.

Nutrition facts per wedge: 114 cal., 4 g total fat (2 g sat. fat), 11 mg chol., 95 mg sodium, 15 g carbo., 1 g fiber, 4 g pro. *Daily values:* 1% vit. A, 19% vit. C, 3% calcium, 6% iron.

PARMESAN POTATO PUFFS

Prep: 30 min. ◆ Bake: 15 min.

6 **medium potatoes, peeled and quartered (2 lb.)**
  ◆◆◆
¼ **cup finely chopped onion**
2 **cloves garlic, minced**
3 **Tbsp. margarine or butter**
¼ **cup fine dry bread crumbs**
¼ **cup finely shredded Parmesan cheese (1 oz.)**
1 **tsp. baking powder**
2 **eggs, beaten**
2 **Tbsp. snipped fresh basil or 1 tsp. dried basil, crushed**

1 Cook potatoes, covered, in boiling salted water 20 to 25 minutes or until tender; drain.

2 Meanwhile, in a small skillet cook onion and garlic in margarine or butter until tender. Mash the drained potatoes with a potato masher or beat with an electric mixer on low speed. Add onion mixture, bread crumbs,

Parmesan cheese, baking powder, ¼ teaspoon *salt,* and ¼ teaspoon *pepper.* Beat in eggs and basil.

3 Drop potato mixture in 8 to 10 mounds onto a well-greased baking sheet. Bake, uncovered, in a 425° oven about 15 minutes or until hot. Makes 8 to 10 servings.

Nutrition facts per serving: 182 cal., 7 g total fat (1 g sat. fat), 56 mg chol., 247 mg sodium, 26 g carbo., 2 g fiber, 5 g pro. *Daily values:* 8% vit. A, 14% vit. C, 8% calcium, 4% iron.

PRIZE TESTED RECIPE WINNER

LEMON-BASIL POTATO PUFF

Prep: 30 min. ◆ **Bake: 45 min.**

The buttery crumb crust adds a crisp coat to this herb-laced mashed potato casserole.

6 medium potatoes, peeled and quartered (2 lb.)

◆◆◆

¾ cup fine dry bread crumbs
3 Tbsp. margarine or butter, melted
1 Tbsp. finely snipped fresh parsley

◆◆◆

3 eggs, separated
¼ cup snipped fresh basil
1 tsp. finely shredded lemon peel
1 tsp. lemon juice
1 cup milk
1½ cups shredded Swiss cheese

1 Cook potatoes, covered, in boiling water for 20 to 25 minutes or until tender; drain. Mash the drained potatoes; set aside.

2 Meanwhile, in a bowl combine bread crumbs, margarine or butter, and parsley. Press mixture onto bottom and up sides of a lightly greased 1½-quart casserole.

3 In a bowl combine egg yolks, basil, lemon peel and juice, ¾ teaspoon *salt,* and ¼ teaspoon *ground white pepper.* Stir in milk and 1 cup of the cheese. Stir milk mixture into mashed potatoes. Beat egg whites until stiff peaks form; fold into potato mixture.

4 Transfer potato mixture to prepared casserole; top with remaining cheese. Bake, uncovered, in a 350° oven about 45 minutes or until a knife inserted in center comes out clean. Garnish with snipped fresh *parsley.* Makes 8 to 10 servings.

Nutrition facts per serving: 296 cal., 13 g total fat (6 g sat. fat), 102 mg chol., 419 mg sodium, 32 g carbo., 13 g pro. *Daily values:* 24% vit. A, 16% vit. C, 23% calcium, 6% iron.

MEXICALI POTATO BRUNCH BAKE

Prep: 20 min. ◆ **Bake: 25 min.**

3 cups refrigerated shredded hash brown potatoes
5 eggs
1 cup shredded Monterey Jack cheese with jalapeño peppers (4 oz.)
½ cup ricotta cheese or cream cheese, softened

◆◆◆

¾ cup milk, half-and-half, or light cream
2 Tbsp. margarine or butter

1 Tbsp. all-purpose flour
1 4-oz. can diced green chili peppers

1 Stir together the potatoes, 1 egg, and ½ cup of the shredded cheese. Spread mixture into bottom of a greased 2-quart square baking dish. Spread with a thin layer of ricotta or cream cheese.

2 Beat together remaining eggs, ¼ cup of the milk, ⅛ teaspoon *salt,* and ⅛ teaspoon *pepper.* In a medium skillet melt 1 tablespoon of the margarine over medium heat; add egg mixture. Cook, without stirring, until mixture begins to set on the bottom and around edge. Using a spatula or a large spoon, lift and fold partially cooked egg mixture so the uncooked portion flows underneath. Continue cooking about 4 minutes or until eggs are cooked through, but are still glossy and moist. Spoon eggs evenly over mixture in dish.

3 In same skillet melt remaining margarine; stir in flour. Add remaining milk and chili peppers; cook and stir until thickened and bubbly. Stir in remaining cheese until melted. Spoon evenly over the eggs. Bake, uncovered, in a 375° oven 25 minutes. Serves 6.

TO MAKE AHEAD

Prepare casserole as directed; cover and chill up to 24 hours. Bake, covered, in a 375° oven for 25 minutes. Uncover and bake for 5 minutes more.

Nutrition facts per serving: 289 cal., 16 g total fat (7 g sat. fat), 203 mg chol., 406 mg sodium, 22 g carbo., 2 g fiber, 16 g pro. *Daily values:* 22% vit. A, 143% vit. C, 23% calcium, 8% iron.

POTATO CRUST VEGETABLE PIZZA

Prep: 20 min. ◆ Bake: 30 min.

Shredded potatoes become the tasty crust for a vegetable-and-cheese-topped pizza.

3 medium baking potatoes, peeled (1 lb.)
1 small onion
1 egg yolk, beaten
2 tsp. all-purpose flour
  Dash salt

◆◆◆

6 tsp. olive oil

◆◆◆

1 cup thinly sliced zucchini
1 cup thinly sliced yellow summer squash
1 small yellow sweet pepper, chopped
1 small red onion, halved and thinly sliced
1 clove garlic, minced

◆◆◆

½ of a 5.3-oz. pkg. soft goat cheese (chèvre)
8 cherry tomatoes, quartered
1 Tbsp. snipped fresh basil
¾ cup shredded mozzarella cheese (4 oz.)
  Fresh basil sprigs (optional)

1 Shred potatoes and onion into a bowl of water; drain well, squeezing out excess moisture. In a medium mixing bowl combine potato mixture, egg yolk, flour, and salt; mix well.

2 In an 11×7×1½-inch baking pan heat 2 teaspoons of the oil in a 500° oven for 1 to 2 minutes. Remove from oven and carefully press potato mixture into bottom and up sides of pan. Brush the top of potato mixture with 2 teaspoons of the oil. Bake in a 500° oven about 30 minutes or until golden brown and crisp.

3 Meanwhile, combine zucchini, yellow squash, yellow pepper, red onion, and garlic. In a large skillet heat remaining oil. Add vegetable mixture and cook until vegetables are crisp-tender, stirring often.

4 Carefully spread goat cheese over potato crust. Top with the cooked vegetables and tomatoes. Sprinkle with snipped basil and mozzarella cheese. If desired, garnish with fresh basil sprigs. Makes 6 to 8 servings.

Nutrition facts per serving: 216 cal., 11 g total fat (4 g sat. fat), 55 mg chol., 169 mg sodium, 21 g carbo., 2 g fiber, 8 g pro. *Daily values:* 11% vit. A, 91% vit. C, 10% calcium, 4% iron.

WASABI MASHED POTATOES

Prep: 15 min. ◆ Cook: 20 min.

Your taste buds will love these mashed spuds that take on a fiery flavor-boost with wasabi—Japanese horseradish. A little dab of the pungent powder or paste will do you, but add more if you really like it hot. (See the photograph on page 40.)

4 medium potatoes (1⅓ lb.)
2 Tbsp. margarine or butter
1 to 2 tsp. wasabi powder or wasabi paste
½ tsp. salt
¼ tsp. pepper
¼ cup milk
  Coarsely ground pepper (optional)

SELECTING AND STORING POTATOES

Choose fresh potatoes with clean, smooth skins, a firm texture, and good shape for the variety. Avoid potatoes with green spots, soft or moldy areas, or wilted skins.

Store fresh potatoes in a well-ventilated, dark place that's cool and humid, but not wet. Lengthy exposure to light will cause greening of the skin, resulting in a bitter flavor. Avoid refrigerating potatoes because they become overly sweet and may darken when cooked. Home freezing of potatoes is not recommended.

1 Peel and quarter potatoes. Cook, covered, in a small amount of boiling salted water for 20 to 25 minutes or until tender; drain.

2 Transfer the potatoes to a large mixing bowl. Mash potatoes with a potato masher or beat with an electric mixer on low speed. Add margarine or butter, wasabi powder or paste, salt, and pepper. Gradually beat in enough of the milk until mixture is light and fluffy. If desired, sprinkle with coarsely ground pepper. Serve potatoes immediately. Makes 4 side-dish servings.

Nutrition facts per serving: 188 cal., 6 g total fat (1 g sat. fat), 1 mg chol., 362 mg sodium, 31 g carbo., 2 g fiber, 3 g pro. *Daily values:* 7% vit. A, 19% vit. C, 2% calcium, 3% iron.

Calabaza (kah-lah-BAH-zah): Spanish for squash, calabaza also is known as West Indian pumpkin. It ranges from cantaloupe- to watermelon-size and has deep orange-yellow flesh with a flavor similar to butternut squash. Prepare it as you would any winter squash.

Celery root: Also known as celeriac, this tuber is cultivated especially for its gnarly-but-nice edible root. It has a mild celerylike flavor and a delightfully crisp texture. Purchase firm, small celery roots because the large roots tend to be woody and tough.

Chipotle (chi-POHT-lay) peppers in adobo sauce: Chipotles are dried smoked jalapeños, typically packed in an adobo sauce made of ground chilies and other seasonings. The combination of spicy adobo sauce with the distinctively smoky peppers makes a fabulous flavor booster for soups, sauces, and stews.

Guava paste: This thick gelatinlike paste, made of pulp from the tropical guava fruit, has a concentrated sweetness. The paste typically is packaged in a round, flat tin and can be found in the gourmet or ethnic sections of grocery stores or in Latin American and Asian markets.

Mexican-style sweet chocolate: Long revered as the key ingredient in making an incredible cup of hot chocolate, Mexican chocolate starts with roasted cocoa beans ground together with cinnamon and sugar. Ground almonds also may be added. The chocolate often is shaped into thick, round blocks and scored in wedges. Find it in Mexican markets.

Mixed peppercorn blend: The spice sections of most grocery stores carry this mix of black, white, red, and/or green peppercorns. Black peppercorns have the strongest flavor; green ones are milder than black; and white peppercorns have a pungent, but subtle flavor. Red and pink "peppercorns" are not really peppercorns, but actually are dried berries with a pepperlike spiciness.

Red bananas: These tropical fruits are popping up in more stores as they gain popularity. They are sweeter, shorter, and chunkier than the typical yellow Cavendish bananas you're used to seeing. Red bananas are best eaten, or used in cooking or baking, when skin is a deep reddish-brown color.

Red chili paste: Red chilies, garlic, vinegar, and other seasonings typically fire up the flavor in this ground paste. The paste can be used as a condiment, like catsup, or stirred into dishes to give them a fiery boost.

Red curry paste: This spicy, salty blend gets its start from ground red chili peppers. The concentrated paste usually is seasoned with lemongrass, shallots, and garlic, along with fish sauce or shrimp sauce. Found in jars in most Asian markets, red curry paste can be used in place of curry powder when making curry sauces.

Udon (oo-DOHN) and soba (SO-buh) noodles: Japanese udon noodles are made from either wheat or corn flour and are shaped round like spaghetti or flat like fettuccine. They're interchangeable with squarish soba noodles made from buckwheat flour. The noodles are available in Asian markets or in ethnic sections of grocery stores.

Wasabi (WAH-sah-bee): Also known as Japanese horseradish, wasabi packs a potent punch. The seasoning comes in two forms: a paste in a tube (like toothpaste) or a fine powder in a small tin or bottle. Both versions are greenish in color and zap the taste buds with a pungent, horseradishlike bite. When stirred into soy sauce, wasabi makes a flavor-packed dipping sauce. You'll find wasabi in Asian sections of large grocery stores or in Asian markets.

Yuca (YOO-kuh): This starchy root vegetable, also called cassava, is not to be confused with yucca (YUH-kuh), the tropical plant that produces white blossoms. The yuca root looks like an elongated potato and can be prepared like potatoes. Be sure to peel yuca's tough brown skin and to remove the woody center string before eating. Store yuca in a cool, dry place for up to 4 days.

YUCA WITH GARLIC AND ROSEMARY

30 MIN. LOW FAT

Prep: 15 min. ◆ Cook: 10 min.

Yuca is a mild-flavored starchy root vegetable with a tough dark skin that is peeled like a potato. Like the potato, yuca can be baked, boiled, dressed up with a sauce, or simmered in a stew. The vegetable's woody center string must be removed before eating. (See the photograph on page 43.)

1 lb. yuca root or medium
    potatoes

❖❖❖

2 cloves garlic, minced
1 Tbsp. margarine or butter
1 tsp. snipped fresh rosemary
    or ¼ tsp. dried rosemary,
    crushed

1 Scrub yuca or potatoes thoroughly with a stiff brush. Peel and cut into 2-inch pieces. If using yuca, remove the fibrous string from the center.

2 In a medium saucepan cook yuca or potatoes, covered, in a small amount of boiling lightly salted water 10 to 12 minutes or until tender; drain. Return yuca or potatoes to saucepan.

3 Meanwhile, in a small skillet cook garlic in margarine or butter over medium heat about 30 seconds. Remove from heat; stir in rosemary. Pour the rosemary mixture over yuca or potatoes, tossing gently to coat. Season to taste with salt and pepper. Makes 4 side-dish servings.

Nutrition facts per serving: 172 cal., 3 g total fat (1 g sat. fat), 0 mg chol., 39 mg sodium, 33 g carbo., 0 g fiber, 4 g pro. *Daily values:* 3% vit. A, 96% vit. C.

**Thai Pork Sandwiches
Au Jus** (see page 30)

◆◆◆

Winter Vegetable Slaw
(see below)

◆◆◆

Pineapple sorbet

◆◆◆

Crisp cookies

ROASTED CALABAZA

LOW FAT

Prep: 15 min. ◆ Bake: 65 min.

Its rich, golden flesh and speckled or striped shell make the calabaza one of those gorgeous vegetables perfect for a still life. And, yes, it tastes as good as it looks. This oversized squash has a flavor similar to other sweet winter squashes. Look for it year-round in Latin markets, or check the produce section of your supermarket for the vegetable. This side dish makes a tasty accompaniment to roasted poultry. (See the photograph on page 42.)

1 3-lb. calabaza

❖❖❖

1 medium onion, cut into
    ½-inch wedges

❖❖❖

2 Tbsp. margarine or butter,
    melted
1 Tbsp. snipped fresh thyme
    or ½ tsp. dried thyme,
    crushed
1 Tbsp. lemon juice
3 cloves garlic, minced
½ tsp. salt
¼ tsp. pepper
⅛ tsp. ground allspice

❖❖❖

Fresh thyme sprigs
    (optional)

1 Cut the calabaza in half and remove the seeds. Cut each portion in half lengthwise; then cut in half crosswise, forming a total of 8 pieces.

2 Place calabaza pieces, cut sides up, in an ungreased 13×9×2-inch rectangular baking dish. Place the onion wedges on top of the calabaza pieces.

3 Stir together the melted margarine or butter, fresh or dried thyme, lemon juice, minced garlic, salt, pepper, and allspice. Drizzle over calabaza and onions.

4 Bake the cabbage and onions, covered, in a 325° oven for 40 minutes. Uncover and continue to bake for 25 to 35 minutes more or until calabaza is just tender. If desired, garnish with sprigs of fresh thyme. Makes 8 side-dish servings.

Nutrition facts per serving: 88 cal., 3 g total fat (1 g sat. fat), 0 mg chol., 173 mg sodium, 16 g carbo., 3 g fiber, 2 g pro. *Daily values:* 103% vit. A, 38% vit. C, 5% calcium, 6% iron.

WINTER VEGETABLE SLAW

Prep: 15 min. ◆ Chill: 2 to 24 hr.

Celery root has a garden-fresh flavor with a mild celery taste. Just peel off the root's tough outer layer and shred the rest as you would carrots.

3 cups packaged shredded
    cabbage with carrot
    (coleslaw mix)
2 cups coarsely shredded
    celery root
¼ cup sliced green onions

2 Tbsp. salad oil
4 tsp. rice vinegar
1 Tbsp. sugar
1½ tsp. toasted sesame oil
1 tsp. soy sauce
½ tsp. dry mustard

1 In a large bowl stir together the shredded cabbage with carrot, celery root, and green onions. Set aside.

2 For dressing, in a screw-top jar combine salad oil, rice vinegar, sugar, sesame oil, soy sauce, and dry mustard. Cover and shake well. Pour dressing over coleslaw mixture. Toss lightly to coat. Cover and chill 2 to 24 hours. If desired, serve slaw with Thai Pork Sandwiches au Jus (see page 30). Makes 4 to 6 side-dish servings.

Nutrition facts per serving: 120 cal., 9 g total fat (1 g sat. fat), 0 chol., 154 mg sodium, 11 g carbo., 2 g fiber, 1 g pro. *Daily values:* 54% vit. A, 53% vit. C, 4% calcium, 5% iron.

VEGETABLE SALAD WITH CHIPOTLE VINAIGRETTE
Prep: 20 min. ◆ Chill: 4 to 24 hr.

You'll get a sensational surprise with each bite of this fresh-tasting veggie combo; the sweet-hot dressing awakens the taste buds.

1 15-oz. can black beans, rinsed and drained
1 8¾-oz. can whole kernel corn, drained
½ cup thin bite-size strips peeled jicama
½ cup chopped green sweet pepper

WHAT'S A MANDOLINE?

The mandoline (MAHN-duh-lihn), long appreciated by cooking professionals, is a small, manually operated slicing tool. Its adjustable blades enable a cook to slice, shred, julienne, and waffle-cut hard-to-cut vegetables and fruits, such as potatoes, carrots, and apples, with uniformity and precision.
◆ Resembling a washboard, a mandoline's long, rectangular body is made of plastic, wood, or stainless steel. This tool is available in a range of qualities and prices. Simple models have a single blade; more expensive models have two blades of different thicknesses or the capacity to adjust the blades for a range of thicknesses. A lid with a knob on a metal carriage glides on tracks, protecting your hand from the blades.
◆ Because each one has slight variations, follow the manufacturer's directions for using and cleaning your mandoline.

4 red pearl onions, thinly sliced or ¼ cup chopped red onion
◆◆◆
2 to 3 canned chipotle peppers in adobo sauce*
3 Tbsp. salad oil
3 Tbsp. vinegar
2 Tbsp. snipped fresh cilantro
2 Tbsp. lime juice

2 tsp. snipped fresh oregano or ½ tsp. dried oregano, crushed
¼ tsp. garlic salt
◆◆◆
Torn mixed salad greens
Chipotle-flavored tostada chips or tortilla chips (optional)

1 In a large bowl stir together the black beans, corn, jicama strips, green pepper, and onions. Set aside.

2 For vinaigrette, in a food processor bowl or blender container combine chipotle peppers, salad oil, vinegar, cilantro, lime juice, oregano, and garlic salt. Cover and process or blend until smooth. Pour vinaigrette over bean mixture. Toss lightly to coat. Cover and chill salad for 4 to 24 hours, stirring occasionally.

3 To serve, line 4 shallow bowls or salad plates with torn mixed greens. Divide bean mixture among the greens-lined bowls or plates. If desired, serve with tostada chips or tortilla chips. Makes 4 servings.

***Note:** If canned chipotle peppers are not available, use 2 to 3 dried chipotle peppers. Cut open and discard stems and seeds. Cut peppers into pieces. Place in a small bowl and cover with boiling water. Let stand 45 to 60 minutes to soften; drain well.

Nutrition facts per serving: 223 cal., 11 g total fat (2 g sat. fat), 0 mg chol., 603 mg sodium, 30 g carbo., 6 g fiber, 9 g pro. *Daily values:* 12% vit. A, 60% vit. C, 4% calcium, 13% iron.

ASIAN CHICKEN NOODLE SOUP

Prep: 15 min. ◆ Cook: 10 min.

Japanese udon and soba noodles traditionally are cooked and served cold with dipping sauces. In this twist on tradition, we've added miso (MEE-soh)—fermented soybean paste—which is rich in flavor, protein, and B vitamins. Find refrigerated miso in health food stores or Asian markets.

2 14½-oz. cans reduced-
    sodium chicken broth
1 cup water
3 oz. udon or soba noodles,
    broken in half (1 cup)

◆◆◆

1 medium red sweet pepper,
    bias-sliced into bite-size
    strips (½ cup)
⅓ cup sliced green onions
1 Tbsp. white miso
1 tsp. grated fresh ginger
⅛ tsp. crushed red pepper
1½ cups chopped cooked
    chicken or turkey
1 cup fresh snow pea pods,
    halved crosswise, or ½ of a
    6-oz. pkg. frozen snow pea
    pods, thawed and halved
    crosswise
    Crushed red pepper
    (optional)

1 In a large saucepan combine chicken broth and water. Bring to boiling. Add noodles. Return to boiling; reduce heat. Simmer, covered, for 6 minutes.

2 Stir the sweet pepper, green onions, miso, fresh ginger, and the ⅛ teaspoon crushed red pepper into the noodle mixture in saucepan. Add chicken or turkey. Return to boiling; reduce heat. Simmer, covered, for 3 minutes. Stir in pea pods. Simmer, uncovered, for 1 minute more or until pea pods are crisp-tender. Ladle soup into bowls. If desired, garnish with crushed red pepper. Makes 4 servings.

Nutrition facts per serving: 225 cal., 6 g total fat (1 g sat. fat), 51 mg chol., 957 mg sodium, 22 g carbo., 2 g fiber, 23 g pro. *Daily values:* 16% vit. A, 75% vit. C, 2% calcium, 13% iron.

PLUM-GLAZED CHILI CHICKEN

Prep: 10 min. ◆ Bake: 45 min.

This family-friendly dish gets a lift with a kicky sauce that includes red chili paste—a spicy blend of ground dried or fresh red chili peppers—and grated gingerroot. Add steamed vegetables and Wasabi Mashed Potatoes (see page 26) for a jazzed-up version of a comfy Sunday supper.
(See the photograph on page 40.)

2½ to 3 lb. meaty chicken pieces
⅓ cup finely chopped green
    onions
2 Tbsp. soy sauce
1 Tbsp. red chili paste
1½ tsp. grated fresh ginger
¼ tsp. garlic salt

◆◆◆

½ cup plum jam
    Green onion strips
    (optional)

1 Rinse chicken; pat dry with paper towels. Arrange chicken pieces in a 15×10×1-inch baking pan, making sure the pieces do not touch. Combine finely chopped green onions, soy sauce, red chili paste, fresh ginger, and garlic salt. Brush the surface of chicken with 2 tablespoons of the mixture. Bake in a 400° oven for 30 minutes.

2 Meanwhile, stir the remaining chili paste mixture into the plum jam. Brush about *half* of the mixture over the chicken. Return chicken to oven; bake for 15 to 20 minutes more or until golden brown and chicken is no longer pink. Heat remaining plum jam mixture. Spoon over chicken before serving. If desired, garnish with green onion strips. Makes 4 to 6 servings.

Nutrition facts per serving: 457 cal., 18 g total fat (5 g sat. fat), 130 mg chol., 885 mg sodium, 30 g carbo., 0 g fiber, 43 g pro. *Daily values:* 6% vit. A, 2% vit. C, 3% calcium, 18% iron.

THAI PORK SANDWICHES AU JUS

Prep: 15 min. ◆ Marinate: 6 to 24 hr.
Roast: 25 min. ◆ Chill: up to 24 hr.

You can roast and slice the pork tenderloin in advance, then assemble the sandwiches the next day if you wish. These hearty sandwiches are great to serve during a break from playing board games or cards on a Sunday afternoon.

1 12-oz. pork tenderloin
¼ cup water
¼ cup reduced-sodium soy
    sauce
¼ cup packed brown sugar
2 Tbsp. red curry paste
2 tsp. bottled minced garlic
1½ tsp. grated fresh ginger
½ tsp. toasted sesame oil

4 French-style rolls, split
1 recipe Winter Vegetable Slaw
(see page 28) (optional)

1 Place pork tenderloin in a heavy plastic bag set in a shallow dish. For marinade, combine water, soy sauce, brown sugar, red curry paste, garlic, grated fresh ginger, and sesame oil. Pour marinade over pork. Close bag; turn to coat meat with marinade. Refrigerate overnight, turning the bag occasionally.

2 Drain pork, reserving marinade. Cover and chill marinade. Place pork on a rack in a shallow roasting pan; cover with foil. Roast in a 425° oven for 15 minutes. Remove foil; roast for 10 to 15 minutes more or until meat thermometer inserted in center registers 160°. Cool slightly; bias-slice into very thin slices. Cover and chill up to 24 hours.

3 To serve, bring marinade to boiling. Add pork slices. Return to boiling; reduce heat. Simmer, uncovered, about 5 minutes or until heated through. Remove pork slices from marinade; arrange on rolls. If desired, top with Winter Vegetable Slaw and serve with individual dishes of marinade for dipping. Makes 4 servings.

Nutrition facts per serving (without slaw): 299 cal., 7 g total fat (2 g sat. fat), 60 mg chol., 650 mg sodium, 33 g carbo., 0 g fiber, 24 g pro.
Daily values: 5% calcium, 20% iron.

Menu

**Guava Barbecued Beef
(see below)**

♦ ♦ ♦

**Roasted Calabaza
(see page 28)**

♦ ♦ ♦

Crusty bread

♦ ♦ ♦

**Salad of mixed greens with
grapefruit sections**

♦ ♦ ♦

**Aztec Chocolate Flans
(see page 45)**

GUAVA BARBECUED BEEF

Prep: 20 min. ♦ Roast: 1¾ hr.
Stand: 15 min.

A winter meal will be especially memorable when the star is a succulent beef roast accompanied by a tropical-inspired sweet 'n' sour barbecue sauce. The sauce goes well with beef ribs or pork ribs, too. (See the photograph on page 42.)

1 2- to 3-lb. beef eye of round
   roast
   Salt and pepper

♦ ♦ ♦

¾ cup unsweetened pineapple
   juice
¾ cup catsup
½ cup guava paste
⅓ cup vinegar
1 Tbsp. brown sugar
2 tsp. prepared horseradish
2 tsp. grated fresh ginger
2 cloves garlic, minced
⅛ tsp. salt
⅛ tsp. ground red pepper

♦ ♦ ♦

   Fresh thyme sprigs
   (optional)

1 Trim fat from meat. Sprinkle the meat with salt and pepper. Place meat on a rack in a shallow roasting pan. Insert a meat thermometer. Roast, uncovered, in a 325° oven for 1¼ hours.

2 Meanwhile, for sauce, in a food processor bowl or blender container combine the unsweetened pineapple juice, catsup, guava paste, vinegar, brown sugar, horseradish, grated ginger, garlic, ⅛ teaspoon salt, and ground red pepper. Cover and process or blend until mixture is smooth. Transfer to a medium saucepan. Bring to boiling; reduce heat. Boil gently, uncovered, about 20 minutes or until desired consistency, stirring occasionally.

3 Brush some of the sauce over meat. Roast 30 to 45 minutes more or until thermometer registers 155° for medium, brushing occasionally with the sauce. Cover with foil; let stand for 15 minutes before carving. (The meat's internal temperature will rise 5° during standing.)

4 Thinly slice meat across the grain. Arrange meat on a platter. Bring remaining sauce to boiling; pour some on top of sliced meat. If desired, garnish with fresh thyme. Pass remaining sauce. Makes 8 to 10 servings.

Nutrition facts per serving: 228 cal., 4 g total fat (1 g sat. fat), 54 mg chol., 408 mg sodium, 28 g carbo., 2 g fiber, 21 g pro.
Daily values: 4% vit. A, 21% vit. C, 1% calcium, 19% iron.

LAMB CHOPS AU POIVRE

Prep: 15 min. ◆ Broil: 10 min.

When you're in a hurry for a fancy feast, this entrée definitely impresses. The secret lies in the mixed peppercorn blend found in the spice or gourmet sections of supermarkets. (See the photograph on page 43.)

8 lamb rib or loin chops, cut 1 inch thick (about 2 lb. total)

◆◆◆

1½ to 2 tsp. dried whole mixed peppercorns
3 Tbsp. coarse-grain brown mustard
1 Tbsp. snipped fresh rosemary or ½ tsp. dried rosemary, crushed
1 clove garlic, minced

⅓ cup soft bread crumbs
Fresh rosemary sprigs (optional)

1 Trim fat from meat. Using a sharp knife, cut a pocket in the fatty side of the meat, cutting almost to the bone.

2 Crush peppercorns with a mortar and pestle. (Or, place in a plastic bag; seal and crush peppercorns with the flat side of a mallet.) In a small bowl combine crushed peppercorns, brown mustard, rosemary, and garlic. Spread about ½ teaspoon of the mustard mixture in the pocket of each chop. Reserve the remaining mustard mixture.

3 Place lamb chops on the unheated rack of a broiler pan. Broil 3 to 4 inches from heat for 5 minutes.

4 Meanwhile, stir bread crumbs into remaining mustard mixture. Turn chops. Broil 2 minutes more. Spread some of the crumb mixture evenly over each chop. Broil for 3 to 4 minutes more for medium doneness. If desired, garnish with fresh rosemary sprigs. Makes 4 servings.

Nutrition facts per serving: 291 cal., 16 g total fat (5 g sat. fat), 103 mg chol., 267 mg sodium, 3 g carbo., 0 g fiber, 33 g pro. *Daily values:* 2% vit. C, 3% calcium, 20% iron.

INDIAN-STYLE RICE PUDDING

Prep: 10 min. ◆ Cook: 30 min.
Cool: 30 min.

Basmati rice works best for authentic Indian rice pudding. Once only available in specialty stores, basmati—or its Texas cousin Texmati—now can be found in many supermarkets.

3 cups milk
⅓ cup basmati or long grain rice

◆◆◆

⅓ cup snipped dried apricots
¼ cup sugar
3 Tbsp. sliced almonds, toasted
1 tsp. rose water or ½ tsp. vanilla
¼ tsp. ground cinnamon
¼ tsp. ground cardamom
2 Tbsp. chopped pistachio nuts, cashews, or almonds
Warm milk (optional)

1 In a heavy medium saucepan bring the 3 cups milk just to boiling; stir in rice. Reduce heat. Cook, covered, over low heat for 30 to 35 minutes or until most of the milk is absorbed, stirring occasionally. (Mixture may appear curdled.) For a thicker pudding, simmer, uncovered, 5 minutes more. Remove from heat.

2 Stir in apricots, sugar, sliced almonds, rose water or vanilla, cinnamon, and cardamom. Cool 30 minutes. Spoon into dessert cups; sprinkle with chopped nuts. If desired, serve with warm milk. Makes 6 servings.

Nutrition facts per serving: 220 cal., 6 g total fat (2 g sat. fat), 11 mg chol., 75 mg sodium, 34 g carbo., 2 g fiber, 8 g pro. *Daily values:* 15% vit. A, 3% vit. C, 17% calcium, 10% iron.

"Be Mine" Lollipops*

30 MIN. NO FAT

Prep: 20 min. ◆ Bake: 6 to 8 min.

Cupid himself would be smitten with these sweetheart sweets. They're easy to make and oh-so-fun to give. Bundle up a bouquet or give them one at a time—either way, there's no better way to say, "Be my valentine."

2½- to 3½-inch round or heart-shaped metal cookie cutters

8 oz. assorted red, pink, and/or clear hard candies

◆◆◆

35 to 60 (2 to 3 oz.) assorted small decorative candies, such as red cinnamon candies, small nonpareils, colored candy hearts, spice drops, and gumdrops

Edible rose petals or other flower petals (optional)

◆◆◆

Lollipop sticks

1 Place unwrapped hard candies in a heavy plastic bag. Place the bag on top of a folded towel and crush candies into small chunks using a meat mallet or small hammer.

2 Make only 3 or 4 lollipops at a time. Line a baking sheet with foil. Place the desired cookie cutters on foil, at least 2 inches apart. Divide the crushed candies evenly among cutters, approximately 1½ to 2 tablespoons per lollipop (a). The candy layer should be ¼ to ½ inch thick. Add small decorative candies or edible rose or other flower petals to crushed candies. (If using flower petals, make sure they are covered with a layer of the crushed candy.)

(a) Fill inside of desired cookie cutters with coarsely crushed candies.

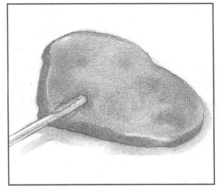

(c) Quickly attach a stick to the base of each melted shape, quickly twisting the stick to cover the end with the melted candy.

3 Bake in a 350° oven for 6 to 8 minutes or until the candies are completely melted. Cool 30 seconds. Remove cookie cutters with tongs (b), allowing melted candy to spread slightly.

4 Quickly attach a stick to the base of each lollipop, twisting the stick to cover lollipop end with melted candy (c). If desired, press more small candies or flower petals into hot lollipops (d). Cool. Peel the foil from lollipops. Makes 8 lollipops.

(b) After melting hard candies in the oven, cool 30 seconds. Then, use tongs to remove cookie cutters, allowing candy to spread.

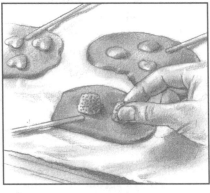

(d) Gently place small candies, colored hearts, and gumdrops on top of melted candy shapes. Allow to cool thoroughly.

*Note: These lollipops are not intended for children under age 3. To prevent children from choking, the Consumer Product Safety Commission says children under age 3 shouldn't handle anything smaller than 2¼×1¼×1¼ inches.

Nutrition facts per lollipop: 137 cal., 0 g total fat (0 g sat. fat), 0 mg chol., 11 mg sodium, 35 g carbo., 0 g fiber, 0 g pro. *Daily values:* 4% iron.

RASPBERRY MERINGUE HEARTS

Prep: 30 min. ◆ Bake: 35 min.
Stand in oven: 1 hr.

*These crispy hearts can be baked a day
ahead. Simply store them overnight in
an airtight container.
(See the photograph on page 44.)*

3 egg whites
1 tsp. vanilla
¼ tsp. cream of tartar
Dash salt
1 cup sugar
⅓ cup very finely chopped
    toasted almonds
    ◆◆◆
3 cups fresh or frozen loose-
    pack raspberries
    ◆◆◆
¼ cup seedless raspberry
    preserves
1 tsp. cornstarch
    ◆◆◆
3 cups raspberry, lemon, or
    papaya sorbet or vanilla or
    chocolate frozen yogurt
⅓ cup sliced almonds, toasted
    Fresh raspberries (optional)

1 Let egg whites stand in a
large mixing bowl at room temperature for 30 minutes. Add the
vanilla, cream of tartar, and salt to
egg whites. Beat with an electric
mixer on medium speed until soft
peaks form (tips curl). Add sugar,
a tablespoon at a time, beating
about 7 minutes on high speed or
until stiff peaks form (tips stand
straight) and sugar is almost dissolved. Fold in very finely
chopped almonds.

2 Cover a large baking sheet
with clean plain brown paper or
parchment paper. Draw six
4-inch-long heart shapes on
paper. Using a pastry bag fitted
with a large star tip, pipe the
meringue onto the hearts on the
paper, building the sides up to
form shells. (Or, use the back of a
spoon to spread the meringue
over the hearts, building up the
sides.) Bake in a 300° oven for
35 minutes. Turn off oven. Let
shells dry in oven, with door
closed, for at least 1 hour.
Remove from paper.

3 Meanwhile, thaw berries, if
frozen. Do not drain. Place half of
the berries in a blender container
or food processor bowl. Cover
and blend or process until berries
are smooth. Press berries through
a fine-mesh sieve; discard seeds.
Repeat with remaining berries.
(Should have about 1¼ cups.)

4 In a medium saucepan stir
together sieved berries, preserves,
and cornstarch. Cook and stir
over medium heat until thickened
and bubbly. Cook and stir for
2 minutes more. Remove from
heat. Cool to room temperature.

5 To serve, scoop sorbet or
frozen yogurt into meringue
hearts. Spoon berry sauce atop.
Sprinkle with sliced almonds. If
desired, garnish with additional
fresh raspberries. Serves 6.

Nutrition facts per serving: 425 cal., 10 g
total fat (2 g sat. fat), 5 mg chol., 84 mg
sodium, 83 g carbo., 4 g fiber, 6 g pro.
Daily values: 2% vit. A, 33% vit. C, 9%
calcium, 7% iron.

LEMON MACAROON TART

Prep: 30 min. ◆ Bake: 15 min.
Chill: at least 2 hr.

1 cup all-purpose flour
⅓ cup cold butter
¼ cup finely chopped toasted
    almonds
¼ cup coconut, toasted
1 beaten egg yolk
2 to 3 Tbsp. cold water
    ◆◆◆
2 beaten eggs
⅔ cup whipping cream
¼ cup sugar
1½ tsp. finely shredded lemon
    peel
¼ cup lemon juice
    ◆◆◆
⅓ cup whipping cream
2 tsp. sugar
1 8-oz. carton lemon-flavored
    yogurt
    ◆◆◆
    **Blueberries, raspberries,
    and/or sliced strawberries**

1 In a medium mixing bowl
place flour. Using a pastry
blender, cut butter into flour
until pieces are pea-size. Stir in
finely chopped almonds and
coconut. Stir together egg yolk
and 1 tablespoon of the cold
water. Gradually stir egg yolk
mixture into flour mixture. Add
remaining water until all the
dough is moistened. Gently
knead the dough just until a ball
forms. If necessary, cover dough
with plastic wrap and refrigerate
for 30 to 60 minutes or until
dough is easy to handle.

2 On a lightly floured surface,
use your hands to slightly flatten
the dough. Roll dough from the
center to edges into a circle

11 inches in diameter. Carefully transfer pastry to a 9-inch tart pan with removable bottom. Press pastry into fluted sides of pan. Trim edges. Line pastry with a double thickness of foil. Bake in a 450° oven for 8 minutes. Remove foil. Bake for 4 minutes more. Cool pastry in pan on a wire rack. Reduce oven temperature to 375°.

3 For filling, in a medium mixing bowl stir together the whole eggs, ⅔ cup whipping cream, ¼ cup sugar, lemon peel, and lemon juice. Pour into baked crust. Bake in a 375° oven about 15 minutes or until set. Cool on a wire rack. Remove sides of pan; transfer to serving platter. Chill at least 2 hours.

4 In a small mixing bowl beat together ⅓ cup whipping cream and 2 teaspoons sugar until soft peaks form. Fold in yogurt.

5 To serve, cut tart into wedges. Top each wedge with fresh berries and yogurt mixture. Makes 8 servings.

Nutrition facts per serving: 366 cal., 24 g total fat (13 g sat. fat), 142 mg chol., 131 mg sodium, 33 g carbo., 2 g fiber, 7 g pro. *Daily values:* 27% vit. A, 15% vit. C, 7% calcium, 8% iron.

BLACK TIE CHEESECAKE

Prep: 30 min. ◆ Bake: 35 min.
Chill: at least 4 hr.

See the photograph on page 42.

1¾ cups finely crushed
    chocolate wafers
    (about 33)
⅓ cup butter, melted

TEST KITCHEN TIP

TESTING THE DONENESS OF CHEESECAKE

Test cheesecake for doneness at the minimum baking time to avoid overbaking, which dries out the cake and causes the center to fall. Gently shake the pan rather than inserting a knife which may start a crack in the cake. The center of the cheesecake should appear nearly set. A 1-inch portion in the center may jiggle slightly even when the cheesecake is done. (If the cheesecake contains sour cream, a slightly larger portion in the center will seem unset but will firm upon cooling.)

3 8-oz. pkg. cream cheese,
    softened
1 cup sugar
2 Tbsp. all-purpose flour
½ tsp. almond or mint extract
2 egg yolks
1 egg
¼ cup half-and-half or light
    cream
1 6-oz. pkg. white chocolate
    baking bars, chopped

◆◆◆

2 Tbsp. light-colored corn
    syrup
1 Tbsp. water
1 Tbsp. butter or margarine
½ cup semisweet chocolate
    pieces
    Whipped cream (optional)
    Chocolate bow ties
    (optional)*

1 For crust, combine cookie crumbs and the ⅓ cup melted butter. Press crumb mixture onto bottom and 2 inches up sides of a 9-inch springform pan. Set aside.

2 For filling, in a large mixing bowl beat cream cheese, sugar, flour, and extract with an electric mixer until combined. Add egg yolks and whole egg all at once, beating on low speed just until combined. Stir in half-and-half and chopped white chocolate.

3 Pour filling into crust-lined pan. Place on a shallow baking pan in oven. Bake in a 375° oven for 35 to 40 minutes or until center appears nearly set when shaken. Cool in pan on a wire rack for 15 minutes. Loosen the crust from sides of pan and cool for 30 minutes more. Remove the sides of the pan; cool cheesecake completely. Cover and chill at least 4 hours before serving.

4 Heat corn syrup, water, and the 1 tablespoon butter until butter melts and mixture just boils. Pour over chocolate pieces in a small bowl; let stand 1 minute. Stir until smooth. Spread over top of cheesecake. Chill 5 to 10 minutes or until chocolate is set. If desired, garnish with whipped cream and bow ties*. Serves 16.

*Note: To make bow ties, melt 3 ounces semisweet chocolate and 1½ teaspoons shortening. Pipe bow tie shapes onto waxed paper. Let stand until set.

Nutrition facts per serving: 405 cal., 28 g total fat (16 g sat. fat), 104 mg chol., 265 mg sodium, 35 g carbo., 0 g fiber, 6 g pro. *Daily values:* 27% vit. A, 5% calcium, 9% iron.

CHOCOLATE-RASPBERRY CHEESECAKE

Prep: 40 min. ◆ Bake: 50 min.
Chill: At least 4 hr.

Two favorite flavors—chocolate and raspberry—meld like magic in this two-layer dessert.
(See the photograph on page 37.)

1½ **cups finely crushed graham crackers**
¼ **cup sifted powdered sugar**
⅓ **cup butter, melted**
2 **cups fresh or frozen loose-pack raspberries, thawed**
½ **tsp. granulated sugar**

◆◆◆

3 **8-oz. pkg. cream cheese, softened**
1 **14-oz. can (1¼ cups) sweetened condensed milk**
4 **eggs**
1 **tsp. vanilla**
1 **6-oz. pkg. semisweet chocolate pieces (1 cup), melted and cooled**

1 For crust, combine crackers and powdered sugar; stir in melted butter. Press onto bottom and 2 inches up the sides of a 9-inch springform pan. Set aside. In a bowl, stir together 1 cup of the raspberries and the granulated sugar; set aside.

2 For filling, in a large bowl beat cream cheese and condensed milk with an electric mixer until combined. Add eggs and vanilla; beat just until combined. Divide batter in half. Stir melted chocolate into half of batter. Pour chocolate batter into crust-lined

pan. Stir raspberry mixture into the remaining batter. Spoon raspberry batter over chocolate batter.

3 Place on a shallow baking pan. Bake in a 350° oven for 50 to 60 minutes or until center appears nearly set when shaken. Cool in pan on a wire rack for 15 minutes. Loosen crust from sides of pan and cool 30 minutes. Remove sides of pan; cool cake completely. Cover and chill at least 4 hours. Serve with remaining raspberries. Makes 16 servings.

Nutrition facts per serving: 382 cal., 26 g total fat (14 g sat. fat), 119 mg chol., 257 mg sodium, 32 g carbo., 8 g pro.
Daily values: 27% vit. A, 7% vit. C, 10% calcium, 9% iron.

RED BANANA UPSIDE-DOWN CAKE

Prep: 25 min. ◆ Bake: 35 min.

The produce sections of most supermarkets now are carrying the honey-scented red bananas, which are typically imported from Jamaica. But, other bananas also are wonderful in this gently spiced cake with its fruity upside-down topping.
(See the photograph on page 37.)

2 **Tbsp. butter or margarine**
¼ **cup cream of coconut**
2 **ripe red bananas or 2 firm large bananas, peeled and bias-sliced ¼ inch thick**

◆◆◆

1½ **cups all-purpose flour**
½ **cup sugar**
¾ **tsp. ground ginger**
½ **tsp. baking soda**
½ **tsp. baking powder**
¼ **tsp. ground allspice**
½ **cup buttermilk**

¼ **cup butter or margarine, softened**
¼ **cup cream of coconut**
1 **egg**

◆◆◆

Coconut curls, toasted*
(optional)

1 Melt the 2 tablespoons butter or margarine in a 9×1½-inch round baking pan. Stir in the ¼ cup cream of coconut. Arrange sliced bananas in the bottom of the baking pan. Set pan aside.

2 In a medium mixing bowl stir together flour, sugar, ginger, baking soda, baking powder, and allspice. Add buttermilk, the ¼ cup butter or margarine, and the ¼ cup cream of coconut. Beat with an electric mixer on low to medium speed about 30 seconds or until combined. Then beat the batter on high speed for 2 minutes, scraping sides of bowl occasionally. Add the egg and beat for 2 minutes more. Spoon the batter into the prepared pan.

3 Bake in a 350° oven about 35 minutes or until a wooden toothpick inserted near the center of the cake comes out clean. Cool the cake in the pan on a wire rack for 5 minutes. Loosen sides; invert the cake onto a serving plate. If desired, garnish with toasted coconut curls. Serve warm. Makes 8 servings.

***Note:** Coconut curls can be purchased at many Asian markets.

Nutrition facts per serving: 349 cal., 19 g total fat (8 g sat. fat), 50 mg chol., 218 mg sodium, 41 g carbo., 1 g fiber, 4 g pro.
Daily values: 9% vit. A, 4% vit. C, 4% calcium, 9% iron.

Top: *Chocolate-Raspberry Cheesecake (page 36)*
Above: *Red Banana Upside-Down Cake (page 36)*

Top: *Right-Bite Finger Sandwiches (page 12)*
Above left: *Vegetable Ribbon Meatballs (page 13), Petite Spring Rolls (page 14)*
Above right: *Quick-Fix Focaccia Wedges (page 12)*

Top: *Crepe Party Purses (page 11)*
Above left: *Mandarin Beef Buns (page 14)*
Above right: *Portobello Pizzettas (page 12)*

Left: *Plum-Glazed Chili Chicken (page 30), Wasabi Mashed Potatoes (page 26)*
Top: *Butternut Squash Compote (page 19)*
Above: *Torn Turkey and Phyllo Pie (page 18)*

Top: *Black Tie Cheesecake (page 35)*
Above: *Guava Barbecued Beef (page 31), Roasted Calabaza (page 28)*
Page 43: *Lamb Chops au Poivre (page 32), Yuca with Garlic and Rosemary (page 28)*

Left: *Raspberry Meringue Hearts (page 34)*
Below: *Aztec Chocolate Flans (page 45)*

AZTEC CHOCOLATE FLANS

Prep: 20 min. ◆ Bake: 30 min.

Mexican chocolate is grainier than most chocolate. If you'd like to take that texture out of your flans, strain the warm chocolate mixture through cheesecloth. (See the photograph on page 44.)

1½ **cups milk**
3 **oz. coarsely chopped Mexican-style sweet chocolate (about ¾ cup)**
2 **inches stick cinnamon**

◆◆◆

⅓ **cup sugar**

◆◆◆

3 **eggs**
⅓ **cup sugar**

◆◆◆

1 **recipe Mexican Chocolate Sauce (see right)**

◆◆◆

Sliced almonds
Orange slices and orange peel (optional)

1 In a heavy medium saucepan combine milk, chocolate, and stick cinnamon. Cook over medium heat until mixture simmers. Remove stick cinnamon; discard. Remove saucepan from heat; set aside.

2 Meanwhile, to caramelize sugar, in a heavy 8-inch skillet cook ⅓ cup sugar over medium-high heat until the sugar begins to melt, shaking the skillet occasionally to heat sugar evenly. Do not stir. Once the sugar starts to melt, reduce heat to low and cook about 5 minutes more or until all of the sugar is melted and golden, stirring as needed with a wooden spoon. Immediately divide the caramelized sugar among four 6-ounce custard cups or ramekins; tilt custard cups or ramekins to coat bottoms of the cups evenly. Let stand 10 minutes.

3 In a large mixing bowl use a rotary beater or wire whisk to lightly beat eggs just until mixed. (Pour chocolate mixture through a strainer lined with 100-percent cotton cheesecloth into a large glass measure, if desired.) Stir chocolate mixture and ⅓ cup sugar into beaten eggs. Beat until well combined but not foamy.

4 Place the custard cups or ramekins in a 2-quart square baking dish on an oven rack. Divide the chocolate mixture evenly among custard cups or ramekins. Pour boiling water into baking dish around custard cups or ramekins to a depth of 1 inch. Bake in a 325° oven for 30 to 35 minutes or until set in centers.

5 Remove cups or ramekins from water. Cool slightly on a wire rack. Cover and chill. To unmold flans, loosen edges with a knife, slipping the point of the knife down the sides to let air in. Invert a dessert plate over each flan; turn custard cup or ramekin and plate over together. Remove cup or ramekin. Drizzle Mexican Chocolate Sauce on top.

FOR SUCCESSFUL FLANS

The secret to a smooth flan is in how you beat the eggs. Using a rotary beater or wire whisk, beat the eggs just until the yolks and whites are blended. Don't beat until foamy or your flan will have bubbles on the surface.

You may be tempted to skip the hot water bath when you're baking flan or custard, but don't. The hot water evens out the heat from the oven so the custard bakes slowly without overcooking the edges.

Once the flans are done, remove them from the water immediately. A jar lifter used for canning makes a wonderful tool for removing the custard cups or ramekins from the boiling water bath.

6 Sprinkle each flan with a few sliced almonds. If desired, garnish with orange slices and orange peel. Makes 4 servings.

Mexican Chocolate Sauce: In a heavy small saucepan melt 1 ounce (¼ cup) grated Mexican-style sweet chocolate over low heat just until melted. Gradually stir in ⅓ cup whipping cream. Cook and stir over medium heat about 3 minutes or until mixture is well combined. Remove from heat. Cool slightly. Makes ½ cup.

Nutrition facts per serving: 441 cal., 23 g total fat (13 g sat. fat), 194 mg chol., 102 mg sodium, 56 g carbo., 2 g fiber, 9 g pro. *Daily values:* 21% vit. A, 1% vit. C, 12% calcium, 8% iron.

CHOCOLATE-PEANUT MOUSSE PIE

Prep: 1¼ hr. ◆ Bake: 5 min.
Chill: 4 to 24 hr.

Your most-special valentines will enjoy sampling this decadent dessert.

1¼ cups crushed chocolate
  graham crackers
3 Tbsp. sugar
⅓ cup butter or margarine,
  melted

◆◆◆

3¾ cups whipping cream
4 oz. bittersweet chocolate,
  finely chopped (about
  ¾ cup)
1 cup chopped peanuts

◆◆◆

1⅓ cups peanut-butter-flavored
  pieces

◆◆◆

Chocolate curls (optional)

1 For crust, combine graham crackers and sugar; stir in butter. Spread onto bottom and up sides of a 9-inch pie plate. Bake in a 375° oven for 5 minutes; cool.

2 Meanwhile, in a saucepan combine ¾ cup of the whipping cream and the chocolate. Stir over low heat until mixture is smooth. Stir in ¾ cup of the peanuts. Pour half the chocolate mixture over crust. Place in freezer and chill about 20 minutes or until set. Transfer to the refrigerator. Cover and refrigerate the remaining chocolate mixture.

3 In another saucepan combine 1 cup of the whipping cream and the peanut butter pieces. Stir over low heat until mixture is smooth. Chill in refrigerator about 30 minutes or until cool but not stiff, stirring occasionally.

4 In a chilled bowl beat the remaining 2 cups whipping cream with chilled beaters on medium speed until soft peaks form. Fold about one-third of the whipped cream into the peanut butter mixture; gently fold in remaining whipped cream. Spoon 2½ cups of the mixture over the chocolate in crust. Place in the freezer for 15 minutes or until set. (Cover and refrigerate remaining peanut butter mixture.) Spread remaining chocolate mixture over peanut butter mixture. Pipe or spoon remaining peanut butter mixture around edge of pie. Sprinkle with remaining nuts. If desired, garnish with chocolate curls. Chill at least 4 hours or overnight. Serves 16.

Nutrition facts per serving: 410 cal., 36 g total fat (20 g sat. fat), 87 mg chol., 185 mg sodium, 20 g carbo., 7 g pro.
Daily values: 28% vit. A, 5% calcium, 5% iron.

SWEET DESSERT BRUSCHETTA

Start to finish: 10 min.

6 slices (about ¾ inch thick)
  Italian country bread or
  crusty sourdough bread
½ cup chocolate hazelnut
  spread*
3 Tbsp. chopped hazelnuts
3 Tbsp. brown sugar

3 medium bananas, thinly
  bias-sliced
2 Tbsp. butter or margarine,
  melted

1 Toast bread and let cool; spread with chocolate hazelnut spread. Combine nuts and sugar; set aside. Layer banana slices on top of spread. Brush banana with melted butter or margarine. Top with 1 tablespoon nut mixture.

2 Broil bruschetta 5 inches from heat 30 seconds or until bananas just begin to glaze and nuts are toasted. If desired, garnish serving plate with sifted *unsweetened cocoa powder, chocolate curls,* and *white chocolate curls.* Makes 6 bruschetta.

***Note:** Chocolate hazelnut spread can be purchased in specialty food stores or large supermarkets.

Nutrition facts per bruschetta: 317 cal., 13 g total fat (3 g sat. fat), 11 mg chol., 236 mg sodium, 47 g carbo., 1 g fiber, 5 g pro.
Daily values: 3% vit. A, 8% vit. C, 3% calcium.

MARCH
Renew Those Resolutions

*C*hart a new course for healthy and thrifty cooking. Economical meats, such as pot roast, swiss steak, and even oxtail are perfect cuts for slow braising on brisk winter days. Meatless main dishes like Chickpea Pita Pockets and Winter Vegetable Stew bring diversity to the table without breaking the budget. Savory Muffins, sparked by red pepper, are versatile accompaniments to any meal. Now is a good time to overhaul breakfast traditions, too, adding nutritionally sound choices such as Double-Cheese Quesadillas, Mushroom and Cheese Strata, and a potato and egg dish made easily in the microwave.

> 30-minute recipes indicated in RED.
> Low-fat and no-fat recipes indicated
> with a ♥.
> Photographs indicated in italics.
> *All new in 1998.

Mushroom and Cheese Strata

Prep: 30 min. ◆ Chill: 2 to 24 hr.
Bake: 55 min.

*Take time to enjoy the beginning of a
new day by assembling this tasty
casserole the night before and baking
just before mealtime.*

½ cup chopped onion
1 clove garlic, minced
2 Tbsp. margarine or butter
4 cups assorted sliced fresh
   mushrooms, such as
   oyster, shiitake, button,
   white, and/or cremini

◆◆◆

½ cup shredded mozzarella
   cheese (2 oz.)
¼ cup shredded fontina cheese
   (1 oz.)
2 Tbsp. assorted snipped fresh
   herbs, such as basil,
   oregano, thyme, and/or
   parsley

◆◆◆

5 cups French or Italian bread
   cubes
2 oz. prosciutto or Canadian-
   style bacon, chopped

◆◆◆

4 beaten eggs or 1 cup frozen
   or refrigerated egg
   product, thawed
1¾ cups milk
½ cup regular or light dairy
   sour cream
1 Tbsp. Dijon-style mustard
⅛ tsp. pepper

1 In a large skillet cook onion
and garlic in hot margarine or
butter over medium heat for
2 minutes. Add mushrooms and
cook about 3 minutes more or
until tender, stirring occasionally.
Remove from heat.

**Orange Breakfast Granola
topped with fresh fruit and
plain or vanilla yogurt
(see right)**

◆◆◆

**English muffins with
strawberry preserves**

◆◆◆

Orange or grapefruit juice

2 In a small mixing bowl
combine the mozzarella, fontina,
and herbs; toss to mix.

3 In a greased 2-quart square
baking dish place half of the bread
cubes. Top with the mushroom
mixture, cheese mixture, and prosciutto or Canadian-style bacon.
Top with remaining bread cubes.

4 In a mixing bowl combine
beaten eggs or egg product, milk,
sour cream, mustard, and pepper.
Pour over layers in dish. Cover
and chill in the refrigerator for
2 to 24 hours.

5 Bake, uncovered, in a 325°
oven for 55 to 60 minutes or until
a knife inserted near the center
comes out clean. Let stand for
10 minutes. To serve, cut into
squares. If desired, garnish with
fresh herb sprigs. Serves 6.

Nutrition facts per serving: 330 cal., 19 g
total fat (7 g sat. fat), 167 mg chol., 582 mg
sodium, 23 g carbo., 1 g fiber, 17 g pro.
Daily values: 23% vit. A, 5% vit. C, 20%
calcium, 14% iron.

Orange Breakfast Granola

Prep: 20 min. ◆ Bake: 30 min.

*"House" granolas are all the rage in
small breakfast spots, and this one is
destined to become a favorite at your
house. To take it beyond breakfast
time, try sprinkling a couple of
spoonfuls over ice cream or frozen
yogurt for dessert.*

3 cups regular rolled oats
½ cup toasted wheat germ
½ cup coarsely chopped
   hazelnuts (filberts) or
   sliced almonds
⅓ cup honey
½ tsp. finely shredded orange
   peel
⅓ cup orange juice
½ tsp. ground cinnamon

◆◆◆

Nonstick spray coating
1 cup flaked or shredded
   coconut

◆◆◆

Any combination of fresh
   fruit, such as blueberries,
   sliced nectarines,
   blackberries, sliced
   strawberries, raspberries,
   and/or sliced, peeled
   peaches (optional)
Plain or vanilla low-fat
   yogurt (optional)

1 In a large mixing bowl stir
together the oats, wheat germ,
and hazelnuts or almonds. In a
small saucepan stir together the
honey, orange peel and juice, and
cinnamon. Heat just until boiling; remove from heat. Add
honey mixture to oat mixture,
tossing gently until coated.

2 Spray a 15×10×1-inch baking pan with nonstick coating.
Spread oat mixture evenly in pan.

SAY CHEESE FOR BREAKFAST

You might expect to see cottage cheese at lunch or dinner, but it's a wise choice for breakfast, too. Half a cup of low-fat cottage cheese has 80 calories, under 2 grams of fat, and 100 milligrams of calcium (10 percent of the daily recommendation). Unfortunately, most of us aren't getting enough calcium—a nutrient that can prevent bone loss later in life. Eating more cottage cheese can help. These simple breakfast ideas are an easy way to start your day with some bone-building calcium.

◆ **Just-Peachy Shake:** In a blender container combine frozen peach slices, cottage cheese, a little milk, and a spoonful of honey. Cover and blend until smooth. To thin as desired, add more milk and blend until smooth. If you like, sprinkle each serving with ground nutmeg or cinnamon.

◆ **Very Cherry Blintz:** Fill purchased crepes with drained cottage cheese. Sprinkle with ground cinnamon. Fold into packets. Microwave on high for about 1 minute or until heated through. Top with a spoonful of warmed cherry or strawberry preserves.

◆ **Honey of a Dip:** In a blender container blend equal amounts of cottage cheese and vanilla yogurt, a spoonful of honey, and a little finely shredded lemon or orange peel. Serve with banana chunks, melon, peach slices, apple wedges, or other pieces of fresh fruit.

◆ **Double-Cheese Quesadillas:** Spread a little cottage cheese onto a flour tortilla. Sprinkle with shredded cheddar cheese and sliced green onion. Top with another tortilla. In a skillet cook the filled tortilla in a little hot cooking oil until it begins to brown, turning once. (Or, microwave on high about 1 minute or until heated through.)

Note: Two kinds of cottage cheese are available in most supermarkets: cream-style and dry curd. For these easy ideas, use cream-style cheese. You can choose from either large or small curd. And, when you're limiting calories or sodium, you can opt for the low-fat or fat-free varieties. Because kids need the calories, you may want to serve them regular cream-style cottage cheese. Dry curd is not recommended for these breakfast foods. Use it only when specified in recipes.

Bake in a 325° oven for 15 minutes. Add coconut to oat mixture and stir. Bake for 15 to 20 minutes more or until lightly browned, stirring once. Remove from oven and immediately turn out onto a large piece of foil; cool. Store in an airtight container at room temperature for up to 2 weeks or in the freezer for up to 3 months. Thaw before serving.

3 To serve, spoon granola into a bowl. If desired, top with fruit and yogurt. Makes about 5 cups (ten ½-cup servings).

Nutrition facts per serving: 224 cal., 8 g total fat (3 g sat. fat), 0 mg chol., 3 mg sodium, 33 g carbo., 1 g fiber, 7 g pro. *Daily values:* 7% vit. C, 2% calcium, 13% iron.

30 MIN. LOW FAT

POTATOES 'N' EGGS

Start to finish: 10 min.

Scramble! If that describes your mornings instead of what you eat, then this hot breakfast is for you.

1 cup frozen loose-pack diced hash brown potatoes with onion and peppers

2 slices turkey bacon, cut into 1-inch pieces

◆◆◆

1 8-oz. carton refrigerated or frozen egg product, thawed, or 4 eggs

⅛ tsp. salt

2 Tbsp. shredded reduced-fat cheddar cheese

2 Tbsp. salsa

1 In a 1-quart microwave-safe casserole mix potatoes and bacon. Cover and microwave on high for 3 to 5 minutes or until tender, stirring once.

2 In a small mixing bowl beat together the eggs and salt; add to potatoes. Microwave, uncovered, on high for 1 to 3 minutes or until almost set, pushing cooked egg to center after 1 minute, then every 15 seconds. Top with cheese; let stand 1 minute. Serve with salsa. Makes 2 servings.

Nutrition facts per serving: 161 cal., 5 g total fat (2 g sat. fat), 14 mg chol., 624 mg sodium, 14 g carbo., 1 g fiber, 17 g pro. *Daily values:* 65% vit. A, 15% vit. C, 9% calcium, 18% iron.

MINIATURE WHEAT AND NUT MUFFINS

Prep: 15 min. ◆ Bake: 10 min.

Try these with the Mushroom and Cheese Strata on page 48. After cooking the strata, increase the oven to 400° before baking these treats.

⅔ cup all-purpose flour
¼ cup whole wheat flour
¼ cup chopped almonds or
    pecans, toasted
1 tsp. baking powder
⅛ tsp. baking soda
⅛ tsp. salt
⅛ tsp. ground nutmeg
◆◆◆
1 beaten egg
⅓ cup milk
3 Tbsp. packed brown sugar
3 Tbsp. cooking oil

1 Grease eighteen 1¾-inch muffin cups or line them with paper bake cups; set aside.

2 In a medium mixing bowl stir together the all-purpose flour, whole wheat flour, almonds or pecans, baking powder, baking soda, salt, and nutmeg. Make a well in the center of the dry mixture; set aside.

3 In a small mixing bowl combine egg, milk, packed brown sugar, and cooking oil. Add egg mixture all at once to the dry mixture. Stir just until moistened (batter should be lumpy).

4 Spoon batter into prepared muffin cups, filling each ⅔ full. Bake in a 400° oven 10 to 12 minutes or until golden. Cool in muffin cups on a rack for 5 minutes. Remove from muffin cups; serve warm. Makes 18 muffins.

TO MAKE AHEAD

Prepare and bake muffins as directed at left; cool completely. Place muffins in a freezer container or bag and freeze for up to 3 months. Before serving, wrap frozen muffins in heavy foil and reheat in a 300° oven for 12 to 15 minutes or until warm.

Nutrition facts per muffin: 65 cal., 4 g total fat (1 g sat. fat), 12 mg chol., 50 mg sodium, 7 g carbo., 0 g fiber, 2 g pro. *Daily values:* 2% calcium, 2% iron.

BASIC SAVORY MUFFINS

Prep: 10 min. ◆ Bake: 20 min.

1¾ cups all-purpose flour
3 Tbsp. sugar
2 tsp. baking powder
¼ tsp. salt
◆◆◆
1 beaten egg
¾ cup milk
¼ cup cooking oil

1 In a medium mixing bowl stir together flour, sugar, baking powder, and salt. Make a well in center of dry mixture; set aside.

2 In a small mixing bowl combine egg, milk, and oil. Add egg mixture all at once to dry mixture. Stir just until moistened (batter should be lumpy).

3 Spoon batter into greased muffins cups, filling each ⅔ full. Bake in a 400° oven about 20 minutes or until golden. Cool in muffin cups on a rack 5 minutes. Remove from muffin cups; serve warm. Makes 10 to 12.

TO MAKE AHEAD

Prepare and bake muffins as directed at left; cool completely. Place muffins in a freezer container or bag and freeze for up to 3 months. Before serving, wrap frozen muffins in heavy foil and reheat in a 300° oven for 15 to 18 minutes or until warm.

Nutrition facts per muffin: 153 cal., 6 g total fat (1 g sat. fat), 23 mg chol., 142 mg sodium, 20 g carbo., 1g fiber, 3 g pro. *Daily values:* 2% vit. A, 7% calcium, 7% iron.

Red Pepper and Mozzarella Muffins: Prepare muffins as directed at left, except fold ½ cup shredded smoked mozzarella cheese, ⅓ cup chopped roasted red sweet pepper, and ¼ teaspoon cracked black pepper into batter. Sprinkle greased muffin cups generously with cornmeal. Fill the muffin cups ⅔ full. Top muffin batter with additional cracked black pepper before baking.

CHICKPEA PITA POCKETS

Start to finish: 20 min.

Packed in a pita, this grape, spinach, and chickpea combo makes a satisfying meatless meal.

1 15-oz. can light or regular chickpeas (garbanzo beans), rinsed and drained
1 cup shredded spinach or lettuce
⅔ cup seedless grapes, halved
½ cup finely chopped red sweet pepper

⅓ cup thinly sliced celery
¼ cup finely chopped onion

♦♦♦

¼ cup mayonnaise or salad
   dressing
2 Tbsp. poppy seed dressing or
   desired creamy salad
   dressing
4 pita bread rounds, split in
   half crosswise
½ cup finely shredded Swiss
   cheese (2 oz.)

1 In a large bowl combine chickpeas, spinach or lettuce, grapes, red sweet pepper, celery, and onion.

2 In a small bowl stir together mayonnaise or salad dressing and poppy seed or desired dressing. Add to chickpea mixture, stirring until combined. Spoon into pita bread halves. Top with cheese. Makes 4 servings.

Nutrition facts per serving: 467 cal., 21 g total fat (5 g sat. fat), 21 mg chol., 586 mg sodium, 57 g carbo., 5 g fiber, 15 g pro. *Daily values:* 19% vit. A, 47% vit. C, 17% calcium, 17% iron.

LOW FAT
WINTER VEGETABLE STEW

Prep: 45 min. ♦ Bake: 1¾ hr.

Be sure to allow time to properly soak the clay pot used to cook this herbed vegetable medley. If you don't have a clay pot, follow the instructions for baking in a Dutch oven.

1 large onion, chopped
2 Tbsp. olive oil
¼ cup snipped fresh parsley
½ tsp. dried sage, crushed
½ tsp. dried thyme, crushed
¼ tsp. dried rosemary, crushed
2 bay leaves

Menu

**Winter Vegetable Stew
(see below)**

♦♦♦

**Multigrain bread with
butter**

♦♦♦

**Salad of Bibb lettuce,
snipped oil-pack dried
tomatoes, feta cheese,
walnuts, and vinaigrette**

♦♦♦

**No-Fret Apple Pie
(see page 67)**

1 14½-oz. can whole tomatoes,
   cut up
¼ cup dry red wine
2 Tbsp. soy sauce
4 cloves garlic, minced

♦♦♦

4 large parsnips (1 to 1½ lb.),
   peeled and cut into 2-inch
   pieces (3 to 4 cups)
2 leeks (white parts only),
   halved lengthwise and cut
   into 1-inch pieces (1 cup)
2 14½-oz. cans great northern
   or navy beans, rinsed and
   drained
1 medium turnip, peeled and
   cut into wedges (1½ cups)
4 oz. shiitake, cremini, brown,
   or button mushrooms,
   halved (1½ cups)
2 small potatoes, quartered
   (1½ cups)

1 Do not preheat oven when using clay pot. Submerge top and bottom of a 2- to 3-quart clay pot (unglazed) in a sink of cool water; allow to soak 30 minutes.

2 In a saucepan cook onion in hot oil over medium-high heat for 12 to 15 minutes or until onions are tender and golden, stirring occasionally. Stir in the parsley, sage, thyme, rosemary, and bay leaves. Add undrained tomatoes, wine, soy sauce, and garlic.

3 Drain the clay pot. Fill with parsnips, leeks, drained beans, turnip wedges, mushrooms, and potatoes (there should be about 10 cups of vegetables). Pour tomato mixture over the vegetables. Put top on clay pot and place in cold oven.

4 Set oven temperature to 350° and bake for 1¾ to 2 hours or until vegetables are tender. Discard bay leaves. If desired, season to taste with salt and pepper and garnish with additional chopped *fresh parsley* and *fresh sage leaves.* Makes 6 servings.

DUTCH OVEN DIRECTIONS

In a large Dutch oven cook onion in hot oil over medium-high heat for 12 to 15 minutes or until the onions are tender and golden, stirring occasionally. Stir in the ¼ cup parsley, dried sage, thyme, rosemary, and bay leaves. Add undrained tomatoes, wine, soy sauce, and garlic. Add parsnips, leeks, turnip, and potatoes to the pot. Cover; bake in a 350° oven for 1 hour. Stir in beans and mushrooms. Bake, covered, about 15 minutes more or until vegetables are tender. Discard bay leaves. Continue as directed above.

Nutrition facts per serving: 304 cal., 6 g total fat (1 g sat. fat), 0 mg chol., 515 mg sodium, 54 g carbo., 12 g fiber, 12 g pro. *Daily values:* 6% vit. A, 62% vit. C, 12% calcium, 32% iron.

OXTAIL RAGOÛT

Prep: 30 min. ◆ Cook: 1½ hr.

Oxtails give a special richness and flavor to this fortifying winter stew. This bony meat cut is available in the meat sections of most supermarkets and needs long, slow cooking. (See the photograph on page 79.)

1 lb. oxtails, cut into 1½- to 2-inch pieces (optional)
1 lb. boneless beef short ribs (if omitting oxtails, use an additional ¼ lb. boneless beef short ribs)
2 Tbsp. cooking oil

2 14½-oz. cans beef broth (about 3½ cups)
½ cup dry red wine or beef broth
½ cup coarsely chopped shallots
4 cloves garlic, minced
2 bay leaves
½ tsp. salt
¼ to ½ tsp. coarsely ground black pepper
◆◆◆
1 lb. carrots, peeled and cut into ¾-inch pieces
1 lb. rutabagas or turnips, peeled and cut into ¾-inch cubes
2 medium onions, peeled and coarsely chopped
◆◆◆
⅔ cup cold water
⅓ cup all-purpose flour
◆◆◆
⅓ cup snipped fresh parsley
Salt (optional)
Coarsely ground black pepper (optional)
◆◆◆
Hot cooked couscous (optional)
Cooked and crumbled bacon (optional)
Flat-leaf parsley (optional)

1 In a 4- to 6-quart Dutch oven brown oxtails and ribs on all sides in hot oil. Drain off fat.

2 To avoid spattering, carefully add the beef broth, red wine or broth, shallots, garlic, bay leaves, the ½ teaspoon salt, and the ¼ to ½ teaspoon pepper to meat in pan. Bring mixture to boiling; reduce heat. Simmer, covered, about 1 hour or until meat is nearly tender.

3 Add the carrots, rutabagas or turnips, and onions to meat mixture in pan. Return to boiling; reduce heat. Cook, covered, for 30 to 45 minutes more or until meat and vegetables are tender. Discard bay leaves. Remove meat; allow to cool slightly.

4 Meanwhile, in a small mixing bowl stir the cold water into all-purpose flour until smooth (or shake together in a screw-top jar). Stir into pan. Cook and stir until thickened and bubbly. Cook and stir for 1 minute more.

5 Cut meat into bite-size pieces, discarding any bones. Return meat to pan; heat through. Stir in snipped parsley. If desired, season to taste with additional salt and pepper.

6 If desired, spoon meat and vegetables over hot cooked couscous and sprinkle with crumbled bacon and flat-leaf parsley. Makes 5 or 6 servings.

Nutrition facts per serving: 441 cal., 27 g total fat (11 g sat. fat), 53 mg chol., 881 mg sodium, 28 g carbo., 6 g fiber, 18 g pro. *Daily values:* 227% vit. A, 48% vit. C, 8% calcium, 24% iron.

KEEPING MEAT AND POULTRY SAFE

Follow these simple practices whenever you handle meat or poultry so you'll know you're serving your family safe, wholesome food.

STORE IT RIGHT

◆ Place fresh meat in your refrigerator (set at 36° to 40°) as soon as possible after purchasing.

◆ Refrigerate meat in the original plastic wrapping, unless the wrapping is torn. If the wrapping is damaged, or the meat was wrapped in paper, rewrap the meat in plastic wrap or foil.

◆ Store fresh meats in the refrigerator under or away from foods that may be eaten without cooking, such as produce. If necessary, place raw meat in a pan or plastic bag. This avoids contamination from the meat dripping onto other foods.

◆ Freeze meat at 0° or below. Prepackaged meat should be overwrapped or rewrapped to prevent freezer burn (drying of the surface). Wrap meat tightly in wrap or bags made especially for freezing, removing as much air as possible.

THAW IT RIGHT

◆ Thaw frozen meat in the refrigerator—never thaw it at room temperature or in warm water. Allow five hours of thawing time for every pound of frozen meat.

◆ Use the "defrost" setting on your microwave oven to thaw meats if you're unable to thaw them in the refrigerator. Check your owner's manual for timings. Cook thawed meat or poultry immediately.

◆ Never thaw frozen ground meat, then refreeze it.

◆ Cook meat as soon after thawing as possible.

COOK AND SERVE IT RIGHT

◆ Cook beef or veal to at least 145° for medium-rare, 160° for medium, and 170° for well done. Cook lamb to at least 150° for medium-rare and 160° for medium. The United States Department of Agriculture cautions that any type of meat cooked to below 145° is considered "unsafe."

◆ Thoroughly cook ground meat to at least 160° before eating. To be sure the meat is fully cooked, make sure no pink remains. (It's OK to eat meat slightly pink that is not in a ground form, such as a pork loin or beefsteaks. However, chicken or turkey meat should not be eaten if it's pink.)

◆ Cook meat completely before adding it to casseroles or make-ahead dishes. Partially cooked meat may promote the growth of harmful bacteria that can make you ill.

◆ Do not allow cooked or raw meat to stand at temperatures above 40° for more than two hours.

◆ Keep foods containing meat at safe temperatures. Keep cold foods containing meat below 45° and hot foods above 140°.

CLEANUP KNOW-HOW

◆ Keep cutting boards and knives clean by washing in hot, soapy water after each use.

◆ After cutting raw meat, wash the knives and cutting boards thoroughly with hot, soapy water before using them to cut up other foods that will not be cooked, such as salad ingredients. Better yet, reserve one cutting board for meats only.

◆ Wash your hands in hot, soapy water before and after handling any raw meat.

COUNTRY SWISS STEAK
Prep: 15 min. ◆ Cook: 1½ hr.

This recipe pays tribute to the hearty taste of sausage, which is one of the basic elements of Swiss cooking. The Swiss don't actually make Swiss Steak, however. The recipe name is believed to be English and likely comes from relating the process of smoothing out cloth between rollers called "swissing" to pounding and flattening of meat.

1 **lb. boneless beef round steak, cut ¾ to 1 inch thick**
2 **Tbsp. all-purpose flour**
¼ **tsp. salt**
¼ **tsp. pepper**

◆◆◆

4 **oz. spicy fresh bratwurst or other sausage, cut into ¾-inch-thick slices**
1 **Tbsp. cooking oil**
1 **14½-oz. can chunky tomatoes with olive oil, garlic, and spices**
1 **small onion, sliced and separated into rings**
1 **tsp. dried thyme, crushed**
2 **cups hot cooked noodles or rice**
   Fresh thyme (optional)

1 Trim fat from meat. Cut meat into 4 serving-size pieces. Combine all-purpose flour, salt, and pepper. With the notched side of a meat mallet, pound flour mixture into both sides of meat (see top right).

2 In a large skillet brown meat and sausage on all sides in hot oil. Drain off fat. Add undrained tomatoes, onion, and dried thyme. Bring to boiling; reduce heat. Simmer, covered, over low heat about 1¼ hours or until meat is tender. Serve with hot cooked

noodles or rice. If desired, sprinkle with thyme. Serves 4.

◼ OVEN DIRECTIONS ◼

Prepare and brown meat as directed. Transfer meat to a 2-quart square baking dish. Drain fat from skillet. In the same skillet combine undrained tomatoes, onion, and thyme. Bring to boiling, scraping up any browned bits. Pour over meat. Cover; bake in a 350° oven for 1 to 1½ hours or until meat is tender. Serve steak as directed.

◼ IN CROCKERY COOKER ◼

Use a 1-inch-thick boneless beef round steak. Trim fat from meat. Cut meat into 4 serving-size pieces. Omit flouring and pounding meat. Brown meat and sausage in hot oil in a skillet. Place onion in a 3½- or 4-quart electric crockery cooker. Sprinkle with the thyme, 2 tablespoons quick-cooking tapioca, salt, and pepper. Pour undrained tomatoes over vegetables. Add meat. Cover and cook on low-heat setting for 10 to 12 hours. Serve as directed.

Nutrition facts per serving: 412 cal., 15 g total fat (4 g sat. fat), 110 mg chol., 755 mg sodium, 32 g carbo., 4 g fiber, 35 g pro. *Daily values:* 7% vit. A, 21% vit. C, 3% calcium, 26% iron.

GARDEN POT ROAST
Prep: 30 min. ◆ Cook: 2½ hr.

In Romania, the national dish is called Ghiveciu National; it celebrates spring by pairing meat with an array of vegetables. We've modified it for American ingredients and methods and substituted beef for the traditional veal.

1 **3-lb. beef bottom round roast**
½ **to 1 tsp. cracked black pepper**
¼ **tsp. salt**
1 **Tbsp. cooking oil**

◆◆◆

1 **cup beef broth**
2 **Tbsp. tomato paste**
1 **medium onion, coarsely chopped (½ cup)**
2 **cloves garlic, minced**
½ **tsp. dried marjoram, crushed**
½ **tsp. dried thyme, crushed**

◆◆◆

⅓ **cup golden raisins**
3 **cups vegetables, such as whole green beans; peeled and cut-up winter squash or parsnips; or cut up celery, broccoli, and/or cauliflower**
1 **cup sugar snap peas**

◆◆◆

1 **Tbsp. cornstarch**
2 **Tbsp. cold water**

1 Trim fat from roast. Sprinkle with cracked pepper and salt. In a large 4- to 6-quart Dutch oven brown roast on all sides in hot oil, about 5 minutes. Drain off fat.

2 Meanwhile, in a small mixing bowl stir together the beef broth and tomato paste; pour over roast. Add the onion, garlic, marjoram, and thyme. Bring to boiling; reduce heat. Simmer, covered, about 2 hours or until meat is tender.

3 Add raisins and green beans (if using), squash, or parsnips. Return to boiling; reduce heat. Simmer, covered, 10 to 15 minutes more or until vegetables are just tender. Stir in sugar snap peas and celery (if using), broccoli, or cauliflower. Cook for 3 to 4 minutes more or until vegetables are crisp-tender. Using a meat fork and slotted spoon, remove meat and vegetables to a serving platter, reserving juices in Dutch oven. Cover meat and vegetables to keep warm.

4 For gravy, strain juices into a glass measuring cup. Skim off fat. Return 1¼ cups of the pan juices to Dutch oven. Discard remaining pan juices.

5 In a small bowl stir cornstarch into cold water until smooth (or shake together in a screw-top jar). Stir into the juices in Dutch oven. Cook and stir until thickened and bubbly. Cook and stir for 2 minutes more. Spoon some of the gravy over meat and vegetables; pass remaining gravy. Makes 6 servings, plus leftover meat.

Nutrition facts per serving: 303 cal., 10 g total fat (3 g sat. fat), 82 mg chol., 277 mg sodium, 23 g carbo., 4 g fiber, 30 g pro. *Daily values:* 20% vit. A, 30% vit. C, 5% calcium, 29% iron.

TEST KITCHEN TIP

BRAISING BASICS

Turn tough—and usually less expensive—cuts of meat into fork-tender morsels with the magic of braising. The secret of this easy technique is the long, slow cooking in just a small amount of liquid.

WHICH MEATS TO BRAISE

Because braising tenderizes meat, choose beef and pork cuts that benefit from long cooking (see below). Never braise a tender, lean cut of meat such as beef or pork tenderloin; long cooking toughens tender meats.

THREE EASY STEPS

1. Brown meat. Using a large ovenproof Dutch oven over medium heat, brown meat on all sides in just enough hot oil to prevent meat from sticking. (Meats with some fat may not require added oil unless they are coated with flour or bread crumbs.) Drain off drippings. Season meat with salt, pepper, herbs, or spices after browning, unless meat has a seasoned flour or crumb coating.

2. Add a small amount of liquid. Water, tomato juice or sauce, broth, wine, or other seasoned liquids are the most common choices. One-quarter to one-half cup liquid is recommended. Cover the Dutch oven with a tight-fitting lid to prevent the liquid from evaporating. Depending on the braising time, you may need to add more liquid during cooking.

3. Simmer on low heat until meat is tender. This may be done on the stove top or in a 300° to 325° oven. The time required will depend on the size of the meat. Check the meat section of a cookbook for guidelines.

BEST CUTS FOR BRAISING

Beef chuck	*Beef rib*
Boneless top blade roast	Back ribs
Shoulder pot roast	*Beef short plate and flank*
Arm pot roast	Flank or skirt steak
Short ribs	Flank steak roll
Beef round	*Beef foreshank and brisket*
Round steak	Corned or fresh beef brisket
Bottom round steak	Shank crosscut
Bottom round roast	
Round tip roast	
Eye of round roast	
Pork shoulder	*Pork loin*
Blade steak or roast	Rib chop
Boneless blade roast	Sirloin chop
Pork side and leg	
Ribs	

PORK WITH MUSHROOM CREAM SAUCE

Start to finish: 25 min.

12 oz. pork tenderloin
3 Tbsp. margarine or butter
♦♦♦
8 oz. mushrooms, sliced ½ inch thick
2 Tbsp. all-purpose flour
½ tsp. multicolored peppercorns, coarsely crushed
¼ tsp. salt
1 cup half-and-half or light cream
¼ cup dry white wine
Hot cooked basmati or long grain rice

1 Cut pork tenderloin crosswise into ½-inch-thick slices. In a large skillet cook pork in 2 tablespoons of the margarine or butter over medium heat for 4 to 6 minutes or until no pink remains, turning once. Remove pork from pan; cover and keep warm.

2 Add remaining margarine and mushrooms to skillet. Cook and stir until mushrooms are tender. Stir in the flour, peppercorns, and salt; cook and stir 1 minute. Gradually stir in half-and-half or light cream. Cook and stir until thickened and bubbly. Add wine and pork; heat through. Serve over hot cooked rice. Garnish with *fresh snipped chives.* Makes 4 servings.

Nutrition facts per serving: 302 cal., 19 g total fat (7 g sat. fat), 83 mg chol., 304 mg sodium, 9 g carbo., 1 g fiber, 22 g pro. *Daily values:* 18% vit. A, 5% vit. C, 6% calcium, 15% iron.

RIBS WITH APPLES AND SAUERKRAUT

Prep: 30 min.
Cook: 8 to 10 hr. (low); 4 to 5 hr. (high)

Quick browning in a skillet seals in natural juices, adding flavor and aroma to the pork country-style ribs.

2½ lb. pork country-style ribs, cut crosswise in half and cut into 1- to 2-rib portions
1 Tbsp. cooking oil
2 medium potatoes, sliced ½ inch thick
2 medium carrots, sliced ¼ inch thick
1 medium onion, thinly sliced
1 8-oz. can sauerkraut, rinsed and drained
½ cup apple cider or apple juice
2 tsp. caraway or fennel seed
⅛ tsp. ground cloves
♦♦♦
1 Tbsp. all-purpose flour
2 Tbsp. cold water
½ of a large apple, cored and thinly sliced
Salt (optional)
Pepper (optional)
1 Tbsp. snipped fresh parsley

1 In a large skillet brown pork ribs on both sides in hot oil over medium-high heat. In a 3½- or 4-quart electric crockery cooker place potatoes, carrots, onion, browned pork ribs, and sauerkraut. In a bowl combine apple cider or juice, caraway seed, and cloves. Pour over sauerkraut.

2 Cover crockery cooker and cook on low-heat setting for 8 to 10 hours or on high-heat setting for 4 to 5 hours.

Menu

Ribs with Apples and Sauerkraut (see left)
♦♦♦
Salad of fresh spinach, sliced fresh mushrooms, thinly sliced red onion, and fruit-flavored vinaigrette
♦♦♦
Rye bread with butter
♦♦♦
Spice cake

3 Remove meat and vegetables to a serving platter, reserving the juices in the crockery cooker. Cover the meat and vegetables to keep warm.

4 For gravy, strain juices into a glass measuring cup. Skim off fat. Measure 1 cup liquid (if necessary, add water); pour into a saucepan. In a small bowl stir all-purpose flour into cold water until smooth (or shake together in a screw-top jar). Stir into the juices in saucepan. Cook and stir until thickened and bubbly. Stir in the apple. Cook and stir for 1 minute more or until heated through. If desired, season to taste with salt and pepper. Stir in parsley just before serving. Serve gravy with ribs and vegetables. Makes 4 servings.

Nutrition facts per serving: 431 cal., 20 g total fat (7 g sat. fat), 103 mg chol., 371 mg sodium, 32 g carbo., 4 g fiber, 31 g pro. *Daily values:* 86% vit. A, 38% vit. C, 4% calcium, 22% iron.

SKILLET ROTINI WITH ZUCCHINI AND SAUSAGE

Start to finish: 30 min.

Cleanup doesn't get any easier—one skillet is all it takes to cook this saucy Italian-style pasta dish.

- 1 lb. bulk pork sausage or ground turkey sausage
- 1 cup chopped onion
- ¾ cup chopped green sweet pepper
- 1 clove garlic, minced

♦♦♦

- 1 15-oz. can low-sodium tomato sauce
- 1 10-oz. can chopped tomatoes and green chili peppers or one 14½-oz. can stewed tomatoes
- ¾ cup water
- 1 Tbsp. snipped fresh oregano or 1 tsp. dried oregano, crushed
- ¼ tsp. pepper
- 1 cup rotini
- 4 cups sliced zucchini
- ½ cup shredded mozzarella cheese (2 oz.)

1 In a 12-inch skillet cook sausage, onion, green pepper, and garlic until meat is brown and vegetables are tender. Drain fat.

2 Stir in the tomato sauce, undrained tomatoes, water, oregano, and pepper. Bring to boiling; stir in uncooked pasta. Simmer, covered, about 10 minutes or until pasta is nearly tender. Add zucchini and simmer, covered, about 5 minutes more or until pasta and zucchini are just tender. Remove from heat. Sprinkle with cheese. Cover and let stand for 1 to 2 minutes or until cheese is melted. Makes 5 servings.

Nutrition facts per serving: 309 cal., 15 g total fat (6 g sat. fat), 42 mg chol., 853 mg sodium, 27 g carbo., 3 g fiber, 16 g pro. *Daily values:* 15% vit. A, 50% vit. C, 11% calcium, 15% iron.

CHICKEN AND RIGATONI WITH ROASTED RED PEPPERS

Start to finish: 30 min.

Made in only minutes, this bistro-style dish is as eye-catching as it is palate-pleasing.

- 1 lb. skinless, boneless chicken breast halves
- ½ cup seasoned fine dry bread crumbs
- 2 Tbsp. grated Parmesan or Romano cheese
- 1 beaten egg
- 1 Tbsp. water

♦♦♦

- 1 7-oz. jar roasted red sweet peppers
  Chicken broth
- 2 tsp. cornstarch

♦♦♦

- 3 cups rigatoni

♦♦♦

- 2 Tbsp. olive oil or cooking oil
- 2 cloves garlic, minced
- 1 cup chopped plum tomatoes
- 2 Tbsp. dry white wine
- 2 Tbsp. snipped fresh basil
- 2 Tbsp. grated Parmesan or Romano cheese

1 Rinse chicken; pat dry. Halve each chicken piece lengthwise. In a shallow bowl combine crumbs and Parmesan or Romano cheese. In another shallow bowl beat together egg and water.

2 Dip each chicken piece in egg and then in crumb mixture, turning to coat all sides. Set chicken aside.

3 Drain peppers, reserving liquid. Add the chicken broth to liquid to equal ⅔ cup; stir in cornstarch. Cut peppers into thin strips; set aside.

4 Cook rigatoni according to package directions; drain.

5 Meanwhile, in a 12-inch skillet cook chicken, uncovered, in hot oil over medium-high heat for 10 to 12 minutes or until tender and no longer pink, turning once. Remove from pan; cover and keep warm.

6 Add garlic to skillet; cook and stir 1 minute. Carefully add the broth mixture; cook and stir until thickened and bubbly. Stir in tomatoes, pepper strips, wine, and basil; cook 1 minute more. Toss mixture with drained rigatoni and 2 tablespoons Parmesan or Romano cheese; arrange chicken atop. Makes 6 servings.

Nutrition facts per serving: 379 cal., 10 g total fat (2 g sat. fat), 79 mg chol., 442 mg sodium, 41 g carbo., 1 g fiber, 24 g pro. *Daily values:* 17% vit. A, 125% vit. C, 7% calcium, 18% iron.

PEPPER AND CHICKEN LINGUINE

Start to finish: 20 min.

8 oz. linguine

♦♦♦

12 oz. skinless, boneless chicken breast halves

⅓ cup bottled Italian salad dressing or other clear salad dressing

2 Tbsp. reduced-sodium soy sauce

1 Tbsp. cornstarch

♦♦♦

1 16-oz. pkg. frozen pepper stir-fry vegetables

2 medium carrots, coarsely shredded

1 Cook linguine according to package directions; drain.

2 Meanwhile, rinse chicken; pat dry. Cut chicken into bite-size strips; set aside. For sauce, stir together ¼ cup of the salad dressing, the soy sauce, cornstarch, and ¼ cup *water*; set aside.

3 Heat remaining salad dressing in a 12-inch skillet over medium heat. Add chicken; stir-fry 3 to 4 minutes or until chicken is no longer pink. Push chicken from center of skillet. Stir sauce; add to skillet. Cook and stir until sauce is bubbly. Cook and stir for 2 minutes. Add vegetables; cook and stir for 3 to 4 minutes or until heated through. Serve over linguine. Makes 4 servings.

Nutrition facts per serving: 455 cal., 13 g total fat (2 g sat. fat), 45 mg chol., 494 mg sodium, 57 g carbo., 3 g fiber, 26 g pro. *Daily values:* 157% vit. A, 60% vit. C, 4% calcium, 23% iron.

NORTH AFRICAN CHICKEN COUSCOUS

Start to finish: 20 min.

Quick-cooking couscous adds the finishing touch to this spiced-up stir-fry specialty.

2 medium onions, cut into thin wedges

2 cloves garlic, minced

1 Tbsp. olive oil

1 lb. skinless, boneless chicken breast halves, cut into bite-size pieces

16 packaged, peeled baby carrots (about ¾ cup)

2½ cups chicken broth

2 medium zucchini, quartered and cut into 2-inch pieces

½ cup raisins

2 to 3 tsp. curry powder

1 tsp. ground cinnamon

½ tsp. salt

♦♦♦

1⅓ cups quick-cooking couscous

¼ cup slivered almonds, toasted (optional)

1 In a large saucepan cook onions and garlic in hot olive oil about 3 minutes or until crisp-tender. Add chicken pieces and carrots. Cook, uncovered, over medium heat for 5 minutes, stirring frequently. Stir in ½ cup of the chicken broth, zucchini, raisins, curry powder, ½ teaspoon of the cinnamon, and salt. Cook, covered, over medium heat 3 to 4 minutes or until chicken is no longer pink and vegetables are crisp-tender.

2 Meanwhile, in a medium saucepan bring the remaining chicken broth and the remaining cinnamon to boiling. Stir in couscous; cover. Remove from heat; let stand 5 minutes. Fluff couscous lightly with fork before serving. To serve, divide couscous among 4 plates. Spoon chicken and vegetables over couscous. If desired, garnish with toasted slivered almonds. Makes 4 servings.

Nutrition facts per serving: 500 cal., 8 g total fat (2 g sat. fat), 60 mg chol., 833 mg sodium, 72 g carbo., 13 g fiber, 34 g pro. *Daily values:* 62% vit. A, 10% vit. C, 6% calcium, 20% iron.

BRAISED CHICKEN WITH MUSHROOMS

Prep: 15 min. ♦ Cook: 50 min.

Slow and steady wins this race for taste. Homey ingredients with a long history of flavor are joined by basil, tomatoes, and a hint of red pepper.

2½ to 3 lb. meaty chicken pieces

2 Tbsp. cooking oil

♦♦♦

3 cups sliced fresh mushrooms

1 large onion, chopped

2 cloves garlic, minced

2 tsp. dried basil, crushed

1 tsp. crushed red pepper

¼ tsp. salt

¼ tsp. pepper

1 cup chicken broth

½ cup dry red wine

1 6-oz. can tomato paste

♦♦♦

1 Tbsp. all-purpose flour

2 Tbsp. cold water

¼ cup snipped fresh parsley
Fresh basil sprigs (optional)

1 In a 12-inch heavy skillet cook chicken in hot oil over medium-high heat about 15 minutes or until well browned on both sides. Set chicken aside. Drain drippings, reserving 1 tablespoon drippings in skillet.

2 In the same skillet cook and stir mushrooms, onion, garlic, the 2 teaspoons basil, crushed red pepper, salt, and pepper over medium heat until vegetables are tender. Stir in chicken broth, red wine, and tomato paste. Return chicken to skillet. Bring to boiling; reduce heat. Simmer, covered, for 30 to 40 minutes or until chicken is tender and no longer pink. Transfer the chicken to a platter, reserving sauce in skillet; Keep chicken warm.

3 In a small mixing bowl stir all-purpose flour into cold water until smooth (or shake together in a screw-top jar). Stir into sauce. Cook and stir until thickened and bubbly. Cook and stir for 1 minute more. Stir in parsley; pour the sauce over the chicken. If desired, garnish with basil sprigs. Makes 4 servings.

Nutrition facts per serving: 458 cal., 20 g total fat (5 g sat. fat), 130 mg chol., 498 mg sodium, 17 g carbo., 3 g fiber, 47 g pro. *Daily values:* 20% vit. A, 46% vit. C, 5% calcium, 32% iron.

LOW FAT BRUNSWICK STEW
Start to finish: 1¼ hr.

Traditionally served at barbecues, this savory adaptation of the time-honored classic is a wonderful way to introduce family members to the flavors of the South. (See the photograph on page 78.)

2 lb. meaty chicken pieces, skinned*
2 smoked pork hocks (12 to 16 oz. each)

3 medium onions, cut into thin wedges
1 14½-oz. can diced tomatoes
½ cup chicken broth
4 cloves garlic, minced
1 Tbsp. Worcestershire sauce
1 tsp. dry mustard
1 tsp. dried thyme, crushed
¼ tsp. pepper
¼ tsp. bottled hot pepper sauce

♦♦♦

2 cups loose-pack frozen cut okra
1 cup loose-pack frozen baby lima beans
1 cup loose-pack frozen whole kernel corn

♦♦♦

¼ cup cold water
2 Tbsp. all-purpose flour
Salt (optional)
Pepper (optional)

1 In a large Dutch oven combine the chicken pieces, pork hocks, onions, undrained tomatoes, chicken broth, garlic, Worcestershire sauce, mustard, thyme, the ¼ teaspoon pepper, and hot pepper sauce. Bring to boiling; reduce heat. Simmer, covered, for 35 to 45 minutes or until chicken is tender and no longer pink. Remove pork hocks (and chicken, if desired); cool slightly.

2 Cut meat from hocks; chop meat and set aside, discarding bone. (Cut chicken into bite-size pieces, if desired.) Add okra, lima beans, and corn to mixture in Dutch oven. Return to boiling; reduce heat. Simmer, covered, for 10 to 15 minutes more or until vegetables are just tender.

3 In a small bowl stir cold water into all-purpose flour until smooth (or shake together in a

WHY IS IT CALLED BRUNSWICK STEW?

Originally a simple combination of squirrel meat and onions, this much-loved dish is claimed by three different areas of the South. The counties of Brunswick, Virginia; Brunswick, North Carolina; and the city of Brunswick, Georgia, all take credit for its creation.

The earliest written record of the dish comes from Virginia in 1828 when a state legislator named Dr. Creed Haskins requested it for a political rally.

Over the years, more and more ingredients have been added and the squirrel meat has been omitted.

screw-top jar). Stir into stew. Cook and stir until thickened and bubbly; cook and stir for 1 minute more. Stir in meat from pork hocks (and chicken, if cut up). If desired, season to taste with salt and pepper. Makes 4 or 5 servings.

***Note:** If desired, brown the chicken pieces before cooking. Heat 2 tablespoons cooking oil in the Dutch oven. Add the chicken pieces and cook over medium heat about 15 minutes, turning to brown the chicken evenly. Drain off fat. Continue as directed.

Nutrition facts per serving: 454 cal., 10 g total fat (3 g sat. fat), 109 mg chol., 794 mg sodium, 44 g carbo., 5 g fiber, 48 g pro. *Daily values:* 12% vit. A, 65% vit. C, 10% calcium, 36% iron.

MAKING THE MOST OF A CHICKEN

I use whole chickens a lot when making meals for my family. It's very economical, and the meat goes a long way. When making soup or stew, after simmering the chicken for the correct time, I separate the breast portion from the rest of the meat. I slice the breast for sandwiches or salads. This is an economical alternative to lunch meat, which can cost as much as $5 a pound or more.

Mary Roth
Indianapolis, Indiana

LOW FAT

OLD ENGLISH CHICKEN

Prep: 25 min. ◆ Bake: 1 hr.

This is an adaptation of an 18th century English recipe called Jugged Hare. In our version, a large pot or Dutch oven stands in for the fragile crockery jug used in the original. (See the photograph on page 82.)

1 tsp. whole juniper berries
1 large bay leaf
1 2½-lb. broiler-fryer chicken or rabbit, cut up and skinned
◆◆◆
2 slices bacon, coarsely chopped
◆◆◆
Cooking oil

2 medium carrots, peeled and coarsely chopped (about 1 cup)
¼ cup finely chopped shallots or onion
¼ cup coarsely chopped celery
½ cup chicken broth
¼ cup dry red wine or port
½ tsp. dried thyme, crushed
¼ tsp. dried rosemary, crushed
¼ tsp. salt
⅛ tsp. pepper
◆◆◆
2 Tbsp. red currant jelly
Salt (optional)
Pepper (optional)
Fresh rosemary leaves (optional)

1 In a small square of 100-percent cotton cheesecloth, tie together juniper berries and bay leaf; set aside. Rinse chicken or rabbit; pat dry with paper towels.

2 In a 4- to 5-quart heavy ovenproof Dutch oven cook bacon over medium heat until crisp, stirring occasionally. Using a slotted spoon, transfer the bacon to paper towels to drain. In the same pan brown the chicken or rabbit (in 2 batches, if necessary) in the hot bacon drippings, turning once. Remove the chicken or rabbit from the pan.

3 Reserve 1 tablespoon bacon drippings in the Dutch oven (if necessary, add cooking oil to make 1 tablespoon fat). Add the carrots, shallots or onion, and celery. Cook about 5 minutes or until vegetables are tender. Add the chicken broth, red wine or port, and the cheesecloth bag. Bring to boiling over high heat, scraping up any brown bits clinging to the bottom and sides of the

pan. Add the thyme, rosemary, salt, and pepper. Return chicken or rabbit and bacon to pan.

4 Bake, covered, in a 350° oven about 1 hour or until the chicken or rabbit is tender. Stir in the currant jelly. If desired, season to taste with salt and pepper and sprinkle with fresh rosemary. Makes 4 servings.

Nutrition facts per serving: 290 cal., 9 g total fat (3 g sat. fat), 95 mg chol., 406 mg sodium, 16 g carbo., 2 g fiber, 32 g pro. *Daily values:* 99% vit. A, 6% vit. C, 3% calcium, 15% iron.

LEMON-TARRAGON CHICKEN

Prep: 20 min. ◆ Bake: 45 min.

Whether you make it in a clay pot or in an ovenproof Dutch oven, this family-pleasing chicken-and-potatoes dish goes together quickly. (See the photograph on page 78.)

1 tsp. dried tarragon, crushed
1 tsp. finely shredded lemon peel
¾ tsp. salt
½ tsp. paprika
⅛ tsp. ground red pepper
4 small potatoes, sliced ¼ inch thick (about 1 lb.)
1 large onion, cut into 8 wedges
2 lb. meaty chicken pieces, skinned, if desired
◆◆◆
1 Tbsp. lemon juice
Lemon peel curls and lemon wedges (optional)
Snipped fresh tarragon (optional)

1 Do not preheat oven when using clay pot. Submerge the top and bottom portions of a 2- to

3-quart clay pot (unglazed) in a sink of cool water; allow to soak for 30 minutes. In a small bowl combine tarragon, lemon peel, salt, paprika, and ground red pepper; set aside. Drain the clay pot. Place potatoes and onion in pot. Sprinkle with about half of the tarragon mixture. Place chicken pieces on top of potatoes and onion. Sprinkle with remaining tarragon mixture. Put top on clay pot; place in cold oven.

2 Set oven temperature to 425° and bake for 45 to 50 minutes or until potatoes are tender and chicken is no longer pink. Drizzle lemon juice over all. If desired, sprinkle with lemon peel curls and snipped fresh tarragon; serve with lemon wedges. Makes 4 servings.

■ DUTCH OVEN DIRECTIONS ■

Preheat oven to 375°. In a small bowl combine tarragon, lemon peel, salt, paprika, and ground red pepper. Place potatoes and onion in a large ovenproof Dutch oven. Sprinkle with about half of the tarragon mixture. Place chicken pieces on top of potatoes and onion. Sprinkle with remaining tarragon mixture.

Bake, covered, 45 to 50 minutes or until potatoes are tender and chicken is no longer pink. Drizzle lemon juice over all. If desired, sprinkle with lemon peel curls and snipped fresh tarragon; serve with lemon wedges.

Nutrition facts per serving: 382 cal., 13 g total fat (4 g sat. fat), 104 mg chol., 500 mg sodium, 29 g carbo., 2 g fiber, 37 g pro. *Daily values:* 5% vit. A, 31% vit. C, 3% calcium, 22% iron.

CURRIED TURKEY MEATBALLS WITH CUCUMBER RAITA

Start to finish: 30 min.

Yogurt salads, known as "raita," are used to tame the spiciness of many Indian dishes.

1 beaten egg white
½ cup chopped green onions
⅓ cup soft bread crumbs (about ½ slice)
3 Tbsp. snipped fresh cilantro
1 tsp. curry powder
½ tsp. ground coriander
½ tsp. ground cumin
½ tsp. salt
1 lb. ground raw turkey

♦♦♦

1 Tbsp. margarine or butter
¼ cup slivered almonds
1 cup basmati rice or long grain rice
2 cups water

♦♦♦

1 small cucumber, seeded and finely chopped (about 1 cup)
½ cup plain low-fat yogurt
½ tsp. honey
Dash ground red pepper

1 In a large mixing bowl combine egg white, ¼ cup of the green onions, the soft bread crumbs, 1 tablespoon of the cilantro, the curry powder, coriander, cumin, and ¼ teaspoon of the salt. Add ground turkey; mix well. Shape into 24 meatballs. Arrange meatballs in a 15×10×1-inch baking pan. Bake in a 350° oven for 15 to 20 minutes or until no pink remains. Drain off fat.

Curried Turkey Meatballs With Cucumber Raita (see left)

♦♦♦

Warm soft pita bread

♦♦♦

Iced tea with lemon slices

♦♦♦

Orange slices drizzled with honey and lightly sprinkled with ground cinnamon

♦♦♦

Crisp ginger or almond cookies

2 Meanwhile, in a small saucepan heat margarine or butter until melted. Add almonds; cook and stir for 1 minute. Add rice; cook and stir about 2 minutes more or until lightly toasted. Carefully add water and remaining salt. Bring to boiling; reduce heat. Simmer, covered, for 15 minutes. Remove from heat; let stand for 5 minutes.

3 In a small mixing bowl stir together the remaining green onions, remaining cilantro, the cucumber, yogurt, honey, and ground red pepper.

4 To serve, spoon rice onto a serving platter or 4 dinner plates; top with turkey meatballs. Spoon cucumber mixture atop. Makes 4 servings.

Nutrition facts per serving: 428 cal., 17 g total fat (4 g sat. fat), 44 mg chol., 413 mg sodium, 45 g carbo., 2 g fiber, 23 g pro. *Daily values:* 7% vit. A, 6% vit. C, 11% calcium, 29% iron.

CUTTING UP IN THE KITCHEN

Even experienced cooks sometimes falter when a recipe asks for "cubed ham" or shortening cut into flour until the pieces are the "size of small peas." To help, we've provided life-size illustrated examples of the most commonly used recipe terms. So put your rulers away.

"Cubed" refers to uniform pieces, usually ½ inch on all sides.

"Chopped" means cut into medium-size irregular pieces. **"Coarsely chopped"** indicates slightly larger pieces.

"Crumbs" indicates crackers or cookies that are crushed finely for cheesecake and tart crusts or for coatings. Use a rolling pin, food processor, or blender.

"Snipped fresh herbs" signifies that scissors should be used to cut the leaves into tiny pieces. For ease, put herbs in a cup, then snip.

"Minced" means cut into tiny irregular pieces. Garlic can be minced by squeezing through a press.

"Diced" means cut into uniform pieces about ¼ inch on each side.

"Until pieces are the size of small peas" refers to shortening, margarine, or butter worked into dry ingredients with a pastry blender so the largest pieces are about ½ inch in diameter.

"Matchsticks" or **"julienne"** refers to strips about 2 inches long and about ¼ inch thick.

"Sliced" means cut crosswise about ¼ inch thick.

MEDITERRANEAN CHICKEN PIZZA

Prep: 15 min. ◆ Bake: 10 min.

For more than mozzarella cheese, try one of the preshredded pizza cheese blends.

1 16-oz. Italian bread shell
   (Boboli)
⅔ cup pizza sauce
   ◆◆◆
8 oz. skinless, boneless chicken
   breast halves
1 tsp. ground cumin
½ tsp. ground coriander
½ tsp. chili powder
¼ tsp. salt
1 6-oz. jar marinated artichoke
   hearts
   ◆◆◆
1 cup sliced fresh mushrooms
1 small red sweet pepper, cut
   into thin strips
1 Tbsp. finely chopped
   shallots
2 cloves garlic, minced
   ◆◆◆
¼ cup sliced pitted ripe olives
1 cup shredded mozzarella
   cheese (4 oz.)

1 Place bread shell on a pizza pan or large baking sheet. Spread pizza sauce atop bread shell, leaving ½ inch border; set aside.

2 Rinse chicken; pat dry. Cut chicken into bite-size strips. In a mixing bowl combine cumin, coriander, chili powder, and salt. Add chicken strips to the mixture, tossing to coat. Set chicken aside. Drain artichokes, reserving marinade. Coarsely chop artichokes; sprinkle atop pizza sauce.

3 In a large skillet heat 2 tablespoons of the reserved artichoke marinade. Add the mushrooms, red sweet pepper, shallots, and garlic. Cook and stir for 2 minutes. Using a slotted spoon, remove vegetables from the skillet and spoon atop pizza.

4 If necessary, add remaining reserved marinade (about 1 tablespoon) to skillet; add chicken. Cook and stir for 3 to 4 minutes or until tender and no longer pink. With the slotted spoon, remove chicken and spoon atop pizza. Sprinkle with olives and cheese. Bake in a 400° oven for 10 to 12 minutes or until cheese is melted. Cut into wedges. Serve immediately. Makes 6 servings.

Nutrition facts per serving: 343 cal., 12 g total fat (2 g sat. fat), 34 mg chol., 784 mg sodium, 41 g carbo., 2 g fiber, 22 g pro. *Daily values:* 20% vit. A, 46% vit. C, 19% calcium, 18% iron.

GINGER AND CILANTRO SCAMPI

Start to finish: 35 min.

Jasmine rice adds a subtle popcorn flavor to the spunky shrimp. You'll find jasmine rice in larger supermarkets as well as Asian and Indian groceries.

1 lb. fresh or frozen peeled
   and deveined medium
   shrimp
2 Tbsp. finely chopped shallot
¼ tsp. ground cumin
1 Tbsp. margarine or butter
2 cups water
¼ tsp. salt
1 cup jasmine rice or long
   grain rice
2 tsp. cornstarch
⅔ cup chicken broth
2 Tbsp. lemon juice
1 Tbsp. margarine or butter
3 cloves garlic, minced
1 Tbsp. grated fresh ginger
¼ tsp. crushed red pepper
   ◆◆◆
¼ cup snipped fresh cilantro

1 Thaw shrimp if frozen; set aside. In a medium saucepan cook and stir shallots and cumin in 1 tablespoon margarine or butter for 1 minute. Carefully add water and salt; bring to boiling. Slowly add rice; return to boiling. Simmer, covered, for 15 minutes. Remove from heat; let stand, covered, for 5 minutes.

2 Meanwhile, in a small mixing bowl stir together the cornstarch, chicken broth, and lemon juice; set aside. In a large skillet heat 1 tablespoon margarine or butter over medium-high heat. Cook and stir shrimp, garlic, gingerroot, and red pepper in hot margarine for 1 to 3 minutes or until shrimp is opaque. Push shrimp to the side of skillet. Add chicken broth mixture to center of skillet. Cook and stir until thickened and bubbly; stir in shrimp. Cook and stir for 2 minutes more.

3 To serve, stir 2 tablespoons of the cilantro into the rice. Spoon rice onto 4 dinner plates. Top with shrimp and sauce and sprinkle with remaining cilantro. Makes 4 servings.

Nutrition facts per serving: 331 cal., 7 g total fat (1 g sat. fat), 174 mg chol., 539 mg sodium, 41 g carbo., 1 g fiber, 23 g pro. *Daily values:* 21% vit. A, 11% vit. C, 5% calcium, 34% iron.

STEAMED CHOCOLATE PUDDING

Prep: 30 min. ◆ Cook: 1½ hr.
Cool: 40 min.

Steamed what? This pudding is much the same as a cake, except it's cooked over water on the stove, making it extra moist and deliciously rich.

1¾ cups all-purpose flour
2 tsp. baking powder
1⅓ cups milk
2 tsp. instant espresso powder or 4 tsp. instant coffee crystals

◆◆◆

½ cup butter
1¼ cups granulated sugar
½ tsp. almond extract
4 eggs
4 oz. unsweetened chocolate, melted and cooled

◆◆◆

½ cup chopped almonds

◆◆◆

Powdered sugar
1 recipe Chocolate Sauce (see top right)
Orange wedges (optional)
Fresh raspberries (optional)
Edible sage blossoms (optional)

1 Grease and flour a 2½-quart heat-proof glass mixing bowl or a 10-cup steamed pudding mold with cover.

2 In a small mixing bowl stir together the all-purpose flour and baking powder; set aside. In another bowl combine milk and espresso powder or coffee crystals, stirring until dissolved; set aside.

3 In a large mixing bowl beat butter with an electric mixer on medium to high speed for 30 seconds. Add granulated sugar and almond extract; beat until well combined. Add eggs, one at a time, beating on low speed after each addition just until combined. Stir in melted chocolate.

4 Add flour mixture and milk mixture alternately to butter mixture, beating on low speed after each addition just until combined. Stir in almonds. Pour batter into prepared bowl or mold. Cover with foil or put lid on mold; press foil tightly against edge of bowl.

5 Place bowl or mold on a rack in a deep kettle. Add boiling water to a depth of about 1 inch up sides of bowl or mold. Cover the kettle and bring water to boiling; reduce heat to simmering. Steam for 1½ to 1¾ hours or until a long wooden pick or skewer inserted in center of pudding comes out clean. Check water level about every 30 minutes, adding additional boiling water to the kettle, as necessary.

6 Remove the bowl or mold from kettle and remove foil or top. Cool pudding for 10 minutes; unmold onto serving platter. Let stand for 30 to 40 minutes on a wire rack to cool slightly. Sift powdered sugar over top of pudding. Serve warm with Chocolate Sauce and, if desired, garnish with orange wedges, raspberries, and edible sage blossoms. Makes 12 servings.

Chocolate Sauce: In a heavy small saucepan over low heat, melt ¾ cup semisweet chocolate pieces and ¼ cup butter. Add ⅔ cup sugar. Gradually stir in one 5-ounce can (⅔ cup) evaporated milk. Bring mixture to boiling; reduce heat. Boil gently over low heat for 8 minutes, stirring frequently. Remove pan from heat. Cool slightly.

▌ TO MAKE AHEAD ▐

Prepare and steam pudding as directed at left. Cool for 10 minutes; unmold onto a wire rack. Cool thoroughly. Wrap tightly; store in the refrigerator for up to 2 weeks. To reheat, return pudding to the same bowl or mold. Cover and steam about 45 minutes or until warm. Unmold and allow pudding to stand until slightly cool for easier slicing.

Nutrition facts per serving: 331 cal., 18 g total fat (8 g sat. fat), 93 mg chol., 174 mg sodium, 41 g carbo., 2 g fiber, 7 g pro. *Daily values:* 12% vit. A, 10% calcium, 13% iron.

OATMEAL-CHEESECAKE-CRANBERRY BARS

Prep: 20 min. ◆ Bake: 55 min.
Chill: at least 3 hr.

Cranberry sauce adds a winning tartness to these special cheesecake-flavored goodies.

2 cups all-purpose flour
1¼ cups quick-cooking rolled oats
¾ cup packed brown sugar
1 cup butter, softened

12 oz. cream cheese, softened
½ cup granulated sugar
2 eggs
2 tsp. lemon juice
1 tsp. vanilla

♦♦♦

1 16-oz. can whole cranberry
 sauce
2 tsp. cornstarch

1 Grease a 13×9×2-inch baking pan; set aside. In a large mixing bowl stir together flour, oats, and brown sugar. Using a pastry blender or two knives, cut in butter until mixture resembles coarse crumbs. Reserve 1½ cups of the crumbs. Press remaining crumbs into the prepared baking pan. Bake in a 350° oven 15 minutes.

2 Meanwhile, for filling, in the same bowl beat the cream cheese and granulated sugar with an electric mixer on medium speed until light and fluffy. Beat in the eggs, lemon juice, and vanilla. Carefully spread filling over crust in baking pan.

3 Stir together the cranberry sauce and cornstarch; spoon carefully over cream cheese layer. Sprinkle with the reserved crumbs. Bake about 40 minutes more or until filling is set. Cool on a wire rack. Cover and chill at least 3 hours. Cut into bars. Makes 36 bars.

Nutrition facts per bar: 161 cal., 9 g total fat (5 g sat. fat), 36 mg chol., 88 mg sodium, 19 g carbo., 1 g fiber, 2 g pro. *Daily values:* 9% vit. A, 1% vit. C, 1% calcium, 4% iron.

THE CLEVER COOK

MOCHA MAGIC

When the directions in a chocolate cake or brownie mix call for water, I blend a teaspoon or so of instant coffee crystals into the water first. This lends a subtle but delicious mocha flavor to my baked treats!

Lenora Dernoga
Laurel, Maryland

PRIZE
TESTED
RECIPE
WINNER

MALTED MOCHA BARS

Prep: 25 min. ♦ Bake: 35 min.
Cool: 2 hr.

Chocolate malted milk powder is the secret ingredient in these rich, brownielike bars.

1¼ cups all-purpose flour
⅔ cup butter, softened
⅔ cup packed brown sugar
 Nonstick spray coating

♦♦♦

3 beaten eggs
⅓ cup granulated sugar
2 tsp. vanilla
1½ cups flaked coconut
¾ cup chocolate malted milk
 powder
¼ cup all-purpose flour
1½ tsp. instant espresso powder
 or instant coffee crystals
¼ tsp. baking powder

1½ cups sifted powdered sugar
3 Tbsp. chocolate malted milk
 powder
1 Tbsp. boiling water
2 tsp. vanilla
½ tsp. instant espresso powder
 or instant coffee crystals

1 In a medium mixing bowl stir together 1¼ cups flour, butter, and brown sugar until smooth. If necessary, gently knead to blend. Spray a 13×9×2-inch baking pan with nonstick spray coating; pat flour mixture into the bottom of pan. Bake in a 350° oven about 15 minutes or until just set.

2 Meanwhile, for filling, in a large mixing bowl beat together the eggs, granulated sugar, and 2 teaspoons vanilla with an electric mixer. Stir in coconut, the ¾ cup malted milk powder, the ¼ cup flour, the 1½ teaspoons espresso powder or coffee crystals, baking powder, and ¼ teaspoon *salt.* Carefully spread mixture on top of baked layer. Bake for 20 to 25 minutes more or until set. Cool on a wire rack.

3 For frosting, in a medium mixing bowl beat together powdered sugar, the 3 tablespoons malted milk powder, boiling water, 2 teaspoons vanilla, and ½ teaspoon espresso powder or coffee crystals. If necessary, beat in a little additional boiling water until frosting is easy to spread. Spread frosting over cooled bars. Makes 36 bars.

Nutrition facts per bar: 146 cal., 6 g total fat (4 g sat. fat), 31 mg chol., 85 mg sodium, 23 g carbo., 2 g pro. *Daily values:* 4% vit. A, 1% calcium, 4% iron.

CHEWY CHOCOLATE PEANUT BUTTER BARS

Prep: 20 min. ◆ Bake: 25 min.

Keep this yummy bar cookie recipe handy. It will be one the kids will request time after time.

- 2 **cups all-purpose flour**
- 2 **cups quick-cooking rolled oats**
- 1½ **cups packed brown sugar**
- 1 **cup butter**

◆◆◆

- 1 **14-oz. can (1¼ cups) chocolate-flavored sweetened condensed milk**
- 2 **Tbsp. butter**
- 1 **cup peanut butter**
- 1 **tsp. vanilla**

1 In a large mixing bowl stir together the flour, oats, and brown sugar. Using a pastry blender or two knives, cut in the 1 cup butter until mixture resembles coarse crumbs. Reserve ¾ cup of crumbs for topping. Press remaining crumbs into the bottom of an ungreased 15×10×1-inch baking pan. Set pan aside.

2 In a medium saucepan combine the sweetened condensed milk and 2 tablespoons butter. Cook over medium-low heat until butter is melted, stirring frequently. Remove from heat. Stir in the peanut butter and vanilla. Carefully spread mixture evenly over crust in pan. Sprinkle with reserved crumbs.

3 Bake in a 350° oven about 25 minutes or until crumbs on top are lightly browned. Cool on a wire rack. Cut into bars. Makes 60 bars.

Nutrition facts per bar: 116 cal., 6 g total fat (3 g sat. fat), 11 mg chol., 68 mg sodium, 14 g carbo., 1 g fiber, 2 g pro. *Daily values:* 3% vit. A, 1% calcium, 3% iron.

MARBLED PEANUT-SESAME BROWNIES

Prep: 20 min. ◆ Bake: 30 min.

Tahini is a thick paste that is made from ground sesame seed. Look for the paste in specialty food stores or Asian markets.

- 8 **oz. semisweet chocolate**
- ¼ **cup butter or margarine**

◆◆◆

- ½ **cup butter or margarine**
- ¼ **cup creamy peanut butter**
- ¼ **cup tahini (sesame butter)**
- ¾ **cup packed brown sugar**
- ½ **cup granulated sugar**
- 2 **tsp. baking powder**
- 3 **eggs**
- 2 **Tbsp. milk**
- 1 **tsp. vanilla**
- 2 **cups all-purpose flour**

◆◆◆

- ½ **cup coarsely chopped unsalted peanuts**
- 2 **Tbsp. sesame seed**

1 In a small saucepan melt the chocolate and ¼ cup butter or margarine over low heat until smooth. Set aside to cool slightly.

2 In a large mixing bowl beat together the ½ cup butter or margarine, the peanut butter, and tahini until combined. Add brown sugar, granulated sugar, and baking powder; beat until combined. Beat in the eggs, milk, and vanilla. Beat in as much of the flour as you can with the mixer. Stir in any remaining flour.

3 Spread half of the peanut butter batter into the bottom of an ungreased 13×9×2-inch baking pan. Spread cooled chocolate mixture atop. Spoon remaining peanut butter batter into small mounds over chocolate mixture. Sprinkle with chopped peanuts and sesame seed.

4 Bake in a 350° oven for 30 to 35 minutes or until a wooden toothpick inserted in center comes out clean. Cool on a wire rack. Makes 48 bars.

Nutrition facts per bar: 115 cal., 7 g total fat (3 g sat. fat), 21 mg chol., 57 mg sodium, 12 g carbo., 1 g fiber, 2 g pro. *Daily values:* 3% vit. A, 2% calcium, 4% iron.

Double Chocolate-Orange Brownies

Prep: 15 min. ◆ Bake: 40 min.

1 cup milk chocolate pieces
¼ cup butter or margarine
2 eggs
½ cup granulated sugar
1 tsp. vanilla
½ cup all-purpose flour
½ cup white baking pieces
⅓ cup chopped pecans, almonds, macadamia nuts, or walnuts

◆◆◆

1 3-oz. pkg. cream cheese, softened
2 Tbsp. granulated sugar
1 egg yolk
2 tsp. finely shredded orange peel

◆◆◆

Sifted powdered sugar (optional)

1 Grease an 8×8×2-inch baking pan; set aside. In a medium saucepan melt milk chocolate and butter or margarine over low heat, stirring constantly. Remove from heat. Stir in whole eggs, ½ cup granulated sugar, and vanilla. Using a wooden spoon, beat lightly just until combined. Stir in flour, white baking pieces, and nuts. Spread chocolate batter in prepared baking pan; set aside.

2 In a small mixing bowl, beat cream cheese for 30 seconds. Add the 2 tablespoons granulated sugar; beat until fluffy. Beat in egg yolk and orange peel. Drizzle cream cheese mixture atop chocolate batter in pan. Using a narrow metal spatula gently cut through batter to marble.

3 Bake in a 350° oven for 40 minutes. Cool on a wire rack. Cut into bars. If desired, sprinkle with sifted powdered sugar just before serving. Makes 16 bars.

Nutrition facts per bar: 201 cal., 12 g total fat (7 g sat. fat), 55 mg chol., 70 mg sodium, 20 g carbo., 0 g fiber, 3 g pro. *Daily values:* 9% vit. A, 3% calcium, 3% iron.

No-Fret Apple Pie

Prep: 40 min. ◆ Bake: 1 hr.

Served upside down on its cheddar crust, this pie tastes best when topped with flavorful cinnamon-flecked whipped cream.

6 cups baking apples, peeled, cored, and sliced ½ inch thick (about 2½ lb.)
¼ cup granulated sugar
¼ cup packed brown sugar
½ tsp. ground cinnamon
2 Tbsp. quick-cooking tapioca
½ cup chopped walnuts
¼ cup raisins

◆◆◆

1 cup all-purpose flour
¼ cup shortening
⅔ cup shredded extra-sharp or sharp cheddar cheese
3 to 4 Tbsp. cold water

◆◆◆

1 Tbsp. margarine or butter, cut into small pieces
1 Tbsp. milk

◆◆◆

1 recipe Cinnamon Whipped Cream (see right)

1 Butter a 9×1½-inch round baking pan; set aside. In a mixing bowl combine apples, sugars, cinnamon, and tapioca. Stir in walnuts and raisins. Let stand at room temperature for 30 minutes.

2 In a medium mixing bowl stir together all-purpose flour and dash *salt*. Using a pastry blender, cut in shortening until pieces are the size of small peas. Stir in cheddar cheese. Sprinkle 1 tablespoon of the water over part of the mixture; gently toss with a fork. Push moistened dough to side of bowl. Repeat, using 1 tablespoon water at a time, until all the dough is moistened. Form dough into ball.

3 On a lightly floured surface use your hands to slightly flatten dough. Roll dough from center to edges into a 10-inch circle.

4 Pour apple mixture into prepared baking pan; dot with margarine or butter. Lay pastry crust over top. Press pastry crust to sides of pan. Brush with milk. Cut 3 parallel slits, 2 inches long, into top of crust to allow for steam to escape.

5 Bake in a 325° oven for 1 to 1¼ hours or until top is golden brown. Cool for 1 hour. To serve, invert onto a 12-inch plate, loosening edges if necessary. Cut into wedges and serve warm with Cinnamon Whipped Cream. Makes 8 servings.

Cinnamon Whipped Cream: In a small chilled bowl combine 1 cup whipping cream, 2 tablespoons granulated sugar, and ½ teaspoon ground cinnamon. Beat with chilled beaters of an electric mixer on medium speed until soft peaks form.

Nutrition facts per serving: 438 cal., 27 g total fat (11 g sat. fat), 50 mg chol., 104 mg sodium, 47 g carbo., 3 g fiber, 6 g pro. *Daily values:* 18% vit. A, 9% vit. C, 9% calcium, 9% iron.

JUMPING BLACK BEAN SALAD

Start to finish: 10 min.

In this main-dish salad, red pepper and cumin add spice, while black beans bring protein to the mix.

1 15-oz. can black beans, rinsed and drained
2 tsp. chili oil or olive oil
½ tsp. ground cumin
2 Tbsp. lime juice
4 cups torn mixed greens
   Chopped tomatoes
   Shredded carrot
   Ground red pepper to taste

1 Mix beans, chili oil, cumin, and lime juice. Toss with greens, tomatoes, carrot, red pepper, and salt to taste. Makes 3 servings.

Nutrition facts per serving: 139 cal., 4 g fat, (0 g sat. fat), 0 mg chol., 406 mg sodium, 23 g carbo., 8 g fiber., 10 g pro. *Daily values:* 5% vit. A, 21% vit. C, 3% calcium, 15% iron.

TURKEY SANDWICH ON THE WING

Start to finish: 10 min.

1 Tbsp. plain fat-free yogurt
2 tsp. horseradish mustard
2 slices multigrain bread, toasted
   Lettuce leaves
2 to 3 oz. sliced cooked fat-free turkey breast
2 slices tomato
1 thin slice yellow sweet pepper
6 fresh snow pea pods

1 Stir together yogurt and mustard. Spread mixture onto one side of each bread slice. On one bread slice layer lettuce, turkey, tomato, yellow pepper, and pea pods. Top with remaining bread. Makes 1 sandwich.

Nutrition facts per sandwich: 229 cal., 3 g fat, (1 g sat. fat), 21 mg chol., 1029 mg sodium, 33 g carbo., 2 g fiber, 19 g pro. *Daily values:* 4% vit. A, 89% vit. C, 8% calcium, 23% iron.

ON THE FLY STIR-FRY

Start to finish: 20 min.

A simple stir-fry can pack a meal's-worth of nutrition into a single dish. Don't want chicken? Substitute lean beef or pork. Whichever one you choose, dinner is on the table with a fast flip of the wrist.

   Nonstick spray coating
8 oz. skinless, boneless chicken breast, cut into thin strips
2 medium carrots, thinly bias-sliced
1½ cups small broccoli florets
2 cloves minced garlic
¼ cup bias-sliced green onion
3 Tbsp. chopped honey-roasted peanuts
1 Tbsp. grated fresh ginger
1 Tbsp. reduced-sodium soy sauce
1 tsp. toasted sesame oil
¼ to ½ tsp. crushed red pepper
¼ cup bottled plum sauce
¼ cup water
   Hot cooked noodles or rice

1 Spray a nonstick wok or large skillet with spray coating. Add chicken, carrots, broccoli, and garlic; stir-fry for 3 minutes. Add green onions, peanuts, fresh ginger, soy sauce, sesame oil, and crushed red pepper. Stir-fry for 2 minutes more. Stir in plum sauce and water; heat through. Serve over hot cooked noodles or rice. Makes 4 servings.

Nutrition facts per serving: 523 cal., 5 g fat, (1 g sat. fat), 30 mg chol., 227 mg sodium, 104 g carbo., 3 g fiber, 14 g pro. *Daily values:* 93% vit. A, 57% vit. C, 5% calcium, 23% iron.

SHAKE, RATTLE, AND POUR SMOOTHIES

Start to finish: 10 min.

A yogurt-berry smoothie is almost a meal in itself. It's perfect as an energy-boosting morning pick-me-up or as an emergency lunch toted in a sport bottle and enjoyed on the run.

2 cups plain fat-free yogurt
2 ripe medium bananas
1 cup sliced fresh strawberries or unsweetened frozen strawberries
1 cup mixed fresh berries, such as raspberries, blueberries, and/or blackberries, or unsweetened frozen mixed berries

1 In a blender container combine yogurt and fruit. Cover and blend until pureed. Serves 3 or 4.

Nutrition facts per serving: 176 cal., 1 g fat, (0 g sat. fat), 3 mg chol., 89 mg sodium, 25 g carbo., 3 g fiber, 10 g pro. *Daily values:* 2% vit. A, 53% vit. C, 19% calcium, 3% iron.

APRIL
Down-Home Baking

*N*othing stirs the appetite like the smell of baked goods wafting from the kitchen. Give your family plenty to anticipate with a month's worth of home-tested recipes. How about Dill and Cheese Beer Bread? (It's great for beginning bakers.) Or Maple-Macadamia Cake? Tender Potato Rolls are foolproof, and Cheese Cracker Delights are homemade treats you can't get anywhere but home. Try starting the day with a warm, gooey slice of Sour Cream Bread and ending it with a slice of airy Strawberry Chiffon Pie. No one will stray far from the kitchen, waiting for the next fragrant offering.

30-minute recipes indicated in RED.
Low-fat and no-fat recipes indicated
with a ♥.
Photographs indicated in italics.
*All new in 1998.

CHOCOLATY PEANUT BUTTER AND BANANA BREAD

Prep: 15 min. ◆ Bake: 45 min.

Start your day with a slice of this stir-together bread or give yourself an energy boost by snacking on it mid-afternoon.

2 slightly beaten eggs
1 cup mashed bananas (2 to 3 medium)
¾ cup sugar
½ cup creamy peanut butter
½ cup milk
2 cups self-rising flour*
¾ cup semisweet chocolate pieces
½ cup chopped peanuts or pecans

1 Grease the bottom and ½ inch up the sides of two 8×4×2-inch or two 7½×3½×2-inch loaf pans; set aside.

2 In a medium mixing bowl stir together the eggs, bananas, sugar, peanut butter, and milk. Stir in the flour just until moistened (batter should be lumpy). Fold in the chocolate pieces and peanuts or pecans.

3 Spoon batter into the prepared pans. Bake in a 350° oven about 45 minutes or until a wooden toothpick inserted near the center comes out clean. Cool in pans on a wire rack for 10 minutes. Remove loaves from pans. Cool completely on a wire rack. Wrap and store overnight for easier slicing. Makes 2 loaves (32 servings).

*Note: Substitute 2 cups all-purpose flour plus 2 teaspoons baking powder, 1 teaspoon salt, and ½ teaspoon baking soda.

Nutrition facts per serving: 117 cal., 5 g total fat (1 g sat. fat), 14 mg chol., 134 mg sodium, 15 g carbo., 1 g fiber, 3 g pro. *Daily values:* 1% vit. C, 3% calcium, 3% iron.

PRIZE TESTED RECIPE WINNER

ISLAND-STYLE BANANA BREAD

Prep: 20 hours ◆ Bake: 50 min.

A nibble is all it takes to wow your taste buds with this tropical teaser.

2 cups all-purpose flour
1½ tsp. ground cinnamon
1 tsp. baking powder
½ tsp. baking soda
¼ tsp. salt

◆◆◆

½ cup butter, softened
½ cup packed brown sugar
2 slightly beaten eggs
1 tsp. vanilla
1 cup mashed ripe banana (2 to 3 medium)
½ cup chopped pecans

◆◆◆

1 8-oz. pkg. reduced-fat cream cheese (Neufchâtel)
1 egg
¼ cup packed brown sugar
½ cup coconut

1 Grease bottom and ½ inch up sides of two 7½×3½×2-inch loaf pans; set aside.

2 In a large mixing bowl stir together the flour, cinnamon, baking powder, baking soda, and salt; set aside.

3 In a large mixing bowl beat butter with an electric mixer on high speed for 30 seconds. Add the ½ cup brown sugar, the 2 eggs, and vanilla; beat until combined. Add dry mixture and mashed banana alternately to beaten mixture, beating on low speed after each addition until combined. Stir in pecans.

4 In a medium mixing bowl beat the cream cheese, egg, and ¼ cup brown sugar on medium speed until almost smooth. Stir in the coconut.

5 Pour one-fourth of the banana batter into each loaf pan. Spoon one-fourth of the cream cheese mixture over each loaf. Using a thin metal spatula or a table knife, cut through the batter to marble. Repeat the 2 layers as above, but do not marble.

6 Bake in a 350° oven about 50 minutes or until a wooden toothpick inserted near the center comes out clean. Cool in pans on a wire rack for 10 minutes. Remove loaves from pans. Cool completely on a wire rack. Wrap and store overnight for easier slicing. Makes 2 loaves (20 slices).

Nutrition facts per slice: 191 cal., 11 g total fat (5 g sat. fat), 53 mg chol., 180 mg sodium, 21 g carbo., 1 g fiber, 4 g pro. *Daily values:* 9% vit. A, 2% vit. C, 3% calcium, 7% iron.

RHUBARB BREAD

Prep: 20 min. ◆ Bake: 50 min.

Harvest a crop of tender new rhubarb and stir it into this coffeecakelike bread.

- 2¾ **cups all-purpose flour**
- 1 **tsp. baking soda**
- 1 **tsp. salt**
- 1 **tsp. ground cinnamon**

◆◆◆

- 1 **slightly beaten egg**
- 1⅓ **cups packed brown sugar**
- 1 **8-oz. carton plain low-fat yogurt**
- ½ **cup bran cereal flakes**
- ⅓ **cup applesauce**
- ¼ **cup cooking oil**
- 2 **cups finely chopped fresh rhubarb**
- 1 **recipe Streusel Topping (see above right)**

1 Grease the bottom and ½ inch up the sides of two 8×4×2-inch loaf pans; set aside.

2 In a large mixing bowl stir together the flour, baking soda, salt, and cinnamon; set aside.

3 In a medium mixing bowl stir together the egg, brown sugar, yogurt, bran cereal flakes, applesauce, and cooking oil. Add egg mixture all at once to dry mixture. Stir just until combined. Gently stir in rhubarb.

4 Spread batter into prepared pans. Sprinkle with Streusel Topping. Bake in a 350° oven about 50 minutes or until a wooden toothpick inserted near center comes out clean. Cool in pans on a wire rack for 10 minutes. Remove bread from pans. Cool completely on a wire rack.

Wrap and store overnight for easier slicing. Makes 2 loaves (32 servings).

Streusel Topping: In a small bowl stir together ¼ cup packed brown sugar, ¼ cup rolled oats, 1 tablespoon all-purpose flour, ¼ teaspoon ground cinnamon, and 2 tablespoons melted butter or margarine.

Nutrition facts per serving: 115 cal., 3 g total fat (1 g sat. fat), 8 mg chol., 130 mg sodium, 21 g carbo., 1 g fiber, 2 g pro. *Daily values:* 1% vit. A, 1% vit. C, 2% calcium, 8% iron.

PRIZE TESTED RECIPE WINNER

PEPPERY CHEESE BREAD

Prep: 15 min. ◆ Bake: 45 min.

Spicy mustard, plenty of pepper, and melted cheese create pleasing flavor contrasts in this loaf.

- 2½ **cups all-purpose flour**
- 1 **Tbsp. sugar**
- 1½ to 2 **tsp. cracked black pepper**
- 1 **tsp. baking powder**
- ¾ **tsp. salt**
- ½ **tsp. baking soda**

◆◆◆

- 2 **beaten eggs**
- 1 **8-oz. carton plain low-fat yogurt**
- ½ **cup cooking oil**
- ¼ **cup milk**
- 1 **Tbsp. spicy brown mustard**
- 1 **cup shredded cheddar cheese (4 oz.)**
- ¼ **cup thinly sliced green onions**

1 Grease the bottom and ½ inch up the sides of an 8×4×2-inch loaf pan; set aside.

2 In a large bowl stir together flour, sugar, pepper, baking powder, salt, and soda. Make a well in center of dry mixture; set aside.

3 In a medium bowl stir together eggs, yogurt, oil, milk, and mustard. Add to dry mixture along with cheese and green onions. Stir just until moistened.

4 Spread batter into prepared pan. Bake for 45 to 50 minutes or until a wooden toothpick inserted near center comes out clean. Cool in pan on a wire rack for 10 minutes. Remove bread from pan. Cool for 1 hour on a wire rack; serve warm. Wrap any leftovers and store in refrigerator for up to 3 days. Makes 1 loaf (16 servings).

Nutrition facts per slice: 179 cal., 10 g total fat (3 g sat. fat), 35 mg chol., 239 mg sodium, 16 g carbo., 1 g fiber, 5 g pro. *Daily values:* 4% vit. A, 1% vit. C, 9% calcium, 7% iron.

Grilled pork chops

♦♦♦

Buttered new potatoes
and peas

♦♦♦

Salad of leaf lettuce, red
seedless grapes, feta cheese,
and poppy seed dressing

♦♦♦

Dill and Cheese Beer Bread
(see below)

LOW FAT DILL AND CHEESE BEER BREAD

Prep: 15 min. ♦ Bake: 45 min.

You don't have to be an experienced bread baker to make this savory loaf. It's as easy as stirring and baking.

- 3 cups self-rising flour*
- ½ cup shredded cheddar cheese (2 oz.)
- ½ cup shredded Monterey Jack cheese with jalapeño peppers (2 oz.)
- 2 Tbsp. sugar
- 1 Tbsp. dillseed
- 1 tsp. dried dillweed
- 1 12-oz. can beer

1 Grease the bottom and ½-inch up the sides of a 9×5×3-inch loaf pan; set aside.

2 In a large mixing bowl stir together the flour, cheddar cheese, Monterey Jack cheese, sugar, dillseed, and dillweed. Add beer and stir until well combined.

3 Spread batter into prepared pan. Bake in a 350° oven about 45 minutes or until bread sounds hollow when lightly tapped. Cool in pan on a wire rack for 10 minutes. Remove bread from pan. Cool completely on wire rack. Serve or wrap and store in the refrigerator for up to 3 days. Makes 1 loaf (16 servings).

*Note: Substitute 3 cups all-purpose flour plus 1 tablespoon baking powder, 1 teaspoon salt, and ¾ teaspoon baking soda.

Nutrition facts per serving: 128 cal., 2 g total fat (1 g sat. fat), 7 mg chol., 373 mg sodium, 21 g carbo., 1 g fiber, 4 g pro. *Daily values:* 2% vit. A, 11% calcium, 8% iron.

PEACH-RASPBERRY UPSIDE-DOWN CAKE

Prep: 15 min. ♦ Bake: 30 min.

Peaches and raspberries, upside down—this cake will be the talk of the town.

- 1 8¼-oz. can peach slices (juice pack)
- 2 Tbsp. margarine or butter
- ⅓ cup packed brown sugar
- ½ cup loose-pack frozen raspberries
- 1 pkg. 1-layer-size yellow cake mix
  Whipped cream (optional)

1 Drain peaches, reserving 1 tablespoon juice. Melt margarine or butter in a 9×1½-inch round baking pan over medium-low heat. Stir in the brown sugar and reserved juice. Arrange peach slices atop sugar mixture in pan. Sprinkle with frozen raspberries.

2 In a medium mixing bowl prepare cake mix batter according to package directions. Carefully pour the cake batter over the peach and raspberry mixture.

3 Bake in a 350° oven for 30 to 35 minutes or until a wooden toothpick inserted near the center comes out clean. Cool in the pan on a wire rack for 10 minutes. Loosen the edges of the cake with a knife; invert cake onto a serving plate. Serve cake warm, topped with a spoonful of whipped cream, if desired. Makes 8 to 10 servings.

Nutrition facts per serving: 215 cal., 6 g total fat (1 g sat. fat), 27 mg chol., 263 mg sodium, 39 g carbo., 1 g fiber, 2 g pro. *Daily values:* 5% vit. A, 5% vit. C, 4% calcium, 6% iron.

MAPLE-MACADAMIA CAKE

Prep: 20 min. ♦ Bake: 35 min.

Lots of nuts and a hint of maple help make this a tasty cake to set on your table.

- 1 pkg. 2-layer-size spice cake mix
- ¼ cup maple-flavored syrup
- 2 medium cooking apples, peeled, cored, and finely chopped (about 2 cups)

♦♦♦

- ½ cup all-purpose flour
- 3 Tbsp. brown sugar
- ¼ cup cold butter or margarine
- 1 cup macadamia nuts, finely chopped

1 Grease and lightly flour a 13×9×2-inch baking pan; set pan aside.

2 In a large mixing bowl, prepare cake mix according to package directions, reducing water called for to 1 cup; stir in syrup. Fold apples into batter. Spread batter evenly into prepared pan. Bake in 350° oven about 15 minutes or until top is just barely set.

3 Meanwhile, in a small mixing bowl stir together flour and brown sugar. Using a pastry blender or two knives, cut in butter or margarine until pieces are the size of small peas. Stir in nuts. Sprinkle crumb mixture evenly over partially baked cake. Continue baking 20 to 25 minutes or until a wooden toothpick inserted near the center comes out clean. Serve warm or cool. Makes 12 servings.

Nutrition facts per serving: 421 cal., 23 g total fat (4 g sat. fat), 53 mg chol., 363 mg sodium, 52 g carbo., 2 g fiber, 4 g pro. *Daily values:* 7% vit. A, 1% vit. C, 10% calcium, 9% iron.

CHOCOLATE-NUT PHYLLO CUPS

Prep: 40 min. ◆ Bake: 10 min.

If you'd rather, fill these crispy nut cups with your favorite ready-made pudding instead of the honey-cream filling.

- 3 **Tbsp. honey**
- 1 **Tbsp. cornstarch**
- 1 **cup half-and-half or light cream**
- 2 **beaten egg yolks**

◆◆◆

- 1 **cup ground pecans**
- 4 **tsp. granulated sugar**
- 4 **sheets frozen phyllo dough (17×12 inches), thawed**
- 3 **Tbsp. butter or margarine, melted**
- 1 **oz. semisweet chocolate, cut up**
- 1 **Tbsp. butter or margarine**
- ¾ **cup sifted powdered sugar**
- ½ **tsp. vanilla**
- 2 **to 3 tsp. hot water Unsweetened cocoa powder**

◆◆◆

- ½ **cup whipping cream**
- ½ **tsp. vanilla Grated semisweet chocolate (optional)**

1 In a heavy small saucepan stir together honey and cornstarch. Add half-and-half or light cream. Cook and stir over medium heat until mixture is thickened and bubbly. Cook and stir for 2 minutes more. Remove from heat. Gradually stir some of the hot mixture into the egg yolks. Return all to saucepan. Bring to a gentle boil; reduce heat. Cook and stir for 2 minutes more. Pour mixture into a bowl. Cover surface with clear plastic wrap. Chill.

2 Grease twelve 2½-inch muffin cups; set aside. In a bowl stir together ground pecans and granulated sugar; set aside. Unfold phyllo. Place one sheet of phyllo on work surface; brush with some of the 3 tablespoons melted butter or margarine. Sprinkle evenly with one-third of the nut mixture. Repeat brushing, sprinkling, and layering 2 times. Cover with remaining sheet of phyllo; brush top with melted butter or margarine. Trim edges. Cut phyllo stack crosswise in fourths, and then lengthwise in thirds, to form twelve 4-inch squares.

3 Gently press phyllo squares into the prepared muffin cups, allowing edges to extend upward.

4 Bake in a 350° oven 10 to 15 minutes or until golden. Cool completely in pan on a wire rack. Carefully remove phyllo cups from pan.

5 To serve, in a small, heavy saucepan melt the 1 ounce chocolate and the 1 tablespoon butter or margarine over low heat, stirring until smooth. Remove from heat. Stir in the powdered sugar and the ½ teaspoon vanilla. Add hot water, 1 teaspoon at a time, until it reaches drizzling consistency. Lightly drizzle melted chocolate on dessert plates. Sift cocoa powder over chocolate. (Chocolate also can be drizzled over edges and insides of cups.)

6 In a small, chilled mixing bowl, beat the whipping cream and ½ teaspoon vanilla with an electric mixer on medium speed until soft peaks form. Fold the chilled egg yolk mixture into the whipped cream. Spoon the cream mixture into each phyllo cup. If desired, top each with grated chocolate. Serve immediately. Makes 12 servings.

■ TO MAKE AHEAD ■

Prepare and bake the phyllo cups. Cool completely. Place in a freezer container and freeze for up to 1 week. To serve, let phyllo cups stand at room temperature 20 to 30 minutes or until thawed. Fill with cream mixture and top with grated chocolate as directed.

Nutrition facts per serving: 243 cal., 18 g total fat (7 g sat. fat), 67 mg chol., 83 mg sodium, 20 g carbo., 1 g fiber, 3 g pro. *Daily values:* 16% vit. A, 3% calcium, 4% iron.

DOWN-HOME BAKING

The first signs of spring in a Southern baker's kitchen are light-as-air creations that match the freshness of the season. We've gathered some flavorful secrets from down South that are sure to make your taste buds bloom. Bread pudding crowded with blueberries, a warm slice of heaven-scent cinnamon bread, a wicker swing swaying 'neath the flowering dogwoods…now that's the epitome of Southern comfort.

Jackie Guice

Jackie Guice of Decatur, Alabama, baked her first corn bread when she was about 9 years old. Her father gobbled it up enthusiastically, and Jackie's been baking ever since. When spring is in the air, the aroma of fresh flavors wafts from Jackie's oven. "Spring is a happy, hopeful time of year," Jackie says. "It's a time when simple things are appreciated." And Jackie's simply sensational baked goods are no exception. Her recipes, some handed down through generations, are loaded with tradition and full of homey goodness. Although good ol' Southern corn bread, time-honored cheese straws, and best-ever biscuits are standard fare in her home, she often tinkers with the ingredients to incorporate shortcuts or to customize the goodies for springtime occasions.

"Hospitality and love go into Southern baking as part of the ingredients," Jackie says. That must be why her friends and family gather to enjoy treasured favorites as often as they can.

½-inch thickness. Cut dough into circles with a floured 2½-inch biscuit cutter.

3 Place biscuits 1 inch apart on a lightly greased baking sheet. Bake in a 425° oven for 10 to 15 minutes or until golden. Remove biscuits from baking sheet and serve hot. Makes 10 to 12 biscuits.

*Note: Substitute 2 cups all-purpose flour plus 2 teaspoons baking powder, 1 teaspoon salt, and ½ teaspoon baking soda.

Nutrition facts per biscuit: 136 cal., 5 g total fat (3 g sat. fat), 13 mg chol., 415 mg sodium, 19 g carbo., 3 g fiber, 3 g pro. *Daily values:* 4% vit. A, 8% calcium, 6% iron.

Pepper Cheese Biscuits: Prepare Flaky Biscuits, except stir ¾ cup shredded Monterey Jack cheese with jalapeño peppers (3 ounces), 2 tablespoons snipped fresh chives, and ⅛ teaspoon ground red pepper into flour and butter mixture.

---

30 MIN. LOW FAT

FLAKY BISCUITS

Prep: 15 min. ◆ Bake: 10 min.

Self-rising flour is the key to these Sunday-best biscuits. This flour has salt and some leavening already added. (See the photograph of Pepper Cheese Biscuits on page 81.)

2 cups self-rising flour*
¼ tsp. baking soda
¼ cup butter or margarine
¾ cup buttermilk

1 In a medium mixing bowl stir together flour and baking soda. With a pastry blender or two knives cut in butter or margarine until mixture resembles coarse crumbs. Make a well in center. Add the buttermilk all at once; stir until moistened.

2 Turn dough out onto a lightly floured surface. Quickly knead dough by gently folding and pressing the dough 10 to 12 strokes or until nearly smooth. Pat or lightly roll dough to

LOW FAT

TENDER POTATO ROLLS

Prep: 20 min.
Rise: 1¼ hr. plus 30 min.
Bake: 15 min.

For oven-fresh rolls without a lot of last-minute fuss, shape dough in advance and let it rise in the refrigerator until the dinner hour approaches.

3 to 3½ cups bread flour or all-purpose flour
1 pkg. active dry yeast
¾ cup water

½ cup milk
⅓ cup shortening
¼ cup sugar
1 tsp. salt
⅓ cup packaged instant
  mashed potato flakes
1 egg

1 In a large mixing bowl stir together 1 cup of the flour and the yeast. In a medium saucepan heat and stir the water, milk, shortening, sugar, and salt just until warm (120° to 130°) and shortening almost melts. Stir in the potato flakes. Let stand for 1 minute. Add milk mixture to dry mixture along with the egg. Beat with an electric mixer on low to medium speed for 30 seconds, scraping sides of bowl. Beat on high speed for 3 minutes. Using a wooden spoon, stir in as much of the remaining flour as you can.

2 Turn dough out onto a lightly floured surface. Knead in enough of the remaining flour to make a moderately stiff dough that is smooth and elastic (6 to 8 minutes total). Shape dough into a ball. Place dough in a lightly greased bowl, turning once to grease surface of the dough. Cover and let rise in a warm place until double in size (about 1¼ hours).

3 Punch dough down. Turn dough onto a lightly floured surface. Divide the dough in half. Cover and let rest for 10 minutes. Lightly grease two 8×8×2-inch or 9×9×2-inch baking pans.

4 On a lightly floured surface, roll each portion of dough to ½-inch thickness. Cut dough with

a floured 2½-inch round cutter. Place rolls in prepared baking pans. Cover and let rise in a warm place until nearly double in size (30 to 40 minutes). (Or, cover shaped rolls in pan with oiled waxed paper, then with plastic wrap. Refrigerate 2 to 24 hours. Remove from refrigerator and let stand, covered, at room temperature for 20 minutes.)

5 Bake in a 375° oven for 15 to 20 minutes or until golden. Immediately remove rolls from pans. Cool the rolls on wire racks. Makes 20 to 24 rolls.

Nutrition facts per roll: 125 cal., 4 g total fat (1 g sat. fat), 11 mg chol., 116 mg sodium, 19 g carbo., 1 g fiber, 3 g pro. *Daily values:* 1% calcium, 5% iron.

THE CLEVER COOK

SHORTENING SAVVY

Do you hate to measure shortening? Here's a surefire way to eliminate the hassle. When a recipe calls for both eggs and shortening, break eggs into the cup for measuring shortening, then remove. Now, fill the cup with shortening; it will slide out.

Ethel Edmonds
Huntington, West Virginia

COMPANY CORN BREAD
Prep: 15 min. ◆ Bake: 20 min.

A cast-iron skillet is a favorite pan for making corn bread because the cast iron is an excellent conductor of heat. That's what gives the corn bread its wonderful crisp, golden crust. A round cake pan works well, too.

1 cup all-purpose flour
¾ cup cornmeal
2 Tbsp. sugar
1 Tbsp. baking powder
¾ tsp. salt
2 beaten eggs
1 cup milk
¼ cup melted shortening or
  cooking oil

1 In a medium mixing bowl stir together the flour, cornmeal, sugar, baking powder, and salt. In another bowl combine eggs, milk, and melted shortening or cooking oil. Add the egg mixture all at once to the dry mixture. Stir just until moistened.

2 If using a cast-iron skillet, place a greased 10-inch cast-iron skillet in a 400° oven for 3 minutes. Remove from oven. Pour the batter into hot skillet. (Or, pour the batter into an unheated, greased 9×1½-inch round baking pan.) Bake about 20 minutes or until light brown. Cool slightly in pan on a wire rack. Cut into wedges; serve warm. Makes 8 to 10 servings.

Nutrition facts per serving: 203 cal., 9 g total fat (2 g sat. fat), 56 mg chol., 368 mg sodium, 26 g carbo., 1 g fiber, 5 g pro. *Daily values:* 4% vit. A, 14% calcium, 10% iron.

CHEESE CRACKER DELIGHTS

Prep: 20 min. ◆ Chill: 1 hr.
Bake: 15 min.

*The dough for these tidbits
can be made in advance and chilled
until nearly serving time. Then
just slice them, bake them, and serve
them fresh from the oven.
(See the photograph on page 77.)*

2 cups shredded sharp cheddar
  cheese (8 oz.)
½ cup butter
1½ cups all-purpose flour
¼ to ½ tsp. salt
¼ tsp. ground red pepper

1 In a large mixing bowl combine shredded cheese and butter;
bring to room temperature (about
1 hour). Beat with an electric
mixer on medium to high speed
until well combined. Stir in flour,
salt, and red pepper. Divide the
dough in half. Shape dough into
two 7-inch logs. Wrap and chill
logs for at least 1 hour.

2 With a knife or a crinkle
cutter, slice the cheese logs into
¼-inch-thick slices. Place slices
on ungreased baking sheets. Bake
in a 350° oven for 15 minutes.
Remove crackers from baking
sheet and cool on a wire rack.
Makes about 4½ dozen crackers.

TO MAKE AHEAD

Prepare the dough and shape
into logs. Wrap in moisture- and
vapor-proof wrap; freeze for up to
1 month. To serve, thaw 30 minutes before slicing and baking.

Nutrition facts per cracker: 44 cal., 3 g total
fat (2 g sat. fat), 9 mg chol., 56 mg sodium,
3 g carbo., 0 g fiber, 1 g pro.
Daily values: 3% vit. A, 2% calcium, 1% iron.

CHOCOLATE-PECAN CHESS PIE

Prep: 25 min. ◆ Bake: 52 min.

*This cross between a chess pie and a
pecan pie—with some chocolate
sprinkled in for good measure—is a
Southern dessert dream.
(See the photograph on page 77.)*

1 recipe Pastry for Single-
  Crust Pie (see bottom
  right)

◆◆◆

1¼ cups sugar
 4 tsp. cornmeal
 4 eggs
⅓ cup half-and-half or light
  cream
 3 Tbsp. butter or margarine,
  melted and cooled
 1 tsp. vanilla
½ cup pecans, toasted and
  chopped

◆◆◆

½ cup miniature semisweet
  chocolate pieces

1 Prepare Pastry for Single-
Crust Pie. On a lightly floured
surface, use your hands to slightly
flatten dough. Roll dough from
center to edges into a circle about
12-inches in diameter.

2 Transfer pastry to a 9-inch
pie plate. (Do not prick.) Trim
pastry to ½ inch beyond edge of
pie plate. Fold under extra pastry.
Flute edges high. If desired, press
the tines of a fork against the fluted edges at evenly spaced intervals. Line pastry with a double
thickness of foil. Bake in a 450°
oven for 8 minutes. Remove foil;
bake for 4 to 5 minutes more or
until set and dry but not brown.

3 Meanwhile, for filling, in a
small mixing bowl stir together
sugar and cornmeal; set aside. In a
large mixing bowl beat the eggs
with an electric mixer on medium
speed 1 minute. Stir in the sugar
mixture. With a wooden spoon or
rubber spatula, gradually stir in
half-and-half, melted butter or
margarine, and vanilla. Stir in
the pecans.

4 Place the partially baked
pastry shell on the oven rack.
Sprinkle the chocolate pieces into
the bottom of the pastry shell.
Carefully pour the filling into the
pastry shell.

5 To prevent overbrowning,
cover edge of pie with foil (being
careful not to let the foil touch the
filling). Reduce oven temperature
to 350° and bake for 30 minutes.
Remove foil. Bake 10 to 15 minutes more or until center appears
nearly set when shaken. Cool on a
wire rack. Refrigerate within
2 hours; cover for longer storage.
Makes 10 servings.

Pastry for Single-Crust Pie:
Stir together 1¼ cups all-purpose
flour and ¼ teaspoon salt. Cut in
⅓ cup shortening until pieces are
the size of small peas. Using a
total of 4 to 5 tablespoons cold
water, sprinkle 1 tablespoon water
over part of the mixture; gently
toss with a fork. Push to side of
bowl. Repeat until all is moistened. Form into a ball.

Nutrition facts per serving: 365 cal., 20 g
total fat (4 g sat. fat), 90 mg chol., 123 mg
sodium, 43 g carbo., 1 g fiber, 5 g pro.
Daily values: 9% vit. A, 2% calcium,
8% iron.

Left: *Cheese Cracker Delights (page 76)*
Below: *Chocolate-Pecan Chess Pie (page 76)*

Top: *Brunswick Stew (page 59)*
Above: *Lemon-Tarragon Chicken (page 60)*
Right: *Oxtail Ragoût (page 52)*

Opposite: *Spectacular Cinnamon-Almond Ring (page 88)*
Above: *Pepper Cheese Biscuits (page 74)*
Right: *Sour Cream Bread (page 89)*

Page 82: *Old English Chicken (page 60)*
Top : *Asparagus Spring Rolls (page 97)*
Above: *Spinach, Sorrel, and Orange Pesto (page 95)*

Top: *Quick Pepperoni Pasta (page 100)*
Above: *Cuban-Style Black Beans and Rice (page 94)*

Left: *Blueberry Bread Pudding (page 88)*
Below: *Strawberry Chiffon Pie (page 85)*

Down-Home Baking

Pat Ross

It's a treat to hang around the kitchen of Pat Ross in Jackson, Mississippi, in the springtime. Although she serves up heaping helpings of hospitality year-round, come spring she rejuvenates beloved baked goods with bursts of new taste sensations. In typical Southern style, Pat can't help but share her creations. "There's something about the smell of home-made baked goods that's utterly heaven," Pat says. "Why not share the joy of good taste?"

When Pat thinks about spring, tiny biscuit bunnies hop into her head. As a child, Pat shaped the little critters from scraps of dough her mother set aside for her. Today she's still tickling family and friends with her baked delights. Her cheery ante-bellum charm seems to be folded right into everything she pops into her oven. Make yourself at home, pull up a comfy chair, and enjoy the melt-in-your-mouth goodness of Pat's fresh, updated versions of old-time favorites.

STRAWBERRY CHIFFON PIE

Prep: 45 min. ◆ Bake: 10 min.
Chill: 4 hr.

Whether you use dried egg whites or whipped cream in this pie, the result will be a billowy beauty.
(See the photograph on page 84.)

1 **recipe Baked Pastry Shell (see above right)**

◆◆◆

1 **envelope unflavored gelatin**
⅓ **cup cold water**
¾ **to 1 cup sugar**
3 **egg yolks**
3 **Tbsp. lemon juice**
2½ **cups fresh strawberries, crushed (about 1½ cups after crushing)**

◆◆◆

Dried egg whites equivalent to 3 fresh egg whites, or 1 cup whipping cream

Halved strawberries (optional)
Strawberry leaves or mint leaves (optional)

1 Prepare Baked Pastry Shell. Set pastry shell aside.

2 In a small saucepan stir gelatin into cold water. Let stand for 1 minute. Add sugar, egg yolks, lemon juice, and a dash *salt.* Cook mixture over medium heat, stirring constantly, until mixture just comes to a boil; remove from heat. Transfer gelatin mixture to a medium bowl; stir in crushed strawberries. Cover and chill until mixture mounds when spooned, stirring occasionally.

3 In a medium mixing bowl prepare and beat dried egg white product to stiff peaks according to package directions, or whip the cream to soft peaks. With a wooden spoon or rubber spatula, gently fold the egg white mixture or whipped cream into strawberry mixture. Spoon the filling into the cooled pastry shell. Cover and refrigerate at least 4 hours or until filling is firm. If desired, garnish with halved strawberries and strawberry or mint leaves. Makes 8 servings.

Baked Pastry Shell: Stir together 1¼ cups all-purpose flour and ¼ teaspoon salt. Cut in ⅓ cup shortening until pieces are the size of small peas. Using a total of 4 to 5 tablespoons cold water, sprinkle 1 tablespoon water over part of the mixture; gently toss with a fork. Push to side of bowl. Repeat until all is moistened. Form into a ball.

On a lightly floured surface use your hands to slightly flatten dough. Roll dough from center to edges into a circle about 12 inches in diameter.

To transfer pastry, wrap it around the rolling pin. Unroll pastry into a 9-inch pie plate. Ease pastry into pie plate, being careful not to stretch pastry. Trim pastry to ½ inch beyond edge of pie plate. Fold under extra pastry. Crimp edge as desired.

Generously prick bottom and sides of pastry in pie plate with a fork. Prick all around where bottom and sides meet. Bake in a 450° oven for 10 to 12 minutes or until golden. Cool on a wire rack.

Nutrition facts per serving: 256 cal., 11 g total fat (3 g sat. fat), 80 mg chol., 95 mg sodium, 36 g carbo., 1 g fiber, 4 g pro. *Daily values:* 12% vit. A, 49% vit. C, 1% calcium, 8% iron.

Fruit Ribbon Cake

Prep: 2 hr. ◆ Bake: 30 min.
Chill fillings: 2 hr.

The homemade fruit fillings in this special-occasion cake are wonderful, but you can save time by using purchased lemon curd and raspberry and apricot spreadable fruit. Be sure to make the Crystallized Flowers in advance.

1 recipe Crystallized Flowers
   (optional) (see top right)

◆◆◆

2¼ cups sifted cake flour or
   2 cups sifted all-purpose
   flour
2¼ tsp. baking powder
½ tsp. salt

◆◆◆

¾ cup shortening
1½ cups sugar
1 tsp. vanilla
3 eggs
¾ cup milk

◆◆◆

1 recipe Raspberry Filling (see
   page 87) or ⅔ cup seedless
   raspberry spreadable fruit
1 recipe Apricot Filling (see
   page 87) or ⅔ cup apricot
   spreadable fruit
1 recipe Lemon Curd (see
   page 87) or ⅔ cup
   purchased lemon curd

◆◆◆

1 recipe Whipped Cream Icing
   (see page 87)

1 If using, make Crystallized Flowers up to 1 week in advance.

2 Grease and lightly flour two 9×1½-inch round baking pans; set aside. Stir together flour, baking powder, and salt; set aside.

3 In a large mixing bowl beat shortening with an electric mixer on medium to high speed 30 seconds. Add sugar and vanilla; beat until well combined. Add eggs, 1 at a time, beating on medium speed 1 minute after each. Add flour mixture and milk alternately, beating on low speed after each addition just until combined.

4 Spread batter into prepared pans. Bake in a 350° oven for 30 to 35 minutes or until a wooden toothpick inserted in centers comes out clean. Cool in pans on wire racks for 10 minutes. Loosen edges. Remove layers from pans. Cool thoroughly on wire racks. When cakes are cool, cut each layer horizontally in half.

5 To assemble cake, place a split cake layer on a serving plate; spread with Raspberry Filling. Top with a second cake layer and spread with Apricot Filling. Add the third cake layer and spread with Lemon Curd. Top with fourth cake layer.

6 Frost cake top and sides with Whipped Cream Icing. (Or, cover and chill cake for up to 24 hours before icing.) Do not overwork icing while spreading it on cake or it may look curdled. If desired, decorate cake with Crystallized Flowers. Serve immediately. Cover and store any leftovers in the refrigerator. Makes 16 servings.

Nutrition facts per serving including fillings and icing: 434 cal., 24 g total fat (11 g sat. fat), 125 mg chol., 164 mg sodium, 51 g carbo., 2 g fiber, 4 g pro.
Daily values: 27% vit. A, 12% vit. C, 8% calcium, 12% iron.

Crystallized Flowers

Prep: 30 min. ◆ Stand: 12 hr.

Look for dried egg whites in large supermarkets, health food stores, gourmet shops, or stores that carry cake-decorating supplies.

2 tsp. dried egg whites
2 tsp. warm water

◆◆◆

Edible flowers (see tip,
   page 87)
Sugar

1 In a small bowl mix dried egg whites and warm water. Using a wire whisk, stir gently for 2 minutes to allow powder to absorb water. Then beat with whisk until powder is completely dissolved and foamy.

2 With a clean artist's brush, lightly coat edible flowers with the beaten egg white mixture (see photo, below); sprinkle lightly with sugar. Let dry on waxed paper overnight before placing on iced cake. Flowers can be made up to 1 week in advance; store in a tightly covered container.

RASPBERRY FILLING

Prep: 15 min. ◆ Chill: 2 hr.

1 10-oz. pkg. frozen
     raspberries in syrup,
     thawed
4 tsp. cornstarch

1 In a small saucepan combine the raspberries and syrup with the cornstarch. Cook and stir over medium heat until thick and bubbly; reduce heat. Cook and stir for 2 minutes more. Remove from heat. Immediately press raspberry mixture through sieve and discard seeds.

2 Transfer filling to a small bowl. Cover surface of filling with plastic wrap or waxed paper. Cool, then chill at least 2 hours. Makes about ⅔ cup.

APRICOT FILLING

Prep: 30 min. ◆ Chill: 2 hr.

⅔ cup snipped dried apricots
¼ cup water
½ tsp. finely shredded orange
     peel
¼ cup orange juice
⅛ tsp. ground cinnamon
     ◆◆◆
3 Tbsp. sugar
1 Tbsp. orange liqueur,
     brandy, or orange juice

1 In a small saucepan combine dried apricots, water, orange peel, orange juice, and cinnamon. Bring to boiling; reduce heat. Simmer, covered, about 10 minutes or until apricots are tender.

2 Stir the sugar and orange liqueur into the apricot mixture. Cover; simmer 10 minutes more. Using a potato masher, mash mixture until nearly smooth.

3 Transfer filling to a small bowl. Cover surface of filling with plastic wrap or waxed paper. Cool, then chill at least 2 hours. Makes about ⅔ cup.

LEMON CURD

Prep:15 min. ◆ Chill: 2 hr.

¼ cup sugar
2½ tsp. cornstarch
3 beaten egg yolks
2 tsp. finely shredded lemon
     peel
¼ cup lemon juice
2 Tbsp. margarine or butter,
     cut up
1 Tbsp. water

1 In a small saucepan stir together the sugar and cornstarch. Add egg yolks, lemon peel, lemon juice, margarine or butter, and water. Cook and stir until thick and bubbly; reduce heat. Cook and stir for 1 minute more. Remove from heat.

2 Transfer filling to a small bowl. Cover surface of filling with plastic wrap or waxed paper. Cool, then chill at least 2 hours. Makes about ⅔ cup.

TEST KITCHEN TIP

EDIBLE FLOWERS

The delicate beauty of just a few edible flowers makes a massive impact on a dessert, a salad, or a main dish. Many grocery stores now carry edible flowers in the produce section. Or, you can pick some from your own backyard if you're sure they haven't been sprayed with chemicals. The flowers are best picked first thing in the morning when the blossoms are fresh. Use the entire blossom or individual petals. Here are just some of the edible flowers you might pick: Apple blossom, tuberous begonia, geranium, Johnny-jump-up/viola, lilac, nasturtium, pansy, rose, and violet.

WHIPPED CREAM ICING

Start to finish: 5 min.

2 cups whipping cream
¼ cup sugar

1 In a chilled medium mixing bowl stir together the whipping cream and sugar. Beat with chilled beaters of an electric mixer on medium speed just until stiff peaks form. Makes about 6 cups.

BLUEBERRY BREAD PUDDING

Prep: 40 min. ◆ Bake: 35 min.

See the photograph on page 84.

1	recipe Golden Dessert Sauce (see right)

◆◆◆

3	Tbsp. butter, softened
¾	cup sugar
3	eggs
2	tsp. vanilla
3½	cups milk
8	cups bread cubes (from New Orleans-style poor boy rolls, hoagie buns, or sourdough loaf)
1¾	cups fresh blueberries

◆◆◆

2	Tbsp. sugar
½	tsp. ground cinnamon

1 Prepare Golden Dessert Sauce; set aside. In a large mixing bowl beat butter and the ¾ cup sugar with an electric mixer on medium to high speed until well combined. Add eggs and vanilla; beat for 2 to 3 minutes or until fluffy. Slowly stir in the milk. Place bread cubes in a large bowl; pour milk mixture over the bread. Let stand for 5 minutes. Stir the blueberries into bread mixture; transfer to an ungreased 3-quart rectangular baking dish.

2 Combine the 2 tablespoons sugar and cinnamon; sprinkle evenly over bread mixture. Drizzle ⅓ cup of the Golden Dessert Sauce over bread mixture. Bake about 35 minutes or until a knife inserted near the center comes out clean. Serve warm with remaining Golden Dessert Sauce. Makes 12 servings.

Golden Dessert Sauce: Combine 3 tablespoons butter and ½ cup sugar. Cook and stir over low heat until butter is melted. Stir in 1 cup whipping cream and, if desired, 3 tablespoons brandy. Bring to boiling; reduce heat. Boil gently, uncovered, 5 to 10 minutes or until mixture is slightly thickened. Chill sauce if not using within 2 hours. Reheat to serve. Makes about 1¼ cups.

Nutrition facts per serving: 344 cal., 16 g total fat (10 g sat. fat), 101 mg chol., 252 mg sodium, 43 g carbo., 1 g fiber, 7 g pro. *Daily values:* 20% vit. A, 5% vit. C, 10% calcium, 5% iron.

SPECTACULAR CINNAMON-ALMOND RING

Prep: 45 min. ◆ Rise: 1 hr. or overnight, plus 45 min.
Bake: 50 min. ◆ Cool: 2 hr.

See the photograph on page 80.

5½	to 6 cups all-purpose flour
2	pkg. active dry yeast
1	cup milk
½	cup water
½	cup butter or margarine, cut up
3	Tbsp. sugar
2	beaten eggs
2	tsp. finely shredded lemon peel
2	tsp. finely shredded orange peel
1	cup sliced almonds

◆◆◆

6	Tbsp. butter or margarine, softened
⅔	cup sugar
1	Tbsp. ground cinnamon

◆◆◆

1	recipe Powdered Sugar Icing (see page 89)

1 In a large mixing bowl stir together 2 cups of the flour and the yeast. In a medium saucepan heat and stir milk, water, the ½ cup butter or margarine, the 3 tablespoons sugar, and 1 teaspoon *salt* just until warm (120° to 130°) and butter almost melts. Add milk mixture to dry mixture along with the eggs, lemon peel, and orange peel. Beat with an electric mixer on low to medium speed for 30 seconds, scraping the sides of the bowl constantly. Beat on high speed for 3 minutes. Using a spoon, stir in almonds and as much of the remaining flour as you can.

2 Turn dough out onto a lightly floured surface. Knead in enough of the remaining flour to make a moderately soft dough that is smooth and elastic (3 to 5 minutes total). Shape dough into a ball. Place dough in a lightly greased bowl, turning once to grease surface. Cover and let rise in a warm place until nearly double in size (about 1 hour). (Or, cover and refrigerate dough up to 24 hours. Remove from refrigerator; let dough stand, covered, at room temperature 15 minutes.)

3 Punch dough down. Turn out onto a lightly floured surface; cover and let rest for 10 minutes. Meanwhile, in a bowl combine the 6 tablespoons softened butter or margarine, the ⅔ cup sugar, and the cinnamon; set aside. Lightly grease a 10-inch fluted tube pan; set aside.

4 On a lightly floured surface roll dough into a 20×12-inch rectangle. Spread filling evenly over dough to within ½ inch of edges. Roll up, jelly-roll style, starting from a long side. Seal seam. Carefully place dough, seam side down, in prepared pan, bringing ends together to form ring. Cover and let rise in a warm place until nearly double (about 45 minutes).

5 Bake in a 350° oven 50 to 55 minutes or until golden, covering with foil the last 15 minutes of baking to prevent overbrowning. Carefully invert baking pan onto a wire rack. Remove bread from pan and cool thoroughly. Drizzle with Powdered Sugar Icing. Makes 16 servings.

Powdered Sugar Icing: In a bowl mix 1 cup sifted powdered sugar, 1 tablespoon milk, and ¼ teaspoon vanilla. Stir in additional milk, 1 teaspoon at a time, until the icing is easy to drizzle.

Nutrition facts per serving: 367 cal., 16 g total fat (7 g sat. fat), 55 mg chol., 253 mg sodium, 50 g carbo., 2 g fiber, 8 g pro. *Daily values:* 11% vit. A, 1% vit. C, 5% calcium, 17% iron.

SOUR CREAM BREAD

Prep: 40 min.
Rise: 1 hr. or overnight, plus 30 min.
Bake: 30 min.

Gooey-good sweetened cream cheese fills this rich and wonderful bread. (See the photograph on page 81.)

2¼ **to 2¾ cups all-purpose flour**
1 **pkg. active dry yeast**
½ **cup dairy sour cream**
¼ **cup sugar**
¼ **cup water**
¼ **cup butter or margarine**
½ **teaspoon salt**
1 **beaten egg**

½ **of an 8-oz. package cream cheese, softened**
⅓ **cup sugar**
1 **tsp. vanilla**

♦♦♦

1 **recipe Powdered Sugar Icing (see left)**
Fresh fruit (optional)

1 In a large mixing bowl stir together 1 cup of the flour and the yeast. In a medium saucepan heat and stir sour cream, the ¼ cup sugar, water, butter or margarine, and salt just until warm (120° to 130°) and butter almost melts. Add sour cream mixture to dry mixture along with the egg. Beat with electric mixer on low to medium speed 30 seconds, scraping bowl. Beat on high speed for 3 minutes. Using a wooden spoon, stir in as much of the remaining flour as you can.

2 Turn dough out onto a lightly floured surface. Knead in enough of the remaining flour to make a moderately soft dough that is smooth and elastic (3 to 5 minutes total). Shape dough into a ball. Place dough in a lightly greased bowl; turn once. Cover and let rise in a warm place until double in size (about 1 hour). (Or, cover and chill dough up to 24 hours. Remove from refrigerator and let stand, covered, at room temperature 20 minutes.)

3 Punch dough down. Turn out onto a lightly floured surface; cover and let rest for 10 minutes. Meanwhile, for filling, in a small mixing bowl stir together cream cheese, ⅓ cup sugar, and vanilla; set aside. Lightly grease a baking sheet; set aside.

4 On a lightly floured surface, roll dough into a 14×10-inch rectangle. Spread filling evenly over dough to within ½ inch of edges. Roll up, jelly-roll style, starting from a long side. Seal seam. Place, seam side down, on prepared baking sheet. Make ¼-inch-deep cuts across top of loaf at 2-inch intervals. Cover; let rise in warm place 30 minutes. Bake in a 350° oven for 30 to 35 minutes or until golden. If necessary, cover with foil the last 15 minutes of baking to prevent overbrowning. Cool slightly on a wire rack. Drizzle with Powdered Sugar Icing. Serve warm with fresh fruit, if desired. Makes 10 servings.

Nutrition facts per serving: 294 cal., 12 g total fat (7 g sat. fat), 51 mg chol., 201 mg sodium, 43 g carbo., 1 g fiber, 5 g pro. *Daily values:* 12% vit. A, 2% calcium, 10% iron.

Stuffed Chicken in Phyllo
(see right)

❖❖❖

Steamed baby carrots and
fresh asparagus

❖❖❖

Fresh spinach salad with
sliced peaches, sesame seed,
and a fruited vinaigrette

❖❖❖

Strawberry Chiffon Pie
(see page 85)

PECAN POPOVERS

Prep: 15 min. ◆ Bake: 40 min.

Serve these pecan-packed marvels immediately after baking to get the full impact of the crisp crunch of the crust in contrast to the soft, inner texture.

2 Tbsp. shortening or
   nonstick cooking spray

❖❖❖

4 eggs
2 cups milk
3 Tbsp. butter, melted
2 cups all-purpose flour
½ tsp. salt
⅓ cup finely chopped pecans

❖❖❖

1 recipe Honey Butter
   (see right)

1 Using ½ teaspoon of shortening for each cup, grease the bottom and sides of twelve 6-ounce custard cups or the cups of popover pans. Or, spray cups generously with nonstick spray coating. Place the custard cups on a 15×10×1-inch baking pan. Set pan aside.

2 In a medium mixing bowl use a wire whisk or rotary beater to beat eggs, milk, and melted butter until combined. Add the flour and salt; beat until smooth. Stir in pecans.

3 Fill prepared cups half full with batter. Bake in a 400° oven about 40 minutes or until firm.

4 Immediately after removing popovers from the oven, use the tines of a fork to prick each popover to let the steam escape. Turn off the oven. For crisper popovers, return the popovers to the oven for 5 to 10 minutes or until desired crispness is reached. Remove popovers from cups and serve immediately with Honey Butter. Makes 12 popovers.

Honey Butter: Stir together ½ cup softened butter or margarine and 2 tablespoons honey. Makes ½ cup.

Nutrition facts per popover (without Honey Butter): 179 cal., 10 g total fat (3 g sat. fat), 82 mg chol., 160 mg sodium, 17 g carbo., 1 g fiber, 6 g pro. *Daily values:* 8% vit. A, 5% calcium, 8% iron.

STUFFED CHICKEN IN PHYLLO

Prep: 40 min. ◆ Bake: 15 min.

There's a satisfying snap as you bite through the crisp phyllo to the filling.

4 skinless, boneless chicken
   breast halves (about 1 lb.
   total)

❖❖❖

Salt and pepper
½ of a 4½-oz. round Brie
   cheese, cut up

¼ cup chopped hazelnuts
   (filberts) or pecans,
   toasted
1 Tbsp. snipped fresh tarragon
   or 1 tsp. dried tarragon,
   crushed

❖❖❖

8 sheets frozen phyllo dough
   (17×12 inches), thawed
⅓ cup butter or margarine,
   melted

❖❖❖

2 Tbsp. butter or margarine
1 cup sliced fresh mushrooms,
   such as oyster, cremini,
   shiitake, or button
1 clove garlic, minced
1 Tbsp. all-purpose flour
2 tsp. snipped fresh tarragon
   or ¼ tsp. dried tarragon,
   crushed
¼ tsp. salt
¼ tsp. pepper
¾ cup milk
2 Tbsp. dry white wine or
   milk

1 Rinse chicken; pat dry. Place each breast half between 2 pieces of plastic wrap. Using the flat side of a meat mallet, pound lightly into a rectangle about ⅛ inch thick. Remove wrap.

2 Sprinkle each chicken piece lightly with salt and pepper. Place one-fourth of the cheese 1 inch from the bottom edge of 1 chicken piece; top with one-fourth of the nuts and one-fourth of the 1 tablespoon snipped tarragon. Fold in the bottom and sides of chicken; roll up jelly-roll style. Repeat with remaining cheese, chicken, nuts, and tarragon.

3 Unfold phyllo dough. Lay 1 sheet of phyllo dough flat on the work surface; cover remaining sheets with plastic wrap. Brush phyllo dough with some of the melted butter or margarine. Remove another sheet of dough from stack and place on top of first sheet. Brush with more melted butter. Add 2 more sheets of dough for a total of 4 sheets, brushing each sheet with butter.

4 Cut phyllo stack into two 14×9-inch rectangles. Discard trimmings. Place 1 chicken roll at an end of each rectangle. Roll up, jelly-roll style, folding in sides. Press ends to seal. Using a sharp knife, make 3 diagonal cuts in the top layers of roll. Repeat with remaining phyllo, butter or margarine, and chicken roll. Place wrapped chicken, seam side down, on a rack in a shallow baking pan. Brush with any remaining melted butter or margarine. Bake in a 400° oven for 15 to 18 minutes or until crisp and golden.

5 Meanwhile, for sauce, in a small saucepan melt the 2 tablespoons butter or margarine. Add mushrooms and garlic. Cook and stir until tender. Stir in flour, the 2 teaspoons tarragon, salt, and pepper. Add the ¾ cup milk all at once. Cook and stir until thickened and bubbly. Cook and stir for 2 minutes more. Stir in white wine or additional milk. Serve sauce with phyllo rolls. Makes 4 servings.

Nutrition facts per serving: 558 cal., 36 g total fat (18 g sat. fat), 135 mg chol., 708 mg sodium, 26 g carbo., 1 g fiber, 31 g pro. *Daily values:* 26% vit. A, 2% vit. C, 10% calcium, 19% iron.

---

30 MIN.

SESAME-CRUSTED SALMON

Prep: 20 min. ♦ Cook: 4 min.

One quick flip in the skillet keeps the fish firm and juicy while enhancing the toasty crunch of the sesame.

1 **16-oz. skinless fresh or frozen salmon fillet, thawed**

♦♦♦

6 **Tbsp. all-purpose flour**
2 **Tbsp. white sesame seed**
¼ **teaspoon salt**
2 **Tbsp. black sesame seed**

♦♦♦

¼ **cup tahini (sesame paste)**
3 **Tbsp. lemon juice**
2 **Tbsp. chopped roasted red sweet pepper**
1 **Tbsp. water**

♦♦♦

¼ **cup milk**

♦♦♦

2 **Tbsp. cooking oil**

1 Rinse fish; pat dry with paper towels. Cut into 4 even fillets. Place 1 fillet at a time between pieces of clear plastic wrap. Using the flat side of a meat mallet, gently pound fish, working from the center to the edges, until an even thickness, about ½ inch. Set fish aside.

2 In a bowl combine half of the flour, the white sesame seed, and half of the salt. In a second bowl, combine remaining flour, salt, and the black sesame seed; set aside.

3 In a blender container combine tahini, lemon juice, roasted red sweet pepper, and water. Cover; blend until smooth. If

---

necessary, add additional water a teaspoon at a time until sauce is a creamy consistency.

4 Place milk in a shallow dish. Dip the salmon fillets in the milk. Firmly press half of each side of the fillet in the white sesame seed mixture. Press the other half of each side of the fillet in the black sesame seed mixture.

5 In a large skillet heat cooking oil over medium-high heat; cook coated fish fillets for 4 to 6 minutes or until fish just flakes, turning once. To serve, spoon tahini sauce on dinner plates; top with fillets. If desired, garnish with *lemon and lime wedges* and *fresh watercress.* Makes 4 servings.

Nutrition facts per serving: 350 cal., 23 g total fat (4 g sat. fat), 21 mg chol., 215 mg sodium, 15 g carbo., 2 g fiber, 22 g pro. *Daily values:* 5% vit. A, 31% vit. C, 11% calcium, 21% iron.

Hidden Treasure Chicken (see below)

♦♦♦

Hot cooked linguine tossed with butter and lemon peel and topped with freshly shredded Parmesan cheese

♦♦♦

Crusty Italian bread

♦♦♦

Dry white wine or iced water with lemon slices

♦♦♦

Mixed fresh berries

HIDDEN TREASURE CHICKEN

Prep: 20 min. ♦ Cook: 25 min.

A rich, creamy filling elevates "plain, old" chicken breasts to elegant company fare.

4 large skinless, boneless chicken breast halves (about 1 lb. total)

♦♦♦

4 oil-packed dried tomato halves, drained and cut into strips

2 oz. mascarpone cheese or feta cheese

4 tsp. snipped fresh herb or ½ tsp. dried herb, crushed, such as oregano, basil, tarragon, or parsley

♦♦♦

2 Tbsp. olive oil

1 Rinse chicken; pat dry. Place chicken breast halves between 2 sheets of waxed paper. With the flat side of a meat mallet, pound chicken to ¼-inch

thickness. Remove and discard waxed paper. Sprinkle chicken lightly with salt and pepper.

2 On each breast, layer some of the tomatoes, cheese, and herb. Fold narrow ends over filling; fold in sides. Roll up each breast half from a short side. Secure with a wooden toothpick.

3 In a medium skillet cook chicken in hot oil over medium-low heat about 25 minutes or until no longer pink, turning to brown evenly. Makes 4 servings.

Nutrition facts per serving: 257 cal., 17 g total fat (6 g sat. fat), 77 mg chol., 114 mg sodium, 2 g carbo., 0 g fiber, 25 g pro. *Daily values:* 1% vit. A, 11% vit. C, 1% calcium, 5% iron.

SAUSAGE AND BISCUIT BREAKFAST PIE

Prep: 25 min. ♦ Bake: 25 min.

Hearty and humble, this quichelike pie is great as morning fare, but it's equally delicious for Sunday supper .

Nonstick spray coating

4 oz. bulk turkey sausage or pork sausage

♦♦♦

1 cup refrigerated shredded hash brown potatoes

1 beaten egg

¾ cup reduced-fat packaged biscuit mix or packaged biscuit mix

¾ cup shredded cheddar cheese (3 oz.)

½ cup chopped red or green sweet pepper

⅓ cup milk

¼ cup thinly sliced green onions or chopped onion

½ tsp. Italian seasoning, crushed

⅛ tsp. black pepper

1 Spray a 9-inch pie plate with nonstick coating; set aside. In a skillet cook sausage until no longer pink. Drain off fat.

2 In a large mixing bowl stir together the turkey or pork sausage, hash brown potatoes, egg, biscuit mix, ½ cup of the cheese, the sweet pepper, milk, green onions, Italian seasoning, and black pepper.

3 Spread mixture into the prepared pie plate. Sprinkle with the remaining cheese. Bake in a 375° oven about 25 minutes or until golden brown and a toothpick inserted near center comes out clean. Cut into wedges. Serve warm. Makes 4 servings.

Nutrition facts per serving: 284 cal., 13 g total fat (6 g sat. fat), 98 mg chol., 613 mg sodium, 27 g carbo., 1 g fiber, 15 g pro. *Daily values:* 20% vit. A, 104% vit. C, 19% calcium, 11% iron.

30 MIN.

TUNISIAN PASSOVER RATATOUILLE

Prep: 25 min. ♦ Cook: 15 min.

Special enough for the holiday—roasted eggplant, ripe red tomatoes, and a spunky blend of seasonings combine to make a Mediterranean classic.

2 medium eggplants (about 1½ lb.)

2 Tbsp. olive oil

♦♦♦

1 Tbsp. olive oil

2 medium tomatoes, quartered

4 cloves garlic, minced
1 Tbsp. snipped fresh
   marjoram or 1 tsp. dried
   marjoram, crushed
1 tsp. coriander seeds, crushed
¼ to ½ tsp. salt
¼ to ½ tsp. crushed red pepper
2 Tbsp. pine nuts, toasted
   Fresh marjoram leaves
   (optional)

1 Peel the eggplant; discard peels. Cut eggplant into 1½-inch cubes. Toss with the 2 tablespoons olive oil and transfer to a shallow roasting pan. Roast, uncovered, in a 425° oven for 10 minutes, stirring once; set aside.

2 In a large skillet heat the 1 tablespoon olive oil. Add the tomatoes, garlic, dried marjoram (if using), coriander, salt, and pepper to the skillet. Cook over medium heat until the tomatoes are just softened, stirring occasionally. Add eggplant; reduce heat to low. Cook, covered, for 10 minutes; stir in pine nuts and fresh marjoram (if using) during the last 3 minutes of cooking.

3 To serve, transfer ratatouille mixture to a serving bowl. If desired, sprinkle with additional fresh marjoram leaves. Makes 6 side-dish servings.

Nutrition facts per serving: 115 cal., 9 g total fat (1 g sat. fat), 0 mg chol., 97 mg sodium, 9 g carbo., 3 g fiber, 2 g pro. *Daily values:* 3% vit. A, 16% vit. C, 1% calcium, 6% iron.

CASTILIAN-STYLE PASSOVER POTATO CASSEROLE

Prep: 55 min. ◆ Bake: 15 min.

Kosher cuisine requires separation of "meat" meals and "dairy" meals. This potato casserole shows there are many tantalizing recipe possibilities, even when ingredients are restricted.

6 medium baking potatoes
   (about 2 lb.)
½ cup plain low-fat yogurt
2 Tbsp. margarine or butter
¼ to ½ tsp. salt
⅛ tsp. ground red pepper
2 beaten eggs
¾ cup herbed feta cheese or
   plain feta cheese
   ◆◆◆
¼ cup water
1 10-oz. pkg. prewashed fresh
   spinach
   ◆◆◆
¼ tsp. paprika

1 Peel and quarter potatoes. In a large saucepan cook potatoes, covered, in a small amount of boiling water about 25 minutes or until tender. Drain potatoes.

2 Mash potatoes with a potato masher or an electric mixer on low speed. Add yogurt, margarine or butter, salt, and red pepper; beat just until combined. Add eggs; beat with an electric mixer on low speed about 1 minute or until fluffy. Fold in ½ cup of the feta cheese.

3 In a 12-inch skillet bring the ¼ cup water to boiling; add spinach. Toss 1 minute or until spinach is slightly wilted; drain. Press out excess liquid. Coarsely chop spinach.

ANOTHER SIDE OF PASSOVER

Passover is a holiday with distinctive food themes, and various rules govern what may be eaten during the eight-day observance.

Yet some Passover dietary rules shift and change according to the background and traditions of the family celebrating the holiday.

In America, most persons who celebrate Passover are of European descent. But an increasing influx of Jews of Arabic descent and Jews of Spanish descent has brought new influences that impart an out-of-the-ordinary side to the traditional foods of the holiday. Their recipes continue to add variety to the inclusive cultural tastes of Passover.

4 Spread half of the potato mixture into a lightly greased 2-quart rectangular baking dish. Layer spinach on top; sprinkle with remaining feta cheese. Spread remaining potato mixture on top and sprinkle with paprika.

5 Bake, uncovered, in a 425° oven about 15 minutes or until top is lightly browned. Makes 8 side-dish servings.

Nutrition facts per serving: 240 cal., 10 g total fat (5 g sat. fat), 76 mg chol., 416 mg sodium, 30 g carbo., 2 g fiber, 9 g pro. *Daily values:* 31% vit. A, 32% vit. C, 16% calcium, 18% iron.

RICE AND BEANS: A DYNAMIC DUO

One plus one equals three when two humble staples are combined to produce good luck, good nutrition, and good eating.

There's a little magic happening in kitchens around the world. Cooks everywhere are waving their spoons over pots of beans and rice to transform these two ingredients into soul-soothing home-cooked meals. In the American South, a mixture of black-eyed peas and rice called Hoppin' John is served on New Year's Day to bring good luck in the coming year. The New Orleans classic, red beans and rice, is a spicy take on this lucky combination. In Cuba, *moros y cristianos,* a blend of black beans and white rice, offers comfort and flavor. For Brazilians, a meaty black bean stew served over rice claims fame as the national dish, *feijoada.*

These combinations of rice and beans result in nutritious complementary proteins. Plant proteins (rice, beans, legumes) are deficient in one or more amino acids, but when eaten in combination their amino acids complement each other to form a complete protein. Serving grains or legumes with small amounts of animal protein further boosts protein content.

Whether you're looking for good luck, good taste, good nutrition, or perhaps all three, these providential pairs are worth a try.

CUBAN-STYLE BLACK BEANS AND RICE

Prep: 30 min. ◆ Soak: 1 hr.
Cook: 1½ hr.

See the photograph on page 83.

1½ cups dry black beans

◆◆◆

1 small onion, halved
2 bay leaves

◆◆◆

2 cups chopped onions
1 to 2 fresh jalapeño peppers, seeded and finely chopped*
3 Tbsp. cooking oil or olive oil
4 cloves garlic, finely chopped
2 tsp. ground cumin
2 tsp. finely shredded lime peel
¾ tsp. salt
¼ tsp. pepper

◆◆◆

Hot cooked brown rice
Fresh cilantro sprigs (optional)
Fresh jalapeño pepper slices (optional)
Lime wedges (optional)

1 Rinse beans. In a large Dutch oven combine beans and 4 cups water. Bring to boiling; reduce heat. Simmer for 2 minutes. Remove from heat. Cover and let stand for 1 hour. (Or, place beans in water in Dutch oven. Cover and let soak in a cool place 6 to 8 hours or overnight.) Drain and rinse beans.

2 Return beans to pan. Add onion, bay leaves, and 4 cups *water.* Bring to boiling; reduce heat. Simmer, covered, for 1¼ to 1½ hours or until beans are tender. Remove and discard onion and bay leaves. Remove about ½ cup of the beans; mash them and return to bean mixture in pan.

3 In a large skillet cook chopped onions and jalapeño in hot oil over medium heat about 8 minutes or until the onions are tender. Add garlic, cumin, lime peel, salt, and pepper; cook and stir for 1 to 2 minutes more.

4 Stir the onion mixture into the bean mixture. Bring to boiling; reduce heat. Simmer, uncovered, for 5 to 10 minutes or until soup thickens slightly.

5 Serve beans with hot cooked rice. If desired, garnish with cilantro and serve with jalapeño pepper slices and lime wedges. Makes 4 main-dish servings.

*Note: Be sure to protect your hands from pungent oils when preparing fresh chili peppers. Put plastic gloves or sandwich bags over your hands so your skin doesn't come in contact with the peppers. Always wash your hands and nails with hot, soapy water after handling chili peppers.

Nutrition facts per serving: 451 cal., 12 g total fat (2 g sat. fat), 0 mg chol., 408 mg sodium, 70 g carbo., 4 g fiber, 18 g pro. *Daily values:* 19% vit. C, 8% calcium, 40% iron.

RED BEANS AND RICE

Prep: 20 min. ◆ Soak: 1 hr.
Cook: 2¼ hr.

1 cup dry red beans

◆◆◆

1 lb. meaty smoked pork hocks
1 cup chopped carrots
1 cup sliced celery
½ cup chopped onion
2 cloves garlic, minced

2 bay leaves
1½ tsp. snipped fresh thyme or
½ tsp. dried thyme,
crushed
1 tsp. bottled hot pepper sauce
1 cup chopped green sweet
pepper

♦♦♦

4 oz. cooked smoked sausage,
sliced
3 cups hot cooked rice

1 Rinse and drain beans. In a large Dutch oven combine beans and 4 cups *water.* Bring to boiling; reduce heat. Cook 2 minutes. Remove from heat. Cover; let stand 1 hour. (Or, place beans in water in pan. Cover and soak in a cool place 8 hours or overnight.) Drain and rinse beans.

2 In same pan combine beans, 3 cups *water,* pork hocks, carrots, celery, onion, garlic, bay leaves, thyme, and hot pepper sauce. Bring to boiling; reduce heat. Simmer, covered, for 2 hours or until beans are tender, adding green pepper the last 30 minutes of cooking, stirring occasionally.

3 Remove and discard bay leaves. Remove the pork hocks. When the pork hocks are cool enough to handle, remove meat from bones. Cut meat into bite-size pieces. Discard bones. Return the meat to the bean mixture; add sausage. Cook, uncovered, about 10 minutes or until desired consistency. Serve over rice. Pass *bottled hot pepper sauce.* Makes 6 main-dish servings.

Nutrition facts per serving: 310 cal., 8 g total fat (3 g sat. fat), 25 mg chol., 502 mg sodium, 44 g carbo., 3 g fiber, 16 g pro. *Daily values:* 54% vit. A, 35% vit. C, 5% calcium, 26% iron.

(30 MIN.) SPINACH, SORREL, AND ORANGE PESTO

Start to finish: 15 min.

See the photograph on page 83.

¼ cup slivered almonds, toasted
1½ cups loosely packed fresh
spinach leaves
1½ cups loosely packed fresh
sorrel, arugula, or
watercress leaves
⅓ cup olive oil
⅓ cup grated Parmesan cheese
or Romano cheese
½ tsp. finely shredded orange
peel
3 Tbsp. orange juice
¼ tsp. ground red pepper

1 Place almonds in a food processor bowl or blender container. Cover and process or blend the almonds until finely chopped. Add the spinach and sorrel or arugula or watercress; cover. With the machine running, gradually add the oil in a thin, steady stream, processing until the mixture is combined and slightly chunky. Add the Parmesan or Romano cheese, orange peel, orange juice, ground red pepper, and ⅛ teaspoon *salt.* Process or blend just until combined.

2 To store, divide pesto into ¼-cup portions and place in airtight containers. Store in the refrigerator for up to 1 week or in the freezer for up to 3 months. To serve, bring pesto to room temperature. Makes ¾ cup.

Nutrition facts per tablespoon: 82 cal., 8 g total fat (1 g sat. fat), 2 mg chol., 80 mg sodium, 1 g carbo., 0 g fiber, 2 g pro. *Daily values:* 6% vit. A, 6% vit. C, 4% calcium, 2% iron.

TEST KITCHEN TIP

CHOOSE A USE FOR PESTO

When you crave the kick of flavor that pesto offers, use your creativity and add a spoonful or two to your food favorites. Here are a few simple ideas to get you started:

1. Swirl about 2 teaspoons pesto into a bowl of your favorite vegetable soup.

2. Lightly spread pesto on one side of a thinly sliced baguette or other French or Italian bread. Place bread slices on the rack of a broiler pan, spread side up, and broil 4 to 5 inches from the heat about 1 minute or until pesto is bubbly and warm.

3. Stir a little pesto into a bowl of hot cooked rice.

4. Spoon about 1 tablespoon pesto into each serving of a creamy pasta dish, such as fettuccine Alfredo.

5. Combine some pesto with equal portions of light dairy sour cream and reduced-calorie mayonnaise for a creamy vegetable dip.

6. Mix pesto into soft cream cheese for a bagel topping.

7. Spread a bit of pesto atop grilled fish, chicken, or turkey.

8. Use pesto in place of a tomato-based pizza sauce. Use about ⅓ cup pesto on top of a 12-inch pizza shell. Add toppings and cheese of your choice.

9. Stuff some pesto under the skin of a whole chicken, then roast.

10. Slather pesto on the bun of a grilled burger or chicken sandwich.

Ironclad Rules for Kids

Don't leave those lovable cartoon-character vitamins out on the table: It could prove to be a fatal mistake. Iron from supplements can kill children if it is taken in excessive amounts. About 10,000 children overdose on iron from supplements each year, resulting in some half-dozen fatalities.

Chewable vitamins made in eye-catching shapes and colors seem harmless enough, but they are potent vitamins—not candy—and should be given only in the amount prescribed. Also, children should have their vitamins handed to them by an adult and be taught the possible dangers of vitamin pills.

As a result of this potential danger, the United States Food and Drug Administration (FDA) is warning parents to keep iron supplements—and all vitamin and mineral supplements, even those with childproof caps—out of the reach of children.

Signs of Iron Toxicity

Symptoms of an iron overdose include nausea and vomiting, lethargy, and headaches. In the event of such occurrences, contact a poison control center immediately. (Most telephone directories include a poison control center number in their list of emergency numbers.)

If no emergency number is in your directory, contact the American Association of Poison Control Centers at 202/362-7217 or call toll-free directory assistance. Keep the number in a prominent place.

Warning Labels

Last year the FDA launched new packaging standards for any supplement containing 30 mg of iron or more. Labels must carry the following warning: "Accidental over-dose of iron-containing products is a leading cause of fatal poisoning in children under six years of age. Keep this product out of reach of children."

LOW FAT

Roasted Garlic and Red Pepper Pesto

Start to finish: 45 min.

The sweet flavor of roasted garlic and the mild bite of red peppers create a pesto that's perfect for beef or lamb.

1 large bulb garlic
1 Tbsp. olive oil

2 large red sweet peppers

◆◆◆

½ cup grated Asiago cheese or Parmesan cheese
¼ tsp. freshly ground pepper
⅛ tsp. salt
2 tsp. snipped fresh thyme or ¼ tsp. dried thyme, crushed

1 Peel away the dry outer leaves of skin from garlic bulb. Leave skins of cloves intact. Use a knife to cut off the pointed top portion (about ¼ inch), leaving the bulb intact but exposing the individual cloves. Place garlic bulb, cut side up, in a small covered baking dish. Drizzle olive oil over garlic; cover and set aside.

2 Halve the sweet peppers; remove stems, membranes, and seeds. Place peppers, cut side down, on a foil-lined baking sheet. Bake peppers and covered garlic in a 425° oven for 20 to 25 minutes or until pepper skins are bubbly and browned and garlic cloves feel soft when pressed. Set garlic aside to cool. Place peppers in a clean brown paper bag; close and let peppers cool. Using a sharp paring knife, carefully remove blackened skin from peppers. Cut peppers into pieces.

3 Remove garlic bulb from oil; reserve oil. Press garlic paste from individual cloves or use the tip of a knife to remove soft garlic paste. In a food processor bowl or blender container combine roasted pepper pieces, garlic paste, reserved oil, cheese, pepper, and salt. Cover and process using several on-off turns until smooth, stopping to scrape down the sides as necessary. Stir in the thyme.

4 To store, divide pesto into ⅓-cup portions and place in airtight containers. Store in the refrigerator for up to 1 week or in the freezer for up to 3 months. To serve, bring pesto to room temperature. Makes 1 cup.

Nutrition facts per tablespoon: 28 cal., 2 g total fat (1 g sat. fat), 2 mg chol., 75 mg sodium, 2 g carbo., 0 g fiber, 2 g pro. *Daily values:* 10% vit. A, 40% vit. C, 4% calcium, 1% iron.

ASPARAGUS SPRING ROLLS

Start to finish: 45 min.

Be a creative spin doctor and roll up these fresh and fun lasagna appetizers. (See the photograph on page 83.)

1 8-oz. pkg. reduced-fat cream cheese (Neufchâtel)
2 Tbsp. snipped fresh chives
2 Tbsp. milk
1 to 2 Tbsp. snipped fresh dill
1 clove garlic, minced
1 Tbsp. lemon juice
½ tsp. freshly ground pepper
◆◆◆
1 Tbsp. olive oil
8 dried lasagna noodles
24 asparagus spears
◆◆◆
6 oz. thinly sliced smoked salmon
8 long fresh chives

1 Mix cream cheese, snipped chives, milk, dill, garlic, lemon juice, and pepper; set aside.

2 In a large Dutch oven bring 3 quarts *water* and the olive oil to boiling; add lasagna noodles and ¼ teaspoon *salt*. Cook for 10 to 12 minutes or until nearly tender. Meanwhile, snap off and discard woody bases of asparagus. If necessary, trim asparagus to 5-inch lengths. Add asparagus to pasta; cook 3 minutes. Drain; rinse with cold water. Drain again; pat pasta dry with paper towels.

3 Spread about 2 tablespoons cream cheese mixture evenly over each lasagna noodle. Divide salmon evenly among noodles, placing a single layer of salmon on each noodle. Place 3 asparagus spears on an end of each noodle, letting tips extend beyond edge. Roll up each noodle. Tie with a fresh chive. Stand spring rolls upright to serve. Makes 8 side-dish servings.

Nutrition facts per serving: 196 cal., 10 g total fat (5 g sat. fat), 27 mg chol., 350 mg sodium, 17 g carbo., 1 g fiber, 10 g pro. *Daily values:* 13% vit. A, 14% vit. C, 3% calcium, 8% iron.

BOW THAI SALAD

Start to finish: 30 min.

3 cups bow tie pasta
8 oz. snow pea pods, trimmed and halved, if desired
8 oz. fresh asparagus, trimmed and cut into 1-inch pieces
1 cup very thinly sliced carrots
◆◆◆
3 Tbsp. reduced-sodium soy sauce
2 Tbsp. creamy peanut butter
1 Tbsp. cooking oil
1 tsp. toasted sesame oil
¼ to ½ tsp. crushed red pepper
1½ cups chopped cooked chicken
2 Tbsp. sesame seed, toasted

1 In a large Dutch oven cook bow ties in lightly salted boiling water 8 minutes. Add pea pods, asparagus, and carrots. Return to boiling. Cook about 3 minutes more or until pasta is tender and vegetables are crisp-tender. Drain and return to pan to keep warm.

2 Meanwhile, for dressing, in a small bowl whisk together soy sauce, peanut butter, cooking oil, sesame oil, and crushed red pepper. Add dressing and chicken to pasta mixture, tossing to coat. Transfer to a serving bowl; sprinkle with sesame seed. Serve warm. Makes 4 to 6 main-dish servings.

Nutrition facts per serving: 469 cal., 17 g total fat (3 g sat. fat), 100 mg chol., 521 mg sodium, 48 g carbo., 5 g fiber, 31 g pro. *Daily values:* 86% vit. A, 58% vit. C, 6% calcium, 34% iron.

CAJUN NOODLE SOUP

Start to finish: 20 min.

To make dinner quickly, warm some flour tortillas in the microwave and toss a green salad to serve alongside this smoky flavored soup.

1 14½-oz. can Cajun-style or Mexican-style stewed tomatoes
3 cups water
1 3-oz. pkg. chicken-flavored ramen noodles
4 oz. fully cooked smoked sausage, thinly sliced
½ medium green sweet pepper, cut into bite-size strips
½ cup shredded Monterey Jack cheese (2 oz.) (optional)

1 Cut up large tomato pieces. In a large saucepan combine the stewed tomatoes, water, seasoning packet from noodles, the sausage, and green pepper. Bring to boiling. Break noodles into quarters; add to saucepan. Return to boiling; cook for 2 minutes. To serve, ladle into 4 soup bowls. If desired, top each serving with cheese. Makes 4 side-dish servings.

Nutrition facts per serving 222 cal., 13 g total fat (3 g sat. fat), 19 mg chol., 1,109 mg sodium, 21 g carbo., 0 g fiber, 8 g pro. *Daily values:* 8% vit. A, 32% vit. C, 3% calcium, 9% iron.

Spring into Summer Swimsuits

Spring is coming and it's time for taking account of things—diet-wise, that is. Too many of us are well-acquainted with hibernation poundage: those extra pounds deposited over fall and winter.

When the sun finally comes out, the snow will melt away, but unwanted weight won't. Don't bank on crash diets and fad programs for the answer: They can be uncomfortable, inconvenient, or downright dangerous.

Health professionals agree that the best way to lose weight—and keep it off—is the slow way, about a pound a week. Starting in early April, you can drop up to 10 or 15 pounds of extra winter baggage and fit into a new swimsuit by summertime. It's simpler than you think, and all it takes are two very basic diet and exercise habits: eating a little bit less and enjoying a little bit more activity. You won't need complicated eating programs, expensive exercise equipment, or intricate calculations and ritual weigh-ins. Here's how it works.

Weight-Loss Ideas to Bank On

Early April is a good time to start losing weight for summer. April 1 to July 4 covers 13 weeks, but look at this time span as 13 pounds. If you approach the weight-loss process by thinking of your body as a bank, you'll find it will be as easy as balancing a checkbook. The way to do this is to take your average dietary intake—that is, the total number of calories you eat each day. Think of them as the "deposit" you make in your bank.

To lose the 13 pounds, you will need to make a "daily withdrawal" of about 500 calories. This adds up to 3,500 calories per week. You'll want to make the withdrawal in the forms of both calorie reduction and calorie burn—that is, food and activity.

Before you begin, you'll need to estimate your energy needs to budget how many calories your body needs to maintain its current weight.

To do this, figure about 13 calories per pound if you are somewhat active and within 20 percent or so of your ideal body weight.

Determining Your Ideal Weight

Use the following equations to estimate—within 10 percent either way—your ideal body weight for optimum health.

Women–Figure 100 pounds for 5 feet in height, then add 5 pounds for each inch over 5 feet tall.

Men–Figure 106 pounds for 5 feet in height, then add 6 pounds for each inch over 5 feet tall.

Next, split the 500 calories per day you plan to decrease into two portions: the part you want to lose through eating less and the part that you want to burn off through a daily activity, such as playing ball, biking, skating, or walking. (These activities burn about 150 calories each per half hour.) By performing these activities with extra vigor, you can double the amount of calorie burn.

Borrowing from the Calorie Bank

Some diets call for meticulous record keeping of all that you eat. Forget that. Instead, look at your daily calorie "bank," that is, your normal daily diet. Borrow a few hundred calories from that calorie bank—and don't pay them back!

For instance, if you are in the habit of having a couple of cans of soda pop each day, switch to a diet beverage or water. Each 12-ounce can of regular soda pop contains about 150 calories. Two of those per day add up to 2,100 calories in one week.

Some sandwich spreads or salad dressings can tally up hundreds of calories every day. If you "borrow" these calories without replacing them, you'll be two-thirds of the way to your weekly weight-loss goal.

Other places where calories tend to tally up include condiments, spreads, and snack foods. Trimming even a few calories here and there ultimately leads to big savings. For example, using one spoon of sugar in your coffee instead of two eventually adds up—just like when you bank a dime here and a nickel there.

Fruits often are recommended as substitutes for candy to fill cravings for sweets, and for a good reason: They're mostly water. But watch out for dried fruits—although virtually fat-free, they are concentrated and can be rich in calories.

When it comes to chocolate, if you can't do without the stuff, enjoy it in smaller disbursements. Two favorites of folks trying to lose weight are miniature-size chocolate bars and milk chocolate kisses. Just be sure to go easy on them.

Trimming calories from snacks, sweeteners, and condiments is a relatively painless diet technique. But to be truly effective, you can't compensate for calories lost in one place by adding them in another: Stick to the same amounts and portions you used to enjoy. If you do away with high-calorie snacks and beverages, yet eat larger lunches and dinners, you're only transferring calories from one account to another. And for overall health, remember: Nothing beats a diet of a wide variety of fruits, vegetables, lean meats, low-fat dairy, and whole grains.

ACCOUNTING FOR EXERCISE

Calorie trimming is only half of the equation; you need exercise, too. But don't panic: You don't have to spend excessive time sweating it out in a gym, climbing mountains, or running marathon races.

Simple, fun stuff—like the aforementioned biking and walking—will use up those calories.

The best motivation for taking walks is having a dog. Enjoying a brisk walk with Rover after dinner can dissolve dozens of calories. You'll both be healthier and happier. (Chasing the dog around the yard doubles the calorie deficit.)

Of course, you don't have to get a dog to take a walk. Motivation to exercise also can come through teamwork. When the whole family goes for a walk or a bicycle ride, you'll do more than burn calories; you'll iron out the day's problems and build family values.

FOR NEXT SUMMER

Once you're in shape for swimsuit season, and you look and feel great, you'll have more incentive to stick with your new habits and avoid banking extra pounds over the next year. Here are a few more things to remember.

◆ Small steps lead to big changes.

◆ Take on weight loss one pound at a time. That way you won't feel overwhelmed trying to lose 10 or 15 pounds as a single-step task.

◆ Keep your calorie "account" in balance with exercise all year. Did you enjoy enough activity today? If in doubt— walk it out. Look at walks as good "exercise insurance."

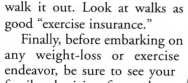

Finally, before embarking on any weight-loss or exercise endeavor, be sure to see your family physician for a clean bill of health.

PENNE WITH ASPARAGUS

Start to finish: 35 min.

2 oz. pancetta or bacon

♦♦♦

12 oz. penne pasta
1 lb. asparagus, trimmed and
    cut into 1-inch pieces

♦♦♦

½ cup chopped onion
3 cloves garlic, minced
½ cup dry white wine or
    chicken broth
½ cup chicken broth
2 large tomatoes, chopped
½ cup snipped fresh basil
½ cup finely shredded
    Parmesan cheese

1 In a large skillet cook pancetta or bacon until crisp; drain on paper towels, reserving 1 tablespoon drippings in skillet. Crumble bacon and set aside.

2 Cook pasta according to package directions, adding the asparagus the last 5 minutes of cooking. Drain and return pasta-asparagus mixture to saucepan to keep warm.

3 Meanwhile, add onion and garlic to reserved drippings in skillet; cook until tender. Carefully stir in wine and broth. Bring to boiling; reduce heat. Simmer, uncovered, over medium-low heat 5 minutes or until reduced by half. Add wine mixture, tomatoes, and basil to pasta; toss. Transfer pasta to a serving dish. Sprinkle with cheese and pancetta. Makes 4 main-dish servings.

Nutrition facts per serving: 481 cal., 9 g total fat (1 g sat. fat), 15 mg chol., 444 mg sodium, 75 g carbo., 3 g fiber, 22 g pro. *Daily values:* 13% vit. A, 66% vit. C, 18% calcium, 30% iron.

QUICK PEPPERONI PASTA

Start to finish: 20 min.

This savory pasta that tastes like pizza is sure to become a mealtime favorite. (See the photograph on page 83.)

6 oz. spaghetti, broken in half
3 cups sliced fresh mushrooms
⅔ cup cubed pepperoni
1 Tbsp. margarine or butter
6 cups lightly packed torn
    fresh spinach

♦♦♦

¼ cup grated Parmesan cheese
2 Tbsp. snipped fresh basil
1 tsp. lemon juice
    Breadsticks (optional)

1 Prepare the pasta according to package directions; drain. Meanwhile, in a 12-inch skillet cook the mushrooms and pepperoni in margarine or butter over medium heat about 5 minutes or until mushrooms are just tender. Drain fat. Stir in spinach. Cook and stir for 1 minute or until spinach begins to wilt. Remove from heat.

2 In a large bowl combine pasta, pepperoni mixture, 3 tablespoons of the Parmesan cheese, basil, and lemon juice. Toss to combine. Sprinkle with remaining Parmesan cheese. If desired, serve with breadsticks. Makes 4 main-dish servings.

Nutrition facts per serving: 344 cal., 14 g total fat (5 g sat. fat), 32 mg chol., 604 mg sodium, 39 g carbo., 2 g fiber, 15 g pro. *Daily values:* 35% vit. A, 9% vit. C, 29% iron.

NUTRITION IN NO TIME

20-MINUTE PASTA

Start to finish: 20 min.

"I've got no time to cook a healthy meal" is no longer an excuse. Zip this fabulous, restaurant-quality pasta dinner from the refrigerator to the table in 20 minutes or less. Then enjoy!

1 9-oz. pkg. refrigerated light
    cheese-filled ravioli

♦♦♦

2 tsp. avocado oil or olive oil
4 plum tomatoes, quartered
1 medium yellow summer
    squash, thinly sliced
1 15-oz. can chickpeas
    (garbanzo beans), rinsed
    and drained
2 cloves garlic, minced
2 tsp. snipped fresh thyme or
    ½ tsp. dried thyme,
    crushed
¼ tsp. crushed black pepper
4 cups shredded fresh spinach

1 Prepare pasta according to package directions.

2 Meanwhile, in a large non-stick skillet heat avocado or olive oil. Add tomatoes, squash, chickpeas, garlic, thyme, and pepper. Cook and stir for 4 to 5 minutes. Add pasta and toss. Serve atop fresh spinach. Serves 4.

Nutrition facts per serving: 334 cal., 8 g total fat (2 g sat. fat), 43 mg chol., 643 mg sodium, 51 g carbo., 10 g fiber, 17 g pro. *Daily values:* 48% vit. A, 85% vit. C, 14% calcium, 37% iron.

MAY
A Fusion of Flavors

30-minute recipes indicated in RED.
Low-fat and no-fat recipes indicated
with a ♥.
Photographs indicated in italics.
*All new in 1998.

*A*s the world becomes smaller, borrowing freely from cuisines opens up exciting culinary cross-pollinations. Think Curry Burritos or Caribbean Slaw with Napa cabbage and mango. Rice travels across many borders, starring in an Italian-inspired risotto, Middle Eastern pilaf, Thai soup, Rice Primavera (made with aromatic jasmine rice), and a skillet of spring herbs and rice that several countries could claim. Fish is a natural partner, whether it be in Salmon-Walnut Rice Pie or Crawfish with Savannah Rice. No matter where you live, far-flung flavors and ingredients can perk up your menus.

CHICKEN WONTONS

Prep: 30 min.
Cook: 2 min. per batch

These crisp appetizers are loaded with ground chicken and other flavorful goodies.

- 1 **green onion, finely chopped**
- 2 **small shallots, finely chopped**
- 2 **Tbsp. finely chopped crystallized ginger**
- 2 **Tbsp. soy sauce or reduced-sodium soy sauce**
- 2 **Tbsp. peanut butter**
- 1 **Tbsp. snipped fresh cilantro**
- 1 **Tbsp. honey**
- 2 **tsp. lime juice**
- ½ **tsp. crushed red pepper**
- 8 **oz. ground raw chicken**
- ¼ **cup chopped peanuts**

♦♦♦

- 22 **wonton wrappers**

♦♦♦

Cooking oil or shortening for deep-fat frying
Bottled sweet-and-sour sauce (optional)

1 In a medium bowl stir together green onion, shallots, ginger, soy sauce, peanut butter, cilantro, honey, lime juice, and red pepper. Add chicken and peanuts; mix well.

2 For each wonton, spoon about 2 teaspoons chicken mixture onto center of each wonton wrapper. Lightly moisten edges of wrapper with water. Fold wrapper over filling to make a triangle; press to seal.

3 In a heavy large skillet heat 1 inch oil or shortening to 365°. Fry wontons, 3 or 4 at a time, in hot oil about 2 minutes or until golden and no pink remains in filling, turning once. Remove wontons from oil. Drain wontons on paper towels. If desired, serve with sweet-and-sour sauce. Makes 22 wontons.

Nutrition facts per wonton: 81 cal., 5 g total fat (1 g sat. fat), 6 mg chol., 166 mg sodium, 7 g carbo., 0 g fiber, 3 g pro. *Daily values:* 1% vit. A, 3% iron.

BAKED CRAB RANGOON-STYLE BUNDLES

Prep: 30 min. ♦ Bake: 8 min.

Brushing with oil helps crisp up the outsides of these traditionally fried Chinese restaurant favorites.

- 1 **egg white**
- 1 **8-oz. tub cream cheese with chive and onion**
- 1 **6- to 7-oz. can crabmeat, drained, flaked, and cartilage removed**
- 1 **tsp. grated fresh ginger**
- 1 **Tbsp. cooking oil**
- 1 **tsp. toasted sesame oil**

♦♦♦

- 30 **wonton wrappers**
Chinese hot mustard sauce or bottled sweet-and-sour sauce

1 In a medium mixing bowl stir egg white into cream cheese. Stir in crabmeat and fresh ginger until combined; set aside. In a small bowl stir together the cooking oil and sesame oil; set aside.

2 To shape each wonton, spoon a scant 2 teaspoons cream cheese mixture onto center of each wonton wrapper. Lightly moisten edges of wrapper with water. Bring up corners of wonton and twist, forming a small bundle. Place bundles on a large baking sheet. Brush with the oil mixture.

3 Bake in a 375° oven for 8 to 10 minutes or until light brown and crisp. Serve warm with hot mustard sauce or sweet-and-sour sauce. Makes 30 appetizers.

Nutrition facts per appetizer: 62 cal., 3 g total fat (1 g sat. fat), 14 mg chol., 107 mg sodium, 5 g carbo., 0 g fiber, 3 g pro. *Daily values:* 1% vit. A, 1% calcium, 2% iron.

CURRY BURRITOS

Prep: 45 min. ♦ Cook: 5 min.

You can find curry paste and rice-paper wrappers at most Asian markets. (See the photograph on page 122.)

- ⅓ **cup chopped onion**
- 2 **cloves garlic, minced**
- 1 **Tbsp. margarine or butter**

♦♦♦

- 1 **cup reduced-sodium chicken broth or purchased coconut milk**
- 2 **Tbsp. all-purpose flour**
- 1 **to 1½ tsp. Thai red curry paste**

♦♦♦

- ¾ **cup cooked purple Thai rice***
- ¾ **cup cooked long grain white rice****
- ¼ **cup chopped peanuts**

♦♦♦

- 8 **8-inch round rice-paper wrappers**

1 medium carrot, cut into thin
    bite-size strips
½ cup snow pea pods, cut into
    thin strips, or quartered
    sugar snap pea pods
½ small summer squash or
    zucchini, cut into thin
    bite-size strips, or one
    whole baby pattypan
    squash, cut into thin,
    bite-size wedges
    ◆◆◆
    Nonstick spray coating
    ◆◆◆
    Slivered snow pea pods
      (optional)
    Plain low-fat yogurt
      (optional)
    Chutney (optional)

1 In a small saucepan cook onion and garlic in hot margarine or butter over medium heat about 3 minutes or until onion is tender.

2 In a small mixing bowl whisk the chicken broth or coconut milk into flour and curry paste. Carefully stir into the hot onion mixture. Cook and stir over medium heat until thickened and bubbly. Cook and stir 1 minute more. Reserve ⅔ cup of the sauce to serve with the burritos.

3 In a medium bowl stir together the cooked purple Thai rice, cooked long grain rice, and peanuts. Add remaining sauce, stirring to mix. Set aside.

4 Carefully dip each rice paper quickly in water and place between paper towels or clean cotton dish towels. Let stand for 10 minutes.

5 Meanwhile, in a large skillet cook the carrot, pea pod strips, and squash in a small amount of boiling water, covered, about 3 minutes or until crisp-tender. Drain and set aside.

6 To assemble each burrito, remove 1 rice paper from between the towels. Place 2 tablespoons cooked vegetable mixture on rice paper about 1 inch from the edge. Spoon 2 to 3 tablespoons of the rice mixture next to the vegetables, still leaving 1 inch of space at the edge of the rice paper. Fold 2 sides of rice paper over vegetables and the rice mixture. Roll up from the bottom to encase filling.

7 Spray a steamer rack with nonstick coating. In a large deep skillet bring ½ inch of water to boiling. Place rolls on rack. Place rack in skillet. Cover and steam for 5 minutes.

8 To serve, cut each roll in half diagonally and serve on a bed of thinly slivered pea pods, if desired. Serve with reserved curry sauce and, if desired, yogurt and/or chutney. Makes 8 appetizer or side-dish servings.

*Note: If desired, substitute ¾ cup cooked long grain white rice for the purple Thai rice. If using 2 colors of rice, cook each separately or the colored rice will tint the long grain white rice.

**Note: To make ¾ cup cooked purple or long grain white rice, bring 1 cup of water to a boil and slowly add ⅓ cup of uncooked rice. Return to boiling; reduce heat to medium-low. Rice should be barely simmering.

For white rice, simmer, covered, about 15 minutes. Remove pan from heat; let stand, covered, for 5 minutes.

For purple rice, simmer, covered, about 25 minutes. Remove pan from heat; let stand, covered, for 10 minutes.

TO MAKE AHEAD

Prepare the burritos up to 8 hours before serving. Place on a plate sprayed with nonstick spray coating; cover and refrigerate. Remove from the refrigerator about 30 minutes before serving and follow the steaming directions.

Nutrition facts per burrito: 164 cal., 4 g total fat (1 g sat. fat), 0 mg chol., 260 mg sodium, 27 g carbo., 1 g fiber, 5 g pro. *Daily values:* 22% vit. A, 5% vit. C, 1% calcium, 6% iron.

THE CLEVER COOK

NAPKINS MAKE SCENTS

Guests love the aroma of napkins stored in an airtight container with simmering-type potpourri chips or dried flower petals.

Germaine Piper
Arvada, Colorado

COCONUT SHRIMP WITH CURRY DIPPING SAUCE

Prep: 30 min. ◆ Chill: 1 to 4 hr.
Fry: 1½ min. per batch

1 lb. fresh or frozen jumbo
    shrimp in shells (15 to 18)
⅔ cup finely chopped, dried
    unsweetened coconut
⅔ cup fine dry bread crumbs
1 beaten egg yolk
¾ cup ice-cold water
1 cup all-purpose flour
½ tsp. baking soda
¼ tsp. salt

◆◆◆

1 Tbsp. finely chopped
    shallots
1 clove garlic, minced
2 tsp. Thai red curry paste
1 tsp. cooking oil
1 Tbsp. cornstarch
1 14-oz. can unsweetened
    coconut milk
1 Tbsp. lime juice
¼ tsp. salt
2 Tbsp. snipped fresh basil or
    1 tsp. dried basil, crushed

◆◆◆

**Cooking oil or shortening
for deep-fat frying**

1 Thaw shrimp, if frozen. Peel and devein shrimp, leaving tails intact; set aside. In a shallow bowl stir together coconut and bread crumbs; set aside. In another bowl whisk together egg yolk and water. Add flour, baking soda, and the ¼ teaspoon salt; whisk until smooth. Dip the shrimp in batter, then in coconut mixture, pressing lightly to coat. Place on a tray. Cover and chill for 1 to 4 hours.

2 For sauce, in a medium saucepan cook shallots, garlic, and curry paste in the 1 teaspoon oil about 2 minutes or until shallots are tender. In a bowl combine cornstarch, coconut milk, lime juice, and ¼ teaspoon salt. Stir milk mixture into shallots in saucepan. Cook and stir until thickened and bubbly. Cook and stir for 2 minutes more. Remove from heat; stir in basil.

3 In a heavy large skillet heat 1 inch oil or melted shortening to 350°. Fry shrimp, 3 to 4 at a time, about 1½ to 2 minutes or until golden. Remove shrimp from oil and drain on paper towels. Serve shrimp warm with sauce. Makes 15 to 18 appetizers.

Nutrition facts per appetizer: 134 cal., 7 g total fat (6 g sat. fat), 49 mg chol., 223 mg sodium, 11 g carbo., 0 g fiber, 6 g pro. *Daily values:* 4% vit. A, 1% vit. C, 1% calcium, 9% iron.

VEGETABLE APPETIZERS

Start to finish: 1 hr.

Crisp vegetables serve as tiny containers for the flavored rice in this fresh spin on sushi. The wasabi used in the sauce is available as either a powder or paste in Asian markets or large supermarkets.

1 recipe Vegetable Bowls
    (see page 105)

◆◆◆

½ cup short grain rice

◆◆◆

1 cup cold water
2 Tbsp. rice vinegar or white
    wine vinegar
¼ tsp. salt
¼ cup finely shredded carrot
1 Tbsp. sugar

1 Tbsp. sake or dry sherry
    (optional)

◆◆◆

1 recipe Wasabi Sauce (see
    page 105)
1 recipe Honey-Ginger Sauce
    (see page 105)
2 Tbsp. white and/or black
    sesame seed, toasted

1 Prepare the Vegetable Bowls; set aside. (Vegetables may be prepared, covered, and chilled for up to 6 hours.)

2 Wash uncooked rice under cold running water, rubbing the grains together with fingers, for about 1 minute or until water runs clear. Drain rice.

3 In a medium saucepan stir together the rinsed, uncooked rice, the 1 cup cold water, vinegar, and salt. Bring to boiling; reduce heat. Cover with a tight-fitting lid. Simmer for 15 minutes. (Rice should be sticky.) Remove from heat; stir in the carrot, sugar, and, if using, sake or dry sherry. Cover and cool to room temperature. (The mixture may be made ahead and chilled.)

4 Prepare Wasabi Sauce and Honey-Ginger Sauce. Use a teaspoon that has been dipped in water to fill Vegetable Bowls with a scant 2 teaspoons of the rice mixture. Place vegetables on a serving platter. Sprinkle with toasted sesame seed and drizzle with Wasabi Sauce or Honey-Ginger Sauce. Serve with remaining sauce. (Serve within 2 hours of filling.) Makes 36 appetizers.

Vegetable Bowls: Mix and match vegetable choices to create 36 "bowls."

For cucumber bowls, peel and cut medium cucumbers crosswise into 1-inch pieces. Use a small melon baller or a small spoon to scoop out centers of cucumber pieces to form a cup (see below).

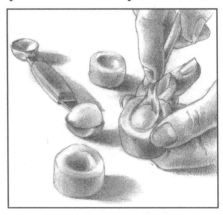

For cherry tomato bowls, cut a very thin slice from the bottoms of tomatoes so they stand upright; then cut a thin slice from the tops. Use a small melon baller or a small spoon to scoop out centers of tomatoes from top (see above).

For romaine lettuce bowls, use the smallest romaine leaves. Rinse leaves in cold water; pat dry.

For baby zucchini bowls, cut baby zucchini in half lengthwise. If necessary, trim a thin slice from bottoms of both halves to keep zucchini upright. Use the tip of a vegetable peeler to slightly hollow out centers of zucchini halves to form "boats." If desired, steam and chill zucchini before stuffing.

For baby pattypan squash bowls, cut pattypan in half lengthwise or crosswise. Use the tip of a vegetable peeler to hollow out centers of squash. If desired, steam and chill squash before stuffing. Replace top of squash after stuffing.

Nutrition facts per appetizer with sauce: 31 cal., 0 g total fat, 0 mg chol., 190 mg sodium, 7 g carbo., 0 g fiber, 1 g pro. *Daily values:* 3% vit. A, 7% vit. C, 2% iron.

WASABI SAUCE

Start to finish: 5 min.

- ¼ **cup soy sauce**
- 1 **tsp. powdered wasabi (Japanese horseradish)**

1 In a small bowl combine soy sauce and wasabi powder. Cover and chill. Makes ¼ cup.

HONEY-GINGER SAUCE

Start to finish: 25 min.

- ⅓ **cup honey**
- ¼ **cup water**
- 2 **Tbsp. plum sauce**
- 2 **Tbsp. soy sauce**
- 1 **2-inch section fresh ginger, peeled and thinly sliced**

1 In a small saucepan combine honey, water, plum sauce, soy sauce, and ginger. Bring just to boiling, stirring frequently. Reduce heat. Simmer, uncovered, for 15 to 20 minutes or until slightly thickened. Strain into a small bowl. Cool, cover, and chill. Makes a scant ¾ cup.

TEST KITCHEN TIP

EASY-TO-COOK RICES

When you're scurrying to fix dinner for your hungry family, quick-cooking rices help save time in the kitchen.

For the best results, be sure to follow the manufacturer's cooking directions.

Instant and quick-cooking rice: Popular because of their short cooking times, instant and quick-cooking rices are partially or fully cooked before they're packaged.

Converted rice: Also called parboiled rice, this white rice is steamed and pressure cooked before it's packaged. This process helps to retain nutrients and keeps the grains from sticking together.

Boil-in-bag rice: Partially cooked parboiled rice is packaged in a heat-proof bag. To prepare the rice, the bag is put into boiling water. It cooks faster than dry rice and holds well if the cook is busy with other parts of the meal. The grains of rice stay very separate. Both white and brown rices are available.

Because these rices are quicker cooking, you'll have a little extra time to jazz them up with some creative add-ins:

◆ Mix in hot cooked vegetables.
◆ Stir in your favorite seasoned salt or salt-free seasoning blend.
◆ Add snipped fresh herbs.
◆ Toss with butter and a bit of grated Parmesan cheese.
◆ Top with shredded cheddar cheese or one of the shredded cheese blends from the store.

THAI RICE MUSHROOM SOUP

Start to finish: 50 min.

Mushrooms pair deliciously with all kinds of rice, as this recipe demonstrates.

⅓   **cup finely chopped onion**
1   **Tbsp. margarine or butter**
1   **49½-oz. can reduced-sodium chicken broth**
¼   **cup brown rice**
¼   **cup wild rice, rinsed**
    ◆◆◆
1   **recipe Spinach and Mushroom Wontons (see right)**
½   **cup thinly sliced carrot**
1   **Tbsp. snipped fresh thyme or ½ tsp. dried thyme, crushed**
    Salt and pepper
    ◆◆◆
    Slivered snow pea pods (optional)
    Fresh thyme sprigs (optional)

1 In a large saucepan cook and stir onion in hot margarine or butter about 3 minutes or until onion is tender. Carefully add broth and bring to boiling. Add uncooked brown rice and uncooked wild rice. Return to boiling; reduce heat. Simmer, covered, for 40 minutes.

2 Return rice mixture to boiling. Add Spinach and Mushroom Wontons, carrot, and thyme to saucepan; reduce heat. Cook, uncovered, for 2 to 3 minutes more or until wontons are done and carrot is crisp-tender. Season to taste with salt and pepper.

3 To serve, ladle soup into individual bowls. If desired, garnish with slivered pea pods and fresh thyme. Makes 6 appetizer or side-dish servings.

Nutrition facts per serving with wontons: 195 cal., 6 g total fat (1 g sat. fat), 3 mg chol., 946 mg sodium, 30 g carbo., 1 g fiber, 7 g pro.
Daily values: 38% vit. A, 6% vit. C, 2% calcium, 11% iron.

SPINACH AND MUSHROOM WONTONS

Start to finish: 25 min.

These quick-to-cook vegetable-filled morsels are used in the Thai Rice Mushroom Soup at left. Another day, try adding the wontons to your favorite broth-based soup.

1   **cup finely chopped fresh mushrooms, such as button, cremini, shiitake, chanterelle, oyster, and/or porcini**
1   **cup fresh baby spinach leaves or chopped spinach leaves**
2   **Tbsp. sliced green onion**
1   **Tbsp. margarine or butter**
2   **tsp. cornstarch**
½   **tsp. snipped fresh thyme or ¼ tsp. dried thyme**
¼   **tsp. salt**
¼   **tsp. pepper**
    ◆◆◆
18   **4-inch wonton wrappers**

1 In a large skillet cook and stir mushrooms, spinach leaves, and green onion in hot margarine or butter about 3 minutes or until liquid is almost gone. Stir in cornstarch, thyme, salt, and pepper. Remove from heat; set aside.

2 Brush edges of each wonton wrapper with water. Spoon

1 scant teaspoon of filling onto center of wonton wrapper. Fold in half diagonally to form triangle, gently pressing sides together to seal in filling. If desired, bring the 2 opposite corners together, overlapping slightly in center. Moisten edges; pinch together. Cover filled wontons with plastic wrap until ready to cook.

PRIZE TESTED RECIPE WINNER

SPRINGTIME SOUP

Start to finish: 25 min.

Garden-fresh asparagus, snow peas, and spinach make this soup a triple treat.

1   **lb. fresh asparagus spears**
    ◆◆◆
½   **cup chopped onion**
3   **cloves garlic, minced**
1   **Tbsp. olive oil**
1   **49½-oz. can chicken broth**
½   **cup orzo or other tiny pasta**
3   **cups snow pea pods, ends and strings removed**
6   **cups torn fresh spinach**
¼   **tsp. pepper**
¼   **cup purchased pesto (optional)**
¼   **cup finely shredded Parmesan cheese**

1 Snap off and discard woody bases from asparagus. If desired, scrape off scales. Bias-slice the asparagus into 1-inch-long pieces. Set asparagus aside.

2 Meanwhile, in a 4-quart Dutch oven cook the onion and garlic in hot oil until tender. Carefully add chicken broth; bring to boiling. Stir in pasta; reduce heat. Boil pasta gently for

5 minutes. Stir in asparagus and snow peas. Return soup to boiling; cook 3 minutes more. Stir in spinach and pepper; cook 1 minute more. Remove soup from heat.

3 To serve, ladle soup into bowls. If desired, swirl 1 to 2 teaspoons pesto into each bowl of soup. Sprinkle Parmesan cheese on top of each serving. Makes 8 side-dish servings.

Nutrition facts per serving: 133 cal., 4 g total fat (1 g sat. fat), 3 mg chol., 634 mg sodium, 15 g carbo., 3 g fiber, 10 g pro. *Daily values:* 31% vit. A, 59% vit. C, 8% calcium, 18% iron.

GREAT GREENS WITH CASHEWS

Prep: 20 min. ◆ Chill: 1 hr.

Ground cashew nuts help create a creamy dressing used as a tasty topper on this salad.

¾ cup lightly salted roasted cashews
½ cup water
1 small clove garlic, halved
¼ tsp. salt
⅛ tsp. onion powder
2 Tbsp. lemon juice

◆◆◆

5 cups assorted baby greens or torn leaf lettuce
1 cup chopped tomato (2 small)
¾ cup shelled fresh peas, cooked and chilled
3 green onions, thinly sliced
Freshly ground pepper (optional)

1 In a blender container or food processor bowl combine ½ cup of the cashews, the water, garlic, salt, and onion powder. Cover and blend or process about 2 minutes or until mixture is smooth and creamy. (Mixture will thicken as it purees.) Stir in the lemon juice. Cover and chill at least 1 hour or up to 3 days.

2 In a salad bowl combine greens, tomato, peas, and green onion. Divide greens mixture among 4 serving plates. Sprinkle with the remaining cashews. Drizzle some dressing over each serving. If desired, sprinkle with freshly ground pepper. Makes 4 side-dish servings.

Nutrition facts per serving: 186 cal., 12 g total fat (2 g sat. fat), 299 mg sodium, 16 g carbo., 3 g fiber, 7 g pro. *Daily values:* 9% vit. A, 37% vit. C, 3% calcium, 13% iron.

CARIBBEAN SLAW

Start to finish: 30 min.

As the temperature heats up, cool down with this refreshing fruit-and-vegetable slaw and one of your grilled poultry or fish favorites. (See the photograph on page 117.)

2 Tbsp. snipped fresh basil or 1 tsp. dried basil, crushed
2 Tbsp. snipped fresh mint or 1 tsp. dried mint, crushed
2 Tbsp. olive oil
2 Tbsp. rice vinegar or white wine vinegar
2 tsp. soy sauce

◆◆◆

4 cups thinly sliced Napa cabbage (about ½ of a small head)

Grilled chicken brushed with apricot or plum preserves

◆◆◆

Caribbean Slaw (see below)

◆◆◆

Sourdough bread with butter

◆◆◆

Angel food cake slices served with fruit sorbet and sprinkled with toasted coconut and almonds

1 mango, peeled, pitted, and sliced; or 2 peaches or nectarines, pitted and sliced
1 large cucumber, peeled, seeded, and cut into pieces
1 small red sweet pepper, cut into matchstick-size pieces
½ of a small red onion, quartered and thinly sliced

1 For dressing, in a screw-top jar combine basil, mint, olive oil, vinegar, and soy sauce. Cover and shake dressing well. Set aside.

2 In a large bowl combine the cabbage, mango, peaches or nectarines, cucumber, sweet pepper, and red onion. Add the dressing, gently tossing to combine. Serve slaw immediately. Makes 5 side-dish servings.

Nutrition facts per serving: 114 cal., 6 g total fat (1 g sat. fat), 146 mg sodium, 16 g carbo., 3 g fiber, 2 g pro. *Daily values:* 39% vit. A, 86% vit. C, 5% calcium, 6% iron.

SEVEN-SPICE RICE PILAF

Prep: 10 min. ◆ Cook: 20 min.

The flavors of spinach, almonds, onions, and raisins are enhanced by a spice mixture called "baharat" from the Middle East country of Oman.

⅓ cup chopped onion
1 Tbsp. cooking oil or olive oil
1 cup long grain rice
½ tsp. ground cardamom
½ tsp. paprika
¼ tsp. ground coriander
¼ tsp. ground cinnamon
¼ tsp. ground cumin
¼ tsp. ground black pepper
⅛ tsp. ground nutmeg
1 14½-oz. can vegetable broth
¼ cup water
◆◆◆
1 cup chopped fresh spinach
¼ cup golden raisins
¼ cup sliced almonds
¼ to ½ tsp. rose water (optional)
    Small fresh spinach leaves (optional)

1 In a medium saucepan cook onion in hot oil until tender. Stir in uncooked rice, cardamom, paprika, coriander, cinnamon, cumin, black pepper, and nutmeg. Cook and stir over medium heat about 5 minutes or until rice is golden. Carefully add the vegetable broth and water. Bring to boiling; reduce heat. Simmer, covered, for 15 minutes.

2 Remove from heat; let stand, covered, for 5 minutes. Stir in chopped spinach, golden raisins, and almonds. If desired, sprinkle with rose water and garnish with small spinach leaves. Makes 4 to 6 side-dish servings.

Nutrition facts per serving:: 290 cal., 9 g total fat (1 g sat. fat), 0 mg chol., 437 mg sodium, 51 g carbo., 2 g fiber, 6 g pro. *Daily values:* 11% vit. A, 8% vit. C, 5% calcium, 22% iron.

SPRING PEAS AND CHICKEN RISOTTO

Start to finish: 30 min.

Showcasing fresh spring produce such as peas and spinach, this creamy Italian-style rice dish is hearty enough for a main course. Add a salad of mesclun greens, some berries, and a vinaigrette along with a thick-crusted loaf of Italian bread and you've got a trattoria-style meal in the comfort of your home.

½ cup chopped onion
2 cloves garlic, minced
2 Tbsp. butter or olive oil
1 cup Arborio rice
◆◆◆
3½ cups reduced-sodium chicken broth
◆◆◆
¾ cup fresh shelled or loose-pack frozen tiny peas
¼ cup shredded carrot
◆◆◆
3 cups shredded fresh spinach
1½ cups chopped smoked chicken breast
¼ cup grated Parmesan cheese
2 Tbsp. snipped fresh thyme

1 In a large saucepan cook onion and garlic in hot butter or olive oil until onion is tender. Add the uncooked rice. Cook and stir over medium heat about 5 minutes or until rice is golden.

2 Meanwhile, in another saucepan bring broth to boiling; reduce heat and simmer. Slowly add 1 cup of the broth to the rice mixture, stirring constantly. Continue to cook and stir over medium heat until liquid is absorbed. Add another 1 cup of the broth to the rice mixture, stirring constantly. Continue to cook and stir until liquid is absorbed. Add another 1 cup broth, ½ cup at a time, stirring constantly until the broth has been absorbed. (This should take about 18 to 20 minutes.)

3 Stir in remaining ½ cup broth, the peas, and carrot. Cook and stir until the rice is slightly creamy and just tender.

4 Stir in the spinach, chicken, Parmesan cheese, and thyme; heat through. Serve immediately. Makes 4 main-dish servings.

Nutrition facts per serving: 371 cal., 10 g total fat (5 g sat. fat), 68 mg chol., 1,351 mg sodium, 48 g carbo., 3 g fiber, 23 g pro. *Daily values:* 57% vit. A, 28% vit. C, 13% calcium, 28% iron.

TWELVE GREAT GRAINS

New varieties of rice are being developed around the world, creating a bonanza for home cooks who want to go beyond basic white. Specialty rices now make up 10 percent of all rice eaten in the United States. There isn't room to list even a fraction of the varieties available, but here are a dozen, including old favorites and some that may not be quite as familiar.

Follow the package directions when cooking colored rices, but test them for doneness before serving: taste a fork full or squeeze a grain between your fingers. Either way, you shouldn't feel a hard center in the rice grain. If you do, a few more minutes on the stove may be needed.

Colored rices often will transfer their hues to the foods they're cooked with, so prepare them in a separate pan if that is a concern.

COLORED RICES

1. Himalayan Red: Salmon pink when cooked, this is one of the more flavorful of the colored rices with a taste similar to wheat or nuts. Its chewy texture serves as a good counterpoint to stir-fries. Available: Asian, Indian groceries; health food and gourmet stores.

2. Chinese Black: Turns a very dark, almost indigo color after cooking with a slightly nutty flavor and a pleasant, almost floral aftertaste. Serve Chinese black rice as a side dish as you would brown rice or in such mixtures as stuffings and puddings. Available: Asian and Indian groceries; health food and gourmet stores.

3. Colusari Red: This chewy rice has a light nutty, popcornlike flavor. It works well as a side dish and in salads and stuffings. Available: Indian Harvest Specialtifoods Inc. (800/294-2433).

4. Black Japonica: This rice has a chewier texture than other rices and a starchy flavor that works well as a side dish and in salads and stuffings. It combines well with other rices. Available: health food and gourmet stores; larger supermarkets.

5. Purple Thai: Also called Purple Thai Sticky Rice, this is a flavorful rice with a faintly fruity taste, though not sweet. Used for rice pudding, but also delicious in savory dishes, such as salads. Available: Asian and Indian groceries; health food and gourmet stores.

SHORT AND MEDIUM GRAIN RICES

6. Short Grain: The rice to use when you prefer a stickier texture and a softer grain after cooking. It pairs well with many Asian dishes and is used in dishes such as paella and risotto. Available: larger supermarkets; gourmet stores; Italian markets.

One popular type of short grain rice is Arborio. Grown in both America and Italy, it sometimes is labeled Risotto Rice and most often is used in the Italian rice dish called risotto. When cooked, Arborio rice produces a slightly chewy, creamy exterior that is firm to the bite. Available: supermarkets; Italian groceries; gourmet and health food stores.

7. Medium Grain: A slightly sticky rice that cooks up tender and plump with a neutral taste. Use this rice in desserts, pancakes, risotto, or paella. Available: supermarkets.

BROWN RICES

8. Brown: With its nutty taste and chewy texture, this unpolished rice tastes best when paired with strong seasonings and sauces. Available: supermarkets; gourmet and health food stores.

9. Brown and Wild Rice Mix: The strong, nutty taste of wild rice (which actually is a long-grain marsh grass native to the U.S.) is mellowed when paired with brown rice. Use it as a side dish for boldly flavored meats. Available: supermarkets.

LONG GRAIN RICES

10. Jasmine: This rice has a mild popcorn aroma. Grains swell lengthwise only; they don't plump up. Jasmine rice is soft and slightly sticky. Use as an accompaniment to stir-fry dishes. Available: larger supermarkets; Asian and Indian groceries; health food and gourmet stores.

11. Basmati: Like jasmine rice, this has a popcorn aroma. When cooked, its long grains separate well. This is an excellent rice to pair with stir-fry dishes and other Asian-inspired meals. Available: larger supermarkets; Asian and Indian groceries; health food and gourmet stores.

12. Long Grain: This rice's neutral taste and firm texture make it a perfect side dish with almost anything. When cooked, grains remain separate and fluffy. Available: supermarkets.

RICE COOKING BASICS

There's no trick to making good rice time after time; it's a matter of measuring carefully and paying attention to timing.

◆ To make white rice, bring 2 cups of water to boiling. Slowly stir in 1 cup uncooked long grain white rice. Return to boiling; reduce heat to medium-low. (Rice should be barely simmering.) Simmer, covered, about 15 minutes or until liquid is absorbed. Remove from heat; let stand, covered, for 5 minutes. Makes 3 cups rice.

◆ To make brown rice, bring 2 cups of water to boiling. Add 1 cup uncooked brown rice. Return to boiling; reduce heat to medium-low. (Rice should be barely simmering.) Simmer, covered, about 35 minutes. Remove from heat; let stand, covered, for 5 minutes. Makes 3 cups rice.

30 MIN.
LOW FAT

SPRING HERB RICE

Start to finish: 30 min.

This recipe brings out the best in short grain rice by cooking it quickly, keeping ingredients simple, and pairing the rice with the freshest of the season's herbs.
(See the photograph on page 123.)

1¾ cups water
1 cup short grain rice

◆◆◆

1 cup chopped onion
1 Tbsp. olive oil
1 Tbsp. margarine or butter

1 cup sliced celery
1 cup sliced fresh mushrooms
½ tsp. salt
¼ tsp. pepper
2 Tbsp. snipped fresh herbs, such as basil, oregano, parsley, thyme, verbena, and/or lemon thyme
1 tsp. snipped fresh rosemary

1 In a saucepan bring water to boiling; stir in uncooked rice. Return to boiling; reduce heat. Simmer, covered, about 15 minutes or until liquid is absorbed. Remove saucepan from heat; let rice stand, covered, for 5 minutes.

2 Meanwhile, in a large skillet cook and stir onion in hot oil and margarine or butter over medium heat for 3 minutes. Add celery, mushrooms, salt, and pepper. Cook and stir for 1 minute more or until vegetables are tender. Remove skillet from heat. Stir in cooked rice, fresh herbs, and rosemary just until combined. Makes 6 side-dish servings.

Nutrition facts per serving: 173 cal., 4 g total fat (1 g sat. fat), 0 mg chol., 224 mg sodium, 30 g carbo., 1 g fiber, 3 g pro. *Daily values:* 3% vit. A, 8% vit. C, 1% calcium, 12% iron.

30 MIN.

GARDEN RISOTTO

Start to finish: 30 min.

Long, slow cooking is the key to producing the creamy results in this classic Italian dish.

1 cup Arborio rice or short grain white rice
2 Tbsp. olive oil or cooking oil
2 cloves garlic, minced

3¼ to 3½ cups reduced-sodium chicken broth or vegetable broth

◆◆◆

1 cup shredded carrot
¼ cup thinly sliced green onions
¼ to ½ cup shredded Parmesan or Romano cheese
2 Tbsp. snipped fresh basil

◆◆◆

Long, thin carrot curls (optional)
Basil leaves (optional)

1 In a large saucepan cook and stir uncooked rice in hot oil over medium heat 5 minutes. Add garlic; cook and stir 1 minute.

2 Meanwhile, in a medium saucepan, bring broth to boiling; reduce heat and simmer. Slowly add 1 cup of the broth to rice mixture (be careful of spattering); stir constantly. Cook and stir over medium heat until broth is absorbed (about 5 minutes).

3 Add 2 more cups of broth, ½ cup at a time, stirring constantly until broth is absorbed. Stir in remaining broth, shredded carrot, and green onions. Cook and stir until rice is creamy and just tender. Stir in Parmesan or Romano cheese and snipped basil.

4 To serve, spoon the rice into bowls. If desired, garnish each serving with some of the carrot curls and the basil leaves. Makes 4 side-dish servings.

Nutrition facts per serving: 289 cal., 10 g total fat (1 g sat. fat), 5 mg chol., 611 mg sodium, 42 g carbo., 1 g fiber, 8 g pro. *Daily values:* 79% vit. A, 6% vit. C, 7% calcium, 14% iron.

FRESH VEGETABLES EN PAPILLOTE

Prep: 30 min. ◆ Bake: 15 min.

As the vegetables bake and let off steam, the paper pouches puff. After the "X" is cut, carefully peel back the paper to reveal the vegetables.

6 10-inch squares parchment
   paper or foil

♦♦♦

1 medium zucchini, quartered
   lengthwise, seeded, and
   thinly sliced (about
   1¼ cups)
1 cup very thinly sliced carrots
1 cup 1-inch pieces trimmed
   asparagus
1 cup thinly sliced leeks (white
   part only)
½ tsp. snipped fresh tarragon
   or ¼ tsp. dried tarragon,
   crushed
½ tsp. snipped fresh dillweed
   or ¼ tsp. dried dillweed,
   crushed
1 clove garlic, minced
⅛ tsp. salt
   Dash pepper

♦♦♦

   Lemon wedges

1 Fold each square of parchment paper or foil in half to form a rectangle. Cut each rectangle into a half-heart shape, about 8 inches long and 4½ inches wide. (When opened, the heart should be 9 inches wide.)

2 Combine zucchini, carrots, asparagus, and leeks. Add tarragon, dillweed, garlic, salt, and pepper, gently tossing to mix. Place one-sixth of the mixture on 1 side of each heart. Fold other half of paper up and over. Crimp edges to seal; twist end several times.

Menu

Poached salmon fillets

♦♦♦

**Fresh Vegetables
En Papillote
(see left)**

♦♦♦

**Arugula and pear salad
topped with toasted nuts**

♦♦♦

Fresh fruit tart

3 Place vegetable packets on an ungreased baking sheet. Bake in a 350° oven for 15 to 20 minutes or until vegetables are just tender. Cut an "X" in the top of each heart to open. Serve with lemon wedges. Makes 6 servings.

Nutrition facts per serving: 38 cal., 0 g total fat, 0 mg chol., 67 mg sodium, 9 g carbo., 3 g fiber, 1 g pro.
Daily values: 55% vit. A, 16% vit. C, 2% calcium, 7% iron.

FONTINA-TOPPED ANGEL HAIR AND VEGETABLE TOSS

Start to finish: 25 min.

Fontina, a smooth and creamy cheese with a mild, nutty flavor, is one of the great cheeses of Italy. Look for this pale yellow cheese with a golden brown rind in the cheese section of large supermarkets or Italian markets. If fontina is not available, substitute Asiago cheese.

1 lb. fresh asparagus spears,
   trimmed and cut into
   1-inch pieces (3 cups)

1½ cups assorted sliced fresh
    mushrooms, such as
    button, shiitake, oyster
1 small red onion, thinly sliced
2 cloves garlic, minced
1 Tbsp. olive oil
¼ cup dry white wine or
   chicken broth

♦♦♦

8 oz. dried angel hair pasta,
   broken in half
2 medium tomatoes, coarsely
   chopped (2 cups)
1 Tbsp. snipped fresh oregano

♦♦♦

½ cup shredded fontina cheese
   (2 oz.)
   Coarsely ground black
   pepper

1 In a large skillet cook asparagus, mushrooms, onion, and garlic in hot olive oil for 3 to 4 minutes or until tender. Carefully stir in wine or broth. Bring to boiling; reduce heat. Simmer, uncovered, 3 minutes or until liquid is almost evaporated.

2 Meanwhile, cook pasta according to package directions. Drain pasta; add to asparagus mixture in skillet. Stir in tomatoes and oregano, tossing to coat.

3 To serve, transfer to a serving platter. Top with fontina cheese and sprinkle with coarsely ground black pepper. Serve immediately. Makes 6 to 8 side-dish servings.

Nutrition facts per serving: 242 cal., 6 g total fat (2 g sat. fat), 11 mg chol., 83 mg sodium, 36 g carbo., 2 g fiber, 10 g pro.
Daily values: 9% vit. A, 35% vit. C, 6% calcium, 15% iron.

SALMON-WALNUT RICE PIE

Prep: 35 min. ◆ Bake: 45 min.
Stand: 10 min.

*When your taste runs to classic comfort fare, try this flavor-packed combination of toasted walnuts, spinach, feta cheese, and salmon baked in a crust made with rice.
(See the photograph on page 123.)*

1	cup water
½	cup long grain rice
¼	tsp. salt

◆◆◆

1	beaten egg
1	cup crumbled feta cheese with basil and tomato or plain feta cheese (4 oz.)

◆◆◆

1	cup milk
1	Tbsp. all-purpose flour
3	beaten eggs
1	8-oz. skinless, boneless salmon fillet, coarsely chopped
1	cup chopped fresh spinach
½	cup crumbled feta cheese with basil and tomato (2 oz.)
¼	cup sliced green onions
1	clove garlic, minced
¼	tsp. salt

◆◆◆

¼	cup coarsely chopped walnuts, toasted*
	Lemon wedges (optional)

1 In a small saucepan bring water to boiling. Stir in uncooked rice and the ¼ teaspoon salt. Return to boiling; reduce heat. Simmer, covered, about 15 minutes or until liquid is absorbed. Remove pan from heat; let stand, covered, for 5 minutes. Allow the rice to cool about 15 minutes.

2 While rice is cooling, preheat oven to 325°. Stir the 1 beaten egg and the 1 cup crumbled feta cheese into the cooled rice.

3 Using your fingers, a spatula, or bottom of a drinking glass, press rice mixture into bottom and up sides of a greased 9-inch glass pie plate, building edges high to keep filling from spilling over during baking. Bake crust 10 minutes or until set.

4 In a medium bowl stir milk into flour until thoroughly combined. Stir in the 3 beaten eggs, the salmon, chopped spinach, the ½ cup feta cheese, the green onions, garlic, and the ¼ teaspoon salt. Pour milk mixture into the prebaked rice crust.

5 Bake pie, uncovered, about 45 minutes or until a knife inserted near the center comes out clean. If necessary, cover the edge of the crust with foil to prevent overbrowning. Let the pie stand 10 minutes before serving. Sprinkle top of pie with walnuts. Cut into wedges. If desired, serve with lemon wedges. Makes 6 main-dish servings.

***Note:** To toast walnuts, spread them in a single layer in a shallow baking pan. Bake in a 350° oven for 5 to 10 minutes or until light golden brown, watching carefully and stirring once or twice to prevent burning.

*Nutrition facts per serving: 368 cal., 22 g total fat (12 g sat. fat), 208 mg chol., 982 mg sodium, 20 g carbo., 1 g fiber, 22 g pro. **Daily values:** 24% vit. A, 6% vit. C, 33% calcium, 15% iron.*

SALMON TERIYAKI

(LOW FAT)

Prep: 10 min. ◆ Marinate: 30 min.
Broil: 8 min.

For a restaurant-style presentation, add a little finely shredded zucchini and carrot to the rice after cooking. Then, make a bed of rice mixture on the dinner plates, top with fish, and carefully spoon thickened teriyaki sauce over fish.

¼	cup reduced-sodium soy sauce
¼	cup rice vinegar
1	Tbsp. sugar
1	Tbsp. cooking oil
1	tsp. dry mustard
1	tsp. ground ginger
¼	tsp. pepper
4	skinless, boneless salmon fillets (about 1 to 1¼ pounds)

◆◆◆

	Hot cooked rice
2	Tbsp. thinly sliced green onion

1 For marinade, stir together soy sauce, vinegar, sugar, oil, mustard, ginger, and pepper. Place fish in a shallow dish. Pour marinade over fish. Cover and let stand at room temperature for 30 minutes, turning once. (Or, cover and chill for up to 1 hour, turning occasionally.) Drain fish, reserving marinade.

2 Place fish on unheated rack of a broiler pan. Broil 4 inches from the heat for 4 to 6 minutes per ½-inch thickness of fish, turning and brushing with marinade once halfway through. Discard remaining marinade.* Serve fish with hot cooked rice. Sprinkle with green onion. Makes 4 main-dish servings.

*Note: If desired, instead of discarding remaining marinade, reserve it. Measure the marinade and add water to equal ½ cup liquid. In a small saucepan, stir marinade mixture into 1¼ teaspoons cornstarch. Cook and stir until thickened and bubbly. Cook for 1 minute more. Spoon sauce over salmon fillets.

Nutrition facts per serving without sauce: 234 cal., 6 g total fat (1 g sat. fat), 20 mg chol., 333 mg sodium, 25 g carbo., 0 g fiber, 19 g pro. *Daily values:* 2% vit. A, 1% vit. C, 1% calcium, 13% iron.

CRAWFISH WITH SAVANNAH RICE

Start to finish: 55 min.

From the South, where nearly 80 percent of America's rice is grown, comes this combination of two regional favorites: rich, tomato-infused rice from Savannah, Georgia, and crawfish étouffée from Louisiana.

| 1 | lb. frozen peeled, cooked crawfish tails or fresh or frozen shrimp in shells |
| 4 | slices bacon |

♦♦♦

½	cup chopped onion
1½	cups water
2	Tbsp. tomato paste
1	tsp. sugar
¼	tsp. salt

♦♦♦

| ¾ | cup long grain rice |

♦♦♦

½	cup chopped celery
½	cup chopped green and/or red sweet pepper
2	cloves garlic, minced

♦♦♦

1	Tbsp. cornstarch
¼ to ½	tsp. ground red pepper
⅛ to ¼	tsp. ground black pepper

1 Thaw crawfish or shrimp, if frozen. In a large skillet cook bacon over medium heat until crisp. Drain bacon on paper towels. Crumble bacon and set aside. Remove all but 1 tablespoon of bacon drippings from skillet. Reserve the remaining drippings.

2 Add onion to skillet. Cook and stir over medium heat until onion is tender. Carefully stir in the water, tomato paste, sugar, and salt. Cook and stir until heated through and tomato paste is dissolved. Remove mixture from heat; set aside.

3 Spoon 3 tablespoons of the uncooked rice in each of four 6-ounce custard cups or four 8-ounce individual soufflé cups. Place cups in a shallow baking pan. Divide the tomato-onion mixture evenly among the custard cups (there should be ½ to ⅔ cup of tomato mixture per custard cup). Cover cups with foil. Bake in a 350° oven 40 minutes or until rice is tender, stirring once.

4 If using shrimp, peel and devein. Rinse shrimp; pat dry. In a 3-quart saucepan bring 4 cups *water* and 1 teaspoon *salt* to boiling. Add shrimp. Cook and stir 1 to 3 minutes or until shrimp turn pink. Drain; set aside.

5 Meanwhile, in a large skillet cook celery, sweet pepper, and garlic in 1 tablespoon of the reserved bacon drippings until vegetables are tender.

6 In a small bowl or cup stir 1 cup *cold water* into cornstarch; add red pepper, black pepper, and

⅛ teaspoon *salt.* Stir into skillet along with the cooked crawfish tails or cooked shrimp and cooked bacon. Cook and stir until thickened and bubbly; cook and stir for 2 minutes more or until heated through.

7 Remove rice from oven. Transfer to a wire rack. Let stand for 10 minutes. To unmold, loosen edges with a knife. Carefully invert rice mixture onto a shallow bowl or dinner plate; spoon a fourth of the crawfish mixture around mounded rice. Repeat with remaining rice and crawfish mixture. Makes 4 main-dish servings.

Nutrition facts per serving: 354 cal., 11 g total fat (4 g sat. fat), 168 mg chol., 506 mg sodium, 36 g carbo., 1 g fiber, 25 g pro. *Daily values:* 5% vit. A, 29% vit. C, 7% calcium, 22% iron.

EASING THE PRESSURE

You can't see it or feel it, but high blood pressure can increase your risk of heart disease, stroke, and kidney disease. Nearly one quarter of Americans—around 50 million people—have hypertension. Except for the common cold, high blood pressure accounts for more doctor visits than any other health condition.

Fortunately, high blood pressure is simple to detect and often easy to control: Eating right is the cornerstone of treatment and prevention. Where do you start? If you're like most people, you probably think the first line of attack is the salt shaker. Not true! There are other health-smart strategies—involving diet and lifestyle as well as losing weight and limiting alcohol intake—that can help keep your blood pressure in check.

MAKING SENSE OF SALT

Only about one in four persons with high blood pressure benefits from a low-sodium diet. These individuals are considered "salt sensitive," meaning that excess dietary sodium can be a factor in driving their blood pressure into the danger zone.

For these salt-sensitive people, "a high-sodium intake is a major component of high blood pressure," according to Dr. Maurizio Trevisan, professor and chairman of the department of social and preventive medicine at the University of Buffalo. Dr. Trevisan further explains that higher sodium intake is more likely to increase the risk for hypertension as we age.

Although it's hard to tell who is salt sensitive, certain populations are more likely to have the condition—people over 65, African Americans, and persons with diabetes. But some medical experts feel that all Americans, whether they have high blood pressure or not, can benefit from cutting back on salt.

On the other side of the salt pillar are researchers who believe that the recommendation for all Americans to reduce sodium intake is unwarranted. They point out that there is insufficient scientific evidence that restricting salt prevents hypertension in healthy people. According to their studies, salt has little or no effect on people with normal blood pressure.

Says Dr. Suzanne Oprial, director of the hypertension program at the University of Alabama at Birmingham and an American Heart Association past president, "Evidence is accumulating that the strategy to reduce salt intake is not worthwhile (in healthy people), that salt restriction has no benefit on cardiovascular disease."

FOOD AS MEDICINE

For years, health experts have urged Americans to watch their fat intake and eat plenty of fruits, vegetables, and whole grains. It is well known that such a diet reduces the risks of many serious illnesses, such as heart disease, cancer, obesity, and diabetes. This same healthy regimen also can be your best medicine in the fight against hypertension.

"Food is very powerful," says Judith Stern, Sc.D., R.D., past president of the American Society for Clinical Nutrition. "We now have significant and important evidence—based on science—that a dietary pattern that emphasizes fresh fruits, vegetables, and low-fat dairy products, plus modest amounts of nuts,

RICE WITH CHICKEN AND SOUR CHERRIES
Start to finish: 40 min.

Short- and medium-grain rices, which are stickier than long grain, create just the right texture to showcase the sweet-tart mixture of cherries and chicken.
(See the photograph on page 122.)

2⅔ cups water
1⅓ cups short or medium grain white rice

12 oz. skinless, boneless chicken breasts or thighs, cut into ½-inch cubes
¼ tsp. salt
¼ tsp. pepper
⅓ cup finely chopped onion,
1 Tbsp. cooking oil or olive oil
◆◆◆
2 Tbsp. margarine or butter
◆◆◆
1⅓ cups dried tart cherries
1 Tbsp. sugar
¼ tsp. ground saffron or turmeric

2 Tbsp. hot water
◆◆◆
2 Tbsp. chopped pistachios and/or slivered almonds
Fresh chive sprigs (optional)
Snipped dried tart cherries (optional)

1 In a medium saucepan bring water, uncooked rice, and ½ teaspoon *salt* to boiling; reduce heat. Simmer, covered, for 15 minutes. Remove from heat; let stand, covered, for 5 minutes.

beans, seeds, fish, poultry, and lean meats, can effectively lower a person's blood pressure."

A new study found that blood pressure can be lowered by a diet low in fat and saturated fat that includes 8 to 10 servings a day of fruits and vegetables and 3 servings a day of low-fat dairy products. This study, called the Dietary Approaches to Stop Hypertension (DASH), was spearheaded by the National Heart, Lung, and Blood Institute.

For about 40 percent of the DASH subjects, results were significant enough that the need for medication was eliminated in as little as two weeks, without changes in weight, sodium intake, or alcohol consumption. It was estimated that if most Americans ate the DASH diet, strokes could drop by 27 percent and coronary disease by 15 percent.

"The DASH study provides the most compelling evidence to date that the foods we eat can help us to reduce our risk of hypertension," says Dr. David McCarron, M.D., a professor of medicine at the Oregon Health Sciences University and a supporting researcher in the DASH study.

OVERWEIGHT AND UNDER PRESSURE

Hypertension experts do agree: Weight loss still is the single most important way to lower blood pressure. Shedding even a few pounds can help because the more overweight you are, the greater your risk for developing hypertension. Says Dr. Oprial, "With a 10-pound weight loss, you can achieve substantial decreases in blood pressure and your responsiveness to hypertension medication improves."

OTHER CONTRIBUTING FACTORS

Blood pressure is also sensitive to alcohol. If you drink, do so in moderation—and opt for red wine instead of beer or liquor. Research shows that up to two glasses of red wine daily could have a beneficial effect on hypertension.

Regular exercise is another key to healthy blood pressure. It lowers weight, improves circulation, and helps regulate key minerals involved in hypertension. Exercise even benefits people with hypertension who are within their ideal body weight. Be sure to consult your physician before starting any exercise program.

For more information on the DASH study, visit the Internet site at http://dash.bwh.harvard.edu.

—Ellen Albertson, M.S., R.D., is an author and journalist specializing in the field of nutrition communication.

OTHER KEY MINERALS

Table salt contains both sodium and chloride. New studies hint that the chloride—not the sodium—may be the high-blood-pressure culprit in salt. Research is still in the preliminary stages, but since most of the chloride we get comes from salt, you still may want to reach for the salt shaker less often if you are prone to hypertension.

While the salt issue may be open to debate, other minerals may have a positive impact on blood pressure: The DASH study showed that potassium, magnesium, and calcium are possible good guys in the hypertension equation, keeping blood pressure from rising even in cases of high salt intake.

2 Meanwhile, sprinkle chicken with salt and pepper. In a large nonstick skillet cook onion in hot oil until tender. Add the chicken; cook and stir for 4 to 5 minutes or until no longer pink. Transfer the chicken and onion to a bowl; set aside.

3 In the same skillet melt the margarine or butter over medium heat. Press half of the cooked rice evenly in skillet using the back of a greased spoon. Cook, uncovered, without stirring, for 8 minutes or until rice is brown and crispy on bottom.

4 Meanwhile, add remaining cooked rice, the 1⅓ cups cherries, and the sugar to the chicken mixture; toss to combine. Spread mixture over top of the rice. Dissolve saffron or turmeric in the hot water; drizzle the saffron or turmeric mixture over top. Cover and cook about 5 minutes or until heated through.

5 Carefully invert rice cake onto a serving platter. Sprinkle nuts on top before serving. Cut into wedges. If desired, garnish with chives and additional dried tart cherries. Serve immediately. Makes 6 main-dish servings.

Nutrition facts per serving: 571 cal., 14 g total fat (3 g sat. fat), 45 mg chol., 516 mg sodium, 86 g carbo., 3 g fiber, 23 g pro. *Daily values:* 31% vit. A, 1% vit. C, 3% calcium, 22% iron.

THAI CHICKEN AND NECTARINE SALAD

Start to finish: 40 min.

A peppery-sweet dressing is the grand finale on this pasta salad standout. (See the photograph on page 117.)

¼ cup reduced-sodium chicken broth
3 Tbsp. reduced-sodium soy sauce
2 Tbsp. bottled hoisin sauce
1 Tbsp. sugar
1 Tbsp. salad oil or olive oil
2 tsp. toasted sesame oil
3 cloves garlic, minced
1½ tsp. grated fresh ginger
1 tsp. crushed red pepper
⅛ tsp. ground black pepper

♦♦♦

12 oz. skinless, boneless chicken breast halves
4 oz. dried angel hair pasta
3 medium nectarines, plums, or peeled peaches, pitted and sliced
2 cups shredded bok choy
2 green onions, thinly sliced

1 In a screw-top jar combine broth, soy sauce, hoisin sauce, sugar, salad or olive oil, sesame oil, garlic, ginger, red pepper, and black pepper. Cover; shake well.

2 Rinse chicken; pat dry. In a large skillet cook chicken in a small amount of boiling water, covered, for 12 to 15 minutes or until no longer pink. Drain; cool slightly and cut into cubes. Cook pasta according to package directions; drain. In a bowl toss pasta with 3 tablespoons of the dressing. Place pasta on 4 serving plates. Top with chicken, fruit, bok choy, and green onion. Drizzle with remaining dressing. Makes 4 main-dish servings.

Nutrition facts per serving: 359 cal., 9 g total fat (2 g sat. fat), 45 mg chol., 644 mg sodium, 46 g carbo., 2 g fiber, 23 g pro. *Daily values:* 17% vit. A, 29% vit. C, 4% calcium, 15% iron.

LOW FAT RICE PRIMAVERA

Prep: 25 min. ♦ Cook: 20 min.

You'll find jasmine rice in larger supermarkets, some Asian and Indian groceries, as well as health food and gourmet stores. (See the photograph on page 117.)

1 cup jasmine rice
3 cups assorted fresh vegetables, such as sugar snap pea pods; asparagus, sliced into 1-inch pieces; red, green, or yellow sweet pepper, cut into 1-inch cubes; and/or cherry tomatoes, quartered
¼ cup finely chopped red onion

♦♦♦

2 tsp. cornstarch
1 tsp. finely shredded lemon peel
1 Tbsp. lemon juice
¼ tsp. ground black pepper
1 cup chicken broth

♦♦♦

3 to 4 Tbsp. shredded fresh basil or purple basil
1 Tbsp. basil oil or olive oil
2 Tbsp. pine nuts, toasted

1 In a saucepan bring 1⅔ cups *water* to boiling. Stir in uncooked rice. Return to boiling; reduce heat. Simmer, covered, 15 minutes or until liquid is absorbed and rice is tender. Meanwhile, in a large saucepan cook vegetables (except cherry tomatoes, if using) and red onion in a small amount of lightly salted boiling water, covered, 2 to 3 minutes or until crisp-tender. Drain; keep warm.

2 In a medium saucepan stir together cornstarch, lemon peel, lemon juice, and black pepper. Stir in chicken broth. Cook and stir over medium heat until thickened and bubbly. Cook and stir 2 minutes more. Remove from heat. Add cooked vegetables and, if using, cherry tomatoes; toss.

3 Toss rice with shredded basil and oil. Divide rice among 6 individual bowls; make an indentation in centers. Fill with vegetable mixture. Sprinkle with pine nuts. If desired, garnish with *purple basil blossoms*. Serve immediately. Makes 6 side-dish servings.

Nutrition facts per serving: 188 cal., 5 g total fat (1 g sat. fat), 0 mg chol., 138 mg sodium, 32 g carbo., 1 g fiber, 6 g pro. *Daily values:* 11% vit. A, 65% vit. C, 2% calcium, 14% iron.

THE CLEVER COOK

FLOWERPOTS FROM DISPOSABLE PANS

I save the disposable pans that come with mixes and dinners and use them to start plants indoors or to grow an indoor herb garden.

Lynette Kittle
Spring Hill, Florida

Above: *Caribbean Slaw*
(page 107)
Left: *Thai Chicken and*
Nectarine Salad (page 116)
Below: *Rice Primavera*
(page 116)

Above: *Roast Beef and Red Pepper Sandwiches (page 140)*
Left: *Overnight Garden Dills (page 138)*
Right: *"Fried" Chicken Salad (page 139) and Summertime Tortellini (page 138)*

Top left: *Berry Delicious White Chocolate Cheesecake*
(page 144)
Above left: *Merry Berry Sorbet (page 145)*
Page 120: *Lemon-Light Shortcakes (page 142)*

Top right: *Mango-Lime Trifles (page 143)*
Above right: *Cherry Cordial Brownie Torte (page 146)*

Above: *Rice with Chicken and Sour Cherries (page 114)*
Right: *Curry Burritos (page 102)*

Left: *Salmon-Walnut
Rice Pie (page 112)*
Above: *Spring Herb
Rice (page 110)*

Left: *Beef and Garlic Rice (page 125)*
Below: *Caramel Rice Pudding (page 126)*

BEEF AND GARLIC RICE

Prep: 25 min. ◆ Bake: 1½ hr.

This homey, hearty combination is bound to become a family favorite. (See the photograph on page 124.)

1 small bulb garlic*
2 tsp. olive oil*

◆◆◆

1¼ lb. boneless beef chuck roast, trimmed of fat and cut into ¾-inch cubes
1 Tbsp. cooking oil
1 14½-oz. can beef broth (1¾ cups)
½ cup water
1 Tbsp. Worcestershire sauce
1 Tbsp. snipped fresh marjoram or 1 tsp. dried marjoram, crushed

◆◆◆

3 small onions, cut into wedges

◆◆◆

2 cups water
1 cup long grain rice
¼ tsp. salt
2 to 3 Tbsp. snipped chives, cut into 1-inch pieces

◆◆◆

¼ cup cold water
2 Tbsp. cornstarch
2 Tbsp. balsamic vinegar or red wine vinegar

1 Remove papery outer layers from garlic bulb. Cut off about ¼ inch from top of bulb, leaving the bulb intact but exposing the individual cloves. Place garlic in center of a 12-inch square of foil. Drizzle garlic with olive oil. Seal foil around garlic; set aside.

Menu

Baked Crab Rangoon-Style Bundles (see page 102)

◆◆◆

Beef and Garlic Rice (see left)

◆◆◆

Hot tea and/or ice water with lemon slices

◆◆◆

Chocolate-dipped fortune cookies or sesame cookies

2 In an ovenproof Dutch oven brown half the beef in hot cooking oil. Remove meat with a slotted spoon; brown remaining meat. Drain off excess fat. Return all meat to Dutch oven. Stir in the beef broth, the ½ cup water, the Worcestershire sauce, and dried marjoram, if using.

3 Cover Dutch oven and bake in a 325° oven along with the wrapped garlic for 35 minutes. Remove the garlic from oven and add onion wedges to meat in Dutch oven. Cover and bake about 55 minutes more or until meat is just tender.

4 After meat has baked about 1 hour, prepare rice. Squeeze garlic from half of the roasted cloves into a medium saucepan; stir in the 2 cups water, the uncooked rice, and the salt. (Refrigerate remaining roasted garlic, covered,

for another use.**) Bring to boiling; reduce heat. Simmer, covered, for 15 minutes. Remove from heat; let stand, covered, for 5 minutes. Stir in chives (and bottled garlic, if using).

5 Remove meat from oven. In a small bowl or cup, stir the ¼ cup cold water into cornstarch; add balsamic or red wine vinegar and mix until well combined. Add to beef along with fresh marjoram, if using. Cook and stir over medium-high heat until thickened and bubbly. Cook and stir for 2 minutes more.

6 To serve, divide garlic rice among 4 bowls or plates. Serve the beef mixture alongside. Makes 4 main-dish servings.

***Note:** If desired, substitute 1 to 2 tablespoons bottled roasted minced garlic for the garlic bulb and olive oil. Add bottled garlic to rice along with the chives.

****Note:** Leftover roasted garlic can be wrapped and refrigerated for a few days. Use roasted garlic as a spread on sandwiches or on toasted French bread slices, added to mashed potatoes or a salad dressing, as a topping for pizza, or tossed with roasted vegetables.

Nutrition facts per serving: 512 cal., 16 g total fat (5 g sat. fat), 103 mg chol., 583 mg sodium, 49 g carbo., 1 g fiber, 39 g pro. *Daily values:* 21% vit. C, 5% calcium, 46% iron.

SIMPLE BERRY SHORTCAKES

Prep: 15 min. ◆ Bake: 13 min.

2 Tbsp. granulated sugar
2 Tbsp. brown sugar
1 tsp. apple pie spice
1 17.3-oz. pkg. (8) refrigerated large southern-style biscuits
2 Tbsp. butter, melted

◆◆◆

2 cups sliced fresh strawberries
1 cup fresh red raspberries
¼ cup seedless strawberry or raspberry preserves
1 cup whipping cream

1 In a shallow dish combine sugars and apple pie spice; set aside. Separate dough into 8 biscuits. Brush tops and sides of each biscuit with butter; dip in sugar mixture. Place 2 inches apart on ungreased baking sheet. Bake in a 375° oven for 13 to 17 minutes or until golden. Remove from baking sheet and cool slightly on a wire rack.

2 Meanwhile, in a bowl gently toss together the berries and preserves. In a chilled mixing bowl beat whipping cream with chilled beaters until soft peaks form.

3 To serve, split biscuits in half crosswise. Spoon fruit and whipping cream between halves. Makes 8 servings.

Nutrition facts per serving: 398 cal., 24 g total fat (12 g sat. fat), 48 mg chol., 666 mg sodium, 42 g carbo., 2 g fiber, 5 g pro. *Daily values:* 16% vit. A, 42% vit. C, 5% calcium, 11% iron.

CARAMEL RICE PUDDING

Start to finish: 40 min.

See the photograph on page 124.

½ cup Arborio rice or short grain rice
1 Tbsp. margarine or butter
3 cups milk
½ tsp. ground cinnamon
1 tsp. vanilla
⅓ cup caramel ice cream topping

◆◆◆

¼ cup sugar
2 drops hot water

1 In a medium saucepan cook and stir uncooked rice in hot margarine or butter for 2 minutes. Carefully stir in milk and cinnamon (mixture may spatter). Bring to a low boil; reduce heat. Cover; cook over low heat about 30 minutes or until most of the milk is absorbed, stirring occasionally. (Mixture may appear curdled.) Remove from heat. Stir in vanilla. Swirl in the ice cream topping. Transfer to 4 bowls. Keep warm.

2 In a small saucepan heat the ¼ cup sugar over medium-high heat until sugar begins to melt, shaking saucepan occasionally to heat sugar evenly. Do not stir until sugar begins to melt. Reduce heat; cook 3 to 5 minutes more or until sugar is melted and golden in color. Remove from heat. Stir in the 2 drops hot water. Quickly drizzle topping over each serving of pudding. Makes 4 servings.

Nutrition facts per serving: 325 cal., 7 g total fat (3 g sat. fat), 14 mg chol., 220 mg sodium, 59 g carbo., 0 g fiber, 8 g pro. *Daily values:* 14% vit. A, 3% vit. C, 20% calcium, 8% iron.

NUTRITION IN NO TIME

FULL-STEAM-AHEAD FISH

Prep: 10 min. ◆ Cook: 6 min.

No need to get steamed when you're in a dinnertime crunch. Steam this basil fish instead. It's quick, ingredients retain their nutrients, and calories from fat are minimal since there's no need to use oil.

2 6-oz. orange roughy or other fish fillets
Whole fresh basil leaves (1 or 2 per cut)
1 garlic clove, minced
2 tsp. shredded fresh ginger

◆◆◆

1 cup thinly sliced sweet peppers
8 oz. fresh asparagus spears

1 Using a sharp knife, make bias cuts about ¾ inch apart into the fish fillets. (Do not cut completely through fish.) Tuck basil leaves into each cut. Rub fillets with garlic and ginger.

2 Place peppers and asparagus in steamer basket. Top with fish. Place basket into a large, deep saucepan or wok in which 1 inch of water is boiling. Cover and steam for 6 to 8 minutes or until fish flakes easily with a fork. Serve immediately.

Nutrition facts per serving: 254 cal., 2 g fat (0 g sat. fat), 37 mg chol., 61 mg sodium, 36 g carbo., 3 g fiber, 21 g pro. *Daily values:* 15% vit. A, 77% vit. C, 3% calcium, 9% iron.

JUNE
Entertaining Style

Graduation open houses, wedding showers, and backyard barbecues all get penciled in on June's calendar. Make it a summertime affair to remember with Pixie Ice Cream Sandwiches made with almond and chocolate cookie dough, Herbed Feta Spread that can be chilled well in advance, and low-fat Gazpacho To Go that's pretty enough to be its own centerpiece. Follow our helpful tips for no-fuss hosting and end on a high note with tangy Blueberry-Rhubarb Crisp or Merry Berry Sorbet, a frosty mix of the season's best berries.

30-minute recipes indicated in RED.
Low-fat and no-fat recipes indicated
with a ♥.
Photographs indicated in italics.
*All new in 1998.

CREAMY SPINACH DIP

Prep: 20 min. ◆ Chill: 2 to 24 hr.

*Jicama, a crisp, mild-tasting
root vegetable, adds a delicate crunch
to this flavorful dip.*

2 8-oz. cartons plain fat-free
   yogurt
1 8-oz. carton light dairy sour
   cream
1 envelope (1.4 oz.) vegetable
   soup mix
◆◆◆
½ of a 10-oz. pkg. frozen
   chopped spinach, thawed
½ cup finely chopped jicama or
   ½ cup canned sliced water
   chestnuts, drained and
   finely chopped
¼ cup finely chopped onion
   Dash ground red pepper
   Assorted vegetable dippers,
      such as carrot sticks, sweet
      pepper strips, zucchini,
      and/or broccoli flowerets;
      or crackers

1 In a mixing bowl stir
together the yogurt, sour cream,
and vegetable soup mix.

2 Squeeze excess liquid from
spinach. Finely chop spinach. Stir
the spinach, jicama or water
chestnuts, onion, and ground red
pepper into yogurt mixture.
Cover; chill 2 to 24 hours before
serving. Serve with assorted vegetable dippers or crackers. Makes
3 cups dip.

Nutrition facts per tablespoon dip: 14 cal.,
0 g total fat, 1 mg chol., 18 mg sodium, 2 g
carbo., 0 g fiber, 1 g pro.

ANTIPASTO WITH TOASTED PITA CRISPS

Start to finish: 45 min.

*Prepare the conserve and pita crisps
ahead of time, then assemble this
antipasto platter just before serving.*

1 recipe Two-Tomato Conserve
   (see recipe, lower right)
◆◆◆
   Fresh mango slices (about
      2 mangoes)
   Thinly sliced prosciutto
      (about 4 oz.)
   Marinated artichoke hearts,
      drained (about two 6-oz.
      jars)
   Seedless red and/or green
      grape clusters
   Green olives and/or Greek
      black olives
1 recipe Toasted Pita Crisps
   (see recipe, below)

1 Transfer conserve to a small
dish. Place on a serving platter or
in a serving basket. Wrap each
mango slice with a slice of prosciutto. Arrange mango slices,
artichoke hearts, grapes, and
olives on the platter or in the basket. Serve with Toasted Pita
Crisps. Makes 15 to 20 servings.

TOASTED PITA CRISPS

Prep: 15 min. ◆ Bake: 10 min.

*To make splitting the pita bread
rounds easier, you can soften them
in the microwave on high power
for 20 to 30 seconds.*

4 large pita bread rounds
¼ cup olive oil
◆◆◆
¼ cup finely shredded
   Parmesan cheese

1 Slice each pita bread round
in half horizontally, separating
into 2 rounds. Brush cut sides of
each sliced pita round with oil.
Cut each sliced round into
6 wedges. On a large baking sheet
spread wedges, cut sides up, in a
single layer.

2 Sprinkle Parmesan cheese
over wedges. Bake in a 350° oven
for 10 minutes. Cool on baking
sheet on a wire rack. Transfer
crisps to an airtight container.
Store at room temperature for up
to 1 week. Makes 48 crisps.

Nutrition facts per pita crisp: 26 cal., 1 g
total fat (0 g sat. fat), 0 mg chol., 36 mg
sodium, 3 g carbo., 0 g fiber, 1 g pro.

TWO-TOMATO CONSERVE

Prep: 45 min. ◆ Chill: up to 2 days
Stand: 30 min.

*Two kinds of tomatoes and a pear?
That's right! One sweet pear mellows
the tart from the fresh vine ripened
tomatoes. Spoon the conserve atop pita
crisps or toasted slices of Italian bread.*

¼ cup boiling water
2 Tbsp. snipped dried
   tomatoes (not oil-packed)
1 Tbsp. margarine or butter
2 small onions, thinly sliced
   and separated into rings
   (1 cup)
2 tsp. brown sugar
◆◆◆
1 lb. Roma or plum tomatoes,
   chopped (2½ cups)

1 **large pear, peeled, cored, and chopped (1 cup)**
¼ **tsp. salt**
⅛ **tsp. freshly ground pepper**

◆◆◆

2 **Tbsp. balsamic vinegar or red wine vinegar**

1 In a small bowl pour boiling water over dried tomatoes; let stand. In a medium saucepan melt margarine or butter. Add onions. Cook, covered, over medium-low heat 10 to 12 minutes or until onions are tender. Uncover; add brown sugar. Cook and stir over medium-high heat for 4 to 5 minutes more.

2 Add the undrained dried tomatoes, Roma tomatoes, pear, salt, and pepper to onions in saucepan. Cook, covered, for 10 minutes. Uncover and cook 5 minutes more or until most of the liquid has evaporated.

3 Add the balsamic or red wine vinegar. Cook and stir for 1 minute more. Remove from heat. Let mixture cool slightly. Place in an airtight container and store in refrigerator up to 2 days. Let conserve stand at room temperature for 30 minutes before serving. Makes 2 cups.

Nutrition facts per 2 tablespoons: 35 cal., 1 g total fat (0 g sat. fat), 0 mg chol., 56 mg sodium, 7 g carbo., 1 g fiber, 1 g pro. *Daily values:* 3% vit. A, 17% vit. C, 2% iron.

Herbed Feta Spread
Prep: 15 min. ◆ Chill: up to 3 days

This is a fast and easy make-ahead recipe to have on hand. Serve the spread with fresh figs.

1 **8-oz. pkg. reduced-fat cream cheese (Neufchâtel)**
1 **4-oz. pkg. crumbled garlic-and-herb feta cheese**
1 **Tbsp. milk**
  Freshly ground pepper

◆◆◆

Fresh figs, halved (optional)
Lemon leaves (optional)
Assorted snipped fresh herbs and/or herb sprigs (optional)

1 In a small mixing bowl combine the cream cheese, feta cheese, milk, and freshly ground pepper. Beat with an electric mixer on medium speed until mixture is well combined and of desired spreading consistency.

2 Line a 1½-cup mold or bowl with plastic wrap. Spoon cheese mixture into mold; evenly spread in mold, removing any air bubbles. Cover the top with plastic wrap and chill until ready to serve, up to 3 days.

3 To serve, unwrap and invert molded cheese mixture onto serving platter. Carefully remove plastic wrap. If desired, surround the molded cheese with halved fresh figs and lemon leaves and garnish with snipped herbs and/or fresh herb sprigs. Makes 15 to 20 appetizer servings.

Nutrition facts per serving: 64 cal., 5 g total fat (3 g sat. fat), 21 mg chol., 150 mg sodium, 1 g carbo., 0 g fiber, 3 g pro. *Daily values:* 4% vit. A, 4% calcium.

Tips for Simple-but-Beautiful Entertaining

Here are some tips to help you with simple-but-beautiful outdoor entertaining:

◆ Buy large quantities of inexpensive, attractive glassware. Once purchased, you can use it again and again.

◆ Reusable cloth napkins also are a cost-saver and are more elegant than paper.

◆ Sheets serve well as tablecloths. Look for flat sheets with great patterns at white sales or on the discontinued tables.

◆ The right lighting can create subtle drama. Keep it soft and simple to flatter your guests. Candles of all sizes help create the mood.

◆ Scale is important. A few oversize platters or baskets on a buffet table look better than several small ones.

◆ Keep buffet fare simple; it should only look like you labored in the kitchen all day. Start with no-fuss food stuffs, such as prepared cheeses, presliced meats, and vegetables; then add finishing touches with fresh herbs and fruit garnishes.

◆ To keep the party lively and traffic circulating, set up separate food and beverage stations, with seating close by to accommodate intimate chats.

◆ Don't try to be perfect. People just like to be included in the fun.

HUMMUS

Start to finish: 10 min.

Nabbing a nutritious nosh is a breeze with this tasty Middle Eastern spread.

1 **15-oz. can chickpeas (garbanzo beans), undrained***
¼ **cup tahini (sesame paste)**
1 **Tbsp. lemon juice**
2 **to 4 cloves garlic**
¼ **tsp. salt**
¼ **to ½ tsp. ground red pepper (optional)**

◆◆◆

Dippers such as Toasted Pita Crisps (see recipe, page 128), whole wheat pita bread wedges, bagel chips, carrot sticks, and/or celery sticks

1 In a food processor bowl or blender container combine the chickpeas, tahini, lemon juice, garlic, salt, and red pepper, if using. Cover and process or blend until smooth.

2 To serve, spoon mixture into a serving bowl. Serve with the desired dippers. Makes 6 to 8 appetizer servings.

*****Note:** For a thicker spread, drain part of the chickpea liquid.

Nutrition facts per serving without dippers: 114 cal., 6 g total fat (1 g sat. fat), 0 mg chol., 71 mg sodium, 12 g carbo., 3 g fiber, 4 g pro. *Daily values:* 7% vit. C, 3% calcium, 12% iron.

UPSIDE-DOWN MARINATED SHRIMP BOWL

Prep: 1 hr. ◆ Chill: 24 hr.

Because the stacked shrimp maintain the shape of the bowl in which they're marinated, the finished creation makes a stunning centerpiece.

5 **lb. fresh large shrimp in shells, peeled and deveined**

◆◆◆

½ **cup olive oil**
½ **cup white or red wine vinegar**
1½ **tsp. finely shredded lemon peel**
¼ **cup lemon juice**
2 **Tbsp. tomato paste**
1 **Tbsp. honey**
3 **cloves garlic, minced**
2 **tsp. grated fresh ginger**
½ **tsp. salt**
¼ **tsp. ground red pepper**

◆◆◆

Assorted fresh greens and herbs (optional)
Lime wedges (optional)
Thinly sliced cucumber or cucumber ribbons (optional)
Thinly sliced red onion, separated into rings (optional)
Yellow pear-shaped tomatoes and cherry tomatoes (optional)

1 In a large Dutch oven bring 5 quarts *water* and 1 teaspoon *salt* to boiling. Add shrimp. Bring to boiling; reduce heat. Simmer, uncovered, 1 to 3 minutes or until shrimp turn pink, stirring occasionally. Drain shrimp. Rinse under cold water; drain again.

2 To arrange shrimp, use a glass bowl that is 7 to 8 inches in diameter and about 4 inches deep. Arrange the shrimp, pointing the tails to the middle (see photo, below), in a circle to make 1 flat layer. (Only the round backs of shrimp should be visible from the outside of the bowl.) Repeat layers until bowl is filled, pressing down every couple of layers with the bottom of a plate that will fit into the bowl. When bowl is full, press down with plate 1 more time.

3 For marinade, in a screw-top jar combine the olive oil, wine vinegar, lemon peel, lemon juice, tomato paste, honey, garlic, ginger, salt, and ground red pepper. Cover and shake well. Pour marinade over shrimp in bowl. Cover and chill overnight, occasionally placing a larger flat plate tightly over the bowl and inverting to redistribute marinade.

4 Before serving, hold the plate off-center and invert bowl slightly to drain off marinade. Repeat inverting and draining until all marinade is drained. Discard the marinade. Place serving platter over bowl; carefully invert bowl to unmold (see illustration, page 131).

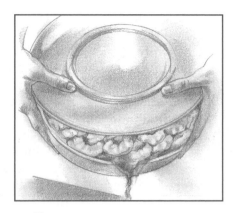

5 If desired, arrange greens, herbs, lime, cucumber, onion, and tomatoes around shrimp. Makes about 20 appetizer servings.

Nutrition facts per serving: 131 cal., 3 g total fat (1 g sat. fat), 222 mg chol., 302 mg sodium, 1 g carbo., 0 g fiber, 24 g pro. *Daily values:* 7% vit. A, 6% vit. C, 3% calcium, 23% iron.

SMOKED SALMON PASTA SALAD

Start to finish: 30 min.

Grab some bakery-fresh bread and you've got a summer-fresh lunch.

2½ cups cavatelli or medium
    shell macaroni
        ◆◆◆
¼ cup lemon juice
3 Tbsp. snipped fresh dillweed
4 tsp. Dijon-style mustard
2 tsp. sugar
¼ tsp. salt
⅛ tsp. pepper
3 Tbsp. peanut oil
6 oz. skinned, boned, and
    flaked hot smoked salmon
½ cup coarsely chopped
    cucumber
¼ cup snipped fresh chives

1 Cook pasta according to package directions; drain. Rinse with cold water; drain again. Return to saucepan; set aside.

2 In a small bowl whisk together the lemon juice, dillweed, mustard, sugar, salt, and pepper. Slowly add peanut oil in a thin, steady stream, whisking constantly. Add the dressing to pasta along with the salmon, cucumber, and chives. Toss mixture to coat well. Serve immediately. Makes 4 main-dish servings.

Nutrition facts per serving: 377 cal., 13 g total fat (2 g sat. fat), 10 mg chol., 591 mg sodium, 48 g carbo., 1 g fiber, 16 g pro. *Daily values:* 2% vit. A, 15% vit. C, 2% calcium, 17% iron.

CRAB AND PAPAYA SALAD

Start to finish: 40 min.

12 oz. fresh or frozen lump
    crabmeat or peeled,
    deveined, cooked shrimp
6 7- to 8-inch flour tortillas
        ◆◆◆
3 medium papayas, peeled,
    seeded, and cubed (about
    3 lb. or 5 cups)
1 cup frozen whole kernel
    corn, thawed
½ cup sliced green onions
½ cup peeled, seeded, and
    chopped cucumber
¼ cup snipped fresh cilantro
        ◆◆◆
⅓ cup plain yogurt
2 tsp. lemon juice
1 tsp. grated fresh ginger
1 tsp. ground cumin
¼ tsp. pepper

1 Thaw crabmeat, if frozen; drain. For tortilla crisps, cut each tortilla into 8 wedges. On a large baking sheet spread wedges in a single layer. Bake in a 350° oven for 5 to 10 minutes or until dry and crisp. Set aside to cool.

2 Combine crabmeat, papayas, corn, green onions, cucumber, and cilantro. Set aside.

3 For dressing, mix yogurt, lemon juice, ginger, cumin, and pepper. Pour over crab mixture; toss to coat. Arrange tortilla crisps on 6 serving plates; spoon salad atop. Makes 6 main-dish servings.

Nutrition facts per serving: 227 cal., 4 g total fat (1 g sat. fat), 57 mg chol., 293 mg sodium, 33 g carbo., 2 g fiber, 16 g pro. *Daily values:* 26% vit. A, 130% vit. C, 12% calcium, 15% iron.

Mexican Sea Breeze Salad

Start to finish: 25 min.

Cumin adds a special zing to the dressing drizzled on this refreshing crab salad.

6 cups mixed baby greens
2 cups fresh cooked lump crabmeat or crab-flavored, chunk-style fish pieces
2 medium tomatoes, cut into wedges
1 medium ripe avocado, peeled, pitted, and sliced
1 4-oz. can diced green chili peppers, drained
2 Tbsp. finely chopped red onion
2 Tbsp. snipped fresh cilantro

◆◆◆

¼ cup white vinegar
2 Tbsp. olive oil or cooking oil
1 Tbsp. sugar
½ tsp. ground cumin

1 Divide baby greens among 6 salad plates. Arrange crabmeat, tomatoes, avocado, and green chili peppers atop greens. Sprinkle with red onion and cilantro.

2 In a screw-top jar combine vinegar, oil, sugar, cumin, and ½ teaspoon *salt*. Cover and shake well. Pour some of the dressing over each salad. If desired, garnish with *yellow sweet pepper rings* and *sliced black olives*. Makes 6 main-dish servings.

Nutrition facts per serving: 173 cal., 11 g total fat (2 g sat. fat), 45 mg chol., 368 mg sodium, 11 g carbo., 3 g fiber, 11 g pro. *Daily values:* 7% vit. A, 36% vit. C, 7% calcium, 10% iron.

Dilled Tuna and Potato Salad

Prep: 30 min. ◆ Cook: 12 min. Chill: 4 to 24 hr.

Keep the fat in check with light mayonnaise dressing or salad dressing and fat-free yogurt.

3 medium red potatoes (about 1 lb.), scrubbed

◆◆◆

½ cup light mayonnaise dressing or salad dressing
½ cup plain fat-free yogurt
4 tsp. snipped fresh dillweed or 1 tsp. dried dillweed
1 Tbsp. milk
½ tsp. lemon-pepper seasoning
¼ tsp. garlic powder
1 cup chopped cucumber
¼ cup sliced green onions
1 9¼-oz. can tuna (water pack), drained and broken into chunks
2 hard-cooked eggs, chopped

Red-tip leaf lettuce leaves
4 cups shredded red-tip leaf lettuce
Sieved hard-cooked egg yolk (optional)
Cucumber spears (optional)
Fresh dill (optional)

1 Cut unpeeled potatoes into ½-inch cubes. In a saucepan cook potatoes, covered, in a small amount of boiling water for 12 to 15 minutes or until just tender. Drain well. Cool slightly.

2 Meanwhile, in a small mixing bowl stir together mayonnaise dressing or salad dressing, yogurt, dillweed, milk, lemon-pepper seasoning, and garlic powder. Stir in cucumber and onion. Add cooked potatoes, tuna, and chopped eggs. Toss lightly to mix. Cover and chill for 4 to 24 hours.

3 To serve, line 4 dinner plates with lettuce leaves and shredded lettuce. Divide tuna mixture among plates. If desired, garnish with sieved egg yolk, cucumber, and fresh dill. Makes 4 main-dish servings.

Nutrition facts per serving: 360 cal., 14 g fat (3 g sat. fat), 127 mg chol., 647 mg sodium, 33 g carbo., 2 g fiber, 25 g pro. *Daily values:* 18% vit. A, 46% vit. C, 12% calcium, 28% iron.

Lemon-Pepper Linguine with Pesto

Start to finish: 25 min.

8 oz. lemon-pepper linguine or plain linguine
12 oz. peeled and deveined medium shrimp

1 7-oz. jar roasted red
   peppers, drained and cut
   into strips
½ cup pitted Greek black
   olives, halved
⅓ cup purchased pesto
1 Tbsp. pine nuts, toasted
1 Tbsp. finely shredded
   Parmesan cheese

1 Cook linguine according to the package directions, adding shrimp the last 2 to 3 minutes, cooking until pasta is tender and shrimp turn pink. Drain; return to saucepan. Stir in roasted peppers, black olives, and pesto until combined. Transfer to a serving platter. Sprinkle with pine nuts and Parmesan cheese. Makes 4 main-dish servings.

Nutrition facts per serving: 486 cal., 20 g total fat (1 g sat. fat), 135 mg chol., 403 mg sodium, 52 g carbo., 2 g fiber, 26 g pro. *Daily values:* 24% vit. A, 172% vit. C, 5% calcium, 34% iron.

MEDITERRANEAN POTATO SALAD

Prep: 10 min. ◆ Cook: 15 min.
Chill: 4 to 24 hr.

Greek black olives, known as kalamata olives, are available in most grocery stores or specialty food markets.

1 lb. whole tiny new potatoes,
   scrubbed
   ◆◆◆
⅓ cup mayonnaise
2 Tbsp. lemon juice
1 clove garlic, minced
¼ tsp. coarsely ground black
   pepper
¼ cup pitted Greek black
   olives, coarsely chopped
1 2-oz. can anchovies, drained
   and chopped
2 Tbsp. capers, drained

2 Tbsp. finely chopped green
   onion
   ◆◆◆
3 hard-cooked eggs, coarsely
   chopped
½ of a small red onion, sliced
   and separated into rings

1 Place potatoes in a medium saucepan; add water to cover and, if desired, ¼ teaspoon *salt*. Bring to boiling; reduce heat. Simmer, covered, for 15 to 20 minutes or until potatoes are just tender. Drain well. Cool slightly. Cut potatoes into quarters and place in a large bowl.

2 Meanwhile, for dressing, in a small bowl stir together the mayonnaise, lemon juice, garlic, and pepper. Stir in the black olives, anchovies, capers, and green onion.

3 Pour dressing over potatoes. Add eggs and red onion. Toss gently to mix. Cover; chill 4 to 24 hours, stirring occasionally. Makes 6 side-dish servings.

Nutrition facts per serving: 222 cal., 14 g total fat (2 g sat. fat), 118 mg chol., 356 mg sodium, 19 g carbo., 1 g fiber, 7 g pro. *Daily values:* 5% vit. A, 21% vit. C, 3% calcium, 13% iron.

CURRIED CHICKEN AND PASTA SALAD

Start to finish: 40 min.

1 cup gemelli or rotini pasta,
   cooked, rinsed, and
   drained
   ◆◆◆
1 small pineapple
1 small papaya
5 cups shredded romaine

½ cup light mayonnaise
   dressing or salad dressing
1 Tbsp. honey
1 Tbsp. rice vinegar or white
   vinegar
1 tsp. curry powder
1 tsp. toasted sesame oil
1 to 2 fresh jalapeño peppers,
   seeded and chopped*
1½ cups cubed cooked chicken
2 Tbsp. cashew halves and
   pieces, toasted

1 Cook pasta according to package directions. Drain pasta. Rinse with cold water; drain again.

2 To prepare pineapple, remove crown. Wash and peel pineapple; remove eyes and core. Slice pineapple; cut slices in half. To prepare papaya, peel, halve, and scoop out seeds. Slice papaya. On a large platter arrange shredded romaine. Arrange pineapple and papaya slices atop romaine.

3 For dressing, stir together mayonnaise dressing or salad dressing, honey, vinegar, curry powder, sesame oil, and jalapeno peppers. Stir in the chicken and cooked pasta; spoon atop fruit on platter. Sprinkle with cashews. Makes 4 main-dish servings.

Note: Hot peppers contain oils that can burn your eyes, lips, and skin. Wear plastic gloves while preparing peppers and be sure to thoroughly wash your hands and nails in hot, soapy water afterward.

Nutrition facts per serving: 411 cal., 18 g total fat (4 g sat. fat), 51 mg chol., 305 mg sodium, 42 g carbo., 3 g fiber, 212 g pro. *Daily values:* 26% vit. A, 103% vit. C, 4% calcium, 20% iron.

A CANCER FIGHTER'S GROCERY LIST

Your risk of cancer could be decreased by 20 percent or more if you eat five servings (½ cup each) of fruits and vegetables each day. Making this simple, good-for-you change could reduce the nation's overall risk of acquiring most forms of cancer, according to the American Institute for Cancer Research and the World Cancer Research Fund.

Turning the wealth of cancer research into news you can use is as easy as going shopping. Availability of fresh and flavorful produce has never been greater. The best news is that all plant foods have some cancer-fighting attributes.

Variety is the key. Statistically, your total fruit and vegetable intake is more closely associated with reduced cancer risk than any individual food. Think of specific foods or types of foods as participants in your total anticancer diet. That said, the following foods have been recognized for having strong cancer-fighting properties.

BOOST YOUR BROCCOLI

The cruciferous vegetables—which include broccoli, kale, cauliflower, and all cabbages—are loaded with phytochemicals (plant chemicals) that have directly reduced cancer by some 60 to 80 percent in animal studies. Fiber, which helps fight colorectal cancer, also is found in abundance in these vegetables.

Broccoli sprouts (they look like bean sprouts and taste like broccoli) are loaded with up to 100 times higher concentrations of these phytochemicals than mature broccoli. Many health food stores and some larger supermarkets now stock broccoli sprouts. If you don't find broccoli sprouts, ask the produce manager at your local supermarket to order them.

◆ **Tip:** Mix broccoli sprouts into your salads or pile them high on sandwiches. Include a large serving—1 cup or more—of broccoli, kale, or other cruciferous vegetables on your menu several times a week. Lightly steam them to obtain the most nutritional benefit, while keeping their flavor and crunch.

CITRUS CRUSH

Oranges, lemons, limes, grapefruit—all citrus fruits are concentrated sources of the antioxidant vitamin C. They also contain other compounds, folate and bioflavonoids, which have an excellent research track record for helping ward off cancer.

Components in citrus fruits scavenge cells to remove elements that cause damage and can trigger tumor development. They also help slow the growth of any early-stage tumorlike cell clusters.

◆ **Tip:** Think of orange or grapefruit juice beyond breakfast: Enjoy a glass or two instead of soda pop or coffee in the middle of the day. Reach for citrus or other fruits instead of candy or chips as a between-meal snack.

TOSS IN A TOMATO

Tomatoes are known for their abundant vitamin C and beta-carotene content. They're also replete with another powerful carotene called lycopene. Carotenes are heat-stable, so cooked tomatoes will provide about the same benefit as raw ones. Tomatoes also are thought to be effective against cancers of the prostate and the digestive system.

◆ **Tip:** Dried tomatoes are concentrated and versatile versions of the fresh fruit. Toss snipped, softened dried tomatoes into salads, or stir them into spreads, sauces, and pastas.

THE MELLOW YELLOWS

Storehouses of cancer-fighting carotenes include carrots, sweet potatoes, and winter squashes, as well as fruits such as mangoes, papayas, cantaloupes, and apricots.

Other compounds in these orange and yellow fruits and vegetables appear to boost the immune system's response against cancerous agents.

◆ **Tip:** Mangoes and papayas once were rare treats. Take advantage of their abundance by adding them to the shopping basket every time you visit your supermarket.

BERRY GOOD NEWS

Blackberries, blueberries, and strawberries are sources of vitamins A and C, but they also contain phytochemical cancer-fighters, such as ellagic acid and anthocyanins.

Berries—especially strawberries—also are rich in the B vitamin folic acid, itself a stalwart cancer preventive.

◆ **Tip:** When craving "grab-and-go" snacks that are small and sweet, think berries. Countries south of the equator grow berries during our winter, so there's hardly a time when you can't find fresh berries.

SOYBEANS, NUTS, AND GRAINS

Soybeans—one of the first and most studied plants in cancer research—and soy products (except for soy oil) have been the center of attention when it comes to disease prevention. Soy and other legumes, such as peas and beans, are generous in the phytochemical department and easy to include in the diet.

Nuts and whole grains also are excellent sources of phytochemicals and of the antioxidants selenium and vitamin E. These are thought to help prevent cancer by capturing molecules that might disrupt a cell's normal processes.

◆ **Tip:** Add roasted soy nuts or cooked whole grains, peas, or beans to salads and soups. Pack a handful of nuts to take with you to work or while running errands.

THE ACTIVE APPROACH

Using fruits, vegetables, beans, and grains as ammunition in the war against cancer helps your odds of fending off the disease.

But in the long run, what you eat is only part of an overall healthy lifestyle necessary for preventing disease: Alcohol and tobacco also play key roles in cancer and health. If you drink alcohol, do so only in moderation, and eschew smoking.

Lastly, no approach to health is complete without at least half an hour of walking, biking, or similar moderate exercise each day.

—Jeanine Barone, M.S., provided additional research for this article.

LET HISTORY BE YOUR GUIDE

Anyone with a family history of cancer should consider eating at least 10 servings of fruits and vegetables a day. That's the recommendation of Dr. George Blackburn of Harvard Medical School. Blackburn also suggests bringing your family history to the attention of your doctor or nutrition specialist, who can help you design a personalized dietary approach to cancer prevention.

"For example," Blackburn says, "if there is a history of prostate cancer, you might want to include more tomatoes and soy in your diet; for colon cancer, you'd need more wheat bran. If it's breast cancer, then lowering fat and calories is more important."

Backyard Barbecue

This menu lets you avoid last-minute fuss. Make the ice cream sandwiches a week or two in advance, then stir up the potato salad and marinate the kabobs the night before your barbecue.

Steak with Roasted Garlic and Herbs
(see lower left)

◆◆◆

Shades of Green Kabobs
(see page 137)

◆◆◆

Mediterranean Potato Salad
(see page 133)

◆◆◆

Pixie Ice Cream Sandwiches
(see lower right)

◆◆◆

Lemonade

STEAK WITH ROASTED GARLIC AND HERBS

Prep: 15 min. ◆ Grill: 30 min.

Whole bulbs of garlic are soft and sweet after roasting, making them a fantastic flavor treat to spread on grilled steak or slices of crusty bread.

1 or 2 **whole garlic bulb(s)**
3 to 4 tsp. **snipped fresh basil or 1 tsp. dried basil, crushed**
1 Tbsp. **snipped fresh rosemary or 1 tsp. dried rosemary, crushed**
2 Tbsp. **olive oil or cooking oil**

◆◆◆

1 1½-lb. **boneless beef sirloin steak or rib eye steaks, cut 1 inch thick**
1 to 2 tsp. **cracked black pepper**
½ tsp. **salt**

◆◆◆

Fresh oregano sprigs (optional)

1 Remove papery outer layers from garlic bulb(s), leaving individual cloves attached to bulb(s). Cut off about ½ inch from top of bulb and discard. Place garlic in center of a 10-inch square cut from a double thickness of heavy foil. Bring foil up around garlic forming a shallow bowl. Sprinkle garlic with basil and rosemary; drizzle with oil.

2 Completely enclose garlic in foil, twisting ends of foil on top. Place foil packet on rack of an uncovered grill over medium coals for 30 minutes or until garlic cloves are soft. Remove garlic from foil packet, reserving herb-oil mixture. Let cool slightly.

3 Meanwhile, trim fat from meat. In a small bowl combine pepper and salt; rub onto both sides of steak. Grill steak alongside the garlic packet to desired doneness, turning steak halfway through desired grilling time. (For sirloin steak allow 14 to 18 min-utes for medium-rare or 18 to 22 minutes for medium. For rib eye steaks allow 8 to 12 minutes for medium-rare or 12 to 15 minutes for medium.)

4 To serve, cut steaks into serving-size pieces. Carefully squeeze the pulp from the garlic cloves onto the steak. Mash pulp slightly with a fork; spread over steaks. Drizzle steaks with the herb-oil mixture. If desired, garnish with oregano sprigs. Makes 6 servings.

Nutrition facts per serving: 251 cal., 15 g total fat (5 g sat. fat), 76 mg chol., 235 mg sodium, 2 g carbo., 0 g fiber, 26 g pro. *Daily values:* 3% vit. C, 2% calcium, 20% iron.

PIXIE ICE CREAM SANDWICHES

Prep: 30 min. ◆ Chill: 1 to 24 hr.
Bake: 8 min. ◆ Freeze: 2 hr. to 2 weeks

Personalize these little dessert treats by using the ice cream flavors your dessert eaters love to lick.

3 cups **mint chip ice cream and/or toasted almond fudge ice cream, softened**

◆◆◆

1 oz. **unsweetened chocolate, cut up**
1 tsp. **instant coffee crystals**

◆◆◆

¼ cup **shortening**
¼ cup **butter**
¼ cup **granulated sugar**
¼ cup **packed brown sugar**
½ tsp. **ground cinnamon**
1 **egg**
½ tsp. **vanilla**
1¼ cups **all-purpose flour**

◆◆◆

½ cup **finely chopped almonds**

1 Line a 9-inch round baking pan with foil. Spread softened ice cream in pan. Cover with plastic wrap or waxed paper and freeze about 2 hours or until firm.

2 Meanwhile, in a small saucepan combine chocolate and coffee crystals. Cook and stir over low heat until chocolate is melted. Set aside.

3 In a large mixing bowl beat shortening and butter with an electric mixer on medium to high speed for 30 seconds. Add granulated sugar, brown sugar, and cinnamon. Beat until combined, scraping sides of bowl. Beat in egg and vanilla until combined. Beat in as much of the flour as you can. Using a wooden spoon, stir in remaining flour. Divide dough into 2 equal parts.

4 Stir chocolate mixture into 1 portion of dough. Stir chopped almonds into remaining dough. Shape each portion of dough into a log that is 2 inches in diameter and about 4 inches long. Wrap in plastic wrap or waxed paper; chill for 5 to 24 hours. (Or, omit shaping dough into logs and simply wrap and chill dough 1 to 2 hours or until easy to handle. Roll chilled dough ¼ inch thick on a lightly floured surface. Cut with a 2-inch round cutter.)

5 Cut each log into ¼-inch-thick slices. Place cookie rounds 1 inch apart on an ungreased cookie sheet. Use a meat mallet to gently create a design on top of each cookie. Bake in a 375° oven for 8 to 10 minutes or until edges are golden. Transfer cookies to a wire rack; let cool.

6 Remove plastic wrap or waxed paper from ice cream. Lift the ice cream from pan using the foil. With a 2-inch scalloped or round cutter, cut out 12 rounds of ice cream. Place an ice cream round on the flat side of half of the cookies. Top with the remaining cookies, flat side toward ice cream. Wrap each ice cream sandwich securely in plastic wrap and freeze for 2 hours or store in the freezer for up to 2 weeks. Makes 12 ice cream sandwiches.

Nutrition facts per almond cookie sandwich: 301 cal., 19 g total fat (7 g sat. fat), 40 mg chol., 64 mg sodium, 28 g carbo., 1 g fiber, 5 g pro. *Daily values:* 6% vit. A, 3% calcium, 8% iron.

Nutrition facts per chocolate cookie sandwich: 261 cal., 16 g total fat (8 g sat. fat), 40 mg chol., 63 mg sodium, 28 g carbo., 1 g fiber, 4 g pro. *Daily values:* 6% vit. A, 1% calcium, 8% iron.

SHADES OF GREEN KABOBS

Prep: 20 min. ◆ Marinate: 1 to 24 hr. Grill: 8 min.

Feel free to create multicolored skewers with the baby veggies of your choice.

   8 **green onions**
  12 **baby green pattypan squash**
  12 **baby zucchini**
   1 **cup sugar snap pea pods**

◆◆◆

  ⅓ **cup olive oil**
  ⅓ **cup grated Parmesan cheese**
   3 **Tbsp. red wine vinegar**

   3 **Tbsp. snipped fresh oregano or 1½ tsp. dried oregano, crushed**
  ¼ **tsp. salt**
  ¼ **tsp. pepper**

1 Rinse and trim vegetables. Cut a 3-inch portion from the bottom of 6 of the green onions. Save remaining onion tops for another use. Place pattypan squash, zucchini, pea pods, and 3-inch green onion portions in a plastic bag set in a shallow dish.

2 Finely chop remaining 2 green onions. For marinade, in a screw-top jar combine oil, Parmesan cheese, vinegar, finely chopped green onion, oregano, salt, and pepper. Cover and shake well. Pour over vegetables in bag. Close bag. Marinate vegetables in the refrigerator for 1 to 24 hours, turning bag occasionally.

3 Drain vegetables, reserving marinade. On 6 long bamboo* or metal skewers, poke vegetables in alternating order. Cook vegetables on the rack of an uncovered grill directly over medium coals for 8 to 10 minutes or until browned and tender, turning and brushing occasionally with reserved marinade. Makes 6 side-dish servings.

*Note: If using bamboo skewers, keep them from catching fire by soaking them in water at least 30 minutes before use.

Nutrition facts per serving: 156 cal., 14 g total fat (3 g sat. fat), 4 mg chol., 194 mg sodium, 6 g carbo., 2 g fiber, 4 g pro. *Daily values:* 5% vit. A, 33% vit. C, 9% calcium, 7% iron.

Special Sunday Spread

Get a jump on this lunch by preparing the Garden Dills, the Summertime Tortellini, and the peanut coating for the "Fried" Chicken Salad a day in advance. The salad greens can be washed, dried, and refrigerated overnight, too. The morning of your meal, stir together the Iced Green Tea and bake the shortcakes (add the berry mixture just before serving). Sauté the chicken and finish the salad just before serving.

Overnight Garden Dills
(see lower left)

◆◆◆

Summertime Tortellini
(see lower right)

◆◆◆

"Fried" Chicken Salad
(see page 139)

◆◆◆

Lemon-Light Shortcakes
(see page 142)

◆◆◆

Iced Green Tea
(see page 139)

***Note:** Hot peppers contain oils that can burn your eyes, lips, and skin. Wear plastic gloves while preparing peppers and be sure to thoroughly wash your hands and nails in hot, soapy water afterward.

Nutrition facts per serving: 28 cal., 0 g total fat, 0 mg chol., 153 mg sodium, 7 g carbo., 2 g fiber, 1 g pro.
Daily values: 67% vit. A, 13% vit. C, 2% calcium, 5% iron.

SUMMERTIME TORTELLINI

Prep: 20 min. ◆ **Chill: 2 to 24 hr.**

Big wedges of yellow sweet peppers can be transformed into whimsical bowls to hold this make-ahead pasta salad. (See the photograph on page 119.)

- 1 to 1½ tsp. finely shredded lemon peel
- 3 Tbsp. lemon juice
- 1 tsp. Dijon-style mustard
- ½ tsp. sugar
- ¼ tsp. salt
- 1 clove garlic, minced

◆◆◆

- 2 9-oz. pkg. refrigerated cheese tortellini
- 1 lb. fresh asparagus spears (about 16 spears), bias-cut into 1-inch pieces
- 1 large yellow sweet pepper, cut into ½-inch pieces

◆◆◆

- 2 Tbsp. olive oil
- ½ cup finely shredded Romano or Parmesan cheese
- 4 green onions, sliced
- ¼ cup pine nuts or chopped almonds, toasted
- Yellow sweet peppers, quartered (optional)

OVERNIGHT GARDEN DILLS

Prep: 25 min.
Marinate: 4½ hr. to 3 days

Show off these crisp vegetable pickles in a favorite glass mug or in a "cup" made of a hollowed-out sweet pepper. (See the photograph on page 118.)

- 8 oz. fresh whole green beans, trimmed (about 2 cups)
- 1½ cups packaged, peeled baby carrots (about 8 oz.)

◆◆◆

- ½ cup cider vinegar
- ¼ cup water
- 1 Tbsp. chopped, seeded fresh red chili peppers*
- 2 cloves garlic, minced
- ½ tsp. salt
- ¼ to ½ tsp. crushed red pepper
- ¼ cup snipped fresh dillweed or 1 Tbsp. dried dillweed

◆◆◆

- 2 pickling cucumbers (each about 4 inches long), cut into spears

1 In a large saucepan cook green beans, covered, in a small amount of boiling water for 2 minutes. Add carrots; continue cooking, covered, for 2 minutes. Drain; transfer to a large bowl.

2 In the same saucepan combine vinegar, water, chili peppers, garlic, salt, and crushed red pepper. Heat just to boiling. Remove from heat; stir in dillweed.

3 Add cucumber spears to green beans and carrots in bowl. Pour hot vinegar mixture over vegetables in bowl. Let stand at room temperature for 30 minutes. Transfer vegetables and vinegar mixture to a plastic bag set in a deep bowl. Close bag.

4 Marinate in the refrigerator for 4 hours or up to 3 days, turning the bag occasionally. Makes 8 to 10 side-dish servings.

1 In a screw-top jar combine lemon peel, lemon juice, mustard, sugar, salt, and garlic. Cover; shake well. Chill until needed.

2 In a large saucepan cook tortellini according to package directions, adding asparagus and yellow sweet pepper pieces for the last minute of cooking. Drain. Rinse tortellini and vegetables with cold water; drain again.

3 In a very large bowl toss tortellini-vegetable mixture with olive oil. Cover and chill for 2 to 24 hours. Just before serving, stir cheese, green onions, and nuts into tortellini mixture. Shake dressing; pour over all, tossing lightly to coat. Let stand 10 minutes before serving. If desired, serve in quartered sweet peppers. Makes 10 main-dish servings.

Nutrition facts per serving: 238 cal., 10 g total fat (3 g sat. fat), 28 mg chol., 347 mg sodium, 27 g carbo., 1 g fiber, 12 g pro. *Daily values:* 6% vit. A, 60% vit. C, 14% calcium, 11% iron.

"FRIED" CHICKEN SALAD

Prep: 35 min. ◆ Cook: 10 min.

See the photograph on page 119.

½ cup finely chopped peanuts
3 Tbsp. fine dry bread crumbs
1 Tbsp. snipped fresh basil
¼ to ½ tsp. crushed red pepper
4 medium skinless, boneless chicken breast halves
2 Tbsp. margarine or butter, melted

◆◆◆

2 Tbsp. cooking oil

8 cups torn mixed greens
3 medium oranges, peeled and sectioned
3 medium tomatoes, cored and cut into wedges
8 oz. fresh mozzarella cheese, cut into ¼-inch-thick slices and quartered
1 recipe Balsamic Vinaigrette (see recipe below)

1 In a shallow dish combine peanuts, bread crumbs, basil, and crushed red pepper. Set aside. Rinse chicken; pat dry. Brush with margarine. Dip in peanut mixture, pressing firmly to coat.

2 In a large skillet cook the chicken breasts in hot oil over medium-low heat 10 to 12 minutes or until chicken is no longer pink, turning once. Cool slightly. Cut into ½-inch-thick slices.

3 Meanwhile, in a very large bowl combine greens, oranges, tomatoes, and cheese. Shake Balsamic Vinaigrette. Drizzle vinaigrette over all; toss to coat. Spoon salad onto large platter. Top with sliced chicken. Makes 6 main-dish servings.

Balsamic Vinaigrette: In a screw-top jar combine 3 tablespoons olive oil or salad oil, 3 tablespoons balsamic vinegar, 1 tablespoon snipped fresh basil, ¼ teaspoon salt, ¼ teaspoon crushed red pepper, and ¼ teaspoon freshly ground black pepper. Cover and shake well.

Nutrition facts per serving: 437 cal., 30 g total fat (8 g sat. fat), 61 mg chol., 384 mg sodium, 15 g carbo., 3 g fiber, 29 g pro. *Daily values:* 19% vit. A, 53% vit. C, 24% calcium, 12% iron.

NO FAT ICED GREEN TEA

Prep: 25 min. ◆ Cool: several hr.

Poke plump strawberries, quartered limes, and orange peel curls onto a long bamboo skewer to create a fruit-laced swizzle stick sure to cause a stir inside your iced tea pitcher.

12 cups water
¼ cup sugar
3 inches fresh ginger, peeled and thinly sliced
12 to 16 green tea bags

◆◆◆

Strawberries
Limes, quartered
Orange peel strips
Ice cubes

1 In a large saucepan combine water, sugar, and ginger. Bring to boiling; reduce heat. Simmer, covered, for 5 minutes. Remove from heat. Add tea bags; let stand, covered, for 3 minutes. Remove tea bags. Strain ginger from tea; discard ginger.

2 Transfer tea to a 2-gallon pitcher or punch bowl. Cover; cool several hours. If desired, chill.

3 Meanwhile, on a 12-inch wooden skewer alternate strawberries, lime quarters, and orange peel strips. Place the skewer inside the pitcher or punch bowl as a decorative swizzle stick. Serve tea in glasses over ice cubes. Makes 12 servings.

Nutrition facts per serving: 24 cal., 0 g total fat, 0 mg chol., 7 mg sodium, 6 g carbo., 0 g fiber, 0 g pro. *Daily values:* 15% vit. C.

Easygoing Picnic

Fix this portable meal the night before traveling so everything is ready to pack up and move to your favorite picnic spot. The gazpacho gains flavor overnight. The Turkey and Chutney Sandwiches, Roast Beef and Red Pepper Sandwiches, and Mango-Lime Trifles keep well when wrapped and chilled.

Roast Beef and Red Pepper Sandwiches (see below)

Turkey and Chutney Sandwiches (see right)

❖❖❖

Pineapple Cream Cheese Sandwiches (see page 141)

❖❖❖

Gazpacho to Go (see page 141)

❖❖❖

Mango-Lime Trifles (see page 143)

❖❖❖

Fruit-flavored sparkling water

ROAST BEEF AND RED PEPPER SANDWICHES

Prep: 25 min. ◆ Chill: up to 24 hr.

See the photograph on page 118.

⅓ cup light mayonnaise dressing or mayonnaise
⅓ cup Dijon-style mustard
2 to 4 Tbsp. prepared horseradish
6 6- or 7-inch Italian bread shells (Boboli) or Italian flatbreads (focaccia)
12 oz. thinly sliced cooked roast beef
1 12-oz. jar roasted red peppers, drained and cut into ¼-inch-wide strips
6 oz. thinly sliced Monterey Jack cheese
2 cups fresh watercress
2 cups fresh spinach

1 In a small bowl combine mayonnaise dressing, Dijon-style mustard, and horseradish. Slice bread shells in half horizontally. For each sandwich, spread 1 side of bread shell with mayonnaise mixture. Top each with roast beef, roasted red peppers, Monterey Jack cheese, watercress, spinach, and remaining half of bread.

2 Wrap sandwiches in plastic wrap and refrigerate up to 24 hours. (Or, serve immediately.) To serve, slice sandwiches in half. Makes 12 servings (half sandwich per serving).

Nutrition facts per serving: 303 cal., 14 g total fat (4 g sat. fat), 41 mg chol., 656 mg sodium, 27 g carbo., 2 g fiber, 20 g pro. *Daily values:* 18% vit. A, 65% vit. C, 15% calcium, 17% iron.

TURKEY AND CHUTNEY SANDWICHES

Prep: 25 min. ◆ Chill: up to 24 hr.

3 medium carrots
½ cup chutney, snipped
⅓ cup light mayonnaise dressing or mayonnaise
6 6- or 7-inch Italian bread shells (Boboli) or Italian flatbreads (focaccia)

❖❖❖

12 oz. thinly sliced cooked turkey
6 oz. thinly sliced smoked Gouda cheese
6 large Romaine leaves
6 fresh tarragon sprigs

1 Peel carrots. Using a vegetable peeler, carefully cut carrots into long, thin ribbons. Place in cold water to crisp. Set aside. In a small bowl stir together the chutney and mayonnaise dressing or mayonnaise. Slice bread shells or flatbreads in half horizontally.

2 For each sandwich, spread 1 cut side of bread shell or flatbread with mayonnaise mixture. Top with the turkey, cheese, a Romaine lettuce leaf, carrot ribbons, a fresh tarragon sprig, and the remaining half of the bread.

3 Wrap sandwiches in plastic wrap; refrigerate up to 24 hours. (Or, serve immediately.) To serve, slice sandwiches in half. Makes 12 servings (half of a sandwich per serving).

Nutrition facts per serving: 283 cal., 10 g total fat (3 g sat. fat), 29 mg chol., 818 mg sodium, 34 g carbo., 2 g fiber, 16 g pro. *Daily values:* 55% vit. A, 5% vit. C, 14% calcium, 11% iron.

PINEAPPLE CREAM CHEESE SANDWICHES

Prep: 25 min. ◆ **Chill:** up to 24 hr.

Consider toting extra dried fruit and seeds in sealed plastic bags, and let the kids add the goodies to their sandwiches at the picnic site.

- 3 medium carrots
  ◆◆◆
- ⅓ cup dried cranberries, raisins, or mixed dried fruit bits
- ¼ cup shelled sunflower seeds
- 6 6- or 7-inch Italian bread shells (Boboli) or Italian flatbreads (focaccia)
- 2 8-oz. tubs cream cheese with pineapple

1 Peel carrots. Cut carrots into long, thin ribbons with a vegetable peeler. Place carrot ribbons in cold water to crisp. Set aside.

2 Combine the cranberries, raisins, or dried fruit bits with sunflower seeds. Slice bread shells or flatbreads in half horizontally. For each sandwich, spread cream cheese with pineapple on both cut sides of bread. Sprinkle fruit-seed mixture onto pineapple cream cheese. Add carrot ribbons. Top with remaining half of bread.

3 Wrap sandwiches in plastic wrap; refrigerate up to 24 hours. (Or, serve immediately.) To serve, slice sandwiches in half. Makes 12 servings (half of a sandwich per serving).

Nutrition facts per serving: 307 cal., 16 g total fat (7 g sat. fat), 36 mg chol., 455 mg sodium, 34 g carbo., 2 g fiber, 9 g pro. *Daily values:* 58% vit. A, 2% vit. C, 7% calcium, 9% iron.

GAZPACHO TO GO

Prep: 30 min. ◆ **Chill:** 2 to 24 hr.

Show off the mosaic of colors in this fresh soup by carrying it to your picnic in a clear plastic storage container. Pack the container in an ice-filled cooler to keep the gazpacho well chilled.

- 1 15-oz. can chunky Italian- or salsa-style tomatoes
- 2 cups quartered yellow pear-shaped and/or halved cherry tomatoes
- 1 15-oz. can chickpeas (garbanzo beans), drained and rinsed
- 1¼ cups hot-style vegetable juice or vegetable juice
- 1 cup beef broth
- ½ cup coarsely chopped, seeded cucumber
- ½ cup coarsely chopped yellow and/or red sweet pepper
- ¼ cup coarsely chopped red onion
- ¼ cup snipped fresh cilantro
- 3 Tbsp. lime juice or lemon juice
- 2 cloves garlic, minced
- ¼ to ½ tsp. bottled hot pepper sauce
  ◆◆◆
- 1 recipe Herbed Crouton Sticks (see recipe, right)

1 In a large mixing bowl combine all ingredients, except for the Herbed Crouton Sticks. Cover and chill for 2 to 24 hours.

2 To serve, ladle soup into bowls or mugs. Serve with Herbed Crouton Sticks. Makes 7 side-dish servings.

Nutrition facts per serving without Herbed Crouton Sticks: 142 cal., 5 g total fat (0 g sat. fat), 0 mg chol., 1,145 mg sodium, 27 g carbo., 5 g fiber, 7 g pro. *Daily values:* 33% vit. A, 131% vit. C, 5% calcium, 24% iron.

HERBED CROUTON STICKS

Prep: 10 min. ◆ **Bake:** 15 min.

For something special to nibble on, bake these king-size croutons. Dunk them in gazpacho or your favorite herb dip.

- 1 8-oz. thin baguette
- ½ cup margarine or butter
- 1 Tbsp. snipped fresh basil or ½ tsp. dried basil, crushed
- ⅛ tsp. garlic powder

1 Using a serrated knife, cut baguette in half horizontally. Cut bread into 12 strips, 1 inch wide by 5½ inches long; set aside. In a 12-inch skillet melt margarine or butter. Stir in basil and garlic powder. Add half the crouton sticks, stirring until coated with margarine mixture.

2 Arrange the crouton sticks in a single layer in a shallow baking pan. Repeat with remaining bread sticks. Bake, uncovered, in a 300° oven for 10 minutes; turn sticks over. Bake about 5 minutes more or until crouton sticks are dry and crisp. Cool completely. Store in an airtight container at room temperature up to 1 week. Makes 12 sticks.

Nutrition facts per stick: 120 cal., 8 g total fat (2 g sat. fat), 0 mg chol., 204 mg sodium, 10 g carbo., 0 g fiber, 2 g pro. *Daily values:* 9% vit. A, 1% calcium, 3% iron.

CITRUS SAMPLER

A bit of finely shredded citrus peel—lemon or orange—is an easy way to add a light, fresh flavor to foods in a flash.

The best part is you can shred it today and use it next month. The next time a recipe calls for shredded citrus peel, shred more than you need. Be careful to shred only the brightly colored layer of the peel, not the bitter, white pith layer beneath the peel. Place any extra in a small freezer container or bag. Seal, label, and freeze. Then go ahead and juice the fruit. Freeze the juice in ice cube trays, then transfer the cubes to a freezer container or bag. Seal, label, and freeze for a future use.

LEMON-LIGHT SHORTCAKES
Prep: 30 min. ◆ Bake: 8 min.

Old-fashioned buttery shortcakes are shaped into petite triangles that sparkle with a sprinkling of coarse sugar. (See the photograph on page 120.)

1½ cups all-purpose flour
2 Tbsp. sugar
1½ tsp. baking powder
⅓ cup butter
◆◆◆
1 slightly beaten egg
⅓ cup half-and-half, light cream, or milk

2 tsp. finely shredded lemon peel
◆◆◆
1 slightly beaten egg white
2 Tbsp. coarse-grain sugar or granulated sugar
◆◆◆
3½ cups sliced fresh strawberries
1½ cups fresh red raspberries
⅓ cup granulated sugar
3 Tbsp. Grand Marnier or orange juice
4 tsp. snipped fresh mint
◆◆◆
½ cup whipping cream, whipped
  Snipped fresh mint

1 For shortcakes, in a medium mixing bowl stir together flour, the 2 tablespoons sugar, and baking powder. Using a pastry blender, cut in the butter until mixture resembles coarse crumbs. Make a well in the center of the dry mixture; set aside.

2 In a small mixing bowl stir together the egg, half-and-half, and lemon peel. Add the egg yolk mixture all at once to the dry mixture. Using a fork, stir just until moistened.

3 Turn the dough out onto a lightly floured surface. Gently knead dough for 10 to 12 strokes or until dough is nearly smooth. Pat the dough into a 6-inch square. Using a floured knife, cut the square into nine 2-inch squares. Then cut each square diagonally in half.

4 Place triangles on an ungreased baking sheet. Brush the tops with beaten egg white; lightly sprinkle with coarse-grain sugar or granulated sugar. Bake in a 450° oven for 8 to 10 minutes or until golden. Remove shortcake triangles from baking sheet; cool on a wire rack.

5 Meanwhile, for topping, in large mixing bowl toss together the strawberries, raspberries, the ⅓ cup sugar, Grand Marnier or orange juice, and the 4 teaspoons snipped mint. Cover and chill for up to 1 hour.

6 For each serving, spoon berry mixture onto a dessert plate. Place 3 shortcake triangles on berry mixture. Top with whipped cream and garnish with additional mint. Makes 6 servings.

Nutrition facts per serving: 431 cal., 21 g total fat (12 g sat. fat), 95 mg chol., 228 mg sodium, 55 g carbo., 4 g fiber, 6 g pro. *Daily values:* 22% vit. A, 98% vit. C, 12% calcium, 15% iron.

TIRAMISU CREAM PIE
Prep: 1¼ hr. ◆ Chill: 4 to 24 hr.

This dreamy, creamy pie is just as luscious when made using reduced-fat cream cheese (Neufchâtel) and fat-free instant vanilla pudding mix.

1½ cups finely crushed chocolate wafers (about 25)
⅓ cup butter, melted
◆◆◆
1 envelope unflavored gelatin
¼ cup sugar

2 tsp. instant coffee crystals
½ cup water

♦♦♦

1 8-oz. container mascarpone cheese* or one 8-oz. pkg. cream cheese, softened
2 cups milk
1 4-serving-size pkg. instant vanilla pudding mix
3 Tbsp. coffee liqueur or milk

♦♦♦

Whipped cream (optional)
Shaved chocolate (optional)

1 In a medium bowl combine crushed wafers and butter. Toss to mix well. Spread crumb mixture evenly into a 9-inch pie plate. Press onto bottom and sides to form a firm, even crust. Chill about 1 hour or until firm.

2 Meanwhile, in a small saucepan combine the gelatin, sugar, and coffee crystals. Stir in the water. Cook and stir over low heat just until gelatin dissolves. Set aside to cool.

3 In a blender container or food processor bowl combine mascarpone cheese or cream cheese, milk, pudding mix, coffee liqueur or milk, and the gelatin mixture. Cover and blend on low speed or process about 30 seconds or until smooth. Let the mixture stand about 5 minutes to thicken slightly. Pour mixture into pie shell. Cover; chill at least 4 hours or overnight.

4 If desired, pipe whipped cream atop pie using a pastry bag fitted with a large star tip, then sprinkle pie with shaved chocolate. To serve, cut into wedges Makes 8 servings.

*Note: Mascarpone cheese is a creamy, soft Italian dessert cheese. You can purchase it in the cheese section at large supermarkets or at Italian markets.

Nutrition facts per serving: 405 cal., 24 g total fat (13 g sat. fat), 63 mg chol., 437 mg sodium, 39 g carbo., 0 g fiber, 10 g pro. *Daily values:* 10% vit. A, 1% vit. C, 6% calcium, 3% iron.

MANGO-LIME TRIFLES
Prep: 20 min. ♦ Chill: 1 to 24 hr.

Lemon yogurt adds a refreshing tang to the fat-free whipped dessert topping in these individual treats. (See the photograph on page 121.)

2 8-oz. cartons lemon yogurt
½ of an 8-oz. container frozen fat-free whipped dessert topping, thawed
1 to 2 tsp. finely shredded lime peel

♦♦♦

12 soft coconut macaroon cookies (two-thirds of a 13¾-oz. pkg.)
6 8- to 10-oz. disposable clear plastic cups
3 mangoes, peeled and chopped (about 2 cups)

♦♦♦

Sliced, peeled mangoes (optional)
Lime peel curls (optional)

1 In a medium mixing bowl fold together the lemon yogurt, whipped topping, and lime peel.

THE CLEVER COOK

COOKBOOK FOR KIDS
When children show an interest in cooking, create a cookbook just for them using favorite recipes that fit their abilities. Use a blank book or notebook and decorate with pictures from magazines. Include personal notes about the origins of the recipes. In addition to passing on your culinary knowledge, you will be creating an heirloom.

Clare Hafferman
Kalispell, Montana

2 To assemble individual trifles, coarsely crumble 1 cookie into each of the 6 cups. Spoon about 3 heaping tablespoons of the yogurt mixture into each cup on top of the crumbled cookie. Spoon about ⅓ cup of the chopped mangoes into each cup. Crumble another cookie into each cup, and top with remaining yogurt mixture (about 3 tablespoons in each cup).

3 Cover trifles and chill for 1 to 24 hours. If desired, garnish with mango slices and lime peel before serving. Makes 6 servings.

Nutrition facts per serving: 356 cal., 10 g total fat (1 g sat. fat), 3 mg chol., 69 mg sodium, 63 g carbo., 4 g fiber, 6 g pro. *Daily values:* 41% vit. A, 49% vit. C, 11% calcium, 3% iron.

Berry Delicious White Chocolate Cheesecake

Prep: 25 min. ◆ Bake: 55 min.
Cool: 1 hr. ◆ Chill: 4 hr.

Be sure to use the reduced-fat cream cheese. Fat-free cream cheese won't give you acceptable results for this party-perfect dessert. When time is short, use the tempting jelly and berry topper to dress up purchased cheesecake. (See the photograph on page 121.)

2   tsp. margarine or butter
¾   cup ground toasted almonds
2   Tbsp. all-purpose flour
        ◆◆◆
1   6-oz. pkg. white chocolate
        baking squares
        ◆◆◆
4   8-oz. pkg. reduced-fat cream
        cheese (Neufchâtel),
        softened
1   cup sugar
2   Tbsp. all-purpose flour
2   tsp. finely shredded lemon
        peel or orange peel
1   tsp. vanilla
5   eggs
½   cup milk
        ◆◆◆
⅓   cup strawberry jelly
        Fresh red raspberries and/or
        blackberries and/or
        blueberries

1 Use the margarine or butter to grease bottom and sides of a 10-inch springform pan. Stir together almonds and the 2 tablespoons flour. Press ground almond mixture onto bottom of springform pan. Set pan aside.

2 In a heavy small saucepan melt the white chocolate baking squares over very low heat, stirring occasionally. Set chocolate aside to cool slightly.

3 Meanwhile, in a large mixing bowl beat cream cheese, sugar, the 2 tablespoons flour, the lemon or orange peel, and vanilla with an electric mixer on medium to high speed until combined. With the mixer running, slowly add the melted white chocolate, beating until combined. Add eggs all at once, beating on low speed just until combined (do not overbeat). Stir in milk.

4 Pour filling into prepared springform pan. Place springform pan in a shallow baking pan. Bake in a 375° oven about 55 minutes or until center appears nearly set when shaken gently. Cool cheesecake in pan on a wire rack for 15 minutes. Use a small metal spatula to loosen cheesecake from sides of pan; cool 30 minutes. Remove sides of pan; cool cheesecake completely.

5 Transfer cheesecake to cake stand or dessert platter. In a small saucepan heat and stir strawberry jelly over low heat until melted. Remove from heat. Using a pastry brush, generously brush some of the jelly over top of the cheesecake. Arrange berries on cheesecake; drizzle with remaining jelly. Cover with plastic wrap; chill at least 4 hours before serving. Makes 16 to 20 servings.

Nutrition facts per serving: 378 cal., 23 g total fat (11 g sat. fat), 122 mg chol., 275 mg sodium, 32 g carbo., 2 g fiber, 11 g pro. *Daily values:* 16% vit. A, 14% vit. C, 7% calcium, 5% iron.

PRIZE
TESTED
RECIPE
WINNER

Blueberry-Rhubarb Crisp

Prep: 20 min. ◆ Bake: 30 min.

A homespun dessert doesn't get much easier than this fruit combo with a streusel topping.

3   cups fresh or frozen
        unsweetened blueberries
2   cups fresh or frozen
        unsweetened sliced
        rhubarb
        ◆◆◆
½   cup regular rolled oats
½   cup all-purpose flour
½   cup packed brown sugar
½   tsp. ground cinnamon
¼   cup butter

1 For filling, thaw fruit if frozen. Do not drain. Place fruit in a 2-quart square baking dish.

2 For topping, in a medium bowl combine the oats, flour, brown sugar, and cinnamon. Using a pastry blender, cut in butter until mixture resembles coarse crumbs. Sprinkle topping over filling.

3 Bake in a 350° oven for 30 to 35 minutes (40 minutes for frozen fruit) or until fruit is tender and topping is golden. Makes 6 servings.

Nutrition facts per serving: 233 cal., 8 g total fat (5 g sat. fat), 20 mg chol., 88 mg sodium, 38 g carbo., 3 g fiber, 3 g pro. *Daily values:* 8% vit. A, 21% vit. C, 5% calcium, 9% iron.

BERRY CHOCOLATE CRUMB TART

Prep: 35 min. ◆ Bake: 20 min.
Chill: 3 hr.

1 cup finely crushed bite-size
   graham snacks or
   chocolate graham crackers
1 Tbsp. sugar
3 Tbsp. butter, melted
   Nonstick spray coating

◆◆◆

1 8-oz. pkg. cream cheese,
   softened
1 8-oz. carton vanilla yogurt
½ cup sliced fresh strawberries
   and/or raspberries
2 Tbsp. all-purpose flour
2 Tbsp. sugar
2 eggs

◆◆◆

⅓ cup miniature semisweet
   chocolate pieces
1 tsp. shortening
1½ cups sliced fresh strawberries
1 cup fresh raspberries

1 For crust, combine crushed graham crackers and 1 tablespoon sugar. Stir in melted butter. Spray a 9-inch fluted tart pan or 9-inch pie plate with nonstick coating. Press the crumb mixture into prepared pan or plate; set aside.

2 Meanwhile, for filling, in a blender container or food processor bowl combine cream cheese, yogurt, ½ cup berries, flour, 2 tablespoons sugar, and eggs. Cover and blend until smooth.

3 Pour the filling into crust. Bake in a 325° oven for 20 to 25 minutes or until filling appears nearly set when shaken. Cool in pan or plate on a wire rack. Cover loosely and chill at least 3 hours before serving.

4 For drizzle, in a small heavy saucepan melt the chocolate and shortening over low heat. Arrange fresh berries over chilled tart. Drizzle with chocolate mixture. Serve immediately. Makes 8 to 10 servings.

Nutrition facts per serving: 333 cal., 22 g total fat (11 g sat. fat), 98 mg chol., 221 mg sodium, 30 g carbo., 2 g fiber, 7 g pro. *Daily values:* 21% vit. A, 42% vit. C, 8% calcium, 8% iron.

MERRY BERRY SORBET

Prep: 20 min. ◆ Chill: 2 hr.
Freeze: 30 min. ◆ Ripen: 4 hr.

A burst of berry flavor tickles your tongue as this frosty creation melts in your mouth.
(See the photograph on page 121.)

1¾ cups water
1 cup sugar
1 cup fresh or frozen
   unsweetened blueberries

◆◆◆

1 cup fresh or frozen
   unsweetened blackberries,
   thawed
¾ cup fresh or frozen loose-
   pack raspberries, thawed

◆◆◆

1 cup orange juice
   Fresh blueberries,
   blackberries, and
   raspberries (optional)

1 In a medium saucepan bring water, sugar, and the blueberries to boiling. Cook and stir for 1 to 2 minutes or until sugar is dissolved and blueberries are tender. Remove from heat. Drain berries, reserving liquid; set aside to cool.

FREEZING BERRIES

Fresh-picked berries can be frozen by arranging washed berries, with stems removed, on a baking sheet. Place in freezer until solid; transfer them to plastic freezer containers or bags, leaving ½-inch headspace. Return to freezer.

2 Meanwhile, in a food processor bowl or blender container combine blackberries and raspberries. Cover and process or blend until smooth. Press pureed berries through fine-mesh sieve; discard seeds. Place the blueberries and ⅓ cup of the reserved cooking liquid (do not discard remaining liquid) in food processor bowl or blender container. Cover and process or blend until almost smooth. Press blueberry mixture through the fine-mesh sieve; discard skins.

3 In a large bowl combine the pureed mixtures, remaining cooking liquid, and orange juice. Cover and chill for 2 hours or until mixture is completely chilled. Freeze mixture in a 4- or 5-quart ice cream freezer according to manufacturer's directions. Ripen 4 hours. Use within 2 days. If desired, serve with fresh berries. Makes about 5 cups (10 servings).

Nutrition facts per serving: 109 cal., 0 g total fat, 0 mg chol., 3 mg sodium, 28 g carbo., 2 g fiber, 0 g pro. *Daily values:* 32% vit. C, 1% iron.

CHERRY CORDIAL BROWNIE TORTE

Prep: 20 min. ◆ Bake: 35 min.
Chill: 30 min.

This impressive torte starts with a brownie mix. Mark it as a good dessert for the wintertime holidays and use dried cranberries instead of cherries. (See the photograph on page 121.)

1   21½-oz. pkg. brownie mix
        ◆◆◆
⅓   cup white baking pieces
1   3-oz. pkg. cream cheese, softened
1   Tbsp. powdered sugar
¼   tsp. almond extract
¼   cup whipping cream
½   cup snipped dried tart red cherries
        ◆◆◆
⅓   cup semisweet chocolate pieces
1   tsp. shortening

1 Lightly grease a 9-inch springform pan; set aside. Prepare brownie mix according to package directions. Spoon batter into the prepared pan, spreading evenly.

2 Bake in a 350° oven for 35 to 40 minutes or until a wooden toothpick inserted near the center comes out clean. Cool in the pan on a wire rack for 30 minutes. Remove sides of pan. Cool completely.

3 Meanwhile, in a small saucepan heat white baking pieces over low heat until melted. Cool slightly. In a medium mixing bowl beat the cream cheese, powdered sugar, and almond extract with an electric mixer on medium speed until combined. Stir in melted white baking pieces. In a small mixing bowl beat whipping cream until soft peaks form. Fold whipped cream and cherries into cream cheese mixture. Spread cream cheese mixture atop cooled brownie. Loosely cover and chill at least 30 minutes before serving.

4 In a small saucepan heat chocolate pieces and shortening over low heat until melted. Cut torte into individual servings and place on serving plates. Drizzle chocolate mixture evenly over individual servings. Makes 12 to 16 servings.

Nutrition facts per serving: 376 cal., 17 g total fat (6 g sat. fat), 52 mg chol., 230 mg sodium, 55 g carbo., 0 g fiber, 4 g pro. *Daily values:* 9% vit. A, 1% calcium, 11% iron.

NUTRITION IN NO TIME

(30 MIN. LOW FAT)

HEALTHY BREAKFAST 1-2-3

Start to finish: 10 min.

You've had to skip enough breakfasts. How about a tasty reprieve from going hungry before noon? This zingy bacon and egg burrito is low in fat, high in protein, and best of all, "ready to wrap" in about 10 minutes.

1   strip turkey bacon, chopped
2   Tbsp. chopped green sweet pepper
⅛   tsp. salt
⅛   tsp. ground cumin
⅛   tsp. crushed red pepper (optional)
2   egg whites or ¼ cup refrigerated egg product
2   Tbsp. chopped tomato
    Few dashes bottled hot pepper sauce (optional)
1   warmed 8-inch fat-free flour tortilla

1 In a medium nonstick skillet cook turkey bacon until crisp. Add the green sweet pepper, salt, cumin, and, if desired, crushed red pepper. Cook and stir for 3 minutes. Add the egg whites or egg product and cook for 2 minutes more. Remove from heat. Stir in the tomato and hot pepper sauce. Spoon and roll into the flour tortilla.

Nutrition facts per serving: 197 cal., 6 g total fat (1 g sat. fat), 9 mg chol., 753 mg sodium, 24 g carbo., 1 g fiber, 14 g pro. *Daily values:* 3% vit. A, 51% vit. C, 5% calcium, 11% iron.

JULY
From Garden & Orchard

30-minute recipes indicated in RED.
**Low-fat and no-fat recipes indicated
with a ♥.**
Photographs indicated in italics.
*****All new in 1998.**

In July, a cascade of fresh fruits and vegetables, from pungent jalapeños to tender, sweet-smelling peaches, fill gardens—and refrigerators. Live a little. Try Spicy Sprouts and Snow Peas, Eggplant and Gouda Sandwiches, or Beer-Barrel Lima Beans. Fish is a fitting counterpoint, be it grilled bass or sizzling shrimp. As the sunsets fade, cool down with exotic frozen confections such as Cactus Fruit Sorbet and no-fat Tequila Sunrise Ice Pops. Or serve iced watermelon and crunchy jicama in an ice bowl dotted with melon seeds.

ICED YELLOW TOMATO SOUP

Prep: 15 min. ◆ Chill: 4 hr.

You can make this recipe with ripe red tomatoes too. For a vegetarian version, substitute equal amounts of vegetable broth for the chicken broth.

2 14½-oz. cans reduced-sodium chicken broth
1½ lb. yellow tomatoes, peeled, seeded, and cut up (about 5 medium)
1 large yellow sweet pepper
2 to 3 yellow banana peppers, seeded and cut up
½ of a small onion
4 cloves garlic, chopped

◆◆◆

1 small Roma tomato, peeled, seeded, and diced
   Fresh whole chives (optional)

1 In a food processor bowl or blender container combine half of each of the following: the broth, tomatoes, sweet pepper, banana peppers, onion, and garlic. Cover and process or blend mixture until smooth. Transfer to a large bowl. Repeat with remaining half of ingredients. Stir into mixture in bowl.

2 Cover soup and chill in the refrigerator for 4 hours. To serve, ladle chilled soup into bowls. Top with diced Roma tomato. If desired, garnish with fresh chives. Makes 8 side-dish servings.

Nutrition facts per serving: 41 cal., 1 g total fat (0 g sat. fat), 0 mg chol., 299 mg sodium, 7 g carbo., 1 g fiber, 2 g pro.
Daily values: 7% vit. A, 107% vit. C, 3% iron.

TEST KITCHEN TIP

ABOUT SPROUTS

Sprouts are "live" and extremely perishable. When purchasing sprouts, buy only those that are fresh. They should smell clean and not have discolorations or feel sticky. Rinse them with cold water and shake or pat dry before using. Keep sprouts refrigerated in a ventilated container and be sure to use within 48 hours.

FARMER'S MARKET MELON SOUP

Prep: 20 min. ◆ Chill: 2 hr.

Use only ripe melons for a smooth-textured soup.
(See the photograph on page 162.)

1 medium golden honeydew melon, Persian melon, or cantaloupe, peeled, seeded, and cut up (about 6 cups)
¾ cup apricot nectar
¾ cup plain nonfat yogurt
1 Tbsp. grated fresh ginger

◆◆◆

2 fresh red and/or green serrano peppers, very thinly bias-sliced (optional)

1 In a food processor bowl or blender container combine half of each of the following: the golden honeydew melon, Persian melon, or cantaloupe; apricot nectar; yogurt; and ginger. Cover and

---

process or blend until smooth. Transfer to a large bowl. Repeat with remaining half of ingredients. Stir into mixture in bowl.

2 Cover soup and chill in the refrigerator for at least 2 hours. Meanwhile, chill desired soup bowls. To serve, ladle the chilled soup into chilled bowls. If desired, garnish each serving with several serrano pepper slices. Makes 8 side-dish servings.

Nutrition facts per serving: 69 cal., 1 g total fat (0 g sat. fat), 1 mg chol., 27 mg sodium, 15 g carbo., 1 g fiber, 2 g pro.
Daily values: 42% vit. A, 97% vit. C, 4% calcium, 2% iron.

SPICY SPROUTS AND SNOW PEAS

Start to finish: 20 min.

The watermelon radish is a mild radish that resembles its namesake. Look for different varieties of radishes at your local farmer's markets.

2 cups fresh snow pea pods
1 cup radish sprouts or alfalfa sprouts
¼ cup very thinly sliced watermelon radishes and/or red radishes

◆◆◆

3 Tbsp. rice vinegar or white balsamic vinegar
1 Tbsp. salad oil
¼ tsp. white wine Worcestershire sauce
⅛ tsp. salt
1 Tbsp. snipped fresh basil

1 Remove tips and strings from snow pea pods; cut lengthwise into very thin strips. In a large bowl toss snow peas with the

---

radish or alfalfa sprouts and radish slices; arrange mixture on salad plates.

2 For dressing, in a screw-top jar combine rice or white balsamic vinegar, salad oil, white wine Worcestershire sauce, and salt. Shake well and drizzle over salad. Sprinkle with basil. Makes 6 side-dish servings.

Nutrition facts per serving: 43 cal., 2 g total fat (0 g sat. fat), 0 mg chol., 49 mg sodium, 4 g carbo., 1 g fiber, 2 g pro.
Daily values: 49% vit. C, 2% calcium, 7% iron.

LOW FAT
BEER-BARREL LIMA BEANS

Prep: 25 min. ◆ Cook: 12 min.

Here's a delicious and whimsical version of the Mexican dish "frijoles borrachos" (drunken beans).

12 oz. shelled fresh baby lima beans or frozen baby lima beans

◆◆◆

1 Tbsp. margarine or butter
1 small fresh poblano pepper, seeded and chopped
¼ cup dark beer
1 small red onion, quartered and sliced
1 tsp. snipped fresh thyme or ¼ tsp. dried thyme, crushed
⅛ tsp. salt

1 In a 2-quart saucepan cook fresh beans, covered, in a small amount of boiling water for 10 to 15 minutes. (Or, cook frozen beans for 6 to 8 minutes or until the beans are just tender.) Drain.

2 In a large skillet heat margarine or butter; add cooked beans and poblano pepper. Cook and stir over medium-high heat for 2 minutes. Carefully stir in beer, onion, thyme, and salt; remove from heat. Makes 4 side-dish servings.

Nutrition facts per serving: 150 cal., 3 g total fat (1 g sat. fat), 0 mg chol., 105 mg sodium, 23 g carbo., 7 g fiber, 7 g pro.
Daily values: 4% vit. A, 76% vit. C, 2% calcium, 15% iron.

RIGATONI WITH FIRE-ROASTED JALAPEÑO PESTO

Start to finish: 50 min.

This pasta packs a pesto that's hotter than the Fourth of July. For a less feisty flavor, use 2 to 3 of the milder green Anaheim peppers. (See the photograph on page 162.)

6 large fresh jalapeño peppers

◆◆◆

¼ cup freshly grated Parmesan or Romano cheese
2 Tbsp. olive oil
¼ tsp. salt

◆◆◆

6 oz. dried rigatoni
2 Tbsp. snipped fresh Italian parsley
Fresh Parmesan curls

1 Pierce wide end of peppers with a long-handled fork; roast peppers over the open fire of a gas burner. (Or, roast peppers on a foil-lined baking sheet in a 425° oven for 25 to 30 minutes or until skin is blackened.) Place the peppers in a new brown paper bag and seal. Let stand for 20 to 30 minutes or until the peppers are cool enough to handle.

TEST KITCHEN TIP

HANDLING HOT PEPPERS

Because chili peppers, such as jalapeños, contain volatile oils that can burn your skin and eyes, avoid direct contact with them as much as possible. When working with chili peppers, wear plastic or rubber gloves. If your bare hands do touch the chili peppers, wash your hands well with soap and warm water.

2 Carefully peel and seed the jalapeño peppers. In a food processor bowl or blender container combine the jalapeños, Parmesan or Romano cheese, olive oil, and salt. Cover and process or blend until almost smooth; set aside.

3 Meanwhile, cook pasta according to package directions. Drain and rinse with cold water. Toss cooked pasta with jalapeño pesto and parsley. Garnish with Parmesan curls. Serve immediately or cover and chill up to 24 hours before serving. Makes 4 side-dish servings.

Nutrition facts per serving: 257 cal., 9 g total fat (1 g sat. fat), 5 mg chol., 253 mg sodium, 35 g carbo., 1 g fiber, 9 g pro.
Daily values: 4% vit. A, 117% vit. C, 8% calcium, 14% iron.

HOLY GUACAMOLE

Avocados have a wonderfully silky texture, subtle aroma, and succulent taste. So it should come as no surprise that the word "avocado" is derived from an ancient Aztec word used for aphrodisiac.

Enjoy avocados in salads or by themselves with just a squeeze of lime juice or lemon juice. For a change of pace, add diced avocados to fruit salad.

One of the most familiar uses for avocados is guacamole—a popular avocado-based dip. To make a simple and delicious Tex-Mex guacamole, mash a couple of peeled and pitted ripe avocados. Combine with a few tablespoons of minced onion; a tablespoon each of snipped cilantro and lime juice; a teaspoon of minced garlic; plus a pinch of salt. Garnish with diced tomatoes and sliced jalapeños or other chili peppers, if desired, and serve with crispy tortilla chips or fresh vegetables for dipping.

The Hass avocado from California is one of the most popular varieties. Its rough, dark-green skin changes to purplish black when the fruit is fully ripe. There are dozens of other varieties of avocados, such as Florida Jumbo, Fuerte, and Cocktail. Some have rough skins, others are smooth in texture, but all have the delicious avocado taste. The water and fat content can differ from variety to variety, but this shouldn't affect most of your avocado recipes.

HEALTHY UNDER THE SKIN

The myth that avocados are unhealthy can be put to rest. Beneath the avocado's tough exterior lies a storehouse of nutritional goodies. Its monounsaturated fats have been found to help decrease the risk of heart disease and stroke. One medium-sized avocado contains generous amounts of protein, folate, fiber, potassium, vitamin B6, niacin, riboflavin, pantothenate, magnesium, and vitamins A, C, and E.

Choose avocados with shiny skins that yield slightly to pressure. Unripe avocados will ripen in a few days stored in a cool, dry, and shaded corner of your kitchen. Keep ripe avocados refrigerated for up to 5 days. To keep cut avocados fresh, brush the cut side with lemon or lime juice, wrap tightly with plastic wrap, and refrigerate for up to 2 days. Avocados should not be frozen.

GRILLED CORN WITH ANCHO-AVOCADO BUTTER

Prep: 30 min. ◆ Grill: 10 min.

The velvety avocado butter melts in your mouth—corn on the cob never had it so good.
(See the photograph on page 162.)

½ **to 1 small dried ancho chili pepper**
2 **Tbsp. lime juice**
3 **Tbsp. butter or margarine, softened**

◆◆◆

½ **of a small avocado, seeded, peeled, and chopped**

◆◆◆

6 **ears white and/or yellow sweet corn**

1 In a small saucepan combine ancho pepper, lime juice, and 2 tablespoons *water*. Cook, covered, on low heat about 10 minutes or until pepper turns soft. Drain and cool. Remove stem and seeds of pepper. Finely chop pepper and combine with softened butter or margarine.

2 Slightly mash avocado with ⅛ teaspoon *salt*. Stir into butter mixture. Cover and chill mixture or spoon it into a small mold or cup lined with plastic wrap; chill.

3 Remove husks and silk from ears of corn. If desired, leave a few leaves of the husks intact for presentation. In a large saucepan cook corn, covered, in a small amount of boiling water for 5 to 7 minutes. Drain. Grill on an uncovered grill directly over medium coals for 10 minutes, turning several times. Remove butter from mold. Remove plastic wrap. Serve corn with ancho-avocado butter. Makes 6 servings.

Nutrition facts per ear of corn with 2 tablespoons ancho-avocado butter: 246 cal., 10 g total fat (2 g sat. fat), 8 mg chol., 125 mg sodium, 40 g carbo., 6 g fiber, 5 g pro. *Daily values:* 10% vit. A, 32% vit. C, 7% iron.

Fresh Ginger Relish

Prep: 20 min. ◆ Chill: 2 hr.

⅓ cup peeled and minced fresh
    ginger
2 Tbsp. minced red sweet
    pepper
2 Tbsp. cider vinegar
2 Tbsp. orange juice
1 to 2 tsp. brown sugar
¼ tsp. salt

1 In a bowl combine ginger, sweet pepper, vinegar, orange juice, brown sugar, and salt. Cover and chill several hours or overnight. Serve as a condiment for grilled or roasted meats or in place of pickle relish. Store in refrigerator for up to 1 week. Makes about ½ cup.

Nutrition facts per tablespoon: 8 cal., 0 g total fat, 0 mg chol., 67 mg sodium, 2 g carbo., 0 g fiber, 0 g pro.
Daily values: 1% vit. A, 8% vit. C.

Red Onion Chutney

Prep: 10 min. ◆ Chill: 2 hr.

2 Tbsp. minced fresh garlic
1 Tbsp. dried currants
3 whole cloves, crushed
2 tsp. cooking oil
1 medium red onion,
    quartered and very thinly
    sliced
2 Tbsp. red wine vinegar
⅛ tsp. salt

1 In a small skillet cook the garlic, currants, and cloves in hot oil over medium heat for 2 minutes, stirring often. Remove from heat. Stir in onion, vinegar, and salt. Transfer to a bowl. Cover and chill for 2 hours or overnight.

Serve as a condiment for grilled meat or fish. Store in refrigerator for up to 1 week. Makes ¾ cup.

Nutrition facts per tablespoon: 14 cal., 1 g total fat (0 g sat. fat), 0 mg chol., 23 mg sodium, 2 g carbo., 0 g fiber, 0 g pro.
Daily values: 1% vit. C.

Classic Tex-Mex Salsa

Prep: 30 min. ◆ Chill: 2 hr.

A Southwestern classic with a fresh taste you'll find addictive. Use as a condiment or serve with tortilla chips for a fast, down-home appetizer.

8 oz. tomatoes, seeded and
    finely chopped
4 oz. tomatillos, husked,
    rinsed, peeled, and finely
    chopped, or one 13-oz.
    can tomatillos, rinsed,
    drained, and finely
    chopped (about 1¼ cups)
1 small red onion, finely
    chopped
2 to 4 fresh serrano, habanero,
    jalapeño, or other hot
    peppers, seeded and finely
    chopped*
4 cloves garlic, finely chopped
2 Tbsp. lime juice
2 Tbsp. snipped fresh cilantro

1 In a bowl combine tomatoes, tomatillos, onion, peppers, garlic, lime juice, cilantro, and ¼ teaspoon *salt.* Cover and chill for 2 hours or for up to 1 week. Makes 2½ cups.

***Note:** For a hotter salsa, leave seeds in peppers before chopping.

Nutrition facts per tablespoon: 3 cal., 0 g total fat, 0 mg chol., 14 mg sodium, 1 g carbo., 0 g fiber, 0 g pro.
Daily values: 4% vit. C.

TEST KITCHEN TIP

Pick a Peck of Peppers

Anaheim. This long, slender pepper comes in both red and green. The texture is crisp, and the flavor is mild. It is similar to the New Mexico pepper, which is slightly hotter and has a more wrinkled shape.

Pasilla. The pasilla is often used in mole sauces. The flavor can be mild to medium-hot.

Poblano. Also known as the relleno pepper for its use in the popular dish Chili Rellenos, the poblano is dark green, crisp, and usually mild. But be careful: Some poblano peppers can be hot, depending on where they are grown.

Ancho. This is the dried form of the poblano. It has a tough skin and a slightly smoky, sweet flavor with hints of chocolate. It, too, is used in moles and has become a popular pepper for many of today's chefs.

Serrano. The little serrano is usually green, but red ones are available. Serranos are hot—slightly hotter than jalapeños. Red ones are hot, but also slightly sweet.

Jalapeño. One of the most popular and utilized peppers in America, the jalapeño can sometimes be found ripened to bright red, but it is mostly available when still green. It is a moderately hot to very hot pepper, with wide variation depending on the plant itself. When smoked and dried, it is called a chipotle.

EGGPLANT AND GOUDA SANDWICHES

Start to finish: 20 min.

Most people think of eggplant as a vegetable, but botanically it's really a fruit.

8 ½-inch-thick slices
   sourdough bread
½ of a small eggplant, peeled,
   if desired (about 6 oz.)
1 clove garlic, minced
1 to 2 Tbsp. cooking oil
   ◆◆◆
¼ cup mayonnaise or salad
   dressing
4 lettuce leaves
4 1-oz. slices Gouda cheese
1 small tomato, sliced

1 Toast sourdough bread slices; set aside. Meanwhile, cut eggplant into ½-inch-thick slices. In a large skillet cook garlic in hot oil for 30 seconds. Add eggplant slices. Cook about 4 minutes or until eggplant is tender, turning once. Drain the eggplant slices on paper towels.

2 For each sandwich, divide 1 tablespoon of mayonnaise between 2 toasted bread slices, spreading evenly. With mayonnaise side up, top 1 bread slice with one-fourth of lettuce, cheese, eggplant, and tomato. Sprinkle with salt and pepper. Add remaining bread slice, mayonnaise side down. Makes 4 sandwiches.

Nutrition facts per sandwich: 387 cal., 24 g total fat (8 g sat. fat), 40 mg chol., 656 mg sodium, 31 g carbo., 2 g fiber, 12 g pro. *Daily values:* 8% vit. A, 9% vit. C, 20% calcium, 11% iron.

CUCUMBER AND APRICOT SANDWICHES

Start to finish: 15 min.

Luscious tree-ripened apricots are a pleasant surprise in a truly picnic-perfect sandwich.

1 large cucumber
½ of an 8-oz. pkg. reduced-fat
   cream cheese (Neufchâtel),
   softened
2 Tbsp. snipped fresh basil
⅛ tsp. salt (optional)
   ◆◆◆
8 slices firm-textured whole-
   wheat bread
2 large apricots or 1 nectarine,
   pitted and thinly sliced
¼ cup assorted sprouts or
   alfalfa sprouts
¼ cup arugula leaves or
   cilantro sprigs

1 Peel cucumber. Cut in half lengthwise and scoop out seeds. Thinly slice cucumber; set aside. In a small bowl combine cream cheese, basil, and, if desired, salt.

2 Spread about 1 tablespoon of the cheese mixture on 1 side of each slice of bread. Top 4 slices with cucumber slices, apricot or nectarine slices, sprouts, and arugula or cilantro. Top with remaining 4 slices of bread, cream cheese side down. Cut each sandwich in half diagonally. Serve immediately or cover and chill for 2 hours before serving. Makes 4 sandwiches.

Nutrition facts per sandwich: 238 cal., 10 g total fat (5 g sat. fat), 25 mg chol., 416 mg sodium, 31 g carbo., 3 g fiber, 9 g pro. *Daily values:* 12% vit. A, 6% vit. C, 6% calcium, 12% iron.

PEAR-CHICKEN MONTE CRISTO

Prep: 20 min. ◆ Bake: 25 min.

Serve this variation of a classic sandwich with a summer salad chock full of cucumbers.

4 to 6 tsp. prepared
   horseradish
8 thick slices firm-textured
   white bread
8 thin slices mozzarella cheese
   (12 oz.)
8 thin slices fully cooked
   chicken or turkey breast
   (12 oz.)
1 to 2 medium pears, cored,
   peeled, and thinly sliced
   ◆◆◆
2 beaten eggs
⅔ cup half-and-half, light
   cream, or whipping cream

1 Spread 1 to 1½ teaspoons horseradish on 1 side of half of the bread slices. Top each with 1 slice of cheese, 1 slice of chicken or turkey, and several pear slices. Add another slice of cheese, and a slice of chicken or turkey. Top with a slice of bread.

2 Meanwhile, in a shallow dish combine eggs and half-and-half, light cream, or whipping cream. Dip both sides of sandwiches in egg mixture, allowing each side of sandwiches to stand about 10 seconds until egg mixture is absorbed. Place sandwiches in a greased 15×10×1½-inch baking pan.

3 Bake in a 350° oven for 15 minutes. Carefully turn the sandwiches over and bake about 10 minutes more or until bread is golden and cheese is just melted. To serve, slice sandwiches into 4 triangles. Makes 8 servings (2 triangles per serving).

Nutrition facts per serving: 321 cal., 16 g total fat (8 g sat. fat), 116 mg chol., 428 mg sodium, 19 g carbo., 1 g fiber, 26 g pro. *Daily values:* 13% vit. A, 2% vit. C, 27% calcium, 9% iron.

GRILLED CHICKEN MOLE SANDWICH

Prep: 25 min. ◆ Grill: 12 min. Chill: 30 min.

The road to Southwestern cuisine is paved with good tiendas (Mexican grocery stores). That's where you'll find the ingredients to make these sandwiches truly authentic. (See the photograph on page 163.)

3 **dried New Mexico peppers or dried pasilla peppers**
¼ **cup chopped onion**
3 **cloves garlic, chopped**
1 **Tbsp. cooking oil**
1½ **oz. Mexican-style sweet chocolate or semisweet chocolate, chopped (about 3 Tbsp.)**
½ **cup water**
◆◆◆
4 **large skinless, boneless chicken breast halves**
◆◆◆
1 **small avocado, halved, seeded, peeled, and mashed**
2 **Tbsp. light mayonnaise dressing**
⅛ **tsp. salt**
¼ **tsp. ground red pepper (optional)**

2 **bolitos, bollilos, or other Mexican rolls or hard rolls, approximately 6 inches in diameter, split**
Baby romaine or other green lettuce leaves
Tomato slices
½ **of a medium papaya, peeled, seeded, and sliced**

1 For mole, remove stems and seeds from peppers; coarsely chop peppers and set aside. In a large skillet cook onion and garlic in hot oil over medium-high heat for 4 to 5 minutes or until onions are brown. Add the dried peppers and water; reduce heat and stir in the chocolate. Cook and stir over medium heat for 3 to 5 minutes or until thickened and bubbly. Cool slightly.

2 Transfer pepper mixture to a food processor bowl or blender container. Cover and process or blend until a smooth paste. Set aside to cool. Reserve 1 to 2 tablespoons mole.

3 Rinse chicken; pat dry with paper towels. If desired, season with salt. Using a sharp knife, carefully butterfly-cut each chicken breast by cutting a slit horizontally two-thirds through. Open each breast piece and spread inside face of each with mole. Fold closed.

4 Rub the outside of each breast with reserved mole. Grill breasts on the rack of an uncovered grill directly over medium coals for 12 to 15 minutes or until tender and no longer pink, turning once halfway through. Cover and chill.

TEST KITCHEN TIP

BETTER HOMES AND GARDENS TEST KITCHEN ®

OLÉ MOLE

The word mole (MO lay) means "mixture." Traditionally, this Mexican-Indian sauce base includes ground roasted pumpkin seeds, onions, herbs, and two or more types of chilies.

Green mole sauces use fresh chilies; brown moles use dried peppers plus a touch of Mexican chocolate—a coarse chocolate with cinnamon and ground almonds. For our recipe for Grilled Chicken Mole Sandwich (see left) we opted for a shorter, user-friendly recipe. Purchased moles are available in Mexican and Central American specialty stores or in larger supermarkets.

5 In a small bowl stir together avocado, light mayonnaise dressing, ⅛ teaspoon salt, and, if desired, the ground red pepper. To serve, slice chicken into ¼- to ½-inch-thick slices. Spread avocado mixture onto split rolls; layer with chicken slices, romaine or other lettuce leaves, and tomato slices. Garnish with papaya slices. Serve sandwiches open-faced. Makes 4 sandwiches.

Nutrition facts per sandwich: 524 cal., 24 g total fat (6 g sat. fat), 59 mg chol., 448 mg sodium, 52 g carbo., 7 g fiber, 28 g pro. *Daily values:* 8% vit. A, 120% vit. C, 7% calcium, 25% iron.

THE MEAL THAT WELCOMES ALL:
COMPANY CHICKEN SUPPER

Company is coming—most unexpectedly. No problem. You won't need a mathematician to calculate changes in the ingredient amounts for this saucy chicken dinner that can be ready on the double.

We've crunched the numbers for you so you'll know what you need, whether you're feeding a couple or a crowd. Just check the chart (below) for the proper proportions.

This quick-and-easy dish works for any occasion, from a casual family meal to a special celebration dinner. The chicken, enhanced with mushrooms, sweet pepper, and an herb, is served with a creamy sauce over egg noodles. To avoid lumps in the sauce, add the liquid slowly to the sour cream mixture and blend thoroughly.

COMPANY CHICKEN SUPPER
Prep: 25 min. ◆ Cook: 30 min.

SERVINGS			INGREDIENTS
2	4	8	
8 oz.	1¼ lb.	2½ lb.	skinless, boneless chicken breast halves or thighs, cut into small pieces
⅛ tsp.	¼ tsp.	½ tsp.	salt
⅛ tsp.	¼ tsp.	½ tsp.	black pepper
			Nonstick spray coating
1 tsp.	2 tsp.	4 tsp.	cooking oil
¾ cup	1½ cups	3 cups	halved fresh mushrooms
½ cup	1 cup	2 cups	chopped red or green sweet pepper and/or sliced celery
¼ cup	½ cup	1 cup	sliced green onions
¾ cup	1½ cups	4 cups	chicken broth
2 tsp.	1 Tbsp.	2 Tbsp.	snipped fresh basil, marjoram, oregano, or thyme
			OR
¼ tsp.	½ tsp.	1 tsp.	dried basil, marjoram, oregano, or thyme (crushed)
1½ cups	3 cups	6 cups	dried egg noodles
¼ cup	½ cup	1 cup	dairy sour cream or light dairy sour cream
1 Tbsp.	2 Tbsp.	¼ cup	all-purpose flour
			Fresh herb sprigs (optional)

1 Rinse chicken; pat dry. Sprinkle with salt and black pepper. Spray a large nonstick skillet with nonstick spray coating. Preheat over medium heat. Cook chicken for 5 minutes, turning to brown evenly. Remove chicken from skillet. Add oil to skillet.

2 Cook mushrooms, sweet pepper and/or celery, and green onions in oil for 5 minutes or until crisp-tender. Drain fat. Carefully add broth and desired herb. Bring to boiling, scraping up browned bits from bottom of skillet. Return chicken to skillet; reduce heat. Simmer, covered, for 10 to 15 minutes or until chicken is tender and no longer pink. Place chicken on serving dish; keep warm. Reserve juices in skillet.

3 Meanwhile, cook noodles according to package directions; drain and keep warm.

4 For sauce, in a medium bowl combine sour cream and flour. Slowly add about half of the reserved pan juices to the sour cream mixture, stirring to combine. Pour sour cream mixture into skillet containing the remaining juices.

5 Cook and stir mixture until thickened and bubbly. Cook and stir for 1 minute more. Serve sauce over chicken and hot cooked noodles. If desired, garnish with fresh herb.

Nutrition facts per serving: 394 cal., 14 g total fat (5 g sat. fat), 109 mg chol., 502 mg sodium, 35 g carbo., 31 g pro.
Daily values: 28% vit. A, 75% vit. C, 5% calcium, 23% iron.

BEEF TENDERLOIN FILLETS WITH HORSERADISH CHILI

Prep: 30 min. ◆ Grill: 18 min.

A bold dry rub seals in the flavor of these thick and juicy steaks. The horseradish chili is a surefire wake-up call for your palate.

1½ lb. beef tenderloin, cut into 4 fillets about 1¼ inches thick

2 tsp. snipped fresh sage or ½ tsp. dried sage, crushed

¼ to 1 tsp. coarsely ground white or black pepper

¼ tsp. salt

2 tsp. cooking oil

1 cup coarsely chopped tomatoes

2 Tbsp. chili seasoning mix

2 cloves garlic, minced

½ cup drained canned red beans, rinsed

¼ to ½ cup grated fresh horseradish root

◆◆◆

Sage leaves (optional)
Steamed vegetables (optional)

1 Rub both sides of fillets with sage, pepper, and salt; set aside. In a heavy skillet heat oil over medium-high heat. Add tomatoes, chili seasoning, and garlic to skillet. Cook for 1 to 2 minutes or until tomatoes just start to soften; reduce heat to medium-low. Add beans and horseradish. Cook and stir for 2 minutes more. Loosely cover chili; keep warm.

2 Grill fillets on the rack of an uncovered grill directly over medium coals for 18 to 20 minutes for medium doneness or to desired doneness. (Or, in a heavy skillet cook fillets in 4 teaspoons hot *cooking oil* over medium heat for 14 to 16 minutes, turning once.) To serve, place a fillet on each plate; spoon warm chili sauce over fillet. If desired, garnish with fresh sage leaves and serve with steamed vegetables. Makes 4 servings.

Nutrition facts per serving: 347 cal., 14 g total fat (5 g sat. fat), 96 mg chol., 759 mg sodium, 18 g carbo., 1 g fiber, 37 g pro. *Daily values:* 15% vit. A, 45% vit. C, 5% calcium, 39% iron.

TEST KITCHEN TIP

HORSERADISH ADDS ZIP

Renowned for its pungent bite, the gnarly horseradish root comes from a plant of the mustard family. Related to radishes, not horses, the naming of the root is a curious tale. It once was called meerrettich, or "sea radish" in German, because it grew by the sea. The English mispronounced it "mareradish," and eventually, the name became horseradish.

You can buy horseradish fresh, grated and refrigerated (labeled "prepared"), or dried (flakes). Also, look for prepared horseradish in beet or mustard flavor.

SNAPPY IDEAS

◆ Spice up barbecue sauce with prepared horseradish.

◆ Mix horseradish into soft-style cream cheese with chives to spread on crackers or toasted bagel chips.

◆ Whisk some beet horseradish into vinaigrette dressing.

◆ Season hollandaise sauce (prepared from a mix) with horseradish. Serve sauce with beef steaks, fish steaks, or assorted hot cooked vegetables.

◆ Stir horseradish mustard into the salad dressings used for meat salads, such as chicken, beef, or ham.

◆ Mix horseradish (mustard, regular, or beet) into melted margarine or butter. Serve over fish or hot cooked vegetables.

KITCHEN TIPS

◆ To grate fresh horseradish, peel off the outer layer. Grate the peeled root in a food processor or blender. (Be careful: The fumes can burn your eyes and nose.)

◆ Grate horseradish in small batches because it loses flavor intensity quickly. Use it within a few days. Or, freeze grated horseradish for up to several months.

◆ Refrigerate any unused horseradish root in a plastic bag for up to 3 weeks.

◆ Use dried horseradish flakes as you would dried onion. Look for it in the spice section of the supermarket.

Menu

Salad of arugula, shaved Asiago cheese, and raspberry vinaigrette

♦♦♦

Grilled Bass with Carambola Salsa (see below)

♦♦♦

Grilled whole tiny new potatoes

♦♦♦

Crusty wheat rolls and butter

LOW FAT

GRILLED BASS WITH CARAMBOLA SALSA

Prep: 25 min. ♦ Grill: 8 min.

Sunny star fruit (carambola) brightens up meaty grilled fish.
(See the photograph on page 157.)

½ to 1 tsp. cumin seed
3 large carambola (star fruit)
1 small lime
½ of a small fresh poblano pepper, seeded and finely chopped
2 Tbsp. snipped fresh cilantro
½ tsp. salt

♦♦♦

1 lb. sea bass or red snapper fillet, cut into 4 fillets about 1 inch thick
¼ tsp. ground red pepper

1 In a dry skillet cook cumin seed, uncovered, over medium-high heat for 1 to 2 minutes or until toasted, shaking the skillet frequently. Set cumin seed aside. Slice 1 carambola; cover and chill.

Chop remaining carambola; set aside. Finely shred lime peel; set aside. Peel, section, and chop lime. In a bowl combine toasted cumin seed, chopped carambola, chopped lime, poblano pepper, cilantro, and ⅛ teaspoon of the salt; cover and chill.

2 Rinse fish fillets; pat dry. Sprinkle with remaining salt, ground red pepper, and lime peel.

3 In a covered grill arrange medium-hot coals around a drip pan. Test for medium heat above the pan. Place fish fillets on the grill rack over drip pan. Cover and grill for 8 to 12 minutes per 1-inch thickness or until fish just begins to flake when tested with a fork. Serve with carambola salsa; garnish with sliced carambola. Makes 4 servings.

Nutrition facts per serving: 143 cal., 3 g total fat (1 g sat. fat), 47 mg chol., 280 mg sodium, 8 g carbo., 1 g fiber, 22 g pro. *Daily values:* 10% vit. A, 54% vit. C, 2% calcium, 5% iron.

SIZZLING SHRIMP WITH TANGY COCONUT SAUCE

Start to finish: 25 min.

The zip in the coconut sauce comes from wasabi (WAH-suh-bee)—also called oriental horseradish. It's a large, pale-green relative of the common horseradish and is purchased in raw, paste, or powder form. Look for tubes of wasabi paste in Asian markets.
(See the photograph on page 157.)

⅓ cup purchased unsweetened coconut milk
1 tsp. cornstarch
2 to 4 tsp. wasabi paste

2 tsp. grated fresh ginger
2 Tbsp. lime juice

♦♦♦

15 to 18 fresh or frozen jumbo shrimp in shells (1 lb.)
2 tsp. cooking oil
1 Tbsp. soy sauce
1 Tbsp. minced garlic
¼ to 1 tsp. crushed red pepper (optional)

1 For dipping sauce, in a small saucepan stir together the coconut milk and cornstarch. Cook and stir over low heat for 3 to 5 minutes. Set mixture aside to cool. Meanwhile, in a small mixing bowl combine the wasabi paste, the grated ginger, and ½ to 1 teaspoon of the lime juice. Stir in thickened coconut milk mixture. Cover and cool mixture in the refrigerator.

2 Peel and devein shrimp, leaving tails on, if desired. In a large skillet or wok heat oil over medium-high heat for 30 seconds. Cook shrimp 2 minutes, turning once. Carefully add soy sauce, garlic, and, if desired, crushed red pepper. Cook for 30 seconds to 1 minute more or until shrimp turn pink.

3 Remove skillet or wok from heat. Sprinkle remaining lime juice over shrimp mixture. Serve with dipping sauce. Makes 4 side-dish servings.

Nutrition facts per serving: 137 cal., 7 g total fat (4 g sat. fat), 131 mg chol., 428 mg sodium, 4 g carbo., 0 g fiber, 15 g pro. *Daily values:* 5% vit. A, 8% vit. C, 2% calcium, 16% iron.

Left: *Grilled Bass with Carambola Salsa (page 156)*
Below: *Sizzling Shrimp with Tangy Coconut Sauce (page 156)*

Above: *Mango Parfaits (page 168)*
Right: *Seaside Dessert Platter (page 188),*
Lemon-Lime Ice Cream Floats (page 189)

Page 160: *Herb-Cured Pork Platter,*
Savory Black Beans (page 179)
Left: *Welcome-Home Apricot-Ginger*
Chicken Dinner (page 182), Honeydew
and Apple Salad (page 183)
Below: *Summer Shrimp and Veggie Boil*
(page 181)

Top left: *Cactus Fruit Sorbet (page 172)*
Above: *Farmer's Market Melon Soup (page 148)*

Top right: *Rigatoni with Fire-Roasted Jalapeño Pesto (page 149)*
Above: *Grilled Corn with Ancho-Avocado Butter (page 150)*
Page 163: *Grilled Chicken Mole Sandwich (page 153)*

Top: *Carrot, Corn, and Bean Salad (page 166)*
Above: *Tandoori-Style Lamb (page 165),*
Mustard Greens Salad (page 166)

TANDOORI-STYLE LAMB

**Prep: 15 min. ◆ Marinate: 4 hr.
Grill: 45 min.**

*See page 151 for the perfect condiments
to go with this Indian-inspired lamb.
(See the photograph on page 164.)*

2 1- to 1½-lb. French-style
    lamb rib roasts (6 to 8 ribs
    each)
4 cloves garlic, minced
2 Tbsp. grated fresh ginger
2 Tbsp. curry powder
2 tsp. ground cumin
½ tsp. salt
1 8-oz. carton plain yogurt

◆◆◆

1 recipe Mustard Greens Salad
    (see page 166) (optional)

1 Trim fat from lamb roasts.
Place lamb rib roasts in a large
glass baking dish. In a small bowl
combine garlic, ginger, curry
powder, cumin, and salt. Wearing
disposable or plastic gloves to
avoid staining hands, rub spice
mixture evenly over meat. Spread
roasts with yogurt to coat. Cover
roasts and refrigerate for 4 to
6 hours or overnight.

2 Insert a meat thermometer
into the thickest part of the roast,
making sure the end of thermometer does not touch bone. In
a covered grill arrange medium
coals around a drip pan. Test for
medium-low heat above the pan.

3 Place roasts, bone side
down, on grill rack over drip pan.
Cover and grill the meat for 45 to
60 minutes or until thermometer
registers 155° for medium doneness. (Or, place bone side down
in a foil-lined shallow roasting
pan. Roast, uncovered, in a 325°
oven for 1 to 1¼ hours or until
thermometer registers 155° for
medium doneness.)

4 Cover meat and let stand
about 10 minutes before serving.
If desired, serve with Mustard
Greens Salad and/or desired
condiments. Serves 6 to 8.

Nutrition facts per serving: 156 cal., 7 g
total fat (3 g sat. fat), 53 mg chol., 246 mg
sodium, 5 g carbo., 1 g fiber, 18 g pro.
Daily values: 1% vit. A, 2% vit. C, 8%
calcium, 18% iron.

PRIZE
TESTED
RECIPE
WINNER

SPICY STUFFED
COLLARD GREENS

Prep: 40 min. ◆ Bake: 25 min.

*Collard greens make tasty wrappers
for a ground beef stuffing loaded
with Mexican flavor.*

12 large collard greens leaves or
    cabbage leaves

◆◆◆

1 lb. lean ground beef
1 cup finely chopped celery
½ cup chopped onion
4 cups salsa
2 cups hot cooked rice

3 Tbsp. taco seasoning mix
    (about half of a 1¼-oz.
    pkg.)

◆◆◆

1 cup shredded Monterey Jack
    cheese with jalapeño
    peppers (4 oz.)

1 Remove center veins from
collard leaves, keeping each leaf in
1 piece. Immerse leaves, 4 at a
time, into boiling water about
4 to 5 minutes or until leaves are
limp. Drain well.

2 For filling, in a large skillet
cook ground beef, celery, and
onion until meat is brown and
onion is tender. Drain off fat. Stir
in 2 cups of the salsa, the hot
cooked rice, and taco seasoning
mix. Mix well.

3 Place ⅓ to ½ cup filling
mixture on each collard leaf. Fold
in sides. Starting at an unfolded
edge, carefully roll up each leaf,
making sure folded sides are
included in the roll. Place stuffed
collard greens in a 3-quart baking
dish. Spoon remaining 2 cups
salsa over stuffed greens. Bake,
uncovered, in a 350° oven for
20 minutes. Top with cheese;
bake about 5 minutes more or
until cheese is melted. Makes
6 main-dish servings.

Nutrition facts per serving: 329 cal., 17 g
total fat (6 g sat. fat), 64 mg chol., 887 mg
sodium, 29 g carbo., 2 g fiber, 23 g pro.
Daily values: 33% vit. A, 72% vit. C, 15%
calcium, 22% iron.

Tandoori-Style Lamb
(see page 165)

♦♦♦

Mustard Greens Salad
(see below right)

♦♦♦

Warm pita bread

♦♦♦

Iced tea

CARROT, CORN, AND BEAN SALAD

Prep: 20 min. ♦ Chill: 4 to 24 hr.

A perfect way to use peak-season sweet corn. You also can bring a taste of summer to your wintertime table by making this salad with frozen corn. (See the photograph on page 164.)

1 lb. carrots, thinly sliced
2 cups fresh or frozen whole kernel corn

♦♦♦

1 15-oz. can kidney or black beans, rinsed and drained
1 medium green or red sweet pepper, cut into thin strips
⅓ cup snipped fresh basil or parsley

♦♦♦

¼ cup olive oil or salad oil
¼ cup vinegar
2 tsp. snipped fresh thyme or ½ tsp. dried thyme, crushed
1 tsp. sugar
¼ tsp. cracked black pepper
¼ tsp. crushed red pepper

1 In a large saucepan cook carrots and corn in a small amount of boiling salted water for 4 minutes. Drain.

2 In a large bowl combine carrots, corn, beans, sweet pepper, and basil or parsley. Set aside.

3 For dressing, in a screw-top jar combine oil, vinegar, thyme, sugar, black pepper, and red pepper. Cover and shake to combine. Add dressing to vegetable mixture, tossing to coat. Cover and chill for 4 to 24 hours. Makes 8 side-dish servings.

Nutrition facts per serving: 165 cal., 7 g total fat (1 g sat. fat), 0 mg chol., 124 mg sodium, 24 g carbo., 5 g fiber, 6 g pro. *Daily values:* 130% vit. A, 36% vit. C, 3% calcium, 9% iron.

MUSTARD GREENS SALAD

Start to finish: 20 min.

Crisp, piquant mustard greens are high in folate and vitamins A and C. (See the photograph on page 164.)

4 cups shredded mustard greens
3 Tbsp. chopped walnuts
1 small red sweet pepper, seeded and cut into long, thin slivers
1 Tbsp. salad oil
2 Tbsp. rice vinegar or white vinegar
4 tsp. green peppercorn mustard, tarragon mustard, or Dijon-style mustard

1 Place greens and walnuts in a salad bowl. In a medium saucepan cook pepper in hot oil for 2 minutes, stirring often.

Carefully stir in the vinegar and mustard. Cook and stir until bubbly; remove from heat. Pour the dressing oven greens and walnuts in bowl, tossing to coat. Serve immediately. Makes 4 to 6 side-dish servings.

Nutrition facts per serving: 98 cal., 8 g total fat (1 g sat. fat), 0 mg chol., 149 mg sodium, 6 g carbo., 3 g fiber, 4 g pro. *Daily values:* 52% vit. A, 98% vit. C, 9% calcium, 8% iron.

SPICY SZECHWAN SUMMER SALAD

LOW FAT

Start to finish: 35 min.

A warm and spicy dressing slightly wilts the crunchy cabbage in this fresh citrusy combo.

4 cups thinly shredded Napa cabbage
2 cups thinly shredded red cabbage
2 cups torn mixed baby greens
1 cup watercress
½ tsp. finely shredded orange peel (set aside)
3 medium oranges, peeled, sectioned, and chopped
2 green onions, cut into thin slivers
½ cup snipped fresh cilantro

♦♦♦

2 Tbsp. toasted sesame oil
2 Tbsp. rice vinegar or cider vinegar
2 Tbsp. frozen orange juice concentrate, thawed
1 tsp. chili garlic sauce, or prepared Chinese-style hot mustard plus 2 cloves garlic, minced
1 tsp. grated fresh ginger
2 Tbsp. sliced almonds, toasted (optional)

1 In a large salad bowl toss together the Napa cabbage, red cabbage, baby greens, watercress, oranges, green onions, and cilantro. Set aside.

2 In a small saucepan combine the sesame oil, vinegar, orange juice concentrate, chili garlic sauce, ginger, and orange peel. Bring mixture just to boiling; remove from heat. Pour dressing over greens in salad bowl, tossing to coat. If desired, sprinkle with almonds. Serve at once. Makes 6 side-dish servings.

Nutrition facts per serving: 85 cal., 5 g total fat (1 g sat. fat), 0 mg chol., 23 mg sodium, 10 g carbo., 2 g fiber, 2 g pro.
Daily values: 11% vit. A, 94% vit. C, 6% calcium, 3% iron.

30 MIN.

MANGO SALAD WITH SMOKED TURKEY

Start to finish: 25 min.

Leave out the turkey and lettuce and cube the mango for a fresh salsa to serve with meat and fish.

6 cups torn mixed greens
4 mangoes, pitted, peeled, and cut into thin slices (see photos, page 168)
8 oz. cooked smoked turkey or chicken, cut into thin bite-size strips; or smoked trout, catfish, or other white fish, crumbled
1 green onion, thinly sliced
¼ cup snipped fresh cilantro
1 recipe Lime Vinaigrette (see right)

◆◆◆

Edible flowers (optional)
Lime wedges (optional)

MAD FOR MANGOES

For a tempting taste of paradise, take a ride on the mango express. The fruit gives an exotic twist to some old favorites.

Cut open a ripe mango and savor a spicy, peachy perfume that's as inviting as a tropical breeze. The first bite of this luscious fruit lets you know that this will be no ordinary experience. Although mango consumption in the United States is growing 10 to 15 percent annually, it still equals less than one pound of fruit per person per year. But don't let the statistics fool you—mangoes are the world's most widely eaten fruit.

Native to India, mango trees *(Mangifera indica)* now are grown all over the world. Most of the fruit sold in the United States is grown here or imported from countries such as Mexico, Brazil, Venezuela, Peru, and Guatemala.

Mangoes are most plentiful and prices are generally lowest from May through September (though they can be found in the produce section of many supermarkets all year).

Buying mangoes is much like buying peaches: The skin should be yellow or red with little or no trace of green, and the flesh at the stem end should be starting to soften.

Beware of really large mangoes, experts say, because they can be all seed with little flesh. Also avoid fruit with bruises or soft spots. You should use your nose before you buy; ripe mangoes should have a sweet, peach-like, fresh-fruit aroma.

If the mango is somewhat hard and needs further ripening, place it in a closed brown paper bag for a day or two. Ripe mangoes can be refrigerated for up to five days.

Because of the mango's tough peel, tenaciously clinging seed, and generous amount of juice, some fans say that the best way to eat a mango is in the bathtub. For a neater way to get the fruit off the seed, see the how-to photographs on page 168.

1 Divide greens among 4 salad plates. Arrange one-fourth of the mango, smoked turkey, and green onion on each plate of greens. Sprinkle with cilantro and drizzle with Lime Vinaigrette.

2 If desired, garnish with edible flowers and lime wedges. Makes 4 main-dish servings.

Lime Vinaigrette: In a screw-top jar combine ¼ cup salad oil, ¼ tsp. finely shredded lime peel, 2 Tbsp. lime juice, and ¼ tsp. grated fresh ginger or dash ground ginger. Cover and shake well. Makes about ⅓ cup.

Nutrition facts per serving: 333 cal., 16 g total fat (3 g sat. fat), 29 mg chol., 582 mg sodium, 39 g carbo., 6 g fiber, 13 g pro.
Daily values: 89% vit. A, 111% vit. C, 4% calcium, 5% iron.

NEATLY DONE

You'll maximize the amount of fruit and minimize the mess if you separate the pit and peel from a mango as shown below. The keys are to have a sharp knife and a steady cutting board. Also, be sure to take it slowly when you're cutting; you'll have an easier time seeing the process and being safer.

Cutting: Grasp a mango firmly, making sure your fingers are out of the path of the knife; cut down the sides of the fruit, sliding the blade next to the seed along one side of the mango. (Be careful not to cut into the pit.) Repeat on other side, then cut away all the meat that remains around the narrow sides.

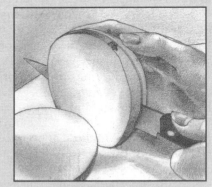

Slicing: If making slices, remove peel from all pieces and slice. If cubes are needed, cut a cross-hatched pattern in the flesh of the two large slices of the mango. The mango flesh shouldn't be tough, so use a light touch and be careful not to cut through the skin or you'll make the next step more difficult.

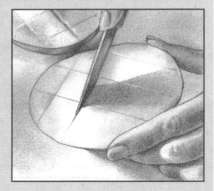

Dicing: Bend the peel back and carefully slide the knife between the peel and the flesh to separate. The cubes will come off ready to use.

MANGO PARFAITS
Prep: 25 min. ◆ Chill: 1 hr.

Update a classic dessert with a new fruit and reduced-fat ingredients. This no-cook dessert is a cool treat on the hottest summer days.
(See the photograph on page 158.)

½ of a 10¾-oz. loaf pound cake or reduced-calorie loaf pound cake, cut into ½-inch cubes
¼ cup amaretto or other almond liqueur, or ¼ cup orange juice plus ¼ tsp. almond extract
1 8-oz. carton fat-free or light dairy sour cream
2 Tbsp. powdered sugar

◆◆◆

2 ripe mangoes, pitted, peeled, and cut into ½-inch pieces (see photos, left)
Fresh fruit, such as sliced kiwifruit, raspberries, or strawberries (optional)

1 In a medium mixing bowl toss cake cubes with half of the amaretto or orange juice/almond extract mixture. In a small mixing bowl combine remaining amaretto or orange juice mixture, sour cream, and powdered sugar.

2 For each serving, place a few cake cubes into the bottom of a parfait glass followed by about 1 tablespoon sour cream mixture. Add a layer of mangoes. Repeat until glass is full. Repeat with 3 more glasses. Cover and chill for up to 1 hour. If desired, garnish with fruit. Makes 4 servings.

Nutrition facts per serving: 320 cal., 8 g total fat (4 g sat. fat), 0 mg chol., 189 mg sodium, 53 g carbo., 2 g fiber, 6 g pro. *Daily values:* 53% vit. A, 47% vit. C, 9% calcium, 4% iron.

LEMON POPPYSEED SHORTCAKES

Prep: 20 min. ◆ Bake: 12 min.
Cool: 30 min.

Choose a variety of peak-season fruits to top these tender, lemony shortcakes.

1   **15.6-oz. pkg. lemon poppyseed quick bread mix**
3   **Tbsp. butter**
1   **slightly beaten egg**
⅓   **cup buttermilk**

◆◆◆

8   **cups assorted fresh fruits, such as sliced nectarines; peeled, sliced peaches; sliced strawberries; sliced bananas; and/or blueberries**
¼   **cup strawberry jelly**

◆◆◆

½   **cup whipping cream, whipped**

1 Grease a large baking sheet; set aside. Pour bread mix into a large mixing bowl. Using a pastry blender cut in butter until mixture resembles coarse crumbs. Combine egg and buttermilk; add to dry mixture. Stir just until moistened.

2 Drop the batter into 12 mounds, 2 inches apart, on the prepared baking sheet. Bake in a 400° oven for 12 to 15 minutes or until golden. Transfer shortcakes to a wire rack and let cool.

3 Meanwhile, in a large mixing bowl combine the fruits. In a small saucepan heat the jelly over low heat just until melted, stirring frequently. Pour jelly over fruit, tossing gently to mix.

4 To serve, place each shortcake in an individual bowl. Divide fruit evenly among bowls and top with whipped cream. Makes 12 servings.*

*Note: If you wish, prepare only half of the fruit and whipped cream. Freeze 6 of the shortcakes for another use. Before serving, thaw shortcakes at room temperature for 1 hour.

Nutrition facts per serving: 294 cal., 12 g total fat (5 g sat. fat), 5 mg chol., 198 mg sodium, 44 g carbo., 2 g fiber, 4 g pro. *Daily values:* 11% vit. A, 28% vit. C, 4% calcium, 8% iron.

SESAME SHORTBREAD BITES

Prep: 15 min. ◆ Bake: 25 min.
Cool: 35 min.

Break time is the right time to serve these crumbly, nutty shortbread bites.

1¼   **cups all-purpose flour**
3   **Tbsp. sugar**
½   **cup butter**
⅓   **cup sesame seeds, toasted**

1 In a medium mixing bowl combine flour and sugar. Using a pastry blender, cut in butter until mixture resembles fine crumbs. Knead in sesame seeds.

2 Form the mixture into a ball and knead just until smooth. On a lightly floured surface, roll the dough into a ½-inch-thick, 8×6-inch rectangle. Cut the dough with decorative 1-inch cookie cutters or slice it into twenty-four 2×1-inch strips.

SWEET SESAME

Popping new flavor into desserts is as easy as saying "open sesame." Sesame seeds have a complex, buttery flavor—just perfect for cookies and shortbread—that is intensified by toasting.

To toast sesame seeds, spread in a thin layer in a dry skillet. Cook over medium heat, stirring often. Or, bake them on an ungreased baking sheet, in a 350° oven, for 5 to 10 minutes, stirring several times.

Lilliputian sesame seeds, which have been cultivated for 8,000 years, come in several colors, such as white, red, brown, and black, but all taste virtually the same. They are rich in oil and turn rancid if not stored in an airtight container. Keep them in a cool, dark pantry for up to 3 months or freeze them for up to 6 months.

3 Place the cut shapes or strips 1 inch apart on an ungreased cookie sheet. If desired, prick the top or score the edge of each cookie with a fork before baking.

4 Bake in a 325° oven about 25 minutes or until bottoms are light brown. Cool for 5 minutes. Transfer cookies to a wire rack; cool for 30 minutes. Store in an airtight container for up to 1 week. Makes 24 cookies.

Nutrition facts per cookie: 74 cal., 5 g total fat (1 g sat. fat), 5 mg chol., 35 mg sodium, 7 g carbo., 0 g fiber, 1 g pro. *Daily values:* 3% vit. A, 1% calcium, 3% iron.

STAR-SPANGLED TART

Prep: 30 min. ◆ Bake: 12 min.
Cool: 1 hr.

*Decorate any cookies that don't
fit on the tart with canned frosting
tinted red or blue.*

1 **20-oz. roll refrigerated sugar
cookie dough**
◆◆◆
Coarse sugar
◆◆◆
1 **14-oz. can (1¼ cups)
sweetened condensed milk
or fat-free sweetened
condensed milk**
½ **cup regular or light dairy
sour cream**
½ **tsp. finely shredded lemon
peel or lime peel**
⅓ **cup lemon juice or lime
juice**
◆◆◆
1 **cup fresh blueberries or
blackberries**
2 **cups fresh red raspberries or
3 cups fresh strawberry
halves**

1 For crust, generously grease
the bottom of an 11×8×1½-inch
rectangular tart pan with a removable bottom or an 11- to 12-inch
pizza pan; lightly grease sides. Set
aside half of dough. With floured
hands, pat remaining dough onto
bottom and up sides of pan.

2 For cookies, on a lightly
floured surface roll out remaining
dough to ⅛- to ¼-inch thickness.
Using small star cutters, cut into
shapes. Place cutouts on an
ungreased baking sheet. Reroll
trimmings and recut. Sprinkle
half of the stars with coarse sugar.

3 Bake crust and cookies in a
375° oven until golden, allowing
4 to 5 minutes for small cookies
and 12 minutes for crust. Cool on
a wire rack.

4 For filling, in a mixing bowl
combine condensed milk, sour
cream, lemon or lime peel, and
juice. Stir about 3 minutes or
until mixture is thickened. Cover;
chill until ready to assemble tart.

5 To assemble, loosen and
remove sides of tart pan from
crust. Transfer crust to a platter,
leaving bottom of pan under
crust. Before serving, spread filling onto crust. Top with berries
and cookies. Cut into 12 pieces.
Makes 12 servings.

Nutrition facts per serving: 325 cal., 13 g
total fat (5 g sat. fat), 27 mg chol., 213 mg
sodium, 48 g carbo., 1 g fiber, 5 g pro.
Daily values: 6% vit. A, 18% vit. C, 11%
calcium, 5% iron.

WHITE CHOCOLATE
FLAN

Prep: 30 min. ◆ Bake: 30 min.
Chill: 1 to 8 hr.

1 **small dried pasilla chili
pepper**
◆◆◆
1½ **cups milk**
3 **oz. white chocolate baking
squares, coarsely chopped**
⅓ **cup sugar**
¼ **tsp. freshly grated nutmeg**
◆◆◆
⅓ **cup sugar**
◆◆◆
3 **slightly beaten eggs**
1 **tsp. vanilla**
◆◆◆
1 **recipe Passion Fruit Cream
(see page 171)
Edible flower petals*
(optional)**

1 Remove stem and seeds
from pepper and discard. Place
pepper in a food processor bowl
or blender container. Cover;
process until ground. Set aside.

2 In a heavy medium saucepan
stir together the milk, chocolate,
the ⅓ cup sugar, and the nutmeg.
Cook over medium heat just to
boiling. Remove from heat; set
aside for 15 minutes.

3 In a heavy 8-inch skillet
cook the ⅓ cup sugar over medium-high heat until it begins to
melt. Shake skillet occasionally to
heat sugar evenly. Do not stir.
Once sugar starts to melt, reduce
heat to low. Cook about 5 minutes more or until all of the sugar
is melted and golden, stirring as
needed with a wooden spoon.
Immediately divide caramelized
sugar among four 6-ounce custard
cups; tilt cups to coat bottoms
evenly. Let stand 10 minutes.

4 In a large mixing bowl slowly stir chocolate mixture into
beaten eggs. Stir in ground pasilla
pepper and vanilla. Beat until
combined, but not foamy. Place
custard cups in a 2-quart square
baking dish and place on an oven
rack. Divide the chocolate mixture evenly among custard cups.

5 Pour boiling water into the
baking dish around custard cups
to a depth of 1 inch. Bake in a
325° oven for 30 to 35 minutes or
until a knife inserted near centers
comes out clean. Remove flans
from baking dish; cool on a wire
rack. Cover and chill 1 to 8 hours.

6 To unmold flans, loosen edges with a knife, slipping the point of the knife down the sides. Invert a dessert plate over each flan; turn cup and plate over together. Remove cup. Spoon Passion Fruit Cream on top. If desired, garnish with edible flower petals. Makes 4 servings.

Passion Fruit Cream: Halve 3 passion fruit; press through a fine sieve. In a chilled mixing bowl beat ¼ cup heavy whipping cream and 1 teaspoon sugar until soft peaks form. Whisk in the strained passion fruit pulp and juice or 2 tablespoons purchased passion fruit pulp. (If desired, substitute 2 teaspoons frozen orange juice concentrate, thawed, for the passion fruit.)

*Note: Edible flowers can be purchased at many supermarkets. If picking wild edible flowers, make sure they are chemical-free.

Nutrition facts per serving: 426 cal., 18 g total fat (10 g sat. fat), 195 mg chol., 126 mg sodium, 56 g carbo., 2 g fiber, 10 g pro. *Daily values:* 20% vit. A, 11% vit. C, 13% calcium, 5% iron.

WHITE NECTARINES WITH RASPBERRY SAUCE

Start to finish: 15 min.

¾ **cup raspberries**
¼ **cup white zinfandel or apple juice**
1 **Tbsp. sugar**
♦♦♦
¼ **cup whipping cream**
3 **white nectarines or peaches**

1 In a blender container or food processor bowl combine raspberries, zinfandel or juice, and sugar. Cover; blend or process until smooth. Strain sauce and discard seeds; set sauce aside.

2 In a small chilled bowl beat cream with chilled beaters until very soft peaks form. Slice nectarines into thin wedges. Divide raspberry sauce onto 4 chilled dessert plates. Arrange nectarine slices on sauce and drizzle cream on top. Makes 4 servings.

Nutrition facts per serving: 135 cal., 6 g total fat (3 g sat. fat), 20 mg chol., 6 mg sodium, 18 g carbo., 2 g fiber, 1 g pro. *Daily values:* 14% vit. A, 18% vit. C, 1% calcium, 2% iron.

WHITE PEACH FROZEN YOGURT

Prep: 40 min. ♦ Freeze: 10 hr.

3 **cups peeled, pitted, and finely chopped white peaches or nectarines**
2 **16-oz. cartons vanilla yogurt**
¼ **cup honey**

1 Place 1½ cups of the chopped peaches in a food processor bowl or blender container with yogurt and honey. Cover; process until smooth. (If using blender, blend small amount at a time and do not overblend.) Stir in remaining chopped peaches. Pour into a 2-quart pan. Cover and freeze 4 hours or until firm.

2 Break the frozen mixture into small pieces and place in a chilled mixing bowl; beat with an electric mixer on medium speed

THE CREAM OF THE CROP

One bite into the dark velvet cover of a white peach and its heady, honey-flavored juice fills the mouth.

Today, a welcome jump in the availability and variety of white peaches (and nectarines) spells easy luxury. There are more than a dozen types from California alone, and the season runs all summer long.

Where white peaches of old were highly perishable and hard to ship, new varieties are more hardy. You'll find white peaches and nectarines beginning in early June and see the last of them by fall. The new varieties are pale on the outside, with roseate patches. If the fruits are not quite ripe when purchased, store them at room temperature, a few at a time, in a loosely closed paper bag. After a couple of days they will yield slightly to touch and be ready to eat.

until fluffy, starting slowly and gradually increasing the speed. Return mixture to pan and freeze, covered, about 6 hours or until firm. Let yogurt stand at room temperature for 10 to 20 minutes before serving. Makes 12 servings.

Nutrition facts per serving: 75 cal., 1 g total fat (0 g sat. fat), 2 mg chol., 22 mg sodium, 16 g carbo., 1 g fiber, 2 g pro. *Daily values:* 3% vit. A, 5% vit. C, 4% calcium.

CACTUS FRUIT SORBET

Prep: 1 hr. ◆ Chill: 1 hr.
Freeze: 6 hr.

*The barbs are off the cactus,
but a little pepper puts some of
the bite back in.
(See the photograph on page 162.)*

**3 to 4 ripe cactus pears
(prickly pears) or 6 ripe
plums (1 lb.)**

◆◆◆

1 cup chopped strawberries
**3 ripe plums, peeled, pitted,
and cut up (about ⅔ cup)**
⅔ cup sugar
⅔ cup water

◆◆◆

**½ tsp. coarsely ground black
pepper (optional)**

◆◆◆

**Cactus pear wedges
(optional)**

1 Peel cactus pears. If using plums, peel and remove pits. Place prepared cactus pears or plums in a food processor bowl or blender container. Cover and process or blend until smooth. Press cactus pear mixture through a sieve, reserving pulp and juice; discard seeds. If using plums, do not sieve. (You should have about 1 cup cactus pear or plum puree.)

2 In a medium saucepan combine cactus pear pulp and juice or plum puree with ¾ cup of the strawberries, cut-up plums, sugar, and water. Bring just to boiling, stirring often. Reduce heat. Cook fruit mixture, uncovered, on low heat for 30 to 45 minutes or until

---

THE CLEVER COOK

NO MESS ICE POPS

To keep kids' hands from getting sticky from melting ice-pop juice or ice cream, cut a slit in the lid of a margarine container. Insert the handle of the ice pop in the slit, and the lid will catch the drips.

Elaine Hagen
Aptos, California

---

liquid is reduced by about one-fourth. If desired, add the black pepper during the last 5 minutes of cooking.

3 Refrigerate mixture for 1 hour or until chilled. Turn the mixture into a 9×9×2-inch pan. Cover and freeze until firm. Break frozen mixture into chunks; turn into a chilled mixing bowl. Beat mixture with an electric mixer on low speed until slightly slushy, then beat on medium-high speed until smooth.

4 Fold in remaining berries. Return to pan. Cover; freeze until firm. Meanwhile, chill desired serving bowls. Scoop and serve several small scoops of sorbet into each bowl. If desired, garnish with cactus pear wedges. Serves 6.

Nutrition facts per serving: 153 cal., 1 g total fat (0 g sat. fat), 0 mg chol., 1 mg sodium, 38 g carbo., 2 g fiber, 1 g pro. *Daily values:* 3% vit. A, 40% vit. C, 0% calcium, 1% iron.

TEQUILA SUNRISE ICE POPS

Prep: 10 min.
Freeze: 1 hr. plus overnight

You can make nonalcoholic ice pops by eliminating the tequila and adding an extra tablespoon each of the cranberry juice cocktail and lime juice.

½ cup cranberry juice cocktail
2 Tbsp. lime juice
2 tsp. honey

◆◆◆

1½ cups orange juice
¼ cup gold tequila

1 In a measuring cup combine cranberry juice cocktail, lime juice, and honey. Using 8 plastic frozen pop molds or 3-ounce paper cups, pour 4 teaspoons of the juice mixture into the bottom of each. Freeze about 1 hour or until firm but not hard.

2 In another liquid measuring cup combine the orange juice and the tequila.

3 Carefully pour orange juice mixture over cranberry mixture. Cover paper cups with foil and insert wooden craft sticks into cups or insert pop mold sticks into pop molds; freeze overnight. Remove pops from molds or tear off paper cups and remove foil before serving. Makes 8 pops.

Nutrition facts per pop: 61 cal., 0 g total fat, 0 mg chol., 1 mg sodium, 12 g carbo., 0 g fiber, 0 g pro. *Daily values:* 49% vit. C.

FRESH FRUIT FREEZE

30 MIN. NO FAT

Start to finish: 15 min.

Cool off with fresh fruits and ice blended into an invigorating beverage. If desired, substitute equal amounts of your favorite fruits for those listed.

1½ cups chilled carbonated water
1½ cups crushed ice
½ cup chopped, peeled, and pitted mango
½ cup sliced fresh strawberries
⅓ cup light rum (optional)
¼ cup honey
¼ cup freshly squeezed lime juice

1 In a blender container combine carbonated water, crushed ice, mango, strawberries, rum (if desired), honey, and lime juice. Cover and blend until well mixed. Pour mixture into tall, chilled glasses. Serve immediately. Makes 6 servings.

Nutrition facts per serving: 58 cal., 0 g total fat, 0 mg chol., 14 mg sodium, 15 g carbo., 1 g fiber, 0 g pro.
Daily values: 5% vit. A, 22% vit. C.

ICED WATERMELON WITH JICAMA

30 MIN. LOW FAT

Prep: 10 min. ◆ Chill: 20 min.

Use both red and yellow watermelon for a more festive look, if desired—and remember to save some of the seeds to make the ice bowl.

4 cups seeded red and/or yellow watermelon cut into 1½-inch cubes

1 small jicama (1 lb.), peeled and cut into ¾-inch cubes
2 Tbsp. balsamic vinegar
1 Tbsp. honey
1 recipe Watermelon-Seed Ice Bowl (see below) (optional)
½ cup nasturtium flowers or other edible flowers* (optional)

1 In a large bowl combine watermelon and jicama. Cover and chill thoroughly in freezer for 20 minutes. (Do not freeze or melon will turn mushy.) Meanwhile, in a small bowl stir together vinegar and honey; cover and chill. Toss melon mixture with vinegar mixture just before serving. If desired, serve in Watermelon-Seed Ice Bowl and garnish with edible flowers. Makes 6 servings.

Nutrition facts per serving: 78 cal., 1 g total fat (0 g sat. fat), 0 mg chol., 3 mg sodium, 18 g carbo., 0 g fiber, 1 g pro.
Daily values: 3% vit. A, 40% vit. C, 5% iron.

Watermelon-Seed Ice Bowl: Line a 9-inch pie plate with plastic wrap. Sprinkle with 3 tablespoons watermelon seeds. Add ½ cup water; freeze until firm.
Pour ½ inch water in a 3-cup bowl. Freeze until firm. Remove from freezer and place a 1-cup bowl on top of the ice layer; add a little water to weight down the bowl. Remove seeded ice from the pie plate and break into pieces; place around small bowl inside the large bowl.
Pour very cold water around seeded ice pieces to fill larger bowl; freeze until firm. To

unmold, run warm water inside small bowl and on the outside of the large bowl.

*Note: Edible flowers can be purchased at many supermarkets. If picking wild edible flowers, make sure they are chemical-free.

SUMMERBERRY COOLER

30 MIN. NO FAT

Start to finish: 10 min.

For best results, keep the berries well chilled before preparing this hits-the-spot beverage.

1 cup fresh strawberries
½ cup fresh raspberries
¼ cup fresh blueberries
¾ cup frozen apple juice concentrate
1⅔ cups chilled carbonated water
1 recipe Berry Ice Cubes (see below)

1 In a blender container combine strawberries, raspberries, blueberries, and apple juice concentrate. Cover and blend until smooth. Pour mixture into pitcher and slowly stir in carbonated water. Pour over Berry Ice Cubes in tall, chilled glasses and serve immediately. Makes 4 servings.

Berry Ice Cubes: Fill 2 ice-cube trays with fresh berries; halve or quarter berries, if necessary. Add water. Freeze until firm.

Nutrition facts per serving: 96 cal., 0 g total fat, 0 mg chol., 15 mg sodium, 24 g carbo., 1 g fiber, 1 g pro.
Daily values: 27% vit. C, 1% calcium.

REALLY HOT ICED COFFEE

Prep: 15 min. ◆ Chill: 1 hr.

⅓ cup ground coffee
2 inches stick cinnamon
¼ to ½ tsp. crushed red pepper
6 pods cardamom, crushed, or
    ¼ tsp. ground cardamom
    Raw sugar or granulated
    sugar (optional)
    Ice
½ cup whipped cream, or
    desired flavored ice cream,
    such as cardamom,
    cinnamon, or vanilla
    (optional)
½ tsp. ground nutmeg
    (optional)

1 Measure coffee into filter-lined coffeemaker basket. Add the cinnamon, pepper, and car-damom. Prepare the coffee according to coffeemaker instructions. Chill for at least 1 hour. If desired, stir in sugar. Pour into ice-filled pitcher. If desired, top with whipped cream or ice cream and sprinkle with nutmeg. (Or, pour into tall, ice-filled glasses and, if desired, top with whipped cream or ice cream and sprinkle with nutmeg.) Makes 10 servings.

Nutrition facts per serving: 5 cal., 0 g total fat, 0 mg chol., 5 mg sodium, 1 g carbo., 0 g fiber, 0 g pro.

SPICED CRANBERRY TEA PUNCH

Prep: 15 min. ◆ Cook: 15 min.
Chill: 4 hr.

4 cups cold water
4 tea bags
2 cups water
2 cups white or red grape juice
2 cups cranberry juice cocktail
½ cup sugar
½ tsp. ground cinnamon
¼ tsp. ground allspice
⅛ tsp. ground cloves

◆◆◆

1 lemon, sliced
1 orange, sliced
    Ice
    Lemon and/or orange
    wedges

1 In a 4-quart Dutch oven bring 4 cups cold water to boil-ing; remove from heat. Add tea bags. Let steep for 3 to 5 minutes. Discard tea bags. Stir in 2 cups water, grape juice, cranberry juice cocktail, sugar, cinnamon, all-spice, and cloves. Bring to boil-ing; reduce heat. Simmer, uncov-ered, for 15 minutes.

2 Add lemon and orange slices to tea mixture. Cover and chill 4 hours. If desired, pour tea through a strainer into a serving pitcher or punch bowl before serving. Pour tea over ice cubes. Garnish each glass with lemon and/or orange wedges. Makes about 10 (8-ounce) servings.

Nutrition facts per serving: 109 cal., 0 g total fat, 0 mg chol., 8 mg sodium, 28 g carbo., 0 g fiber, 1 g pro.
Daily values: 55% vit. C, 1% calcium, 2% iron.

APRICOT-MINT TEA

Prep: 20 min. ◆ Chill: 4 hr.

To release the fresh mint flavor, crush leaves slightly with the back of a spoon.

4 cups cold water
10 tea bags
4 12-oz. cans apricot nectar
½ cup fresh mint leaves,
    slightly crushed
¼ cup sugar

◆◆◆

    Ice
    Fresh mint (optional)

1 In a 4-quart Dutch oven bring cold water to boiling; remove from heat. Add tea bags. Let steep for 3 to 5 minutes. Discard bags. Stir in nectar, mint, and sugar. Cover; chill 4 hours.

2 Pour tea through a strainer into a serving pitcher or punch bowl before serving. Pour tea over ice cubes. If desired, garnish with additional mint leaves. Makes about 10 (8-ounce) servings.

Nutrition facts per serving: 98 cal., 0 g total fat, 0 mg chol., 8 mg sodium, 25 g carbo., 1 g fiber, 1 g pro. *Daily values:* 19% vit. A, 5% vit. C, 1% calcium, 8% iron.

AUGUST
Harvest Happy Eaters

30-minute recipes indicated in RED.
Low-fat and no-fat recipes indicated
with a ♥.
Photographs indicated in italics.
*All new in 1998.

A zucchini invasion? An avalanche of tomatoes? You'll want to hang on to every last fruit from the garden when you can transform them into Zucchini Blini, Squash Strudel, or Chunky Homemade Salsa. Step-by-step canning tips give you fresh-tasting chopped tomatoes that are welcome year-round. The end of summer is the time to celebrate desserts that combine cake and ice cream, such as Candy-Bar Cake (a marriage of pound cake, chocolate, caramel, and ice cream), and Tropical Angel Cake (angel cake meets sherbet). Or conjure up the tropics with rum-infused Piña-Colada Upside-Down Cake.

SAUCY SQUASH OVER POLENTA

Prep: 10 min. ◆ Cook: 10 min.

1 16-oz. tube refrigerated cooked polenta (plain or with mushrooms)

◆◆◆

2 medium zucchini, quartered lengthwise and sliced ¼ inch thick
1 medium yellow summer squash, quartered lengthwise and sliced ¼ inch thick
1 Tbsp. snipped fresh basil or ½ tsp. dried basil, crushed
2 tsp. snipped fresh oregano or ½ tsp. dried oregano, crushed
1 Tbsp. olive oil or cooking oil
¾ cup chicken broth
1 Tbsp. cornstarch
½ tsp. lemon-pepper seasoning
1½ cups cherry tomatoes, quartered

1 Cut polenta into 12 rounds. Heat polenta according to package directions.

2 Meanwhile, in a large saucepan cook zucchini and yellow squash, and, if using, dried basil and oregano in oil over medium heat for 2 to 3 minutes or until vegetables are nearly crisp-tender. Combine chicken broth and cornstarch; stir into squash mixture in saucepan along with lemon-pepper seasoning and, if using, fresh herbs. Cook, stirring gently, until mixture is thickened and bubbly. Reduce heat and cook for 2 minutes more. Gently stir in quartered cherry tomatoes; heat through.

Spoon thickened vegetable mixture over the heated polenta slices. Makes 6 side-dish servings.

Nutrition facts per serving: 119 cal., 3 g total fat (0 g sat. fat), 0 mg chol., 488 mg sodium, 20 g carbo., 4 g fiber, 4 g pro. *Daily values:* 6% vit. A, 22% vit. C, 1% calcium, 3% iron.

EMERALD PANCAKES

Prep: 25 min.
Cook: 4 min. per batch

Use a leftover baked potato to get these pancakes off to a speedy start.

1 large (8 oz.) potato, baked, peeled, and shredded (1½ cups)
1½ cups shredded zucchini
1 cup shredded yellow summer squash
1 cup shredded carrots (2)
½ cup finely chopped onion
3 lightly beaten eggs
¾ cup matzo meal
¼ cup snipped fresh cilantro
¾ tsp. salt
¼ tsp. pepper

◆◆◆

Applesauce (optional)
Dairy sour cream (optional)

1 In a large mixing bowl combine potato, zucchini, yellow squash, carrots, and onion; set aside. In a large mixing bowl combine eggs, matzo meal, cilantro, salt, and pepper. Stir in vegetable mixture until combined.

2 For each pancake, spoon about ¼ cup batter onto a hot, lightly greased griddle or heavy skillet. Flatten cakes to about 3 inches in diameter. Cook over medium heat about 2 minutes on each side or until pancakes are

golden brown, turning to second sides when edges are slightly dry. If desired, serve warm with applesauce and sour cream. Makes 8 side-dish servings.

Nutrition facts per serving: 115 cal., 2 g total fat (1 g sat. fat), 80 mg chol., 231 mg sodium, 19 g carbo., 2 g fiber, 5 g pro. *Daily values:* 43% vit. A, 8% vit. C, 2% calcium, 6% iron.

ZUCCHINI BLINI

Prep: 15 min.
Cook: 2 min. per batch

½ cup cornmeal
½ cup all-purpose flour
2 tsp. baking powder
¼ tsp. salt
2 lightly beaten eggs
1 cup milk
1 cup finely shredded zucchini
3 to 4 Tbsp. finely chopped onion

◆◆◆

½ cup dairy sour cream
1½ tsp. snipped fresh dill or ½ tsp. dried dillweed
½ tsp. wasabi paste or wasabi powder
4 oz. thinly sliced smoked salmon (optional)
Capers

1 In a medium bowl combine cornmeal, flour, baking powder, and salt. In a small bowl combine eggs and milk; stir into the cornmeal mixture just until combined. Stir in the zucchini and onion just until combined. For each blini, pour about 1 tablespoon of batter onto a hot, lightly greased nonstick griddle or skillet. Cook over medium heat about 1 to 1½ minutes on each side or until golden brown, turning to second sides when surfaces are bubbly and edges are slightly dry.

2 Meanwhile, in a small bowl stir together sour cream, dill, and wasabi paste or powder. If desired, top each blini with a small slice of salmon. Dollop with sour cream mixture and add a few capers. Makes about 30.

Nutrition facts per blini: 34 cal., 1 g total fat (1 g sat. fat), 17 mg chol., 63 mg sodium, 4 g carbo., 0 g fiber, 1 g pro. *Daily values:* 2% vit. A, 1% vit. C, 3% calcium, 2% iron.

SQUASH STRUDEL

Prep: 40 min. ◆ Bake: 50 min.
Stand: 10 min.

Phyllo dough and feta cheese infuse a Greek flavor into this dish full of summer squash.

5 cups coarsely shredded
  zucchini (1½ lb.)
5 cups coarsely shredded
  yellow summer squash
  (1½ lb.)
  ◆◆◆
8 beaten eggs
2 Tbsp. snipped fresh parsley
  or 2 tsp. dried parsley
  flakes
2 cloves garlic, minced
1 Tbsp. finely chopped onion
1 Tbsp. snipped fresh dill or
  ½ tsp. dried dillweed
¼ tsp. pepper
8 oz. crumbled feta cheese
  ◆◆◆
5 sheets frozen phyllo dough,
  thawed
¼ cup margarine or butter,
  melted

1 In a large mixing bowl combine shredded zucchini, summer squash, and ½ teaspoon *salt.* Let stand 15 minutes. Place mixture in colander and squeeze to drain.

2 In same bowl combine beaten eggs, snipped parsley or parsley flakes, garlic, onion, fresh dill or dried dillweed, and pepper. Stir in squash mixture and feta cheese. Spoon evenly into an ungreased 13×9×2-inch baking pan.

3 Cut phyllo sheets in half crosswise. Lightly brush a sheet of phyllo with some of the melted margarine or butter. Place phyllo sheet on squash mixture. Top with another sheet of phyllo. Brush with more margarine. Add remaining phyllo, brushing each sheet with margarine. With a sharp knife score through phyllo, making 16 pieces. Bake in a 350° oven for 50 to 55 minutes or until a knife inserted near the center comes out clean. To prevent overbrowning, cover strudel with foil the last 10 minutes of baking. Let strudel stand 10 minutes before serving. Makes 16 side-dish servings.

Nutrition facts per serving: 132 cal., 9 g total fat (4 g sat. fat), 119 mg chol., 319 mg sodium, 5 g carbo., 1 g fiber, 6 g pro. *Daily values:* 12% vit. A, 7% vit. C, 8% calcium, 6% iron.

KALE PIE

Prep: 40 min. ◆ Bake: 25 min.
Stand: 10 min.

1 unbaked 9-inch pastry shell
  ◆◆◆
2 cups chopped fresh kale or
  spinach
1 small yellow sweet pepper,
  chopped (½ cup)
1 small onion, chopped
  (⅓ cup)
1 small carrot, shredded
  (⅓ cup)
2 cloves garlic, minced
1 Tbsp. olive oil
  ◆◆◆
1 3-oz. package cream cheese,
  cubed and softened
4 beaten eggs
½ cup milk
¼ cup finely shredded
  Parmesan cheese
¼ cup snipped fresh basil
¼ tsp. salt

1 Line unpricked pastry shell with a double thickness of foil. Bake in a 450° oven for 8 minutes. Remove foil and bake for 4 to 5 minutes more or until pastry is set. Remove from oven; reduce oven temperature to 350°.

2 Meanwhile, in a large skillet cook kale, yellow pepper, onion, carrot, and garlic in hot olive oil, covered, about 10 minutes or until kale is just tender, stirring occasionally.

3 Remove from heat; stir in cream cheese until melted. In a mixing bowl combine eggs, milk, Parmesan cheese, basil, and salt. Stir in kale mixture; spread in baked crust. Bake about 25 minutes or until set and knife inserted off-center comes out clean. Cool on wire rack about 10 minutes before cutting into wedges to serve. Makes 6 side-dish servings.

Nutrition facts per serving: 355 cal., 24 g total fat (8 g sat. fat), 163 mg chol., 337 mg sodium, 24 g carbo., 2 g fiber, 11 g pro. *Daily values:* 49% vit. A, 50% vit. C, 10% calcium, 13% iron.

SO-SWEET SQUASH PICKLES

Prep: 1¾ hr. ◆ Chill: 24 hr.

These sweet-sour specials are bursting with flavor. Try them solo or on a sandwich.

3 small yellow summer squash, sliced ½ inch thick (about 3 cups)
½ cup chopped onion
1 large red sweet pepper, cut into ¼-inch-wide strips
1 Tbsp. salt
◆◆◆
1 cup sugar
¾ cup white vinegar
¾ tsp. mustard seed
¾ tsp. celery seed
¼ tsp. ground mustard

1 In a large nonmetal bowl combine squash, onion, and sweet pepper. Sprinkle salt over vegetables; stir to combine. Cover and refrigerate for 1 hour. Drain off liquid.

2 In a 3-quart saucepan combine sugar, vinegar, mustard seed, celery seed, and ground mustard. Heat to boiling. Add squash mixture. Return to boiling; remove from heat. Ladle mixture into 2 clean pint jars. Cool 30 minutes. Cover and refrigerate at least 24 hours before serving. Store pickles in refrigerator up to 1 month. Makes 2 pints.

Nutrition facts per ¼-cup serving: 57 cal., 0 g total fat, 0 mg chol., 201 mg sodium, 15 g carbo., 0 g fiber, 0 g pro.
Daily values: 4% vit. A, 15% vit. C, 1% calcium, 1% iron.

NUT 'N' SQUASH CORN BREAD DRESSING

Prep: 20 min. ◆ Bake: 25 min.

Accompany roast poultry with this baked-in-a-dish dressing.

4 small yellow crookneck squash, chopped (4 cups)
½ cup chopped onion
½ cup chopped celery
⅓ cup butter
◆◆◆
4 cups crumbled corn bread
½ cup chopped pecans, toasted
1 tsp. dried leaf sage, crushed
¼ tsp. salt
¼ tsp. pepper
⅛ tsp. ground nutmeg
1 beaten egg
2 to 6 Tbsp. chicken broth

1 In a large skillet cook squash, onion, and celery in hot butter until onion is tender but not brown.

2 Remove from heat; stir in corn bread, pecans, sage, salt, pepper, and nutmeg. Add egg and enough chicken broth to moisten. Turn into a greased 2-quart square baking dish.

3 Bake, uncovered, in a 350° oven for 25 to 30 minutes or until heated through. Makes 6 side-dish servings.

Nutrition facts per serving: 362 cal., 22 g total fat (8 g sat. fat), 89 mg chol., 665 mg sodium, 36 g carbo., 2 g fiber, 7 g pro.
Daily values: 17% vit. A, 10% vit. C, 17% calcium, 16% iron.

POLENTA WITH SPINACH

30 MIN.

Prep: 20 min. ◆ Cook: 10 min.

Serve the vegetable mixture over slices of lightly browned polenta.

1 16-oz. tube refrigerated cooked polenta (desired flavor)
2 Tbsp. olive oil
◆◆◆
⅓ cup chopped onion
3 cups shredded fresh spinach
1 Tbsp. white balsamic vinegar
2 medium tomatoes, seeded and finely chopped
1 Tbsp. snipped fresh basil
◆◆◆
¼ cup finely shredded Parmesan cheese
Cracked black pepper

1 Slice polenta ½ inch thick. In a large skillet cook polenta in 1 tablespoon of the oil over medium-high heat about 6 minutes or until lightly browned. Remove to a serving platter; keep warm.

2 In same skillet cook onion in remaining oil until tender. Add spinach. Cook and stir about 2 minutes or until spinach is slightly wilted. Add vinegar; toss to coat. Stir in tomatoes and basil.

3 Serve spinach mixture over polenta. Sprinkle with shredded Parmesan cheese and cracked pepper. Makes 4 side-dish servings.

Nutrition facts per serving: 222 cal., 9 g total fat (1 g sat. fat), 5 mg chol., 562 mg sodium, 29 g carbo., 5 g fiber, 8 g pro.
Daily values: 35% vit. A, 47% vit. C, 9% calcium, 11% iron.

VEGGIE-STUFFED CHICKEN BREASTS

Prep: 35 min. ◆ Bake: 55 min.

6 medium bone-in chicken
    breast halves (about 3 lb.)
½ cup finely chopped
    mushrooms
¼ cup thinly sliced green onion
1 Tbsp. margarine or butter
1 cup shredded zucchini or
    yellow summer squash
½ cup shredded carrot
1 Tbsp. snipped fresh basil or
    1 tsp. dried basil, crushed
1 tsp. lemon-pepper seasoning
1½ cups crumbled corn bread
¼ cup grated Parmesan cheese
2 Tbsp. coarsely chopped
    almonds, toasted
1 beaten egg

1 Rinse chicken; pat dry. Loosen the skin on one side of each breast half, leaving other sides attached to form a pocket; set aside. In a large skillet cook mushrooms and green onion in hot margarine for 2 minutes. Add squash, carrot, basil, and lemon-pepper seasoning. Cook and stir for 2 minutes more. Remove from heat; stir in corn bread, Parmesan, almonds, and egg until combined. Stuff each chicken pocket with about ⅓ cup of the stuffing mixture. Place chicken, skin side up, in a 3-quart rectangular baking dish. Bake, uncovered, in a 375° oven for 55 to 60 minutes or until chicken is tender and no pink remains. Makes 6 servings.

Nutrition facts per serving: 246 cal., 10 g total fat (3 g sat. fat), 106 mg chol., 474 mg sodium, 11 g carbo., 1 g fiber, 27 g pro.
Daily values: 33% vit. A, 6% vit. C, 11% calcium, 11% iron.

HERB-CURED PORK PLATTER

Prep: 15 min. ◆ Marinate: 24 hr.
Grill: 1 hr.

See the photograph on page 160.

1 Tbsp. snipped fresh thyme
    or ¾ tsp. dried thyme,
    crushed
1 Tbsp. snipped fresh sage or
    ¾ tsp. dried sage, crushed
1 Tbsp. snipped fresh
    rosemary or ¾ tsp. dried
    rosemary, crushed
2 cloves garlic, minced
1½ tsp. coarsely ground black
    pepper
1 to 1½ tsp. coarse salt
½ tsp. crushed red pepper
1 2- to 3-lb. boneless pork
    top-loin roast (single loin)
    ◆ ◆ ◆
1 large pineapple
1 Tbsp. cooking oil
    ◆ ◆ ◆
1 recipe Savory Black Beans
    (see right)

1 In a small bowl combine thyme, sage, rosemary, garlic, black pepper, salt, and crushed red pepper. Rub onto pork loin; place in baking dish. Cover tightly; refrigerate 24 hours.

2 In a grill with a cover, arrange preheated coals around a drip pan; test for medium-slow heat above the pan (see Testing Temperature, page 180). Insert a meat thermometer into the center of meat. Place meat on grill rack directly over drip pan, not coals. Cover; grill 1 to 1¼ hours or until meat thermometer registers 160°.

3 Meanwhile, to prepare pineapple, cut lengthwise into 4 to 8 wedges, leaving leaves on fruit. Cut away center core. The last 15 minutes of grilling the meat, brush pineapple with oil and place directly over coals. Grill, turning occasionally, about 15 minutes or until tender. To serve, loosen pineapple peel by cutting between peel and fruit. Slice pork; arrange slices on platter with pineapple and Savory Black Beans. Serves 6 to 8.

Nutrition facts per serving with Savory Black Beans: 407 cal., 21 g total fat (5 g sat. fat), 76 mg chol., 646 mg sodium, 32 g carbo., 7 g fiber, 30 g pro.
Daily values: 6% vit. A, 46% vit. C, 4% calcium, 22% iron.

SAVORY BLACK BEANS

Start to finish: 15 min.

See the photograph on page 160.

2 15-oz. cans black beans
1 clove garlic, minced
1 tsp. ground cumin
1 medium avocado, halved,
    seeded, peeled, and cubed
½ cup crumbled feta cheese,
    crumbled semifirm goat
    cheese, or shredded
    Monterey Jack cheese
1 small tomato, seeded and
    chopped

1 Drain and rinse 1 of the cans of black beans. In a medium saucepan combine both the drained and undrained black beans, garlic, and cumin. Heat through, stirring occasionally, being careful not to mash beans. Just before serving, place beans in serving bowl; sprinkle with avocado, cheese, and chopped tomato. Serve with Herb-Cured Pork Platter. Makes 6 to 8 servings.

TESTING TEMPERATURE

When grilling, to test the temperature of coals on the grill, carefully hold your hand, palm side down, above coals in the same location you plan to place the food for cooking. Count "one thousand one, one thousand two," etc., for as long as you can hold your hand there.

If you need to remove your hand after:

◆ 2 seconds, the coals are hot.
◆ 3 seconds, the coals are medium-hot.
◆ 4 seconds, the coals are medium.
◆ 5 seconds, the coals are medium-slow.
◆ 6 seconds, the coals are slow.

STEAK-LOVER'S PLATTER

Prep: 30 min. ◆ Marinate: 4 to 6 hr.
Grill: 14 min.

A backyard dinner for hearty appetites.

½ cup cider vinegar
¼ cup dark beer or dark or amber nonalcoholic beer
5 Tbsp. snipped fresh marjoram or 3 tsp. dried marjoram, crushed
2 Tbsp. olive oil or salad oil
1 clove garlic, minced
2 lb. boneless beef top-sirloin steak, 1¼ to 1½ inches thick

◆◆◆

3 medium baking potatoes, cut lengthwise into 8 wedges (about 1 lb. total)

4 small zucchini, halved lengthwise (about 1 lb. total)
3 medium yellow, orange, green, or red sweet peppers, seeded and cut into 1-inch-wide rings
2 Tbsp. olive oil or cooking oil

◆◆◆

1 recipe Onion Sauce (see below right)

1 In a bowl mix together vinegar, beer, 2 tablespoons of the fresh marjoram or 2 teaspoons of the dried marjoram, the first 2 tablespoons oil, garlic, ½ teaspoon *salt,* and ½ teaspoon *black pepper.* Place steak in a self-sealing plastic bag or shallow glass baking dish large enough to hold the meat flat. Add vinegar-beer mixture. Close bag, or if using a baking dish, cover tightly with plastic wrap. Marinate the meat in the refrigerator for 4 to 6 hours, turning meat once or twice.

2 In a medium saucepan cook potato wedges, covered, in boiling water for 4 minutes; drain. In a large bowl stir together potato wedges, zucchini halves, and sweet pepper rings. In a small bowl stir together remaining 2 tablespoons oil, 1 tablespoon of the fresh marjoram or 1 teaspoon of the dried marjoram, ¼ teaspoon *salt,* and ¼ teaspoon *black pepper;* sprinkle seasoning mixture over vegetables. Toss to coat.

3 Drain meat; discard marinade. Arrange meat, potatoes, zucchini, and sweet peppers on greased rack of an uncovered heated grill. Grill directly over

medium coals (see Testing Temperature, left). Allow 14 to 18 minutes for medium-rare meat or 18 to 22 minutes for medium meat, or cook meat until desired doneness, turning meat and vegetables once. Meanwhile, prepare Onion Sauce.

4 Carve beef across grain into ¼-inch slices. Remove beef to a platter and arrange potatoes, zucchini, and peppers around meat.

5 Drizzle with half the Onion Sauce; pass remaining sauce. Sprinkle with remaining fresh marjoram, if using. Serves 6.

Note: If all the food won't fit on your grill at the same time, cook it in 2 batches, vegetables first. If vegetables get too cool while remainder of food is cooking, rewarm them on the grill while you slice the meat.

Nutrition facts per serving with Onion Sauce: 510 cal., 23 g total fat (6 g sat. fat), 101 mg chol., 445 mg sodium, 34 g carbo., 2 g fiber, 39 g pro.
Daily values: 38% vit. A, 165% vit. C, 4% calcium, 41% iron.

ONION SAUCE

Start to finish: 15 min.

1 cup chopped onion
1 clove garlic, minced
1 Tbsp. margarine or butter
½ cup dark beer or dark or amber nonalcoholic beer
½ cup beef broth
1 Tbsp. Worcestershire sauce
1 Tbsp. cornstarch

1 In a small saucepan cook onion and garlic in hot margarine or butter over medium heat for 4 minutes or until onions are tender but not brown. In a small bowl gradually stir beer, broth, and Worcestershire sauce into cornstarch. Add to saucepan. Cook and stir over medium heat until thickened and bubbly. Cook and stir 2 minutes more. Remove from heat. Serve with Steak-Lover's Platter. Makes 1⅓ cups.

SUMMER SHRIMP AND VEGGIE BOIL

Start to finish: 45 min.

Skewering the shrimp before boiling allows you to easily remove them from the pot and serve. (See the photograph on page 161.)

1   lb. fresh or frozen large shrimp, peeled and deveined
4   12-inch bamboo skewers
2   Tbsp. dried dillweed
3   bay leaves
4   cloves garlic
1   tsp. cracked black pepper
◆◆◆
8   cups water
⅓   cup white vinegar
1   lemon, cut into quarters
1   recipe Lemon Dill Sauce (see right)
◆◆◆
3   leeks, cleaned and cut into 2-inch pieces
8   baby artichokes, cleaned and halved, or one 9-oz. package frozen artichoke hearts
2   cups packaged peeled baby carrots
1   lb. small new potatoes
4   ears fresh corn (shucked and cut into 6-inch portions, if desired)

1 Thread shrimp onto bamboo skewers. Set aside. Place dillweed, bay leaves, garlic, and pepper in the center of an 8-inch square piece of 100 percent cotton cheesecloth. Tie closed with kitchen string.

2 In a 12-quart Dutch oven combine water, vinegar, lemon quarters, herb bundle, and 1 teaspoon *salt;* cover and bring to boiling. Meanwhile, prepare Lemon Dill Sauce. Set sauce aside and keep warm.

3 Once water is boiling, add leeks, fresh artichokes (if using), carrots, and potatoes gradually to avoid splashing. Return to boiling; reduce heat. Cover and simmer 10 minutes. Add corn and, if using, frozen artichokes. Cover and simmer 5 minutes or until vegetables are just tender. Add shrimp; cover and cook 1 to 3 minutes more or until shrimp turn opaque. Stir occasionally. Remove shrimp skewers with tongs. Carefully drain vegetables in a colander. Discard lemon quarters and herb bundle.

4 To serve, arrange skewered shrimp and vegetables on a large platter; drizzle with a small amount of the Lemon Dill Sauce. Pass remaining Lemon Dill Sauce. Makes 4 servings.

Nutrition facts per serving with Lemon Dill Sauce: 447 cal., 15 g total fat (7 g sat. fat), 162 mg chol., 992 mg sodium, 65 g carbo., 11 g fiber, 22 g pro.
Daily values: 177% vit. A, 56% vit. C, 9% calcium, 41% iron.

◆◆◆
Summer Shrimp and Veggie Boil (see left)
◆◆◆
Lemon Dill Sauce (see below)
◆◆◆
Crusty hard rolls
◆◆◆
Tropical Angel Cake (see page 191)

LEMON DILL SAUCE

Start to finish: 8 min.

¼   cup butter
1½ tsp. cornstarch
½   cup reduced-sodium chicken broth
½   tsp. finely shredded lemon peel
2   Tbsp. lemon juice
2 to 3 Tbsp. snipped fresh dillweed or 2 tsp. dried dillweed

1 In a small saucepan melt butter over medium heat. Stir in cornstarch. Stir in chicken broth until well combined. Cook and stir until thickened and bubbly. Cook and stir for 2 minutes more. Stir in lemon peel, lemon juice, and dillweed. Cover and remove from heat. Serve with Summer Shrimp and Veggie Boil. Makes about ¾ cup sauce.

Menu

Sizzling Salmon with Minted Lentils (see below)

◆◆◆

Cucumber Sauce (see right)

◆◆◆

Rye rolls

◆◆◆

Blueberry Citrus Cake (see page 191)

SIZZLING SALMON WITH MINTED LENTILS

Prep: 45 min. ◆ Chill: 2 hr.
Cook: 20 min. ◆ Grill: 6 to 9 min.

Make the Cucumber Sauce ahead so it's ready to use with beans and lentils.

1 **recipe Cucumber Sauce (see top right)**
4 **6- to 8-oz. fresh or frozen salmon steaks**

◆◆◆

12 **oz. green beans or long beans**

◆◆◆

1 **14½-oz. can reduced-sodium chicken broth**
⅔ **cup dry lentils, rinsed and drained**

◆◆◆

Salt and pepper

◆◆◆

Lemon wedges (optional)
Mint sprigs (optional)

1 Prepare Cucumber Sauce; cover and chill. Thaw fish, if frozen. Rinse fish; pat dry with paper towels.

2 In a large saucepan bring 8 cups *lightly salted water* to boiling. Add beans. Cook, covered, for 4 minutes or until crisp-tender. Drain beans well. In a medium mixing bowl combine the cooked beans with ½ cup of the Cucumber Sauce. Set aside while preparing lentils and salmon.

3 In a medium saucepan bring broth and lentils to boiling; reduce heat. Cover and simmer for 20 to 25 minutes or until lentils are tender. Drain and discard any liquid. Return lentils to saucepan; stir in half of the remaining Cucumber Sauce (about 1 cup); set aside.

4 Sprinkle salmon with salt and pepper. Grill salmon on greased rack of an uncovered grill directly over medium coals (see Testing Temperature, page 180) for 6 to 9 minutes or until fish just flakes easily with a fork, turning halfway through grilling time. (Or, place fish on the greased, unheated rack of a broiler pan. Broil 4 inches from the heat for 6 to 9 minutes or until fish just flakes easily with a fork.)

5 To serve, place lentil mixture in a serving bowl; place bowl on platter. Arrange bean mixture and salmon on platter. Serve with Cucumber Sauce. If desired, garnish with lemon wedges and mint sprigs. Makes 4 servings.

Nutrition facts per serving with Cucumber Sauce: 397 cal., 14 g total fat (1 g sat. fat), 31 mg chol., 308 mg sodium, 34 g carbo., 6 g fiber, 37 g pro.
Daily values: 13% vit. A, 51% vit. C, 7% calcium, 44% iron.

CUCUMBER SAUCE

Start to finish: 15 min.

2 **medium cucumbers (about 7 inches long), seeded and chopped**
¼ **cup snipped fresh parsley**
¼ **cup lemon juice**
2 **Tbsp. salad oil**
2 **Tbsp. thinly sliced green onion**
2 **Tbsp. snipped fresh mint**
¼ **tsp. salt**

1 In a medium bowl combine cucumber, parsley, lemon juice, salad oil, green onion, mint, and salt. Cover and chill at least 2 hours. (Mixture may be made the night before and chilled, if desired.) Serve alongside Sizzling Salmon with Minted Lentils. Makes about 2½ cups.

WELCOME-HOME APRICOT-GINGER CHICKEN DINNER

Start to finish: 1½ hr.

Use precut chicken tenderloins and quick-cooking rice to save time. (See the photograph on page 161.)

1 **recipe Honeydew and Apple Salad (see page 183)**
1½ **lb. skinless, boneless chicken breast halves**

◆◆◆

3 **Tbsp. chunky peanut butter**
3 **Tbsp. apricot jam**

◆◆◆

1½ **cups shredded coconut**
¾ **cup packaged cornflake crumbs (or 2 cups cornflakes, crushed)**

1 Tbsp. curry powder
1 tsp. ground ginger
⅛ to ¼ tsp. ground red pepper

❖❖❖

5 cups hot cooked rice
¼ tsp. ground cinnamon
¾ cup snipped chutney
3 Tbsp. orange juice

1 Prepare Honeydew and Apple Salad; cover and chill. Rinse chicken; pat dry with paper towels. Cut into 1½-inch strips; place in a medium bowl.

2 In a small saucepan stir together peanut butter and jam. Melt over low heat. Add to chicken; toss to coat.

3 In a plastic bag or shallow dish combine the coconut, cornflake crumbs, curry powder, ginger, and ground red pepper. Add chicken, a few pieces at a time, and shake or toss to coat. Place chicken in a lightly greased 15×10×1-inch baking pan. Bake in a 400° oven for 8 minutes. Turn chicken pieces. Bake 8 minutes more or until chicken is tender and no longer pink.

4 Mound cooked rice in center of a platter. Sprinkle rice with cinnamon. Arrange chicken and Honeydew and Apple Salad around the rice. Stir together chutney and orange juice. Spoon into a small bowl for dipping. Makes 6 servings.

Nutrition facts per serving with Honeydew and Apple Salad: 604 cal., 14 g total fat (8 g sat. fat), 59 mg chol., 303 mg sodium, 92 g carbo., 7 g fiber, 28 g pro.
Daily values: 17% vit. A, 57% vit. C, 4% calcium, 26% iron.

30 MIN.

HONEYDEW AND APPLE SALAD

Start to finish: 20 min.

See the photograph on page 161.

½ medium honeydew melon, peeled, seeded, and cut into thin slices
2 medium tart apples, cored, halved lengthwise, and cut into bite-size pieces
2 medium peaches, pitted and cut into strips
1 cup golden or red raspberries

❖❖❖

2 Tbsp. low-fat vanilla yogurt
2 Tbsp. apricot jam
1 Tbsp. snipped chutney

1 In a large bowl toss together honeydew, apples, peaches, and the raspberries.

2 For dressing, stir together yogurt, jam, and chutney. Add to fruit mixture; toss to coat. Cover and chill until serving time. Serve with Welcome-Home Apricot-Ginger Chicken. Serves 6.

BURGERS BORRACHOS

Prep: 15 min. ♦ Marinate: up to 24 hr.
Grill: 14 to 18 min.

¼ cup finely chopped onion
4 cloves garlic, minced
2 Tbsp. tomato paste
½ tsp. salt
½ tsp. pepper
½ tsp. dried rosemary, crushed
¼ tsp. ground allspice
1½ lb. lean ground beef

1½ cups beer
6 hamburger buns, toasted
1 recipe Mustard Sauce (see below)
Shredded lettuce (optional)
Onion slices (optional)

1 In a large mixing bowl combine onion, garlic, tomato paste, salt, pepper, rosemary, and allspice. Add ground beef; mix well.

2 Shape mixture into six ¾-inch-thick patties. Place in a shallow baking dish. Pour beer over burgers, reserving 1 tablespoon beer for Mustard Sauce. Cover dish tightly with plastic wrap. Marinate in refrigerator up to 24 hours; turn burgers once.

3 Remove burgers from refrigerator; pour off any excess liquid and discard. Grill burgers on the grill rack of an uncovered grill directly over medium coals (see Testing Temperature, page 180) for 14 to 18 minutes or until no pink remains, turning once halfway through grilling time.

4 Serve on toasted buns with Mustard Sauce. If desired, serve with shredded lettuce and onion slices. Makes 6 servings.

Mustard Sauce: In a bowl combine 3 tablespoons stone-ground mustard with the reserved 1 tablespoon beer and ¾ teaspoon Worcestershire sauce. Cover; chill until needed. Serve with Burgers Borrachos.

Nutrition facts per serving: 324 cal., 13 g total fat (5 g sat. fat), 71 mg chol., 547 mg sodium, 24 g carbo., 1 g fiber, 24 g pro.
Daily values: 1% vit. A, 8% vit. C, 4% calcium, 23% iron.

A HEALTHY DASH OF SPICE

The development of modern drugs came from the need to mimic helpful compounds already found in nature.

Long before pills and shots, the family medicine chest was indistinguishable from the pantry. In a way, so is today's medicine chest. According to the American Pharmaceutical Association, about 25 to 50 percent of prescription drugs contain at least one component derived from or modeled after a known plant.

Herbal remedies have seen more scientific scrutiny than skeptics might realize. The modern pharmacy was derived from herbal traditions and the need to mimic these helpful natural compounds that were hard to find or utilize. Although some plants used for drugs are rare denizens of tropical rain forests, many common ones—sitting in your pantry as spices—have value beyond boosting flavor. A number of studies, including some human trials, indicate that specific medicinal benefits may be tucked away in certain spices and herbs.

SPICES AS MEDICINE

As a remedy, there are no established doses for any one herb or spice—science still needs to catch up with anecdotal and cultural evidence. Differences between people, the varying qualities of individual plants, and other factors make it hard for researchers to reach precise conclusions. "Spices and herbs contain thousands of compounds each and are chemically complicated," notes E. John Staba, professor emeritus of pharmacognosy at the University of Minnesota. "People shouldn't jump to conclusions that aren't based on solid research. Certainly plants can do good things, but some spices in large amounts can be toxic. In moderation, herbs and spices are useful and have benefit."

The following are some common spices and what we know so far about their benefits, plus tips for ways to use these common spices.

ALLSPICE, CINNAMON, CLOVES, MACE, AND NUTMEG

These apple-pie spices contain potent antioxidants, known to protect against cancer and heart disease.

They also have an ability to fight microorganisms, such as E. coli, listeria, staphylococcus, and streptococcus; and fungus, such as Candida albicans. This quality led to the early use of these spices in dry rubs for meat and poultry, although they are by no means substitutes for good kitchen hygiene and safe handling.

Clove oil has an extensive track record of use by dentists, mainly for easing pain. In some cases, clove oil ointment eases arthritis inflammation, and some clove compounds act as blood thinners and antihistamines. Nutmeg stopped migraines in one study, and in another it increased the duration of deep sleep in animals.

Add these spices, freshly ground, to smoothies, stewed fruits, or fruit salads.

FULL OF GINGER

Recorded use of ginger as a medicinal in China, India, and the Middle East stretches back 5,000 years. Ginger contains formidable cancer-fighting antioxidants, and reduces factors that cause blood clots and arterial plaque to form. This spice also shows promise as a reducer of cholesterol.

Ginger also appears to enhance insulin, which could lead to its eventual use in diets for persons with noninsulin-dependent diabetes. In some cases, this pungent root offers relief in controlling nausea for patients undergoing minor surgery and chemotherapy, and for nausea associated with pregnancy.

To help ease minor bouts of nausea, gently simmer 1 inch of fresh ginger—peeled and thinly sliced—in 2 cups of water for 5 minutes. Let steep for another 10 minutes; strain and sip.

CARDAMOM, CORIANDER, CUMIN, SAFFRON, AND TURMERIC

The flavorings used in Indian cuisine guard against cancer of the digestive system, and the phytoestrogens in turmeric are thought to protect against breast cancer. In one animal study, cardamom was an

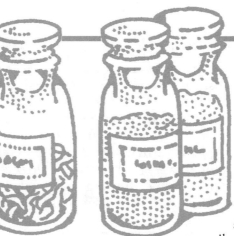

effective anticonvulsant. These spices also inhibit bacteria, one reason they were historically used to preserve foods.

Try these spices simmered in hot beverages or freshly ground in dips and spreads.

PASS THE PEPPER, PLEASE

One of the most common of spices, black pepper has been effective in stemming tumor development and protecting against certain cancers because of its concentration of antioxidants. Animal studies show black pepper to be effective against certain types of seizures.

Capsaicin, the component that makes hot chili peppers hot, is one of the most studied—and most useful—spice compounds. Chilies are loaded with phytochemicals. Also, a wealth of scientific data shows that hot chili peppers can soothe digestion, ease pain, and destroy bacteria.

In countries with hotter climes, spicy foods are considered a great way to beat the heat. The foods provide a sense of coolness to the skin by raising perspiration, and give a greater feeling of satiety by making the stomach feel fuller with smaller amounts of food.

In a recent experiment, small amounts of hot red pepper in food reduced the risk of aspiration pneumonia in elderly persons. The capsaicin in red pepper also is useful as a painkiller. Many pharmacies sell capsaicin-containing ointments to relieve the pain and inflammation of arthritis and other inflammatory diseases as well as simple muscle pain from exercise or trauma.

Peppers are versatile enough to use in a variety of dishes, from chili to salsas.

BASIL, THYME, AND SAGE

The herbs in your pizza and pasta dishes also contain phytoestrogens. Preliminary studies further reveal that extracts of basil and thyme have natural blood-sugar-lowering effects.

In Europe, one successful over-the-counter cold and cough remedy relies on extract of thyme for effectively treating symptoms of bronchitis. Thyme oil also inhibits H. pylori—those nasty bacteria that often are associated with stomach ulcers.

Add snipped herbs to salads, soups, and sandwiches. To ease head and chest cold discomfort, toss fresh or dried sage and mint leaves into boiling water and carefully (to avoid burns) inhale the steam.

ROSEMARY AND FENNEL

Phytochemical-rich rosemary has been researched for abilities ranging from cancer and tumor prevention to killing bacteria and combating the human immunodeficiency virus that causes AIDS. Fennel also is a source for phytochemicals; its seeds have long been used to ease nausea.

Rosemary and fennel seed add a wonderfully fresh flavor to homemade breads. Chewing lightly toasted fennel seeds after a large meal helps to ease digestion.

THE SPICE IS RIGHT

Should you want to try herbal remedies for a particular illness or condition, Dr. Staba recommends seeking out only qualified, licensed health professionals who have studied both mainstream and alternative medicines, and who maintain an objective approach. "Nothing," cautions Dr. Staba, "should be used as medicine unless there is a great assurance that it is risk-free or has a risk-benefit ratio highly in favor of the individual for whom it has been prescribed."

SUPERMARKET PLATTER

Prep: 15 min. ◆ Bake: 20 min.

Pull together a quick meal from the salad bar and deli counter.

- ½ **tsp. sugar**
- ½ **tsp. chili powder**
- ½ **tsp. lemon-pepper seasoning**
- ¼ **tsp. garlic powder**
- ¼ **tsp. salt**
- ¼ **tsp. paprika**
- 1 **purchased whole roasted chicken (2 to 2½ lb.)**
- 1 **Tbsp. cooking oil**

◆◆◆

- 1 **lb. purchased (from deli) marinated vegetable salad in vinaigrette dressing (about 2½ cups)**
- 2 **Tbsp. snipped fresh basil**
- ¼ **tsp. black pepper**
- 1 **lb. purchased pasta salad with vinaigrette dressing (about 2½ cups)**

◆◆◆

- 2 **or 3 nectarines or peeled peaches, pitted and halved or quartered lengthwise**

1 In a small bowl stir together sugar, chili powder, lemon-pepper seasoning, garlic powder, salt, and paprika; set aside. Cut chicken into quarters; discard backbone. Brush chicken with oil. Sprinkle sugar mixture evenly over chicken. Place quartered chicken on baking sheet, skin side up. Bake in a 350° oven for 20 minutes or until heated through.

2 Meanwhile, drain marinated vegetables, reserving dressing in a small bowl. Add basil and black pepper to dressing; set dressing aside. Combine pasta salad and marinated vegetables; stir gently.

3 To serve, arrange pasta salad mixture in a bowl and place on small serving platter. Place chicken on platter alongside salad. Place small platter on larger platter. Arrange the fruit on large platter; drizzle with 2 tablespoons of the reserved dressing. Drizzle remaining dressing over salad mixture. Makes 4 servings.

Nutrition facts per serving: 734 cal., 46 g total fat (9 g sat. fat), 133 mg chol., 969 mg sodium, 70 g carbo., 6 g fiber, 39 g pro. *Daily values:* 213% vit. A, 150% vit. C, 6% calcium, 25% iron.

TURKEY TENDERS WITH SWEET-PEPPER-CITRUS SALSA

Prep: 15 min. ◆ Marinate: 2 to 4 hr. Grill: 12 to 15 min.

- 6 **turkey breast tenderloin steaks (about ½ inch thick)* (about 1½ lb. total)**

◆◆◆

- ⅓ **cup olive oil**
- ¼ **cup lemon juice**
- 1 **tsp. finely shredded orange peel**
- ¼ **cup orange juice**
- 4 **cloves garlic, minced**
- ¼ **tsp. salt**
- ¼ **tsp. pepper**

◆◆◆

- 1 **recipe Sweet-Pepper-Citrus Salsa (see right)**
  Bibb lettuce (optional)

1 Place turkey in a heavy plastic bag set in a large mixing bowl.

2 For marinade, in a small bowl combine oil, lemon juice, orange peel and juice, garlic, salt, and pepper; pour over turkey in

bag. Close bag; turn turkey to coat well. Marinate in refrigerator 2 to 4 hours; turn occasionally.

3 Remove turkey from bag, reserving marinade. Grill turkey directly over medium coals for 12 to 15 minutes or until no pink remains, brushing with marinade during the first 6 minutes and turning once. Serve with Sweet-Pepper-Citrus Salsa. If desired, garnish with lettuce. Serves 6.

*Note: Precut turkey breast tenderloin steaks are available in some areas. If you find only the large whole tenderloins, slice them horizontally into ½-inch-thick steaks.

Nutrition facts per serving: 206 cal., 10 g total fat (2 g sat. fat), 50 mg chol., 107 mg sodium, 6 g carbo., 1 g fiber, 22 g pro. *Daily values:* 11% vit. A, 122% vit. C, 2% calcium, 10% iron.

SWEET-PEPPER-CITRUS SALSA

Prep: 10 min. ◆ Chill: 30 min.

- 1 **7-oz. jar roasted red sweet peppers, drained and chopped**
- 1 **orange, peeled, seeded, and cut up**
- 2 **sliced green onions**
- 1 **Tbsp. snipped fresh basil or 1 tsp. dried basil, crushed**
- 2 **Tbsp. balsamic vinegar**

1 Combine all ingredients. Cover; chill. Makes 1½ cups salsa.

Nutrition facts per ¼-cup serving: 16 cal., 0 g total fat (0 g sat. fat), 0 mg chol., 1 mg sodium, 4 g carbo., 1 g fiber, 0 g pro. *Daily values:* 11% vit. A, 110% vit. C, 3% iron.

TERRIFIC TOMATOES

When your garden or farmer's market becomes flush with summer-fresh tomatoes, it's time to get out those canning jars, buy new lids, and brush up on the latest canning techniques. You'll love having garden-ripened tomatoes year-round to enjoy in soups, stews, or sauces.

EQUIPMENT BASICS

♦ A large, deep kettle with a lid and a rack or a basket (or any large kettle that's deep enough to allow 1 inch of water to boil freely over the jar tops).

♦ Clean quart or pint canning jars. Commercial mayonnaise jars are not recommended.

♦ Purchased canning lids and screw bands.

♦ A canning funnel.

♦ Clean kitchen towels and hot pads.

♦ A jar lifter.

TOMATO PREPARATION

♦ Select firm, plump, fully ripe, unbruised tomatoes that are about the same size.

♦ Plan on 2½ to 3½ pounds of tomatoes per quart of canned product.

♦ Wash tomatoes thoroughly to remove any dirt.

♦ Canned tomatoes must be peeled. Dip the tomatoes in boiling water for about 30 seconds. (The water must be kept at or near the boiling point.) Remove tomatoes with a long slotted spoon and dip them quickly in cold water.

♦ Peel and core the washed tomatoes with a small sharp knife.

♦ Cut large tomatoes in quarters or eighths.

♦ If desired, use a spoon to scrape out the excess seeds from the tomatoes.

STEP-BY-STEP CANNING

To make 6 quarts or 12 pints, you'll need lemon juice or citric acid, granulated sugar, salt, and 15 pounds of tomatoes.

♦ In an 8- to 10-quart kettle, place peeled, chopped tomatoes and just enough water to cover the tomatoes.

♦ Bring to boiling, stirring constantly but gently. Boil gently for 5 minutes, stirring occasionally.

♦ Add 2 tablespoons bottled lemon juice or ½ teaspoon citric acid to each hot, clean quart jar. For pint jars, use 1 tablespoon bottled lemon juice or ¼ teaspoon citric acid (do not substitute ascorbic acid for the citric acid).

♦ Ladle tomatoes and some of the cooking liquid into the hot jars, leaving a ½-inch headspace.

♦ Add 1 teaspoon salt to each quart jar or ½ teaspoon to each pint jar. You also can add 1 teaspoon sugar to each quart jar or ½ teaspoon to each pint jar for flavor.

♦ Place the lids on the jars following manufacturer's directions.

♦ Fill canner half full of water; heat to 180° on high heat.

♦ Set each filled jar into the canner, making sure jars don't touch. Add additional hot water until water is 1 inch over jar tops. Cover; bring to a vigorous boil. Reduce heat to maintain a gentle boil.

♦ Process jars in a boiling water bath allowing 45 minutes* for quarts and 40 minutes* for pints (start timing when water boils after adding jars).

Note: For high altitudes, add an additional 2 minutes of cooking time for every 1,000 feet above sea level.

TIPS FOR PERFECT CANNED TOMATOES

♦ Use a canning funnel when packing each jar.

♦ Wipe the rims of the filled jars with a damp cloth before putting on the lids.

♦ Check seals after cooling. Press the center of each lid. It is sealed if the dip in the lid holds. If the dip bounces, it isn't sealed. (Reheat and reprocess the contents. Use a clean jar and a new lid.)

♦ Dry jars. Remove screw bands after 24 hours. Label and store in a cool (50° to 70°), dry, dark place.

CANNING TIPS

◆ Wash canning jars in hot, sudsy water; rinse well. Pour boiling water over jars. Allow jars to stand in the water until you're ready to fill them.

◆ For canning, use a large, deep kettle with a lid and a rack or basket to hold the jars. Any large kettle will work if it's deep enough for 1 inch of water to boil freely over the jar tops.

◆ Use a canning funnel set atop the canning jar to make filling the jars easier.

◆ Wipe the rims of the jars with a damp cloth to remove any food particles so that jar will seal.

◆ Place a lid on each jar. Screw a band onto each jar following the manufacturer's directions.

◆ Fill canner half full of water; heat over high heat. Set each filled jar into the canner; make sure jars don't touch. Add more hot water to reach 1 inch over jar tops. Process the jars for the time specified in the recipe. Remove jars from canner and place them on a towel to cool.

◆ After cooling, press the center of each lid. The jar is sealed if the dip in the lid holds. If the lid bounces, it isn't sealed. (Reprocess using a clean jar and a new lid.)

◆ Wipe jars and lids. Remove screw bands after 24 hours. Store in a cool (50° to 70°), dry, dark place.

CHUNKY HOMEMADE SALSA

NO FAT

Prep: 1 hr. ◆ Cook: 45 min.
Process: 35 min.

For a spicier version, use the poblano and serrano chili peppers.

20 red medium tomatoes (7 lb.)
10 fresh Anaheim chili peppers or poblano chili peppers, seeded and chopped* (about 3 cups)
3 fresh jalapeño peppers or serrano chili peppers, seeded and chopped* (about ⅓ cup)
2 cups coarsely chopped onion
½ cup snipped fresh cilantro or parsley
5 cloves garlic, minced
½ cup vinegar
1 Tbsp. sugar
1 tsp. salt
1 tsp. black pepper

1 Peel, seed, and coarsely chop tomatoes (you should have about 14 cups). Place tomatoes in a large colander; let drain 30 minutes. Place tomatoes in an 8-quart Dutch oven. Bring to boiling; reduce heat. Simmer, uncovered, for 45 to 50 minutes or until thickened (consistency of chunky salsa); stir frequently. Add remaining ingredients. Return to boiling. Remove from heat.

To can salsa: Ladle mixture into hot, clean pint jars, leaving a ½-inch headspace. Place lids on jars following manufacturer's directions. Process pint jars in a boiling water bath (see Canning Tips, left) for 35 minutes (start timing when water boils after adding jars).

To freeze salsa: Prepare salsa as directed except after removing from heat, set the Dutch oven or kettle of tomato mixture in a large sink of ice water to cool quickly. When cooled, spoon salsa into freezer-safe containers; leave ½-inch headspace. Freeze for up to 6 months. Makes 4 pints.

*Note: When preparing fresh chili peppers, avoid direct contact with the peppers. They contain oils that can burn your skin and eyes. Wear plastic or rubber gloves or work under cold running water. If your skin touches the peppers, wash the area well with soap and water.

Nutrition facts per tablespoon: 10 cal., 0 g total fat, 0 mg chol., 25 mg sodium, 2 g carbo., 0 g fiber, 0 g pro.
Daily values: 7% vit. A, 24% vit. C, 1% iron.

SEASIDE DESSERT PLATTER

Prep: 25 min. ◆ Bake: 18 min.

See the photograph on page 158.

3 Tbsp. finely chopped pecans (optional)
◆◆◆
⅓ cup butter
⅓ cup shortening
¾ cup sugar
¾ tsp. baking powder
1 egg
1 tsp. vanilla
2 cups all-purpose flour
1 tsp. finely shredded lemon peel
◆◆◆
1 to 1½ cups coconut, toasted
1 recipe Strawberries with Lime Dipping Sauce (see page 189)

1 recipe Lemon-Lime Ice-Cream Floats (optional) (see below right)

1 Grease and flour a large shell-shaped pan (12×11×1¾-inch) or the wells of madeleine or star cookie pans. If desired, sprinkle with finely chopped pecans.

2 In a mixing bowl beat butter and shortening on medium to high speed of an electric mixer for 30 seconds. Add sugar, baking powder, and a dash *salt*. Beat until combined, scraping bowl. Beat in egg and vanilla. Beat in as much of the flour as you can with the mixer. By hand, stir in lemon peel and remaining flour. Drop dough in small mounds on top of nuts in the prepared pan(s). Press dough with fingers, filling the shell, madeleine, or star pans about three-fourths full. (This recipe makes about 28 madeleines or 40 stars.)

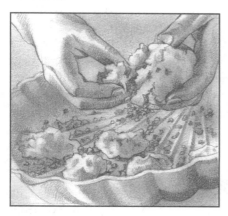

3 Bake in a 350° oven for 18 to 20 minutes in the large shell pan, 10 to 12 minutes in the madeleine pans, or about 12 minutes in the star pans or until cookie edges are lightly browned. Cool large shell in pan on a wire rack. When completely cooled, invert large shell onto a wire rack.

Remove madeleines and stars from pans when hot, and cool on a wire rack.

4 To serve, sprinkle serving tray with toasted coconut. Place large shell cookie in middle of tray or scatter madeleines or stars on tray. Arrange bowls of Strawberries with Lime Dipping Sauce on the platter. Serve with Lemon-Lime Ice-Cream Floats.

5 If you don't have a shell-shaped pan, madeleine pan, or star pan, follow these directions: Roll out dough, half at a time, on a lightly floured surface to ¼ inch thick. Cut into 2-inch rounds. If desired, sprinkle with pecans. Bake cutouts in a 375° oven for 8 to 9 minutes or until edges of cookies are lightly browned. Makes 8 servings.

Nutrition facts per serving with Strawberries with Lime Dipping Sauce and Lemon-Lime Ice-Cream Floats: 585 cal., 24 g total fat (12 g sat. fat), 53 mg chol., 197 mg sodium, 89 g carbo., 2 g fiber, 6 g pro. *Daily values:* 14% vit. A, 5% vit. C, 8% calcium, 11% iron.

30 MIN.

STRAWBERRIES WITH LIME DIPPING SAUCE

Start to finish: 10 min.

1   8-oz. carton dairy sour cream
2   Tbsp. powdered sugar
2   tsp. finely shredded lime peel
1   Tbsp. lime juice
    Lime slices (optional)

♦♦♦

3   cups small strawberries

1 In a bowl stir together sour cream, powdered sugar, lime peel, and lime juice. If desired, line a small serving bowl with lime slices; spoon in the sour cream-lime mixture.

2 Wash strawberries, but do not remove stems. Drain on several layers of paper towels. Arrange berries in a medium serving bowl. Serve with sauce. Makes 8 servings.

LEMON-LIME ICE-CREAM FLOATS

Start to finish: 5 min.

See the photograph on page 159.

1   pint lemon sorbet, ice cream, or sherbet

♦♦♦

    Citrus wedges (optional)

♦♦♦

2   liters lemon-lime carbonated beverage, chilled

1 Place 8 scoops of sorbet, ice cream, or sherbet onto a baking sheet; cover with plastic wrap and freeze until serving time.

2 If desired, thread citrus wedges on a bamboo skewer. Set fruit aside.

3 Pour 3 inches of the carbonated beverage into a pitcher. Garnish with skewered citrus wedges. Carefully place frozen scoops of ice cream into pitcher. Add additional carbonated beverage as necessary to fill pitcher. Makes 8 servings.

ITALIAN RASPBERRY TORTE

Prep: 20 min. ◆ Bake: 35 min.
Cool 2 hr. ◆ Chill: 4 hr.

A ruby crown of berries tops this glorious dessert—a cross between cheesecake and torte.

1¼ cups all-purpose flour
½ tsp. baking soda
½ tsp. baking powder
¼ tsp. salt
◆◆◆
⅔ cup sugar
¾ cup dairy sour cream
½ cup butter, melted
2 eggs
½ tsp. vanilla
¼ tsp. almond extract
◆◆◆
1 8-oz. pkg. cream cheese, softened
¼ cup sugar
¼ tsp. almond extract
2 cups raspberries
Fresh mint sprigs (optional)

1 Grease a 9-inch springform pan; set aside. Combine flour, baking soda, baking powder, and salt; set aside.

2 In a large mixing bowl combine the ⅔ cup sugar, ½ cup of the sour cream, melted butter, eggs, vanilla, and ¼ teaspoon almond extract with an electric mixer until combined. Add flour mixture to sugar mixture; beat until combined. Pour batter into prepared pan. Bake in a 350° oven for 15 minutes. Remove partially baked cake from oven and place on a wire rack.

TEST KITCHEN TIP

SOFTENING ICE CREAM

Some dessert recipes, such as pies, bombes, and cakes, specify softening ice cream before spreading or stirring in additional flavorings. To accomplish this task without melting the ice cream, chill a mixing bowl in the refrigerator or freezer. Working quickly, use a spoon to stir and the back of the spoon to press ice cream against the sides of the bowl. Soften the ice cream just until it is pliable and not melted. Use a wooden spoon for more comfortable stirring.

3 In a bowl beat cream cheese and the ¼ cup sugar with an electric mixer until smooth. Beat in remaining ¼ cup sour cream and the ¼ teaspoon almond extract. Spoon cream cheese mixture over top of partially baked cake, spreading mixture carefully to edges. Return cake to oven. Bake for 20 to 25 minutes more or until top is set and edges are brown. Place cake on wire rack. Mound berries on cake, pressing some of the berries gently into cake top. Cool 10 minutes. Loosen sides of cake from pan. Cool 30 minutes more. Remove sides of pan. Cool completely; serve chilled. Add mint sprigs, if desired. Makes 12 to 16 servings.

Nutrition facts per serving: 291 cal., 18 g total fat (11 g sat. fat), 83 mg chol., 264 mg sodium, 28 g carbo., 1 g fiber, 4 g pro. *Daily values:* 20% vit. A, 8% vit. C, 4% calcium, 7% iron.

CANDY-BAR CAKE

Prep: 30 min. ◆ Freeze: 6 hr.

1 10¾-oz. frozen loaf pound cake
3 cups (1½ pints) ice cream
⅓ cup caramel ice-cream topping
◆◆◆
⅓ cup whipping cream
2 tsp. light corn syrup
⅔ cup (4 oz.) semisweet chocolate pieces
1 Tbsp. shortening
◆◆◆
1 oz. white baking bar
1 oz. milk chocolate
2 tsp. shortening

1 Let cake stand 10 minutes. Slice in half horizontally; slice each half horizontally, making a total of 4 layers. Line an 8×4×2-inch loaf pan with plastic wrap, extending over sides. Place 1 cake slice in pan. Soften ice cream (see Softening Ice Cream, left). Quickly spread one-third of the ice cream atop cake in pan. Drizzle with a third of the caramel topping; top with another cake slice. Repeat twice, ending with cake. Cover with foil; freeze until firm, 5 hours or overnight.

2 Meanwhile, for glaze, in a small heavy saucepan stir together cream and corn syrup. Bring to boiling; reduce heat. Cook and stir for 2 minutes. Remove from heat. Add chocolate pieces and 1 tablespoon shortening; stir until melted. Cool.

3 Remove frozen cake from pan; remove wrap. Trim edges. Place cake on a freezer-proof serving plate. Coat with glaze, lifting and tilting to cover top and sides of cake. Return to freezer; freeze about 1 hour or until firm.

4 In separate small saucepans melt white baking bar and milk chocolate, each with 1 teaspoon of the shortening. Drizzle atop glazed cake. Serve immediately or store, covered, in the freezer for up to 6 months. Slice frozen cake to serve. Makes 8 servings.

Nutrition facts per serving: 401 cal., 23 g total fat (7 g sat. fat), 22 mg chol., 192 mg sodium, 48 g carbo., 1 g fiber, 4 g pro. *Daily values:* 7% vit. A, 5% calcium, 4% iron.

TROPICAL ANGEL CAKE

Prep: 20 min. ◆ Freeze: 2 hr.

1 8- to 9-inch or one 15-oz. purchased angel food cake
3 cups fruit-flavored sherbet
¼ cup frozen juice concentrate
1 cup whipping cream, whipped
Coconut (optional)

1 Slice cake in half horizontally. Hollow out insides, leaving two 1-inch-thick shells. Spoon sherbet into bottom shell. Set top half, hollow side down, over bottom. Poke holes in top. Drizzle with juice concentrate.

2 Frost with whipped cream. If desired, sprinkle with coconut. Cover loosely with foil; freeze up to 1 week. Let stand for 10 minutes before serving. Slice to serve. Makes 10 servings.

Nutrition facts per serving: 315 cal., 10 g total fat (6 g sat. fat), 36 mg chol., 123 mg sodium, 52 g carbo., 5 g pro. *Daily values:* 11% vit. A, 22% vit. C, 4% calcium, 3% iron.

PRIZE TESTED RECIPE WINNER

BLUEBERRY CITRUS CAKE

Prep: 20 min. ◆ Bake: 35 min.
Cool: 1 hr.

Transform a cake mix into a delectable treat by stirring in berries and other goodies.

1 pkg. 2-layer-size lemon cake mix
½ cup orange juice
½ cup water
⅓ cup cooking oil
3 eggs
1½ cups fresh or frozen blueberries
1 Tbsp. finely shredded orange peel
1 Tbsp. finely shredded lemon peel

◆◆◆

1 recipe Citrus Frosting (see below right)
Orange peel curls (optional)

1 Grease and lightly flour two 8×1½-inch or 9×1½-inch round baking pans; set aside. In a large mixing bowl combine cake mix, orange juice, water, oil, and eggs. Beat with an electric mixer on low speed for 30 seconds. Increase speed to medium; beat for 2 minutes. Gently fold in blueberries, orange peel, and lemon peel. Pour batter into prepared pans.

2 Bake in a 350° oven for 35 to 40 minutes or until a wooden toothpick inserted near centers comes out clean. Cool layers in pans on wire racks for 10 minutes. Remove cakes from pans. Cool thoroughly on racks. Frost with Citrus Frosting. If desired,

THE CLEVER COOK

LEMON SLICES NICE WHEN ICED

Although I love to add slices of fresh lemon to glasses of ice water, I'm not always able to use the entire lemon at once. So I place the remaining lemon slices in a plastic freezer bag and put it in the freezer. When I want ice water with lemon, I just remove a lemon slice from the freezer and drop it into my glass for a refreshing treat.

Denise Ernstberger
Jeffersonville, Indiana

garnish with orange peel curls. Store frosted cake in the refrigerator. Makes 12 servings.

Citrus Frosting: In a medium bowl beat together one 3-ounce package softened cream cheese and ¼ cup softened butter until fluffy. Add 3 cups sifted powdered sugar and 2 tablespoons orange juice. Beat until combined. In a small bowl beat 1 cup whipping cream to soft peaks; add to cream cheese mixture. Add 2 tablespoons finely shredded orange peel and 1 tablespoon finely shredded lemon peel. Beat on low speed until combined.

Nutrition facts per serving: 493 cal., 25 g total fat (11 g sat. fat), 98 mg chol., 345 mg sodium, 66 g carbo., 1 g fiber, 4 g pro. *Daily values:* 18% vit. A, 12% vit. C, 9% calcium, 5% iron.

PIÑA-COLADA UPSIDE-DOWN CAKE

Prep: 25 min. ◆ Bake: 40 min.

This cake has all the flavors—pineapple, coconut, and rum—of the popular tropical beverage.

1 8-oz. can pineapple tidbits (juice pack)
1 Tbsp. butter, melted
⅓ cup toasted coconut
⅓ cup cream of coconut
2 Tbsp. rum
◆◆◆
⅓ cup butter, softened
¾ cup sugar
1 egg
1½ tsp. vanilla

1½ cups all-purpose flour
2½ tsp. baking powder
¼ tsp. salt

1 Drain pineapple, reserving juice. Add enough water to reserved pineapple juice to equal ⅔ cup. Place melted butter in a 9×1½-inch round baking pan; tip pan to evenly coat. In a small mixing bowl combine drained pineapple, toasted coconut, cream of coconut, and rum; spread evenly in prepared pan. Set aside.

2 In a medium mixing bowl beat ⅓ cup butter and sugar until combined. Add egg and vanilla; beat until fluffy. Stir together flour, baking powder, and salt; add to beaten mixture alternately with the ⅔ cup pineapple liquid. Carefully spoon batter atop mixture in baking pan.

3 Bake in a 350° oven about 40 minutes or until a wooden toothpick inserted near center comes out clean. Cool in pan on a wire rack 5 minutes. Loosen sides; invert cake onto serving plate. Serve warm. Makes 8 servings.

Nutrition facts per serving: 358 cal., 18 g total fat (7 g sat. fat), 51 mg chol., 291 mg sodium, 45 g carbo., 1 g fiber, 3 g pro. *Daily values:* 9% vit. A, 4% vit. C, 10% calcium, 10% iron.

FRENCH PLUM CAKE

Prep: 1 hr. ◆ Bake: 20 min.

¼ cup butter, softened
¼ cup sugar
1 egg
1 cup all-purpose flour
1 tsp. baking powder
¼ tsp. ground nutmeg
⅓ cup milk

2 lb. red plums, halved and pitted
2 Tbsp. sugar
1 Tbsp. all-purpose flour
¼ tsp. ground nutmeg
◆◆◆
½ cup sugar
¼ cup water

1 In a mixing bowl beat together butter and the ¼ cup sugar until fluffy. Beat in egg. Combine the 1 cup flour, the baking powder, and the ¼ teaspoon nutmeg; add alternately with milk to beaten mixture. Spread batter in a greased 9×1½-inch round baking pan.

2 Arrange half of the plum halves, cut side up, atop batter. Stir together the 2 tablespoons sugar, 1 tablespoon flour, and the ¼ teaspoon nutmeg. Sprinkle mixture over plums and batter in pan. Bake in a 375° oven for 20 to 25 minutes or until a wooden toothpick inserted near center of cake comes out clean and cake is lightly brown. Cool slightly.

3 Meanwhile, chop remaining plums (you should have about 3 cups). In a medium saucepan combine the ½ cup sugar and the water. Add chopped plums. Bring to boiling; reduce heat and boil gently, uncovered, about 30 minutes or until mixture is reduced to 1½ cups, stirring occasionally to prevent sticking. Cool slightly. Cut cake into wedges to serve. Spoon sauce over wedges on serving plates. Makes 8 servings.

Nutrition facts per serving: 270 cal., 8 g total fat (2 g sat. fat), 35 mg chol., 111 mg sodium, 49 g carbo., 3 g fiber, 4 g pro. *Daily values:* 11% vit. A, 18% vit. C, 5% calcium, 6% iron.

SEPTEMBER
Superlative Snacks

30-minute recipes indicated in RED.
Low-fat and no-fat recipes indicated with a ♥.
Photographs indicated in italics.
*All new in 1998.

*S*hort on time doesn't have to mean short on imagination. Mushroom "Risotto" is a sleight-of-hand quickie, using orzo instead of rice. Chicken 'n' Dumpling Soup and Sautéed Green Tomato Pasta are other speedy surprises, each ready in 30 minutes. And if you're eating on the run, consider calzones—baked half-circles of bread filled with anything from chicken alfredo to curried vegetables. Even awe-inspiring desserts can be quickly prepared. Try Towering Brownie Sundaes, a delicious improvement on a banana split. Or end with a spun sugar fantasy called Raspberries on a Citrus Cloud, a show-stopper that takes only 20 minutes.

CATCHING UP ON CATSUP

Catsup is queen of the condiments with a sweet-sour tang and rich tomato flavor that commands attention at all three meals. And what could be more flattering to a queen than a gift of spices. In the recipe below we've bestowed the smoky bite of chipotle chili pepper (chi-POT-lay)—a smoked form of the jalapeño that's becoming more common in supermarkets around the country.

Add the vivid flavors of this sauce to french fries, scrambled eggs, or other dishes you normally liven up with catsup. Or for a delicious reminder of how many of our favorite foods come from Central and South America, we've included a Mexican-influenced french-fry recipe that confers alluring foreign mystery on what we think of as an all-American staple. Tomatoes and potatoes originated in Peru, while chili peppers and cocoa both are native to Mexico and its southerly neighbors.

CHIPOTLE CATSUP

NO FAT

Start to finish: 1¾ hr.

Heat lovers can use up to 4 chipotles for a more fiery sauce. Look for dried chipotle chili peppers in the produce or spice section of the grocery store.

4 lb. ripe tomatoes
    (12 medium)
½ cup chopped onion
    (1 medium)
1 or 2 dried chipotle chili peppers, crumbled*

◆◆◆

½ cup sugar
½ cup white vinegar
1 Tbsp. snipped fresh marjoram or 1 tsp. dried marjoram, crushed
1 tsp. salt

1 Core and quarter tomatoes; drain. In a large saucepan combine tomatoes, onion, and chipotle chili peppers. Bring to boiling, stirring often; reduce heat. Simmer, covered, for 15 minutes. Press through food mill or sieve. Discard seeds and skins.

2 Return tomato mixture to saucepan; stir in sugar. Bring to boiling; reduce heat. Simmer, uncovered, for 45 to 60 minutes or until reduced by half, stirring occasionally. (Use a clean wooden or metal ruler to measure depth of mixture before and after cooking to determine when it is reduced by half.) Add vinegar, marjoram, and salt to mixture. Simmer, uncovered, about 30 minutes or to desired consistency, stirring often. Makes about 2 cups.

***Note:** When working with chili peppers, wear gloves or put hands in plastic bags. Do not touch eyes or face and wash hands with soap and water immediately when finished.

Nutrition facts per tablespoon: 25 cal., 0 g total fat, 0 mg chol., 72 mg sodium, 6 g carbo., 1 g fiber, 1 g pro.
Daily values: 3% vit. A, 20% vit. C, 2% iron.

SPICY FRENCH FRIES

Prep: 20 min. ◆ Bake: 30 min.

The spice coating on these potatoes overcomes a problem with oven fries, the lack of browning. Try them with Chipotle Catsup (see recipe, left).

1 tsp. dried marjoram or oregano, crushed
1 tsp. unsweetened cocoa powder
½ tsp. onion powder or garlic powder
½ tsp. paprika
¼ tsp. salt
⅛ tsp. pepper
½ of a 24-oz. pkg. frozen potato wedges or 2 medium potatoes, each cut into 8 wedges (about 12 oz. total)
Nonstick spray coating

◆◆◆

Lime wedges (optional)

1 In a small bowl combine marjoram or oregano, cocoa powder, onion or garlic powder, paprika, salt, and pepper. Spray potatoes with nonstick coating and place in a plastic bag. Add spice mixture and shake to coat.

2 Spray a 15×10×1-inch baking pan with nonstick coating. Place potatoes in a single layer on baking sheet. If using frozen potatoes, bake according to package directions. If using fresh potatoes, bake in a 450° oven about 30 minutes or until potatoes are tender. Serve with Chipotle Catsup and lime wedges, if desired. Makes 2 or 3 servings.

Nutrition facts per serving: 229 cal., 7 g total fat (0 g sat. fat), 0 mg chol., 317 mg sodium, 39 g carbo., 0 g fiber, 2 g pro.
Daily values: 3% vit. A, 9% vit. C, 1% calcium, 7% iron.

CARAMELIZED SWEET POTATOES

Start to finish: 30 min.

Just like other potatoes, sweet potatoes can be baked, mashed, or hashed, but are sweetly sublime when sautéed with onions and brown sugar, as in this side dish. (See the photograph on page 200.)

2 large red or white onions, cut into ¾-inch chunks
4 tsp. margarine or butter
2 large sweet potatoes, peeled and sliced ½ inch thick (about 1 lb.)
2 Tbsp. brown sugar
¾ tsp. snipped fresh rosemary or ¼ tsp. dried rosemary, crushed
Snipped fresh rosemary (optional)

1 In a large skillet cook onions in hot margarine or butter over medium-high heat for 3 to 4 minutes or until onions are nearly tender, stirring frequently. Stir in sweet potatoes and ¼ cup *water*. Cook, covered, over medium heat for 10 to 12 minutes or until sweet potatoes are nearly tender, stirring occasionally.

2 Uncover skillet; add brown sugar and the ¾ teaspoon fresh or ¼ teaspoon dried rosemary. Cook, stirring gently, over medium-low heat for 4 to 5 minutes or until onions and sweet potatoes are glazed. If desired, garnish with additional fresh rosemary. Makes 4 side-dish servings.

Nutrition facts per serving: 173 cal., 4 g total fat (1 g sat. fat), 0 mg chol., 57 mg sodium, 33 g carbo., 4 g fiber, 2 g pro. *Daily values:* 197% vit. A, 41% vit. C, 3% calcium, 4% iron.

BAKED SWEET POTATO FRIES

Prep: 15 min. ◆ Bake: 20 min.

Move over, fast food. Here's a rival for your best-seller.

Nonstick spray coating
4 small sweet potatoes (about 1 lb.)
1 Tbsp. margarine or butter, melted
¼ tsp. seasoned salt
Dash ground nutmeg

1 Spray a 15×10×1-inch baking pan with nonstick coating. Scrub potatoes; cut lengthwise into quarters. Cut each quarter into 2 wedges. Arrange potatoes in a single layer in pan. Combine margarine or butter, salt, and nutmeg. Brush onto potatoes. Bake in a 450° oven about 20 minutes or until brown and tender. Makes 4 side-dish servings.

Nutrition facts per serving: 117 cal., 3 g total fat (1 g sat. fat), 0 mg chol., 122 mg sodium, 22 g carbo., 3 g fiber, 2 g pro. *Daily values:* 196% vit. A, 36% vit. C, 2% iron.

SWEET POTATO GNOCCHI

Start to finish: 1 hr.

Should you not want to serve all of this recipe at once, cool the cooked gnocchi. Place them in a single layer on a baking sheet, and freeze until firm. Store the gnocchi in a freezer bag for up to 2 months.

4 medium sweet potatoes, peeled and quartered
♦♦♦
1 cup ricotta cheese
½ tsp. salt

½ tsp. ground nutmeg (optional)
2 cups all-purpose flour
Melted butter, grated Parmesan cheese, and/or freshly ground pepper (optional)

1 In a large saucepan cook sweet potatoes, covered, in enough boiling salted water to cover for 25 to 35 minutes or until tender. Drain well; return to the same pan. Over low heat, mash potatoes with a potato masher until smooth, allowing any extra moisture to evaporate.

2 Transfer potatoes to a large bowl. Stir in ricotta cheese, salt, nutmeg (if using), and 1½ cups of the flour. On a well-floured surface, knead in the remaining flour, kneading for 2 to 3 minutes or until dough forms a soft ball. Divide into 8 pieces. With well-floured hands, roll each piece of dough into a 12-inch-long log (about 1 inch in diameter). Cut logs crosswise into 1-inch pieces. With a floured finger, make a dimple in center of each piece.

3 Cook gnocchi, several at a time, in a large pot of boiling salted water for 3 to 4 minutes or until gnocchi rise to surface of the water. (Do not overcook.) Drain on paper towels. Cover to keep warm while cooking remaining gnocchi. If desired, top gnocchi with melted butter, Parmesan cheese, and/or pepper. Makes 16 side-dish servings.

Nutrition facts per serving: 116 cal., 1 g total fat (1 g sat. fat), 5 mg chol., 90 mg sodium, 22 g carbo., 2 g fiber, 4 g pro. *Daily values:* 92% vit. A, 16% vit. C, 6% iron.

Roasted pork loin and whole tiny new potatoes

❖❖❖

Red Cabbage with Fennel (see below right)

❖❖❖

Tossed green salad

❖❖❖

Rye bread with butter

MUSHROOM "RISOTTO"

Start to finish: 30 min.

Quick-cooking orzo, also called rosamarina, makes this a speedy side dish. Pair it with poultry for a fast and flavorful meal.
(See the photograph on page 197.)

¾ **cup dried orzo**

❖❖❖

1 **lb. fresh mushrooms, such as button, chanterelle, and/or shiitake, sliced**
1 **clove garlic, minced**
1 **Tbsp. margarine or butter**
1 **tsp. cornstarch**
¼ **tsp. salt**
⅛ **tsp. pepper**
½ **of a 12-oz. can (¾ cup) evaporated fat-free milk**
½ **cup shredded fontina cheese (2 oz.)**
¼ **cup slivered almonds**
¼ **to ½ tsp. dried tarragon, crushed**
1 **Tbsp. snipped fresh chives**

1 Cook orzo according to package directions. Drain and keep warm.

2 Meanwhile, in a large skillet cook mushrooms and garlic in margarine or butter over medium-high heat about 5 minutes or until tender and most of the liquid has evaporated, stirring occasionally. Stir in cornstarch, salt, and pepper. Stir in evaporated milk all at once. Cook and stir over medium heat until thickened and bubbly. Cook and stir for 1 minute more. Add fontina cheese, almonds, and tarragon; cook and stir until cheese is melted. Stir in cooked orzo.

3 Transfer to a serving bowl; sprinkle with snipped chives. Makes 4 to 6 side-dish servings.

Nutrition facts per serving: 322 cal., 13 g total fat (4 g sat. fat), 18 mg chol., 340 mg sodium, 39 g carbo., 2 g fiber, 16 g pro. *Daily values:* 14% vit. A, 9% vit. C, 21% calcium, 24% iron.

RED CABBAGE WITH FENNEL

Start to finish: 30 min.

Fennel's feathery green tops look like fresh dill but have a delicate anise flavor.
(See the photograph on page 197.)

2 **heads fennel (about 2 lb.)**

❖❖❖

½ **cup apple juice**
¼ **cup cider vinegar**
1 **tsp. instant chicken bouillon granules**
3 **cloves garlic, minced**

❖❖❖

1 **Tbsp. cooking oil**
1 **10-oz. pkg. shredded red cabbage (about 4 cups)**

2 **Tbsp. brown sugar**
¼ **tsp. fennel seed, crushed**

1 Cut off and discard upper stalks of fennel. Snip 2 teaspoons of the leafy fennel tops; set aside along with a few sprigs of the leafy tops. Cut off a thin slice from base of fennel heads; remove wilted outer layers of stalks. Wash fennel and cut each bulb into quarters lengthwise.

2 In a small bowl combine apple juice and vinegar. In a medium saucepan combine the fennel bulbs, ½ cup of the apple juice mixture, bouillon granules, and garlic. Bring to boiling; reduce heat. Cover and simmer for 14 to 16 minutes or until fennel wedges are tender.

3 Meanwhile, in a large skillet or wok preheat oil over medium-high heat. Add cabbage and stir-fry for 3 to 5 minutes or until cabbage is crisp-tender. Combine remaining ¼ cup of the apple juice mixture and brown sugar; stir into cabbage with fennel seed. Cook and stir 1 minute more or until heated through.

4 Transfer cabbage to a serving platter. Remove fennel bulbs from liquid with a slotted spoon. Place on top of cabbage. Garnish with reserved snipped fennel leaves and sprigs. Makes 4 to 6 side-dish servings.

Nutrition facts per serving: 107 cal., 4 g total fat (1 g sat. fat), 0 mg chol., 258 mg sodium, 19 g carbo., 13 g fiber, 2 g pro. *Daily values:* 2% vit. A, 83% vit. C, 6% calcium, 6% iron.

Right: *Mushroom "Risotto"* *(page 196)*
Below: *Red Cabbage with Fennel*
(page 196)

Page 198: *Sausage, Beans, and Greens (page 208)*
Top: *Salmon with Blackberry Sauce (page 207)*
Above: *Sautéed Green Tomato Pasta (page 210)*

Above: *Caramelized Sweet Potatoes (page 195)*
Left: *Pork and Pear Au Jus (page 208)*
Right: *Greek Leeks and Shrimp Stir-Fry (page 206)*

Top: *Carrot and Chili Pepper Soup*
(page 205)
Above: *Chicken 'n' Dumpling Soup*
(page 205)

FIESTA SALSA

Prep: 20 min. ◆ Chill: 4 to 24 hr.

Fruity flavors and racy hot peppers make this a zingy accompaniment to poultry or pork.

8 oz. cranberries, chopped (2 cups)
1 small apple, peeled, cored, and finely chopped
1 small pear, peeled, cored, and finely chopped
1 orange, peeled, seeded, sectioned, and finely chopped
1 shallot, finely chopped
1 green onion, thinly sliced
1 to 2 fresh jalapeño peppers, seeded and finely chopped*
⅓ cup sugar
1 Tbsp. lime juice
1 Tbsp. white wine vinegar

1 In a medium nonmetal bowl combine cranberries, apple, pear, orange, shallot, green onion, and jalapeño peppers. Stir in the sugar, lime juice, and vinegar. Cover and chill for 4 to 24 hours. Stir before serving. Makes about 3 cups salsa.

***Note:** Hot peppers contain oils that can burn. Wear plastic gloves while preparing peppers and thoroughly wash your hands when finished.

*Nutrition facts per ¼-cup serving: 43 cal., 0 g total fat, 0 mg chol., 0 mg sodium, 11 g carbo., 1 g fiber, 0 g pro.
Daily values: 1% vit. A, 13% vit. C.*

---

30 MIN. LOW FAT

CARROT AND CHILI PEPPER SOUP

Start to finish: 30 min.

Sweet baby carrots take on a whole new identity when turned into a special soup revved up with chili peppers and a hint of cumin. (See the photograph on page 204.)

2 14½-oz. cans vegetable broth
16 oz. packaged, peeled baby carrots
1 large onion, chopped
1 4-oz. can diced green chili peppers
1 tsp. chili powder
½ tsp. ground cumin
◆◆◆
1 cup half-and-half or light cream
◆◆◆
Fresh purple basil leaves (optional)

1 In a large saucepan or Dutch oven combine broth, carrots, onion, chili peppers, chili powder, and cumin. Bring mixture to boiling; reduce heat. Simmer, covered, 12 minutes or until carrots are very tender.

2 In a food processor bowl or blender container process half of the mixture until smooth. Repeat with remaining mixture. Return all to saucepan. Stir in half-and-half or light cream. Heat through.

3 To serve, ladle soup into bowls. If desired, garnish each serving with purple basil. Makes 8 side-dish servings.

*Nutrition facts per serving: 75 cal., 4 g total fat (2 g sat. fat), 11 mg chol., 510 mg sodium, 10 g carbo., 2 g fiber, 2 g pro.
Daily values: 133% vit. A, 11% vit. C, 6% calcium, 5% iron.*

---

30 MIN.

CHICKEN 'N' DUMPLING SOUP

Start to finish: 30 min.

See the photograph on page 204.

12 oz. boneless chicken strips for stir-frying
1 Tbsp. olive oil or cooking oil
2 Tbsp. all-purpose flour
¼ tsp. dried marjoram, crushed
1 14½-oz. can chicken broth
1 medium onion, cut into wedges
1 cup fresh green beans, trimmed and halved
1 cup purchased julienne or coarsely shredded carrots
⅔ cup reduced-fat packaged biscuit mix
⅓ cup yellow cornmeal
¼ cup shredded cheddar cheese
½ cup milk

1 Season chicken with salt and pepper. In saucepan cook and stir chicken in hot oil 2 minutes or until browned. Sprinkle flour and marjoram over chicken. Stir in broth, vegetables, and 1 cup *water.* Bring to boiling; reduce heat. Simmer, covered, 5 minutes.

2 Combine biscuit mix, cornmeal, and cheese. Stir in milk just until mixture is moistened. Drop batter onto hot liquid, making 8 dumplings. Return to boiling; reduce heat. Simmer, covered, for 10 to 12 minutes until dumplings test done. (Do not lift cover while simmering.) Makes 4 servings.

*Nutrition facts per serving: 345 cal., 11 g total fat (3 g sat. fat), 55 mg chol., 716 mg sodium, 35 g carbo., 3 g fiber, 25 g pro.
Daily values: 87% vit. A, 8% vit. C, 13% calcium, 18% iron.*

THE CLEVER COOK

PEARS AS SUBSTITUTES

I make pear sauce just like apple sauce and use it for the shortening called for in my banana bread recipe. The bread is tasty, moist, and low in fat.

Linora Terwilliger
Scotia, New York

PRIZE TESTED RECIPE WINNER

GINGERED PUMPKIN-PEAR SOUP

Start to finish: 25 min.

A swirl of lime-laced sour cream adds a burst of flavor to this smooth autumn soup.

½ cup chopped sweet onion
2 tsp. grated fresh ginger
1 Tbsp. margarine or butter
3 pears, peeled, cored, and sliced
1 15-oz. can pumpkin
1½ cups vegetable broth
1 cup milk

❖❖❖

¼ cup light dairy sour cream
½ tsp. finely shredded lime peel
1 Tbsp. lime juice
Lime peel (optional)

1 In a large saucepan cook onion and ginger in hot margarine until onion is tender. Stir in pears; cook 1 minute. Stir in pumpkin and vegetable broth. Bring mixture to boiling; reduce heat. Simmer, covered, 5 minutes more or until pears are tender. Cool slightly. In a food processor bowl or blender container, cover and process or blend half of the pumpkin mixture at a time about 1 minute or until smooth. Return mixture to saucepan; stir in milk. Heat through. Season to taste with salt and pepper.

2 Meanwhile, stir together sour cream, the ½ teaspoon lime peel, and lime juice. Drizzle some sour cream mixture over each serving of soup. If desired, garnish with additional lime peel. Makes 6 side-dish servings.

Nutrition facts per serving: 129 cal., 4 g total fat (1 g sat. fat), 4 mg chol., 310 mg sodium, 24 g carbo., 5 g fiber, 3 g pro. *Daily values:* 162% vit. A, 13% vit. C, 7% calcium, 8% iron.

LOW FAT

AUTUMN HARVEST SOUP

Prep: 15 min. ◆ Cook: 35 min.

1½ cups peeled and cubed sweet potato
1¼ cups peeled and cubed butternut squash
1½ cups chicken broth or vegetable broth
1 medium cooking apple, peeled, cored, and chopped
1 medium pear, peeled, cored, and chopped

❖❖❖

⅓ cup apple cider or apple juice
2 Tbsp. dry sherry (optional)
⅛ tsp. ground cinnamon
¼ cup whipping cream
Ground cinnamon (optional)

1 In a medium saucepan combine sweet potato, squash, and broth. Bring to boiling; reduce heat. Simmer, covered, for 10 minutes. Add apple and pear. Return to boiling; reduce heat. Simmer, covered, 10 to 15 minutes more or until very tender. Remove from heat; cool slightly.

2 In a food processor bowl or blender container, cover and process mixture, one-third to half at a time, until smooth. Return mixture to saucepan. Stir in apple cider, sherry (if using), and the ⅛ teaspoon cinnamon. Bring just to boiling; stir in whipping cream. Heat through. If desired, sprinkle each serving with a dash of ground cinnamon. Makes 6 to 8 side-dish servings.

Nutrition facts per serving: 122 cal., 4 g total fat (2 g sat. fat), 14 mg chol., 202 mg sodium, 20 g carbo., 3 g fiber, 2 g pro. *Daily values:* 91% vit. A, 23% vit. C, 2% calcium, 4% iron.

30 MIN. LOW FAT

GREEK LEEKS AND SHRIMP STIR-FRY

Start to finish: 30 min.

See the photograph on page 201.

1¼ lb. fresh or frozen peeled, deveined medium shrimp
⅓ cup lemon juice
2 tsp. cornstarch
¾ tsp. bouquet garni seasoning or dried oregano, crushed

❖❖❖

1 cup quick-cooking couscous

❖❖❖

1 Tbsp. olive oil
4 medium leeks, thinly sliced
½ cup crumbled feta cheese
10 pitted kalamata olives, quartered

1 Thaw shrimp, if frozen. Rinse shrimp; pat dry with paper towels. In a bowl combine ⅔ cup *water*, lemon juice, cornstarch, and ¼ teaspoon of bouquet garni or oregano. Set the mixture aside.

2 In a bowl combine the couscous, remaining bouquet garni or oregano, and ¼ teaspoon *salt*. Pour 1½ cups *boiling water* over the couscous. Let stand, covered, for 5 minutes. Fluff with a fork.

3 Meanwhile, heat oil in wok or large skillet over medium-high heat. Stir-fry leeks in hot oil 2 to 3 minutes or until leeks are tender. Remove from wok; set aside. Stir lemon juice mixture; add to wok and bring to boiling. Add shrimp; cook 3 minutes or until shrimp turn pink. Stir in cooked leeks and ¼ cup of the feta cheese. Serve shrimp mixture over couscous; top with quartered kalamata olives and remaining feta cheese. If desired, garnish mixture with whole kalamata olives. Serves 4.

Nutrition facts per serving: 412 cal., 10 g total fat (3 g sat. fat), 230 mg chol., 609 mg sodium, 49 g carbo., 11 g fiber, 33 g pro. *Daily values:* 11% vit. A, 28% vit. C, 14% calcium, 36% iron.

SALMON WITH BLACKBERRY SAUCE

Start to finish: 30 min.

The intense heat of broiling leaves the surface of the fish sizzling with flavor and keeps the interior moist. (See the photograph on page 199.)

4 **fresh or frozen salmon or halibut steaks, 1 inch thick (about 1½ lb.)**

2 **Tbsp. margarine or butter, melted**
¼ **tsp. salt**
⅛ **tsp. pepper (optional)**

◆◆◆

½ **cup blackberry or apricot jam or preserves**
2 **Tbsp. finely chopped onion**
1 **small clove garlic, minced**
1 **tsp. snipped fresh thyme or ¼ tsp. dried thyme, crushed**
1 **tsp. Dijon-style mustard**

◆◆◆

Lemon wedges
Fresh blackberries (optional)
Fresh thyme sprigs (optional)

1 Thaw fish, if frozen. Rinse fish; pat dry with paper towels. Place fish on the greased unheated rack of a broiler pan. Lightly brush fish with about half of the melted margarine or butter. Sprinkle with salt and, if desired, pepper. Broil fish 4 inches from the heat for 5 minutes. Using a wide metal spatula, carefully turn fish over. Lightly brush with remaining melted margarine. Broil for 3 to 7 minutes more or until fish just flakes when tested with a fork.

2 Meanwhile, for sauce, in a small saucepan combine jam or preserves, onion, garlic, the snipped fresh thyme or dried thyme, and mustard. Bring just to boiling, stirring frequently; reduce heat. Simmer, uncovered, about 10 minutes or until sauce is slightly thickened. Remove from heat; set aside.

3 To serve, spoon 2 tablespoons of the blackberry or apricot sauce onto each of 4 dinner plates. Place a fish steak on each pool of sauce. Serve with lemon wedges and, if desired, fresh blackberries and fresh thyme sprigs. Makes 4 servings.

Nutrition facts per serving: 319 cal., 12 g total fat (2 g sat. fat), 31 mg chol., 339 mg sodium, 29 g carbo., 0 g fiber, 25 g pro. *Daily values:* 10% vit. A, 2% vit. C, 2% calcium, 10% iron.

TEST KITCHEN TIP

MAKE IT QUICK

When there's no time to dawdle before dinner, some of these shortcuts may come in handy.

◆ If dried beans are called for in a recipe, consider reaching for a can of beans instead. You'll eliminate the time it takes to soak and cook the dried varieties.

◆ Assemble and measure all your ingredients before starting to cook.

◆ Cooking pasta and vegetables in the same hot water saves some time when you're making a veggie-topped pasta. Just drain cooked pasta and vegetables as usual and toss with warm garlic butter or seasoned olive oil for a simple meal.

◆ Buy produce or meat and poultry that has already been cut to the appropriate size for your recipe.

◆ Leave the skins on potatoes when you use them in a dish that calls for sliced or chopped potatoes, such as potato salad or potato soup.

SAUSAGE, BEANS, AND GREENS

30 MIN.

Start to finish: 25 min.

Escarole, a type of endive, typically is used in salads, but it makes a great addition to this one-pot dish. (See the photograph on page 198.)

- 8 oz. hot or mild fresh Italian sausage links, bias-sliced into ½-inch pieces
- ½ cup chopped onion
- 2 19-oz. cans white kidney beans (cannellini), rinsed and drained
- 2 cups coarsely chopped escarole or fresh spinach
- ¾ cup reduced-sodium chicken broth
- ¼ cup dry white wine or reduced-sodium chicken broth
- 2 Tbsp. snipped fresh thyme or 1 tsp. dried thyme, crushed
  ❖❖❖
- ¼ cup finely shredded Parmesan cheese (optional)

1 In a large saucepan cook sausage and onion over medium heat 5 minutes or until onion is tender. Drain off excess fat. Add beans, escarole or spinach, chicken broth, wine, and thyme. Bring to boiling; reduce heat. Simmer, covered, for 5 minutes.

2 To serve, ladle mixture into serving bowls. If desired, sprinkle with Parmesan. Makes 4 servings.

Nutrition facts per serving: 309 cal., 12 g total fat (4 g sat. fat), 32 mg chol., 921 mg sodium, 39 g carbo., 13 g fiber, 24 g pro. *Daily values:* 5% vit. A, 4% vit. C, 7% calcium, 26% iron.

LOW FAT

FIVE SPICE PORK

Prep: 10 min. ◆ Stand: 30 min. Grill: 25 min.

Rub an aromatic Asian blend of spices over the tenderloin's surface before roasting. Use the remaining spice blend in other recipes calling for five-spice powder.

- 3 Tbsp. ground cinnamon
- 2 tsp. anise seed
- 1½ tsp. whole black peppercorns
- 1 tsp. fennel seed
- ½ tsp. ground cloves
- 1 12-oz. pork tenderloin
- 3 cloves garlic, quartered (optional)
  Cooking oil

1 For five-spice powder, in a blender container combine cinnamon, anise seed, peppercorns, fennel seed, and cloves. Blend until powdery. Make random cuts about ½ inch deep in meat. If desired, insert garlic slices into cuts in meat. Brush meat with oil; rub about 1 tablespoon of the seasoning blend over tenderloin. Let meat stand 30 minutes before grilling. Insert a meat thermometer near center of the tenderloin.

2 In a grill with a cover, arrange medium-hot coals around a drip pan; test for medium heat over drip pan. Place pork over drip pan. Cover and grill for 25 to 30 minutes or until meat thermometer registers 160° and juices run clear. Remove pork from grill and cover with foil. Let stand 5 minutes before slicing. Makes 4 servings.

Nutrition facts per serving: 133 cal., 6 g total fat (1 g sat. fat), 60 mg chol., 44 mg sodium, 1 g carbo., 0 g fiber, 19 g pro. *Daily values:* 1% vit. C, 2% calcium, 10% iron.

---

30 MIN.

PORK AND PEAR AU JUS

Start to finish: 30 min.

Cuts of pork from the center loin are quite tender, making them ideal for this fast skillet method of cooking. (See the photograph on page 200.)

- 2 small pears, each cored and cut into 8 wedges
- 1 cup pear nectar or apple juice
- 2 tsp. grated fresh ginger
- ¼ tsp. ground cinnamon
  ❖❖❖
- 4 pork loin rib chops, cut ¾ inch thick (about 2 lb.)

2 tsp. cracked black pepper
¼ tsp. salt
1 Tbsp. cooking oil

♦♦♦

2 tsp. cornstarch

1 In a medium saucepan combine pear wedges, pear nectar or apple juice, fresh ginger, and cinnamon. Bring to boiling; reduce heat. Simmer, covered, for 2 to 3 minutes or until fruit is tender. Remove pear wedges with a slotted spoon, reserving liquid. Pour liquid into a glass measure. If necessary, add enough additional pear nectar or apple juice to equal 1¼ cups; set aside.

2 Trim fat from meat. Use your fingers to press pepper onto both sides of chops. Sprinkle with salt. In a skillet cook chops in hot oil over medium to medium-high heat for 8 to 10 minutes or until no pink remains and juices run clear, turning once. Remove chops from skillet and keep warm, reserving the drippings in the skillet.

3 For the sauce, stir cornstarch into the reserved drippings in the skillet. Stir in the reserved cooking liquid. Cook and stir until thickened and bubbly. Cook and stir for 1 minute. Add pears. Cook and stir for 1 minute more.

4 Serve pears with chops, drizzling sauce on top of chops. Makes 4 servings.

Nutrition facts per serving: 354 cal., 14 g total fat (4 g sat. fat), 98 mg chol., 226 mg sodium, 25 g carbo., 3 g fiber, 32 g pro. *Daily values:* 9% vit. C, 1% calcium, 11% iron.

Low Fat

Pork Tenderloin With Nutty Pear Stuffing

Prep: 20 min. ♦ Roast: 35 min.

½ cup chopped pear
¼ cup chopped hazelnuts or almonds, toasted
¼ cup finely shredded carrot
¼ cup soft bread crumbs
2 Tbsp. chopped onion
1 tsp. grated fresh ginger
1 12-oz. pork tenderloin

♦♦♦

Cooking oil
2 Tbsp. orange marmalade

1 For stuffing, in a medium bowl combine pear, nuts, carrot, bread crumbs, onion, ginger, and ¼ teaspoon each *salt* and *pepper;* set aside. Butterfly the tenderloin by making a lengthwise slit down the center to within ½ inch of underside. Open flat and pound pork with a meat mallet to about ¼-inch thickness. Spread stuffing mixture atop butterflied tenderloin; roll up from a long side, tucking in ends, and secure with kitchen string.

2 Place on a rack in a shallow roasting pan. Brush lightly with oil. Insert meat thermometer into center of pork roll. Roast, uncovered, in a 425° oven for 30 to 40 minutes or until thermometer registers 155°. Brush marmalade over top. Roast about 5 minutes more or until temperature reaches 160°. Let stand 5 minutes before slicing. Makes 4 servings.

Nutrition facts per serving: 225 cal., 10 g total fat (2 g sat. fat), 60 mg chol., 196 mg sodium, 14 g carbo., 2 g fiber, 20 g pro. *Daily values:* 19% vit. A, 4% vit. C, 2% calcium, 10% iron.

The Incredible Crumb

Bread pudding, apple betty, crispy catfish, meatballs, stuffing, and other favorite foods owe it all to versatile crumbs. The type of crumbs used varies as much as the variety of their uses. In general, crumbs come in handy for thickening, coating, or holding together other ingredients in a recipe.

Typically, fine dry bread crumbs are used to produce a crisp coating for fish, poultry, or beef. Prepared fine dry bread crumbs—plain or seasoned—are available in the supermarket. Or, you can make your own by placing very dry bread in a plastic bag and crushing it into a fine consistency with a rolling pin. One slice of bread yields about ¼ cup fine dry crumbs.

Soft bread crumbs bind ingredients to each other and retain moisture, helping keep meatballs and similar dishes from falling apart and drying out. To make soft bread crumbs, use a food processor or blender to break fresh bread into fluffy crumbs. You also can tear bread into small pieces, or use a serrated knife to cut bread into ½-inch cubes. One slice of bread yields ¾ cup soft bread crumbs.

For bread pudding and stuffing, dry bread cubes are handy. Cubes can be purchased at the supermarket—plain or seasoned—or made at home. To do it yourself, cut bread into ½-inch cubes. Spread cubes in a single layer in a shallow baking pan. Bake in a 300° oven for 10 to 15 minutes or until dry, stirring twice during baking. Or, let bread cubes stand, covered, at room temperature 8 to 12 hours.

Sautéed Green Tomato
Pasta
(see below)

♦♦♦

Hearts of romaine with
Italian vinaigrette and
crumbled blue cheese

♦♦♦

Focaccia bread with olive
oil for dipping

♦♦♦

Poached Pears in Marsala
(see page 219)

SAUTÉED GREEN TOMATO PASTA

Start to finish: 30 min.

Take a close look at the orecchiette and you'll see why it means "little ears" in Italian. You can substitute other small pasta, such as bow tie, radiatore, or gemelli for orecchiette.
(See the photograph on page 199.)

1 **cup dried orecchiette or
bow ties**

♦♦♦

2 **cloves garlic, minced**
1 **Tbsp. olive oil**
2 **medium green tomatoes,
coarsely chopped into
1-inch chunks**
1 **cup whipping cream**
2 **Tbsp. snipped fresh Italian
parsley**
¼ **tsp. pepper**

♦♦♦

⅓ **cup finely shredded
Parmesan cheese**

1 **oz. thinly sliced prosciutto
or ham, chopped
Finely shredded Parmesan
cheese (optional)**

1 Cook pasta according to package directions. Drain and keep warm.

2 Meanwhile, in a large skillet cook garlic in hot oil over medium-high heat for 30 seconds. Add green tomatoes; cook 3 to 4 minutes or until heated through, stirring often. Stir whipping cream, parsley, and pepper into tomato mixture. Cook over medium heat for 5 to 8 minutes or until slightly thickened, stirring occasionally. Remove from heat.

3 Stir the ⅓ cup Parmesan cheese and the prosciutto or ham into sauce. Serve sauce over orecchiette. If desired, top with additional Parmesan cheese. Makes 4 main-dish servings.

Nutrition facts per serving: 398 cal., 30 g total fat (14 g sat. fat), 89 mg chol., 277 mg sodium, 22 g carbo., 1 g fiber, 11 g pro. *Daily values:* 32% vit. A, 29% vit. C, 12% calcium, 8% iron.

RIB EYE GRILL

Start to finish: 30 min.

4 **medium red, yellow, and/or
green sweet peppers,
seeded and cut into
1½-inch cubes**
1 **medium onion, cut into
wedges**
2 **cloves garlic, minced**
2 **Tbsp. olive oil**

1 **Tbsp. balsamic vinegar**
¼ **tsp. salt**
⅛ **tsp. freshly ground black
pepper**

♦♦♦

2 **12-oz. beef rib eye steaks,
cut 1 inch thick**
1 **tsp. garlic and pepper salt-
free seasoning blend
(or your favorite seasoning
blend)**
¼ **tsp. salt**

1 In a medium bowl combine the sweet peppers, onion, and garlic. Drizzle with olive oil and balsamic vinegar. Sprinkle with ¼ teaspoon salt and the black pepper; toss to coat. Place sweet pepper mixture in center of an 18-inch square of double thickness heavy foil. Bring foil up around pepper mixture, forming a cup. Twist the ends of the foil to completely enclose mixture in the foil packet.

2 Trim fat from meat. Stir together the seasoning blend and ¼ teaspoon salt; sprinkle over both sides of steaks. Grill steaks and pepper packet on the rack of an uncovered grill directly over medium coals to desired doneness, turning halfway through. (Allow 8 to 12 minutes for medium rare and 12 to 15 minutes for medium.) Cook peppers for 20 minutes.

3 To serve, cut steaks into serving-size pieces. Serve the pepper mixture alongside steaks. Makes 4 servings.

Nutrition facts per serving: 391 cal., 24 g total fat (8 g sat. fat), 100 mg chol., 362 mg sodium, 8 g carbo., 1 g fiber, 35 g pro. *Daily values:* 54% vit. A, 211% vit. C, 2% calcium, 25% iron.

ROASTED VEGETABLE PIZZA

Prep: 30 min. ◆ Rise: 45 min.
Roast: 40 min. ◆ Bake: 15 min.

1⅓ cups bread flour or
      all-purpose flour
1 pkg. active dry yeast
1 tsp. sugar
1 tsp. salt
1¼ cups warm water (120° to
      130°)
2 tsp. olive oil
1⅓ cups semolina flour

◆◆◆

2 medium zucchini, cut into
   ½-inch cubes
1 medium sweet potato, cut
   into ½-inch cubes
2 whole tiny new red potatoes,
   cut into ½-inch cubes
1 cup chopped onion
2 cloves garlic, minced
1 Tbsp. olive oil
¼ cup snipped fresh basil
1 Tbsp. snipped fresh sage

◆◆◆

1 cup pasta-ready tomato
   sauce
1 cup finely shredded
   Parmesan cheese

1 For crust, in a bowl combine 1⅓ cups bread or all-purpose flour, the yeast, sugar, and salt. Add warm water and the 2 teaspoons olive oil. Beat with an electric mixer on low speed for 30 seconds, scraping bowl. Beat on high speed 3 minutes. Stir in semolina flour. Turn dough out onto a lightly floured surface. Knead in additional bread flour or all-purpose flour, if necessary, to make a moderately stiff dough that is smooth and elastic (6 to 8 minutes total). Shape dough into a ball. Place in a lightly greased bowl; turn once. Cover; let rise in a warm place until double in size (45 to 60 minutes).

2 In a greased 13×9×2-inch baking pan combine vegetable cubes, onion, garlic, and, if desired, ⅛ teaspoon each *salt* and *pepper*. Drizzle 1 tablespoon oil over vegetables; toss to coat. Roast, covered, in a 325° oven for 30 minutes; stir once. Increase oven temperature to 425°. Roast, uncovered, for 10 to 15 minutes more or until tender; stir occasionally. Add basil and sage.

3 Punch dough down; divide into 4 equal portions. Cover; let rest 10 minutes. On a lightly floured surface roll each portion into a 6- to 8-inch round. Build up edges slightly. Transfer dough rounds to greased baking sheets. Spread tomato sauce on each crust. Top sauce with vegetables. Sprinkle each pizza with Parmesan cheese. Bake 15 to 20 minutes or until crusts are golden brown. Makes 4 pizzas.

Nutrition facts per pizza: 626 cal., 15 g total fat (1 g sat. fat), 20 mg chol., 934 mg sodium, 98 g carbo., 5 g fiber, 27 g pro. *Daily values:* 75% vit. A, 30% vit. C, 24% calcium, 37% iron.

FIVE FABULOUS PIZZAS

Make your own pizza in less time than it takes to order out. For starters, pick up a prebaked Italian bread shell, such as Boboli brand, from the grocery store. Pile on one of these tasty topper combinations, pop it in a 400° oven about 12 minutes (15 to 20 minutes if crust is frozen), and sit down to a piping-hot pizza.

Hawaiian Delight: Top an Italian bread shell with pizza sauce and layers of sliced and quartered Canadian-style bacon; canned pineapple tidbits, drained; sliced pitted ripe olives; and shredded Swiss or mozzarella cheese.

Smoky Vegetarian: Season a little olive oil with chopped fresh basil, minced garlic, and a pinch of crushed red pepper; brush atop an Italian bread shell. Top with a combination of roasted sweet pepper strips, thin red onion wedges, thinly sliced zucchini, and plum tomato slices. Sprinkle with a handful of shredded smoked cheese.

Southwestern Special: Spoon your favorite salsa atop an Italian bread shell. Add cooked black beans (rinse and drain, if canned), sliced green onion, chopped tomatoes, jalapeño pepper slices, and shredded cheddar cheese. If desired, spoon dairy sour cream atop the cooked pizza.

Presto Pesto and Chicken: Spread an Italian bread shell with a thin layer of purchased pesto. Top with cooked bite-size chicken pieces; marinated dried tomatoes, drained and cut into strips; and equal parts of shredded or grated Parmesan cheese and shredded Monterey Jack cheese.

Little Italy: In a nonstick skillet cook ground turkey sausage, strips of green pepper, and chopped onion until sausage is brown and vegetables are tender. Add crushed red pepper (to taste) to spaghetti sauce with mushrooms and spread the sauce atop an Italian bread shell. Top with the sausage mixture and sprinkle with your favorite shredded cheese.

APPETIZER SPINACH AND WALNUT CALZONES

Prep: 1¼ hr. ◆ Bake: 10 min.

2½ to 2¾ cups all-purpose flour
½ cup whole wheat flour
¼ cup nonfat dry milk powder
1 pkg. active dry yeast
1 Tbsp. snipped fresh oregano
   or 1 tsp. dried oregano,
   crushed
1 tsp. salt
1 cup warm water (120°
   to 130°)
¼ cup olive oil or cooking oil
   ◆◆◆
1 cup chopped red onion
3 cloves garlic, minced
6 cups torn fresh spinach
1 cup shredded Gruyère or
   Swiss cheese (4 oz.)
½ cup chopped walnuts,
   toasted
¼ tsp. salt
¼ tsp. ground nutmeg
⅛ tsp. ground red pepper
   ◆◆◆
1 beaten egg
   Purchased spicy red pepper
   or spaghetti sauce

1 In a large mixing bowl combine 1 cup of the all-purpose flour, the whole wheat flour, nonfat dry milk, yeast, oregano, and the 1 teaspoon salt. Add water and 3 tablespoons of the oil. Beat with an electric mixer on low speed for 30 seconds, scraping sides of bowl. Beat on high speed for 3 minutes. Stir in as much of the remaining all-purpose flour as you can.

2 Turn the dough out onto a lightly floured surface. Knead in enough of the remaining flour to make a moderately stiff dough

that is smooth and elastic (6 to 8 minutes total). Divide dough in half. Cover and set aside.

3 In a large skillet cook onion and garlic in remaining 1 tablespoon oil until onion is tender. Stir in spinach; cover and cook 2 to 3 minutes or until spinach is wilted. Remove from heat. In a colander drain excess liquid from spinach mixture. Transfer spinach to medium bowl and stir in Gruyère or Swiss cheese, walnuts, ¼ teaspoon salt, the nutmeg, and ground red pepper.

4 On a lightly floured surface roll half of the dough at a time to ¼-inch thickness. Cut into 3-inch diameter rounds. Reroll scraps of dough. Place a rounded teaspoon of filling in the center of rounds. Brush edges of each round with water. Fold dough in half over filling. Seal edges with the tines of a fork. Prick tops with tines of fork in a decorative pattern. Brush with egg. Place on greased baking sheets. Bake in a 425° oven for 10 to 12 minutes or until golden. Serve with a purchased spicy red pepper or spaghetti sauce. Makes 16 calzones.

▌ TO MAKE AHEAD ▐

Prepare and bake calzones as directed, except cool completely. Place calzones in a freezer container and freeze for up to 1 month. To reheat, place frozen calzones on a baking sheet. Bake in a 375° oven for 8 to 10 minutes or until heated through.

Nutrition facts per calzone: 178 cal., 9 g total fat (2 g sat. fat), 21 mg chol., 209 mg sodium, 19 g carbo., 2 g fiber, 6 g pro. *Daily values:* 13% vit. A, 3% vit. C, 9% calcium, 11% iron.

CHICKEN ALFREDO CALZONES

Prep: 20 min. ◆ Bake: 25 min.

½ tsp. dried rosemary, crushed
1 6- to 6½-oz. pkg. pizza crust
   mix
   ◆◆◆
1 cup chopped cooked chicken
½ cup chopped red or green
   sweet pepper
⅓ cup light alfredo sauce
¼ cup finely shredded
   Parmesan cheese
¼ cup chopped pecans
2 Tbsp. snipped fresh basil or
   1 tsp. dried basil, crushed
⅔ cup light alfredo sauce,
   heated (optional)

1 Add rosemary to pizza crust mix and prepare according to package directions. Let rest for 5 minutes. Divide dough into 4 equal portions. On a lightly floured surface roll each portion of dough into a 7-inch circle.

2 Combine chicken, sweet pepper, the ⅓ cup alfredo sauce, Parmesan cheese, pecans, and basil. Divide mixture evenly among dough circles. Brush edges with water. Fold dough in half over filling. Seal edges with the tines of a fork. Prick tops 3 or 4 times with the tines of a fork. Place on a greased baking sheet. Bake in a 375° oven about 25 minutes or until golden. If desired, serve warm alfredo sauce with calzones. Makes 4 calzones.

Nutrition facts per calzone: 357 cal., 14 g total fat (3 g sat. fat), 49 mg chol., 617 mg sodium, 38 g carbo., 1 g fiber, 20 g pro. *Daily values:* 13% vit. A, 35% vit. C, 10% calcium, 14% iron.

HAM AND CHARD CALZONES

Prep: 20 min. ◆ Bake: 25 min.

*Purchased frozen pizza dough
is a step-saver for these filled pockets
that make a meal.*

**4 cups torn Swiss chard, ribs
removed**

◆◆◆

**1 frozen pizza dough round,
thawed (about 18 oz.)**
3 cloves garlic, minced
**1 tsp. dried Italian seasoning,
crushed**
**1 cup fat-free ricotta cheese or
fat-free cottage cheese,
well drained**
**4 oz. thinly sliced, extra-lean
ham, chopped (1 cup)**
**4 oz. thinly sliced, reduced-fat
Swiss cheese**

◆◆◆

**1 cup reduced-fat, pasta-ready
tomato sauce, heated**

1 Pour enough boiling water
over Swiss chard to cover. Let
stand for 5 minutes. Drain well,
squeezing out the excess liquid;
set aside.

2 Divide pizza dough into
4 equal portions. On a lightly
floured surface roll each portion
of dough into a 7-inch circle.
Brush each circle with the minced
garlic. Sprinkle with Italian seasoning. Divide ricotta cheese or
drained cottage cheese evenly
among circles, spreading only on
half of each crust and to within
½ inch of edges. Layer the Swiss
chard, ham, and Swiss cheese atop
ricotta cheese.

3 Moisten edges of dough
with water. Fold dough in half
over filling. Seal edges with the
tines of a fork. Prick tops 3 or
4 times with the tines of a fork.
Place calzones on a lightly greased
baking sheet. Bake in a 400° oven
about 25 minutes or until golden.
Serve warm tomato sauce alongside calzones. Makes 4 calzones.

Nutrition facts per calzone: 536 cal., 11 g
total fat (4 g sat. fat), 42 mg chol., 1,244
mg sodium, 75 g carbo., 2 g fiber, 39 g pro.
Daily values: 28% vit. A, 19% vit. C, 41%
calcium, 35% iron.

CURRIED CHICKEN AND VEGETABLE CALZONES

Prep: 35 min. ◆ Bake: 20 min.

*An Italian favorite takes an Oriental
turn with bits of sesame chicken
and assorted vegetables nestled in a
pizzalike crust.*

**1 16-oz. loaf frozen bread
dough, thawed**

◆◆◆

2 tsp. curry powder
¼ tsp. salt
⅛ tsp. ground red pepper
2 tsp. toasted sesame oil
**12 oz. skinless, boneless chicken
breast halves, cut into
bite-size pieces**

◆◆◆

1 Tbsp. cooking oil
**1 stalk celery, cut into ¼-inch
slices (½ cup)**
**1 small zucchini, halved
lengthwise and thinly
sliced (1 cup)**
**1 small red or yellow sweet
pepper, cut into thin bite-
size strips (¾ cup)**
**4 green onions, cut into
matchstick-size pieces**

**1 egg white
Sesame seed (optional)**

1 For crust, divide dough into
4 equal portions. Cover; let rest
while preparing filling.

2 For filling, in a medium
bowl combine curry powder, salt,
and ground red pepper. Stir in the
sesame oil. Add the chicken, tossing to coat. Set aside.

3 Heat cooking oil in a large
nonstick skillet over medium-
high heat. Add celery; cook and
stir for 2 minutes. Add zucchini,
sweet pepper, and green onions;
cook and stir 3 minutes more.
Transfer vegetable mixture to a
medium mixing bowl. Reduce
heat to medium. Add chicken to
skillet; stir-fry for 2 to 3 minutes
or until chicken is no longer pink.
Add chicken to vegetable mixture, tossing to combine.

4 On a lightly floured surface
roll each portion of dough into a
7-inch circle. Divide chicken
mixture evenly among the circles.
Brush edges with water. Fold
dough in half over filling. Seal
edges with the tines of a fork.
Prick tops 3 or 4 times with the
tines of a fork. Place on a greased
baking sheet. Combine egg white
and 1 tablespoon *water*. Brush
egg white mixture over tops of
calzones. If desired, sprinkle with
sesame seed. Bake in a 375° oven
for 20 to 25 minutes or until
golden. Makes 4 calzones.

Nutrition facts per calzone: 428 cal., 8 g
total fat (1 g sat. fat), 45 mg chol., 204 mg
sodium, 51 g carbo., 1 g fiber, 26 g pro.
Daily values: 13% vit. A, 42% vit. C, 10%
calcium, 9% iron.

SAUSAGE AND EGG BREAKFAST PIZZAS

Prep: 25 min. ◆ Bake: 8 min.

One of these deliciously topped pita pizzas is perfect for a hearty morning appetite, but if you plan to serve them for a brunch with other foods along the side, half of a pizza will be plenty.

1 Tbsp. margarine or butter
4 slightly beaten eggs
¼ cup milk
¼ tsp. seasoned salt
◆◆◆
8 oz. bulk pork sausage
2 Tbsp. all-purpose flour
1 cup milk
¼ cup sliced green onions
◆◆◆
4 large pita bread rounds
½ cup chopped green sweet pepper
1 medium plum tomato, seeded and chopped

2 tsp. snipped fresh basil or
½ tsp. dried basil, crushed
1 cup shredded Havarti or Gouda cheese (4 oz.)

1 Melt margarine or butter in a medium skillet over medium heat. In a medium mixing bowl combine eggs, the ¼ cup milk, and seasoned salt. Add the mixture to the skillet. Cook without stirring until mixture begins to set on bottom and around edge. Lift and fold partially cooked eggs so uncooked portion flows underneath. Continue cooking until just set. Remove eggs from skillet; keep warm.

2 Crumble pork sausage into skillet; cook and stir until browned. Drain in a colander; return to skillet. Stir in flour until blended. Add the 1 cup milk. Cook and stir until thickened and bubbly; cook and stir 1 minute more. Remove from heat. Carefully fold the cooked eggs into sausage mixture along with green onions.

3 Arrange pita bread rounds on a large baking sheet. Spoon egg and sausage mixture atop pita rounds. Sprinkle with green pepper, tomato, dried basil (if using), and cheese. Bake in a 400° oven for 8 to 10 minutes or until heated through. Sprinkle with fresh basil, if using. Makes 4 pizzas.

Nutrition facts per pizza: 545 cal., 29 g total fat (6 g sat. fat), 276 mg chol., 1,017 mg sodium, 43 g carbo., 1 g fiber, 26 g pro. *Daily values:* 26% vit. A, 49% vit. C, 28% calcium, 20% iron.

FRESH TOMATO SAUCE WITH PASTA

Prep: 20 min. ◆ Cook: 25 min.

Choose fresh-from-the-vine, ripe red tomatoes when making this classic summertime pasta sauce.

¼ cup finely chopped onion
2 cloves garlic, minced
1 Tbsp. olive oil, margarine, or butter
4 cups peeled, seeded, and chopped ripe fresh tomatoes (about 3 lb.)
½ tsp. salt
¼ tsp. pepper
¼ cup sliced pitted ripe olives
¼ cup snipped fresh basil or 2 tsp. dried basil, crushed
◆◆◆
6 oz. dried capellini or spaghetti
Freshly shredded Parmesan cheese

1 For sauce, in a medium saucepan cook the onion and garlic in hot olive oil, margarine, or butter until onion is tender. Stir in 2 cups of the tomatoes, the salt, and pepper. Bring to boiling; reduce heat. Simmer, uncovered, for 15 minutes, stirring occasionally. Stir in the remaining tomatoes, ripe olives, and fresh or dried basil. Heat through.

2 Meanwhile, cook pasta according to package directions. Drain. Serve tomato sauce over pasta. Sprinkle with Parmesan. Makes 6 side-dish servings.

Nutrition facts per serving: 202 cal., 6 g total fat (1 g sat. fat), 5 mg chol., 298 mg sodium, 31 g carbo., 2 g fiber, 8 g pro. *Daily values:* 10% vit. A, 48% vit. C, 6% calcium, 12% iron.

TOMATO TIME

Whether you're preparing our favorite Fresh Tomato Sauce with Pasta (see recipe, page 214), a family-pleasing soup, or side dishes, the detailed steps that follow will guide you with the greatest of ease. Don your aprons … let's get cooking!

By late August or early September the farm stands and garden markets are overflowing with ripe and juicy fresh tomatoes. Here's how to choose and store the tomatoes at their very best.

Selection: Choose plump, well-shaped, fairly firm-textured tomatoes with bright color. Ripened tomatoes will yield slightly to gentle pressure. Avoid bruised or cracked tomatoes.

Storing: If fresh tomatoes need to ripen, store them at room temperature in a brown paper bag (plastic won't work) or in a fruit-ripening bowl. Skip the temptation to stand tomatoes in the sun to ripen—they will become mushy. And, store only ripe tomatoes in a refrigerator because the chill puts the brakes on further ripening. Freezing is ideal for stretching the season. Enjoy frozen homegrown tomatoes during the cold winter months in soups, stews, and casseroles.

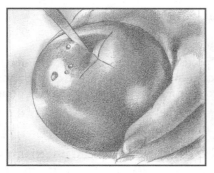

1 Simple Beginnings
Peel a fresh tomato if you plan to use it cooked in recipes, such as the Fresh Tomato Sauce on page 214. First, make a shallow X on the bottom of the tomato.

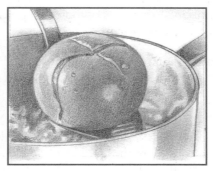

2 Basic Blanching
Place the scored tomato on a slotted spoon; dip into a pan of boiling water for 15 seconds. Rinse with cold water. A mesh colander works well for dipping large quantities.

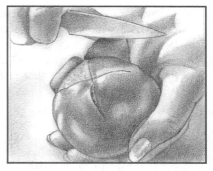

3 Perfect Peeling
After blanching the tomato, allow it to cool slightly until you can handle it. Use a paring knife to gently pull on peel where the scored skin has begun to split apart. The skin will slip off easily.

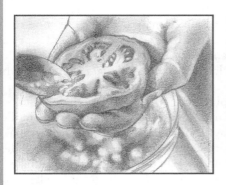

4 Simple Seeding
Not everyone loves seeds. To remove them, cut the tomato in half crosswise. Holding one half over a bowl, use the tip of a spoon to remove the seeds.

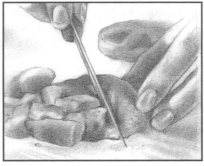

5 Clever Chopping
Place a tomato half, cut side down, on a cutting board. With a sharp knife, cut the tomato half crosswise and lengthwise into pieces of desired size.

6 Foolproof Straining
If the tomato is especially juicy, place chopped pieces in a strainer or colander set over a bowl. Allow tomato pieces to drain 10 to 15 minutes to remove excess juices.

SOUND BITES FOR SNACKING

When students forage for after-school snacks, they're too hungry to ponder nutrition, according to our teen tasters. But, they vote thumbs up for great-tasting, healthy snacks.

The grab-and-gobble snacking technique used by many teens leaves little time for them to consider the nutritional impact of the food they eat. If it looks edible and can go from hand to mouth in seconds, teens will eat it, they tell us.

Nonetheless, parents of "starving" snackers needn't despair: Snacking can offer an excellent opportunity for teenagers to boost the nutrients in their diet, according to Sheah Rarback, registered dietitian and spokesperson for the American Dietetic Association.

To find out what tempts the teen tummy, we assembled a panel of pros—six voracious teens—who agreed they'd be happy to switch from eating junk food to nutritionally sound snacks that taste good and are easy to prepare.

VEGGING OUT

Because about 25 percent of a youth's daily calorie intake comes from snacking, it's wise to be sure those calories come in a nutritionally sound package, Rarback says. You can keep the kids away from a frivolous feeding frenzy by loading the pantry and the fridge full of healthy foods to munch. Stock up on your teenager's favorite raw vegetables. Many teens will happily crunch away on fresh green beans, peas, broccoli, carrots, and celery.

Although the celery-and-carrot routine might sound humdrum, our panel of teens took to the treat, especially the popular "baby" carrots, when served with a calcium-packed, yogurt-based dip. Just one medium carrot—or nine baby carrots—supplies nearly twice the recommended requirements of vitamin A for teens and adults. And two stalks of celery have about 1 g of fiber and 15 percent of the recommended daily intake of vitamin C.

"The majority of kids aren't getting enough vegetables, but if they do get a vegetable, it's in the form of French fries," Rarback says. "That's not necessarily a good thing because French fries are not a nutrient powerhouse."

Instead, fries are loaded with fat. One medium serving of French fries from a fast food restaurant contains almost one-fourth of a teen's daily fat limit.

MOO JUICE AND MORE

The teen and preteen years are important times for loading up on calcium, says Dr. Bess Dawson-Hughes, who's concerned that adolescents aren't getting enough of that essential mineral. Bone density reaches its peak at about age 21. Scientists believe lack of adequate amounts of calcium during the teen years increases the risk of developing bone fractures due to osteoporosis.

Dawson-Hughes, a professor of medicine at Tufts University, worked on the National Academy of Sciences committee that updated calcium guidelines last year. The new guidelines boosted the recommended intake of calcium for teens from 1,200 mg to 1,300 mg in hopes of preventing bone fractures as well as osteoporosis.

"Teens are in a stage when their bodies are adding a lot of mineral to their skeleton," she says.

But teens don't always have a clue about their daily calcium needs. Only two of every 10 girls and four out of 10 boys manage to meet the daily requirement of 1,300 mg of calcium, according to data gathered by the U.S. Department of Agriculture.

"Boys are doing better than girls on calcium intake," Dr. Dawson-Hughes says. "As teens, girls switch to diet drinks and away from milk. If we can somehow make it 'cooler' to drink milk and less cool to drink diet (soda), that could have an impact on calcium intake."

It takes a little more than four 8-ounce glasses of milk to meet daily calcium requirements for adolescents. Moo juice, as teens call it, also provides vitamin D, potassium, and magnesium, which are essential for building healthy bones. Other calcium-rich foods include cheese, yogurt, and ice cream. Although there are nondairy sources, three-quarters of calcium consumed in the United States is in the form of dairy products, Dr. Dawson-Hughes says. Nondairy sources include green leafy vegetables, navy beans, tofu, and calcium-fortified orange juice and cereals.

Iron Workers

In addition to calcium, the need for iron is high during periods of rapid growth. "The teen years are high-energy times when adequate iron intake is extremely important," Sheah Rarback says. For females, iron is needed to replace red blood cells lost during menstruation. Teen girls need about 15 mg of iron per day while teen boys need about 12 mg, requirements that easily can be met through food sources. Dried fruit and nut mixtures are teen-friendly sources of iron. Most dried fruits have about 1 mg iron per ounce.

Other iron-rich foods include beef, pork, chicken, chickpeas, raisins, pumpkin seeds, spinach, sunflower seeds, and fortified breads. A 3½-ounce broiled ground beef patty supplies about 2 mg of iron. A whole wheat bun adds 1 mg more.

Other iron options include a slice of most breads or an ounce of peanuts—each have 1 mg iron.

Eating foods rich in vitamin C helps increase the absorption of iron. For example, more iron is absorbed from a piece of enriched bread when eaten with an orange or glass of orange juice.

Mega-Quick Munchies

Here are some quick and healthy munchies that were highly rated by our Teen Taste Panel. The members told us they wouldn't hesitate to nibble away on these snacks if such good eats were waiting in the fridge. The unanimous favorite was Tropical Treat, a twosome of calcium-fortified orange juice and icy yogurt cubes.

Terrific Tortillas

Make up a batch of Crunchy Cream Cheese for your kids to slather on fat-free tortillas along with salsa as a speedy after-school treat. For the creamy spread, stir together finely chopped or shredded veggies such as broccoli and carrots in half a tub of cream cheese with chive and onion. Then add a sprinkling of seasoning—such as chili powder—and stir it all together. Cover and label the container and pop it in the fridge for up to three days. Make sure the spread is in a prominent spot in the fridge so your famished teen can easily find it. Stock up on colorful, flavored tortillas to use as a base for the veggie spread. Or spread it on crackers.

Tropical Treat

Combine equal amounts of nonfat plain yogurt and thawed frozen pineapple-orange-apple juice concentrate or frozen orange juice concentrate. Freeze the mixture in ice cube trays. Plop several of the cubes into a tall glassful of calcium-fortified orange juice. Let juice stand for a minute, then crush the yogurt cubes with a spoon for a slushy refresher.

Serve-Yourself Smoothie

Blend together favorite fruits and/or yogurt with fat-free milk or pineapple juice.

Mini Tacos

Fill mini taco shells with a combination of shredded cooked pork, turkey, or chicken; chopped mango or peaches; and shredded lettuce. A drizzle of your teen's favorite low-fat dressing can top the tacos, if desired.

There is plenty of opportunity to work calcium into the diet. Teens need about 1,300 mg of calcium daily.

Yogurt, fruit-flavor, 8 oz.	314 mg
Fat-free skim milk, 8 oz.	302 mg
Orange juice, calcium-fortified, 8 oz.	240 mg
Mozzarella cheese, part skim, 1 oz.	183 mg
Bread, calcium-fortified, 2 slices	160 mg
Cottage cheese, 1 percent fat, 1 cup	138 mg
Pizza, cheese, 1 slice	116 mg
Ice cream, vanilla soft-serve, ½ cup	113 mg
Ice cream, vanilla (10 percent fat),
½ cup	85 mg

RASPBERRIES ON A CITRUS CLOUD

Start to finish: 20 min.

A little practice is all it takes to master the technique of creating a caramelized sugar filigree. The golden threads add elegance to any dessert.
(See the photograph on page 202.)

2 cups fresh red raspberries
4 tsp. raspberry liqueur (optional)

❖❖❖

1 8-oz. carton lemon-flavored yogurt
¼ of an 8-oz. container frozen fat-free whipped dessert topping, thawed

❖❖❖

3 Tbsp. sugar

1 Reserve ¼ cup raspberries. In a medium bowl gently toss remaining raspberries with liqueur, if desired.

2 In a small bowl stir together yogurt and whipped dessert topping. Spoon berry-liqueur mixture into 4 dessert dishes. Spoon yogurt mixture onto berries. If not serving immediately, cover dishes and chill for up to 4 hours.

3 Before serving, place sugar in a heavy saucepan. Heat over medium-high heat until sugar begins to melt, shaking pan occasionally to heat sugar evenly. (Do not stir.) Once the sugar starts to melt, reduce heat to low and cook about 5 minutes more or until all of the sugar is melted and golden, stirring as needed with a wooden spoon. Remove pan from heat. Let stand for 1 minute. Dip a fork into caramelized sugar and let syrup run off tines of fork for several seconds before shaking fork over dessert, allowing thin strands of caramelized sugar to drizzle over berries. If sugar starts to harden in the pan, return to heat, stirring until melted. Top with reserved berries. Serve immediately. Makes 4 servings.

Nutrition facts per serving: 148 cal., 1 g total fat (0 g sat. fat), 2 mg chol., 41 mg sodium, 32 g carbo., 3 g fiber, 3 g pro. *Daily values:* 1% vit. A, 26% vit. C, 8% calcium, 2% iron.

TOWERING BROWNIE SUNDAES

Start to finish: 30 min.

The smaller the brownies, the quicker they bake. The individual mini brownies used in this recipe bake in just 15 minutes.
(See the photograph on page 203.)

Nonstick spray coating
¼ cup butter
1 oz. unsweetened chocolate, cut up
½ cup sugar
1 egg
½ tsp. vanilla
⅓ cup all-purpose flour
¼ cup coarsely chopped peanuts

❖❖❖

1 cup chocolate-fudge ice cream topping
2 Tbsp. peanut butter
1 quart tin roof sundae ice cream or vanilla ice cream
Banana slices (optional)
Chocolate-covered peanut butter cups, chopped (optional)
Peanuts (optional)

1 Lightly spray twelve 1¾-inch muffin cups with nonstick coating; set aside. In a medium saucepan melt butter and chocolate over low heat. Remove from heat. Cool 3 minutes. Stir in sugar. Add egg and vanilla, beating lightly with a spoon just until combined. (Don't overbeat.) Stir in flour and the ¼ cup peanuts.

2 Divide batter evenly among prepared muffin cups, filling each nearly full. Bake in a 350° oven 15 minutes or until set (toothpick will not come out clean, nor will brownies spring back). Cool brownies 3 minutes in pan; remove to a wire rack to cool.

3 Meanwhile, in a heavy small saucepan stir ice cream topping and peanut butter over medium-low heat until smooth. Remove saucepan from heat. Divide ice cream into 6 serving containers. Top each serving with 2 brownies, and, if desired, banana slices. Drizzle with chocolate-peanut-butter sauce. If desired, top with peanut butter cups and additional peanuts. Makes 6 servings.

Nutrition facts per serving: 640 cal., 36 g total fat (18 g sat. fat), 95 mg chol., 299 mg sodium, 77 g carbo., 1 g fiber, 12 g pro. *Daily values:* 21% vit. A, 16% calcium, 12% iron.

APPLE AND HONEY CAKE

Prep: 20 min. ♦ Bake: 35 min.

2 cups all-purpose flour
1½ tsp. baking powder
1½ tsp. apple pie spice
½ tsp. baking soda
¼ tsp. ground cardamom
½ cup margarine or butter

1 cup honey
2 eggs
1 cup orange juice

❖❖❖

½ cup snipped dried apples
3 Tbsp. honey

1 Grease a 2-quart baking dish; set aside. Stir together flour, baking powder, apple pie spice, soda, and cardamom; set aside. In a mixing bowl beat margarine with an electric mixer on medium speed for 30 seconds. Add the 1 cup honey and eggs; beat until smooth. Add flour mixture and orange juice alternately to the beaten mixture, beating on low speed until just combined. Pour batter into prepared baking dish. Bake in a 325° oven 20 minutes.

2 Meanwhile, pour boiling water over apples to cover. Let stand 15 minutes; drain well. Sprinkle cake with apples. Bake 15 to 20 minutes more or until a wooden toothpick inserted in center comes out clean. In a small saucepan heat the 3 tablespoons honey just until warm; drizzle over cake. Cool completely. Makes 16 servings.

Nutrition facts per serving: 204 cal., 7 g total fat (1 g sat. fat), 27 mg chol., 152 mg sodium, 35 g carbo., 1 g fiber, 2 g pro. *Daily values:* 8% vit. A, 13% vit. C, 3% calcium, 7% iron.

LOW FAT

POACHED PEARS IN MARSALA

Start to finish: 40 min.

¾ cup orange juice
¾ cup sweet marsala or cream sherry
½ cup sugar

3 inches stick cinnamon

❖❖❖

4 Bosc pears (see tip, right)

❖❖❖

¼ cup dairy sour cream or light dairy sour cream
1 Tbsp. brown sugar

1 For poaching syrup, in a 4-quart saucepan combine orange juice, marsala, sugar, and cinnamon. Bring to boiling, stirring occasionally; remove from heat.

2 With an apple corer, remove core from bottom end of each pear, leaving stem end intact. Immediately after coring, dip the pear bottom in poaching syrup to retard browning, then transfer to a piece of waxed paper.

3 Add all pears to the saucepan, coating them completely in poaching liquid and arranging them stem end up. Cover; simmer 15 to 20 minutes or until tender. While poaching, occasionally spoon the syrup over the pears (this helps keep a ring from forming on pears where the syrup stops).

4 With a slotted spoon, remove pears; set aside. Discard cinnamon stick. Bring poaching syrup to boiling. Continue to boil gently until reduced to 1 cup or until syrupy (about 10 minutes). Cool (the syrup will thicken slightly as it cools). Serve immediately or transfer poaching syrup and pears to separate containers; chill up to 4 hours. Serve warm, at room temperature, or chilled.

5 To serve, stir together sour cream and brown sugar. Place pears on plates and drizzle with

TOP PEAR PICKS

Poached pears are only as good as the pears themselves. Our first choice is the Bosc variety. These golden brown pears with a long neck hold their shape well during poaching, and the skin retains its autumnlike color. The flesh remains somewhat firm, even when ripe. To test for ripeness, gently press the stem end, which should yield to the pressure if ripe. Bosc pears are in season from August through May.

Bartlett pears also can be used. To retard the skin from darkening, turn Bartlett pears frequently while poaching (or peel them before cooking). You'll find Bartletts from August through December. When ripe, the skin of Bartlett pears turns from green to bright yellow and yields to gentle pressure. Red Bartletts turn from dark red to vibrant red as they ripen. Unfortunately, the skin of these beautiful red-skinned Bartlett pears tends to turn brown when cooked.

Whichever variety of pears you choose, use ripe fruit.

poaching syrup. Spoon sour cream alongside each pear. Makes 4 servings.

Nutrition facts per serving: 211 cal., 3 g total fat (1 g sat. fat), 6 mg chol., 11 mg sodium, 43 g carbo., 4 g fiber, 1 g pro. *Daily values:* 2% vit. A, 29% vit. C, 3% calcium, 3% iron.

HOT CIDER NEWS

The latest word on drinking unpasteurized apple juice is: Don't.

Food safety watchdogs tracking foodborne illnesses warn consumers to drink only pasteurized juices. About 5 to 10 percent of juices sold are not treated for harmful microorganisms. (Some apple juice and cider production facilities are state-certified for cleanliness, but this does not mean the product is pasteurized.)

Originally, experts limited their warning to children, the elderly, and people with weakened immune systems. But information about a nasty strain of the E. coli bacteria prompted health experts to issue the blanket recommendation.

The bacteria—called 0157 H7—is especially hardy and particularly virulent. It is harbored in animal and human feces and can survive temperatures as low as 36 degrees—lower than many home refrigerators. Treating fruits and vegetables with chlorinated water kills only about 60 percent of these invisible creatures. And E. coli isn't only a problem in produce. Any raw food can act as a vehicle to ferry this or other nasty bugs, such as salmonella and listeria, into your system.

When a 1991 E. coli outbreak was traced to unpasteurized apple juice, many producers changed processing methods and no longer use apples that have fallen on the ground before harvest. In spite of such efforts, in 1996 another E. coli outbreak was traced to unpasteurized apple juice. If you buy fresh apple cider or other juice from a farm market or roadside stand and it's not labeled "pasteurized," bring it just to boiling before serving or chilling.

each side or until golden, turning once with a slotted spoon. Drain on paper towels. Repeat with remaining fritters. If desired, sprinkle fritters with powdered sugar. Cool on wire racks. Makes 12 fritters.

Nutrition facts per fritter: 91 cal., 6 g total fat (1 g sat. fat), 19 mg chol., 18 mg sodium, 9 g carbo., 1 g fiber, 2 g pro. *Daily values:* 1% vit. A, 2% vit. C, 1% calcium, 3% iron.

NUTRITION IN NO TIME

30 MIN. LOW FAT

FRESH FRUIT SUNDAE SNACKS

Start to finish: 15 min.

Entirely edible, a crispy waffle cone serves as a cup for fruit and topping.

- 1½ **cups hulled, cut-up strawberries**
- 3 **cups cut-up fruits, such as apples, bananas, cherries, seedless red grapes, kiwifruit, and/or peaches**
- 5 **giant waffle ice-cream cones**
- 2 **Tbsp. finely shredded jicama (optional)**

1 In a blender container puree strawberries; set aside. Spoon cut-up fruit into waffle cones. Drizzle with the blended strawberries. If desired, top with finely shredded jicama. Makes 5 servings.

Nutrition facts per serving: 160 cal., 1 g total fat (0 g sat. fat), 0 mg chol., 27 mg sodium, 38 g carbo., 3 g fiber, 3 g pro. *Daily values:* 93% vit. A, 157% vit. C, 5% calcium, 23% iron.

30 MIN.

AUTUMN APPLE FRITTERS

Start to finish: 25 min.

See the photograph on page 203.

- 2 **tart, medium cooking apples, such as Jonathan or Granny Smith**
- ⅔ **cup all-purpose flour**
- 1 **Tbsp. powdered sugar**
- ½ **tsp. finely shredded lemon peel**
- ¼ **tsp. baking powder**
- 1 **egg**
- ½ **cup milk**
- 1 **tsp. cooking oil**

**Shortening or cooking oil for deep-fat frying
Powdered sugar (optional)**

1 Core apples and cut each apple crosswise into 6 rings. In a medium bowl combine flour, the 1 tablespoon powdered sugar, the lemon peel, and baking powder. In a bowl use a wire whisk to beat egg, milk, and the 1 teaspoon cooking oil until combined. Add egg mixture all at once to flour mixture; beat until smooth.

2 Using a fork, dip apple rings into batter; drain off excess batter. Fry 2 or 3 fritters at a time in deep hot oil (365°) about 1 minute on

OCTOBER
Recipe Makeovers

30-minute recipes indicated in RED.
Low-fat and no-fat recipes indicated with a ♥.
Photographs indicated in italics.
*All new in 1998.

*T*each an old standby new tricks! You've made coleslaw, but have you tried Jicama Coleslaw? Barbecue may be old hat, but not when it's Pulled Pork with Root Beer Barbecue Sauce. Bread pudding has been your friend since nursery school, but try its grown-up cousin, Peanut Brittle Bread Pudding. Adding a few imaginative ingredients gives time-honored recipes new zip. Try cardamom in applesauce, rice bran in pancakes, mushrooms in fritters, and pale ale in homestyle potatoes. These recipe makeovers are tailor-made for families who want to try new foods and turn the familiar into the fabulous.

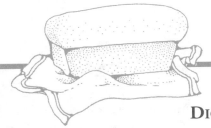

DICK AND JANE, EAT YOUR GRAINS

Sit up straight, kids, and take note. You need to eat at least six servings of breads, cereals, pasta, and grains each day for good health. Kids over the age of 6 and teenage girls need about nine servings to fuel their growing bodies. Teenage boys need even more—as many as 11 servings from this food group. Try to reach for one or more of these high-carb servings every time you eat.

First thing in the morning:
Slice of toast or half of an English muffin or bagel
½ cup cooked cereal, such as oatmeal
½ cup flaked cereal
Small bran muffin
2 small pancakes
1 small waffle

At lunch or dinner:
½ cup cooked pasta (such as macaroni or spaghetti)
½ cup chow mein noodles
1 small flour or corn tortilla
½ of a hamburger or hot dog bun
⅛ of a small pizza
2 breadsticks

1 biscuit
¼ cup bread stuffing
⅓ cup cooked rice

When you're starving for a snack:
2 to 3 cups popcorn
3 graham cracker squares
6 saltine crackers
8 animal crackers
3 gingersnap cookies
6 vanilla wafers
1 plain granola bar
10 pretzels
3 rice or popcorn cakes

---

30 MIN. LOW FAT

PICK-A-GRAIN FRUIT PANCAKES

Prep: 4 min.
Cook: 4 min. per pancake

Look for the different grains in the baking or cereal sections of your supermarket or at a health-food store.

1¾ cups all-purpose flour
2 Tbsp. sugar
1 Tbsp. baking powder
1 tsp. ground cinnamon (optional)
¼ tsp. salt
 ◆◆◆
1 slightly beaten egg
1½ cups milk
3 Tbsp. cooking oil
 Desired fruit (see options, right)
 ◆◆◆
 Margarine or butter (optional)

Maple- or fruit-flavored syrup (optional)

1 In a large mixing bowl combine flour, sugar, baking powder, cinnamon (if desired), and salt.

2 In another mixing bowl stir together the egg, milk, and cooking oil. Add egg mixture to flour mixture all at once; stir just until blended but slightly lumpy. Stir in desired fruit.

3 For each pancake, pour about ¼ cup batter onto a hot, lightly greased griddle or skillet. Cook over medium heat until bubbly and edges are slightly dry. Turn and cook until golden. If desired, serve with margarine and syrup. Makes 12 pancakes.

Fruit options: Stir one of the following fruits into the pancake batter: ½ cup chopped fresh apples, apricots, peaches, nectarines, or pears; ½ cup fresh or frozen blueberries; ⅓ cup chopped fresh cranberries; or ¼ cup chopped dried apples, pears, apricots, raisins, currants, dates, cranberries, blueberries, cherries, or mixed fruit.

Rye Pancakes: Prepare pancakes as directed, except decrease all-purpose flour to ¾ cup. Add 1 cup rye flour. Try with apples, pears, raisins, dates, or peaches.

Whole Wheat Pancakes: Prepare as directed, except decrease all-purpose flour to ¾ cup. Add 1 cup whole wheat flour.

Buckwheat Pancakes: Prepare pancakes as directed, except decrease all-purpose flour to ¾ cup. Add 1 cup buckwheat flour. Try with blueberries, cherries, or dried fruit.

Cornmeal Pancakes: Prepare pancakes as directed, except use 1¼ cups all-purpose flour. Add ½ cup cornmeal.

Oat Bran Pancakes: Prepare pancakes as directed, except use 1½ cups all-purpose flour. Add ¼ cup oat bran.

Wheat Bran Pancakes: Prepare pancakes as directed, except use 1½ cups all-purpose flour. Add ¼ cup wheat bran.

Triticale Pancakes: Prepare pancakes as directed, except decrease the all-purpose flour to ¾ cup. Add 1 cup triticale flour. Try stirring in some dried fruit.

Rice Bran Pancakes: Prepare pancakes as directed, except use 1½ cups all-purpose flour. Add ¼ cup rice bran.

Wheat Germ Pancakes: Make pancakes as directed, except use 1½ cups all-purpose flour. Add ¼ cup toasted wheat germ.

Bulgur Pancakes: Prepare as directed, except cook ¼ cup bulgur in ½ cup water for 12 to 15 minutes or until tender. For ½ cup of the all-purpose flour, substitute cooked bulgur.

Nutrition facts per plain pancake made with fresh apples: 130 cal., 5 g total fat (1 g sat. fat), 21 mg chol., 138 mg sodium, 18 g carbo., 1 g fiber, 3 g pro. *Daily values:* 3% vit. A, 1% vit. C, 11% calcium, 5% iron.

MEXICAN-STYLE BREAKFAST STRATA
Prep: 30 min. ◆ Chill 4 hr.
Bake: 40 min.

1 large green sweet pepper, chopped (1 cup)
1 large red sweet pepper, chopped (1 cup)
1 large onion, chopped (1 cup)
1 tsp. chili powder
2 Tbsp. margarine or butter
1 cup frozen whole kernel corn
1 4-oz. can diced green chili peppers
½ tsp. salt
¼ tsp. black pepper

◆◆◆

8 slices white and/or wheat bread, cubed (6 cups)
1 cup shredded cheddar cheese (4 oz.)
6 eggs
2 cups milk

◆◆◆

Salsa (optional)

1 Grease a 3-quart baking dish; set aside. In a large skillet cook sweet peppers, onion, and chili powder in hot margarine until onion is tender. Stir in corn, undrained chili peppers, salt, and black pepper.

2 In a large mixing bowl combine bread cubes, vegetable mixture, and ½ cup of the cheese; toss gently. Transfer to prepared baking dish. In a medium bowl combine eggs and milk; pour evenly over the bread and vegetables mixture. Sprinkle with remaining ½ cup cheese. Cover and chill for 4 hours or overnight.

3 Bake, uncovered, in a 325° oven for 40 to 45 minutes or until a knife inserted near the center comes out clean. Let stand for 15 minutes before serving. If desired, serve with salsa. Makes 10 servings.

Nutrition facts per serving: 215 cal., 11 g total fat (5 g sat. fat), 143 mg chol., 409 mg sodium, 19 g carbo., 1 g fiber, 11 g pro. *Daily values:* 24% vit. A, 49% vit. C, 16% calcium, 9% iron.

POTATO PIZZA
Prep: 20 min. ◆ Bake: 19 min.

See the photograph on page 240.

1 10-oz. pkg. refrigerated pizza dough

◆◆◆

1 Tbsp. olive oil
1 Tbsp. minced fresh garlic
1 8-oz. pkg. shredded four- or five-cheese blend pizza cheese
2 medium red potatoes, cooked and cut into ¼-inch slices
2 to 3 tsp. snipped fresh rosemary or 1 tsp. dried rosemary, crushed

1 Lightly grease a 15×10×1-inch baking pan. Unroll pizza dough onto greased pan, pressing out dough to a 12×10-inch rectangle. Build up edges slightly. Bake in a 425° oven 7 minutes.

2 Meanwhile, combine olive oil and garlic; brush over hot crust. Sprinkle with half of the cheese. Arrange potatoes over all. Sprinkle with remaining cheese and rosemary. Bake 12 to 15 minutes or until crust is golden. Makes 10 appetizer servings.

Nutrition facts per serving: 206 cal., 8 g total fat (4 g sat. fat), 16 mg chol., 304 mg sodium, 25 g carbo., 1 g fiber, 9 g pro. *Daily values:* 2% vit. A, 12% vit. C, 11% calcium, 5% iron.

HOT ARTICHOKE AND ROASTED PEPPER DIP

Prep: 12 min. ◆ Bake: 20 min.

See the photograph on page 240.

- 1 medium leek, thinly sliced and quartered, or ⅓ cup sliced green onions
- 2 tsp. margarine or butter
- 1 14-oz. can artichoke hearts, drained and coarsely chopped
- 1 cup grated Parmesan cheese
- 1 7-oz. jar roasted red sweet peppers, drained and coarsely chopped
- 1 cup mayonnaise, salad dressing, or light mayonnaise dressing*
- ⅛ tsp. ground black pepper

◆◆◆

- 1 Tbsp. snipped fresh parsley
- 2 Tbsp. grated Parmesan or Romano cheese

◆◆◆

  Assorted vegetable dippers, flat breads, or assorted crackers

1 In a skillet cook sliced leek or onion in hot margarine or butter until tender but not brown. Remove from heat. Stir in artichoke hearts, the 1 cup Parmesan cheese, roasted red peppers, mayonnaise or salad dressing, and black pepper.

2 Transfer mixture to an 8-inch quiche dish or 9-inch pie plate, spreading evenly. Sprinkle with parsley and the 2 tablespoons Parmesan cheese.

3 Bake, uncovered, in a 350° oven about 20 minutes or until heated through. Or, microcook on medium-high power for 6 to 8 minutes or until heated through, turning dish halfway through cooking time. Serve with assorted cut-up raw vegetable dipping sticks, flat breads, or crackers. Makes about 3½ cups.

*Note: Do not make with fatfree mayonnaise dressing or salad dressing. Dip will not set.

| TO MAKE AHEAD |

Prepare dip as directed; do not bake. Cover and chill up to 24 hours. Bake as directed.

Nutrition facts per tablespoon: 40 cal., 4 g total fat (1 g sat. fat), 4 mg chol., 71 mg sodium, 1 g carbo., 0 g fiber, 1 g pro. *Daily values:* 2% vit. A, 10% vit. C, 3% calcium.

SOFT PRETZELS WITH THREE MUSTARDS

LOW FAT

Prep: 20 min. ◆ Rise: 1¼ hr.
Shape: 30 min. ◆ Bake: 14 min.

A brew-pub favorite.
(See the photograph on page 238.)

- 4 to 4½ cups all-purpose flour
- 1 pkg. active dry yeast
- 1½ cups milk
- ¼ cup sugar
- 2 Tbsp. cooking oil
- 1 tsp. salt

◆◆◆

- 1 slightly beaten egg white
- 1 Tbsp. water

◆◆◆

  Coarse salt, sesame seed, or poppy seed
- 1 recipe Pecan Mustard (see page 225)
- 1 recipe Black and Tan Mustard (see page 225)
- 1 recipe Mole Mustard (see page 225)

1 In a large mixing bowl stir together 1½ cups of the flour and the yeast; set aside. In a medium saucepan heat and stir milk, sugar, oil, and the 1 teaspoon salt until warm (120° to 130°). Add milk mixture to flour mixture. Beat with an electric mixer on low to medium speed for 30 seconds, scraping sides of bowl constantly. Beat on high speed for 3 minutes. Stir in as much of the remaining flour as you can.

2 Turn the dough out onto a lightly floured surface. Knead in enough of the remaining flour to make a moderately stiff dough that is smooth and elastic (6 to 8 minutes total). Shape the dough into a ball. Place dough in a lightly greased bowl, turning once to grease surface of dough. Cover and let rise in a warm place until double in size (about 1¼ hours).

3 Punch dough down. Turn dough out onto a lightly floured surface. Cover; let rest 10 minutes. In a small bowl stir together the egg white and water; set aside.

4 To make diamond-shaped pretzels: Roll dough into a 14×12-inch rectangle. Cut into sixteen 7×1½-inch strips. With a sharp knife or pizza cutter, make a slit lengrhwise down center of each strip, beginning and ending ¾ inch from each end. Place strips 3 inches apart on ungreased baking sheet. Pull center apart to form a diamond shape; gently push ends toward one another to form the final shape.

5 Or, for twist-shaped pretzel sticks, roll dough into a 14×12-inch rectangle. Cut into twenty-four 7×1-inch strips. Holding a strip at both ends, carefully twist in opposite directions twice. Place strips 1½ inches apart on an ungreased baking sheet, pressing both ends down.

6 Bake in a 475° for 4 minutes. Remove from oven. Reduce oven temperature to 350°. Brush pretzels with the egg white mixture. Sprinkle pretzels lightly with coarse salt, sesame seed, or poppy seed. Bake about 10 minutes more or until golden brown. Remove from baking sheet; cool on wire racks. Serve with mustards. Makes 16 to 24 pretzels.

Nutrition facts per pretzel: 145 cal., 2 g total fat (1 g sat. fat), 2 mg chol., 148 mg sodium, 26 g carbo., 1 g fiber, 4 g pro. *Daily values:* 1% vit. A, 2% calcium, 9% iron.

Pecan Mustard: In a small bowl stir together ¼ cup coarse-grain brown mustard; ¼ cup chopped pecans, toasted; 2 teaspoons water; and 1 teaspoon lemon juice. Season to taste with salt and pepper. May be made up to 2 weeks ahead. If mustard is to be made ahead, stir in pecans just before serving. Store, covered, in refrigerator. Serve with Soft Pretzels. Makes ⅓ cup.

Nutrition facts per tablespoon: 48 cal., 4 g total fat (0 g sat. fat), 0 mg chol., 188 mg sodium, 2 g carbo., 0 g fiber, 1 g pro. *Daily values:* 1% vit. C, 1% calcium, 2% iron.

Black and Tan Mustard: In a small bowl stir together 2 tablespoons Dijon-style mustard, 2 tablespoons brown sugar, 1 tablespoon dry mustard, and 1 tablespoon stout (a type of ale) or dark beer until smooth. Store, covered, in the refrigerator up to 2 weeks. Serve with Soft Pretzels. Makes ½ cup.

Nutrition facts per tablespoon: 19 cal., 0 g total fat, 0 mg chol., 95 mg sodium, 3 g carbo., 0 g fiber, 0 g pro.

Mole Mustard: Stir 2 tablespoons prepared mole sauce into ¼ cup coarse-grain mustard. Add 3 tablespoons water, 1 tablespoon sugar, and 1 teaspoon unsweetened cocoa powder; stir until combined. Allow to stand overnight. Store, covered, in the refrigerator up to 2 weeks. Serve with Soft Pretzels. Makes ½ cup.

Nutrition facts per tablespoon: 15 cal., 1 g total fat (0 g sat. fat), 0 mg chol., 124 mg sodium, 2 g carbo., 0 g fiber, 1 g pro. *Daily values:* 1% calcium, 1% iron.

MUSHROOM FRITTERS

Prep: 15 min. ◆ Cook: 20 min.

You can also serve fritters with your favorite bottled ranch salad dressing. (See the photograph on page 239.)

- **1 cup all-purpose flour**
- **2 tsp. baking powder**
- **½ tsp. salt**
- **1 beaten egg**
- **⅔ cup milk**
- **12 oz. fresh button mushrooms, sliced (4½ cups)**

◆◆◆

Cooking oil for deep-fat frying

Green onion (optional)
1 recipe Havarti-Pepper Dip (see below)

1 To make fritters, in a medium bowl stir together flour, baking powder, and salt. In a small bowl combine egg and milk. Pour milk mixture all at once into flour mixture; stir just until moistened. Fold in mushrooms.

2 In large saucepan or deep-fat fryer, heat 3 to 4 inches oil to 365°. Carefully drop mushroom mixture by tablespoons into oil. Fry a few fritters at a time, for 3 to 4 minutes or until golden, turning once. Remove fritters using slotted spoon. Drain on paper towels. If desired, garnish with green onion. Serve immediately with Havarti-Pepper Dip. Makes 6 appetizer servings.

▮ TO MAKE AHEAD ▮

Make and drain fritters as directed. Wrap fritters and chill for up to 2 days. To reheat, place on a baking sheet. Bake, uncovered, in a 375° oven about 10 minutes or until hot and crisp.

Havarti-Pepper Dip: In a blender container or food processor bowl combine one 8-ounce carton dairy sour cream, ¾ cup shredded Havarti cheese, 1 to 2 tablespoons cracked black pepper, and ⅛ teaspoon salt. Cover; blend or process until smooth. Serve with Mushroom Fritters.

Nutrition facts per serving: 362 cal., 27 g total fat (7 g sat. fat), 72 mg chol., 459 mg sodium, 22 g carbo., 2 g fiber, 9 g pro. *Daily values:* 14% vit. A, 6% vit. C, 23% calcium, 16% iron.

TOPS IN HOPS

One of the great things about brew pubs, microbreweries, and regional breweries is how much they've expanded the range of thirst-quenching libations—both with and without alcohol. Follow this guide to pick a drink that will appeal to your taste buds.

BEERS

Beer names range from whimsical: "Rogue Dead Guy Ale" and "Snake River Zonker Stout," to completely straightforward: "Brooklyn Lager." Although this quirky way of naming brews can be confusing, if you first decide what you want in a beer, the choice is really a matter of a style.

There are basically two types of beers: ales and lagers. For a hearty beer with complex tastes and aromas, choose an ale. Or, for a beer that's crisp, light, smooth, and subtle with more carbonation, choose a lager. And for both types, the darker beers tend to have stronger flavors and often more sweet-malt or roasted-malt flavors. Hops—the green flowers of the hop vine—contribute a fruity, floral flavor and aroma, especially pronounced in darker beers. Malt, which is the dried or roasted sprouts of barley or other grains, adds a sweet, breadlike aroma and taste. Depending on how the malt is processed, it also can bring in such flavors as toffee, nuts, caramelized sugar, coffee, and chocolate.

Matching food with beer is easy to do. For fish, pasta, pizza, poultry, and Asian and Mexican foods, think about choosing a light ale or lager that will cut through the sharp tastes of these foods. For beef, pork, sausages, and game, try dark ales and lagers to match the foods' heavier flavors.

Whatever beer you choose, refrigerate it and drink it within 3 months of purchase. Unlike wine, beers deteriorate as they age.

To aid you in your beer hunt, here are the basic types identified by the Institute for Brewing Studies and other experts in the brew business.

LAGERS

American amber and red lagers. Amber to light reddish in color, often with caramel and light hop flavors. Great with the Tenderloin Sandwich on page 245 and Jicama Coleslaw on page 231.

Bocks. Ranging from light "helles" (pale) and "maibocks" (beers celebrating the month of May) to darker and more potent "doppelbocks" (very strong bocks). Often strong with flavors of malt, chocolate, and caramel. A good match for sausages.

Dark lagers. Dark amber to brown with a caramel or chocolate flavor and low or medium hop character. Offer with the Beer-Glazed Potatoes on page 231.

European pale lagers. The more flavorful forebears of most of America's mass-market beers. These brews range from the hoppier Pilsners to maltier "helles" and "export" styles. An excellent choice for the Pulled Pork with Root Beer Barbecue Sauce on page 236.

German Oktoberfest, Märzen, and Vienna lagers. Amber to reddish in color with a toasty malt character and low to medium hops. A perfect mate to the Potato Pizza on page 223.

Pale or American lagers. The beers sold by America's largest breweries. Made with rice or corn in addition to barley malt, they have clean, refreshing, mild tastes with a subtle and very balanced blend of hops and malt. These beers are popular because they go with just about everything.

Pilsners. Generally light amber to golden colored, crisp and slightly bitter. Light hop flavor, some maltiness. Serve with Mushroom Fritters on page 225.

Steam beer or California common beer. Amber to copper colored, with emphatic hop flavor and subtle bitterness, medium body. The perfect food companion: braised meats or the Sausage Pie on page 234.

ALES

Amber or red ales. Red to amber colored, sweet or nutty with a range of hop flavor from light to heavy. Brewers sometimes use the terms "amber" and "red" to indicate a beer with a higher percentage of caramel malt. Try these with Fish Fillet Muffuletta on page 236.

Barley wines or strong ales. One of the beers highest in alcohol; copper to medium brown with a rich malty flavor frequently balanced with heavy hop bitterness. These go best with salted nuts, sausages, and smoked fish and meats or desserts. Barley wines also can be served as an after-dinner drink.

Bitters. Amber to copper colored with a moderate to strong level of bitterness in a variety of styles from light to heavy. The name reflects a time when hops first came into use by English brewers. Food suggestion: Barbecued Chicken Pizza, page 234.

Brown ales. Light and slightly malty with sweet or slightly tangy overtones; can sometimes have a pronounced hop flavor. Best with Chicken in Ale, page 234.

German ales. Sometimes labeled as "altbiers" or "alts," these are amber to copper colored with medium to high maltiness and medium to high bitterness. These work well with the Four-Onion Steak on page 245.

Pale ales. A wide variety of beers ranging from the lightly hopped "cream ales" to the "India pale ales," which have very heavy hop flavor. Often, they're fruity, with nutty and toasty malt flavors, and are golden to copper colored. A natural with Sausage Pie on page 234.

Porters. These range from light brown to black with a full taste and some sweetness. They also can include chocolatelike and dark-grain flavors, and are not as bitter as a stout. Perfect with the Double-Chocolate Lava Baby Cakes on page 246.

Stouts. Some of the darkest, most heavy-bodied of beers. They can be sweet, with flavors of toast, coffee, and hops. Like porter, stouts go well with chocolate desserts or the Corn Pudding on page 232.

OTHER STYLES

Flavored beers. Raspberry, cherry, blueberry, lemon, peach, and other fruits are the most common, but this is a broad category that includes both ales and lagers. Other flavors include cinnamon, chilies, spices, and herbs. At the holidays, pumpkin pie spice is sometimes used. Some traditional beers use malt that has been smoked over either hardwoods or peat. These go best with more neutral foods such as the Soft Pretzels with Three Mustards, page 224.

Wheat beer or white ales. Made with a portion of malted or unmalted wheat; usually brewed in summer and often served unfiltered (and therefore cloudy); it has a lemony, citrusy aftertaste. German-style wheat beer may have an aroma of banana; Belgian-style white beer typically is flavored with coriander and orange peel. Try these with New Crab Cakes, page 229.

SOFT DRINKS

Birch beer. Carbonated, flavored with bark and twigs of the birch tree; flavor is similar to root beer. Because they don't have the bitterness or hops of beers, soft drinks will pair well with almost any "pub-style" food.

Cream soda. Very sweet carbonated soft drink; predominant taste is vanilla.

Root Beer. Originally made from the bark of the roots of the sassafras tree, its clean, strong flavors complement bold tastes.

Sarsaparilla. Sweet, root beer or gingerlike flavors, with carbonation.

Menu

Curried Split Pea Soup
(see below)

◆◆◆

Multigrain bread or rolls
with butter

◆◆◆

Double-Chocolate Lava
Baby Cakes
(see page 246)

---

cranberries, bay leaves, curry powder, marjoram, and pepper. Add water. Cover and cook soup on low-heat setting for 10 to 12 hours or on high-heat setting for 5 to 6 hours.

2 Remove ham bone or pork hocks from crockery cooker. Remove meat from bone; discard bone. Chop meat and return to soup. Remove bay leaves; discard. To serve, ladle soup into bowls. Makes 6 main-dish servings.

Nutrition facts per serving: 376 cal., 4 g total fat (1 g sat. fat), 25 mg chol., 626 mg sodium, 58 g carbo., 6 g fiber, 29 g pro. *Daily values:* 55% vit. A, 25% vit. C, 7% calcium, 34% iron.

CURRIED SPLIT PEA SOUP

Prep: 10 min. ◆ Cook: 10 hr. on low-heat setting or 5 hr. on high-heat setting

A Christmas ham glazed with curried cranberries inspired this winning soup.

1 lb. dry green split peas, rinsed and drained
1 1-lb. meaty ham bone or 1 lb. smoked pork hocks
1½ cups cubed ham
1½ cups chopped celery
1 cup chopped onion
1 cup chopped carrot
⅓ cup dried cranberries
2 bay leaves
4 tsp. curry powder
1 Tbsp. dried marjoram, crushed
¼ tsp. pepper
6 cups water

1 In a 3- or 4-quart electric crockery cooker combine the split peas, ham bone or smoked pork hocks, ham, celery, onion, carrot,

---

TOMATO AND VEGETABLE SOUP

Prep: 15 min. ◆ Cook: 55 min.

Take the chill off a fall day and serve a cup of this piping hot vegetable-packed soup with your favorite sandwich.

1 medium onion, finely chopped
1 medium carrot, finely chopped
1 stalk celery, finely chopped
3 cloves garlic, minced
2 cups water
2 14½-oz. cans reduced-sodium chicken broth
1 28-oz. can crushed tomatoes
⅓ cup pearl barley
1 tsp. sugar
1 tsp. dried basil, crushed
¼ tsp. pepper
2 cups firmly packed torn fresh spinach

1 In a Dutch oven combine onion, carrot, celery, garlic, and water. Bring to boiling; reduce

---

heat. Simmer, covered, 5 minutes. Add the chicken broth, undrained tomatoes, barley, sugar, basil, and pepper. Return to boiling; reduce heat. Simmer, covered, 50 minutes or until barley is done.

2 Just before serving, stir spinach into soup. Ladle into bowls. Makes 6 side-dish servings.

Nutrition facts per serving: 97 cal., 1 g total fat (0 g sat. fat), 0 mg chol., 637 mg sodium, 18 g carbo., 4 g fiber, 5 g pro. *Daily values:* 47% vit. A, 45% vit. C, 6% calcium, 12% iron.

GREEN CHILI STEW

Prep: 15 min. ◆ Cook: 2 hr.

Using medium green salsa instead of mild will add an extra kick to this hearty stew.

2 lb. beef stew meat
¼ cup all-purpose flour
¼ cup margarine or butter
6 cloves garlic, minced
3 cups beef broth
1 12-oz. bottle dark (Mexican) beer
1 cup mild or medium green salsa
2 Tbsp. snipped fresh oregano or 2 tsp. dried oregano, crushed
1 tsp. ground cumin

◆◆◆

3 cups cubed potatoes
1 14½-oz. can hominy, drained
2 4-oz. cans diced green chili peppers, drained
12 green onions, bias-sliced into 1-inch pieces
½ cup snipped fresh cilantro

1 Toss beef cubes with flour. In a 4½-quart Dutch oven brown the beef cubes, half at a time, in melted margarine or butter. Using a slotted spoon remove meat from pan. Add garlic to pan; cook for 1 minute. Carefully add beef broth, beer, salsa, oregano, and cumin. Return meat to pan. Bring to boiling; reduce heat. Simmer, covered, about 1¼ hours or until meat is nearly tender.

2 Add potatoes to the Dutch oven. Simmer, covered, about 30 minutes more or until meat and potatoes are tender. Add the hominy, green chili peppers, green onions, and cilantro; heat through. To serve, ladle into bowls. Makes 8 main-dish servings.

Nutrition facts per serving: 392 cal., 16 g total fat (4 g sat. fat), 82 mg chol., 720 mg sodium, 28 g carbo., 1 g fiber, 32 g pro. *Daily values:* 15% vit. A, 49% vit. C, 7% calcium, 38% iron.

NEW CRAB CAKES
Start to finish: 25 min.

These balance tender crab with the crunch of potato chips. (See the photograph on page 243.)

1 beaten egg
½ cup finely crushed potato chips
2 Tbsp. shredded coconut, toasted
2 Tbsp. finely chopped green onion
2 Tbsp. mayonnaise or salad dressing
1 Tbsp. snipped fresh parsley
½ tsp. ground coriander

6 oz. cooked crabmeat, cut into bite-size pieces, or one 6-oz. can crabmeat, drained, flaked, and cartilage removed

◆◆◆

2 Tbsp. cooking oil
1 recipe Herb Sauce (see below)
Shredded lemon peel (optional)

1 In a medium mixing bowl combine egg, ¼ cup of the crushed potato chips, the coconut, green onion, mayonnaise or salad dressing, parsley, and coriander. Stir in crabmeat; mix well. Shape mixture into eight ½-inch-thick patties. Coat patties with remaining crushed potato chips.

2 In a large skillet heat oil. Add crab cakes. Cook over medium heat 2 to 3 minutes on each side or until golden and heated through. Add additional oil if necessary. Serve immediately with Herb Sauce. If desired, garnish with shredded lemon peel. Makes 8 crab cakes.

Herb Sauce: In a small bowl combine ¼ cup mayonnaise or salad dressing, 1 tablespoon snipped fresh cilantro, and 1 teaspoon finely shredded lemon peel. Cover and refrigerate 1 hour to allow flavors to mellow.

Nutrition facts per crab cake with 2 teaspoons sauce: 178 cal., 16 g total fat (2 g sat. fat), 54 mg chol., 163 mg sodium, 4 g carbo., 0 g fiber, 6 g pro. *Daily values:* 2% vit. A, 9% vit. C, 2% calcium, 3% iron.

FULL-OF-BEANS CHILI
Prep: 10 min. ◆ Cook: 1¼ hr.

2 lb. ground beef
1 cup chopped onion
2 Tbsp. chili powder
2 Tbsp. ground cumin
2 cups water
1 16-oz. jar thick and chunky salsa
1 16-oz. can refried beans
1 12-oz. can beer
1 or 2 canned chipotle peppers in adobo sauce, chopped
2 15¾-oz. cans chili beans with chili gravy
2 Tbsp. lime juice

◆◆◆

Dairy sour cream (optional)
Finely shredded lime peel (optional)

1 In a Dutch oven cook beef and onion until meat is brown and onion is tender, stirring occasionally, leaving a few larger pieces of beef. Drain fat. Stir in chili powder and cumin; cook and stir for 2 minutes more.

2 Add the water, salsa, refried beans, beer, and chipotle peppers to the Dutch oven. Bring to boiling; reduce heat. Simmer, covered, for 1 hour. Stir in undrained chili beans and lime juice. Cook, covered, for 15 minutes more.

3 To serve, ladle chili into bowls. If desired, garnish with a spoonful of sour cream and finely shredded lime peel. Makes 8 to 10 main-dish servings.

Nutrition facts per serving: 469 cal., 19 g total fat (6 g sat. fat), 97 mg chol., 1,108 mg sodium, 43 g carbo., 9 g fiber, 34 g pro. *Daily values:* 28% vit. A, 66% vit. C, 10% calcium, 52% iron.

A Blender Revival

1 Blending a couple different batches of soup or sauce? Not a problem! New quick-clean buttons allow you to rinse the jar without taking the unit apart. Simply pour in 2 cups warm water and add a drop of liquid dishwashing detergent. Cover and whirl for ten seconds. Discard soapy water and rinse again with clean water—you're ready to blend again.

2 Tired of high-tech looks in your country kitchen? Gleaming chrome and a classic beehive shape bring back a touch of nostalgia. A single two-speed toggle switch gives control over tasks such as chopping, pureeing, and emulsifying.

3 Need a burst of power? Button options that give short bursts of power, no matter what the speed, help churn up chunks of potatoes or root vegetables for creamier soups, casseroles, and spreads. And, ice-crushing capabilities make quick work of cubes without the usual fuss.

4 Looking for a shot of color? Nowadays, blenders come in bright yellows, lime greens, cool blues, and vibrant reds—they're just right for party tables where ice cold drinks steal the show.

5 Do messy drips get in the way? Wipe spills easily from this flat control pad.

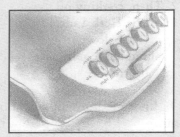

Roasted Red Pepper Soup

Start to finish: 1 hr.

- 4 medium red sweet peppers
- 1 small yellow sweet pepper
- 1 to 2 small fresh red serrano peppers
- 3 cloves garlic
- 1 Tbsp. olive oil

◆◆◆

- 1 14½-oz. can chicken broth
- ½ cup whipping cream

◆◆◆

Fresh basil leaves

1 Remove stems, membranes, and seeds from sweet and serrano peppers. Place peppers, cut side down, on a foil-lined baking sheet. Add garlic. Brush peppers and garlic with oil. Roast in a 425° oven for 20 to 25 minutes or until skins are bubbly. Wrap peppers in foil; let stand for 20 to 30 minutes or until cool. Using a paring knife, pull skins off peppers.

2 In a saucepan combine the red sweet and serrano peppers and chicken broth. Bring to boiling; reduce heat. Simmer, uncovered, about 7 minutes or until liquid is reduced by a third. Cool slightly. Meanwhile, in blender container combine roasted yellow pepper and ¼ cup of the cream. Cover and blend until pureed. Transfer to small bowl. Cover and chill pepper mixture. Rinse and dry the blender.

3 In same blender container blend half the cooked red pepper mixture at a time until smooth. Strain. Place strained mixture in same large saucepan. Stir in remaining cream. Cook and stir until heated through.

4 To serve, ladle soup into bowls. Swirl 2 tablespoons yellow pepper cream into each serving. Top with basil leaves. Makes 4 side-dish servings.

Nutrition facts per serving: 192 cal., 16 g total fat (8 g sat. fat), 41 mg chol., 340 mg sodium, 9 g carbo., 1 g fiber, 4 g pro. *Daily values:* 68% vit. A, 295% vit. C, 3% calcium, 4% iron.

JICAMA COLESLAW

Prep: 20 min. ◆ Chill: 2 to 24 hr.

See the photograph on page 244.

  3 **Tbsp. vinegar**
  3 **Tbsp. salad oil**
  1 **Tbsp. honey**
  ¼ **tsp. salt**
  ⅛ **to ¼ tsp. black pepper**
    Several dashes bottled hot pepper sauce (optional)
  ◆◆◆
  1 **lb. jicama, peeled and cut into thin, match-like strips about 2 inches long (4 cups)**
  1 **cup shredded red or green cabbage**
  1 **cup shredded carrots**
  ¼ **cup thinly sliced green onions**

1 In a screw-top jar combine vinegar, oil, honey, salt, black pepper, and, if desired, hot pepper sauce. Cover and shake well.

2 Combine jicama, cabbage, carrots, and green onions. Pour dressing over jicama mixture. Toss to coat. Chill 2 to 24 hours. Makes 4 to 6 side-dish servings.

Nutrition facts per serving: 117 cal., 7 g total fat (1 g sat. fat), 0 mg chol., 145 mg sodium, 14 g carbo., 1 g fiber, 1 g pro. *Daily values:* 52% vit. A, 41% vit. C, 1% calcium, 5% iron.

LOW FAT

POTATO-APPLE SALAD

Prep: 30 min. ◆ Cook: 20 min.
Chill: 6 to 24 hr.

  6 **medium potatoes (2 lb.)**
  ◆◆◆
  ½ **cup light mayonnaise dressing or salad dressing**
  1 **medium apple, coarsely shredded**
  2 **Tbsp. snipped fresh cilantro**
  ½ **tsp. dry mustard**
  ¼ **tsp. salt**
  ¼ **tsp. ground cumin**
    Dash ground red pepper
  1 **cup chopped carrots**
  1 **cup chopped celery**
  2 **hard-cooked eggs, coarsely chopped**
  ◆◆◆
    Milk
  1 **medium tomato, chopped**

1 Wash potatoes; cook, covered, in a small amount of lightly salted boiling water for 20 to 25 minutes or just until tender. Drain well; cool. Peel and cube the potatoes.

2 Meanwhile, for dressing, in a large mixing bowl combine the mayonnaise, apple, cilantro, dry mustard, salt, cumin, and red pepper. Stir in carrots, celery, and eggs. Gently stir in the potatoes. Cover and chill for 6 to 24 hours.

3 If mixture appears dry after chilling, stir in a little milk to moisten. Before serving, sprinkle with tomato. Makes 12 side-dish servings.

Nutrition facts per serving: 134 cal., 4 g total fat (1 g sat. fat), 36 mg chol., 189 mg sodium, 21 g carbo., 1 g fiber, 3 g pro. *Daily values:* 35% vit. A, 22% vit. C, 1% calcium, 107% iron.

BEER-GLAZED POTATOES

Prep: 25 min. ◆ Cook: 25 min.

Just a little beer brings out the best in these home-style potatoes. (See the photograph on page 239.)

  2 **Tbsp. olive oil, margarine, or butter**
  4 **medium potatoes, cut into ½-inch wedges (about 1¼ lb.)**
  ½ **tsp. salt**
  ¼ **tsp. black pepper**
  ◆◆◆
  1 **medium green sweet pepper, cut into ½-inch wedges**
  ½ **cup chopped onion**
  ¼ **cup pale ale or lager or amber non-alcoholic beer**
  ¼ **cup beef broth or chicken broth**
  1 **Tbsp. brown sugar**

1 In a 12-inch skillet heat olive oil, margarine, or butter over medium heat. Layer potatoes into skillet, sprinkling with the salt and black pepper. Cook, uncovered, over medium heat for 15 minutes, turning occasionally. (If potatoes begin to stick, add additional oil to skillet.)

2 Stir sweet pepper and onion into skillet. Cook and gently stir for 5 to 10 minutes more or until the vegetables are tender. Add pale ale or beer, beef or chicken broth, and brown sugar. Cook, uncovered, for 3 to 5 minutes more or until the beer has thickened slightly. Makes 4 to 6 side-dish servings.

Nutrition facts per serving: 226 cal., 7 g total fat (1 g sat. fat), 0 mg chol., 328 mg sodium, 37 g carbo., 2 g fiber, 4 g pro. *Daily values:* 1% vit. A, 54% vit. C, 2% calcium, 17% iron.

SAUERKRAUT AND ONIONS

Start to finish: 15 min.

- 2 Tbsp. brown sugar
- 2 Tbsp. water or beer
- 1 Tbsp. cooking oil
- ½ tsp. caraway seed
- ⅛ tsp. pepper
- 1 onion, cut into thin wedges
- 1 14½-oz. can sauerkraut, rinsed and drained

1 In a large skillet combine the brown sugar, water or beer, oil, caraway seed, and pepper. Stir in the onion wedges. Bring to boiling; reduce heat. Simmer, covered, for 7 to 8 minutes or until the onion is crisp-tender, stirring often. Add the sauerkraut; heat through. Makes 4 side-dish servings.

Nutrition facts per serving: 88 cal., 4 g total fat (1 g sat. fat), 0 mg chol., 588 mg sodium, 14 g carbo., 3 g fiber, 1 g pro. *Daily values:* 25% vit. C, 3% calcium, 10% iron.

CORN PUDDING

Prep: 30 min. ◆ Bake: 30 min.

Choose this side dish to serve with flavorful microbrewery beers. (See the photograph on page 241.)

- 3 egg whites
- 3 egg yolks

◆◆◆

- 1½ cups water
- 1 cup yellow cornmeal
- 1 tsp. instant beef bouillon granules
- ½ tsp. ground cumin
- ¼ tsp. salt
- 1 cup milk

A TOAST TO OCTOBERFEST

Raise your stein and don your lederhosen for Oktoberfest, a rollicking German festival. For two weeks in late September, revelers down steins of German beer and eat platefuls of grilled chicken, sausages, oxen, and fish. You don't have to fly to Munich to try these easy-to-make foods. Instead, ice down a selection of German beers, grill a chicken, and stir up some sauerkraut. Gut Appetit!

- 2 tsp. sugar
- 1 tsp. baking powder
- 1 tsp. dry mustard
- ½ of a 2½-oz. jar (about ⅓ cup) sliced dried beef, finely chopped
- 2 Tbsp. margarine or butter, melted
- 1 Tbsp. snipped flat-leaf parsley

◆◆◆

Sliced dried beef
Snipped fresh parsley (optional)
Flat-leaf parsley leaves (optional)

1 Allow egg whites and yolks to stand at room temperature for 30 minutes. In a large bowl beat egg whites with an electric mixer on high speed until stiff peaks form (tips stand straight); set aside. In a medium bowl beat egg yolks with an electric mixer on high speed about 5 minutes or until thick and lemon-colored. Set bowl of egg yolks aside.

2 In a medium saucepan combine water, cornmeal, beef bouillon granules, cumin, and salt. Cook and stir over medium-high heat until mixture bubbles around edges. Remove from heat. Stir in the milk, sugar, baking powder, and mustard. Stir in the dried beef, margarine or butter, and the 1 tablespoon snipped parsley. Stir in egg yolks. Gradually pour cornmeal-beef mixture over stiffly beaten egg whites, folding to combine. (Batter will be thin with small pockets of egg white showing.)

3 Pour mixture into 8 greased 1- to 1¼-cup soufflé dishes.* Bake in a 325° oven for 25 minutes. Arrange a slice of dried beef on top of each. Bake for 5 to 10 minutes more or until a knife inserted near center comes out clean. If desired, sprinkle with additional snipped fresh parsley and garnish with parsley leaves. Serve immediately. Makes 8 side-dish servings.

*****Note:** Or, pour the mixture into a greased 2-quart square baking dish. Bake for 30 minutes. Arrange slices of dried beef on top. Bake for 5 to 10 minutes more. Serve immediately.

Nutrition facts per serving: 204 cal., 8 g total fat (4 g sat. fat), 131 mg chol., 796 mg sodium, 22 g carbo., 1 g fiber, 10 g pro. *Daily values:* 23% vit. A, 2% vit. C, 10% calcium, 14% iron.

ROAST HERBED CHICKEN

Prep: 15 min. ◆ **Grill: 1 hr.**

Grilled or roasted, the flavorful juices get locked in and the meat is tender and moist.

- 1 2½- to 3-lb. broiler-fryer chicken
- 2 Tbsp. margarine or butter
- 3 Tbsp. lemon juice
- 1 tsp. dried thyme, savory, or sage, crushed
- 3 cloves garlic, minced
- ¼ tsp. salt
- ¼ tsp. pepper
  Fresh thyme (optional)

1 Rinse chicken; pat dry with paper towels. Skewer neck skin to back; tie legs to tail. Twist wing tips under back. Melt margarine or butter; stir in lemon juice, herb, garlic, salt, and pepper. Brush margarine mixture onto chicken. Grill or roast as directed below. Brush occasionally with remaining herb mixture during the first 45 minutes.

2 To serve, cut into pieces. If desired, garnish with fresh thyme. Makes 4 to 6 servings.

To grill indirect: In a covered grill arrange medium-hot coals around a drip pan. Test for medium heat above the pan. Place the chicken, breast side up, on the grill rack over the drip pan but not over the preheated coals. Lower the grill hood. Grill for 1 to 1¼ hours or until no longer pink and the drumsticks move easily in their sockets. Add more coals to maintain heat as necessary.

To roast: Place chicken, breast side up, on a rack in a shallow roasting pan. Roast, uncovered, in a 375° oven for 1¼ to 1½ hours or until no longer pink and the drumsticks move easily in their sockets.

Nutrition facts per serving: 237 cal., 16 g total fat (4 g sat. fat), 66 mg chol., 262 mg sodium, 2 g carbo., 0 g fiber, 21 g pro. *Daily values:* 10% vit. A, 10% vit. C, 1% calcium, 8% iron.

PRIZE TESTED RECIPE WINNER

TAILGATE CHICKEN AND TUSCAN RICE SALAD

Prep: 35 min. ◆ **Chill: 4 to 24 hr.**

Hungry fans will cheer this portable rice salad flavored with feta cheese and veggies. If transporting to a game, pack with an ice pack in an insulated cooler.

- 1 cup long grain rice
- 2 cups water
- 1 2.25-oz. can sliced ripe olives, drained
- ½ cup roasted sweet peppers, drained and chopped
- ½ cup cooked or canned garbanzo beans, drained
- ¼ cup thinly sliced green onions
- 1 6- or 6½-oz. jar marinated artichoke hearts

◆◆◆

- 12 oz. skinless, boneless chicken breasts
- 2 tsp. chili powder
- ½ tsp. dried rosemary, crushed
- ½ cup crumbled feta cheese with basil and tomato or plain crumbled feta

1 In a medium saucepan, combine rice and water. Bring to boiling; reduce heat. Simmer, covered, about 15 minutes or until water is absorbed. Place rice in colander; rinse with cold water. Set aside to drain. In a large mixing bowl combine olives, roasted sweet peppers, garbanzo beans, and green onions. Drain artichokes, reserving marinade. Chop artichokes; add to salad mixture along with cooked rice.

2 Cut chicken into bite-sized strips. Sprinkle with chili powder and rosemary. In a large nonstick skillet cook chicken in 1 tablespoon of the reserved artichoke marinade over medium heat for 3 to 4 minutes or until no pink remains in chicken. Add chicken to rice mixture along with remaining marinade. Add feta cheese, tossing gently to combine. Cover and chill for 4 to 24 hours. Makes 6 main-dish servings.

Nutrition facts per serving: 264 cal., 8 g total fat (2 g sat. fat), 38 mg chol., 376 mg sodium, 33 g carbo., 2 g fiber, 16 g pro. *Daily values:* 13% vit. A, 71% vit. C, 7% calcium, 19% iron.

Menu

**Sausage Pie
(see below right)**

♦♦♦

**Mixed green salad with
dried tomatoes, crumbled
feta or blue cheese, pine
nuts, and a vinaigrette**

♦♦♦

Pale ale

BARBECUED CHICKEN PIZZA

Prep: 20 min. ♦ Bake: 19 min.

*A favorite at brew pubs all over the
country, this easy main dish is a
natural for parties.
(See the photograph on page 243.)*

1   **10-oz. pkg. refrigerated
    pizza dough**

♦♦♦

½   **of a 32-oz. container (about
    2 cups) shredded cooked
    chicken in barbecue sauce**

1   **8-oz. pkg. shredded four-
    or five-cheese blend pizza
    cheese**

¼   **cup snipped fresh cilantro**

1 Lightly grease a 15×10×1-
inch baking pan. Unroll the pizza
dough into greased pan, pressing
out the dough with your hands to
a 12×10-inch rectangle. Build up
the edges slightly. Bake dough in
a 425° oven 7 minutes. Remove
from oven.

2 Spread the shredded cooked
chicken in barbecue sauce evenly
over the hot crust. Sprinkle cheese
and cilantro over chicken. Bake

12 to 15 minutes or until lightly
browned. Cut into wedges. Makes
6 main-dish servings.

*Nutrition facts per serving: 324 cal., 13 g
total fat (6 g sat. fat), 39 mg chol., 683 mg
sodium, 33 g carbo., 1 g fiber, 20 g pro.
Daily values: 9% vit. A, 13% vit. C, 19%
calcium, 9% iron.*

LOW FAT

CHICKEN IN ALE

Start to finish: 35 min.

*To make sure pasta and chicken are
done at the same time, start water
boiling for the fettuccine before you put
the chicken on to cook.
(See the photograph on page 243.)*

6   **skinless, boneless chicken
    breast halves (about 1½ lb.
    total)**

⅓   **cup chopped onion**

4   **tsp. cooking oil**

2½ **cups chopped mixed fresh
    mushrooms (such as
    white, chanterelle,
    cremini, and shiitake)**

1¼ **cups chicken broth**

⅓   **cup brown ale or beer or
    amber non-alcoholic beer**

4   **tsp. white wine
    Worcestershire sauce**

1   **Tbsp. snipped fresh thyme
    or ½ tsp. dried thyme,
    crushed**

¼   **tsp. salt**

¼   **tsp. pepper**

♦♦♦

12 **oz. dried fettuccine**

♦♦♦

3   **Tbsp. all-purpose flour
    Fresh thyme sprigs
    (optional)**

1 Rinse chicken; pat dry. In a
large skillet brown chicken breasts
and onion in hot oil over medium-high heat, turning chicken

once to brown both sides (about
2 minutes per side). Add mushrooms, ¾ cup of the chicken
broth, the ale or beer,
Worcestershire sauce, thyme, salt,
and pepper. Bring to boiling;
reduce heat. Cook, covered,
about 5 minutes or until chicken
is tender and no longer pink.

2 Meanwhile, cook the fettuccine according to package directions. Drain well. Set aside and
keep warm. Remove chicken
breasts to a serving platter and
keep warm.

3 In a screw-top jar shake
together flour and remaining
chicken broth; add to skillet.
Cook and stir until thickened and
bubbly. Cook and stir for
1 minute more. Serve chicken
and sauce over fettuccine. If
desired, garnish with sprigs of
thyme. Makes 6 servings.

*Nutrition facts per serving: 413 cal., 8 g
total fat (2 g sat. fat), 60 mg chol., 336 mg
sodium, 52 g carbo., 1 g fiber, 32 g pro.
Daily values: 3% vit. C, 2% calcium,
26% iron.*

SAUSAGE PIE

Prep: 40 min. ♦ Bake: 45 min.

*The perfect hearty dish for brisk
autumn evenings.
(See the photograph on page 244.)*

1   **16-oz. pkg. hot roll mix**

♦♦♦

1   **lb. bulk sweet or hot Italian
    sausage**

4   **cups sliced fresh mushrooms**

1   **cup chopped onion**

1   **cup chopped red sweet
    pepper**

2   **cloves garlic, minced**

1 **8-oz. can pizza sauce**

◆◆◆

2 **cups shredded smoked
mozzarella or provolone
cheese (8 oz.)**

◆◆◆

1 **egg**
1 **Tbsp. water**

1 Prepare hot roll mix according to package directions through the kneading step. Cover; let dough rest for 5 to 10 minutes.

2 In a large skillet cook sausage over medium heat until meat is brown. Drain off fat, reserving 1 tablespoon fat in skillet. Add mushrooms, onion, red pepper, and garlic. Cook over medium heat until vegetables are tender. Drain off any liquid. Stir in pizza sauce. Set mixture aside.

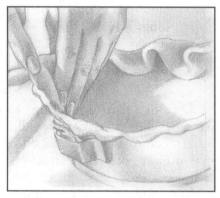

3 Grease the bottom and sides of a 9-inch springform pan. On a lightly floured surface roll three-fourths of the dough into a 15-inch circle. Fit into the bottom and press up the sides of the springform pan (see photo, above). Sprinkle bottom of dough with ½ cup of the mozzarella or provolone cheese. Spoon meat mixture over cheese. Sprinkle remaining cheese over meat. Press lightly into meat filling.

4 On a lightly floured surface roll the remaining dough into a 9-inch circle; place on top of meat-cheese mixture. Fold edge of bottom dough over top dough; pinch to seal.

5 In a small bowl beat together egg and water. Brush top of pie with egg-water mixture; allow to dry 5 minutes. With a sharp knife, score top of pie in a diamond pattern but do not cut all the way through the dough.

6 Bake in a 350° oven for 45 to 50 minutes or until golden brown. Cool in pan on a wire rack 20 minutes. To serve, use a small spatula or table knife to loosen pie from sides of pan; remove pan sides. Cut pie into wedges. Makes 8 main-dish servings.

Nutrition facts per serving: 482 cal., 20 g total fat (7 g sat. fat), 100 mg chol., 1,057 mg sodium, 50 g carbo., 0 g fiber, 25 g pro. *Daily values:* 23% vit. A, 49% vit. C, 17% calcium, 17% iron.

PAN-FRIED TROUT

Start to finish: 35 min.

1 **lb. fresh or frozen rainbow
trout fillets**
¼ **cup milk**
⅓ **cup ground hickory nuts or
hazelnuts (filberts)**
⅓ **cup cornmeal**
½ **tsp. onion salt**

◆◆◆

¼ **cup cooking oil**
1 **recipe Corn and Zucchini
Relish (see right)**

1 Thaw fish, if frozen. Rinse fish; pat dry. Cut fish into 4 serving-size pieces, if necessary. Measure thickness of fish. Put

milk in a shallow dish. In a second shallow dish combine nuts, cornmeal, and onion salt.

2 Dip each piece of fish in the milk, then in the nut mixture. In a 12-inch skillet heat oil over medium heat. Add fish fillets in a single layer. Fry fish on 1 side until golden. Turn carefully. Fry until second side is golden and fish flakes easily with a fork. Allow 2 to 3 minutes per side for ½-inch-thick fillets. Drain on paper towels. Serve with Corn and Zucchini Relish. Serves 4.

Nutrition facts per serving with ½ cup Corn and Zucchini Relish: 450 cal., 25 g total fat (4 g sat. fat), 66 mg chol., 375 mg sodium, 31 g carbo., 2 g fiber, 28 g pro. *Daily values:* 9% vit. A, 28% vit. C, 9% calcium, 22% iron.

CORN AND ZUCCHINI RELISH

Prep: 10 min. ◆ Chill: 4 hr.

1 **cup frozen whole kernel corn**
1 **medium zucchini, chopped**
¼ **cup finely chopped red sweet
pepper**
¼ **cup vinegar**
3 **Tbsp. sugar**
½ **tsp. dried dillweed**
¼ **tsp. salt**
¼ **tsp. dry mustard
Corn husks (optional)**

1 In a bowl combine corn, zucchini, red sweet pepper, vinegar, sugar, dillweed, salt, and mustard. Cover and chill at least 4 hours. To serve, with a slotted spoon place relish into corn husks, if desired. Serve alongside Pan-Fried Trout. Or, spoon relish atop Pan-Fried Trout.

PULLED PORK WITH ROOT BEER BARBECUE SAUCE

**Prep: 15 min.
Cook: 8 hr. (low) or 4 hr. (high)**

Find root beer concentrate in the spice section of supermarkets. (See the photograph on page 237.)

1 2½- to 3-lb. pork sirloin roast
½ tsp. salt
½ tsp. pepper
1 Tbsp. cooking oil
2 medium onions, cut into thin wedges
1 cup root beer*
2 Tbsp. minced garlic

◆◆◆

2 12-oz. cans or bottles root beer* (3 cups)
1 cup bottled chili sauce
¼ tsp. root beer concentrate (optional)
 Several dashes bottled hot pepper sauce (optional)

◆◆◆

8 to 10 hamburger buns, split (and toasted, if desired)
 Lettuce leaves (optional)
 Tomato slices (optional)

1 Trim fat from meat. If necessary, cut roast to fit into crockery cooker. Sprinkle meat with the salt and pepper. In a large skillet brown roast on all sides in hot oil. Drain. Transfer meat to a 3½-, 4-, or 5-quart electric crockery cooker. Add onions, the 1 cup root beer, and garlic. Cover and cook on low-heat setting for 8 to 10 hours or on high-heat setting for 4 to 5 hours.

GREAT CASUAL NAPKINS

For wonderful, easy-to-care-for dinner napkins, purchase inexpensive fingertip towels in colors to match casual tablecloths. They do a great job on the messiest of hands.

Betty Haeberle
Grove, Oklahoma

2 Meanwhile, for sauce, in a medium saucepan combine the 2 cans or bottles of root beer and bottled chili sauce. Bring to boiling; reduce heat. Boil gently, uncovered, stirring occasionally, about 30 minutes or until mixture is reduced to 2 cups. If desired, add root beer concentrate and bottled hot pepper sauce,

3 Transfer roast to a cutting board or serving platter. With a slotted spoon remove onions from juices and place on serving platter. Discard juices. Using 2 forks, pull meat apart into shreds. To serve, line buns with lettuce leaves and sliced tomatoes, if desired. Add meat and onions; spoon on sauce. Makes 8 to 10 main-dish servings.

*Note: Do not substitute diet root beer.

Nutrition facts per serving: 356 cal., 10 g total fat (3 g sat. fat), 59 mg chol., 786 mg sodium, 44 g carbo., 1 g fiber, 22 g pro. *Daily values:* 4% vit. A, 9% vit. C, 4% calcium, 13% iron.

FISH FILLET MUFFULETTA

Start to finish: 25 min.

To keep fish captivatingly crisp, assemble these hearty meal-size sandwiches just before serving. (See the photograph on page 237.)

4 frozen battered or breaded fish fillets
3 Tbsp. mayonnaise or salad dressing
1 tsp. finely shredded lime peel
2 tsp. lime juice
1 cup packaged shredded cabbage with carrots (cole-slaw mix)
2 Tbsp. capers, drained (optional)
4 individual French-style or club rolls (3½ to 4 inches long)
½ cup salsa
½ cup sliced pitted kalamata olives

1 Cook fish according to package directions. Meanwhile, in a medium bowl stir together mayonnaise or salad dressing, lime peel, and lime juice. Add cabbage and, if desired, capers. Stir until well combined. Set aside. Split rolls horizontally. Hollow out the inside of top halves of rolls, leaving a ½-inch-thick shell. Spoon cabbage mixture on the bottom half of each roll. Top with a piece of fish and salsa. Sprinkle with olives. Add top of roll. Makes 4 servings.

Nutrition facts per serving: 447 cal., 25 g total fat (4 g sat. fat), 26 mg chol., 937 mg sodium, 45 g carbo., 1 g fiber, 14 g pro. *Daily values:* 5% vit. A, 35% vit. C, 6% calcium, 16% iron.

Right: *Fish Fillet Muffuletta*
(page 236)
Below: *Pulled Pork with Root Beer*
Barbecue Sauce (page 236)

Left: *Beer-Glazed Potatoes (page 231)*
Below: *Mushroom Fritters (page 225)*
Page 238: *Soft Pretzels with Three Mustards (page 224)*

Above: *Hot Artichoke and Roasted Pepper Dip (page 224)*
Left: *Potato Pizza (page 223)*
Page 241: *Corn Pudding (page 232)*

Left: *Chicken in Ale (page 234)*
Below: *Barbecued Chicken Pizza (page 234)*
Bottom: *New Crab Cakes (page 229)*
Page 242: *Peanut Brittle Bread Pudding (page 246)*

Right: *Four-Onion Steak (page 245)*
Below: *Tenderloin Sandwich (page 245),*
Jicama Coleslaw (page 231)
Bottom: *Sausage Pie (page 234)*

TENDERLOIN SANDWICH

Start to finish: 35 min.

*Big, hearty sandwiches like these are
what makes brew-pub food so popular.
Jicama is a root vegetable with brown
skin, crisp flesh, and a sweet, nutty
flavor. It is available in the produce
aisle of most supermarkets.
(See the photograph on page 244.)*

12 oz. pork tenderloin

♦♦♦

3 Tbsp. all-purpose flour
**¼ tsp. onion powder or garlic
        powder**
¼ tsp. ground red pepper
¼ tsp. black pepper

♦♦♦

2 Tbsp. cooking oil

♦♦♦

4 slices Muenster cheese (4 oz.)
**4 kaiser rolls, sourdough rolls
        or large buns, split and
        toasted**
    Red onion slices (optional)
**1 recipe Jicama Coleslaw
        (see page 231)**
    **Mustard, catsup, green
        onions, and/or dill pickle
        slices (optional)**

1 Cut pork crosswise into
4 pieces. Place 1 piece between
2 pieces of clear plastic wrap.
Working from center, pound
lightly with the flat side of a mallet to ¼-inch thickness. Remove
plastic wrap. Repeat with remaining pork pieces.

2 In a shallow dish combine
flour, onion or garlic powder,
ground red pepper, and black
pepper. Dip meat into the flour
mixture to coat.

3 In a 12-inch skillet cook
pork in hot oil over medium heat

for 6 to 8 minutes or until no
pink remains and juices run clear,
turning once. Remove from skillet. (If all slices won't fit in skillet,
fry in 2 batches, adding additional oil if necessary.)

4 Place cheese and pork on
roll bottoms. Top with onion
slices (if desired), about ¼ cup of
the Jicama Coleslaw, and roll
tops. Serve additional Jicama
Coleslaw as a side dish. If desired,
pass mustard, catsup, green
onions, and/or dill pickle slices.
Makes 4 servings.

*Nutrition facts per serving (without
coleslaw):* 460 cal., 21 g total fat (8 g sat.
fat), 87 mg chol., 532 mg sodium, 35 g
carbo., 0 g fiber, 32 g pro.
Daily values: 10% vit. A, 22% calcium,
21% iron.

FOUR-ONION STEAK

Prep: 20 min. ♦ Cook: 14 min.

*Top loin steaks go by different names
including New York steaks, strip steaks,
shell steaks, Delmonico steaks, and
Kansas City (strip) steaks.
(See the photograph on page 244.)*

**2 12-oz. boneless beef top
        sirloin steaks cut 1 inch
        thick**
¾ tsp. garlic salt
½ tsp. chili powder
¼ tsp. pepper
⅛ tsp. ground cinnamon
1 Tbsp. cooking oil

♦♦♦

**1 large white onion, thinly
        sliced**
**1 medium leek, thinly sliced
        (⅓ cup)**
2 shallots, chopped (¼ cup)
½ cup beef broth
1 tsp. Worcestershire sauce
½ cup sliced green onions

**Four-Onion Steak served
atop a piece of toasted
country-style bread
(see below left)**

♦♦♦

Potato chips

♦♦♦

German ale

♦♦♦

Apple spice cake

1 Cut steaks into 4 portions.
Combine garlic salt, chili powder,
pepper, and cinnamon. Use your
fingers to press mixture onto both
sides of each steak portion. In a
large skillet cook steaks in hot oil
over medium heat to desired
doneness, turning once. (Allow
8 to 11 minutes for medium rare
or 12 to 14 minutes for medium.)
Transfer steaks to a serving platter,
reserving the drippings in the skillet. Keep warm.

2 For sauce, add white onion,
leek, and shallots to skillet. Cook
and stir over low heat about
5 minutes or until onions are tender. Carefully add beef broth and
Worcestershire sauce. Cook and
stir for 1 to 2 minutes more or
until broth is slightly reduced.
Add green onions. Spoon onion
mixture over steaks. If desired,
garnish with additional *green
onion pieces.* Makes 4 servings.

Nutrition facts per serving: 274 cal., 11 g
total fat (4 g sat. fat), 69 mg chol., 580 mg
sodium, 8 g carbo., 2 g fiber, 34 g pro.
Daily values: 16% vit. A, 14% vit. C, 3%
calcium, 24% iron.

DOUBLE-CHOCOLATE LAVA BABY CAKES

Prep: 20 min. ◆ Bake: 15 min.

This is a two-fork dessert—so rich it can easily be shared. Though it looks complicated, this is basically a brownie recipe with a little fun added. (See the photograph on page 2.)

- ¾ cup butter
- 1 6-oz. pkg. (1 cup) semisweet chocolate pieces

◆◆◆

- 1 recipe Praline Sauce (see right)
- 3 eggs
- 3 egg yolks
- ⅓ cup sugar
- 1½ tsp. vanilla
- ⅓ cup all-purpose flour
- 3 Tbsp. unsweetened cocoa powder

◆◆◆

- ⅓ cup pecan halves, toasted

1 Lightly grease and flour six 1- to 1¼-cup soufflé dishes or six 10-ounce custard cups. Place soufflé dishes or custard cups in a shallow baking pan and set pan aside. In a heavy small saucepan melt butter and semisweet chocolate over low heat, stirring constantly. Remove from heat; cool.

2 Meanwhile, prepare Praline Sauce. Cover and keep sauce warm until needed. In a bowl beat whole eggs, egg yolks, sugar, and vanilla with an electric mixer on high speed 5 minutes or until thick and lemon-colored. Beat in cooled chocolate mixture on medium speed. Sift flour and cocoa powder over chocolate mixture; beat on low speed just until combined. Spoon into prepared dishes or cups.

3 Bake in a 400° oven for 10 minutes. Pull cakes out of oven. Using a table knife, carefully puncture top of each partially cooked cake. Slowly spoon about 1 tablespoon Praline Sauce into center of each cake. Return cakes to oven. Bake about 5 minutes more or until the cakes feel firm at the edges.

4 Cool cakes in soufflé dishes or custard cups on a wire rack for 3 minutes. Using a table knife, loosen edge of cakes from side of dish or cup and slip cakes out upright on a serving platter or individual dessert plates.

5 Stir the toasted pecan halves into remaining Praline Sauce. If necessary, stir 1 to 2 teaspoons *hot water* into remaining sauce to thin. Spoon warm Praline Sauce on top of cakes. If desired, garnish with *edible flowers.* Serve immediately. Makes 6 servings.

Praline Sauce: In a heavy medium saucepan combine ½ cup granulated sugar, ⅓ cup packed brown sugar, and 2 tablespoons dark-colored corn syrup. Stir in ½ cup whipping cream. Cook over medium-high heat until mixture boils, stirring constantly to dissolve sugar. Reduce heat. Cook, uncovered, about 10 minutes or until thickened, stirring occasionally.

Nutrition facts per serving with 2½ tablespoons sauce: 700 cal., 48 g total fat (21 g sat. fat), 302 mg chol., 281 mg sodium, 67 g carbo., 1 g fiber, 8 g pro. *Daily values:* 51% vit. A, 7% calcium, 17% iron.

PEANUT BRITTLE BREAD PUDDING

Prep: 25 min. ◆ Bake: 40 min.

This scrumptious variation on the original also can be made with chopped pecan pralines or other candied nuts. (See the photograph on page 242.)

- 2¼ cups milk
- 4 beaten eggs
- ½ cup sugar
- 1 Tbsp. vanilla
- 1 tsp. finely shredded orange peel
- ½ tsp. ground cinnamon
- 4 cups dry French, Italian, or sourdough bread cubes*
- 1 cup coarsely chopped peanut brittle

1 recipe Bananas Foster Sauce
   (see below)
   Vanilla ice cream (optional)

1 In a large mixing bowl beat together milk, eggs, sugar, vanilla, orange peel, and cinnamon. Place bread cubes in an ungreased 2-quart square baking dish. Pour egg mixture evenly over bread cubes. Sprinkle with chopped peanut brittle.

2 Bake in a 350° oven for 40 to 45 minutes or until a knife inserted in center comes out clean. Cool slightly. To serve, spoon warm bread pudding into bowls. If desired garnish with long, fine *orange peel shreds.* Top with Bananas Foster Sauce and, if desired, vanilla ice cream. Serves 8.

*Note: To dry bread cubes, place cubes in a large pan and bake in a 350° oven for 10 to 15 minutes or until dry but not brown, stirring twice.

Bananas Foster Sauce: In a large skillet melt ⅓ cup margarine or butter over medium heat. Stir in ⅓ cup packed brown sugar until melted. Add 2 medium bananas, sliced; cook and gently stir over medium heat about 1 minute or until heated through. Remove from heat. Stir in ⅛ teaspoon ground cinnamon; 1 tablespoon rum or orange juice; and 1 tablespoon banana liqueur, crème de cacao, or orange juice. Serve immediately.

Nutrition facts per serving with 3 tablespoons sauce: 364 cal., 14 g total fat (7 g sat. fat), 132 mg chol., 255 mg sodium, 50 g carbo., 1 g fiber, 9 g pro.
Daily values: 16% vit. A, 6% vit. C, 10% calcium, 9% iron.

PRIZE TESTED RECIPE WINNER

WINTER FRUIT COMPOTE

Prep: 20 min. ◆ **Cook: 3 hr. (low)**

The spicy-sweet aroma and flavor makes this apple-pear combo an irresistible winter treat.

3 medium cooking apples, cored and sliced
2 medium pears, cored and sliced
1 16-oz. can whole cranberry sauce
¼ cup water
½ tsp. grated fresh ginger
½ tsp. finely shredded lemon peel
½ tsp. ground cinnamon
◆◆◆
Toasted angel food cake (optional)

1 In a 3½- to 4-quart electric crockery cooker combine the apples, pears, cranberry sauce, water, ginger, lemon peel, and cinnamon. Cover and cook on the low-heat setting for 3 to 4 hours.

2 To serve, spoon warm fruit mixture over toasted angel food cake pieces, if desired. Or, serve in individual compote dishes. Makes 8 to 10 servings.

Nutrition facts per serving: 135 cal., 0 g total fat, 0 mg chol., 17 mg sodium, 35 g carbo., 3 g fiber, 0 g pro.
Daily values: 10% vit. C, 2% iron.

RASPBERRY-SAUCED FRUIT CRISP

Prep: 15 min.
Cook: 3 hr. (low) plus 10 min. (high)

This crisp—tender fruit topped with a buttery crunch—is made easily in a crockery cooker.

1 10-oz. pkg. frozen red raspberries in syrup, thawed
2 Tbsp. sugar
4 tsp. quick-cooking tapioca
1 16-oz. pkg. frozen unsweetened peach slices
3 medium cooking apples, peeled, cored, and sliced
¼ cup dried tart red cherries or dried cranberries
◆◆◆
1½ cups granola
2 Tbsp. flaked coconut, toasted
2 Tbsp. butter, melted
   Vanilla ice cream (optional)

1 In a 3½- to 4-quart electric crockery cooker stir together the raspberries in syrup, sugar, and tapioca. Add peach slices, apple slices, and dried cherries or cranberries. Stir gently to coat fruit. Cover and cook on the low-heat setting for 3 hours.

2 Meanwhile, stir together the granola, coconut, and melted butter. Turn crockery cooker to the high-heat setting. Stir the fruit mixture. Sprinkle granola mixture atop fruit. Cover and cook for 10 minutes more. To serve, spoon crisp into bowls. If desired, top with ice cream. Makes 8 servings.

Nutrition facts per serving: 250 cal., 7 g total fat (4 g sat. fat), 8 mg chol., 76 mg sodium, 46 g carbo., 4 g fiber, 3 g pro.
Daily values: 8% vit. A, 19% vit. C, 2% calcium, 7% iron.

THE APPLE CORPS

For the best applesauce, select your apples from among the following varieties.

Crispin: Green color with a pink blush. Sweet, juicy flavor.

Golden Delicious: Yellow to light green skin. Mellow, with juicy flavor.

Jonagold: Yellow and red skin. Sweet and juicy flavor.

Jonathan: Light red stripes over a golden yellow or deep-red skin. Semi-tart flavor.

McIntosh: Mixed red and green color. Tart, tender, and juicy flavor.

Rome Beauty: Red and red-striped skin. Firm. Medium-tart to sweet.

Winesap: Deep purplish-red, thick skin. Tangy, wine-like flavor.

LOW FAT

CARDAMOM-GINGER APPLESAUCE

Prep: 45 min. ◆ Cook: 8 min.

Store this sauce in your refrigerator for up to a week, or freeze it for 8 months.

½ **of a 3-inch stick of cinnamon, broken up**

½ **tsp. whole cardamom seeds (without pods)**

¼ **tsp. anise seed**

1 **½-inch piece fresh ginger**

3 **lb. cooking apples, peeled, cored, and quartered**

⅔ **cup water**

⅓ **to ½ cup sugar**

◆◆◆

Ground cinnamon (optional)

1 On a piece of 100-percent cotton cheesecloth combine stick cinnamon, cardamom, anise seed, and ginger. Bring up corners of cheesecloth; tie with a string.

2 In a 4½-quart Dutch oven combine apples, water, sugar, and spice bag. Bring to boiling; reduce heat. Simmer, covered, for 8 to 10 minutes or until apples are tender, adding more water, if necessary. Remove from heat.

3 Remove the spice bag. Mash with a potato masher or 2 large forks until mixture reaches desired smoothness. (Or, blend or process apples in a blender or food processor or press through a food mill or sieve.) Serve warm or chilled; stir before serving. If desired, sprinkle each serving with a little ground cinnamon. Makes 8 servings.

Nutrition facts per serving: 108 cal., 1 g total fat (0 g sat. fat), 0 mg chol., 2 mg sodium, 28 g carbo., 1 g fiber, 0 g pro. *Daily values:* 2% iron.

Easy Applesauce: Prepare as directed, except substitute ⅛ teaspoon each of ground cinnamon, ground cardamom, and ground ginger for the bag of spices. The applesauce will be darker in color.

NUTRITION IN NO TIME

30 MIN. LOW FAT

QUICK AND HEALTHY PIZZA

Prep: 10 min. ◆ Bake: 12 min.

Pizza crust can be a canvas for appetizing art. Try this fast fix-up as a start. Then, mix and match your favorite vegetables and pre-cooked lean meats.

1 **12-inch Italian flat bread (focaccia)**

2 **14½-oz. cans Italian-style stewed tomatoes, chopped and well drained**

3 **cups chopped fresh or frozen broccoli flowerets**

4 **oz. sliced fat-free roasted chicken breast**

2 **Tbsp. finely shredded Parmesan cheese**

½ **tsp. dried Italian seasoning, crushed**

¼ **cup shredded reduced-fat mozzarella cheese (1 oz.)**

1 Place Italian flat bread on a baking sheet. Arrange on top the tomatoes, broccoli, chicken, Parmesan cheese, Italian seasoning, and mozzarella cheese.

2 Bake in a 350° oven for 12 to 15 minutes or until heated through. Let stand for 5 minutes. To serve, cut into wedges. Makes 3 main-dish servings.

Nutrition facts per serving: 447 cal., 6 g total fat (0 g sat. fat), 33 mg chol., 2,022 mg sodium, 77 g carbo., 4 g fiber, 27 g pro. *Daily values:* 46% vit. A, 139% vit. C, 26% calcium, 17% iron.

NOVEMBER
Classics with a Twist

IN THIS CHAPTER

30-minute recipes indicated in RED.
Low-fat and no-fat recipes indicated with a ♥.
Photographs indicated in italics.
*All new in 1998.

Looking for tasty alternatives for your Thanksgiving menu? Serve Herb-Rubbed Turkey with Pear Stuffing. Or expand your family's horizons with Pomegranate-Glazed Goose. With it, introduce a stuffing with a whole new twist. Mediterranean Fig Dressing combines dried figs, specialty breads, and snipped herbs for great results. It's the season to cook with wheat berries, bulgur, walnuts, and squashes of all persuasions. Fresh flavors in baking include marbled Two-Corn Corn Bread and popovers stuffed with savory mushrooms. Fall's sweet bounty comes inside with desserts like Persimmon-Streusel Cake and Cranberry Harvest Tart.

ROSEMARY "BRAIDSTICKS"

Prep: 40 min. ◆ Rise: 1¼ hr.
Bake: 15 min.

For faster shaping, cut rolled dough into 1-inch-wide strips. Holding a strip at both ends, carefully twist in opposite directions two or three times. Place on greased baking sheet, pressing both ends down. Repeat with remaining strips. Let rise and bake as directed.
(See the photograph on page 280.)

1 to 1¼ cups all-purpose flour
1 pkg. active dry yeast
1 Tbsp. snipped fresh
    rosemary or ½ tsp. dried
    rosemary, crushed
¼ tsp. coarsely ground pepper
¾ cup milk
2 Tbsp. margarine or butter
1 Tbsp. sugar
½ tsp. salt
   ◆◆◆
1 cup semolina pasta flour
   ◆◆◆
1 egg white
1 Tbsp. water

1 In a mixing bowl combine ¾ cup of the all-purpose flour, the yeast, rosemary, and pepper. In a saucepan heat the milk, margarine or butter, sugar, and salt just until warm (120° to 130°) and butter almost melts.

2 Add milk mixture to dry mixture. Beat with an electric mixer on low to medium speed for 30 seconds, scraping the sides of the bowl constantly. Beat on high speed for 3 minutes. Using a wooden spoon, stir in semolina

pasta flour. Let stand 1 minute. Stir in as much of the remaining all-purpose flour as you can.

3 Turn the dough out onto a lightly floured surface. Knead in enough of the remaining all-purpose flour to make a stiff dough that is smooth and elastic (8 to 10 minutes total). Shape into a ball. Place the dough in a lightly greased bowl, turning once to grease surface of dough. Cover and let rise in a warm place until dough is nearly double (about 45 to 60 minutes).

4 Punch dough down. Turn dough out onto a lightly floured surface. Divide dough in half. Cover and let rest for 10 minutes. Lightly grease a large baking sheet; set aside.

5 On a lightly floured surface, roll 1 portion of the dough into a 10×9-inch rectangle. Cut the rectangle into thirty-six 10×¼-inch strips.

6 For each breadstick, pinch together ends of 3 strips. Braid the strips of dough. Pinch the other ends together. Tuck under the thin, pinched ends. Place on the prepared baking sheet. Repeat with remaining portion of dough. Cover and let rise in a warm place until nearly double (about 30 minutes).

7 In a small bowl beat together egg white and water; brush on breadsticks. Bake in a 375° oven about 15 minutes or until golden. Remove from baking sheet and cool slightly on a wire rack. Serve warm. Makes 24 breadsticks.

Prepare dough as directed. Cover and freeze in an airtight container for up to 3 weeks. To use, thaw dough overnight in the refrigerator. Shape dough and let it rise as directed at left. Bake breadsticks in a 350° oven for 20 minutes.

Nutrition facts per breadstick: 58 cal., 1 g total fat (0 g sat. fat), 0 mg chol., 60 mg sodium, 10 g carbo., 0 g fiber, 2 g pro. *Daily values:* 1% vit. A, 1% calcium, 3% iron.

SWEET POTATO BREAD

Prep: 40 min. ◆ Rise: 1¼ hr.
Bake: 35 min.

Serve this sweet, spicy bread for a special breakfast treat. Slices also can be used to make French toast.

1¼ cups water
1 cup cubed, peeled sweet
    potato
   ◆◆◆
1 cup buttermilk
¼ cup granulated sugar
2 Tbsp. margarine or butter
2 tsp. salt
   ◆◆◆
6¼ to 6¾ cups all-purpose flour
2 pkg. active dry yeast
   ◆◆◆
½ cup granulated sugar
½ cup chopped toasted walnuts
2½ tsp. pumpkin pie spice
   ◆◆◆
1 recipe Powdered Sugar Icing
    (see page 251) (optional)

1 In a medium saucepan combine the water and sweet potato. Bring to boiling; reduce heat. Simmer, covered, about 12 minutes or until sweet potato is very tender. Do not drain. With a potato masher, mash the sweet potato in the water. Measure the sweet potato mixture. If necessary, add additional water to make 1¾ cups total mixture.

2 Return sweet potato mixture to saucepan. Stir in buttermilk, the ¼ cup granulated sugar, margarine or butter, and salt. (The mixture may appear curdled.) Heat or cool and stir as necessary until warm (120° to 130°); set aside.

3 In a large mixing bowl combine 2 cups of the flour and the yeast. Add the sweet potato mixture. Beat with an electric mixer on low to medium speed for 30 seconds, scraping the sides of the bowl. Beat on high speed for 3 minutes. Using a wooden spoon, stir in as much of the remaining flour as you can.

4 Turn the dough out onto a lightly floured surface. Knead in enough of the remaining flour to make a moderately stiff dough that is smooth and elastic (6 to 8 minutes total). Shape dough into a ball. Place dough in a lightly greased bowl, turning once to grease the surface of the dough. Cover and let rise in a warm place until double (45 to 60 minutes). (When poked with 2 fingers, dough will dent in and dents will not spring back.)

5 Punch dough down. Turn dough out onto a lightly floured surface. Divide dough in half. Cover and let rest for 10 minutes. Lightly grease two 8×4×2- or two 9×5×3-inch loaf pans; set aside.

6 On a well-floured surface roll out 1 portion of dough into a 15×10-inch rectangle. Combine the ½ cup sugar, walnuts, and pumpkin pie spice. Brush half the dough (about 10×7½ inches) with water.

7 Using about one-fourth of the granulated sugar mixture, sprinkle mixture over the surface brushed with water. Fold the unbrushed portion of dough over the sugar mixture, making a 10×7½-inch rectangle. Roll out to a 12×8-inch rectangle. Brush surface lightly with water. Sprinkle with another one-fourth of sugar mixture to about 1 inch from edges.

8 Roll up, jelly-roll style, starting from a short side. Pinch seam and ends to seal. Place, seam side down, in a prepared loaf pan. Repeat rolling, filling, folding, and shaping with remaining dough and granulated sugar mixture. Place seam side down in a prepared loaf pan. Cover and let dough rise in a warm place about 30 minutes or until nearly double in size.

9 Bake in a 375° oven about 35 minutes or until bread sounds hollow when tapped. (If necessary, cover loosely with foil the last 15 minutes of baking to prevent overbrowning.) Remove bread from pans; cool completely on wire racks. If desired, drizzle loaves with Powdered Sugar Icing. Cover and store at room temperature for up to 3 days. Makes 2 loaves (about 32 servings).

THE CLEVER COOK

SWEET POTATO SECRET

Purchased caramel apple dip makes a wonderful topping for sweet potatoes. Prepare sweet potatoes according to your usual recipe and spoon warm caramel apple dip on top. Sprinkle toasted pecans on top to add tasty crunch to this special dish.

Betty Furanek
Fairfield, Nebraska

Powdered Sugar Icing: In a small mixing bowl combine 1 cup sifted powdered sugar, 1 tablespoon milk, and ¼ teaspoon vanilla. Stir in additional milk, 1 teaspoon at a time, until icing is of drizzling consistency.

TO MAKE AHEAD

Prepare and bake bread as directed; cool completely and do not drizzle with icing. Place loaves in a freezer container or bag and freeze up to 3 months. Before serving, thaw bread at room temperature for 2 hours. If desired, drizzle with icing when thawed.

Nutrition facts per serving without icing: 133 cal., 3 g total fat (0 g sat. fat), 0 mg chol., 150 mg sodium, 24 g carbo., 1 g fiber, 3 g pro.
Daily values: 8% vit. A, 1% vit. C, 1% calcium, 7% iron.

TWO-CORN CORN BREAD

Prep: 15 min. ◆ Bake: 20 min.

The marbling of blue and white cornmeal turns this easy recipe into an eye-catching classic. If blue cornmeal is not available, substitute yellow. (See the photograph on page 280.)

1 cup all-purpose flour
3 Tbsp. sugar
4 tsp. baking powder
¼ tsp. salt
⅛ tsp. pepper
2 beaten eggs
1 cup milk
¼ cup cooking oil
½ cup finely chopped pecans
◆◆◆
½ cup blue cornmeal
½ cup white cornmeal

1 Grease twelve 4-inch fluted individual tube pans, a 9- or 9½-inch cast iron skillet, or an 8×8×2-inch baking pan. Set pan aside.

2 In a medium mixing bowl combine flour, sugar, baking powder, salt, and pepper. In another bowl combine eggs, milk, and cooking oil. Add egg mixture all at once to dry mixture, beating by hand or with a wire whisk just until smooth. Stir in pecans.

3 Transfer half of the batter to another bowl. To 1 portion, stir in blue cornmeal; to the other portion, stir in white cornmeal. Pour the blue batter into the prepared pan(s). Gradually pour the white batter over the top. Stir slightly with a toothpick or a blade of a table knife to marble.

4 Bake in a 425° oven for 20 to 25 minutes or until tops are golden and a wooden toothpick inserted in the center comes out clean. Cool slightly on wire rack; serve warm. Makes 12 muffins, 8 wedges, or 9 squares.

Nutrition facts per muffin: 183 cal., 9 g total fat (1 g sat. fat), 37 mg chol., 187 mg sodium, 22 g carbo., 1 g fiber, 4 g pro. *Daily values:* 3% vit. A, 12% calcium, 9% iron.

MOSTLY MUSHROOMS POPOVERS

LOW FAT

Prep: 15 min. ◆ Bake: 35 min.

The key to airy popovers is not overbeating the batter. (See the photograph on page 281.)

Nonstick spray coating
⅓ cup dried mushrooms, such as shiitake or porcini
◆◆◆
½ tsp. salt
¼ tsp. dried thyme leaves
⅛ tsp. pepper
1 cup milk
2 beaten eggs
1 Tbsp. cooking oil
1 cup all-purpose flour

1 Spray the cups of a popover pan or six 6-ounce custard cups with nonstick coating. Place the custard cups on a 15×10×1-inch baking pan; set side. In a small bowl pour boiling water over the dried mushrooms to cover; let stand for 5 minutes. Drain, pressing out the excess liquid. Finely chop mushrooms.

2 In a mixing bowl combine chopped mushrooms, salt, thyme, and pepper. Add milk, eggs, and oil. Beat with a rotary beater until well mixed. Add flour. Beat just until mixture is smooth.

3 Fill cups about half full with batter. Bake in a 400° oven about 35 to 40 minutes or until very firm. Remove from oven. Immediately prick each popover with a fork to let steam escape. Loosen edges. Remove popovers from cups. Serve immediately. Makes 6 popovers.

Nutrition facts per popover: 150 cal., 5 g total fat (1 g sat. fat), 74 mg chol., 219 mg sodium, 20 g carbo., 1 g fiber, 6 g pro. *Daily values:* 5% vit. A, 5% calcium, 8% iron.

NUTTY WHEAT-BERRY MUFFINS

LOW FAT

Prep: 25 min. ◆ Cook: 45 min.
Bake: 15 min.

If you have difficulty finding wheat berries, substitute ½ cup chopped mixed nuts. (See the photograph on page 280.)

3 Tbsp. wheat berries
◆◆◆
1¼ cups all-purpose flour
½ cup whole wheat flour
2 Tbsp. sugar
2 tsp. baking powder
◆◆◆
1 beaten egg
¾ cup milk
¼ cup margarine or butter, melted
¼ cup raisins or dried currants
◆◆◆
Milk
1 recipe Apricot Butter (optional) (see page 253)

1 In a small saucepan bring 1 cup *water* just to boiling. Add wheat berries. Reduce heat; simmer, covered, for 45 minutes or until just tender. Drain; set aside.

2 Grease twelve 2½-inch muffin cups; set aside. In a medium bowl stir together the flours, sugar, baking powder, and ½ teaspoon *salt*. Make a well in center of dry ingredients; set aside.

3 In another bowl combine the egg, ¾ cup milk, and margarine. Add all at once to dry ingredients. Stir just until moistened (batter should be lumpy.) Fold in wheat berries and raisins. Spoon into prepared muffin cups, filling three-fourths full.

4 Brush tops lightly with additional milk. Bake in a 400° oven for 15 to 20 minutes or until golden. Cool in muffin pan on a wire rack for 5 minutes; remove from pan. If desired, serve warm with Apricot Butter. Makes 12.

Nutrition facts per muffin: 135 cal., 5 g total fat (1 g sat. fat), 19 mg chol., 208 mg sodium, 20 g carbo., 1 g fiber, 3 g pro. *Daily values:* 6% vit. A, 7% calcium, 7% iron.

APRICOT BUTTER

Prep: 8 min. ◆ Chill: 1 hr.

If made ahead, let stand for 15 to 30 minutes before serving.

3 Tbsp. snipped dried apricots
½ cup butter or margarine, slightly softened
2 tsp. sugar
1½ tsp. grated fresh ginger or ½ tsp. ground ginger

1 In a small bowl pour boiling water over apricots to cover; let stand 5 minutes. Drain well. In a mixing bowl combine drained apricots, softened butter, sugar, and ginger. Beat on medium to high speed until light and fluffy.

A BERRY GOOD BERRY

During the early 1900s, husked wheat kernels, called wheat berries, secured a place on pantry shelves as a standard staple. Over time, they lost their spot as processed foods became the darlings of the day. Because of their nutritional perks, wheat berries are again finding a place on our menus.

You can add cooked wheat berries to salads, casseroles, soups, breads, or even meat loaf for a crunchy whole-grain flavor. You also add fiber (½ cup cooked wheat berries contains 2 grams dietary fiber), protein, plus vitamins and minerals.

HOW TO USE WHEAT BERRIES

◆ Buy berries that do not have wheat husks (papery covering) attached. The husks are inedible. Also, avoid damp or spotted kernels, which indicate spoilage.

◆ Presoak wheat berries to cut cooking time in half. Place ¾ cup berries (for salad recipe on page 265) in 2½ cups water in the refrigerator for 6 to 24 hours. Do not drain. To cook, bring water to boiling; reduce heat. Simmer, covered, for 30 minutes or until berries are tender but firm.

◆ To skip the soaking step, cook each cup of berries in 3½ cups of water about 60 minutes or until tender; drain. Berries will double in volume with cooking.

◆ Cook wheat berries before adding to salads, breads, or stuffings. Use them in place of rice in salads. Try adding about ½ cup of cooked wheat berries to a favorite yeast dough. Or, substitute the cooked berries for nuts in a bread stuffing.

◆ Freeze cooked wheat berries to add as desired to soups or casseroles. To prepare berries for the freezer, place the cooked, drained, and cooled berries in airtight freezer containers or plastic freezer bags. Freeze berries in desired serving amounts for up to 6 months. To thaw, place the container in a bowl of warm water for 1 hour, stirring occasionally to break up the mixture. Or, micro-thaw on high (100% power) for 2 minutes, stirring twice.

◆ Store uncooked wheat berries in a container with a tight-fitting lid. Place them in a cool, dry place (60° or less) or in the freezer. Wheat berries stored in a cool, dry place will keep indefinitely.

2 Cover and chill until mixture begins to firm up, stirring once or twice. Serve immediately or store, covered, for up to 1 week in refrigerator. Makes ¾ cup.

Nutrition facts per teaspoon: 25 cal., 3 g total fat (2 g sat. fat), 7 mg chol., 26 mg sodium, 1 g carbo., 0 g fiber, 0 g pro. *Daily values:* 3% vit. A, 1% calcium.

ACORN SQUASH MUFFINS

Prep: 15 min. ◆ Bake: 18 min.

Acorn squash gives these muffins a delicate flavor and texture. Freeze extras, tightly wrapped in foil, and reheat when desired.

1⅔ cups all-purpose flour
2 tsp. baking powder
1¼ tsp. ground cinnamon
½ tsp. ground allspice
¼ tsp. salt

◆◆◆

2 beaten eggs
1 cup mashed cooked acorn, butternut, or other squash (one 12-oz. squash)
¾ cup pure maple syrup or maple-flavored syrup
⅓ cup cooking oil
1 tsp. vanilla
½ cup chopped pecans
½ cup raisins

◆◆◆

Butter or margarine (optional)

1 Lightly grease eighteen 2½-inch muffin cups; set side. In a large bowl stir together flour, baking powder, cinnamon, allspice, and salt; make a well in the center and set aside.

2 In a medium bowl combine eggs, squash, syrup, cooking oil, and vanilla. Add all at once to the dry mixture. Stir just until moistened (batter should be lumpy). Fold in pecans and raisins.

3 Fill each muffin cup about three-fourths full with batter. Bake in a 375° oven for 18 to 20 minutes or until a wooden toothpick inserted near the centers comes out clean. Remove

---

MAKING CRUMBS

Crumbs often are used as a coating, thickener, or binder. Bread crumbs can be either soft or fine and dry, and usually are not interchangeable in recipes.

For 1 cup of cracker crumbs, you'll need 28 saltine crackers, 14 graham crackers, or 24 rich, round crackers.

To make soft bread crumbs, use a blender or food processor to break fresh bread cubes into fluffy crumbs.

To make fine dry bread crumbs, place very dry bread in a plastic bag and finely crush it with a rolling pin. You also can buy fine dry bread crumbs; store the opened canister in the refrigerator indefinitely.

from muffin pan and cool slightly on a wire rack. If desired, serve warm with butter or margarine. Makes 18 muffins.

TO MAKE AHEAD

Prepare and bake muffins as directed; cool completely. Place muffins in a freezer container or bag and freeze for up to 3 months. Before serving, wrap the frozen muffins in foil and reheat in a 300° oven for 15 to 18 minutes or until muffins are heated through.

Nutrition facts per muffin: 154 cal., 7 g total fat (1 g sat. fat), 24 mg chol., 96 mg sodium, 22 g carbo., 1 g fiber, 2 g pro. *Daily values:* 5% vit. A, 2% vit. C, 4% calcium, 5% iron.

FENNEL AND ARTICHOKE DRESSING

Start to finish: 25 min.

6 cups Italian bread cubes

◆◆◆

1 medium fennel bulb, trimmed and chopped
½ cup chopped onion
3 Tbsp. olive oil
½ of a 9-oz. pkg. frozen artichoke hearts, thawed and coarsely chopped
1½ cups chicken broth
½ tsp. ground sage
½ tsp. dried basil, crushed
½ tsp. dried oregano, crushed
½ cup chopped, pitted kalamata or ripe olives

◆◆◆

½ cup chopped walnuts, toasted

1 Place bread cubes in a single layer in a 15×10×1-inch baking pan. Bake in a 375° oven about 10 minutes or until golden, stirring once or twice. Set aside.

2 In a large saucepan cook and stir fennel and onion in hot oil 3 minutes. Add artichokes; cook and stir 2 minutes more. Stir in broth, sage, basil, oregano, and ¼ teaspoon *pepper*. Bring to boiling; reduce heat. Cook, covered, 2 minutes. Stir in bread cubes and olives. Remove from heat. Cover; let stand 5 minutes.

3 To serve, fluff with a fork. Season to taste with salt and pepper. Sprinkle with nuts. Serves 8.

Nutrition facts per serving: 201 cal., 12 g total fat (2 g sat. fat), 0 mg chol., 369 mg sodium, 19 g carbo., 4 g fiber, 5 g pro. *Daily values:* 5% vit. C, 4% calcium, 9% iron.

MOROCCAN-STYLE STUFFING

Start to finish: 20 min.

Take a stuffing mix from simple to sensational by adding flavor-packed dried fruits.

1 6-oz. pkg. chicken-flavored
    stuffing mix
1 to 1¼ cups chicken broth
2 Tbsp. margarine or butter
¾ cup snipped pitted prunes
¾ cup snipped dried apricots
½ cup dried cranberries

◆◆◆

⅓ cup pine nuts or chopped
    almonds, toasted
2 Tbsp. lemon juice
1 Tbsp. snipped fresh mint or
    ½ tsp. dried mint, crushed

1 In a 2-quart saucepan combine the seasoning packet from stuffing mix, 1 cup of the broth, margarine or butter, prunes, apricots, and cranberries. Bring to boiling; reduce heat. Simmer, covered, for 6 minutes. Remove from heat.

2 Stir in the stuffing mix, pine nuts or almonds, lemon juice, and mint. Add the remaining ¼ cup broth to moisten, if necessary. Cover and let stand for 5 minutes. Before serving, fluff with fork. Makes 8 servings.

Nutrition facts per serving: 234 cal., 7 g total fat (1 g sat. fat), 11 mg chol., 499 mg sodium, 40 g carbo., 2 g fiber, 6 g pro. *Daily values:* 15% vit. A, 5% vit. C, 3% calcium, 17% iron.

MEDITERRANEAN-STYLE DRESSING

Prep: 20 min. ◆ Bake: 50 min.

The splash of lemon makes this a refreshing home-style side for fresh fish.

8 cups Italian bread cubes

◆◆◆

¾ chopped red or yellow sweet
    pepper
½ cup chopped onion
3 cloves garlic, minced
¼ cup olive oil
1 Tbsp. lemon juice
1 tsp. dried rosemary, crushed
⅛ tsp. ground red pepper
¼ cup snipped fresh parsley
1 to 1¼ cups chicken broth

1 Place bread cubes in a single layer in a 15×10×1-inch baking pan. Bake in a 375° oven 10 minutes or until golden, stirring once or twice; set aside. Reduce oven temperature to 350°.

2 In a medium skillet cook the pepper, onion, and garlic in hot olive oil about 4 minutes or until vegetables are tender; remove from heat. Stir in the lemon juice, rosemary, and ground red pepper. In a large mixing bowl toss together the bread cubes, cooked vegetable mixture, and parsley. Add broth and toss to moisten. Transfer mixture to a 2-quart round casserole.

3 Bake, covered, for 20 minutes. Uncover and bake about 20 minutes more or until heated through. Makes 8 servings.

Nutrition facts per serving: 150 cal., 8 g total fat (1 g sat. fat), 0 mg chol., 264 mg sodium, 16 g carbo., 0 g fiber, 3 g pro. *Daily values:* 8% vit. A, 33% vit. C, 2% calcium, 7% iron.

DRIED TOMATO STUFFING

Prep: 15 min. ◆ Bake: 40 min.

6 cups French bread cubes

◆◆◆

⅓ cup oil-packed dried
    tomatoes
½ cup chopped onion
2 Tbsp. butter
3 cloves garlic, minced
½ cup chopped walnuts or
    pecans
¼ cup snipped fresh basil or
    1 Tbsp. dried basil,
    crushed
¼ cup grated Parmesan cheese
½ to ¾ cup reduced-sodium
    chicken broth

1 Place bread cubes in a single layer in a 15×10×1-inch baking pan. Bake in a 375° oven about 10 minutes or until golden, stirring once or twice. Set aside.

2 Drain oil from tomatoes; reserving 1 tablespoon. Transfer reserved oil to a large skillet. Add onion, butter, and garlic; cook and stir over medium heat until onion is tender. Add nuts; cook and stir 1 minute. Remove from heat. Stir in basil, Parmesan, and ⅛ teaspoon *pepper.* In a large bowl toss together bread cubes and onion mixture. Snip tomatoes; add to bowl. Drizzle with enough broth to moisten; toss lightly. Transfer to a 2-quart casserole.

3 Bake stuffing, covered, for 30 to 35 minutes or until heated through. Makes 8 to 10 servings.

Nutrition facts per serving: 178 cal., 9 g total fat (3 g sat. fat), 10 mg chol., 348 mg sodium, 19 g carbo., 0 g fiber, 6 g pro. *Daily values:* 3% vit. A, 3% vit. C, 6% calcium, 6% iron.

Salad of mixed greens, apple slices, toasted walnuts, and crumbled blue cheese

◆◆◆

Roast pork

◆◆◆

Autumn Corn Bread Stuffing
(see page 257)

◆◆◆

Buttered green beans or broccoli

◆◆◆

Country Pumpkin Torte
(see page 285)

JAZZY JAMAICAN STUFFING

Prep: 25 min. ◆ Bake: 1 hr.

5   cups bread cubes

◆◆◆

½   cup chopped onion
⅓   cup margarine or butter
2   tsp. Jamaican jerk seasoning
1   15½-oz. can crushed pineapple
2   cups cooked white rice
1   15-oz. can black beans, rinsed and drained
3   Tbsp. snipped fresh cilantro

1 Place bread cubes in a single layer in a 15×10×1-inch baking pan. Bake in a 375° oven 10 minutes or until golden, stirring once or twice. Set aside. Reduce oven temperature to 325°.

2 In a large skillet cook onion in margarine or butter until tender. Add jerk seasoning; cook for 1 minute more. Stir in undrained pineapple, cooked rice, black beans, and cilantro.

3 In a large bowl combine bread cubes and pineapple mixture; toss to mix. Transfer stuffing to a 2-quart casserole. Bake, covered, for 40 minutes. Uncover and bake 10 minutes more or until heated through. Makes 10 servings.

Nutrition facts per serving: 205 cal., 7 g total fat (1 g sat. fat), 0 mg chol., 307 mg sodium, 32 g carbo., 3 g fiber, 5 g pro. *Daily values:* 9% vit. A, 8% vit. C, 4% calcium, 10% iron.

PRIZE TESTED RECIPE WINNER

MEDITERRANEAN FIG DRESSING

Prep: 25 min. ◆ Bake: 55 min.

Figs, pita bread, plus a wonderful herb combination send your taste buds on a savory trip.

1   cup coarsely chopped dried figs
2   Tbsp. brandy or desired wine
3   cups pita bread rounds, cut into thin strips
3   cups Italian bread cubes

◆◆◆

2   cloves garlic, minced
⅓   cup margarine or butter
1   Tbsp. snipped fresh rosemary or ½ tsp. dried rosemary, crushed
1   Tbsp. snipped fresh thyme or 1 tsp. dried thyme, crushed

◆◆◆

1   cup chopped Spanish or yellow onion
½   cup chopped walnuts
1   to 1¼ cups chicken broth Fresh thyme sprigs (optional)

1 In a small bowl combine figs and brandy or wine; set aside. Place pita bread strips and Italian bread cubes in a shallow baking pan; set aside.

2 In a large skillet cook garlic in margarine or butter for 1 minute; reserve 3 tablespoons of the margarine mixture in skillet. Drizzle the remaining margarine mixture over bread strips and cubes; sprinkle with rosemary and thyme. Bake in a 350° oven for 15 to 20 minutes or until bread is toasted, stirring once.

3 Meanwhile, cook onion in the reserved 3 tablespoons of margarine or butter until tender; set aside. In a large bowl combine bread cube mixture, fig mixture, cooked onion mixture, and the walnuts. Drizzle with enough chicken broth to moisten. Transfer stuffing to a 1½-quart casserole. Bake, covered, for 40 to 45 minutes or until heated through. If desired, garnish with thyme sprigs. Makes 8 servings.

Nutrition facts per serving: 254 cal., 13 g total fat (2 g sat. fat), 0 mg chol., 357 mg sodium, 28 g carbo., 2 g fiber, 5 g pro. *Daily values:* 10% vit. A, 4% vit. C, 5% calcium, 10% iron.

BLACK WALNUT DRESSING

Prep: 25 min. ◆ Bake: 30 min.

Wild game such as turkey or pheasant pair perfectly with the earthy flavors of wild rice, black walnuts, and a medley of vegetables in this satisfying side dish.

10 cups wheat bread cubes

◆◆◆

1 cup chopped onion
1 cup sliced celery
1 cup chopped carrot
¼ cup margarine or butter
½ tsp. dried tarragon, crushed
¼ tsp. dried sage, crushed
¼ tsp. pepper

◆◆◆

2 cups cooked wild rice
½ cup chopped black walnuts or toasted walnuts
1 to 1½ cups reduced-sodium chicken broth

1 Place bread cubes in a 15×10×1-inch baking pan. Bake in a 375° oven about 10 minutes or until golden, stirring once or twice; set aside.

2 Meanwhile, in a large skillet cook the onion, celery, and carrot in hot margarine or butter until vegetables are tender. Stir in tarragon, sage, and pepper. Remove from heat.

3 In an extra large bowl combine the bread cubes, cooked wild rice, walnuts, and vegetable mixture. Drizzle with enough broth to moisten; toss to combine.

4 Use to stuff one 8- to 10-pound turkey. Place any remaining stuffing in a casserole.* Bake, covered, about 30 minutes or until hot. Makes 15 servings.

*Note: If desired, place all of the stuffing in a 3-quart casserole. Cover and bake in a 375° oven for 40 to 45 minutes or until stuffing is heated through.

Nutrition facts per serving: 151 cal., 7 g total fat (1 g sat. fat), 0 mg chol., 232 mg sodium, 20 g carbo., 3 g fiber, 5 g pro. *Daily values:* 25% vit. A, 2% vit. C, 2% calcium, 8% iron.

AUTUMN CORN BREAD STUFFING

Prep: 25 min. ◆ Bake: 40 min.

Fix up a mix with some fruits, sausage, and nuts and you have a homemade stuffing in minutes.

8 oz. bulk pork sausage
½ cup chopped onion
3 Tbsp. butter
1 medium pear, peeled, cored, and chopped (1 cup)
1 medium apple, peeled, cored, and chopped (⅔ cup)
¼ tsp. salt

◆◆◆

1 8-oz. pkg. corn bread stuffing mix
¼ cup raisins
½ cup chopped walnuts, toasted
¾ to 1 cup water

1 In a large skillet cook the sausage and onion until sausage is no longer pink. Drain off fat. Add butter, pear, apple, and salt; cook and stir 1 minute more.

2 In a large bowl stir together stuffing mix, raisins, and walnuts. Add the sausage mixture to the stuffing mixture; toss to coat. Add enough water to moisten.

TEST KITCHEN TIP

STUFFING REMINDERS

Remember to use these safety tips from the United States Department of Agriculture (USDA) when you're stuffing your poultry.

◆ Prepare stuffing immediately before using in bird. Don't place the stuffing in the bird until just before roasting. (Ingredients may be assembled ahead of time and kept covered in the refrigerator, but keep wet and dry ingredients separate.)

◆ Don't pack the bird; a loose stuffing cooks more thoroughly. (The USDA suggests ¾ cup stuffing per pound of poultry.)

◆ Don't roast stuffed poultry at oven temperatures lower than 325°.

◆ The temperature of the meat should reach 180°, as measured by a meat thermometer inserted into the inner thigh of the bird. The cooked stuffing temperature, measured from the center, should reach at least 165°.

3 Transfer stuffing to a 2-quart casserole. Bake, covered, in a 325° oven about 40 minutes or until heated through. Makes 10 servings.

Nutrition facts per serving: 226 cal., 11 g total fat (4 g sat. fat), 18 mg chol., 482 mg sodium, 27 g carbo., 1 g fiber, 6 g pro. *Daily values:* 3% vit. A, 3% vit. C, 1% calcium, 7% iron.

BULGUR WHEAT STUFFING

LOW FAT

Prep: 45 min. ◆ Bake: 30 min.

For turkey roasting timings, see the chart on page 268.

 3 cups chicken broth
1½ cups bulgur wheat
1½ cups dried apricots, snipped
 1 cup pitted dates, snipped
 2 to 3 tsp. snipped fresh rosemary or ½ to ¾ tsp. dried rosemary, crushed
 2 tsp. shredded orange peel
1½ tsp. snipped fresh thyme or ½ tsp. dried thyme, crushed
 ¼ to ½ tsp. crushed red pepper
 ¼ tsp. salt

◆◆◆

 2 Tbsp. cooking oil
 1 large onion, chopped
 1 medium carrot, finely chopped

1 In a saucepan bring broth to boiling. In a large mixing bowl combine bulgur, apricots, dates, rosemary, orange peel, thyme, crushed red pepper, and salt.

2 Pour hot broth into bulgur mixture and stir; let stand about 30 minutes or until liquid is absorbed. In a small saucepan heat oil; cook onion and carrot for 5 minutes. Cool slightly; stir into bulgur mixture. Rinse poultry; pat dry with paper towels.

3 Use to stuff one 9- to 12-pound turkey or two 5- to 6-pound geese. Place any remaining stuffing in a casserole. Cover and chill; add to oven during last 30 to 45 minutes of roasting time. Or, use a microwave-safe casserole and cook on high

TEST KITCHEN TIP

ROASTING PUMPKIN SEEDS

Roasting pumpkin seeds after carving is a fall tradition. Did you know you can do that with any squash seeds? Simply rinse the seeds under running water to clean off the attached pulp, shake off excess water, and spread on a lightly greased baking sheet.

If desired, let stand for 24 to 48 hours to dry. Lightly salt and bake in a 350° oven about 15 minutes or until browned. Roasted squash seeds are an excellent high-protein snack.

(100% power) for 5 to 8 minutes or until heated through. Makes 14 servings.

Nutrition facts per serving: 152 cal., 3 g total fat (0 g sat. fat), 0 mg chol., 212 mg sodium, 31 g carbo., 6 g fiber, 4 g pro. *Daily values:* 21% vit. A, 2% vit. C, 1% calcium, 9% iron.

CANDIED BUTTERNUT SQUASH

LOW FAT

Prep: 15 min. ◆ Bake: 55 min.

Any winter squash can be used with this recipe, but you'll love the satiny texture of butternut squash.

 3 medium butternut squash (about 4½ lb. total)

◆◆◆

 ⅓ cup packed brown sugar
 2 Tbsp. molasses

 2 Tbsp. margarine or butter, softened
 1 tsp. finely shredded orange peel
 ½ tsp. ground cinnamon
 ¼ tsp. ground cloves

◆◆◆

 Brown sugar (optional)
 Ground cloves (optional)
 Orange peel curls (optional)

1 Scrub squash; halve lengthwise and remove seeds. Place halves, cut side up, in a large roasting pan.

2 In a mixing bowl combine sugar, molasses, margarine or butter, orange peel, cinnamon, and cloves. Spoon spice mixture into squash halves.

3 Bake squash, covered, in a 350° oven for 40 minutes. Stir sugar mixture; uncover and bake about 15 minutes more or until squash is tender. If desired, sprinkle with additional brown sugar and ground cloves, and garnish with orange peel curls. Serves 5.

Nutrition facts per serving: 189 cal., 4 g total fat (2 g sat. fat), 10 mg chol., 53 mg sodium, 41 g carbo., 6 g fiber, 2 g pro. *Daily values:* 181% vit. A, 64% vit. C, 10% calcium, 14% iron.

AUTUMN PUMPKIN RISOTTO

Prep: 20 min. ◆ Cook: 33 min. Stand: 10 min.

A side dish of sumptuous risotto makes an alluring companion for slow-roasted meat dishes or holiday turkey.

1½ cups fresh pumpkin or winter squash, peeled, seeded, and cubed

½ cup chopped peeled parsley
   root or parsnip
¼ cup chopped hazelnuts
   (filberts)
¼ tsp. ground white pepper
 2 Tbsp. cooking oil
⅔ cup Arborio rice or medium
   grain rice
 1 14½-oz. can reduced-sodium
   chicken broth
¼ cup water

♦♦♦

 2 tsp. snipped fresh chervil or
   parsley
 1 tsp. grated fresh ginger
   Fresh chervil or parsley
   sprigs

1 In a medium saucepan cook and stir pumpkin or winter squash, parsley root or parsnip, hazelnuts, and pepper in hot oil for 5 minutes. Stir in rice and cook for 3 minutes more, stirring often. Carefully stir in broth and water and bring just to boiling; reduce heat. Simmer, covered, for 25 minutes, stirring occasionally.

2 Remove from heat and gently stir in snipped chervil or parsley and grated ginger. Let stand, covered, for 10 minutes. Rice should be tender but firm and mixture should be slightly creamy. Serve garnished with chervil or parsley sprigs. Makes 4 to 6 servings.

Nutrition facts per serving: 263 cal., 12 g total fat (2 g sat. fat), 0 mg chol., 296 mg sodium, 35 g carbo., 3 g fiber, 5 g pro. *Daily values:* 31% vit. A, 16% vit. C, 4% calcium, 13% iron.

SQUARED AWAY ON SQUASHES

Here are a few of the many varieties of squash you can find from early fall through winter.

Turban. These squashes do indeed look like turbans. They have a buttery flavor and a slightly floral aroma.

Hubbard. The rough-skinned hubbard has a thick, orange pulp. Quarter, season, and bake, covered, for best results.

Banana. This giant squash, red-orange in color, has a flavor and texture similar to the butternut squash. Peel, cut into slices, and steam it. Then brush with margarine or butter and grill.

Buttercup. Similar to acorn squash, the buttercup is rounder and larger. Prepare this great green globe the same way you would a hubbard squash or an acorn squash.

Spaghetti. When cooked, the inside pulp of this oblong yellow squash really does resemble spaghetti. Toss with a little tomato sauce, grab a fork, and twirl away.

Acorn. An annual holiday favorite, the acorn squash has a soft and sweet golden flesh. Halves of this small squash make perfect single servings.

Butternut. The cooked pulp of this beige, bottle-shaped squash is very smooth. Steam it and mash it with a little olive oil, margarine, or butter for rich flavor. Or, use it to make a delectable soup.

Turban

Hubbard

Banana

Buttercup

Spaghetti

Acorn

Butternut

Country Barley Pilaf

Prep: 10 min. ◆ Cook: 20 min.

For added holiday pizzazz, serve this wholesome and hearty side dish in roasted white or yellow acorn squash halves. (See the photograph on page 279.)

2 medium fennel bulbs with tops
3 oz. fresh oyster mushrooms or button mushrooms
◆◆◆
1 14½-oz. can chicken broth
1 cup water
1½ cups quick-cooking barley
◆◆◆
2 Tbsp. olive oil
4 medium carrots, thinly sliced
1½ tsp. dried thyme, crushed
   Salt (optional)
   Pepper (optional)

1 Snip enough of the fennel leaves from the tops to measure 2 tablespoons; set aside. Finely chop fennel bulbs; measure 1½ cups. Cut any large mushrooms into bite-size pieces; set fennel and mushrooms aside.

2 In a medium saucepan bring broth and water to boiling. Stir in barley. Return to boiling; reduce heat. Simmer, covered, about 10 minutes or until barley is tender, stirring occasionally. Remove from heat. Let stand, covered, for 5 minutes.

3 Meanwhile, in a large skillet heat oil over medium-high heat. Add chopped fennel, carrots, mushrooms, and thyme. Cook and stir for 5 to 6 minutes or

until vegetables are tender. Drain any free liquid from barley. Stir in cooked vegetable mixture and snipped fennel leaves. If desired, season to taste with salt and pepper. Makes 6 to 8 servings.

Nutrition facts per serving: 259 cal., 6 g total fat (1 g sat. fat), 0 mg chol., 278 mg sodium, 45 g carbo., 17 g fiber, 8 g pro. *Daily values:* 114% vit. A, 11% vit. C, 3% calcium, 10% iron.

Sweet Potatoes

Once a year—twice at most—sweet potatoes appear at our tables, shrouded beneath clouds of golden-brown marshmallows and basking in a steamy, rich sea of butter and brown sugar. They're devoured, and then we spend the next 12 months wondering why we don't eat more of them. That's unfortunate, because few foods match this edible root for versatility and concentration of nutrients, including potassium and vitamins A and C.

Now is the ideal time to track them down; supply is greatest and prices are lowest in fall and winter. When shopping, look for small- to medium-size potatoes that are firm and free of soft spots and blemishes. Certain varieties of sweet potatoes are sometimes sold in supermarkets as yams—either can be used in these recipes.

Sweet Potatoes Roasted with Bacon

Prep: 15 min. ◆ Roast: 55 min.

Sweet potatoes and bacon are a down-home combination. This version has been fortified with shallots and white wine.

2 lb. sweet potatoes, peeled and cut into 1-inch pieces
½ cup dry vermouth or white wine
⅓ cup very finely chopped shallots
1 Tbsp. margarine or butter, melted, or cooking oil
6 slices bacon, crisp-cooked, drained, and crumbled
1 Tbsp. snipped fresh parsley
◆◆◆
1 Tbsp. margarine or butter, melted (optional)
   Parsley sprigs (optional)

1 In a shallow roasting pan combine sweet potatoes, vermouth or wine, shallots, and the 1 tablespoon margarine, butter, or oil. Bake, covered, in a 400° oven for 30 minutes. Stir; roast, uncovered, for 15 minutes more. Stir in bacon and snipped parsley; continue to roast 10 to 15 minutes more or until sweet potatoes are lightly brown and tender.

2 To serve, transfer potatoes to a serving dish. If desired, toss potatoes with the 1 tablespoon of melted margarine or butter and garnish with parsley sprigs. Makes 6 servings.

Nutrition facts per serving: 194 cal., 5 g total fat (1 g sat. fat), 5 mg chol., 138 mg sodium, 30 g carbo., 4 g fiber, 4 g pro. *Daily values:* 270% vit. A, 54% vit. C, 3% calcium, 5% iron.

CORN AND POLENTA BAKE

Prep: 15 min. ◆ Bake: 45 min.

Thanksgiving grew out of the Native American corn harvest celebration, which included dishes made with the best of the year's corn crop. This casserole features both cornmeal in the polenta and corn kernals. (See the photograph on page 278.)

- 2 **fresh ears of corn or 1 cup frozen corn**
- 1 **Tbsp. cooking oil**
- ½ **cup chopped green sweet pepper**
- ¼ **cup chopped onion**
- 2 **cloves garlic, minced**
- ¼ **tsp. coarsely ground pepper**
  ◆◆◆
- 1 **16-oz. tube refrigerated cooked polenta**
- 3 **slightly beaten eggs**
- 4 **tsp. stone-ground mustard or Dijon-style mustard**
- ½ **tsp. sugar**
  ◆◆◆
- ¾ **cup soft bread crumbs (1 slice)**
- 1 **Tbsp. stone-ground mustard or Dijon-style mustard Corn husks (optional)**

1 If using fresh corn, cut kernels from ears (you should have about 1 cup). In a medium saucepan heat oil. Cook corn, green pepper, onion, garlic, and ground pepper in hot oil about 5 minutes or until just tender.

2 Crumble the polenta (should have about 3½ cups); set aside. In a large mixing bowl combine eggs, the 4 teaspoons mustard, and the sugar. Stir in the cooked vegetable mixture and crumbled polenta. Spoon polenta mixture into a lightly greased 1-quart casserole.

3 In a small mixing bowl combine bread crumbs and the 1 tablespoon mustard. Sprinkle over top of polenta mixture. Bake in a 350° oven about 45 minutes or until knife inserted near center comes out clean. If desired, serve in cleaned, organic corn husks. Makes 6 servings.

Nutrition facts per serving: 180 cal., 6 g total fat (1 g sat. fat), 107 mg chol., 437 mg sodium, 26 g carbo., 3 g fiber, 7 g pro. *Daily values:* 6% vit. A, 13% vit. C, 2% calcium, 5% iron.

30 MIN.

FARM-STYLE BRAISED LEEKS

Start to finish: 30 min.

A velvety Havarti cheese sauce with caraway drapes the braised fresh leeks. To toast caraway seeds, spread desired amount on an ungreased baking sheet. Bake in a 400° oven about 10 minutes or just until toasted, shaking once. (See the photograph on page 279.)

- 8 to 12 **small leeks (about 1¾ lb.)**
  ◆◆◆
- 2 **Tbsp. margarine or butter**
- 2 **Tbsp. all-purpose flour**
- ⅛ **tsp. white pepper**
- ¾ **cup milk**
- ½ **cup shredded Havarti or Muenster cheese (2 oz.)**
- ½ **tsp. caraway seed, toasted**
- 2 **tsp. snipped fresh chives**

1 Trim leeks, discarding the first 2 inches of the ends, and the first inch and outer leaves of the tough green tops. Wash well. Using a sharp kitchen knife, slash remaining green tops lengthwise several times. In a large skillet cook leeks, covered, in a small amount of boiling lightly salted water for 6 to 8 minutes or until just tender.

2 Meanwhile, in a small saucepan melt margarine or butter over medium heat. Stir in flour and white pepper until blended. Add milk all at once. Cook and stir until the mixture is thickened and bubbly. Cook and stir for 1 minute more. Add cheese. Heat and stir just until cheese is melted. Serve with leeks. Top with toasted caraway seeds and chives. Makes 4 servings.

Nutrition facts per serving: 224 cal., 13 g total fat (2 g sat. fat), 21 mg chol., 185 mg sodium, 24 g carbo., 8 g fiber, 7 g pro. *Daily values:* 13% vit. A, 18% vit. C, 17% calcium, 19% iron.

THE CLEVER COOK

FREEZING BACON

When I purchase a pound of bacon, and don't plan to use it all at once, I lay it in strips on baking parchment. I then roll the paper and cut in half. The bacon is then stored in a self-sealing plastic freezer bag in the freezer, and individual strips peel off easily.

Tanya D. Seale
Ballwin, Missouri

GRANDMA'S PENICILLIN

Got a cold? Take a nice, hot bowl of chicken soup.

Outside, the rumblings of winter will come battering at your door, bringing yet another cold and flu season.

When colds or the flu attack, we turn to the treatments that provide comfort: warm blankets, soap operas, and, of course, hot chicken soup—sometimes called "Grandma's penicillin." But there's more in that pot of soup than meets the eye—or nose and throat.

MAGIC FROM THE PAST

With chicken soup, you have more than a simple folksy tradition—you have a full-blown anti-misery strategy with 2,000 years of scrutiny behind it. An ancient Greek treatise described how chicken soup could be used to treat respiratory disorders. In the twelfth century, physician and scholar Moses Maimonides wrote that chicken soup suppresses some symptoms associated with colds, flu, and asthma.

Research is bringing scientific credibility to the longstanding assertion that chicken soup can help cure a common cold or an upper respiratory tract infection. It's comforting to know that this centuries-old heritage appears to have significant scientific substance.

To get an idea how chicken soup works its magic, it helps to understand what happens when you get a cold. A cold virus makes itself at home in your upper respiratory system—the nose, sinuses, and throat. The virus causes inflammation wherever it resides because the body's immune system rushes to the scene to fend off infection. This causes swelling of the membranes, specifically those that line the nose, throat, and sinuses. The results: You end up with a cold. The symptoms are all too familiar—congestion, sore throat, coughing, headaches, fatigue, and (occasionally) a low-grade fever.

FIVE OUT OF FIVE DOCTORS

Anything that helps to thin congestion and move it out of your system is considered by all doctors an ally on the road to better health. In a controlled experiment, physicians at Mount Sinai Hospital in Miami, Florida, found that hot chicken soup cleared the congestion that accompanies a cold.

It's not only the steam from hot liquids—soup, tea, or any other concoction—that helps clear up sinus blockage. Chicken soup contains compounds that seem to block the movement of inflammation-causing white blood cells in the windpipe. The exact chemistry of these compounds and how they work is still a mystery. But it is known, according to Dr. Stephen Rennard of the University of Nebraska, that the compounds help protect the sinus membranes.

Perhaps the most compelling evidence for chicken soup's efficacy in fighting colds comes from the University of California, Los Angeles. Dr. Irwin Ziment, a pulmonary specialist at the university, found that acetylcysteine, a prescription medicine used to combat congestion, is chemically similar to the amino acid cysteine—which happens to be abundant in the proteins in chicken soup.

Dr. Rennard found that the medicinal effect wasn't noticeable unless the chicken soup was made with carrots, onions, sweet potatoes, turnips, and parsnips. Although the reason for this is not entirely understood, scientists speculate that it may have to do with phytochemicals—healthful compounds that are found in all plant foods.

ASTHMA, TOO

A cold is not the only instance where chicken soup can lend a helping hand. Asthma involves a narrowing in the bronchial tubes that carry air in and out of the

lungs, resulting in labored breathing and wheezing. Coughing and congestion often complicate the picture, so a critical aspect of asthma therapy is to open up the airways and clear the lungs.

In a recent study, scientists investigated the effects of drinking hot chicken soup on patients suffering exercise-induced asthma. They believe that aromatic compounds in chicken soup act in tandem with the soup's hot steam to help clear the bronchial tracts. Given chicken soup's purported ability to clear these airways, it certainly has all the earmarks of a worthy ally—no matter what the mechanism.

WHAT'S GOOD FOR THE SOUL

Can we legitimately call chicken soup "penicillin?" Of course not. Chicken soup doesn't have bacteria- or virus-killing abilities. But it can provide relief from the symptoms of these diseases. So go ahead, enjoy chicken soup, knowing that you are doing something good for your body as well as your soul. In fact, why wait until you're not feeling well? Have a bowl anyway—it would make your Grandma proud.

A "CURE" FOR WHAT AILS YOU

There isn't one single recipe for "medicinal" chicken soup. Methods of making chicken soup have been adapted by cultures around the world, with chicken soup recipes in countless variations being passed from generation to generation. All will work in the face of minor illness. The basic recipe usually involves nothing more than putting a chicken into a large pot with various vegetables. My vote for the best chicken soup of all time goes to my mother Ruth's recipe (below), adapted from her grandmother's chicken soup.

—Ed Blonz, Ph.D. is a former professor of biochemical nutrition and the author of several books on nutrition and health, including Power Nutrition.

GREAT-GRANDMOTHER GOLD'S "ROMANIAN GOLD"

1 2½- to 3-lb. chicken, cut into pieces
6 cups water (or enough to just cover chicken pieces in pot)
1 large onion, cut up
3 stalks of celery
3 medium carrots
4 sprigs parsley
1½ tsp. salt

Combine chicken and onion in a large stock pot. Add water. Bring just to boiling. Cover and cook on medium heat for 1 hour. Add celery, carrots, parsley, and salt. Cook on low heat for 2 hours or until chicken is tender and falling off the bone. Strain the soup through a colander. Skim off the fat before serving. If desired, serve with noodles, rice, matzo balls, or crackers. Makes 5 cups.

THE NOBLE QUINCE

In medieval times, the quince symbolized love, joy, and harmony. Today, this often unnoticed and underappreciated fruit is poised for a renaissance—it's time the quince, that unsung Cinderella of the winter harvest, was invited to the ball.

Quinces can be eaten right off the tree, but they taste better cooked. The fruit's delicate, floral flavor and heady perfume belie its natural hardiness. Available fresh from late August through February, quinces keep for two months stored in the refrigerator or a cool, dry place. Use quinces in preserves, pastries, pies, stuffings, and salsas.

DOWN-SOUTH GREEN BEANS

Start to finish: 20 min.

The flavor of fresh green beans is at its best when they're cooked just enough to stay crisp-tender—about 5 to 10 minutes, as in this recipe.

1 **lb. fresh green beans or one 16-oz. pkg. frozen whole green beans (about 4 cups)**
¼ **to ½ tsp. finely snipped dried chipotle pepper**
◆◆◆
2 **tsp. garlic-flavored olive oil**
½ **cup pecan halves, coarsely chopped**
  Edible flowers (optional)

1 In a medium saucepan cook fresh green beans and chipotle pepper, covered, in a small amount of lightly salted water for 5 to 10 minutes or until just crisp-tender (cook frozen beans, if using, for 5 minutes). Drain.

2 Meanwhile, in a large skillet, heat oil over medium heat. Add pecans. Cook and stir for 30 seconds. Add drained beans. Heat and stir for 1 to 2 minutes more or until nuts are toasted and beans are just heated through. If desired, garnish with edible flowers. Makes 6 servings.

Nutrition facts per serving: 101 cal., 8 g total fat (1 g sat. fat), 0 mg chol., 15 mg sodium, 8 g carbo., 3 g fiber, 2 g pro.
Daily values: 6% vit. A, 12% vit. C, 3% calcium, 7% iron.

"GRANBERRY" SAUCE

Start to finish: 40 min.

Traditional cranberry sauce gets a sweet makeover with plump and juicy seedless red grapes. (See the photograph on page 279.)

½ **cup water**
½ **cup white zinfandel wine or cranberry juice cocktail**
⅓ **to ⅔ cup sugar**
1½ **cups cranberries**
¾ **cup seedless red grapes**
½ **tsp. grated fresh ginger or ½ tsp. snipped fresh mint Dash ground cloves**

1 In a medium saucepan combine water, wine or juice, and sugar. Bring to boiling, stirring occasionally, until sugar is dissolved. Add cranberries, grapes, grated ginger, if using, and cloves. Return to boiling; reduce heat.

Cook, covered, for 15 minutes, stirring occasionally. Uncover and cook 10 minutes more, stirring occasionally. Stir in mint just before serving, if using. Serve warm or chilled with roast goose or turkey. Makes 6 servings.

Nutrition facts per serving: 84 cal., 0 g total fat, 0 mg chol., 2 mg sodium, 18 g carbo., 1 g fiber, 0 g pro.
Daily values: 9% vit. C, 1% iron.

BUTTERNUT SQUASH WITH CRANBERRIES

Start to finish: 30 min.

Expand your use of tart cranberries by including them in vegetable side dishes, such as this simmered butternut squash. (See the photograph on page 281.)

2 **lb. butternut squash or sweet potatoes**
◆◆◆
¼ **tsp. ground cloves**
2 **Tbsp. margarine or butter**
◆◆◆
1 **to 1½ cups cranberries**
½ **cup cranberry juice cocktail or apricot nectar**
1 **tsp. finely shredded orange peel**
⅓ **cup pure maple syrup**
¼ **cup chopped walnuts or hazelnuts (filberts), toasted**
  Orange peel strips (optional)

1 Peel squash or sweet potatoes. Halve squash lengthwise and remove seeds. Slice squash or sweet potatoes crosswise into ½-inch slices.

2 In a large skillet cook the squash or potatoes and cloves in the melted margarine or butter, covered, over medium heat for 8 minutes or until nearly tender, stirring occasionally.

3 Add cranberries, cranberry juice or apricot nectar, and shredded orange peel. Heat to boiling; reduce heat. Simmer, covered, for 5 to 10 minutes or until squash is just tender, stirring once or twice. Remove from heat. Gently stir in maple syrup and, if desired, walnuts or hazelnuts. If desired, garnish with orange peel strips. Serve immediately. Makes 6 to 8 servings.

Nutrition facts per serving: 180 cal., 7 g total fat (1 g sat. fat), 0 mg chol., 53 mg sodium, 31 g carbo., 4 g fiber, 2 g pro.
Daily values: 88% vit. A, 47% vit. C, 4% calcium, 7% iron.

QUINCE-APRICOT COMPOTE

Start to finish: 35 min.

Warm this piquant compote and spoon over thick slices of pound cake.

3 to 4 medium quinces (about 1 lb.)
1 large apple

♦♦♦

1 cup apricot nectar or orange juice*
½ cup sugar
½ cup dried apricots, halved
1 tsp. ground cinnamon
¼ tsp. ground cloves

1 Peel quinces and apple; core and cut into bite-size pieces. (You should have about 5 cups cut-up fruit total.)

2 In a large saucepan combine quince, apple, nectar or orange juice, sugar, apricots, cinnamon,

and cloves. Bring to boiling, stirring to dissolve sugar; reduce heat. Simmer, covered, about 20 minutes or until fruit is just tender, stirring occasionally. Serve warm or cover and store for up to 5 days in the refrigerator. Use as a side dish, a condiment for roasted meats, or a topping for cake or ice cream. Makes 4 cups.

***Note:** If using orange juice, increase amount of sugar slightly.

Nutrition facts per ¹⁄₂-cup serving: 127 cal., 0 g total fat, 0 mg chol., 4 mg sodium, 33 g carbo., 2 g fiber, 1 g pro.
Daily values: 10% vit. A, 33% vit. C, 1% calcium, 6% iron.

FENNEL AND WHEAT BERRY SALAD

Prep: 15 min. ♦ Cook: 1 hr. Chill: 4 to 24 hr.

Look for hints and tips about wheat berries on page 253.

¾ cup wheat berries
¼ cup long grain rice

♦♦♦

1 11-oz. can mandarin orange sections, drained
1 cup packaged shredded broccoli (broccoli slaw mix)

♦♦♦

¼ cup balsamic vinegar or white wine vinegar
3 Tbsp. salad oil
1 tsp. sugar
1 tsp. fennel seed, crushed Cabbage leaves (optional)

1 In a 2-quart saucepan combine wheat berries, 4½ cups *water,* and ½ teaspoon *salt.* Bring to boiling; reduce heat. Simmer, covered, for 40 minutes. Add rice. Cover and cook 20 minutes more

TEST KITCHEN TIP

QUINCE HINTS

Quinces are ripe when they are still quite firm, but no longer rock-hard, and have a strong, flowery aroma. Introduce yourself to the aromatic fruit by combining it with—or using it in place of—apples and pears. Prepare quinces as you would extra-hard pears, allowing a little extra cooking time.

To enjoy quinces raw, let them sit at room temperature for a few days until they are softened slightly.

Even in season, not all supermarkets carry quinces. However, most stores will order them on demand. And, since they keep so well, don't be afraid to order a couple of pounds to have on hand.

or until rice is tender. Drain off any excess liquid. Cool mixture.

2 Gently combine the wheat berry-rice mixture, orange sections, and broccoli mix. Set aside.

3 For dressing, in a screw-top jar combine vinegar, oil, sugar, and fennel seed. Pour dressing over wheat berry mixture; toss lightly to coat. Cover and chill for 4 to 24 hours. If desired, line 6 salad bowls with cabbage leaves. Spoon salad onto leaves. Serves 6.

Nutrition facts per serving: 212 cal., 7 g total fat (1 g sat. fat), 0 mg chol., 196 mg sodium, 34 g carbo., 2 g fiber, 4 g pro.
Daily values: 2% vit. A, 37% vit. C, 2% calcium, 11% iron.

HERB-RUBBED TURKEY WITH PEAR STUFFING

Prep: 45 min. ◆ Roast: 3½ hr.
Stand: 15 min.

*The dried herb coating and
unique pilaf-style stuffing add old-
world appeal to Thanksgiving's
familiar center of attention.*

  3 Tbsp. dried sage leaves
  3 Tbsp. dried savory leaves
1½ tsp. whole white or black
      peppercorns
  1 tsp. celery salt
  1 tsp. paprika
  1 10- to 12-lb. turkey

◆◆◆

  1 recipe Pear Stuffing
      (see right)

◆◆◆

    Cooking oil or olive oil

◆◆◆

¼ cup all-purpose flour
    Chicken broth or water

Autumn fruits, such as pears, crab apples, and Lady apples, and assorted fresh herbs, such as tri-color sage, sage, or bay laurel (optional)

1 In a clean dry blender container combine sage, savory, peppercorns, celery salt, and paprika. Cover and blend until coarsely ground; set aside. Rinse turkey and pat dry with paper towels.

2 Lightly spoon Pear Stuffing into neck and body cavities. Pull neck skin of turkey to back and fasten with a skewer. If a band of skin crosses the tail, tuck the ends of the drumsticks under band. If there is no band, tie drumsticks to the tail. Twist wing tips under the back. Place any remaining stuffing in a casserole; cover and chill.

3 Brush turkey with cooking oil or olive oil. Rub ground herb mixture over entire bird. If desired, loosen skin from breast and rub mixture over meat under breast skin (this will infuse flavor from rub into meat). Place bird, breast side up, on a rack in a shallow roasting pan. Insert a meat thermometer into the center of an inside thigh muscle. (The bulb should not touch the bone.) Cover turkey loosely with foil. Roast in a 325° oven 2¼ hours.

4 Cut band of skin or string between the drumsticks so the thighs will cook evenly. Continue roasting for ¾ to 1¼ hours more, or until thermometer registers 180° to 185° and stuffing registers 170°. Uncover for the last 30 minutes of roasting. Cover turkey; let stand 15 to 20 minutes before carving. Bake any remaining stuffing, covered, the last 45 minutes of turkey roasting.

5 Transfer turkey to a serving platter. Pour pan drippings into a large measuring cup, scraping the browned bits into the cup. Skim and reserve fat from drippings. Pour ¼ cup of the fat into a medium saucepan; discard the remaining fat. Stir in flour. Add enough chicken broth or water to remaining drippings to make 2 cups. Add all at once to flour mixture in saucepan. Cook and stir over medium heat until thickened and bubbly. Cook and stir for 1 minute more. If desired, season to taste with salt and pepper. If desired, garnish serving platter with fall fruits and assorted fresh herbs. Makes 12 to 14 servings.

Pear Stuffing: Rinse and drain ½ cup uncooked wild rice. In a medium saucepan cook the rice in 2 tablespoons margarine or butter over medium heat for 2 minutes. Add two 14½-ounce cans chicken broth. Bring mixture to boiling; reduce heat. Simmer, covered, for 30 minutes. Add 1¼ cups orzo pasta. Return to boiling; reduce heat. Simmer mixture, covered, for 10 to 12 minutes more. Remove from heat. Stir in 2 medium red pears, cored and cut into ½-inch cubes; ¾ cup toasted chopped hazelnuts; ½ cup sliced green onions; ½ cup golden raisins; and 1 tablespoon grated fresh ginger.

Nutrition facts per serving: 520 cal., 24 g total fat (5 g sat. fat), 121 mg chol., 593 mg sodium, 39 g carbo., 2 g fiber, 43 g pro. *Daily values:* 13% vit. A, 5% vit. C, 7% calcium, 31% iron.

A Bird to Boast About

Roasting a perfect turkey is easy when you come to the kitchen equipped with two things: a little patience and this guide. Patience, because it takes about an hour to make stuffing and get a turkey ready for roasting; this guide, because it will tell you what you need to know to make your meal a success.

Buying: With birds that weigh 12 pounds or less, allow 1 pound per adult family member. With birds that weigh more than 12 pounds, count on ¾ pound for each serving. If you're serving boneless turkey breast, figure ½ pound per person. For leftovers, buy a bird that is 2 to 4 pounds larger than you need.

In the store, look for the "sell by" date on the label of fresh turkey. This date is the last day the turkey should be sold by the retailer. The unopened turkey should maintain its optimal quality and be safe to use for 1 or 2 days after the "sell by" date.

For frozen turkey products, look for packaging that is clean, undamaged, and free of frost.

Thawing safely: Allow plenty of time to thaw the bird. For a whole frozen turkey, leave the bird in its wrapping and place on a tray in the refrigerator for 2 to 5 days. Plan on at least 24 hours for every 5 pounds—and remember, don't count the day you will be roasting the bird. Thawed birds will keep for 1 or 2 days in the refrigerator.

If your turkey is not completely thawed on the day you plan to roast it, place the bird in a clean sink full of cold water. Change the water every 30 minutes. Do not thaw at room temperature, in the microwave, or in warm water; those methods will allow harmful bacteria to grow quickly to dangerous levels.

The bird is thawed and ready for roasting if the giblets can be removed easily, and there are no ice crystals in the body and neck cavities. If the center is still frozen, the bird will cook unevenly. After thawing, remove the giblets and neck from the interior cavity. Rinse bird and pat dry with paper towels.

Safe stuffing: If you don't have an accurate meat thermometer, consider cooking the stuffing in a covered casserole alongside the bird. Mix the stuffing just before you stuff and roast the bird.

To stuff, first measure out the amount of stuffing that will go into the bird, allowing ¾ cup per pound of bird. (That's 9 cups for a 12-pound bird.) Release drumsticks from band of skin, unhooking the tail or leg clamp if one is provided. Spoon some stuffing loosely into neck cavity. Pull the neck skin over stuffing; fasten to back with a short skewer.

Loosely spoon stuffing into body cavity; do not pack or stuffing won't be fully cooked and safe to eat by the time the turkey is done. Spoon any remaining stuffing into a casserole; cover and chill until ready to bake. (For an unstuffed bird, place quartered onions and celery in body cavity to add flavor to drippings used in gravy. Pull neck skin to back; fasten with a short skewer.) Tuck drumsticks under band of skin that crosses tail or reset into leg clamp. If there isn't a band or if you've removed clamp, tie drumsticks with kitchen string to tail. Twist wing tips under back.

Oven roasting: Place oven rack in its lowest position and preheat oven to 325°. Place turkey, breast side up, on a rack in a shallow pan. To enhance browning, brush with cooking oil. Push a meat thermometer into the center of an inside thigh muscle. Cover turkey loosely with foil, pressing it over drumsticks and neck. Roast, using timings in chart (see page 268) as a guide.

When bird has been in the oven for two-thirds of the cooking time, cut band of skin or string holding legs or release leg clamp. Remove foil the last 30 to 45 minutes. When done, the thigh meat should be 180° and the stuffing should be at least 170°. The temperature will rise about 5° after the bird comes out of the oven.

When the turkey is done, the drumsticks should move very easily in their sockets and their thickest parts should feel soft when pressed. In addition, juices from the thigh should run clear when pierced deeply with a long-tined fork. Remove turkey from the oven and cover loosely with foil. Let stand for 20 minutes. Remove stuffing before carving.

Leftovers: Do not allow turkey to remain at room temperature more than 2 hours after it comes out of the oven. Cooked turkey and stuffing may be covered and refrigerated separately for up to 2 days.

STUFFED WHOLE TURKEY ROASTING GUIDE

Ready-to-cook turkey weight	Oven temperature	Roasting time
8 to 12 lb.	325°	3 to 3½ hr.
12 to 14 lb.	325°	3½ to 4 hr.
14 to 18 lb.	325°	4 to 4¼ hr.
18 to 20 lb.	325°	4¼ to 4¾ hr.
20 to 24 lb.	325°	4¾ to 5¼ hr.

For unstuffed turkeys of the same weight, reduce the total cooking time by 15 to 30 minutes.

POMEGRANATE-GLAZED GOOSE

Prep: 40 min. ◆ Roast: 2 hr.
Stand: 15 min.

This recipe also works well with domestic duck. For a 4- to 5-pound duckling, roast for 1¾ to 2¼ hours or until thermometer registers 180° and drumsticks move easily in sockets. (See the photograph on page 278.)

1 7- to 8-lb. domestic goose
1 tsp. dried marjoram, crushed
¼ to ½ tsp. coarsely ground black pepper
1 medium unpeeled orange, cut into wedges
1 stalk celery, cut up

◆◆◆

1 lb. parsnips, peeled and cut into 1½-inch pieces
2 large quinces, quartered (core, if desired)

3 large pomegranates

◆◆◆

1 18-oz. jar plum jam
⅓ cup apple cider or apple juice
3 Tbsp. soy sauce
1½ tsp. shredded lemon peel

◆◆◆

Fresh herbs, such as sage, opal basil, or tarragon (optional)
Whole or sliced apples (optional)
Edible flowers (optional)

1 Rinse goose; pat dry with paper towels. Sprinkle body cavity, and rub outside of skin, with marjoram and pepper; stuff cavity with orange wedges and celery. Skewer neck skin to back of bird; tie legs to tail using 100 percent cotton string. Twist wings under back. Prick the entire surface of the skin with a fork.

2 Place goose, breast side up, on a rack in a shallow roasting pan. Insert a meat thermometer into thigh meat. (The bulb should not touch the bone.)

3 Roast, uncovered, in a 350° oven for 2 to 2½ hours, or until the thermometer registers 180°, drumsticks move easily in sockets, and juices run clear. Using a basting bulb, carefully discard the hot, liquid fat as it accumulates during roasting. Place parsnips and quince alongside goose on the rack. Roast with goose during last 45 minutes of roasting.

4 Meanwhile, for glaze, halve pomegranates. Using the tip of a spoon, remove 2 tablespoons of the pomegranate seeds; set aside. Squeeze remaining pomegranates with a hand juicer. You should have about ½ cup of juice.

5 In a medium saucepan combine pomegranate juice, jam, apple cider or juice, soy sauce, and lemon peel. Bring just to boiling; reduce heat. Simmer, uncovered, for 15 minutes or until reduced to 1½ cups, stirring frequently as mixture thickens. Strain mixture through a sieve set over a bowl.

6 Baste goose with about ½ cup of the strained glaze mixture during the last 15 minutes of roasting; reserve remaining glaze. Reheat glaze to serve as a sauce. Cover goose; let stand for 15 minutes before carving.

CARVING MADE EASY

Even a novice can do a great job carving the holiday turkey with a well-sharpened knife and these directions. If you are a rookie, reduce the pressure on yourself and carve in the kitchen rather than at the table in front of guests.

When the turkey is done, remove it from the oven and cover with foil. Let it stand for 15 to 20 minutes before beginning to carve. Standing lets the bird's flesh firm up, allowing easier carving and ensuring the carved slices hold together better.

Place the bird on a serving platter or large cutting board. If stuffed, spoon out stuffing and remove to a serving bowl; keep warm. Have a platter standing by to receive the carved meat. Grasp the tip of one drumstick (using a paper towel if it's too hot to handle) and pull it away from the body. Cut through the skin and meat between the thigh and the body (see photo 1). With the tip of the knife, separate the thighbone from the backbone by cutting through the joint. Repeat with the other drumstick and thigh. To separate the thighs and drumsticks, cut through the joints where the drumstick bones and the thighbones meet.

Next, carve the meat from the drumsticks, hold each drumstick vertically by the tip with the large end resting on the serving platter. Then slice the meat parallel to the bone and under some tendons, turning the leg to get even slices. Slice the thigh meat the same way.

Finally, carve the breast meat. Steady turkey with a carving fork in the center of the breast and make a deep horizontal cut into the breast above each wing (see photo 2). This cut marks the end of each breast meat slice. Beginning at the outer top edge of each breast, cut slices from the top down to the horizontal cut and place on serving platter (see photo 3). Cut the final smaller slices following the curve of the breastbone.

Remove wings by cutting through joints where wing bones and backbone meet. Place whole wings on the serving platter.

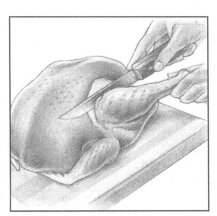

1. Pull a leg away from the bird; cut through the meat between the thigh and the body.

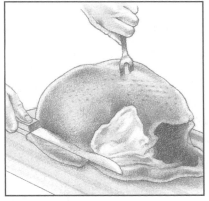

2. Steady the bird with a large fork. Make a deep cut into the breast just above each wing.

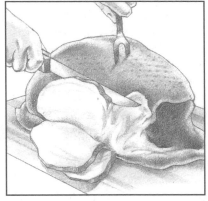

3. Cut from the top down to the deep horizontal cut, cutting thin, even slices from the breast.

7 Transfer goose to serving platter. If desired, surround with fresh herbs, whole or sliced apples, or edible flowers. To serve, carve the goose. Spoon remaining glaze over slices of goose and sprinkle the reserved pomegranate seeds on top of each serving. Serve with roasted parsnips and quinces. Makes 12 servings.

Nutrition facts per serving: 503 cal., 23 g total fat (7 g sat. fat), 93 mg chol., 344 mg sodium, 48 g carbo., 3 g fiber, 27 g pro. *Daily values:* 2% vit. A, 21% vit. C, 3% calcium, 26% iron.

GIBLET GRAVY

Start to finish: 20 min.

Giblets are the edible internal organs of poultry. If you don't want to use them, substitute canned chicken broth for the giblet broth called for in the recipe.

**Giblets and neck from
turkey or roasting chicken**

2 **stalks celery with leaves, cut
up**

1 **small onion, cut up**

◆◆◆

**Pan drippings from roasted
turkey or chicken**

◆◆◆

⅓ **cup all-purpose flour**

½ **tsp. freshly ground pepper**

2 **cloves garlic, minced**

1 **Tbsp. snipped fresh sage or
thyme or 1 tsp. dried leaf
sage or thyme, crushed
Kitchen Bouquet (optional)**

1 Rinse giblets and neck. Wrap liver; chill until needed. In a medium saucepan combine remaining giblets, neck, celery, onion, 2½ cups *water,* and ¼ teaspoon *salt.* Bring to boiling; reduce heat. Cover and simmer about 1 hour or until tender. Add liver; simmer 20 to 30 minutes more for turkey (5 to 10 minutes more for chicken) or until tender. Remove neck and giblets from broth. Discard neck; finely chop giblets. Strain broth, discarding vegetables. Cover and chill giblets and broth until needed.

2 After transferring roasted poultry to a platter, pour pan drippings into a glass measuring cup. Skim off and reserve ¼ cup fat from drippings. Transfer fat to a medium saucepan; set aside. (Discard any remaining fat.) Measure pan drippings; add as much reserved giblet broth as needed to equal 2½ cups liquid.

3 Stir the flour, pepper, and ¼ teaspoon *salt* into fat in saucepan until completely smooth. Cook and stir over medium heat for 1 minute. Pour broth-dripping mixture all at once into flour mixture. Stir in garlic and sage. Cook and stir over medium heat until thickened and bubbly; reduce heat. Cook and stir for 1 minute more. Stir in chopped giblets and, if desired, a few drops of Kitchen Bouquet. Makes 3 cups (8 to 10 servings).

Nutrition facts per serving: 97 cal., 7 g total fat (2 g sat. fat), 40 mg chol., 92 mg sodium, 5 g carbo., 0 g fiber, 3 g pro. *Daily values:* 18% vit. A, 1% vit. C, 6% iron.

CANDIED ORANGE PEEL

Prep: 15 min. ◆ Cook: 15 min.

Prepare a batch of this old-fashioned sweet and put it in the candy dish for satisfying guests' sweet tooths.

2 **medium oranges**

◆◆◆

1⅓ **cups sugar**

⅓ **cup water**

◆◆◆

Sugar

1 Cut peels of the oranges lengthwise into quarters, cutting just through the pulp to the surface of the fruit. Pry back the quartered peel with a spoon. Scrape away the soft, white part on the inside of the peel. If left on, the peel will be bitter. Cut peel into ⅜-inch-wide strips. Wrap and refrigerate peeled fruit for another use.

2 In a 2-quart saucepan combine the 1⅓ cups of sugar and the water. Cover and bring to boiling. Add the orange peel strips. Return to boiling, stirring constantly to dissolve sugar; reduce heat. Cook orange peel mixture, uncovered, over medium-low heat. Mixture should boil at a moderate, steady rate over entire surface. Cook, stirring occasionally, for 15 to 20 minutes or until peel is almost translucent.

3 Using a slotted spoon remove peel from syrup, allowing it to drain. Transfer peel to a wire rack set over waxed paper. Set cooked peel aside until cool enough to handle but still warm and slightly sticky. Roll peel in additional sugar to coat. Continue drying on the rack for 1 to 2 hours. Store, tightly covered, in a cool, dry place for up to 1 week. Makes about 48 pieces.

▌ TO MAKE AHEAD ▐

Prepare and dry orange peel as directed. Place in a freezer container or bag and freeze for up to 6 months. To serve, thaw at room temperature.

Nutrition facts per piece: 7 cal., 0 g total fat 0 mg chol., 0 mg sodium, 2 g carbo., 0 g fiber, 0 g pro. *Daily values:* 3% vit. C.

CRANBERRY HARVEST TART

Prep: 40 min. ◆ Bake: 35 min.

A golden, nutty streusel crowns the top of a bright, jewel-tone red fruit filling.

1¼ cups all-purpose flour
2 Tbsp. granulated sugar
¼ tsp. salt
⅓ cup butter
4 to 5 Tbsp. water

◆◆◆

¾ cup packed brown sugar
4 tsp. cornstarch
½ cup light-colored corn syrup
2 tsp. finely shredded lemon
　　peel
2 Tbsp. lemon juice
2 cups cranberries
2 medium cooking apples,
　　peeled, cored, and
　　chopped
⅓ cup golden raisins
¾ cup chopped walnuts

◆◆◆

½ cup granulated sugar
½ cup all-purpose flour
½ tsp. ground cinnamon
¼ cup butter

1 For crust, in a medium mixing bowl combine the 1¼ cups flour, the 2 tablespoons granulated sugar, and the salt. Using a pastry blender, cut in the ⅓ cup butter until pieces are pea-size. Sprinkle 1 tablespoon of the water over part of the mixture; gently toss with a fork. Push moistened dough to the side of the bowl. Repeat moistening dough, using 1 tablespoon water at a time, until all the dough is moistened. Form dough into a ball. If necessary, cover and chill about 1 hour or until easy to handle.

2 On a lightly floured surface roll dough from center to edges into a circle 13 inches in diameter. Ease pastry into an 11-inch tart pan with removable bottom. Trim pastry even with sides of pan. Line pastry with a double thickness of foil. Bake in 400° oven for 8 minutes. Remove foil and bake for 5 to 6 minutes more or until golden. Set crust aside. Reduce oven temperature to 350°.

3 For filling, in a large saucepan stir together the brown sugar and cornstarch. Stir in the corn syrup, lemon peel, and juice. Add cranberries. Cook and stir until mixture boils; reduce heat. Simmer, covered, for 2 minutes. Add apples, raisins, and ½ cup of the walnuts. Simmer, uncovered, for 5 minutes more. Remove from heat. Pour cranberry mixture into baked pastry shell.

4 For topping, in a small bowl combine the ½ cup granulated sugar, ½ cup flour, and ground cinnamon. Using a pastry blender, cut in the ¼ cup butter until crumbly. Stir in remaining ¼ cup walnuts. Sprinkle atop tart.

5 Bake in a 350° oven for 35 to 40 minutes or until topping is lightly browned and mixture is bubbly. Cool on a wire rack. Before serving, remove sides of pan. Cut into wedges. Makes 12 servings.

Nutrition facts per serving: 348 cal., 14 g total fat (6 g sat. fat), 24 mg chol., 149 mg sodium, 56 g carbo., 2 g fiber, 3 g pro. *Daily values:* 8% vit. A, 8% vit. C, 2% calcium, 13% iron.

TEST KITCHEN TIP

PIE CRUST POINTERS

The crust makes the pie, as any baker knows. These Test Kitchen secrets are essential to crisp, flaky results.

Water lightly. Add the least amount of water possible. (Too much can make pastry tough.) If the dough is crumbly, add a teaspoon of water at a time, just until you can form a ball.

Avoid a sticky situation. Use a pastry cloth and a rolling pin cover. Before rolling, lightly sprinkle the cloth and the cover with flour.

Don't stretch. Roll the dough to a bigger circle than you need so you won't stretch the pastry. (Stretched pastry will shrink during baking.)

Use a light touch. To transfer, drape pastry over a rolling pin, unroll onto the pie plate, and ease it in without stretching. Press against the pan to prevent air pockets.

Patch it up. Pastry with cracks and holes can absorb the filling and get soggy. Fill any cracks with trimmings. If you're baking a pie with a filling, do not prick the pastry.

Bake without bubbles. Before baking an unfilled crust, prick the bottom and sides. Line with a double thickness of heavy-duty foil.

Don't get steamed. For double-crust pies, make a few slits in the top crust so it doesn't get soggy.

SEASON'S EATINGS TO ALL

Ahh...the golden turkey with buttery mashed potatoes and gravy. Ohh...the vegetables drizzled with cheese sauce. Mmm...the pumpkin pie with whipped cream. Argh...the calories, the cholesterol, the fat.

Contrary to public opinion, the annual foray into season's eatings can bring pleasure without adding pounds. Our favorite yuletide treats can indeed stay on the holiday menu, say nutrition experts. Moderation is the key.

"All foods can fit into a healthy-eating plan. There really are no bad foods, whether it's holiday time or the rest of the year," says Edith Howard Hogan, registered dietitian and spokesperson for the American Dietetic Association (ADA). But before you head for the fridge to forage for that leftover roast duck to nibble while you're sipping a mug of hot buttered rum, heed some advice from the ADA. Here are some of the association's best tips to get you through the holiday season without discarding those good eating habits you've cultivated all year long. Bear in mind that an occasional indulgence isn't all bad. Sometimes it's nice to be naughty. Just don't make a habit of it.

KEEP AN EYE ON YOUR FOOD BANK

Just as you balance your checkbook, you need to balance your nutritional account. If you know you're going to a dinner or party where extra calories cry out for attention, plan to eat low-fat or fat-free foods the rest of the day or week. The day of the event, eat a light breakfast and lunch. Or, fix yourself a bowl of oatmeal to quell your appetite before a party. One cup of oatmeal cooked with water contains only 2 grams of fat and 146 calories. It just might fill you up enough to prevent you from reaching for a second piece of pumpkin pie with whipped cream, which has 16 grams of fat and 315 calories per slice.

FOCUS ON FLAVOR

There are plenty of flavors that add flair to your holiday festivities without adding fat and calories. Here are some options:

◆ Offer gingerbread cookies or sugar cookies instead of pies or cakes. One 5- or 6-inch gingerbread boy has 157 calories and 6 grams of fat, compared to a piece of pecan pie which has 541 calories and 30 grams of fat.

◆ Fix a lighter version of traditional eggnog by combining purchased low-fat eggnog with skim milk. Or, serve hot spiced cider instead of eggnog.

◆ Substitute refrigerated or frozen cholesterol-free egg products and low-fat turkey sausage when you're fixing a holiday breakfast that calls for eggs and sausage.

◆ Satisfy cravings for rich food by searching out more healthful recipes such as low-fat cheesecake made with reduced-fat cream cheese and refrigerated or frozen egg product.

◆ Bake or poach whole pears until tender and drizzle with a little chocolate-flavored syrup (most syrups are fat free). Serve warm for an elegant dessert.

◆ Go ahead and splurge occasionally on whipped cream, but use a teaspoon of whipped cream to top off each dessert instead of a tablespoon. One teaspoon of whipped cream contains 9 calories; a tablespoon has 27.

◆ Stir a bit of your favorite liqueur into low-fat or nonfat whipped topping and float it on a steaming mug of coffee. Serve it with a gingersnap cookie for a simple finale to a cozy winter dinner.

CREATE A HELP-YOURSELF SHELF
Encourage healthful snacking, even when decadent temptations abound, with some of these simple ideas.

Instead of discouraging your family from gobbling up the goodies you've prepared in advance for a special gathering, encourage them to grab a healthy snack. Set aside a help-yourself shelf in the refrigerator entirely for grazing. Keep the shelf stocked with fresh fruit, low-fat yogurt, reduced-fat cheeses, and raw veggies. You can even keep pretzels, gingersnaps, and individual boxes of cereal in the fridge so they're handy for nibbling.

Or, display some healthful, edible decor, such as a big bowl of shiny red apples and gorgeous golden pears, throughout the living areas of your home. Encourage your family and holiday visitors to sample the edible art.

TAKE A HIKE
After a holiday dinner that leaves you with a tranquil smile on your face, push yourself away from the table, put the food away, and convince your family and friends to take a stroll around the neighborhood. A brisk 15-minute walk in the invigorating fresh air will perk you up and burn about 85 calories (almost the amount in the dinner roll).

MAGNIFICENT MASHED POTATOES
Help yourself to potatoes at your holiday meal, says Dr. John McDougall, medical director of a nutrition program at St. Helena Health Center in California. They'll help fill you up so you won't eat so much of those rich, fatty foods on the holiday buffet table. McDougall, whose program emphasizes a low-fat, complex carbohydrate-based diet, takes his mashed potatoes without added fat—sour cream, butter, or cheese. Instead, there are plenty of flavor secrets to enhance the simple spuds.

◆ Toss a few cloves of peeled garlic into the water when you are boiling your potatoes. Drain the potatoes, reserving the water. Then mash the garlic cloves along with the potatoes, adding enough of the reserved potato water to make them light and fluffy. To enrich the flavor and boost the calcium, mix about 2 tablespoons instant dry milk powder with each ½ cup of potato water before adding it to the potatoes. Each tablespoon of instant dry milk powder contains 60 mg calcium and no fat.

◆ Mash the potatoes along with broccoli, rutabaga, or carrots that have been cooked until tender. They'll add a different flavor and some color.

◆ Replace milk or cream with evaporated skim milk or reduced-sodium chicken broth when you mash the potatoes.

◆ Use nonfat dairy sour cream in place of regular sour cream for a creamy texture and a pleasant tang. For each pound (3 medium potatoes) of peeled, cooked, and mashed potatoes, beat in 2 to 4 tablespoons nonfat dairy sour cream and enough cooking liquid (2 to 4 tablespoons) to make potatoes light and fluffy. Stir in snipped chives or finely chopped green onions for added flavor.

◆ Add a generous dash of your favorite herb. If you're using fresh herbs, stir them into the mashed potatoes so the delicate flavor won't cook away.

Sweet Potato and Hazelnut Pie

Prep: 55 min. ♦ Bake: 40 min.
Cool: 2 hr.

A traditional favorite of the South meets the preferred nut of the Pacific Northwest. The result is a pie that you'll add to the menu every year. (See the photograph on page 277.)

3 **medium white or orange sweet potatoes, peeled and quartered (about 1 lb.)**
¼ **cup milk**

♦♦♦

2 **slightly beaten eggs**
1 **14-oz. can (1¼ cups) sweetened condensed milk**
2 **tsp. pumpkin pie spice**
1 **unbaked 9-inch pastry shell**

♦♦♦

1 **cup chopped hazelnuts (filberts)**
⅓ **cup packed brown sugar**
¼ **cup margarine or butter, melted**

1 In a medium saucepan cook potatoes, covered, in 2 cups boiling *water* for 30 to 35 minutes or until tender; drain. Mash or, using an electric mixer, beat potatoes until almost smooth (you should have about 1½ cups). Add milk and beat until smooth.

2 In a large mixing bowl combine eggs, sweetened condensed milk, and pumpkin pie spice. Add potato mixture. Stir to combine. Turn into pastry shell.

3 In a small mixing bowl combine hazelnuts, brown sugar, and margarine or butter. Sprinkle hazelnut mixture evenly over pie. Cover the edge of pie with foil. Bake in a 375° oven for 25 min-

utes. Remove foil; bake for 15 to 20 minutes more or until a knife inserted near the center comes out clean. Cool on a wire rack for 2 hours before serving. Cover and refrigerate to store. Serves 10.

Nutrition facts per serving: 432 cal., 23 g total fat (6 g sat. fat), 57 mg chol., 179 mg sodium, 49 g carbo., 3 g fiber, 8 g pro. *Daily values:* 89% vit. A, 16% vit. C, 14% calcium, 10% iron.

PRIZE TESTED RECIPE WINNER

Macaroon Brownie Pie

Prep: 25 min. ♦ Bake: 45 min.
Chill: 3 to 24 hr.

Chocolate-covered cherries with a tropical twist come to mind with this moist, chewy treat.

1¼ **cups all-purpose flour**
1 **Tbsp. sugar**
⅛ **tsp. salt**
6 **Tbsp. butter**
1 **beaten egg**

♦♦♦

½ **cup light-colored corn syrup**
½ **cup sugar**
4 **oz. semisweet chocolate, coarsely chopped**
¼ **cup butter**
3 **beaten eggs**
¾ **cup coconut**
1 **Tbsp. maraschino cherry juice**
¼ **tsp. almond extract**

♦♦♦

Chocolate shavings (optional)
Sweetened whipped cream (optional)
Whole maraschino cherries (optional)

1 In a medium bowl stir together flour, the 1 tablespoon sugar, and the salt. Using a pastry blender, cut butter into mixture until pieces are pea-size. Gradually stir the 1 beaten egg into flour mixture until most of dough is moistened. Gently knead until a ball forms. If necessary, cover dough with plastic wrap and refrigerate for 30 to 60 minutes or until the dough is easy to handle.

2 On a lightly floured surface, slightly flatten dough; roll into a 12-inch circle. Transfer pastry into a 9-inch pie plate. Trim pastry to ½ inch beyond edge of pie plate. Fold under; crimp edge. Do not prick pastry. Set aside.

3 For filling, in a medium saucepan combine corn syrup and the ½ cup sugar. Cook and stir over medium heat until mixture begins to boil. Remove from heat and stir in chocolate, butter, the 3 beaten eggs, coconut, cherry juice, and almond extract. Pour filling into prepared pastry shell.

4 Bake in a 350° oven about 45 minutes or until filling sets (filling puffs during baking and falls when cool). Cool completely on a wire rack. Chill for 3 to 24 hours. Let stand 30 minutes before serving. If desired, sprinkle chocolate shavings on each plate and serve with whipped cream garnished with whole cherries. Makes 10 servings.

Nutrition facts per serving: 355 cal., 19 g total fat (12 g sat. fat), 116 mg chol., 181 mg sodium, 44 g carbo., 1 g fiber, 5 g pro. *Daily values:* 14% vit. A, 2% calcium, 14% iron.

FESTIVE CRANBERRY-APRICOT PIE

Prep: 25 min. ◆ Bake: 50 min.

1 15-oz. pkg. folded
  refrigerated unbaked pie
  crust (2 crusts)
½ cup sugar
3 Tbsp. cornstarch
1½ tsp. pumpkin pie spice
3 15¼-oz. cans apricot halves,
  drained and quartered
½ cup dried cranberries,
  snipped

◆◆◆

1 egg white
1 Tbsp. milk
1 Tbsp. sugar
¼ tsp. pumpkin pie spice

1 Line a 9-inch pie plate with 1 of the crusts according to package directions. Fold edge under; set aside. In a mixing bowl combine the ½ cup sugar, cornstarch, the 1½ teaspoons pumpkin pie spice, and ¼ teaspoon *salt*. Stir in apricots and cranberries. Spoon mixture into prepared crust.

2 Place remaining crust on a lightly floured surface. Cut with 2-inch-long leaf cutter or other desired cutter to make 18 to 20 leaves. In a small bowl stir together egg white and milk. Brush mixture over leaves; reserve remaining egg white mixture. Combine the 1 tablespoon sugar and ¼ teaspoon pumpkin pie spice. Sprinkle half of the leaves with the sugar mixture. Arrange 6 to 8 leaves, alternating brushed and sprinkled leaves, in a circle in

center of the top of pie filling. Brush edge of crust with remaining egg white mixture. Evenly distribute the remaining leaves around edge of crust. Cover edge lightly with foil. Bake pie in a 375° oven 35 minutes. Remove foil. Bake 15 minutes more. Cool on wire rack. Makes 8 servings.

Nutrition facts per serving: 454 cal., 15 g total fat (0 g sat. fat), 15 mg chol., 302 mg sodium, 78 g carbo., 3 g fiber, 3 g pro. *Daily values:* 18% vit. A, 7% vit. C, 1% calcium, 5% iron.

CORDIALLY YOURS

Cordials are such a—well—cordial way to end an evening. As guests gather in the living room for coffee, set out a collage of homemade after-dinner spirits.

The procedure for making cordials is simple and the list of ingredients is short and sweet: a bottle of vodka, sugar, water, and the fruit of your choice. The only commodity that may be hard to commandeer is patience—for the flavors take up to three weeks to marry.

Serving protocol needn't be a big deal. You can pour an ounce or two into cordial glasses, small wine glasses, or brandy snifters; fill glasses two-thirds full to allow space for the aroma to collect and greet you. Or, pour cordials over crushed ice to reduce the cordials' sweetness and alcohol and increase the richness of the aroma. Cordials also make an elegant addition to coffee.

FRUIT CORDIAL

In a small saucepan heat together 1½ cups sugar and 1 cup water, stirring until sugar is dissolved. Remove from heat; cool. Pour sugar syrup into a 2-quart glass jar. Add desired fruit and one 750-ml bottle vodka (3½ cups); stir gently. Cover the jar with a tight-fitting lid or cork; let stand (steep) in a cool place for time suggested for each fruit.

After steeping, use a wire strainer and strain liquid through several thicknesses of 100 percent cotton cheesecloth or coffee filters into a large bowl. Using a funnel, transfer mixture to a bottle. Seal and label. Store at room temperature. Makes about 5 cups.

Orange Cordial: With a sharp knife or vegetable peeler, remove the thin orange layer of peel from 3 oranges, taking care to avoid the bitter white layer. Use peel to prepare cordial (reserve fruit for another use); steep the mixture for 3 weeks.

Banana Cordial: Peel and thinly slice 1 ripe large banana; steep the mixture for 1 week.

Mango Cordial: Peel, pit, and chop 2 ripe mangoes; steep the mixture for 1 to 2 weeks.

Pear Cordial: Peel, core, and thinly slice 6 medium pears; steep the mixture for 3 weeks.

PERSIMMON-STREUSEL CAKE

Prep: 25 min. ◆ Bake: 40 min.

Choose fruits that have smooth, bright skins and green caps.
(See the photograph on page 277.)

- 2 large Hachiya or Fuyu persimmons (about 1 lb.)
- ¼ cup sugar
- ¾ tsp. pumpkin pie spice or apple pie spice

◆◆◆

- 1½ cups all-purpose flour
- 1½ tsp. baking powder

◆◆◆

- ⅓ cup margarine or butter, softened
- ⅔ cup sugar
- 1 egg
- 1 tsp. vanilla
- ¼ cup milk

◆◆◆

- ¼ cup all-purpose flour
- ¼ cup sugar
- 2 Tbsp. margarine or butter

1 If using Hachiya persimmons, cut in half and scoop out pulp, discarding skin and seeds. Mash with fork until smooth (you should have about 1 to 1¼ cups). For Fuyu persimmons, rinse; discard stem end and seeds. Cut into ½-inch-thick slices (you should have about 2 cups). Combine persimmon, ¼ cup sugar, and ¼ teaspoon of the pie spice; set aside.

2 Grease bottom and about ½ inch up sides of an 8×8×2-inch baking pan; set aside. Combine the 1½ cups flour and the baking powder; set aside.

3 In a medium mixing bowl beat the ⅓ cup margarine with an electric mixer on medium speed

30 seconds. Add the ⅔ cup sugar. Beat on medium to high speed until well combined. Add egg and vanilla; beat well. Add flour mixture and milk alternately, beating on low speed after each addition just until smooth.

4 Spread about three-fourths of the batter into prepared pan. Spoon persimmon mixture evenly over batter. Using a spoon, drop remaining batter into small mounds atop filling, forming a diagonal pattern.

5 Combine the ¼ cup flour, the ¼ cup sugar, and the remaining ½ teaspoon pumpkin pie spice. Cut in the 2 tablespoons margarine or butter until mixture resembles coarse crumbs. Sprinkle over fruit mixture.

6 Bake in a 350° oven for 40 to 45 minutes or until golden and a wooden toothpick inserted in center comes out clean. Let stand for 10 minutes. To serve, cut into squares. If desired, serve warm with *whipped cream* and chopped *persimmon*. If desired, garnish with *mint leaves*. Serves 9.

Nutrition facts per serving: 309 cal., 10 g total fat (2 g sat. fat), 24 mg chol., 182 mg sodium, 52 g carbo., 1 g fiber, 4 g pro. *Daily values:* 23% vit. A, 6% vit. C, 6% calcium, 8% iron.

NUTMEG-SOUR CREAM DROP COOKIES

Prep: 20 min.
Bake: 8 min. per batch

See the photograph on the cover.

- 2½ cups all-purpose flour
- 1 tsp. baking soda
- ½ tsp. baking powder

- ¼ tsp. ground nutmeg
- 1½ cups packed brown sugar
- ¾ cup shortening
- 2 slightly beaten eggs
- 1 tsp. finely shredded lemon peel
- 1 Tbsp. lemon juice
- ⅔ cup dairy sour cream
- ⅔ cup chopped walnuts

◆◆◆

- 1 recipe Browned Butter Frosting (see below)
  Walnut halves (optional)

1 Stir together flour, soda, baking powder, nutmeg, and ¼ teaspoon *salt*; set aside. In a large mixing bowl beat brown sugar and shortening with an electric mixer on medium to high speed until combined. Beat in eggs, peel, and juice. Alternately add flour mixture and sour cream, beating well after each addition. Stir in chopped walnuts.

2 Drop dough by rounded teaspoons 2 inches apart onto greased cookie sheets. Bake in a 375° oven for 8 to 10 minutes or until edges are lightly browned. Transfer cookies to a wire rack and let cool. Spread cooled cookies with Browned Butter Frosting. If desired, top each with a walnut half. Makes about 60 cookies.

Browned Butter Frosting: In a small saucepan heat and stir 3 tablespoons butter until browned. Remove from heat. Slowly beat in 2 cups sifted powdered sugar, 2 tablespoons milk, and 1 teaspoon vanilla until smooth and creamy.

Nutrition facts per cookie: 92 cal., 5 g total fat (1 g sat. fat), 10 mg chol., 44 mg sodium, 12 g carbo., 0 g fiber, 1 g pro. *Daily values:* 1% vit. A, 1% calcium, 2% iron.

Right: *Sweet Potato and Hazelnut Pie* (page 274)
Below: *Persimmon-Streusel Cake* (page 276)

Top: *Corn and Polenta Bake (page 261)*
Above: *Pomegranate-Glazed Goose (page 268)*
Page 279: *"Granberry" Sauce (page 264), Country Barley Pilaf (page 260),*
Farm-Style Braised Leeks (page 261)

Top: *Mostly Mushrooms Popovers (page 252)*
Above: *Butternut Squash with Cranberries (page 264)*
Page 280: *Nutty Wheat-Berry Muffins (page 252),*
Rosemary "Braidsticks" (page 250), Two-Corn Corn Bread (page 252)

Right: *Twinkly Star Cut-Outs*
(page 286)
Below: *Marbled Holiday Wishes*
(page 286)
Page 282: *Frosty Snow Balls (page 286)*

Left: *Autumn Fruits with Cinnamon Custard (page 285)*
Below: *Country Pumpkin Torte (page 285)*

AUTUMN FRUITS WITH CINNAMON CUSTARD

30 MIN. LOW FAT

Start to finish: 25 min.

If Lady apples and Seckel pears aren't available, don't worry—this recipe works with any fall fruit. (See the photograph on page 284.)

⅔ cup white vermouth, apple
  cider, or apple juice
6 Seckel or Forelle pears,
  quartered lengthwise*
6 Lady apples, halved
  crosswise*
3 whole star anise
3 Tbsp. sugar
1 recipe Cinnamon Custard
  (see below)

1 In a large skillet bring vermouth, cider, or juice just to boiling; reduce heat. Gently add pears, apples, and star anise to hot liquid. Sprinkle sugar over fruit. Cook, covered, about 5 minutes or until fruit is just tender. Using a slotted spoon, carefully transfer fruit to individual dessert bowls. Discard poaching liquid. Drizzle fruit with custard. Serves 6.

Cinnamon Custard: In a heavy small saucepan combine 1 beaten egg, ⅔ cup milk, and 4 teaspoons sugar. Cook and stir over medium heat until mixture just coats back of a spoon; stir in ½ teaspoon vanilla and a dash of ground cinnamon. Remove from heat. If desired, place in a pan of ice water to stop cooking process.

*Note: If desired, core fruit.

Nutrition facts per serving: 188 cal., 2 g total fat (1 g sat. fat), 38 mg chol., 25 mg sodium, 36 g carbo., 4 g fiber, 3 g pro. *Daily values:* 3% vit. A, 14% vit. C, 4% calcium, 4% iron.

COUNTRY PUMPKIN TORTE

Prep: 40 min. ◆ Bake: 22 min.
Cool: 1 hr.

You can make the cake, icing, and Candied Orange Peel ahead of time for later assembly so you can take a well-deserved break. (See the photograph on page 284.)

2⅔ cups all-purpose flour
1 Tbsp. baking powder
1 tsp. pumpkin pie spice
¾ tsp. baking soda
¾ tsp. salt
¾ tsp. ground cloves
  ◆◆◆
1 cup shortening
1 cup packed brown sugar
¼ cup dark-flavored molasses
4 eggs
1 cup milk
¾ cup canned pumpkin
1 Tbsp. grated fresh ginger
  ◆◆◆
1 recipe Cream Cheese
  Frosting (see right)
  Candied Orange Peel
  (see recipe, page 270)

1 Grease and lightly flour three 9×1½-inch or 8×1½-inch round baking pans; set aside. In a medium mixing bowl combine flour, baking powder, pumpkin pie spice, baking soda, salt, and cloves; set aside.

2 In a large mixing bowl beat shortening with an electric mixer on medium to high speed for 30 seconds. Add brown sugar and molasses; beat until smooth. Add eggs, 1 at a time, beating for 1 minute after each addition. In a small bowl combine milk, pumpkin, and ginger. Add flour mixture and pumpkin mixture alternately to beaten mixture, beating

on low speed after each addition until just combined. Pour batter evenly into prepared pans.

3 Bake in a 350° oven for 22 to 28 minutes or until a wooden toothpick inserted near the center comes out clean. (If all 3 layers won't fit in oven at the same time, or if you do not have 3 pans, one-third of the batter may be covered and chilled for up to 45 minutes before baking.) Cool cakes in pans on wire racks for 10 minutes. Remove cakes from pans. Cool thoroughly on wire racks.

4 To assemble, place 1 cake layer on serving plate; spread with one-third of the Cream Cheese Frosting. Top with second layer cake; spread with one-third of the frosting. Top with third cake layer and remaining frosting. If desired, arrange Candied Orange Peel on top. Cover and store in the refrigerator. Makes 16 servings.

Cream Cheese Frosting: In a large mixing bowl beat one 8-ounce package softened cream cheese, ½ cup softened butter, and 2 teaspoons vanilla with an electric mixer on medium speed for 30 seconds. Slowly add 2 cups sifted powdered sugar and 1 tablespoon lemon juice, beating well.

Add 2 cups additional sifted powdered sugar, beating well. If necessary, beat in additional powdered sugar or lemon juice until the frosting is easy to spread.

Nutrition facts per serving: 467 cal., 25 g total fat (11 g sat. fat), 85 mg chol., 356 mg sodium, 56 g carbo., 1 g fiber, 5 g pro. *Daily values:* 40% vit. A, 2% vit. C, 11% calcium, 14% iron.

Frosty Snow Balls

Prep: 20 min.
Bake: 20 min. per batch

Edible sparkles add color to a classic.
(See the photograph on page 282.)

1 **cup butter, softened**
⅓ **cup granulated sugar**
1 **Tbsp. water**
1 **tsp. vanilla**
2¼ **cups all-purpose flour**
1 **cup chopped pecans**
♦♦♦
1 **cup sifted powdered sugar**
Green, pink, and purple
edible cake sparkles or
colored sugar

1 In a large mixing bowl beat butter with an electric mixer on medium speed for 30 seconds. Add the granulated sugar. Beat until combined, scraping bowl. Beat in water and vanilla until combined. Beat in as much of the flour as you can with the mixer. Stir in the remaining flour and chopped pecans.

2 Shape dough into 1-inch balls. Place 1 inch apart on ungreased cookie sheets. Bake in a 325° oven about 20 minutes or until bottoms are lightly browned. Transfer cookies to a wire rack and let cool.

3 In each of 3 small bowls combine ⅓ cup of the sifted powdered sugar and green, pink, or purple edible cake sparkles or colored sugar. Gently roll and shake cooled cookies in desired powdered sugar mixture. Makes about 36 cookies.

Nutrition facts per cookie: 110 cal., 7 g total fat (3 g sat. fat), 14 mg chol., 52 mg sodium, 11 g carbo., 0 g fiber, 1 g pro.
Daily values: 4% vit. A, 2% iron.

Twinkly Star Cut-Outs

Prep: 35 min.
Bake: 6 min. per batch

See the photograph on page 283.

1 **cup butter**
¾ **cup granulated sugar**
1 **egg**
3 **cups all-purpose flour**
♦♦♦
1 **recipe Powdered Sugar Glaze**
(see right)
1 **recipe Decorative Frosting**
(see page 287)

1 In a large mixing bowl beat butter with an electric mixer on medium speed for 30 seconds. Add sugar and beat until combined. Add egg and beat until combined. Beat in as much flour as you can. Stir in any remaining flour. Divide dough in half.

2 On a lightly floured surface, roll half of the dough at a time to ⅛-inch-thickness. Shape with star cutters; reroll trimmings. Arrange cutouts on greased cookie sheets. Bake in a 375° oven for 6 to 8 minutes or until edges are firm and bottoms are very lightly browned. Transfer cookies to wire racks and let cool.

3 To decorate, glaze with white or tinted Powdered Sugar Glaze. Let dry. Prepare Decorative Frosting. Pipe dots or lines with white or tinted Decorative Frosting. Let dry. Or, for swirled tops, glaze cookies as above. Using 1 teaspoon of milk at a time, thin some of the white or tinted Decorative Frosting until drizzling consistency. Scatter dots of thinned frosting on top of freshly glazed stars. To swirl, pull pick through dots. Let dry. Makes about 36 cookies.

Powdered Sugar Glaze: In medium mixing bowl combine 4 cups sifted powdered sugar and ¼ cup milk. Stir in additional milk, 1 teaspoon at a time, until glaze is easy to drizzle. Tint as desired with pink, violet, leaf green, or lemon yellow food coloring paste. (To make green color shown in photo, combine leaf green and lemon yellow.)

▐ **PACKAGING TIP** ▌

Showy clear boxes and streamers of iridescent ribbons add sparkle and appeal to this gift of cookies.

Customize each cookie constellation as you please, filling each gift box with a mix of sizes, colors, and decorative patterns.

Nutrition facts per cookie: 185 cal., 5 g total fat (3 g sat. fat), 20 mg chol., 55 mg sodium, 34 g carbo., 0 g fiber, 1 g pro.
Daily values: 5% vit. A, 3% iron.

Marbled Holiday Wishes

Prep: 90 min.
Bake: 7 min. per batch

See the photograph on page 283.

1 **cup butter, softened**
⅔ **cup shortening**
2 **cups granulated sugar**
⅔ **cup dairy sour cream**
2 **eggs**
1½ **tsp. baking powder**
1 **tsp. vanilla**
½ **tsp. baking soda**
⅛ **tsp. salt**
5 **cups all-purpose flour**

Rose petal, violet, leaf green, or lemon yellow food coloring paste

❖❖❖

½ tsp. **peppermint extract**
½ tsp. **almond extract**
1 tsp. **finely shredded lime peel**
1 recipe **Decorative Frosting (see below right)**

1 In a large mixing bowl beat butter and shortening with an electric mixer on medium speed for 30 seconds. Add the sugar, sour cream, eggs, baking powder, vanilla, baking soda, and salt; beat until combined. Beat in as much flour as you can with the mixer. Stir in remaining flour. Divide dough into 6 portions. If necessary, wrap dough in waxed paper or clear plastic wrap and chill for 30 to 60 minutes or until dough is easy to handle.

2 Using 4 wooden picks, dip tip of each pick into 1 of the food colors, placing a generous dot of paste on each pick. Use picks to tint 1 portion dough rose pink, 1 portion violet, and 1 portion lime green. Knead dough gently until it is tinted evenly throughout. (To make the green color shown in the photograph on page 283, combine leaf green and lemon yellow.) Leave 3 portions of the dough untinted.

3 To flavor doughs, add peppermint extract to pink dough, almond extract to purple dough, and lime peel to green dough. To marble, choose one portion of plain dough and one portion of colored dough. Break off pieces of each; place pieces alternately on floured pastry cloth to form

11×7-inch rectangle, pressing pieces together. Roll dough into a 12-inch square, ¼ inch thick, to create a marble effect. Using a pastry wheel, trim edges of square; cut into forty-eight 1×3-inch rectangles.

4 Place cookies 1 inch apart on ungreased cookie sheets. Bake in a 375° oven for 7 to 8 minutes or until edges are firm. Transfer cookies to a wire rack and let cool. Repeat with remaining dough, using 1 portion colored dough with 1 portion plain dough.

5 Use Decorative Frosting to pipe "Peace," "Noel," or "Joy" onto each cookie. Let frosting dry. Makes 144 cookies.

Nutrition facts per cookie: 59 cal., 3 g total fat (1 g sat. fat), 7 mg chol., 25 mg sodium, 9 g carbo., 0 g fiber, 1 g pro.
Daily values: 1% vit. A, 1% iron.

◼ TO MAKE AHEAD ◼

Prepare and bake cookies as directed, except do not pipe on frosting. Place in a freezer container or bag and freeze for up to 1 month. To serve, thaw cookies at room temperature for 30 minutes. Pipe on frosting as directed.

◼ PACKAGING TIP ◼

Sweet, handwritten greetings and pretty paper snowflakes add simple holiday style to this tempting special delivery.

For extra charm, color-coordinate stacks of marble cookie bars and parade them in a neat and orderly row.

COOKIE PACKING TIPS

◆ Before packaging your cookies in gift boxes, be sure to allow the cookies to stand until glazes and frostings are completely dry.

◆ Don't rush the surprise! Before wrapping, decorated cookies may be stored in a tightly covered container or sealed plastic bags at room temperature for up to 3 days. To ensure absolute freshness, prepare and wrap cookies as close to the giving date as possible.

DECORATIVE FROSTING
Start to finish: 10 min.

Pipe this creamy frosting on any favorite holiday treats.

4 cups **sifted powdered sugar**
3 Tbsp. **milk**
Pink, violet, leaf green or lemon yellow food coloring paste

1 In a medium mixing bowl stir together the powdered sugar and the 3 tablespoons milk until smooth. Stir in additional milk, 1 teaspoon at a time, until frosting is easy to pipe. Tint frosting as desired with pink, violet, leaf green, and lemon yellow food coloring paste. (To make the green color shown in the photograph on page 283, combine leaf green and lemon yellow.) Fill pastry bags, fitted with #2 or #3 tips. Use to decorate Twinkly Star Cut-Outs and Marbled Holiday Wishes (see recipes, page 286). Makes 1 cup.

HANDY CANDY-MAKING TIPS

Candy recipes call for a little more precision than most recipes. Try the following tips for foolproof results:

◆ Candy mixtures should be cooked to the exact temperatures the recipe calls for. A good candy thermometer is a worthwhile investment. Before you start, test your thermometer with boiling water.

◆ Use only wooden spoons for stirring candy mixtures.

◆ Make homemade candy on a dry day. Candy mixtures react to the humidity in the air. If the humidity goes to 60 percent or higher, your candy may not set properly.

◆ Only butter should be used in candy recipes unless the recipe specifically allows for margarine to be used instead. If using margarine, make sure it is not a reduced-fat variety.

NUT ROCHA
Start to finish: 40 min.

The toffee stacks easily in airtight containers, making it a perfect pack-and-mail present.

2 **cups butter**
2 **cups sugar**
2 **Tbsp. light-colored corn syrup**
⅓ **cup water**

◆◆◆

1 **11½-oz. pkg. (1¾ cups) milk chocolate pieces**

1 **cup finely chopped, toasted nuts (such as almonds, pecans, walnuts, and/or cashews)**

1 Line a 15×10×1-inch baking pan with foil, extending over edges; set aside.

2 In a 3-quart saucepan melt butter. Stir in sugar, corn syrup, and water. Cook over medium-high heat to boiling, stirring until sugar is dissolved. Avoid splashing onto sides of pan. Clip candy thermometer to pan. Be sure bulb is well covered and not touching bottom of pan. Cook over medium heat, stirring frequently until thermometer registers 290° (soft-crack stage), about 15 minutes. (It should boil at a moderate, steady rate over entire surface.) The mixture will turn golden brown.

3 Remove from heat; remove thermometer. Pour candy mixture into prepared pan; spread evenly. Cool about 5 minutes or until top is just set. Sprinkle chocolate pieces atop; let stand 2 minutes. Spread chocolate onto toffee. Top with nuts; press into chocolate. Cool several hours or until set. If necessary, place in refrigerator.

4 Holding foil, lift candy out of the pan. Break into pieces. To store, layer candy in an airtight container between sheets of waxed paper. Makes about 2½ pounds (40 servings).

Nutrition facts per serving: 181 cal., 13 g total fat (7 g sat. fat), 25 mg chol., 128 mg sodium, 16 g carbo., 0 g fiber, 1 g pro. *Daily values:* 9% vit. A, 2% calcium, 1% iron.

BUTTERY CASHEW BRITTLE
Start to finish: 1 hr.

2 **cups sugar**
1 **cup light-colored corn syrup**
1 **cup butter**

◆◆◆

3 **cups (about 12 oz.) raw cashews**
1 **tsp. baking soda, sifted**

1 In a 3-quart saucepan combine sugar, corn syrup, and ½ cup *water*. Cook and stir until sugar dissolves. Bring syrup to boiling; add butter and stir until butter is melted. Clip candy thermometer to pan. Be sure bulb is well covered and not touching bottom of pan. Cook over medium-low heat, stirring occasionally, until thermometer registers 280° (soft-crack stage), about 35 minutes. (It should boil at a moderate, steady rate over entire surface.)

2 Stir in nuts; continue cooking over medium-low heat, stirring frequently until thermometer registers 300° (hard-crack stage), 10 to 15 minutes more. Remove from heat; remove thermometer. Quickly stir in the baking soda, mixing thoroughly. Pour mixture onto 2 buttered baking sheets or two buttered 15×10×1-inch pans.

3 As brittle cools, stretch it out by lifting and pulling with 2 forks from edges. Loosen from pans as soon as possible; pick up sections and break into bite-size pieces. Store tightly covered. Makes 2½ pounds (72 servings).

Nutrition facts per serving: 90 cal., 5 g total fat (2 g sat. fat), 7 mg chol., 47 mg sodium, 11 g carbo., 0 g fiber, 1 g pro. *Daily values:* 2% vit. A, 3% iron.

DECEMBER
Entertaining Thoughts

IN THIS CHAPTER

Question: What's a one-word antidote to holiday entertaining stress? Answer: appetizers. Plan an appetizer buffet, with alluring choices like Dried Cherry Chutney, Basil and Tomato Cream Cheese Spiral, and Mushroom-Spinach Pinwheels. Many can be made ahead, and others put together in a jiffy. Holiday gifts of food are true gifts from the heart—especially if its low-fat Holiday Surprise Bread or no-fat Peppery Peach Sauce. Amid the gifts and glitz, take care of day-to-day meals with baked egg frittatas and stratas.

30-minute recipes indicated in RED.
Low-fat and no-fat recipes indicated
with a ♥.
Photographs indicated in italics.
*All new in 1998.

Menu

Baked Sunrise Frittata
(see below)

❖❖❖

Fresh fruit bowl

❖❖❖

Assorted muffins and
breads

❖❖❖

Fruit juice and/or coffee

LOW FAT

BAKED SUNRISE FRITTATA

Prep: 20 min. ◆ Bake: 25 min.
Stand: 5 min.

*A frittata is similar to an omelet,
except that in a frittata, the filling
ingredients are mixed through the eggs
and the dish is served open faced. (In
an omelet, fillings are added to the top
just before the eggs are folded over.)*

1½ cups potatoes, cut in ½-inch
    cubes
 1 Tbsp. cooking oil
1½ cups finely chopped cooked
    ham
 ¾ cup shredded cheddar cheese
    (3 oz.)

❖❖❖

 2 8-oz. cartons refrigerated or
    frozen egg product,
    thawed, or 8 slightly
    beaten eggs
 ⅓ cup milk
 1 4-oz. can diced green chili
    peppers
 ¼ cup finely chopped green
    onions
 2 tsp. snipped fresh oregano
    or ½ tsp. dried oregano,
    crushed

 ½ of a 7-oz. jar roasted red
    sweet peppers, cut into
    thin strips

❖❖❖

1½ cups salsa
 ¼ cup snipped fresh cilantro
    Sliced green onion (optional)
    Shredded Parmesan cheese
    (optional)

1 In a 10-inch oven-safe skillet cook potatoes in hot oil, uncovered, over medium heat for 5 minutes, stirring occasionally. Cover and cook 5 minutes more or until tender, stirring once. Remove from heat. Sprinkle ham and ½ cup of the cheddar cheese over the potatoes.

2 In a large mixing bowl stir together egg product or eggs, milk, chili peppers, chopped green onions, oregano, and ¼ teaspoon *salt*. Pour into skillet.

3 Arrange the roasted pepper strips spoke-fashion on top of frittata. Bake, uncovered, in a 350° oven for 25 to 30 minutes or until center is just set and knife inserted in center comes out clean. Sprinkle top with the remaining ¼ cup cheddar cheese. Let stand for 5 minutes.

4 Meanwhile, in a small saucepan stir together salsa and cilantro; heat through. To serve, cut frittata into wedges. Serve with salsa mixture and, if desired, sprinkle with some sliced green onion and Parmesan cheese. Makes 8 servings.

Nutrition facts per serving: 196 cal., 10 g total fat (3 g sat. fat), 26 mg chol., 762 mg sodium, 11 g carbo., 0 g fiber, 17 g pro. *Daily values:* 25% vit. A, 67% vit. C, 12% calcium, 18% iron.

BAKED DENVER STRATA

Prep: 25 min. ◆ Bake: 35 min.
Stand: 10 min.

 6 English muffins, split and
    quartered

❖❖❖

 9 eggs
 1 cup milk
 1 4-oz. can diced green chili
    peppers, drained
 ¼ tsp. salt
 ¼ tsp. black pepper
 1 cup diced cooked ham
 ½ cup sliced pitted ripe olives
 ½ cup finely chopped green
    onions
 1 7-oz. jar roasted red sweet
    peppers, drained and cut
    into strips
1½ cups shredded provolone
    cheese (6 oz.)
 ½ cup shredded cheddar cheese
    (2 oz.)

1 Grease a 3-quart rectangular baking dish. Arrange English muffin quarters in baking dish.

2 In a large mixing bowl beat together the eggs, milk, chili peppers, salt, and black pepper. Pour egg mixture over muffin quarters; let stand for 10 minutes. Sprinkle with ham, olives, green onions, red pepper, provolone cheese, and cheddar cheese.

3 Bake, uncovered, in a 350° oven for 35 to 40 minutes or until a knife inserted near the center comes out clean. Let stand 10 minutes before serving. Makes 6 to 8 servings.

Nutrition facts per serving: 463 cal., 23 g total fat (10 g sat. fat), 365 mg chol., 1,159 mg sodium, 33 g carbo., 1 g fiber, 30 g pro. *Daily values:* 40% vit. A, 134% vit. C, 42% calcium, 24% iron.

PRIZE TESTED RECIPE WINNER

MEDITERRANEAN STRATA

Prep: 20 min. ◆ Bake: 35 min.
Stand: 5 min.

The flavors of olives and feta cheese make this brunch dish a standard.

Nonstick spray coating
3 cups cubed Italian bread

◆◆◆

2 large onions, thinly sliced
2 tsp. bottled minced garlic
2 Tbsp. olive oil
½ cup chopped roasted red sweet peppers
½ cup chopped pitted green olives
½ cup crumbled feta cheese (2 oz.)

◆◆◆

6 eggs
1 14½-oz. can chicken broth
¼ cup dry white wine
¼ tsp. black pepper

1 Spray a 10-inch quiche dish with nonstick spray coating. Arrange the bread cubes in dish; set aside.

2 In a large skillet cook onions and garlic in hot oil over medium heat about 10 minutes or until onions are golden, stirring frequently. Remove from heat. Stir the roasted red peppers and olives into mixture in skillet. Evenly spoon mixture over bread cubes in dish. Sprinkle with the feta cheese.

3 In a large bowl beat together eggs, chicken broth, wine, and black pepper. Pour egg mixture over bread mixture in dish.

4 Bake in a 350° oven for 35 to 45 minutes or until a knife inserted near the center comes out clean. Let strata stand for 5 to 10 minutes before serving. Makes 8 servings.

Nutrition facts per serving: 173 cal., 11 g total fat (3 g sat. fat), 166 mg chol., 515 mg sodium, 11 g carbo., 1 g fiber, 8 g pro. *Daily values:* 12% vit. A, 46% vit. C, 6% calcium, 9% iron.

TEST KITCHEN TIP

USING EGGS SAFELY

Great egg dishes depend on eggs that are in top condition. Here are some egg-handling pointers to remember.

◆ Select clean, fresh eggs from refrigerated display cases. Don't use dirty, cracked, or leaking eggs. They may have become contaminated with harmful bacteria.

◆ When you come home from the grocery store, promptly refrigerate the eggs with the large ends up. Store them in their cartons because eggs easily absorb refrigerator odors. Fresh eggs can be refrigerated for up to 5 weeks after the packing date (a number stamped on the carton from 1 to 365, with 1 representing January 1 and 365 representing December 31).

◆ To store raw egg whites, refrigerate them in a tightly covered container for up to 4 days. Refrigerate raw yolks covered with water in a tightly covered container for up to 2 days. Refrigerate hard-cooked eggs in their shells for up to 7 days.

◆ When cracking eggs, avoid getting any eggshells in with the raw eggs. Also, when separating eggs, don't pass the yolk from shell half to shell half. Instead, use an egg separator so if bacteria are present on the shell, they won't contaminate either the yolk or the white.

◆ Be sure to wash your hands, utensils, and countertop after working with eggs.

◆ Serve hot egg dishes as soon as they're cooked. Refrigerate cold egg dishes immediately. Chill leftovers promptly and reheat thoroughly before serving.

◆ Eating uncooked or slightly cooked eggs may be harmful because of possible bacterial contamination. The individuals most susceptible include the elderly, infants, pregnant women, and those who are already ill. Check with your doctor to see if you are at risk. If you are, you probably should avoid eating foods that contain raw or partially cooked eggs. Healthy people should eat raw eggs with discretion.

For more information on handling eggs safely, call the U.S. Department of Agriculture Meat and Poultry Hotline at 800/535-4555.

BLUEBERRY CHEESECAKE FLAPJACKS

Prep: 25 min. ◆ Cook: 4 min. per flapjack

Frozen berries will deepen the color of the syrup in these special breakfast or brunch treats.

1 8-oz. pkg. cream cheese, softened
½ of an 8-oz. carton frozen whipped dessert topping, thawed

◆◆◆

1 cup pure maple syrup or maple-flavored syrup
½ cup fresh or frozen blueberries, thawed

◆◆◆

1 cup all-purpose flour
½ cup graham cracker crumbs
1 Tbsp. sugar
1 tsp. baking powder
½ tsp. baking soda
¼ tsp. salt
2 beaten eggs
1¼ cups buttermilk
¼ cup margarine or butter, melted
1 cup fresh or frozen blueberries, thawed

1 In a medium bowl beat cream cheese with an electric mixer on medium speed for 30 seconds. Beat in whipped topping just until smooth. Cover and chill until serving time.

2 Meanwhile, in a small saucepan combine maple syrup and the ½ cup berries; heat just to boiling. Remove from heat.

3 In a large mixing bowl stir together flour, graham cracker crumbs, sugar, baking powder, baking soda, and salt; set aside. In another bowl combine eggs, buttermilk, and melted margarine or butter. Add egg mixture to flour mixture; stir just until moistened. Stir in the 1 cup blueberries.

4 For each flapjack, pour about ¼ cup batter onto a hot, lightly greased griddle or heavy skillet. Cook over medium heat 2 minutes on each side or until flapjacks are golden brown, turning when flapjacks have bubbly surfaces and edges are slightly dry.

5 For each serving, stack 3 or 4 flapjacks, spreading a little cream cheese mixture between each. Top with blueberry syrup. Cover and refrigerate any remaining cream cheese mixture for up to 7 days. Makes 4 to 5 servings.

Nutrition facts per serving: 558 cal., 25 g total fat (10 g sat. fat), 130 mg chol., 751 mg sodium, 73 g carbo., 2 g fiber, 12 g pro. *Daily values:* 28% vit. A, 11% vit. C, 18% calcium, 20% iron.

NO FAT
QUINCE MARMALADE

Prep: 10 min. ◆ Cook: 25 min.

1 to 1¼ lb. quinces (2 medium)
1 cup water
¾ cup sugar
2 tsp. sliced fresh ginger (optional)
2 Tbsp. lemon juice
½ tsp. cardamom seeds

1 Peel, halve, and seed quinces, removing and discarding cores. Shred quince halves. In a large saucepan combine quinces, water, and sugar. Bring to boiling, stirring to dissolve sugar; reduce heat. Simmer, uncovered, 10 to 15 minutes, stirring occasionally. Add ginger (if desired), lemon juice, and cardamom. Simmer for 10 minutes more or until mixture thickens. Ladle into 2 hot, clean half-pint jars, leaving ¼ inch of headspace. Loosely cover and chill. Secure lids and store in refrigerator for up to 2 weeks. Makes about 2 half-pints.

Nutrition facts per tablespoon: 30 cal., 0 g total fat, 0 mg chol., 1 mg sodium, 8 g carbo., 0 g fiber, 0 g pro. *Daily values:* 4% vit. C.

BASIL AND TOMATO CREAM CHEESE SPIRAL

Prep: 20 min. ◆ Chill: 3 to 24 hr.

1 8-oz. pkg. cream cheese, softened
¼ cup oil-packed dried tomatoes, drained and snipped
1 Tbsp. snipped fresh basil or ½ tsp. dried basil, crushed
⅛ tsp. pepper

◆◆◆

3 Tbsp. purchased pesto
1 small plum tomato, thinly sliced
Basil leaves
Assorted crackers

1 In a medium bowl combine cream cheese, dried tomatoes, the 1 tablespoon basil, and the pepper until well-combined. Place the cream cheese mixture between 2 pieces of waxed paper. Roll the mixture into a 10×7-inch rectangle. (If mixture seems too soft to roll out easily, place in freezer for a few minutes to stiffen slightly.)

2 Remove top piece of waxed paper. Spread rectangle lightly with pesto, leaving a ½-inch border. Roll up, jelly-roll style, starting from a long side, and using the waxed paper to guide. Wrap roll in waxed paper or plastic wrap. Chill for 3 to 24 hours or until firm. Transfer cheese log to serving platter. Arrange tomato slices and basil leaves on platter. Serve with assorted crackers. Serves 24.

Nutrition facts per serving: 50 cal., 5 g total fat (2 g sat. fat), 11 mg chol., 46 mg sodium, 1 g carbo., 0 g fiber, 1 g pro. *Daily values:* 4% vit. A, 2% vit. C.

CRANBERRY TOAST

Prep: 30 min. ◆ **Bake:** 40 min.
Chill: 12 hr. ◆ **Toast:** 15 min.

When toasted, the thin slices make an ideal base for Country Pâté (see recipe, page 295).

2½ cups all-purpose flour
⅓ cup sugar
⅓ cup cornmeal
1 Tbsp. baking powder
½ tsp. salt
¼ tsp. baking soda

◆◆◆

1 beaten egg
1⅔ cups milk
¼ cup cooking oil
1 tsp. finely shredded orange peel
¾ cup coarsely chopped cranberries
½ cup chopped pecans or walnuts

1 Grease the bottoms and ½ inch up the sides of two 8×4×2-inch loaf pans; set aside. In a large mixing bowl stir together flour, sugar, cornmeal, baking powder, salt, and baking soda. Make a well in center; set aside.

2 In a medium mixing bowl combine egg, milk, cooking oil, and orange peel. Add egg mixture all at once to flour mixture. Stir just until moistened. Fold in cranberries and nuts. Spoon batter into the prepared pans.

3 Bake in a 350° oven for 40 to 50 minutes or until a wooden toothpick inserted near centers comes out clean. Cool in pans on a wire rack for 10 minutes. Remove loaves from pans. Cool completely on wire rack. Wrap and store overnight in the refrigerator before toasting.

4 To serve, trim ends from loaf with a serrated knife; cut each loaf into 18 slices. Lay slices on 2 large baking sheets. Bake in a 425° oven for 15 to 18 minutes or until crisp, turning slices once. Makes 36 servings.

Nutrition facts per serving: 73 cal., 3 g total fat (1 g sat. fat), 7 mg chol., 76 mg sodium, 10 g carbo., 0 g fiber, 2 g pro. *Daily values:* 1% vit. A, 3% calcium, 3% iron.

SAVORY NUTS

Start to finish: 25 min.

Combine the flavors and colors of macadamia nuts and walnuts, and add seasonings for a simple snack.

2 cups macadamia nuts and/or walnuts
2 Tbsp. white wine Worcestershire sauce
1 Tbsp. olive oil
2 tsp. snipped fresh thyme
1 tsp. snipped fresh rosemary
¼ tsp. salt
⅛ tsp. ground red pepper

1 Spread nuts in a 13×9×2-inch baking pan. In a small bowl stir together the Worcestershire sauce, olive oil, thyme, rosemary, salt, and red pepper. Drizzle oil mixture over nuts; toss to coat.

2 Bake in a 350° oven for 12 to 15 minutes or until nuts are toasted, stirring occasionally. Spread on foil; cool. Store in an airtight container. If desired, garnish serving dish with a sprig of *fresh thyme.* Makes 2 cups.

Nutrition facts per ¼-cup serving: 253 cal., 26 g total fat (4 g sat. fat), 0 mg chol., 100 mg sodium, 5 g carbo., 3 g fiber, 3 g pro. *Daily values:* 2% calcium, 5% iron.

DRIED CHERRY CHUTNEY

Prep: 30 min. ◆ **Chill:** 2 to 24 hr.

Serve this glossy, jewel-like, ginger-flavored accompaniment with cream cheese or other soft cheeses and crackers.

½ cup dried tart red cherries
¼ cup water
2 Tbsp. sugar
1 Tbsp. finely chopped fresh ginger
¾ cup chutney

1 In a small saucepan combine cherries, water, sugar, and ginger. Bring to boiling. Cover and remove from heat. Let stand for 15 minutes. Snip any large pieces of chutney. Stir chutney into cherry mixture. Cover and chill for 2 to 24 hours. Makes about 1⅓ cups.

Nutrition facts per tablespoon: 37 cal., 0 g total fat, 0 mg chol., 2 mg sodium, 9 g carbo., 0 g fiber, 0 g pro. *Daily values:* 2% vit. A.

Holiday Cheese Tray
(see below)

◆◆◆

Country Pâté
(see page 295)

◆◆◆

Cranberry Toast
(see page 293)

◆◆◆

Savory Nuts
(see page 293)

◆◆◆

Roasted Red Pepper Tart
(see page 296)

◆◆◆

Festive Apple Wedges
(see page 298)

TIMETABLE FOR THE BUFFET
Set aside a half-day to do as much of the work ahead as possible for this appetizer spread. Then, tuck the items away in the refrigerator.

The day before: Start with the Country Pâté. While it bakes, prepare the Festive Apple Wedges—cover and chill the pancetta, beet-carrot mixture, and poached apples. Chill the pâté overnight after cooling slightly.

◆ Prepare the Dried Cherry Chutney and Cheese Spread Duo. Cover and chill for 2 to 24 hours.

◆ Bake bread for Cranberry Toast; wrap and chill overnight.

◆ Prepare and bake the Savory Nuts. Store covered in an airtight container at room temperature.

◆ Make the Herb Pastry for the Roasted Red Pepper Tart; wrap ball of dough, and chill overnight.

◆ Set out serving containers and serving utensils and determine where each appetizer will be placed on the table.

Before the party: Transfer Savory Nuts to serving bowl.

◆ Prepare and bake Roasted Red Pepper Tart so it is warm when served.

◆ While the tart bakes, arrange the Holiday Cheese Tray with the Cheese Spread Duo and the Dried Cherry Chutney.

◆ Assemble the Festive Apple Wedges. (Apples can be assembled and chilled for up to 1 hour before serving.)

◆ Slice the Country Pâté and finish making the Cranberry Toast.

of tangy blue or Gorgonzola cheese, soft Brie or Camembert, creamy mascarpone, two-color colby-Monterey Jack, red-wax-coated Edam, a wedge of cheddar, plain or flavored cream cheese, and Swiss cheese. Check out the cheese counter for some specialty cheeses as well, such as peppered Brie, layered Muenster-cheddar cheese, and cheddar with claret. For some of the firmer cheeses, cut into thin slices and the trim edges with a fluted pastry wheel. Leave other cheeses in large chunks for slicing.

2 Intersperse cheese slices, chunks, and Cheese Spread Duo with fresh fruit, such as grape clusters, stem-on strawberries, kumquats, seckel pears, and lady apples. Add a container of Dried Cherry Chutney and garnish with a sprig or 2 of fresh herb.

3 If desired, serve with crisp crackers or breadsticks, melba toast rounds, toasted baguette-style French bread slices, or sliced party rye or pumpernickel bread.

HOLIDAY CHEESE TRAY
Start to finish: 30 min.

Want an easy appetizer suggestion? Purchase a variety of cheeses at the supermarket or specialty cheese store and artfully arrange on a tray.

Assorted cheeses
1 **recipe Cheese Spread Duo**
   (see right)

Assorted fresh fruit
1 **recipe Dried Cherry Chutney**
   (see page 293)
Fresh herb sprigs

◆◆◆

**Assorted crackers,
   breadsticks, and breads**

1 Select cheeses of different flavors, colors, shapes, and textures. Suggestions include a wedge

CHEESE SPREAD DUO
Prep: 25 min. ◆ Chill: 24 hr.

*Start with a basic cheese mixture, divide it in half, and turn each portion into a flavorful spread.
(See the photograph of the dried tomato version on page 317.)*

1 **3-oz. pkg. cream cheese,
   softened**
7 **oz. goat cheese (chèvre)**
⅓ **cup mascarpone cheese**
¼ **cup finely chopped shallots
   or onion**

¼ cup snipped fresh basil
2 Tbsp. well-drained and
    chopped oil-packed dried
    tomatoes*
    Few dashes bottled hot
    pepper sauce
½ cup crumbled Stilton,
    Gorgonzola, or blue cheese

♦♦♦

Dried tomato strips
    (optional)
Parsley sprigs
¼ cup toasted pine nuts
    Radicchio leaves

1 Line two 1-cup molds or 10-ounce custard cups with plastic wrap; set aside. In a medium mixing bowl beat the cream cheese, goat cheese, and mascarpone cheese with an electric mixer on medium speed until smooth. Stir in shallots or onion.

2 Divide mixture in half. To 1 portion stir in the basil, chopped tomatoes, and hot pepper sauce. To the other portion stir in the Stilton, Gorgonzola, or blue cheese. Spoon each portion into a lined mold or cup. Cover and refrigerate for up to 24 hours.

3 To serve, unmold the cheese mixtures. If desired, garnish the top of dried tomato cheese spread with dried tomato strips. Trim with parsley sprigs. Press the pine nuts into the molded Stilton cheese spread and garnish with radicchio leaves. Makes about 1 cup of each spread.

*Note: If necessary, pat tomatoes dry with a paper towel.

Nutrition facts per tablespoon of dried tomato cheese spread: 49 cal., 5 g total fat (2 g sat. fat), 10 mg chol., 43 mg sodium, 1 g carbo., 0 g fiber, 2 g pro.
Daily values: 3% vit. A, 1% vit. C, 1% iron.

Nutrition facts per tablespoon of blue cheese spread: 50 cal., 4 g total fat (3 g sat. fat), 13 mg chol., 93 mg sodium, 0 g carbo., 0 g fiber, 2 g pro.
Daily values: 4% vit. A, 1% vit. C, 2% calcium.

COUNTRY PÂTÉ

**Prep: 20 min. ♦ Bake: 1½ hr.
Chill: 12 hr.**

This colorful, easy-to-slice baked pâté makes the perfect accompaniment to slices of Cranberry Toast (see recipe, page 293) or thin slices of French bread.

Nonstick spray coating

♦♦♦

1 **beaten egg**
¾ **cup dried cranberries**
½ **cup chopped shallots**
½ **cup pistachio nuts**
⅓ **cup port wine or cranberry
    juice**
¼ **cup fine dry bread crumbs**
¼ **cup half-and-half or light
    cream**
2 **tsp. dried sage leaves,
    crushed, or ¼ tsp. ground
    sage**
2 **cloves garlic, minced**
1 **tsp. salt**
1 **tsp. coarsely ground black
    pepper**
1 **lb. lean ground beef**
1 **lb. ground pork**

1 Lightly spray a 9×5×3-inch loaf pan with nonstick spray coating; set aside.

2 In a large mixing bowl combine the egg, cranberries, shallots, pistachio nuts, port wine, bread crumbs, half-and-half or cream, sage, garlic, salt, and pepper. Add the ground beef and pork. Mix well. Press the meat mixture into the prepared pan.

3 Cover pan tightly with foil. Bake in a 350° oven for 1½ hours.

4 Remove pan from oven. Cool slightly on a wire rack. Carefully pour off drippings. Cover pâté loosely with foil. Place several heavy cans of food in another 9×5-inch loaf pan to serve as weights; place on top of the covered pâté. Chill overnight.

5 Remove weights and foil. Loosen sides, if necessary. Invert pâté onto a serving platter. Cut in half lengthwise and then into thin slices. Makes 24 servings.

▌ TO MAKE AHEAD ▐

Prepare pâté as directed. Chill overnight. Wrap pâté and store in the refrigerator for up to 2 days. Slice before serving.

Nutrition facts per serving: 98 cal., 5 g total fat (2 g sat. fat), 31 mg chol., 116 mg sodium, 6 g carbo., 1 g fiber, 7 g pro.
Daily values: 5% vit. A, 1% vit. C, 1% calcium, 5% iron.

ROASTED RED PEPPER TART

Prep: 45 min. ◆ Bake: 38 min.
Stand: 10 min.

3 cups sliced fresh
  mushrooms, such as
  shiitake, cremini,
  chanterelle, and/or button
1 cup coarsely chopped red
  onions
2 cloves garlic, minced
1 Tbsp. olive oil
◆◆◆
1 recipe Herb Pastry (see
  below right)
◆◆◆
1 cup shredded smoked Swiss
  cheese, or smoked Swiss
  and cheddar cheese (4 oz.)
4 tsp. all-purpose flour
1 beaten egg
⅓ cup half-and-half, light
  cream, or milk
1 12-oz. jar roasted red sweet
  peppers, well drained and
  chopped (about 1¼ cups)
1 Tbsp. snipped fresh basil or
  1 tsp. dried basil, crushed
½ tsp. coarsely ground black
  pepper
¼ tsp. salt
◆◆◆
  Roasted red pepper strips
  (optional)
  Fresh basil (optional)

1 In a large saucepan cook mushrooms, onions, and garlic in hot olive oil over medium-high heat for 4 to 5 minutes or until mushrooms are tender, stirring occasionally. Remove from heat. Drain off any excess liquid. Pat mixture dry with paper towels.

2 On a lightly floured surface, roll Herb Pastry into a 14×11-inch rectangle. Ease pastry into an 11×8×1-inch tart pan with removable bottom. Press pastry into fluted sides of tart pan; trim edges. (Or, line an 11×7½×1½-inch baking pan with foil, extending foil over edges; ease pastry into pan and up sides.) Do not prick pastry. Line pastry with a double thickness of foil. Bake in a 450° oven for 8 minutes. Remove foil. Bake for 5 to 6 minutes more or until pastry is golden. Remove pan from oven. Reduce oven temperature to 350°.

3 Toss together the cheese and flour; sprinkle over baked pastry. In a medium mixing bowl combine the egg and half-and-half. Stir in the mushroom mixture, chopped roasted red peppers, basil, black pepper, and salt. Spoon mixture evenly into crust.

4 Bake in a 350° oven about 25 minutes or until custard is set. Let stand for 10 minutes. To serve, cut tart into appetizer-size pieces. Serve warm. If desired, garnish with additional strips of roasted peppers and fresh basil. Makes 12 appetizer servings.

Herb Pastry: In a medium mixing bowl combine 1⅓ cups all-purpose flour; 1 tablespoon snipped fresh basil or 1 teaspoon dried basil, crushed; ½ teaspoon snipped fresh rosemary or ¼ teaspoon dried rosemary, crushed; and ¼ teaspoon salt. Using a pastry blender, cut in ⅓ cup cold butter until pieces are the size of small peas.

In a small mixing bowl combine 1 beaten egg yolk and 1 tablespoon cold water. Gradually stir the yolk mixture into the flour mixture. Add 3 to 4 tablespoons additional cold water, 1 tablespoon at a time, until all of the dough is moistened. Using your fingers, gently knead the dough for a few strokes just until a ball forms.

Nutrition facts per serving: 175 cal., 11 g total fat (6 g sat. fat), 60 mg chol., 175 mg sodium, 15 g carbo., 1 g fiber, 6 g pro. *Daily values:* 20% vit. A, 87% vit. C, 9% calcium, 9% iron.

PRIZE
TESTED
RECIPE
WINNER

HERBED LEEK TART

Prep: 15 min. ◆ Bake: 15 min.
Stand: 5 min.

Ready-made dough is a time-saver in this savory appetizer seasoned to perfection.

1 10-oz. pkg. refrigerated
  pizza dough
◆◆◆
6 medium leeks, thinly sliced
3 cloves garlic, minced
2 Tbsp. olive oil
1 tsp. dried herbes de Provence
  or dried basil, crushed
2 Tbsp. Dijon-style mustard
1 Tbsp. water
1 cup shredded Gruyère or
  Swiss cheese (4 oz.)
¼ cup pine nuts or chopped
  almonds, toasted

1 Unroll pizza dough onto a greased baking sheet; press to form a 12×9-inch rectangle. Bake in a 425° oven for 7 minutes.

2 Meanwhile, in a large skillet cook leeks and garlic in olive oil about 5 minutes or until tender. Remove from heat. Stir in herbes de Provence or basil. Stir together mustard and water; spread over prebaked crust. Top with leek mixture, cheese, and nuts.

3 Bake about 8 minutes more or until cheese is bubbly. Before serving, let stand 5 minutes. Cut into 24 squares. If desired, garnish with *fresh savory*. Makes 24 appetizer servings.

Nutrition facts per serving: 74 cal., 4 g total fat (1 g sat. fat), 5 mg chol., 88 mg sodium, 7 g carbo., 1 g fiber, 3 g pro.
Daily values: 1% vit. A, 2% vit. C, 5% calcium, 5% iron.

PRIZE TESTED RECIPE WINNER

MUSHROOM-SPINACH PINWHEELS

Prep: 30 min. ◆ Chill: 30 min. for dough; 1 hr. for logs ◆ Bake: 20 min.

For an appetizing head start, freeze the unbaked slices up to 3 months, then bake as directed.

1   8-oz. pkg. reduced-fat cream cheese (Neufchâtel), softened
⅔   cup butter, softened
1   cup all-purpose flour
1   cup self-rising flour

◆◆◆

1   10-oz. pkg. frozen chopped spinach
2   Tbsp. butter or margarine
2½   cups chopped fresh mushrooms
1   cup chopped onions
1   Tbsp. all-purpose flour
½   tsp. dried oregano, crushed
½   tsp. salt
½   tsp. lemon juice
⅛   tsp. garlic powder
¼   cup grated Parmesan cheese

1   egg white
1   Tbsp. water

1 In a large bowl beat together cream cheese and ⅔ cup butter. Add the 1 cup all-purpose flour and the self-rising flour; beat well. Divide dough into 2 balls; wrap and refrigerate 30 to 60 minutes or until dough is easy to handle.

2 For filling, cook spinach according to package directions; drain. Squeeze out excess liquid; set aside. In a large skillet melt the 2 tablespoons butter. Add mushrooms and onions. Cook and stir over medium heat about 3 minutes or until onions are tender. Add spinach, the 1 tablespoon flour, oregano, salt, lemon juice, and garlic powder. Cook and stir until mixture thickens. Stir in Parmesan cheese; set aside to cool.

3 On a floured surface, roll 1 pastry ball into a 12×7-inch rectangle. Spread dough with half the spinach mixture, leaving a ½-inch border around edges. Roll up dough and filling, jelly-roll style, starting from a short side. Moisten edges with water; pinch to seal. Cover; chill for 1 hour. Repeat with remaining pastry.

4 Slice logs into ½-inch-thick slices. Place on ungreased baking sheets. Combine egg white and water. Brush slices with egg mixture. Bake in a 400° oven about 20 minutes or until golden. Transfer pinwheels to wire racks and let cool. Makes 30 pinwheels.

Nutrition facts per pinwheel: 101 cal., 7 g total fat (4 g sat. fat), 19 mg chol., 190 mg sodium, 8 g carbo., 1 g fiber, 2 g pro.
Daily values: 11% vit. A, 2% vit. C, 2% calcium, 4% iron.

NUTRITION IN NO TIME

30 MIN. LOW FAT

HOISIN CHICKEN CANAPÉS

Start to finish: 20 min.

Part of the "hoopla" of the holiday season is the balancing act between time spent in the kitchen and time enjoying the company of friends and family. Being a good holiday host is easier with these quick, crunchy—and positively yummy—appetizers.

⅔   cup finely chopped cooked chicken
⅔   cup packaged shredded cabbage with carrot (coleslaw mix)
2   Tbsp. bottled hoisin sauce
1   Tbsp. chopped peanuts
    Few dashes bottled hot pepper sauce
12   Belgian endive leaves; 2 red or yellow sweet peppers, cut into wedges; or 2 medium cucumbers, cut in half lengthwise, then cut into thirds, seeds removed

1 In a bowl stir together the chicken, cabbage mixture, hoisin sauce, peanuts, and hot pepper sauce. Spoon chicken mixture onto the endive leaves or vegetables cups. Makes 12 canapés.

Nutrition facts per canapé: 34 cal., 1 g total fat (0 g sat. fat), 0 mg chol., 66 mg sodium, 3 g carbo., 0 g fiber, 3 g pro.
Daily values: 3% vit. A, 11% vit. C, 1% iron.

THE CLEVER COOK

PERSONALIZED PLACE CARDS

When I have a dinner party, I use photographs of my guests in antique-looking frames as place cards. It's fun to see if they recognize themselves and what memories the pictures invoke.

Mrs. Marie T. Gasperin
Greensburg, Pennsylvania

LOW FAT

FESTIVE APPLE WEDGES

Prep: 45 min. ◆ Chill: 2 to 24 hr.

If small cans of beets and carrots are unavailable, use about 1 cup from larger cans of the julienne vegetables. (See the photograph on page 317.)

- 2 oz. pancetta or 3 slices thick-sliced bacon
- 1 8¼-oz. can julienne beets, drained
- 1 8¼-oz. can julienne carrots, drained
- ¼ cup Raspberry Vinaigrette (see below right, or use purchased)
  ◆◆◆
- 6 small apples or 12 Lady apples
- 4 cups water
- ¼ cup lemon juice
  ◆◆◆
- ¼ cup crumbled goat cheese (chèvre) with chives

Lettuce cup (optional)
Fresh rosemary sprigs (optional)

1 Cut pancetta into ¼-inch pieces or bacon into ¼-inch strips. Cook until crisp. Drain, wrap, and chill. In a medium bowl combine beets and carrots. Toss with the ¼ cup Raspberry Vinaigrette. Cover and marinate in the refrigerator for 2 to 24 hours, stirring occasionally.

2 Meanwhile, core and quarter the small apples or core and halve the lady apples. (If desired, leave stem on a portion of the apple.) Cut a very thin slice from rounded side of each apple portion to prevent rolling. In a large saucepan bring the water and lemon juice to boiling; add apples. Cook apples about 3 to 4 minutes or until just tender (don't overcook); drain. When cool enough to handle, use a melon baller to hollow out the center of each fruit quarter or half. Cover and chill.

3 Shortly before serving, drain beet mixture; stir pancetta or bacon into beet mixture. Crumble a small amount of cheese into apple quarters or halves. Top with a small spoonful of the beet mixture. Cover and chill up to 1 hour. If desired, serve any remaining beet-carrot mixture in a lettuce cup; garnish apples with rosemary sprigs. Makes 24 servings.

Raspberry Vinaigrette: In a food processor bowl or blender container combine 1 cup fresh or frozen raspberries, thawed, and ¼ cup red wine vinegar. Cover

and process or blend about 30 seconds or until raspberries are pureed. Press through a sieve, discarding seeds. Transfer the pureed raspberry mixture to a small mixing bowl. Stir in ¼ cup salad oil, 1 tablespoon sugar, and ¼ teaspoon ground cinnamon. Cover and chill. Use remaining vinaigrette with other salads. Makes about ¾ cup.

Nutrition facts per serving: 33 cal., 2 g total fat (1 g sat. fat), 3 mg chol., 60 mg sodium, 4 g carbo., 1 g fiber, 1 g pro.
Daily values: 8% vit. A, 5% vit. C, 1% iron.

HOLIDAY WREATH SLAW

Prep: 50 min. ◆ Chill: 2 hr.

To make thin, evenly sliced fruits and vegetables for the salad, use a mandoline—a food preparation utensil with adjustable blades.

- 2 tsp. finely shredded blood orange peel or orange peel
- ⅔ cup blood orange juice or orange juice
- ½ cup salad oil
- 2 Tbsp. white wine vinegar
- 2 Tbsp. honey
- 2 tsp. anise seed, crushed
- ¼ tsp. salt
  ◆◆◆
- 2 medium fennel bulbs
  ◆◆◆
- 3 red apples, cored and cut into thin wedges
- 2 Tbsp. lemon juice
- 6 cups shredded green or red cabbage
- 5 blood oranges or oranges, peeled and thinly sliced
- 2 English cucumbers, thinly sliced

1 In a screw-top jar combine orange peel and juice, salad oil, vinegar, honey, anise seed, and salt. Cover and shake well. Chill for up to 3 days.

2 Cut off and discard upper stalks of fennel. Remove any wilted outer layers; cut off a thick slice from fennel base. Wash and thinly slice fennel.

3 In a bowl toss together the apple slices and lemon juice. Line a serving platter with deep sides with shredded cabbage. Arrange the orange slices, cucumber slices, fennel slices, and apple wedges to resemble a wreath on the cabbage-lined platter.

4 Pour half of the dressing over salad. Cover salad with plastic wrap and chill for up to 2 hours. Pour remaining dressing in a decorative long-neck bottle with a lid; chill until ready to serve. To serve, shake remaining dressing; pour over salad. Makes 10 to 12 side-dish servings.

To transport: Place the salad in a basket that fits closely around platter to avoid sliding around. Just before serving, remove plastic wrap from salad. Shake remaining dressing and pour over salad.

Nutrition facts per serving: 178 cal., 11 g total fat (2 g sat. fat), 0 mg chol., 74 mg sodium, 20 g carbo., 8 g fiber, 2 g pro. *Daily values:* 3% vit. A, 98% vit. C, 5% calcium, 5% iron.

SALADS WITH PASTRY PACKAGES

Prep: 30 min. ◆ Bake: 10 min.

Stuffed inside each salad "package" is a flavor-packed cheese and grape mixture surprise.

1½ **cups seedless red grapes, halved**
½ **cup crumbled Gorgonzola cheese or blue cheese**
½ **cup chopped walnuts**

◆◆◆

6 **sheets frozen phyllo dough (17×12-inch rectangles), thawed**
3 **Tbsp. margarine or butter, melted**

◆◆◆

⅓ **cup balsamic vinegar or cider vinegar**
1 **clove garlic, minced**
½ **tsp. dried thyme, crushed**
¼ **cup salad oil**
Salt

◆◆◆

4 **cups torn fresh spinach or mixed salad greens**
4 **cups torn red-tip leaf lettuce or radicchio**
Coarsely ground pink peppercorns
Small clusters of seedless red grapes (optional)
Fresh chives (optional)

1 In a small bowl combine the 1½ cups halved grapes, the Gorgonzola or blue cheese, and walnuts. Set aside.

2 For pastry packages, unfold phyllo dough. Cover phyllo with a slightly damp cloth to help keep it from drying out; remove sheets as needed. Brush 1 phyllo sheet with some of the melted margarine or butter. Top with another sheet of phyllo and brush with some of the melted margarine. Add 1 more sheet for a total of 3 sheets, brushing each sheet with margarine. Use remaining phyllo and melted margarine to make a second 3-layer stack of phyllo. Trim each stack into a 14-inch square; cut each large square into four 7-inch squares.

3 Place about ¼ cup of the grape-cheese mixture onto the center of one 7-inch square. Fold 2 opposite sides of phyllo over filling; fold remaining 2 sides of phyllo over, forming a square package. Press edges lightly to seal. Place seam side down on a lightly greased baking sheet or 15×10×1-inch baking pan. Repeat with remaining squares. Brush with any remaining melted margarine. Bake in a 400° oven about 10 minutes or until golden.

4 For dressing, in a food processor bowl or blender container combine vinegar, garlic, and thyme. With food processor or blender running, slowly add the salad oil; process or blend until combined. Add salt to taste.

5 To serve, for each salad, place a pastry package in the center of a salad plate. Surround with spinach or salad greens and red-tip lettuce or radicchio. Drizzle with 1 tablespoon of the dressing. Sprinkle with ground pink peppercorns. If desired, garnish with clusters of grapes and chives. Makes 8 side-dish servings.

Nutrition facts per serving: 262 cal., 19 g total fat (4 g sat. fat), 6 mg chol., 283 mg sodium, 19 g carbo., 1 g fiber, 5 g pro. *Daily values:* 26% vit. A, 24% vit. C, 7% calcium, 12% iron.

CAULIFLOWER CROWNS WITH PESTO AND PROSCIUTTO

Start to finish: 30 min.

Instead of breaking cauliflower into small florets, break each head into six to eight large clusters so they look like "crowns."

2 heads cauliflower (about
   1½ lb. each)

♦♦♦

1 cup snipped fresh parsley
½ cup smoked walnuts or
   almonds
½ cup olive oil
2 Tbsp. fresh tarragon
2 cloves garlic
1 tsp. red wine vinegar
2 Tbsp. butter, melted
2 Tbsp. diced prosciutto
   (1 oz.)
   Fresh parsley sprigs
   (optional)

1 Wash cauliflower heads and remove leaves and woody stems. Break each cauliflower head into 6 to 8 clusters. In a 6-quart Dutch oven cook cauliflower, covered, in a small amount of boiling salted water about 8 to 10 minutes or until crisp-tender. Drain. Arrange the cauliflower crowns in a large shallow serving dish, floret side up. Keep warm.

2 Meanwhile, for pesto, in a food processor bowl or blender container combine snipped parsley, walnuts or almonds, oil, tarragon, garlic, and vinegar. Cover and process or blend until smooth. Spoon half of the pesto around base of cauliflower. Drizzle cauliflower with melted butter and sprinkle with diced prosciutto. Pass remaining pesto. If desired, garnish with parsley sprigs. Serve immediately. Makes 12 side-dish servings.

*Note: If not serving immediately, cover and refrigerate pesto and cauliflower in separate containers. About 1 hour before serving, remove pesto and cauliflower from refrigerator and allow to come to room temperature.

To transport: Carry cauliflower and pesto in separate containers. Just before serving, drizzle melted butter over cauliflower and sprinkle with prosciutto. Pour half of pesto around base of cauliflower and pass the remaining pesto.

Nutrition facts per serving: 155 cal., 15 g total fat (3 g sat. fat), 5 mg chol., 69 mg sodium, 5 g carbo., 2 g fiber, 3 g pro. *Daily values:* 4% vit. A, 75% vit. C, 2% calcium, 5% iron.

SAVORY OLIVE LOAF

Prep: 45 min. ♦ Rise: 1¾ hr.
Bake: 30 min.

While it looks like a country-style pie, the round loaf tastes like a hearty yeast bread chockful of onions and olives. Serve small wedges for an appetizer or larger pieces as bread with a meal.

2 to 2½ cups all-purpose flour
1 pkg. active dry yeast
1 cup warm water (120° to
   130°)
1 Tbsp. olive oil or cooking
   oil
¾ tsp. salt

♦♦♦

3 cups slivered red or yellow
   onions
4 cloves garlic, minced
2 Tbsp. olive oil
1 6-oz. can pitted ripe green
   olives, drained and halved
2 to 3 Tbsp. snipped fresh
   sage

♦♦♦

1 egg yolk
1 Tbsp. water

♦♦♦

Fresh sage sprigs (optional)

1 In a large mixing bowl combine 1 cup of the flour and the yeast. Add the warm water, the 1 tablespoon olive oil or cooking oil, and the salt to the flour mixture. Beat with an electric mixer on low to medium speed for 30 seconds, scraping sides of bowl. Beat on high speed for 3 minutes. Stir in as much of the remaining flour as you can.

2 Turn dough out onto a lightly floured surface. Knead in enough of the remaining flour to make a stiff dough that is smooth and elastic (8 to 10 minutes total). Shape dough into a ball. Place in a lightly greased bowl; turn once to grease surface of dough. Cover and let rise in a warm place until double in size (about 1 hour).

3 Punch dough down; divide into 2 equal portions. Turn dough out onto a lightly floured surface. Cover and let rest for 10 minutes.

4 Just before shaping bread, in a large skillet cook onions and garlic in the 2 tablespoons olive oil until onion is tender but not brown. Remove from heat and cool slightly. Stir in olives and the snipped sage; set aside.

5 Grease a 9-inch pie plate. On a lightly floured surface, roll 1 portion of dough into a 12-inch circle. Line prepared pie plate with dough. Spoon onion mixture over dough.

6 On a lightly floured surface, roll the remaining portion of dough into a 10-inch circle. Cut the dough into ¾-inch-wide strips. To make lattice top, lay half of the dough strips on top of filling at 1-inch intervals. Fold alternate dough strips back halfway. Place another dough strip in the center of loaf across the strips already in place. Unfold folded strips; fold back remaining strips. Place another dough strip parallel to strip in center. Repeat weaving steps on both sides of center strip until lattice covers filling. Brush edges lightly with water. Press ends of strips into crust rim. Fold bottom dough over strips; seal and crimp edge.

7 Cover and let rise in a warm place until nearly double (45 to 60 minutes). Press the tines of a fork into the center of each flute on edge of loaf.

8 In a small bowl combine egg yolk and water; brush over top of loaf. Bake in a 350° oven for 30 to 35 minutes or until done. If necessary, cover with foil the last 10 minutes of baking to prevent overbrowning. Remove from oven; cool slightly on wire rack. Just before serving, cut into wedges. If desired, garnish with sprigs of fresh sage. Makes 8 to 12 servings.

To transport: Cover the pie plate with plastic wrap. Put the covered pie plate in a pie carrier to protect edges.

Nutrition facts per serving: 203 cal., 9 g total fat (1 g sat. fat), 27 mg chol., 634 mg sodium, 28 g carbo., 3 g fiber, 5 g pro. *Daily values:* 4% vit. A, 4% vit. C, 2% calcium, 13% iron.

LOW FAT

MORE-THAN-CANDIED SWEET POTATOES

Prep: 40 min. ◆ Bake: 40 min.

Homemade chutney adds a new twist to traditional candied sweet potatoes.

12 **medium white sweet potatoes or orange sweet potatoes, peeled and cut into 1-inch pieces (about 4 lb.)**

◆ ◆ ◆

⅓ **cup packed brown sugar**
¼ **cup margarine or butter**
2 **Tbsp. pineapple juice or apple juice**

◆ ◆ ◆

1 **recipe Pineapple-Cherry Chutney (see right)**

1 In a Dutch oven cook sweet potatoes, covered, in enough boiling water to cover, about 10 minutes or until crisp-tender. Drain and place cooked sweet potato pieces in a 3-quart casserole.

2 Meanwhile, in a small saucepan combine brown sugar, margarine or butter, and pineapple juice or apple juice. Heat and stir until margarine is melted. Bring to boiling; reduce heat. Cook and stir over medium heat about 5 minutes or until syrupy. Remove from heat. Pour over sweet potatoes in casserole.

3 Bake, uncovered, in a 375° oven for 20 minutes. Gently stir about half of the chutney mixture into the potatoes. Continue baking about 15 minutes more or until potatoes are just tender and glazed. Spoon remaining chutney on top of potatoes and bake about 5 minutes more to heat through. Makes 10 to 12 side-dish servings.

To transport: Cover the hot dish with foil, then wrap in a towel. Place in an insulated container to keep warm. Serve within 2 hours. To serve, remove foil.

Pineapple-Cherry Chutney: In a medium saucepan combine 2 cups chopped fresh pineapple or canned unsweetened pineapple, ½ cup golden raisins, ½ cup dried tart red cherries, and 3 tablespoons finely chopped onion. Add ½ cup granulated sugar, ½ cup white wine vinegar, 3 tablespoons lemon juice, 3 tablespoons finely chopped crystallized ginger, and ¼ teaspoon ground cinnamon. Heat mixture over medium heat to boiling; reduce heat. Boil gently, uncovered, about 30 minutes or until syrup is slightly thickened. Cool slightly. (If desired, chutney may be made ahead, covered, and chilled for up to 2 days.)

Nutrition facts per serving: 321 cal., 5 g total fat (1 g sat. fat), 0 mg chol., 73 mg sodium, 70 g carbo., 6 g fiber, 3 g pro. *Daily values:* 317% vit. A, 72% vit. C, 5% calcium, 11% iron.

MUSHROOMS IN CHIVE CREAM

Start to finish: 20 min.

Although this recipe requires last-minute preparation, it's an elegant first course to begin the holiday meal.

24 whole 2- to 2½-inch
    diameter fresh
    mushrooms, stems
    trimmed (about 2 lb.)
3 Tbsp. margarine or butter
    ♦♦♦
1 cup whipping cream
2 Tbsp. snipped fresh chives
1 Tbsp. finely shredded lemon
    peel
    Salt and pepper (optional)
    ♦♦♦
⅓ cup crushed croutons

1 In a 12-inch nonstick skillet cook the mushrooms, covered, in hot margarine or butter for 5 to 7 minutes or until tender, stirring twice. Remove the mushrooms with a slotted spoon; set aside and keep warm.

2 Stir the cream, chives, and lemon peel into the skillet. Bring the mixture to boiling; reduce heat. Simmer, uncovered, about 5 minutes or until the mixture is slightly thickened and bubbly. Stir in the reserved mushrooms; heat through (do not cook longer or mushrooms will thin sauce). If desired, season mushroom mixture with some salt and pepper.

Menu

**Mushrooms in Chive Cream
(see left)**

♦♦♦

**Salads with Pastry Packages
(see page 299)**

♦♦♦

**Raspberry-Pepper Glazed
Ham
(see page 304)**

♦♦♦

**Stuffed Pumpkin Shell
Potatoes
(see page 303)**

♦♦♦

**Nutty Brussels Sprouts
(see page 303)**

♦♦♦

**Cinnamon-Apple Spice Cake
(see page 305)**

♦♦♦

Coffee

TIMETABLE FOR THE FEAST

One week ahead: Check the candle supply and decide on the centerpiece, place cards, and other table decorations.

♦ Pull out tablecloth and cloth napkins and freshen with an iron.

♦ Search for miniature pumpkins, if planning to use.

♦ Shop for all of the nonperishable items.

Two days ahead: Decide on serving containers and utensils. Get out a cutting board, carving knife, and meat fork to carve the ham.

♦ Purchase perishable foods.

One day ahead:

♦ Prepare Cinnamon-Apple Spice Cake; cover and store at room temperature.

♦ If desired, prepare mashed potato mixture and chill, covered, in a casserole.

Day of the feast—about 3 hours before dinner:

♦ Bake mini pumpkin shells.

♦ When pumpkins are tender, place glazed ham in oven.

♦ Meanwhile, start mashed potato mixture if not made ahead.

♦ Prepare either the ham sauce or glaze and start Nutty Brussels Sprouts. Don't forget to glaze the ham. Add the Stuffed Pumpkin Shell Potatoes to the oven at the appropriate time.

♦ Prepare Mushrooms in Chive Cream.

♦ While ham is standing before being carved, increase oven temperature; bake pastries for Salads with Pastry Packages and arrange salads. Place food in serving containers; bring all food to table.

3 To serve, for each appetizer sprinkle about 2 teaspoons of crushed croutons on each plate or bowl. Top croutons with 3 mushrooms and about 1 tablespoon of the cream sauce. Makes 8 appetizer servings.

Nutrition facts per serving: 171 cal., 16 g total fat (8 g sat. fat), 41 mg chol., 76 mg sodium, 7 g carbo., 1 g fiber, 3 g pro.
Daily values: 18% vit. A, 8% vit. C, 2% calcium, 10% iron.

NUTTY BRUSSELS SPROUTS

Prep: 30 min. ◆ Cook: 11 min.

Update Brussels sprouts with a pine nut and dried tomato topping.

1½ lb. fresh Brussels sprouts or three 10-oz. pkg. frozen Brussels sprouts

◆◆◆

   Boiling water
⅓ cup dried tomatoes (not oil-packed), snipped

◆◆◆

2 Tbsp. margarine or butter
1 cup chopped onions
   Salt and pepper
¼ cup pine nuts, toasted

1 Trim stems and remove any wilted outer leaves from fresh Brussels sprouts; wash. Cut any large fresh sprouts in half lengthwise; set aside.

2 In a bowl pour boiling water over the dried tomatoes. Let stand for 2 minutes or until softened. Drain well; set aside.

3 In a large skillet melt margarine or butter over medium heat. Add Brussels sprouts and onions. Cook, covered, about 10 minutes (15 minutes, if using frozen sprouts) or until Brussels sprouts are nearly tender, stirring occasionally. (If necessary, reduce heat to medium-low to prevent overbrowning.) Uncover and cook for 1 to 2 minutes more or until Brussels sprouts are just tender. Season with salt and pepper.

4 To serve, spoon Brussels sprouts into a serving dish. Sprinkle with the tomatoes and pine nuts. Makes 8 to 10 side-dish servings.

Nutrition facts per serving: 100 cal., 6 g total fat (1 g sat. fat), 0 mg chol., 117 mg sodium, 12 g carbo., 4 g fiber, 4 g pro. *Daily values:* 10% vit. A, 98% vit. C, 3% calcium, 10% iron.

STUFFED PUMPKIN SHELL POTATOES

Start to finish: 1 hr.

Looking for a new twist on mashed potatoes? Stir in canned pumpkin (not the pie filling kind) and smoked cheese. (See the photograph on page 317.)

8 miniature pumpkins

◆◆◆

2 lb. medium baking potatoes, such as russet, round white, or yellow potatoes
1 cup canned pumpkin
2 Tbsp. margarine or butter
⅛ to ¼ tsp. ground nutmeg
½ cup milk, half-and-half, or light cream
1 cup shredded smoked Jarlsberg or smoked cheddar cheese (4 oz.)
   Salt and pepper (optional)

1 Cut ¼ inch off tops of pumpkins; discard tops. Remove seeds and fibrous strings from insides of pumpkins. Place pumpkins, cut side down, on an ungreased baking sheet. Bake in a 325° oven for 20 to 25 minutes or just until pumpkins can be easily pierced with a fork.

2 Meanwhile, peel and quarter potatoes. Cook, covered, in a small amount of boiling lightly salted water for 20 to 25 minutes or until tender; drain. Mash with a potato masher or beat with an electric mixer. Beat in canned pumpkin, margarine or butter, and nutmeg. Gradually beat in milk, half-and-half, or light cream to make light and fluffy. Stir in Jarlsberg or cheddar cheese. If desired, season to taste with salt and pepper.

3 Spoon mashed potatoes into empty pumpkin shells, spooning any remaining potato mixture into a small casserole. Place pumpkin shells on a 15×10×1-inch baking pan. Cover loosely with foil. Bake for 15 to 20 minutes or until heated through. (Or, omit pumpkin shells and spoon all of the potato mixture into a greased 1½-quart casserole. Bake, covered, about 1 hour or until heated through.) Makes 8 side-dish servings.

▌ TO MAKE AHEAD ▐

Omit miniature pumpkins. Prepare mashed potato mixture and spoon into a greased 1½-quart casserole. Cover and chill for up to 24 hours. Before serving, heat in a 325° oven for 1½ hours.

Nutrition facts per serving: 194 cal., 7 g total fat (3 g sat. fat), 14 mg chol., 85 mg sodium, 26 g carbo., 2 g fiber, 7 g pro. *Daily values:* 75% vit. A, 16% vit. C, 14% calcium, 5% iron.

RASPBERRY-PEPPER GLAZED HAM

Prep: 20 min. ◆ Bake: 1¾ hr.
Stand: 15 min.

Consider your guests' tolerance for heat by selecting either the peppery Raspberry Sauce or the milder Chutney Glaze to flavor the ham. The Raspberry Sauce makes enough to pass so guests can add extra "hotness." (See the photograph on page 317.)

1 9- to 10-lb. cooked bone-in ham (rump half or shank portion)

◆◆◆

1 recipe Raspberry Sauce or Chutney Glaze (see right)
1 Tbsp. pink or black peppercorns, coarsely cracked

◆◆◆

Fresh raspberries and fresh herb sprigs (optional)

1 If desired, score ham by making diagonal cuts in fat in a diamond pattern. Place ham on a rack in a shallow roasting pan. Insert a meat thermometer into the thickest portion of the meat that is not touching bone. Bake in a 325° oven until the thermometer registers 130°. Allow 1½ to 2¼ hours. Prepare desired sauce or glaze.

2 Brush the ham with some of the sauce or glaze. Bake ham for 15 to 20 minutes more or until the thermometer registers 135°, brushing once or twice with additional sauce or glaze. Remove from oven. Sprinkle with the peppercorns. Cover the ham with foil and let stand for 15 minutes. (Temperature of meat will rise 5° during standing.)

3 Just before serving, carve the ham. Reheat any of the remaining Raspberry Sauce and pass with ham. If desired, garnish with raspberries and herbs. Makes 16 to 20 servings.

Nutrition facts per serving with Raspberry Sauce: 250 cal., 7 g total fat (2 g sat. fat), 68 mg chol., 1,676 mg sodium, 15 g carbo., 0 g fiber, 31 g pro. *Daily values:* 2% vit. A, 1% vit. C, 1% calcium, 8% iron.

Nutrition facts per serving with Chutney Glaze: 230 cal., 7 g total fat (2 g sat. fat), 68 mg chol., 1665 mg sodium, 8 g carbo., 1 g fiber, 31 g pro. *Daily values:* 4% vit. C, 1% calcium, 9% iron.

RASPBERRY SAUCE

Start to finish: 10 min.

1½ cups seedless raspberry preserves
2 Tbsp. white vinegar
2 or 3 canned whole chipotle peppers in adobo sauce, drained and chopped
3 cloves garlic, minced

1 In a saucepan stir together the preserves, vinegar, chipotle peppers, and garlic. Bring just to boiling; reduce heat. Simmer, uncovered, for 5 minutes. Makes about 1¾ cups.

CHUTNEY GLAZE

Start to finish: 10 min.

1 12-oz. jar chutney
1 tsp. finely shredded orange peel
2 Tbsp. orange juice
1 Tbsp. stone-ground mustard

1 In a food processor bowl or blender container combine chutney, orange peel and juice, and mustard. Process until almost smooth. Makes about 1 cup.

MACADAMIA-ORANGE PIE

Prep: 18 min. ◆ Bake: 40 min.

3 beaten eggs
1 cup sugar
½ cup light-colored corn syrup
¼ cup butter or margarine, melted
1 tsp. finely shredded orange peel
3 Tbsp. orange juice
1 cup coarsely chopped macadamia nuts or almonds
1 unbaked 9-inch pie shell

◆◆◆

Whipped cream (optional)

1 In a large mixing bowl combine the eggs, sugar, corn syrup, melted butter or margarine, orange peel, and orange juice. Stir in macadamia nuts or almonds. Carefully pour mixture into unbaked pie shell.

2 Bake in a 375° oven for 30 minutes. Cover loosely with foil. Bake for 10 to 15 minutes more or until slightly puffed in center. Cool on a wire rack. To serve, cut into wedges. If desired, serve with whipped cream. Cover and store any remaining pie in the refrigerator. Makes 10 servings.

Nutrition facts per serving: 397 cal., 23 g total fat (7 g sat. fat), 76 mg chol., 131 mg sodium, 46 g carbo., 2 g fiber, 5 g pro. *Daily values:* 7% vit. A, 4% vit. C, 2% calcium, 12% iron.

CINNAMON-APPLE SPICE CAKE

Prep: 30 min. ◆ Bake: 25 min.
Frost: 20 min.

Spiced apple rings add flecks of red and a cinnamon flavor to this cake. (See the photograph on page 318.)

1   14- to 14½-oz. jar spiced apple rings
2   cups all-purpose flour
1½ tsp. baking powder
1   tsp. ground cinnamon
½   tsp. baking soda
½   tsp. salt
◆◆◆
½   cup butter, softened
1¼ cups granulated sugar
1   tsp. vanilla
3   eggs
¾   cup buttermilk or sour milk*
◆◆◆
1   recipe Buttercream Frosting
    (see right)
    Cookie Rounds (see
    Victorian Cookie
    Ornaments recipe, page
    309) (optional)

1 Grease and lightly flour two 8×8×2-inch square baking pans; set pans aside.

2 Drain apple rings; discard syrup. Place apples in a food processor bowl or blender container. Cover and process or blend until almost smooth (should have about ¾ cup apple puree); set aside. Combine the flour, baking powder, cinnamon, baking soda, and salt; set aside.

3 In a large mixing bowl beat butter with an electric mixer on medium to high speed for 30 seconds. Add sugar and vanilla. Beat until well combined. Add eggs, one at a time, beating well after each. Add flour mixture and buttermilk alternately to beaten mixture, beating on low speed after each addition just until combined. Fold in the processed apples. Divide batter evenly between prepared pans.

4 Bake in a 350° oven for 25 to 30 minutes or until a wooden toothpick inserted near center comes out clean. Cool layers in pans on wire racks for 10 minutes. Remove layers from pans. Cool thoroughly on wire racks.

5 To assemble, place 1 cake layer on a cake plate. Spread some of the frosting atop layer. Top with remaining cake layer. Frost top and sides. If desired, decorate cake with Cookie Rounds. Makes 12 to 16 servings.

*Note: To make sour milk, place 2 teaspoons lemon juice or vinegar in a glass measuring cup. Add enough milk to make ¾ cup total liquid; stir. Let stand 5 minutes before using.

Buttercream Frosting: In a mixing bowl beat ½ cup butter with an electric mixer on medium to high speed until fluffy. Gradually add 3 cups sifted powdered sugar, beating well on low speed. Slowly beat in ⅓ cup milk and 2 teaspoons vanilla. Gradually beat in 3½ cups sifted powdered sugar. If necessary, beat in additional milk to make frosting easy to spread.

Nutrition facts per serving: 554 cal., 17 g total fat (10 g sat. fat), 95 mg chol., 382 mg sodium, 99 g carbo., 1 g fiber, 4 g pro. *Daily values:* 16% vit. A, 7% calcium, 8% iron.

POACHED RED PEAR ZINFANDEL

Start to finish: 40 min.

4   large ripe red pears or other pear variety
1½ cups white zinfandel or rosé wine
1   vanilla bean, split lengthwise, or 1 teaspoon vanilla
◆◆◆
⅓   cup sugar
◆◆◆
4   tsp. honey

1 Core pears from bottom, leaving stem intact. Slice bottoms off pears. Stand pears up in the bottom of a large saucepan; add wine and vanilla bean or liquid vanilla. Bring mixture just to boiling; reduce heat. Simmer pears, covered, for 10 to 15 minutes or until pears are just tender.

2 Using a slotted spoon, transfer pears to individual serving dishes. Reserve cooking liquid in saucepan. Add sugar to liquid in pan. Bring to boiling; reduce heat. Simmer pear liquid, uncovered, for 12 to 15 minutes or until the liquid is reduced to ⅔ to ¾ cup and has the consistency of a thin sauce (it should coat the back of a spoon).

3 To serve, spoon sauce over pears. Drizzle with honey. Serve warm or chilled. If desired, garnish each plate with several *fresh mint leaves*. Makes 4 servings.

Nutrition facts per serving (one pear): 247 cal., 1 g total fat (0 g sat. fat), 0 mg chol., 5 mg sodium, 48 g carbo., 5 g fiber, 1 g pro. *Daily values:* 11% vit. C, 2% calcium, 4% iron.

PUMPKIN-PEAR TRIFLE

Prep: 55 min. ◆ Chill: 24 hr. (pears and sauce); 4 to 6 hr. (trifle)

This dessert looks more interesting if you don't make perfectly even layers of bread, sauce, and fruit.
(See the photograph on page 320.)

- 1 14-oz. pkg. pumpkin quick bread mix or 1 loaf purchased pumpkin bread, cut into 1-inch cubes (8 cups)
- 1 recipe Custard Sauce (see right)

◆◆◆

- 1¼ cups sweet white wine such as Sauterne or Riesling
- ⅓ cup sugar
- 1½ tsp. finely shredded lemon peel
- ½ tsp. ground nutmeg
- ¼ tsp. ground cinnamon

◆◆◆

- 4 large ripe pears, peeled, cored, and cut into ½-inch slices

◆◆◆

Lemon peel curls (optional)

1 Prepare pumpkin bread, if using a mix. Chill Custard Sauce.

2 In a large skillet stir together wine, sugar, lemon peel, nutmeg, and cinnamon. Cook and stir over low heat until sugar is dissolved. Bring mixture to boiling; reduce heat. Simmer, uncovered, about 10 minutes or until reduced by half.

3 Carefully stir pear slices into wine mixture, stirring to coat. Bring to boiling; reduce heat. Simmer, covered, for 3 to 5 min-

utes or until pears are tender, stirring occasionally. Using a slotted spoon, remove pears from skillet; discard any cooking liquid. Cover and chill pears for up to 24 hours.

4 In a 2-quart serving bowl alternate layers of the pumpkin bread cubes, custard, and poached pear slices. Cover and chill for 4 to 6 hours. If desired, garnish with lemon peel curls. Makes 10 to 12 servings.

Custard Sauce: In a heavy saucepan stir together ¾ cup sugar, ¼ cup all-purpose flour, ¼ teaspoon salt, and ¼ teaspoon ground nutmeg. Gradually stir in 2¾ cups milk, 4 beaten egg yolks, and 1 teaspoon vanilla. Cook and stir over medium heat until thickened and bubbly. Cook and stir for 2 minutes more. Remove from heat. Cover surface with plastic wrap and chill in the refrigerator up to 24 hours.

Nutrition facts per serving: 446 cal., 11 g total fat (2 g sat. fat), 133 mg chol., 334 mg sodium, 72 g carbo., 3 g fiber, 8 g pro. *Daily values:* 22% vit. A, 6% vit. C, 10% calcium, 10% iron.

PEAR-APRICOT COMPOTE

Prep: 15 min. ◆ Cook: 10 min.

This spicy fruit mixture is great over cake, but equally delicious atop a scoop of French vanilla ice cream.

- 1 large Bosc or other pear variety, thinly sliced
- 2 large apricots, pitted and sliced

- 2 small cinnamon sticks (about 1½-inches)
- 2 tsp. margarine or butter
- 3 Tbsp. dried tart red cherries or dried cranberries
- ¼ tsp. ground cloves

◆◆◆

- ⅔ cup sweet vermouth or cherry cider
- 2 Tbsp. brown sugar
- 1 tsp. finely shredded orange peel

◆◆◆

- 2 slices purchased pound cake or reduced-calorie pound cake

Orange peel curls (optional)

1 In a large skillet cook pear and apricot slices with cinnamon sticks, uncovered, in hot margarine or butter over medium heat for 3 to 4 minutes. Add cherries or cranberries and cloves. Cook for 3 minutes more.

2 Reduce heat. Add vermouth or cider, brown sugar, and shredded orange peel. Simmer fruit mixture, uncovered, for 10 to 12 minutes or until pears are tender and cherries soften. Remove and discard cinnamon sticks.

3 To serve, arrange pound cake slices on individual dessert plates. Spoon fruit mixture over each pound cake slice. If desired, garnish with orange peel curls. Makes 2 servings.

Nutrition facts per serving: 431 cal., 10 g total fat (4 g sat. fat), 0 mg chol., 175 mg sodium, 62 g carbo., 4 g fiber, 3 g pro. *Daily values:* 25% vit. A, 14% vit. C, 3% calcium, 8% iron.

SHORTBREAD STICKS

Prep: 45 min.
Bake: 18 min. per batch

*Vary the appearance of shortbread
by cutting into cookie
sticks and decorating with almonds
and candied cherries.
(See the photograph on page 319.)*

1½   **cups all-purpose flour**
½   **cup sifted powdered sugar**
⅔   **cup butter**
2   **Tbsp. finely chopped
crystallized ginger**

◆◆◆

¼   **cup sliced almonds, finely
chopped**
¼   **cup finely chopped candied
red cherries**
1   **Tbsp. granulated sugar**

1 In a medium mixing bowl
stir together the flour and powdered sugar. Using a pastry
blender, cut in the butter until the
mixture resembles fine crumbs
and starts to cling. Stir in the crystallized ginger. Form the mixture
into a ball and knead gently in the
bowl until smooth. On a lightly
floured surface, roll the dough
into a 14×6-inch rectangle (about
¼ inch thick).

2 In a small bowl stir together
the almonds, candied cherries,
and granulated sugar. Sprinkle
evenly over the dough and press
in lightly. Using a knife or pizza
cutter, cut the rectangle into
twenty to twenty-eight 6×½- to
¾-inch strips. Place the strips
about ½ inch apart on an
ungreased cookie sheet.

3 Bake in a 325° oven about
18 minutes or until bottoms of
cookies just start to brown. Cool
on cookie sheet 5 minutes.
Transfer cookies to wire racks and
let cool. Makes 20 to 28 sticks.

PEERLESS PEARS

The very shape of a pear speaks of
its luscious nature. When ripe and
ready to eat, the pear has a hon-
eyed flavor and beckoning perfume that bewitch your senses.
Numerous varieties and extended
growing seasons mean pears of all
sizes and colors are pyramiding in
the produce aisles of supermarkets
year-round. Simple recipes are the
best ones for highlighting this sen-
suous fruit. Although you can use
any variety of pear in most
recipes, use fruit that is still slightly firm for the best results.

BUYING AND RIPENING PEARS
At the supermarket, look for pears
that are free from bruises and cuts.
If you plan to bake the pears,
select those that are fairly firm.

To ripen pears, place them in a
paper bag at room temperature for
2 to 3 days or store them in the
fruit bowl in a cool, dark place.
For most varieties, test for ripeness
by applying a little pressure to the
stem end. A ripe pear will yield.
Yellow Bartletts are one variety
that become a bright yellow when
they are fully ripe. Ripe pears can
be kept in the refrigerator for
several days.

PICK YOUR PEAR
Pears come in a variety of shapes,
sizes, and colors, from tiny Seckels
to long-necked Boscs to colorful
Red Bartletts. Use this guide to
check shape as well as season for
the most available pear varieties.

Red Bartlett. Firm, red, and
juicy; very sweet when ripe. Available August through December.

Forelle. Larger than a Seckel;
freckled skin and red blush. Available October through February.

Seckel. A small, firm, sweet
pear; like a miniature Bosc.
Available August through January.

Asian. Flavor of this light, crisp
fruit is like a cross between an
apple and a pear. The texture is
similar to that of a water chestnut.
Generally available year-round.

Anjou. Firm and green, even
when ripe. Great for eating
and baking. Available October
through June.

Bosc. Softer than a Bartlett; this
long-neck pear with golden brown
skin is very juicy when ripe.
Available August through May.

Bartlett. One of the most common pears, firm and bell-shaped;
sometimes takes on a red blush.
Available July through December.

Nutrition facts per stick: 113 cal., 7 g total
fat (4 g sat. fat), 16 mg chol., 63 mg
sodium, 12 g carbo., 0 g fiber, 1 g pro.
Daily values: 5% vit. A, 4% iron.

TIERED MERINGUE TREE

Prep: 1¾ hr.
Bake: 20 min. per batch

If you like, top off this airy tree with a sparkly ornament instead of the final meringue sandwich. (See the photograph on page 319.)

3 egg whites
1 tsp. vanilla
¼ tsp. cream of tartar
¼ tsp. peppermint extract
1½ cups granulated sugar

♦♦♦

1 recipe Pink Icing (see right)

1 Lightly grease cookie sheets; set aside. For meringue, in a large mixing bowl beat the egg whites, vanilla, cream of tartar, and peppermint extract with an electric mixer on high speed until soft peaks form (tips curl). Add the sugar, 1 tablespoon at a time, beating until stiff peaks form.

2 Spoon meringue into a large pastry bag fitted with a large star tip. Pipe small mounds (about 130 meringues, 1 inch in diameter) 1 inch apart onto the prepared cookie sheets.

3 Bake in a 300° oven about 20 minutes or until firm and bottoms are very lightly browned. Transfer meringues to wire racks and let cool. Spread the bottoms of half of the meringues with about 1 teaspoon of the Pink Icing. Gently press bottom sides of remaining meringues into icing to form meringue sandwiches.

4 Dot icing in an 8-inch circle on a serving plate. Arrange about 15 meringue sandwiches on their sides in a circle on the icing, with points of 1 side of the meringue sandwiches facing the edge of plate; place 10 sandwiches in the center. Continue stacking the sandwiches on their sides in smaller circles to form a tree or cone shape. Use small amounts (about ½ teaspoon) of icing to attach each meringue sandwich to the previous layer, forming 5 to 6 layers of meringue sandwiches (25 in the first layer, 15 in the second, 13, 7, 4, and 1 in the following consecutive layers). Makes 65 meringue sandwiches.

Pink Icing: In a small mixing bowl combine 3 cups sifted powdered sugar, 3 tablespoons softened butter, and 1½ teaspoons vanilla. Add 1 or 2 drops red food coloring to tint a light pink color. Stir in ¼ cup finely chopped candied red cherries. Stir in 1 to 2 tablespoons milk until icing is smooth and easy to spread.

Nutrition facts per meringue sandwich: 43 cal., 1 g total fat (0 g sat. fat), 1 mg chol., 8 mg sodium, 10 g carbo., 0 g fiber, 0 g pro.

GIANT GINGER COOKIES

Prep: 20 min.
Bake: 12 min. per batch

These irresistibly chewy and delicious cookies are giant in size and giant in snappy ginger flavor. Be sure to use only shortening to make them rise to the occasion.

4½ cups all-purpose flour
4 tsp. ground ginger
2 tsp. baking soda
1½ tsp. ground cinnamon
1 tsp. ground cloves
¼ tsp. salt

♦♦♦

1½ cups shortening
2 cups granulated sugar
2 eggs
½ cup molasses

♦♦♦

¾ cup coarse sugar or granulated sugar

1 In a medium mixing bowl stir together the flour, ginger, soda, cinnamon, cloves, and salt. Set aside.

2 In a large mixing bowl beat shortening with an electric mixer on low speed for 30 seconds to soften. Gradually add the 2 cups granulated sugar; beat until fluffy. Add eggs and molasses; beat well. Add half of the flour mixture; beat until combined. Stir in the remaining flour mixture with a wooden spoon.

3 Shape into 2-inch balls using ¼ cup dough (or measure using a #20 ice cream scoop). Roll in the ¾ cup coarse or granulated sugar. Place dough balls on an ungreased cookie sheet about 2½ inches apart.

4 Bake in a 350° oven for 12 to 14 minutes or until cookies are light brown and puffed. (Do not overbake.) Let the cookies stand for 2 minutes before transferring to a wire rack to cool. Makes 25 four-inch cookies.

Nutrition facts per serving: 293 cal., 13 g total fat (3 g sat. fat), 17 mg chol., 129 mg sodium, 42 g carbo., 1 g fiber, 3 g pro.
Daily values: 1% calcium, 9% iron.

Victorian Cookie Ornaments

Prep: 1 hr. ◆ Chill: 3 hr.
Bake: 6 min. per batch

See the photograph on page 320.

½ cup shortening
¾ cup sugar
½ tsp. baking powder
¼ tsp. ground nutmeg
1 egg
1 Tbsp. milk
1 tsp. finely shredded orange
    peel
½ tsp. vanilla
2 cups all-purpose flour

◆◆◆

1 recipe Royal Icing (see right)
  Small red candies
24 36-inch lengths white string
    or narrow ribbon

1 Beat shortening on medium to high speed for 30 seconds. Add sugar, baking powder, nutmeg, and dash *salt*. Beat until combined, scraping bowl. Beat in egg, milk, orange peel, and vanilla. Beat in as much of the flour as you can. Stir in remaining flour. Divide dough in thirds. If necessary, cover and chill dough 3 hours or until easy to handle.

2 On a lightly floured surface, roll a third of dough into a 9-inch circle. Trim to an 8-inch circle with a fluted pastry wheel. Cut into 8 pie-shaped wedges. Carefully transfer to an ungreased cookie sheet, placing about 1 inch apart. Using a straw, make a hole about 1 inch from the bottom point. Make 1 hole about ¼ inch from the top corners and then 1 more hole on each side that is midway between the top and bottom holes and about ¼ inch from sides (3 holes total on each side). Bake cookies in a 375° oven 6 to 8 minutes or until edges are firm. Cool on a wire rack. Repeat with remaining dough.

3 Decorate with white Royal Icing, using icing to attach the small red candies. Let stand until icing has dried and candies are secure. After icing has dried, lace 3 cookies together with string or ribbon. Tie three 36-inch lengths of string together about 4 inches from an end and then 1 inch above that, forming a tassel. Place 2 of the cookies together at a slight angle, matching up the holes. Starting from the bottom point, lace 1 long string end through the holes in the 2 cookies. (Note: Use a large eyed needle for lacing.) Double lace through the top holes. Add a third cookie and lace it together with the other 2 cookies (see below). Bring 3 strings and tie in another knot at the top to make a hanger.

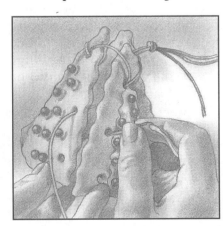

4 On the day of the party, fill each ornament with a small *Lady apple*. Or, fill ornaments with *hard candies* and wrap in cellophane, if desired. Hang by the top knot. Makes 24 cookies (enough for 8 ornaments).

Royal Icing: In a large mixing bowl combine 3 tablespoons meringue powder, ⅓ cup warm water, 4½ cups (1 pound) sifted powdered sugar, 1 teaspoon vanilla, and 1 teaspoon lemon juice. Beat with an electric mixer on low speed until combined. Beat on high speed for 7 to 10 minutes or until very stiff. For Cookie Rounds, tint half of the frosting pink using liquid or paste food coloring. If desired, thin some of the icing with water to a glazing consistency. Use icings to decorate Victorian Cookie Ornaments or Cookie Rounds. Keep icing covered to prevent it from drying out. If necessary, store overnight in the refrigerator in a tightly covered container.

Nutrition facts per cookie: 175 cal., 5 g total fat (1 g sat. fat), 9 mg chol., 14 mg sodium, 32 g carbo., 0 g fiber, 1 g pro.
Daily values: 3% iron.

Cookie Rounds: (See photograph on page 318.) Prepare cookie dough; roll half of the dough at a time ⅛-inch thick on a lightly floured surface. Using a round cookie cutter or cardboard pattern, cut out rounds about 4 or 5 inches in diameter; transfer to a cookie sheet with a large spatula. Cut a ¾-inch square of dough from dough trimmings and overlap about ¼ inch on 1 side of the round, forming the "hanger." Using a small straw, make 1 or 2 holes in the hanger so that cookie ornament can be threaded with narrow ribbon after baking. Bake cookies in a 375° oven for 8 to 10 minutes. Cool completely. Frost the cookie rounds with white and pink icing; let dry. Decorate as desired. Makes about 12 cookie rounds.

DOUBLE-DIPPED RED PEARS

Start to finish: 2½ hr.

These pears are so luscious and loaded with caramel, chocolate, and nuts that each is large enough to cut into wedges for sharing. (See the photograph on page 320.)

6 large firm red and/or green pears with stems

1 cup coarsely chopped nuts, such as cashews, hazelnuts (filberts), almonds, or pecans

♦♦♦

1 14 oz. pkg. vanilla caramels or chocolate caramels

2 Tbsp. water

♦♦♦

⅔ cup semisweet chocolate pieces

2 tsp. shortening

♦♦♦

½ cup white baking pieces

1½ tsp. shortening

1 Wash and dry pears. Leave stems intact. Place pears on a buttered baking sheet. Place chopped nuts in a shallow dish; set aside.

2 Unwrap caramels. In a medium saucepan heat and stir caramels and water over medium-low heat just until caramels melt.

3 Using a fork to prop pear on and holding onto the stem, carefully dip each pear into hot caramel mixture, spooning caramel evenly over the bottom half of the pear (do not dip entire pear). Allow excess caramel to drip off. Briefly set bottom or coated pear in nuts. Place pear on prepared baking sheet and let stand about 30 minutes or until

firm. Repeat with remaining pears, caramel, and nuts.

4 In a small saucepan stir semisweet chocolate pieces and the 2 teaspoons shortening over low heat until melted. Drizzle chocolate over stem end of pears allowing excess chocolate to drip down sides of pears, but not cover all of the peel of the pears.* Place pears on prepared baking sheet and let stand about 30 minutes or until chocolate is set.

5 In a small saucepan stir white pieces and the 1½ teaspoons shortening over low heat until melted. Drizzle mixture over each pear, but do not completely cover semisweet chocolate.* Let pears stand 1 hour or until chocolate is set. Chill, if desired, in a covered container up to 2 days. To serve, cut pears into quarters. Makes 6 pears (serves 24).

***Note:** If you like, place melted chocolate in self-sealing bags.

Snip off a corner of each bag and use to drizzle chocolate onto the pears.

TO PRESENT AS A GIFT

Place each coated pear on an inexpensive, pretty compote or dish and overwrap in cellophane. Tie with a ribbon and attach a gift card or petite ornament.

Nutrition facts per quarter: 170 cal., 8 g total fat (2 g sat. fat), 1 mg chol., 81 mg sodium, 26 g carbo., 2 g fiber, 2 g pro. *Daily values*: 2% vit. C, 3% calcium, 4% iron.

PEPPERY PEACH SAUCE

Prep: 30 min. ♦ Cook: 15 min.
Process: 15 min.

Make the spicy sauce with fresh peaches when they are in season or use frozen peaches other times of the year. Serve sauce with pork, ham, or poultry.

4 lb. fresh peaches or three 16-oz. pkg. frozen unsweetened peach slices, thawed

♦♦♦

2 cups sugar

1 5½-oz. can peach or apricot nectar

¼ cup cider vinegar

1 Tbsp. lemon juice

2 cloves garlic, minced

1 fresh red chili pepper or habanero chili pepper, seeded and very finely chopped* (about 1 tablespoon)

1½ cups fresh raspberries

1 Wash fresh peaches, if using. Peel and pit peaches. Place half of the fresh or frozen peaches in a food processor bowl or blender container. Cover and process or blend until peaches are very finely chopped. Transfer chopped peaches to a 6-quart Dutch oven or kettle. Repeat with remaining peaches. (You should have 5 cups pureed peaches.)

2 Add sugar, nectar, vinegar, lemon juice, garlic, chili pepper, and ½ teaspoon *salt* to Dutch oven. Bring to boiling; reduce heat. Simmer, uncovered, 15 to 20 minutes or until desired consistency, stirring occasionally. Remove from heat. Stir in berries.

3 Process sauce in standard canning jars following directions below, or ladle into decorative jars and store in the refrigerator for up to 1 week before using.

4 To process the sauce, immediately ladle hot sauce into hot, clean half-pint canning jars, leaving ¼-inch headspace. Wipe rims and adjust lids. Process jars in a boiling-water canner 15 minutes (start timing when water begins to boil). Remove jars from canner; cool on racks. Stir sauce before serving. Makes 8 half-pint jars.

*Note: Hot peppers contain oils that can burn eyes, lips, and sensitive skin. Wear plastic gloves while preparing peppers and be sure to thoroughly wash your hands afterward.

▮ TO PRESENT AS A GIFT ▮

Tie a ribbon around jar; label with contents and serving suggestions. If you like, use a ribbon to tie a small spoon onto jar.

Nutrition facts per 2-tablespoon serving: 39 cal., 0 g total fat, 0 mg chol., 17 mg sodium, 10 g carbo., 1 g fiber, 0 g pro. *Daily values:* 1% vit. A, 5% vit. C.

LOW FAT

HOLIDAY SURPRISE BREAD

Prep: 20 min. ◆ Rise: about 2½ hr. Bake: 30 min.

Look for one-of-a-kind gift plates at local flea markets or antique shops.

- 3¾ to 4¼ cups all-purpose flour
- 2 pkg. active dry yeast
- ¾ cup milk
- ⅓ cup margarine or butter
- ⅓ cup sugar
- 1 tsp. salt
- 2 eggs
- 4 oz. semisweet chocolate, coarsely chopped (do not use semisweet chocolate pieces)
- ¾ cup chopped candied red cherries
- ¼ cup diced candied orange peel
- 2 tsp. finely shredded orange peel

1 In a large mixing bowl combine 1½ cups of the all-purpose flour and the yeast. In a medium saucepan heat and stir milk, margarine or butter, sugar, and salt just until warm (120° to 130°) and margarine almost melts. Add milk mixture to flour mixture along with the eggs. Beat with an electric mixer on low to medium speed for 30 seconds, scraping sides of bowl constantly. Beat on high speed for 3 minutes. Using a wooden spoon, stir in the chocolate, candied cherries, candied orange peel, shredded orange peel, and as much of the remaining flour as you can.

2 Turn dough out onto a lightly floured surface. Knead in enough of the remaining flour to make a moderately soft dough that is smooth and elastic (3 to 5 minutes total). Shape dough into a ball. Place in a lightly greased bowl; turn once to grease surface of dough. Cover and let rise in a warm place until double in size (1½ to 2 hours).

3 Punch dough down. Turn dough out onto a lightly floured surface. Divide dough in half. Cover; let rest for 10 minutes. Grease 2 baking sheets.

4 Shape each portion of dough into a round loaf. Place on the prepared sheets. Press to flatten each to a 6-inch-diameter round. Cover and let rise in a warm place until nearly double (about 50 to 60 minutes).

5 Using a sharp knife, cut an "X" about ½ inch deep in top of each loaf. Bake in a 325° oven for 30 minutes or until bread sounds hollow when tapped. If necessary, cover loosely with foil the last 10 minutes of baking to prevent overbrowning. Transfer loaves to wire racks and let cool. Makes 2 loaves (12 servings each).

▮ TO PRESENT AS A GIFT ▮

Wrap cooled loaf with cellophane and place on a plate. Tie a ribbon around wrapped loaf and plate. If desired, tuck in a fresh evergreen sprig.

Nutrition facts per serving: 147 cal., 5 g total fat (2 g sat. fat), 18 mg chol., 124 mg sodium, 24 g carbo., 1 g fiber, 3 g pro. *Daily values:* 3% vit. A, 1% calcium, 7% iron.

Dinner Café Style

Start with candlelight and flowers. Add chic tablesettings. Serve sophisticated bistro fare. Enjoy.

**Chicken and Rigatoni with
Roasted Red Peppers (page 57)**

◆◆◆

**Salad of fresh pear and cantaloupe slices
wrapped with prosciutto and served
atop leaf lettuce and very lightly drizzled
with balsamic vinegar and olive oil.**

◆◆◆

Peppery Cheese Bread (page 71)

◆◆◆

**Peanut Brittle Bread Pudding
(page 246)**

3 hours ahead:
◆ Make and bake bread; cool.

1½ hours ahead:
◆ Make bread pudding.
◆ Prepare salad (except dressing).

30 minutes before:
◆ Prepare pasta.

Just before serving:
◆ Dress salad; slice bread.

Game Day Gathering

Spread out on a tailgate or TV tray, this barbecue-based meal will get the crowd cheering.

**Pulled Pork with Root Beer
Barbecue Sauce (page 236)**

◆◆◆

**Potato-Apple Salad (page 231) and/or
Jicama Coleslaw (page 231)**

◆◆◆

Assorted fresh vegetable crudités

◆◆◆

Assorted chips

◆◆◆

**Beer (such as European pale lagers) and
other desired beverages**

◆◆◆

**Nutmeg-Sour Cream Drop Cookies
(page 276)**

The day before:
◆ Prepare Potato-Apple Salad and Jicama
Coleslaw; cover and chill.
◆ Make, bake, and frost cookies. Cover to store.

8 hours before:
◆ Prepare meat in crockery cooker.

1 hour before:
◆ Make barbecue sauce.
◆ Prepare vegetable crudités.

Just before serving:
◆ Transfer salads to serving bowls; garnish.
◆ Shred pork and assemble sandwiches.

Note: If you plan to serve this meal away from
home, make sure you pack it to keep hot
foods hot and cold foods cold.

A Meal of Heart-Warming Foods

Soothing and substantial, comfort foods recall fond memories.
Use them to create new memories around the family table.

Garden Pot Roast (page 54)

◆◆◆

Buttered whole tiny new potatoes

◆◆◆

**Mixed fresh fruit salad
served atop fresh greens**

◆◆◆

**Tender Potato Rolls
(page 74)**

◆◆◆

No-Fret Apple Pie (page 67)

6 hours before:
◆ Make, bake, and cool pie.

3 hours before:
◆ Prepare and cook pot roast.

1 hour before:
◆ Let rolls rise; bake.

30 minutes before:
◆ Cook potatoes; toss with butter.
◆ Arrange salads on individual plates.

Up to 24 hours before:
◆ Prepare and shape rolls; cover and chill.

Just before serving:
◆ Make gravy.

Special Occasion Brunch

Produce a feast for the eyes, as well as the palate, that celebrates any noteworthy day in high style.

Mushroom and Cheese Strata (page 48)

◆◆◆

**Baked ham slices and/or
cooked sausage links**

◆◆◆

**Miniature Wheat and Nut Muffins
(page 50)**

◆◆◆

Fresh fruit bowl

◆◆◆

**Apricot-Mint Tea (page 174)
and/or coffee**

The day before:
◆ Assemble strata; cover and chill.

Several hours before:
◆ Prepare tea; cover and chill.

1¼ hours before:
◆ Bake strata; let stand and cut into squares.

30 minutes before:
◆ Make and bake muffins.
◆ Prepare fruit bowl.
◆ Heat ham slices.

Just before serving:
◆ Strain tea into a pitcher or bowl.

Trio-of-Salads Luncheon

Hit a triple with three tasty make-ahead salads. Your guests will consider it a grand slam.

Crisp Apple-Rice Salad (page 19)
◆◆◆
Mediterranean Potato Salad (page 133)
◆◆◆
Carrot, Corn, and Bean Salad (page 166)
◆◆◆
Assorted fresh breads
◆◆◆
Strawberry Chiffon Pie (page 85)

1 day before:
◆ Prepare Crisp Apple-Rice Salad (do not add apple); cover and chill.

◆ Prepare potato salad and bean salad; cover and chill.

6 hours before:
◆ Make pie; cover and chill.

Just before serving:
◆ Toss rice salad with apple.
◆ Transfer salads to platter or bowls.

Between courses:
◆ Cut pie into wedges; garnish with strawberries and strawberry or mint leaves.

Picnic on the Patio

Grilled meat is the centerpiece, but this outdoor meal includes a bouquet of fresh greens and vegetables, and a fruit-studded cake that's both sweet and tangy.

Sweet Red Pepper Bruschetta (page 24)
◆◆◆
Steak Lover's Platter with Onion Sauce (page 180)
◆◆◆
Salad of fresh spinach greens, tomato slices, sliced fresh mushrooms, and vinaigrette
◆◆◆
Blueberry Citrus Cake (page 191)
◆◆◆
Iced Tea

Up to 8 hours before:
◆ Make, bake, and cool cake. Frost cake; cover and store in the refrigerator.

Up to 6 hours before:
◆ Prepare marinade. Add meat; cover and chill.

1 hour before:
◆ Prepare salad (except vinaigrette).
◆ Precook vegetables.
◆ Grill bread slices.
◆ Grill meat and vegetables.
◆ Prepare Onion Sauce.

Just before serving:
◆ Top grilled bread slices; dress salad.
◆ Arrange meat and vegetables on platter.

Between courses:
◆ Slice cake into wedges.

Movie Night Supper

When movie buffs gather to watch an epic, the script calls for "reel" food:
a hearty meat pie and a sweet, happy ending.

Sausage Pie (page 234)
◆◆◆
Assorted vegetable crudités with dip
◆◆◆
Towering Brownie Sundaes (page 218)
◆◆◆
Milk

Up to 3 days before:
◆ Make and bake brownies; cool. Cover and store at room temperature.

1½ hours before:
◆ Make and bake Sausage Pie.
◆ Prepare crudités.

Just before serving:
◆ Cut pie into wedges.

Between courses:
◆ Prepare sauce and assemble sundaes.

Fall Harvest Dinner

Plucked from the fields, and gathered from the garden, fall's harvest shows up in fresh, inventive dishes.

Pomegranate-Glazed Goose (or Duck) (page 268)
◆◆◆
Salad of mesclun greens with apple slices, toasted black walnuts, and a fruit-flavored vinaigrette
◆◆◆
Salad of fresh spinach greens, tomato slices, sliced fresh mushrooms, and vinaigrette
◆◆◆
Rosemary "Braidsticks" (page 250)
◆◆◆
Sweet Potato and Hazelnut Pie (page 274) and/or Festive Cranberry-Apricot Pie (page 275)

Up to 3 weeks before:
◆ Prepare "braidstick" dough; cover and freeze.

1 day before:
◆ Remove dough from freezer; thaw in the refrigerator.

Up to 8 hours before:
◆ Make and bake pie(s); cool, cover, and chill.

3 hours before:
◆ Prepare and roast goose.

2 hours before:
◆ Shape, rise, and bake "braidsticks."
◆ Prepare pomegranate glaze.

Just before serving:
◆ Prepare salad.
◆ Carve goose.

Outdoor Appetizer Party

Update the picnic with an array of savory hors d'oeuvres and dainty, individual desserts.

Curry Phyllo Triangles (page 11)

◆◆◆

**Upside-Down Marinated
Shrimp Bowl (page 130)**

◆◆◆

Herbed Feta Spread (page 129)

◆◆◆

**Antipasto with Toasted
Pita Crisps (page 128)**

◆◆◆

Cappuccino Brownie Cups (page 22)

◆◆◆

Jelly Roll Dainties (page 22)

◆◆◆

Spiced Cranberry Tea Punch (page 174)

◆◆◆

Champagne, wine, and/or beer

Up to 1 week before:
◆ Bake Toasted Pita Crisps; cover and store.
◆ Prepare phyllo triangles (do not bake);
cover and freeze.

Up to 3 days before:
◆ Prepare Herbed Feta Spread; cover and chill.

Up to 2 days before:
◆ Prepare the Two-Tomato Conserve
(for the Antipasto); cover and chill.

The day before:
◆ Prepare shrimp bowl; cover and chill.
◆ Bake brownies; cool. Cover to store.
◆ Bake jelly roll; roll up and cool. Cover to store.
◆ Prepare punch; cover and chill.

1 hour before:
◆ Assemble individual jelly rolls.

30 minutes before:
◆ Arrange antipasto on a serving platter.
◆ Cut brownies; pipe in filling.

Just before serving:
◆ Bake phyllo triangles.
◆ Strain tea into a pitcher or bowl.
◆ Arrange appetizers on platters, in bowls,
and/or baskets.

Top left: *Cheese Spread Duo (page 294)*
Top right: *Festive Apple Wedges (page 298)*
Above: *Raspberry-Pepper Glazed Ham (page 304), Stuffed Pumpkin Shell Potatoes (page 303)*

Right: *Shortbread Sticks (page 307)*
Below: *Tiered Meringue Tree (page 308)*
Page 318: *Cinnamon-Apple Spice Cake (page 305),*
Victorian Cookie Ornaments (page 309)

Far left: *Double-Dipped
Red Pears (page 310)*
Left: *Victorian Cookie
Ornaments (page 309)*
Below: *Pumpkin-Pear
Trifle (page 306)*

MAIN INDEX

Main Index **329**

EMERGENCY SUBSTITUTIONS

IF YOU DON'T HAVE:	SUBSTITUTE:
1 teaspoon baking powder	½ teaspoon cream of tartar plus ¼ teaspoon baking soda
1 tablespoon cornstarch (for thickening)	2 tablespoons all-purpose flour
1 package active dry yeast	1 cake compressed yeast
1 cup buttermilk	1 tablespoon lemon juice or vinegar plus enough milk to make 1 cup (let stand 5 minutes before using); or 1 cup plain yogurt
1 cup whole milk	½ cup evaporated milk plus ½ cup water; or 1 cup water plus ⅓ cup nonfat dry milk powder
1 cup light cream	1 tablespoon melted butter or margarine plus enough whole milk to make 1 cup
1 cup dairy sour cream	1 cup plain yogurt
1 whole egg	2 egg whites, 2 egg yolks, or 3 tablespoons frozen egg product, thawed
1 cup margarine	1 cup butter; or 1 cup shortening plus ¼ teaspoon salt, if desired
1 ounce semisweet chocolate	3 tablespoons semisweet chocolate pieces; or 1 ounce unsweetened chocolate plus 1 tablespoon granulated sugar
1 ounce unsweetened chocolate	3 tablespoons unsweetened cocoa powder plus 1 tablespoon cooking oil or shortening, melted
1 cup corn syrup	1 cup granulated sugar plus ¼ cup liquid
1 cup honey	1¼ cups granulated sugar plus ¼ cup liquid
1 cup molasses	1 cup honey
1 cup granulated sugar	1 cup packed brown sugar or 2 cups sifted powdered sugar
1 cup beef broth or chicken broth	1 teaspoon or 1 cube instant beef or chicken bouillon plus 1 cup hot water
2 cups tomato sauce	¾ cup tomato paste plus 1 cup water
1 cup tomato juice	½ cup tomato sauce plus ½ cup water
¼ cup fine dry bread crumbs	¾ cup soft bread crumbs, ¼ cup cracker crumbs, or ¼ cup cornflake crumbs
1 small onion, chopped (⅓ cup)	1 teaspoon onion powder or 1 tablespoon dried minced onion
1 clove garlic	½ teaspoon bottled minced garlic or ⅛ teaspoon garlic powder
1 teaspoon lemon juice	½ teaspoon vinegar
1 teaspoon poultry seasoning	¾ teaspoon dried sage, crushed, plus ¼ teaspoon dried thyme or marjoram, crushed
1 teaspoon dry mustard (in cooked mixtures)	1 tablespoon prepared mustard
1 tablespoon snipped fresh herb	½ to 1 teaspoon dried herb, crushed
1 teaspoon dried herb	½ teaspoon ground herb
1 teaspoon grated gingerroot	¼ teaspoon ground ginger
1 teaspoon apple pie spice	½ teaspoon ground cinnamon plus ¼ teaspoon ground nutmeg, ⅛ teaspoon ground allspice, and dash ground cloves or ginger
1 teaspoon pumpkin pie spice	½ teaspoon ground cinnamon plus ¼ teaspoon ground ginger, ¼ teaspoon ground allspice, and ⅛ teaspoon ground nutmeg